CW01513017

You Must Get Them All
The Fall On Record

Steve Pringle

[signature: Steve Pringle]

route

First published by Route in 2022
info@route-online.com
www.route-online.com

ISBN : 978-1901927-88-7

First Edition

Steve Pringle asserts his moral
right to be identified as the author of this book

Cover Design:
John Sellards

Typeset in Bembo by Route

Printed and bound by CPI Group (UK) Ltd, Croydon, CR0 4YY

For Kirsty, for putting up with it all…

People write to me and say, 'I heard The Fall, which record should I get?' And I never have any hesitation in telling them: you must get them all, because it's impossible to pick one. You have to have them all, you do. And you have to have any new record that comes out... Live in Nova Scotia 1984... *even if the sound quality's terrible, and he was pissed, or he'd just fired half the band or whatever, you still have to have them. You do. So there is no answer to that... and in fact I'll go further. I say: anybody who can tell you the five best Fall LPs, or the five best Fall tracks, has missed the point, really. It's the whole body of the work that is to be applauded.*

John Peel (1939 – 2004)

Foreword

As you're about to see, this book represents the first serious attempt to document in print all of The Fall's recorded output. *You Must Get Them All* is a satisfyingly unique excursion that will take you from the group's earliest bootlegs to *New Facts Emerge*, the last record to be released while The Fall still existed, and beyond. And unlike some other books, there's no bias towards certain periods or line-ups. It's all here.

Perhaps what John Peel should have said in relation to the vast expanse of Fall material out there was 'you must know about them all'. Because personally, even as he said it, I don't think he meant you must buy all Fall records that exist. (If he did, he was wrong.) And even he probably didn't know about *all* of them. There is a famous picture of him holding *Hip Priest And Kamerads*, so presumably some compilations were part of his brief. He was also fond of the live albums (the *Live in Nova Scotia 1984* that he mentions seems to have been a particular favourite, despite the possibly pertinent fact that it doesn't exist). But even someone as zealous as he was surely wouldn't bother with *Nord-West Gas* (an utterly pointless précis of the two Fall albums that immediately preceded it) for instance. We'll have to speculate where he actually drew the line, because everyone draws it somewhere.

But telling someone that they have to purchase every Fall record on the right side of wherever that line ends up is throwing down quite a serious gauntlet – not least because when John Peel said it, the group was still regularly issuing records, with no sign of letting up. And don't forget, back then 'getting' an album was an actual thing, a process, involving such antiquated concepts as bus rides, record shops, and cash, not to mention storage space. That's quite a chunk of change, and quite a drain on your time.

It's all different now. If you want to listen to everything released in The Fall's name, there's really no need to 'get' anything – I found 'Laptop Dog' on my iPhone and 'Quit iPhone' on my laptop in less than the time it took me to type this sentence – and listening to both will cost me nothing at all.[i] It's all there, for free, at the touch of a button, with no effort, outlay or ownership required.

In some ways the argument for collecting this information in a book echoes the argument about buying albums – if it's all on the internet, why should I buy it in physical form? So I'm happy to reassure you that Mr Pringle's creation is more than capable of answering that particular question. *You Must Get Them All* is an old-fashioned, honest-to-goodness book. It's not *Wikipedia*, it's not even the blog of the same name that spawned it. It is, at the end of the day, an extended love letter to The Fall, and everyone prefers to get love letters on paper rather than by text.

Within this hefty tome you will find considered evaluation, and where appropriate re-evaluation, of everything released under The Fall's name. That is, by anyone's reckoning, an epic undertaking. And that's not just because The Fall lasted a long time. By way of an example, the period between 1985 and 1988 saw nine official Fall albums released,[ii] and though that was an unusually prolific period, it was by no means unique. There's a hell of a lot to cover here, and I can only applaud Steve's stamina in getting it all done. Never forget that this is a man who, by way of meticulous research, has listened to 'Crew Filth' more than once so that you don't have to. Most importantly of all, in his quest to encompass everything, he never forgets to be entertaining, and we can only thank him for that.

The perennially humourless Frank Zappa would have it that 'writing about music is like dancing about architecture', which is wrong on just about every level. Writing about music is like writing about everything else; it stands and falls on the quality of the words therein. Someone else's opinion about a subject you care about, if well argued, can be boundlessly entertaining, especially

---

[i] In light of this astonishing technological advancement, many have gone back to buying vinyl again, either as comfortable nostalgia for simpler times, or as a noble attempt to rightfully recompense the artist concerned. Whether they actually listen to their purchases is a different matter. These days buying records is as irrelevant to music appreciation as stamp collecting is to posting your Christmas cards.

[ii] *Hip Priest And Kamerads, This Nation's Saving Grace, Nord-West Gas, The Fall* (a US compilation of recent singles), *Bend Sinister, The 'Domesday Pay-Off' Triad-Plus!, Palace of Swords Reversed, The Frenz Experiment* and *I Am Kurious Oranj.*

if you disagree with them. And though you will undoubtedly find things to disagree with here, you will find little to refute, and also tons of stuff you didn't know. You can't really ask for more than that. And anyway Frank, if you can dance about the sectarian rivalry between King James II and William of Orange, you can certainly dance about architecture.

If I were to offer you some advice as you stand poised to dive into the fast-flowing river that is the recorded output of The Fall, it would be to put aside notions of 'good' or 'bad', at least while you're reading.[iii] Just ask if it's interesting. If you only seek out the good stuff you'll miss a hell of a lot, as even the most superfluous records included here have definite points of interest. Of course, sometimes much of that interest is centred on determining the thought process that lead to such shoddy product seeing the light of day. But so what? Like many a modern TV show, discussing some Fall records is more fun, and more worthy of our time, than actually listening to them. Which is probably why so much of this discussion still goes on. *Thefall.org*, *The Mighty Fall* FB page, *The Annotated Fall*, and myriad others you'll read about later, continue this discourse on a daily basis. No doubt even more dialogue and debate will ensue once the members of those sites get their hands on this book. Mark E Smith was right – The Fall will outlive your sins.

However much ex-members like me insist that The Fall was a group, rather than Mark E Smith and some backing musicians, it's utterly inconceivable that The Fall could ever reform, and none of those ex-members have any say about what will get released or re-released in the future. The Fall now belongs almost entirely to its fans, to people like Steve Pringle. As you'll see, it's in safe hands. If it's testament to the significance of The Fall that people continue to be fascinated by the group and its records, then it's even more of a testament that they can inspire a work as thorough and enjoyable as *You Must Get Them All*.

Paul Hanley

[iii] Apart from 'Crew Filth', obviously.

Introduction

'It's difficult to overstate the significance of The Fall
in my life; they are the air I breathe.'

This book strives to tell the fascinating, complex and often downright strange story of The Fall, principally framed around the 32 albums[1] that they released between 1979 and 2017, but also taking in a series of important diversions down the side roads of their bewildering array of singles, EPs, compilations and live albums.

The Fall's back catalogue is frequently (and not unreasonably) described as 'daunting'. A partial explanation for this can be found in Appendices 2 and 3 of this book, which catalogue the sheer volume of live and compilation LPs released in the group's name.[2] But The Fall's importance should not be assessed in such simplistic terms as the number of releases. It is a *significant* body of work: it has weight; a level of cultural import that exceeds those of most, if not all of their contemporaries. A well-known trope has it that The Velvet Underground sold a limited number of records, but that everyone who bought one formed a band.[3] The Fall should be judged in similar terms. A huge array of artists have taken inspiration from not only the group's sound (which is in any case hard to define, given the breadth of their output), but from their attitude and ethos – and that includes many artists who never really

---

[1] If you're already rolling your sleeves up for an argument, be patient – I'll get to the 'is *Slates* an LP/EP/maxi-single/mini-album?' debate in due course.
[2] I refer to The Fall throughout this book as a 'group' rather than a 'band'. This was Mark E Smith's preference (although he himself wasn't always consistent in his terminology). He explained the distinction whilst answering fan questions for an *Uncut* interview in 2015: 'It's like when you play Jools Holland – they're all [cue withering disdain] "bands" and they've all been to music college. They've all studied to be in a "band", they've all got degrees to be in "bands". You understand? It's true: they've all done courses. I don't know, to me a band's like, 26 musicians. The Fall's different. The Fall's a group.'
[3] Variations on this quotation abound. It probably has its origins in an interview Brian Eno did for the *Los Angeles Times* in May 1982: 'I was talking to Lou Reed the other day, and he said that the first Velvet Underground record sold only 30,000 copies in its first five years. Yet, that was an enormously important record for so many people. I think everyone who bought one of those 30,000 copies started a band!'

13

actually sounded like The Fall, the influence being more subtle and pervasive than that. Furthermore, vocalist and frontman Mark E Smith left behind a unique collection of rich, complex lyricism. Encompassing pithy wit, cuttingly precise observation, opaque abstraction, furious tirades and a myriad of cultural references (from Sartre to *Neighbours*) – all steeped in a distinctive sense of proud yet cynical northern identity – his lyrical output is more than worthy of the critical analysis afforded to Dylan or Lennon. 'I'll tell you the history of English letters,' novelist Michael Nath comments, 'Chaucer, Shakespeare, Dickens, The Fall.'

In addition to the records themselves, much of the source material for this book comes from the obvious places: interviews, articles, reviews; a substantial proportion also comes from books written about The Fall. First-hand accounts by ex-members of the group were particularly useful in understanding the experience of life on the road and in the studio: Steve Hanley's *The Big Midweek*; Brix Smith Start's *The Rise, The Fall, and The Rise*; Simon Wolstencroft's *You Can Drum But You Can't Hide*; Paul Hanley's *Have A Bleedin Guess*. Although they occasionally differ regarding the finer details, this set of memoirs provide a consistent narrative, at least up until the late 90s, when the last of the autobiographers quit the group. They are all contradicted frequently by Smith's entertaining if not always reliable memoir, *Renegade*, but, as will become apparent, MES generally inhabited his own alternative narrative anyway. Another invaluable source of information was Simon Ford's *Hip Priest: The Story of Mark E Smith and The Fall*. It's the only traditionally structured long-term history of the group published so far (although it only extends as far as 2001) and is measured, objective and generally accurate.[4]

As invaluable as these traditional sources are, if you really want to get to the heart of The Fall's story, then you have to dig deeper – into the online Fall community itself. During The Fall's 1994 US tour, long-serving bassist Steve Hanley noted the increasing influence of the internet on ticket sales, and from this point onwards, online interaction would play a crucial role in the

---

[4] Although he does fall for a spoof story from the fanzine *The Biggest Library Yet* which suggested that Lisa Riley of *Emmerdale* and *You've Been Framed* fame was Marc Riley's sister.

group's story. The history of the Fall online community is – like that of the group itself – a complex one, and what follows is only a summative overview.

The first online presence was the *FallNet* mailing list, established in the early 90s, followed by the *Lyrics Parade* and *Fall News*. In the late 90s, Stefan Cooke began compiling the group's gigography, later expanding his site to include a comprehensive collection of interviews, reviews and articles about the group. Other Fall-related online resources included *The Biggest Library Yet*, *The Pseud Mag* and *Reformation Post-TPM* ('post-The Pseud Mag', later renamed *The Track Record*). In 1998, the *Lyrics Parade* and the gig- and bibliographies were combined – with Smith's agreement – to form the first official Fall website, which was later renamed *The Fall Online*.

Both *The Fall Online* and *The Track Record* contain a wealth of information about every one of The Fall's hundreds of releases and nearly every one of the roughly 1700 gigs they played between 1977 and 2017.[5] These resources – especially those covering the live performances – are constructed from the real-life accounts of the diehard Fall fans: those who experienced the highs and lows of The Fall live experience and came back for more, regardless of whether their most recent encounter was an uplifting triumph or a disappointing shambles; those who spent, queued, watched, listened and posted.[6] Their story lies, alongside that of the group itself, at the heart of this book.

The Fall Online hosts the *Fall Online Forum*.[7] Like most other online forums devoted to musical acts, the 'FOF' is home to a myriad of debates and discussions relating to the group and pretty much any other topic you might think of. Of course, most forums

---

[5] At a rate of roughly a gig every eight and a half days – not bad over a 40 year stretch.

[6] ...and recorded. Amongst these hardcore fans is a dedicated set of bootleggers who recorded and shared The Fall's gigs throughout their career. Some of the most prolific include Alex Staszko, 'Big Crashing Beat' (Graeme Semple), 'Tock' and 'QTarquin'. In the last ten years of the group's career, Mark Howard aka 'hanleyfender', became one of the best-known bootleggers, recording performances via his distinctive headgear known as the 'dalek hat'.

[7] *The Fall Online Forum* is run on a day-to-day basis by a team of moderators these days, but overall supervision still rests with founder Conway Paton. Conway first encountered The Fall in 1980 whilst a student at Auckland University. He took over responsibility for the lyrics section of the official site in 2002, and has subsequently worked with the Voiceprint, Sanctuary and Cherry Red labels on various Fall re-issues.

of this nature tend to feature hotly-debated and often eccentric opinions, squabbles, insults and feuds. The FOF, however, is especially rich in all these elements. In particular, members have a seemingly unending capacity to home in on what might seem to an outsider to be an arcane, insignificant detail and devote thousands of increasingly vehement words to it. Notable examples include whether or not Smith actually says 'Oprah Winfrey – she studied bees' in the song 'Two Librans', what the two words following 'M. R. James' are in the track 'Spectre vs. Rector', and the highest-profile debate of all: is *Slates* an album, and if not what is it?

The history of the online Fall community has always echoed the regular upheavals and conflicts of the group's own story. On Valentine's Day 2006, Smith suddenly demanded that the *Official Fall Website* be taken offline immediately, having 'taken exception to one or more posts on the forum'. Cooke and Paton refused, and the site continued as an unofficial one, which was then renamed in 2007 as *The Fall Online*.[8]

Smith – as he did with many things – had a complicated and often contradictory attitude to the online world and technology in general. He described the internet as 'the tongue of Satan', and several latter-day songs cast a withering glance at specific aspects of new technologies. At times, however, he displayed a certain pride in the fanbase's online presence, even making the unlikely claim that 'Fall fans invented the Internet... they were on there in 1982'. Speaking to *The Independent* in 2004, he was a little more ambivalent about the website: 'I never read it... though I know it's the envy of a lot of groups... Most of it's all right, but this culture where you have to explain everything all the time... puts a clamp on you. It's a bit of a trap.' In retrospect, it seems inevitable that Smith would eventually turn against something so important to Fall fans that he had no control over, the type of situation that he never enjoyed. Becoming 'unofficial' did little harm to the site and its forum; throughout the rest of the group's career, they remained at the centre of news and reviews about The Fall.

[8] Smith poached *The Fall Online*'s UK editor, Clayton Hayward, for a short-lived official site. Another official site was eventually created (*thefall.xyz*) which posted news about concerts and releases; its discussion forum, however, was rarely used.

In 2013, a new website emerged that was to offer a whole new level of Fall-related analysis. 'bzfgt'[9] is a philosophy teacher at a community college in New Jersey, where he was born and raised. A lifelong and passionate fan of The Grateful Dead, he didn't come across The Fall until 2010, when an acquaintance made him a 5-CD compilation of the group. He played it through twice, declared himself both overwhelmed and mystified, and then left it on a shelf for the next two years. In 2012, having completed his doctorate in philosophy, he decided to return to the compilation and listened to nothing else for two weeks. 'It was just as well my dissertation was finished,' he reflects, 'because after two weeks with these CDs in my car, I was not thinking about much else besides The Fall.'

Intrigued by the lyrics in particular, he began to frequent the *Fall Online Forum*, discovering that 'some of the mysteries found in The Fall's lyrics turn out to have simple explanations, whereas others remain inscrutable'. He decided that, for him, two factors underpinned the impenetrable nature of Smith's words: the cultural chasm between north-east America and north-west England, and the fact that some were simply 'downright abstruse'. As a 'Deadhead', he was familiar with David Dodd's site, *The Annotated Grateful Dead Lyrics*. 'It seemed clear to me,' he explains, 'that something of this nature was needed for the lyrics of The Fall.' And so, in 2013 — a year in which bzfgt listened to no music other than The Fall's — *The Annotated Fall* was born. The site is a sprawling labyrinth of analysis, research, philosophising and occasionally fanciful conjecture that has rapidly come to be regarded as one of the most important Fall resources. Although at the outset it was very much bzfgt's solo project, its growing strength — like *The Fall Online*'s gigography pages — comes from its ethos of community collaboration, a multitude of Fall fans chipping in with newly-discovered references from films, TV shows, books, poems and other songs.

The site's most regular contributor is 'dannyno', recognised

---

[9] There's no secret meaning to the name, it's just a random conglomeration of letters. Even bzfgt himself has no idea how it should be pronounced, although I'm probably not alone in rendering it as 'buzz-fidget'.

by Paul Hanley in *Have A Bleedin Guess* for his 'sterling detective work'. 'The editorial voice is mine,' bzfgt notes, 'but much of the legwork is Dan's.' A librarian by profession, Dan is not a record-collecting completist, and although a regular attendee at Fall gigs from 1990 onwards, is not one of those fans who followed the group around the country and saw hundreds of performances. 'My obsessions,' he explains, 'take a different form.' The form that they take is the application of his research skills to unearthing the most obscure details of The Fall's performance history and, in particular, the specific books, poems, TV shows, films, adverts, articles and other miscellaneous sources that inspired Smith's lyrics. Some of his more notable achievements include identifying the *Open University* episode that interrupts 'Paintwork' and the newspaper article about an obscure Catholic sect that informed the lyrics of 'Hostile'. His crowning achievement was tracking down the magazine article that Smith quotes in the 2000 song 'Dr. Bucks' Letter'. 'There's an obsessive madness to that twenty-year search,' he admits, 'but it was definitely worth it.'

Dan's excavations and those of many others mean that the collective Fall knowledge pool continues to grow. For the record, throughout this book, there are references to the number of gigs that The Fall played and how often each song was performed live. This is far from an exact science. There is occasionally some doubt – especially in the group's early years and with foreign tours – about precisely which performances took place. Moreover, discoveries are still being made regarding advertised concerts that never actually took place and gigs that were hitherto unknown. Regarding the number of occasions each song was played live, I can only refer to the number of known performances, as there are some gigs where there is no recording available; even where a copy of the setlist has survived, there can be no guarantee that this was the actual set of songs that were performed. Where there is doubt, I have gone with the number given on *The Track Record* as this is generally regarded as the most accurate source.

Although Mark E Smith died in 2018, the online community that obsess and argue about The Fall has barely diminished.

Fall-related Facebook groups such as *The Mighty Fall* and *It's not Repetition, it's Discipline* maintain healthy membership levels (nearly 7,000 each). Even in 2020, there was still sufficient appetite for Fall-related discussion to support the foundation of new platforms. Facebook group *HIP PRIESTS – every album by The Fall* was set up by Jonny Swift. Jonny, like many other casual Fall listeners, had always enjoyed what he'd heard, but was daunted by the sheer size and diversity of the group's back catalogue. 'The Fall were always a band I wanted to discover more of,' he explains, 'but it was a bit like having to clean your house – you don't know where to start so you just keep putting if off.' Seeing the 2020 COVID lockdown as his opportunity to address this, he set up a group that aimed to listen in depth to each of the albums a week at a time in order to understand the wider context of the group's history and development. 'For me,' he says, 'this project has been really life changing. A band that I liked and wanted to hear more of has turned into an obsession! I never knew the full extent of what an amazing band they were both lyrically and musically.'

This book is framed around the remarkable, diverse, frustrating, intriguing, uneven, inspiring and unique collection of records that The Fall released between 1978 and 2017.[10] It tells, I hope, a fascinating story whilst never losing sight of what matters: the amazing music that the group created over their 40-year career. None of this would have been possible without the talent, creativity and dedication of Mark E Smith and the extensive cast of musicians who played in The Fall. But it also owes a huge debt to those who posted gig reviews, scanned articles, noted references in films and TV shows or penned passionate defences or acerbic rebuttals; the people who go on caring about this crazy, unique group; those who feel, like dannyno, that 'it's difficult to overstate the significance of The Fall in my life; they are the air I breathe'.

---

[10] MES would, of course, have disapproved strongly of this approach. Speaking to Mick Middles about his book *The Fall*, Smith said 'I don't want it going from album to album… that would be so dull. Who would want to read that?'

Before The Witch Trials

*'There was something special going on there, but
nobody could quite put a finger on exactly what it was.'*

Mark Edward Smith was born on Tuesday 5th March 1957 in
Crumpsall Hospital,[11] the first child of Irene and John Edward
Smith. They would subsequently have three further children, all
girls: Barbara, Suzanne and Caroline. Smith grew up in Sedgley
Park in Prestwich, which became part of the Metropolitan Borough
of Bury, Greater Manchester in 1974. He attended Stand Grammar
School in Whitefield then enrolled at St John's College in 1973.
His college experience didn't last long: after three months he
dropped out and found employment at a meat factory and then as
a clerk at Manchester docks. Smith's girlfriend at the time was Una
Baines, who he had met at a fair in Heaton Park.[12] Baines, a student
psychiatric nurse at Prestwich Hospital, rented a flat on nearby
Kingswood Road, and before long Smith had moved in with her.

In 1975, the couple were introduced to two of Barbara's friends,
Martin Bramah (real name Martin Beddington) and Tony Friel,
both of whom had attended Heys Road Boys' secondary school in
Prestwich. The four of them, inspired by their love of The Velvet
Underground and The Stooges, became determined to form a
band. 'It started with me on guitar and reading poems,' Smith
described. 'Just as a hobby. That's where The Fall began. Me, a
guitar and a few scribbled words.' The roughly sketched line-up
for the as yet nameless group was Bramah on vocals, Smith on
guitar, Friel on bass and Baines on drums. Smith himself thought
Bramah the obvious choice for frontman, given his good looks
and charisma. Although the notion of forming a band was at the

---

[11] Although Smith frequently stated that he was born in Salford, Crumpsall had been
part of the City of Manchester since 1890.
[12] Several sources suggest that Smith and Baines attended St John's College together,
but according to MES (speaking to Mick Middles): 'I was working as a clerk... then
I went to St John's College for about three weeks, doing A-levels. Una wasn't there...
That just isn't true.'

heart of the foursome's discussions, a lot of the activity at the Kingswood Road flat revolved around drugs. Speed, LSD and mushrooms were the stimulants of choice – Smith claimed to have taken acid before he ever smoked cigarettes – but pot was dismissed as being 'for hippies'.

A lack of clear aims – and, more importantly, musical equipment – might have condemned their notion of forming a band to no more than an idle dream. Impetus, however, was provided in the summer of 1976 by the Sex Pistols. The Pistols' performance at Manchester's Lesser Free Trade Hall on 4th June 1976 was one of the most influential concerts in rock history, one that hundreds have claimed to have attended, even though it's likely that only around 40 actually did. The Buzzcocks' Howard Devoto and Pete Shelley (who organised the gig), Richard Boon (who would go on to be the Buzzcocks' manager), Morrissey, Bernard Sumner, Peter Hook and music journalist Paul Morley were there. It's not entirely clear whether Smith and co. attended this performance,[13] although they certainly were there when the Pistols returned to the same venue on 20th July, this time supported by Buzzcocks and Slaughter and the Dogs (a glam-influenced outfit from Wythenshawe who were one of the first punk bands to sign to a major label). Whilst the nascent Fall were pretty impressed with what they saw – Bramah even described himself as 'bowled over' – Smith was convinced that they could do better.

In practical terms, however, what the group needed more than anything else was a drummer. Una Baines did not have the means to buy a drum kit, and was unable to do any more than bash biscuit tins. So, with the aid of a bank loan, she ordered a 'Snoopy' keyboard instead.[14] The unlikely short-term solution to the drummer problem was a bald, Tory-supporting insurance salesman called Steve Ormrod. This obscure character from the

[13] Martin Bramah, speaking on the *Oh! Brother* podcast in July 2021, insisted that they did, although several other sources suggest otherwise.
[14] Manufactured by Italian company Elgam, the Snoopy had only three sounds and little sustain. On 28th May 1977 – around the time Baines ordered it – the instrument received a highly critical review from Julian Colbeck in *Sounds*. In the review (entitled 'Snoopy: a toy by name and nature') Colbeck declared that he 'fail[ed] to see who is likely to buy it'. He could only suggest 'a musical housewife who's living with her in-laws perhaps?'

group's early history was referred to as 'Dave' for many years, the only known fact about him being that he had offered the group a pro-Tory song called 'Landslide Victory', unsurprisingly never played. However, in 2010, whilst researching his book *The Fallen*, journalist Dave Simpson unearthed the mystery drummer's identity. Ormrod, who had been sectioned in the early 90s, committed suicide in 1994.

Smith's inability to learn the guitar led to him and Bramah swapping roles. Another issue was what to call the group. The first choice was The Outsiders, taken from the Albert Camus novel *L'Étranger*. Finding that this name was already taken, they switched to another Camus title, *La Chute (The Fall)*. Tony Friel has indicated that this was his idea; Smith claimed at least some of the credit.

> It was me and Tony who decided to call it The Fall... He wanted to call it The Outsiders at first... but I'd read *The Outsider* and didn't particularly like it. I thought *The Fall* was a better book. But for a period of time we were The Outsiders until I found a seven-inch... by a 60s band called The Outsiders... So that meant we were The Fall.[15]

It was, as Simon Ford comments, a perfect fit for the new group:

> Simple, distinctive and evocative of the withering social and moral critiques that would come to define Smith's lyric writing... The high-brow literary connections instantly set the group apart from the many... joke and ephemeral 'punk' names such as the Vibrators and Ed Banger and the Nosebleeds.

This distancing of The Fall from the contemporary punk/ new wave scene was from the outset a crucial part of the group's identity. Smith never saw The Fall as part of 'the whole punk thing' – 'Simple fact: we weren't a punk band.' In *Renegade*, he

---

[15] Smith's memories are confused. Whilst there was a UK group called The Outsiders (who released two albums in the late 70s), the single that he goes on to mention, 'A Question of Temperature', was actually a 1967 release by New Jersey garage-psych outfit The Balloon Farm.

identified this as a factor behind the group's longevity. Punk was short-term attention-grabbing: 'When you're dealing in slogans like The Clash and The Pistols it's hard to keep that shit fresh.'

In December 1976, Smith drafted a potential setlist for the group's first performance. The set ('approx 47 minutes') included a handful of soon to be recorded originals ('Psycho Mafia', 'Frightened', 'Repetition') as well as several covers (The Stooges' 'Not Right', 'Louie Louie', 'Brand New Cadillac' and 'You're Driving Me Insane', a pre-Velvet Underground Lou Reed song recorded by The Roughnecks). 'Drugs Or Something' – according to Bramah, 'just a mantra sung over a "Waiting For The Man" hammered piano drone' – was never recorded or performed. Other ideas that never saw the light of day included 'Outsiders', 'Don't Think About It', 'Chile's Dead' and 'Coupla Punks'.

Theory was first put into practice on 23rd May 1977. Dick Witts, a percussionist with the Hallé Orchestra, and Trevor Wishart, composer-in-residence for North-West Arts Association, had established the Manchester Musicians' Collective in early 1977. It aimed to support local bands through sharing equipment and providing a venue at the NWAA basement at King Street on Monday nights. Tony Friel made contact with Witts to organise the first Fall gig. The venue itself was an unusual one. Friel remembers it being 'like a fashionable restaurant in the late 1970s, with everything white. It was done out like a small white cave. Mark and Martin, who were taller than the others, had to kneel down because of the low ceiling.' Una Baines was still without an instrument to play, so watched from the audience, which mainly consisted of other musicians. Steve Ormrod made his solitary appearance. The other acts that played were, Smith remembered, 'a socialist brass band... and a guy who made symphonies out of bird noises' (this latter act was probably Trevor Wishart). The Fall's set included 'Hey! Fascist', 'Bingo Master's Breakout' and 'Repetition'. It also featured the only ever performance of simplistic rant 'Race Hatred'.[16] Contemporary accounts focus

---

[16] 'What yer gonna do when the blacks get you / What yer gonna do when the P*kis get you / What yer gonna do when the chinks get you / What yer gonna do when the commies break through / Yeah, race hatred...'

on the intensity of Smith's performance. Bramah described how Smith 'just sort of reached into the audience and virtually poked his finger up Howard Devoto's nose'.[17] According to Witts, Smith 'howled the place down... There was something special going on there, but nobody could quite put a finger on exactly what it was.' Martin Bramah remembers the gig being taped, but given that no recording has emerged in over 40 years this seems unlikely.

Steve Ormrod was clearly no more than a temporary stopgap. His replacement, Karl Burns, had been in a band called Nuclear Angel with Bramah and Friel and was a talented drummer and guitarist. Persuaded by Bramah to join The Fall, he made his debut on 3rd June at The Squat on Devas Street in Manchester. This was a 'Stuff the Jubilee' festival at which The Fall played alongside local punk bands The Drones and The Worst as well as Warsaw, soon to become Joy Division. Una Baines, now equipped with her new keyboard, played the national anthem.

During the summer of 1977, The Fall recorded three tracks that would first see the light of day on the bootleg single *Rehearsal Early '77 (Vol.1)*. Released in 1987 on Total Eclipse Records, this 7" is often described as a 'home recording', but it's more likely that it was recorded in a rehearsal room. A-side 'Dresden Dolls' ('Dresdon Dolls' on the label) is a jagged, mid-paced lope with a hint of reggae that sees Smith sneer at fashion-conscious punks: 'on plastic bars they sit and pose'. The B-side, described on the label as 'More songs from the front parlour', contained rough but enthusiastic takes of 'Psycho Mafia' and 'Industrial Estate'.

In what would turn out to be a significant moment in the group's history, that summer also saw Kay Carroll became part of The Fall circle. Carroll, born in 1948, had grown up in North Manchester and married young. When her marriage broke down, she began a career in nursing, studying at Prestwich Hospital. This brought her into contact with Una Baines, and when Carroll split up with her boyfriend (another fellow nurse) she began to

---

[17] Several accounts suggest that the Buzzcocks were present at The Fall's debut gig, which seems unlikely as they were on tour supporting The Clash at the time. However, the gig they were scheduled to play on the 23rd (in Stafford) was cancelled, so it's not impossible. Devoto had left the band in February, so it is certainly plausible that he was there.

spend a substantial amount of time at the Kingswood Road flat. By the end of the year, Baines and Smith had separated and he and Carroll became a couple.

Details about early Fall gigs are a little sketchy, but they had probably played around a dozen times by the time they appeared at The Electric Circus on 2nd October 1977. The Electric Circus was a venue in Collyhurst, north-east Manchester. It opened in October 1976, but only lasted a year before being forced to close due to pressure from the local council and the fire service. This weekend bill included Warsaw, The Worst, Buzzcocks and the debut appearance of Howard Devoto's new band Magazine. Two tracks from The Fall's set, 'Stepping Out' and 'Last Orders', became the first of their songs to be released on record. Both are relatively melodic pacey thrashes, the prominence of Baines's discordant keyboards steering them clear of a predictable punk sound. They also contain two of the group's most straightforward lyrics. The play on words in 'Last Orders' sees the usual meaning of 'closing time' being subverted as Smith declares that he's not going to be told what to do any more.[18] The optimistic tone of 'Stepping Out' ('I used to stay in the house and never go out / but now I'm stepping out') represented the positive flipside to the dark paranoia of 'Frightened', which would go on to open the group's debut album.[19]

The Fall's first experience of studio recording came on 9th November 1977. Richard Boon financed the session, which took place at Indigo Studios on Manchester's Gartside Street. Housed in crumbling Georgian building full of 'tawdry lo-fi teak', it had been the venue for the recording of the Buzzcocks' era-defining *Spiral Scratch* EP 11 months earlier. The Fall recorded four tracks, although one ('Frightened') was never released.[20] Smith later admitted to being 'fucking terrified' about the experience, and

---

[18] In a 2006 interview, Tony Friel claimed to have written most of the lyric, MES adding 'a few lines'.

[19] At the Tower Club, Oldham on 21st August 1978 (the performance captured on the 2005 release *Live From The Vaults – Oldham 1978*), Smith introduced 'Stepping Out' as 'a sequel to the last one' ('Frightened').

[20] A 2007 4-CD punk compilation, *Babylon's Burning – The Rough'n'Ready Rise Of PUNK RAWK 1973-1978* (which also contained 'Repetition' and 'Bingo-Master') included 'Frightened (1st E.P. Outtake)', but this is in fact just the album version.

did not enjoy being 'completely at the mercy of the engineers'. Although his retrospective account is obviously coloured by hindsight, he was already starting to adopt the attitude to the studio process that would inform his whole career:

> The fact was we were paying them, they were working for us and they had no right to cock a fucking sneer at us... You have to make that clear from the start when you go in a recording studio. You have to know what you want, in terms of raw sound, and simply go for it... You are in charge. It's your sound. If they want to use high levels of technology, then fine... just as long as it all leads to the sound that you have in your head.

Towards the end of 1977, Kay Carroll became The Fall's manager. Smith's friend, music journalist Mick Middles commented that, 'The first I knew about this was following a... gig at St John's College, Manchester [16th December] after which Mark stated... "Kay is now the manager and things will change".' One of the first performances with her at the helm took place at Stretford Civic Theatre on 23rd December – a 'Rock Against Racism' benefit. Whilst sympathetic to RAR's cause, even at this early stage of the group's career Smith was already uneasy about being too closely aligned with any political movement. Earlier that year, the *NME*'s Tony Parsons and Julie Burchill had approached the group to offer them a front cover with the headline 'The band that stands against the National Front'. After travelling to London with Carroll to meet the duo, Smith turned down the opportunity: 'I could see very clearly that they were going to use this band, y'know, chew'em up, spit'em out.'

The support acts at Stretford were John Cooper Clarke and The Worst; Piccadilly Radio's Roger Day was the DJ.[21] The promoter, RAR's Bernie Wilcox, recalled the venue's bar manager ignoring his advice to use plastic glasses. 'When The Fall came on someone slung a pint pot over at Mark. Then everyone else slung their pots

---

[21] Day, a rather unlikely choice for the event, had previously worked on Radio Caroline and Radio Luxembourg. Three years later, Smith referred to him in a performance of 'The N.W.R.A.'.

over and we had to close the safety curtain, but The Fall carried on playing behind it, good lads that they were.' The Stretford gig would prove to be a notable one. Firstly, it was to be Friel's last performance, the bassist's departure being announced somewhat sarcastically before the final song, 'Louie Louie'.[22] His decision to leave was largely a reaction to Carroll's increasing influence on the group: 'Mark got me in to fuck off Friel,' she confessed, 'and it worked.' After issuing a 'her or me' ultimatum, Friel left to form The Passage with Dick Witts.[23] The second notable thing about this performance is that it is the earliest known full recording of a Fall gig. Chris Hewitt (the organiser of the Deeply Vale festivals, at which the group would perform the following year) was in charge of the PA and gave Bernie Wilcox a recording of the gig on a C90 which he eventually passed on to Smith. According to Wilcox, 'Years later, [Smith] found it at the bottom of his wardrobe.' It received an official release in 2000 as *Live 1977*.[24]

To say that the *Live 1977* is lo-fi is an understatement. Friel's bass is often inaudible, and Baines's keyboards make only sporadic appearances. The other instrumentation is at points little more than a harsh, homogeneous buzz. Throughout, the vocals are startlingly overloaded and distorted and frequently dominate, but they do capture the intensity and aggression as well as the sarcastic humour of Smith's delivery. The first sound you hear is the alarmingly raw, primal scream that introduces 'Psycho Mafia'. It's closely followed by MES uttering the phrase with which he would introduce every performance over the next four decades: 'Good evening, we are The Fall'. Here, he follows it up with a tarot reference, 'the ace of ones'. (Smith claimed to be an accomplished tarot reader: 'When people did a tarot with me they'd walk away with their life changed... I got quite a reputation for it.')

Even if The Fall were avowedly not a punk band, Bramah's

---

[22] MES: 'This is the bass player's last gig. Give him a round of applause.' Bramah: 'It's like losing your left leg.'

[23] The highlight of the band's brief career was reaching number 41 in John Peel's Festive Fifty in 1982.

[24] The front cover says *Live 1977*; everywhere else on the release the title is given as *Live 77*. Song titles given here are as spelled on the sleeve.

remonstration with the audience at the end of the first song shows that some of those attending thought they were a punk audience: 'Will you stop fucking spitting, you stupid bastards!' Smith is a little more sanguine. Over Friel's intro to 'Last Orders', he remarks sardonically, 'the spit in the sky falls in your eye...' The line is adapted from a Jamaican proverb, 'pit inna de sky, it fall inna yuh y'eye', meaning that your actions can be the cause of your own downfall. This is one of only four known live performances of the song. Friel, perhaps a little demob-happy, sneaks in a little bass solo at the end of which Smith doubtless disapproved. Another rarely-heard track – this was one of only three known performances (although there may possibly have been a fourth) – 'Dresden Dolls' is a little sluggish here, despite Burns's energetic fills.

Despite the nature of the event, Smith has little to say between songs about racism beyond a couple of remarks about National Front leader John Tyndall. One of these ('he thinks we are jungle negro music'[25]) comes in the introduction to 'Hey Fascist'. Presumably the song that attracted the attention of Parsons and Burchill, its aggressive lyric ('you're gonna get it through the head... I pick up a knife, I flip my lid') represents the type of direct political message that Smith soon abandoned. As early as 1978, he stated that 'I don't write songs like that anymore. We've done our bit for the left.' Originally titled 'Hey! Student',[26] Smith claimed that the change in title was because it had 'become very trendy to bash students', although the fact that students made up an increasingly substantial proportion of The Fall's audience at the time must also have been a factor. 'Stepping Out' is the one moment where the group sound slightly hesitant and awkward. The notion that it was some sort of sequel to 'Frightened' is reinforced here by an extra verse that includes the line 'I'm not frightened any more'. The spitting was evidently still going on. 'We have mouth trouble at the front of the stage,' Smith drawls, 'our saliva cannot be kept in its mouth.' The glasses were clearly

---

[25] Whilst you can't imagine any artist performing at an anti-racist event these days using the word 'negro', the sarcastic intent is perfectly clear here – more so than is the case with 'The Classical' (see Chapter 5).

[26] It would be revived under its original name 17 years later (see Chapter 17).

also flying around during a breakneck 'Industrial Estate', although Smith seems more offended by the waste of alcohol than the throwing: 'You must have plenty of money, you lot, the amount of fucking beer you're throwing over 'ere. If you don't want your drink, just give it me.'

Bramah's guitar is conspicuously out of tune from 'Frightened' onwards, but you frequently can't distinguish it from the shapeless overall noise anyway. The second half is not without historical interest, however, featuring two tracks that made their debut that night but then wouldn't be performed again for several years. 'Cop It' has the stronger melody of the two. 'Oh Brother' (introduced by MES as 'pop music for today's people; the same fried egg') would go on to be one of the group's lightest, poppiest tracks; here, it's rather a tuneless dirge, and has an ending that sounds distinctly under-rehearsed. The other notable track is the finale, a cover of 'Louie Louie'. Featuring vocals from John the Postman,[27] it rapidly descends into an unholy mess. By this stage, the sound quality has plummeted to the very depths of hell; it sounds as if the participants are taking turns trying to actually ingest the microphone.

The Fall's back catalogue is littered with poorly recorded live albums, but in terms of sonic fidelity, *Live 1977* undoubtedly rates as one of the worst. It's most definitely not an LP to play to the recently initiated (it might put them off for life), but it does provide some interesting context for those already immersed. It is an invaluable record of one the group's earliest incarnations, and captures a moment – one of what would prove to be many – where a key member left The Fall.

[27] Jonathan Ormrod (known as both Jon and John the Postman) was a well-known figure on the punk scene in Manchester in the late 70s. His first public appearance came at a Buzzcocks gig at Manchester's Band on the Wall in May 1977 when he spontaneously jumped on stage after the final song and sang an a cappella version of 'Louie Louie'. His first album, *John the Postman's Puerile*, was released on 17th June. It opened with a 13-minute version of 'Louie Louie' that featured a spoken introduction by MES – Smith's first appearance on a record.

Live At The Witch Trials
Recorded: Camden, London, 15th-16th December 1978
Released: 16th March 1979

Personnel:
Mark E Smith – vocals, guitar ('Live At The Witch Trials'), tapes ('Music Scene')
Martin Bramah – guitar, backing vocals
Marc Riley – bass
Karl Burns – drums
Yvonne Pawlett – keyboards

Chapter 1: Live At The Witch Trials

'You can dance to it and pretend it's avant-garde.'

Articles about The Fall often emphasise the 'revolving door' nature of the group's line-up, often forgetting the periods where they enjoyed relative stability. Nonetheless, it is true that by the time you get to their debut album, The Fall were on version six of their line-up. Tony Friel's replacement, Jonnie Brown, only lasted a couple of weeks (the group having discovered that his unreliability was due to his heroin habit) before he was replaced by Eric 'The Ferret' McGann. McGann's nickname came from his previous involvement in a band called The Ferrets; his real name was Anthony McGann and he also went by the name Rick Goldstraw. Brown's most notable contribution to the group was the drawing that featured on the cover of their first EP, *Bingo-Master's Break-Out!* The Smith / Bramah / Brown / Baines / Burns line-up played the first Fall gig of 1978, at Huddersfield Polytechnic on 13th January. A poor-quality bootleg recording exists that features the sole performance of 'You Don't Turn Me On', written by Bramah and Baines. Less than 30 seconds of the song are captured, a fairly bog-standard three-chord thrash. Danny Baker's review of the gig described 'Repetition' as 'one of the greatest songs I've ever witnessed. Simple as that.'

Later that year, Una Baines left the group. She'd had a brief, torrid relationship with Brown, and suffered a drug-induced nervous breakdown. Her last gig with the group was in Manchester on 30th April, where she simply stood and stared at her keyboards. She was replaced by Yvonne Pawlett, who had advertised her services as a pianist in the *NME*. Her first gig was in Croydon on 7th May, where The Fall supported Siouxsie and the Banshees. Smith was unimpressed by the headliners: 'They're all art students. They come from nice families and they put on this fucking rebellious... con, and they all pretend they are working class and

33

it's all really funny.' A week later, The Fall supported John Cooper Clarke at London's Goldsmith's College. The *NME*'s Geoff Hill described them as 'a conventional new wave outfit – loud, cumbersome... [I] thought a Boeing had crash-landed... [Smith's vocals] make Arthur Mullard sound like Julie Andrews'.

At the end of May, the group recorded the first of what was to become a record-breaking series of Peel sessions. Peel's close friend and long-serving producer John Waters had invited them to record for the show after attending the Croydon gig. For the session, Smith recruited an extra musician. Conga player Steve Davies was a Prestwich resident, had been in the navy, done time in prison and 'wasn't a usual Faller'. Marc Riley, a roadie for The Fall at the time, suggested that Smith recruited him in order to increase the BBC's session fee, although the fact that he owned the van that transported the group to Maida Vale is possibly more pertinent. His involvement led to yet another line-up change. McGann, offended by Davies's Hawaiian shirt and perturbed by the prospect of him playing congas on the session, declined to travel. As a result, Bramah played both guitar and bass on the session. He performed the guitar parts with the rest of the group, then – on a bass guitar borrowed from Tony Friel – overdubbed the bass.[28] On all four songs – 'Rebellious Jukebox', 'Mother-Sister!', 'Industrial Estate' and 'Futures And Pasts' – the group's level of casual confidence is striking, especially considering that they'd only played around 30 gigs at this point and this was only their second experience of studio recording. The songs are exuberant, bursting with energy, yet sharp and precise. In general, they weren't radically different from the versions that would appear on their debut album, although on 'Rebellious Jukebox' the vocals are treated with rather unnecessary reverb; this is also the song where Davies's congas are most audible.

Following McGann's exit, 16-year-old Marc Riley became the new bass player. Riley had been in a band called The Sirens with schoolmates Steve Hanley and Craig Scanlon. They only ever played one gig, at Pips, a venue on Fennel Street near Manchester

---

[28] Despite his left-handedness, Bramah didn't re-string Friel's bass, he simply played it upside down.

Cathedral where Warsaw had made their debut. They had met The Fall at T. J. Davidson's, a rehearsal space also used by Joy Division, and, at Kay Carroll's invitation, had become unofficial roadies. 'One day I invited them to come and help us load and unload the equipment,' she told Simon Ford, 'after that they just ended up coming to lots of gigs… and they would roadie. We couldn't pay them much… but God did they work hard for us.'

In June 1978, the October 1977 recordings of 'Stepping Out' and 'Last Orders' appeared on *Short Circuit – Live At The Electric Circus*, an eight-track 10" released on Virgin that also included tracks from Joy Division, Steel Pulse and Buzzcocks. While reviews of the release as a whole were mixed (*Sounds'* Jon Savage thought it 'disgustingly shoddy') The Fall's contribution was singled out for praise: Savage felt it exhibited 'signs of greatness to come'; the *NME* called it 'intense, promising and defiant'. Two months later, the Indigo sessions from the previous November finally saw the light of day. Richard Boon, who had paid for the studio time, had intended to release them on his New Hormones label, but had found it impossible owing to the increasing demands on his time caused by the rising popularity of Buzzcocks. When the recordings were finally released, it was by Step-Forward, a label that had been founded by Miles Copeland III. Copeland, as well as being the brother of Police drummer Stewart, was the son of a CIA officer and a British intelligence agent and had started his first label BTM in 1974. 'It was Danny Baker, actually, who got us that deal,' Smith explained. 'He had seen us at that Huddersfield gig. He was the one who went in and told Miles Copeland that he should release this record by The Fall.' The deal with Step-Forward prioritised independence over financial reward. Kay Carroll 'refused large amounts of money from any record contracts… I didn't want to be beholden to anyone'. She claimed, for example, that Virgin had offered the group £26k on the condition that they re-recorded Friel's bass part. 'The trade-off,' as she put it, 'was total creative control.' This included the choice of studio and producer, press releases, advertising and artwork. Carroll also ensured that publishing rights to the songs would revert to the group after a fixed period of time.

Bingo-Master's Break-Out! was released on 11th August. The almost–title track ('Bingo-Master' on the sleeve; 'Bingo Master' on the label) opens with a hesitantly plodding bass drum but soon launches into a hectic, staccato riff. According to the press release that accompanied the EP, this was only track from this session that received a second take, the 'mis/tuned guitar being a deliberate rejection of the 1st take which was much more melodic'. It suggests too that 'the lyrics tell a good story also'. The tale in question is that of a depressed bingo caller: bored of reading out 'numbers that rhyme [to a] hundred blank faces', he has a breakdown and ends his life 'with wine and pills'.[29] 'Psycho Mafia', one of the few Fall songs to give Friel a writing credit, takes a sharp adrenalin-rush approach. Baines's keyboard work in particular distinguishes it from the punk herd, although Smith's vocals see him come as close as he ever would to aping John Lydon. Bramah's single–chord 'solo' towards the end sees him – not for the last time – give a nod to The Velvet Underground. The press release stated that it 'started out as a tribute to a local street–gang, but on completion of the lyrics, it took on a sinister aura – an aura of oppression, a sort of sub-conscious manifestation of events which were happening around the writer at the time'.[30]

The final track, 'Repetition', was influenced by Smith's interactions with psychiatric patients. When Smith and Baines lived next to Prestwich Hospital, they would occasionally invite patients to their flat for a cup of tea ('sit them down, play them some rock and roll, a bit of telly. Sometimes I think I did more good than all the nurses put together'). Smith explained that the lyric ('mental hospitals / they put electrodes in your brain / and you'll never be the same') was about those on 'heavy downers' such as Largactil and Mandrax. Perhaps a more notable

---

[29] The line 'holiday in Spain fell through' possibly refers to John Goodall. In May 1974, the *Daily Mail* reported that Goodall, who was working as a bingo caller at a hotel on the Costa Brava, was arrested by Spanish detectives in relation to a bank robbery.
[30] In *Renegade*, Smith describes being 'into causing trouble, forming gangs and things like that. I used to have a few – Psycho Mafia, the Barry Boy gang. We'd fight other gangs. It was quite interesting; there used to be Irish gangs and Orthodox Jewish gangs. But the Psycho Mafia was a real melting pot, and I was the vice president.'

aspect of the song, however, was its identification of what was to become a cornerstone of the group's philosophy: 'The three "R"s – Repetition, Repetition, Repetition'. 'Repetition' is, however, actually a loose-limbed and light-hearted lope, its sardonic humour most clearly expressed in the sneering parody of Richard Hell and the Voidoids' 'Blank Generation'. The press release called it 'an instant converter – there is a point in the song where every body gets into it, a turning point from non-interest to mass hypnosis'. Although *Sounds'* Vivien Goldman enjoyed 'Repetition', he described the other two tracks as 'hideous'. The *NME* and *Melody Maker* were more positive, the latter describing the EP as 'amazing'.

There are three official live releases that capture the group's performances in the summer of 1978. *Live At Deeply Vale*, released in 2005, is a recording of their first performance at an outdoor festival, at which Smith first met Grant Showbiz, at that time the soundman for space-rockers and Gong collaborators Here & Now. The Free People's Festival took place over six days (20th-25th July) with The Fall playing on Saturday the 22nd – a 'New Wave' day compèred by Tony Wilson. Other acts billed on the day included The Durutti Column and Alternative TV. Accounts estimate attendance at anywhere between 3,000 and 20,000. According to one, it was a less than friendly scene: 'Hell's Angels drove through the middle of the site on motorbikes and generally behaved aggressively. Looking into people's tents, looking for Punks to beat up. Police turned up on site. Things got a bit threatening.' The sound on *Deeply Vale* is horribly tinny and features a layer of hiss that suggests it's from a second or third-generation tape. Its most interesting feature is the brief medley of studio outtakes ('Psycho Mafia', 'Dresden Dolls' and 'Industrial Estate') tacked onto the end.[31] *Liverpool 78*, released in 2001, was recorded at Mr Pickwick's on 22nd August. It's only marginally better in terms of sound quality: most of the time, the bass is ludicrously prominent and the drums are almost non-existent. The pick of the three is

[31] It was re-released (with this medley omitted and two extra live tracks included) for Record Store Day in 2016 as *Bingo Masters At The Witch Trials*, featuring what is arguably the worst Fall album cover of all time (see Appendix 3).

Live From The Vaults – Oldham 1978, recorded at the Tower Club the night before the Liverpool gig and released in 2005. Bramah's playing is expansive and exuberant, especially on 'Frightened' and a lengthy 'Repetition'. The introduction to 'Music Scene' (unfortunately cut off in its prime) sees an interesting exchange between Smith and Bramah: 'Mark's just putting his make-up on, it slipped in the heat, y'know'; 'Thank you Martin – man of the people. The next one is "Music Scene": you asked for this, ten minutes of this at least.'

September saw The Fall play their first London date as headliners, at the Marquee on the 8th. They were supported by Bristol band Gardez Darkx and the admission price was 75p. The following day, they recorded what was to be their second release at Surrey Sound Studios, a converted dairy in Leatherhead. 'It's The New Thing' was released in November. A cynical swipe at the shallowness of the music business ('phoney advertising quotes that make you buy some / raise your hopes'), 'New Thing' is centred around Pawlett's off-kilter keyboards and Bramah's scrabbling guitar. The 'crash, smash' elbows-on-the-keyboard breakdowns give it a refreshingly original and brash quality. It was only played live 17 times (possibly 18), all in 1978 and 1979. Although The Fall's output up to this point had already indicated that they were far from just another punk/new wave band, B-side 'Various Times' was arguably the first sign of just how different from their contemporaries they were. Here, they maintain a dark, aggressive tone throughout, and there's a carefully controlled balance between the relentless three-note bassline, the skittering guitar and Burns's flamboyant yet tight drumming. It's also an intriguing lyric. Divided into three sections (past / present / future), it's narrated by a disillusioned German WW2 prison guard, a 'No Man' who despairs of his contemporaries ('everyone I meet's the same now / no brains or thought') and a dystopian future character who complains 'the beer is so weak' and, mysteriously, how 'they got rid of time around here'. It's an incredibly intense and accomplished piece for a group this early in their career.

A mere six months after their BBC debut, The Fall returned to Maida Vale for their second Peel session, recorded on 27th

November and broadcast nine days later. 'No Xmas For John Quays' and 'Like To Blow' are fairly similar to their album counterparts. 'Put Away', however, is rather different from the version that would eventually appear on *Dragnet* (see Chapter 2). The highlight of the session was 'Mess Of My'. Written by Eric the Ferret, its transitions give it an almost prog-like feel, and like 'Various Times' clearly marked the group out as much more inventive and experimental than many of their peers. Live, the introductory line, 'A note of your own choice, boys and girls' was usually followed by discordant cacophony, as the musicians did exactly as instructed; on the Peel version, however, they found themselves randomly in harmony with each other. 'I remember Mark looking round at us thinking that we'd engineered this,' Marc Riley said, 'but we hadn't!' 'Mess Of My' was performed 15 times 1978-79, but never received another studio recording.

Live At The Witch Trials

The group recorded their debut album in Camden Town Suite on the 15-16th December. They had originally been booked into the studio for five days, but as Smith was ill, they spent the first three recuperating from their recent Scottish dates supporting Here & Now. Smith had visited a doctor because he'd lost his voice. 'He had a sore throat,' Bramah explained, 'the doctor said it was psychosomatic. Which meant there was nothing wrong with him, he was just nervous.' Simon Ford suggests that Smith wasn't the only one suffering, describing the whole group as 'exhausted, sick and half-starved'. All of the tracks were recorded on the 15th, and the album was mixed the day after by Bob Sargeant, who had also produced the group's second Peel session. The stark, monochrome cover was provided by John Wriothesley.

Frightened

An intense, creepy account of drug-related paranoia ('amphetamine frightened'), in which Smith captures vividly the effects of speed: 'I'm in a trance / and I sweat'; 'I look to the sky / my lips are dry'. The reference to 'the time when I was sixteen' is explained by his claim that he wrote it at that age; Smith's curious pronunciation of 'faeces' ('fay-sees') is less explicable. The menacing tone of the music matches the theme perfectly, Bramah's prickly guitar seeming to climb the studio walls. It's a bold choice for album opener, especially given that the track that followed it seemed custom-built for the role, but then not doing the obvious thing came to be one of the defining characteristics of The Fall. After being played 16 times in 1977–78, it was dropped from the set for over a year, before being given two (possibly three) further outings in early 1980. According to Paul Hanley, this was because Tony Friel had been claiming in the music press that he'd written the song, and Smith wanted to point out that the 'Frightened' riff was actually derived from '(I'm Not Your) Steppin' Stone'.[32]

Crap Rap 2/Like To Blow

A more obvious choice for opening track, given the clear statement of intent of 'Crap Rap' – not just the oft-quoted 'we are The Fall / northern white crap that talks back', but perhaps even more pertinently, 'no boxes for us'. There are occasions on *Witch Trials* where the 'zooming' of Burns's drums between the stereo channels verges on a distraction, but here it adds to the air of chaos that is brought abruptly into sharp focus by the staccato 'sucker...' intro. The sharp, lurching riff of 'Like To Blow' is full of lop-sided vigour although the chorus flirts with predictability. The concise lyric captures the drug-fogged existence of a 'happy no-hoper' living 'on snacks; potatoes in packs'. 'Blow' didn't last long on the setlist, its twelfth and final performance coming the day after the album was recorded. On stage, variations on 'Crap Rap' popped up in several later songs, although the resemblance was often limited to the 'northern white crap' phrase. It was last spotted in February 1981 at Queen Mary's College in London.

Rebellious Jukebox

A cleaner, crisper take than the Peel session version, shorn of the congas and excessive vocal reverb. 'Jukebox' is the poppiest and

---

[32] 'And if you dissect the riff of this song, you'll find it's "Steppin' Stone" slowed down.' (MES, Birmingham University, 18th March 1980.)

most straightforwardly new wave song on the album – it's perhaps surprising that it didn't become a single. The lyric seems to be narrated by a sentient jukebox ('I sidled up to a fruit machine'). Played live around 30 times, 1978-80, it got a surprise one-off revival in 2009 (see Chapter 28).

No Xmas For John Quays

An intriguing intro finds Smith explaining the word 'Xmas' ('the X... is a substitute crucifix for Christ') over Pawlett's sparse keyboards. Bramah's oddly discordant riff was allegedly written by Smith on a plastic toy guitar. In a 1979 interview, Smith described the song as 'anti-drugs': 'there was this guy – not called John Quays – who just kept wanting things. It's about him really. He was a real bastard.' It stayed in the set until 1982, was dropped for 17 years, and then appeared four more times – once each in 1999, 2007, 2008 and 2014.

Mother-Sister!

The verse is based around a straightforward three-chord keyboard part written by Una Baines (who received a songwriting credit) augmented by an astringent guitar riff – 'I was trying to make it Beefheart, more angular' – courtesy of Bramah (who didn't). The off-kilter reggae-ish verse makes an interesting contrast to the aggressive chorus. It was played only eight times, all in 1978. Despite the opening exchange – 'err, what's this song about? / err, nothing' – according to Martin Bramah, the lyric is about his mother:

> I grew up with my mum... when I was younger, I lived with my gran, and I'd see my mum at weekends. They'd tell me that this was quite common then, in Manchester in those days, in the sixties. But for kids who didn't know who the father was, they'd say your gran was your mum, and your mum was your sister, and your great-gran was your gran, et cetera... they'd move the generation up a notch to explain the lack of a father. So when I was young, I thought my gran was my mum, because that's who I lived with, and I thought my mum was my sister.

Industrial Estate
Harsh guitar harmonics, aggressive string-bending and Burns's thunderous drums make for a striking introduction. Bramah's caustic riff and Pawlett's metronomic keyboard provide what Smith described as a 'Stooges without the third chord' backing for his 'hard poem' about working-class life on the docks. Whilst the song has an undoubted aggressive energy, it doesn't quite hit the 'American rocky' sound Smith was aiming for; the repeated deadpan 'yeah, yeah' refrain in particular makes 'Industrial Estate' the Fall song that could most easily slot into a British punk compilation alongside Sham 69 and the Angelic Upstarts. That said, there's a hint of sardonic irony in Smith and Bramah's vocal delivery that sets them apart from Jimmy Pursey et al.[33] Played 13 times in 1977–78, it got a three-gig revival in April 1998.

Underground Medecin
The opening finds a double-tracked MES deploying the type of unusual emphasis ('under-*ground* medi-*sun*) that would be a career-long trademark. The references to 'medicine', 'the nervous system' and the 'spark inside [that] hits the mind' suggests another drug-related lyric. Smith also alludes to the medical issues that delayed the recording: 'I had a psychosomatic voice.' The motive behind quoting religious standard 'I Believe' ('every time I hear a new baby cry') is not as clear. It's just as brisk as 'Industrial Estate' (both only just make it past the two-minute mark) but is much less traditionally structured, scampering about in all sorts of unexpected directions. Bramah's guitar work, an explosive blues-garage-punk-surf-rock hybrid, is a particular highlight. Played live 13 times, its last performance was in November 1980.

Two Steps Back
A distinct change of pace, 'Two Steps Back' is a stealthy, menacing prowl: Burns and Riley are measured and understated, giving

---

[33] The chorus also brings to mind Jilted John's eponymous single. Released in 1978 and featuring the famous 'Gordon is a moron' chant, it was itself a light-hearted pastiche of contemporary British punk. Jilted John was Graham Fellows, who went on to have a well-regarded career as comedy character John Shuttleworth.

Bramah free rein to let loose with spiky bursts of guitar that once again demonstrates a Velvet Underground influence. The lyric suggests that the drugs mentioned ('I don't need the acid factories / I've got mushrooms in the fields') were sold to the group by Julian Cope[34] – 'Julian said "How was the gear?"'. Cope was delighted by the reference but denies ever supplying the group with drugs: 'Although Mark and I talked a lot about drugs in a purely theoretical sense, I was actually very straight-edge at the time. So I never sold him anything. I'm sorry if that's disappointing.' The song was played live 13 times, all in 1978-79.

Live At The Witch Trials
The first in a long line of experimental interludes that would come to be a regular feature of Fall albums. There's not much to it, less than a minute's worth of guitar noodling over which Smith talks about his belief in the 'R and R dream'. The line 'R and R as primal scream' was the inspiration behind the band Primal Scream's name, Bobby Gillespie commenting that the phrase was 'punk and post-punk, and therefore perfect'. Interviewed a month after the LP's release, Smith said that he regretted including the track: 'It came over more serious than I thought it would. But it's true. I still believe in a kind of purity, that we come from a long line of people who've tried to do things like that – like Gene Vincent – people who were in rock'n'roll 'n' doing it well but whose attitude was different.'

Futures And Pasts
'Futures And Pasts' sees the group return to full-throttle aggression, led by Bramah's slashing chords. Although the chord progression is a tad obvious, the variations in tempo give it an innovative, unpredictable feel. It is, however, the most notable example of the over-fussy production of Burns's drumming, which lurches between the channels in an unnecessarily distracting fashion. The 'lousy lives' and 'ugly face lines' of the middle-aged couple echo

[34] Cope, like Ian McCulloch, was a loyal supporter of the group at the time. Kay Carroll described the pair as 'really good friends... [they] would just start helping us with the gear without me even asking...'

the grim existence of the workers in 'Industrial Estate'. It didn't last long on the setlist, not being performed after 1978 and failing to reach double figures.

Music Scene

Although echoes of the contemporary punk/new wave scene can be heard in parts of *Witch Trials*, this is certainly not the case with the album's expansive finale. Supported by Riley's steady, loping bassline,[35] the cut-up tape samples give it a touch of the avant-garde and Bramah once again demonstrates a regard for The Velvet Underground with flurries of hectic, trebly guitar. There's also a lyrical reference ('Aye you're a good lad / oh here is a pound note') to VU's 'The Murder Mystery' ('oh you're such a good lad, here's another dollar'). The sparse arrangement and gentle tempo give Smith the time and space to deride the shallow and vicious nature of the music business ('the choosy scene'). The meandering conclusion, in which a voice from the studio booth declares 'OK, studio, that's plenty' provides both humour and irony.[36] As Martin Bramah put it, 'On "Music Scene", about the authoritarian hand of the music business, the studio engineers are telling us to stop playing. It was so funny, we used it.' It was played live a dozen (possibly 13) times in 1978-79. Live versions often saw the group start the song with a brief a cappella burst of 'Ding-A-Dong', the winning entry in the 1975 Eurovision Song Contest.

Reviews and Reissues

The *NME*'s Graham Lock found *Live At The Witch Trials* 'a mixture of the good, the slight and the slightly scrappy'. He thought that Burns's drumming 'rescues it from the possibility of formless repetition' and pondered how the group would cope without him (the drummer left the group shortly after the album was recorded). Lock also suggested that 'you can dance to it and

[35] Several sources suggest that the bass part is adapted from 'Fodderstompf' by PiL (the closing track on their 1978 debut album *First Issue*), but this is a rather loose comparison. Melodically, the song is more closely related – via the 'ooh-ooh' backing vocals – to Queen's 'We Will Rock You'.
[36] The voice is that of the group's driver, Michael Adamson (son of Peter, who played Len Fairclough in *Coronation Street*).

pretend it's avant-garde'. Chris Westwood's verdict in *Record Mirror* was that the album 'sometimes comes over as rehearsed incompetence... but is more often stylised, electric, invigorating, appealing rock music'. Although the album didn't trouble the charts (the independent chart wouldn't come into existence for another nine months), it sold a respectable 10,000 copies.

The US version (released in September 1979) had a different sleeve – a smudgy, red-tinged photo of the group on stage – and replaced 'Mother-Sister!' with 'Various Times'. A 2002 reissue included the three tracks from the *Bingo* EP. The 2004 Sanctuary reissue was a much more comprehensive package, featuring both 1978 single/EP releases, the *Short Circuit* tracks, the first two Peel sessions plus *Liverpool 78*. It also included the three tracks that appeared on the bootleg single *Rehearsal Early '77 (Vol.1)*.

Evaluation

Witch Trials was a remarkably assured and confident debut, especially in light of the fact that the group had only made its live debut 18 months earlier, had only had four previous experiences of studio recording and – in particular – recorded the whole thing in a single day. Bob Sargeant's crisp production gives the album a sharpness that, in the main, provides a taut, assertive energy, although it occasionally results in a slightly cold and clinical atmosphere. The treatment of Karl Burns's drumming is a notable feature of the album's production. An undoubtedly accomplished performer, his drumming is technically impressive throughout *Witch Trials*, but the overuse of stereo separation often distracts rather than enhances. Yvonne Pawlett's keyboard work is an important feature of *Witch Trials* that is often overlooked. It broadens the texture of the album, and her often simple, almost metronomic contributions[37] provide Bramah with the space to wander and improvise.

An occasional criticism levelled at *Witch Trials* is that it sticks

[37] Her playing style was undoubtedly influenced by the technical limitations of the Snoopy keyboard that she had inherited from Una Baines. Paul Hanley, describing Marc Riley's use of the same instrument, commented that 'none of the sounds had much sustain, which meant Marc had to play as fast as he could with two fingers on the same key to achieve long notes'.

too closely to contemporary punk tropes and reveals a group that hadn't yet established its own distinctive voice. This has been a source of regular and vigorous debate on the *Fall Online Forum*. In general, those who were of record-buying and gig-attending age at the time of *Witch Trials'* release tend to dismiss this hypothesis; they saw The Fall as significantly different from the outset. Those born later either lack contextual understanding or have a more objective standpoint, depending on your point of view. It is true that a few of the songs could conceivably have slotted quite happily into contemporary punk compilations. Nonetheless, it can't be denied that *Witch Trials* is a refreshingly acerbic and articulate challenge to music business and fashion norms.

Dragnet
Recorded: Cargo Studios, Rochdale, 2nd–4th August 1979
Released: 26th October 1979

Personnel:
Mark E Smith – vocals
Marc Riley – guitar, vocals
Craig Scanlon – guitar, keyboards
Steve Hanley – bass, vocals
Mike Leigh – drums

With:
Kay Carroll – vocals

Chapter 2: Dragnet

'Dragnet *is white crap let loose in a studio but still in control. Sung in natural accents in front of unAFFECTed music.*'

Live At The Witch Trials featured the sixth line-up of The Fall; by the time they got to *Dragnet*, they were on version nine. After *Witch Trials* had been recorded, Karl Burns played three more gigs (on the 17th, 28th and 30th December[38]) before ending the first of several stints in the group. Paul Hanley suggested that the drummer felt that he could earn more money elsewhere; Bramah thought his departure was due to Smith's disapproval at what he saw as Burns's over-elaborate style; according to Simon Ford, Burns's 'chief complaint was Smith's apparent lack of appreciation and respect for him'.

His replacement was Mike Leigh. Previously the drummer for rockabilly outfit The Velvet Collars, Leigh was an unlikely choice, not only in terms of musical background but also sartorially (favouring the teddy boy look) and recreationally (a teetotal non-drug user). He did, however, have a van: a key factor for a band at this stage of its career. To be fair, Leigh's van wasn't the only factor behind his recruitment. 'Mike was... the strength we needed,' Smith explained, 'there was a lot of opposition, 'cos Mike doesn't play conventionally, he plays his drums, he doesn't knock shit out of them.' Martin Bramah commented that Leigh 'didn't really know what the hell he'd got into, but he became very loyal'. Leigh's debut came at Bowdon Vale Youth Club in Altrincham on Valentine's Day 1979. The Fall played two sets, the first being for under 18s. *The Track Record* describes this as 'an important gig as the transition from the *LATWT* sound to a nascent version of the

---

[38] At the first of these, at the Marquee Club, the group opened their set with an untitled, quirky instrumental that they would perform half a dozen more times in 1979 but never recorded. Marc Riley would later use the riff for his 1984 single 'Jumper Clown'.

Dragnet sound' and notes that 'the key component of this being Mike Leigh's drum styling which is altogether more effortless, and less rocky than Burns's powerhouse approach. The importance of this is that the non-percussion instruments have to "up the game" to balance out the sound. Bramah's guitar, for example, feels fuller and less "spidery" than in the preceding year.'

Over the next two months – during which *Live At The Witch Trials* was released – this line-up played a further 18 gigs, including a support slot for Generation X at the London Lyceum in February. They returned to the venue the following month as part of a line-up that also included The Human League, Stiff Little Fingers and Gang Of Four. This performance provides a significant marker of how far The Fall had by now diverged from accepted punk approaches. Writing in the *NME*, Charles Shaar Murray described the gig as 'a watershed between the seventies and the eighties... some of the audience sniffing around looking for the eighties the way dogs look for bones and some looking for 1977 (if they find it, they pogo; if they don't, they throw things)'. The latter bunch were very much in evidence during The Fall's set, the group being pelted with cans and glasses and a 'spiky psycho' running on stage and punching Smith. The Fall, Murray wrote, 'are not just alienated from... society but from standard rock, and that includes punk'.

In describing Leigh's appointment to the group, Smith's use of the phrase 'there was a lot of opposition' is pertinent: despite the rest of the group's reservations, it was his opinion that prevailed. Smith's increasing level of control over the group's direction was one of the factors that led to Martin Bramah's departure; another was the tension caused by the guitarist's relationship with Una Baines, which had begun the previous December. The final straw came when, after Bramah missed a rehearsal in order to accompany his girlfriend to a hospital appointment, Kay Carroll accused Baines of ruining the band. 'Kay came round and was screaming and shouting at Una for leading me astray,' Bramah recalled, 'I left because I was sick of us being treated like children.' The guitarist quit The Fall that night (20th April 1979, at an Iggy Pop gig at the Factory in Hulme), leaving Smith as the only remaining founder member. In his own account of the making of

Dragnet, 'Through A Glass Darkly', Bramah claims that Smith was 'mortified' at his decision to leave. 'He thought it was a terrible thing and tried to convince me of my folly. He was unprepared for it, obviously. He knew we were a strong band, and I was an innovative guitarist, so he was quite upset.'

A major reshuffle was required. Marc Riley moved to guitar and two new members were recruited. Riley's schoolmates and fellow Sirens Craig Scanlon and Steve Hanley had, after his elevation to full Fall member, continued as Staff 9, who had supported both The Fall and Joy Division. A typically abrupt phone call from Carroll saw the two of them invited to join the group. 'Do you want to play the fucking bass or not?... Get your arse down to the rehearsal rooms with Craig. He'll be on guitar as well.' Although Bramah's departure was significant, the elevation of Hanley and Scanlon from fans/roadies to group members was a pivotal moment in the group's history. Many people over the years would make important contributions to the Fall sound, but nobody other than Smith himself would ever play as crucial a role as these two.

Their first appearance on a Fall record came in July 1979 with the release of the group's next single, 'Rowche Rumble', recorded at Rochdale's Cargo studios. 'A great dance number,' according to the press release, it features an unforgettable thumping/chanting intro that morphs into a dissonant guitar riff (perhaps influenced by The Stooges' 'Shake Appeal'). The song was about Valium[39] and was inspired by Smith's experiences as a shipping clerk when most of an accidental overorder of the drug ('I sent 70 pounds instead of 70p to pharmaceutical company Rowche AG'[40]) ended up stuffed in his bottom drawer. The single received positive reviews and was made joint single of the week in both *Sounds* and the *NME*, sharing the honour with Disco Spectacular's 'Aquarius' (*NME*) and Racey's 'Boy Oh Boy' (*Sounds*). In *Smash Hits*, guest reviewer Andy Partridge of XTC seemed to be auditioning for the job of writing The Fall's sleeve notes:

[39] The line 'wives need their pill' echoes the Rolling Stones' 1966 track 'Mother's Little Helper' – 'Mother needs something today to calm her down / and though she's not really ill, there's a little yellow pill... mother's little helper... gets her through her busy day'.
[40] The pharmaceutical company is actually called Roche.

Sounds like the cover, cheap biro lines, bad relationships... Great chemist's organ sound. Not one for young girls to make zips or brassieres mindlessly to on the factory floor. Good sound, bad song (down with pills). B-side 'In My Area' suffocating ill music, felt like I had flu, blanket over the head tunes.[41]

B-side 'In My Area' is a rather slight bluesy trundle, but Pawlett gives it an interestingly unhinged tone. This was her last contribution to the group. Her departure is often attributed to her need to care for her dog – Simon Ford, for example, states that 'her reason for leaving was refreshingly unique: she jacked in life as a rock'n'roll star to look after her sick dog' – but both Paul Hanley and Pawlett herself indicate that she left simply because she felt that she didn't fit in.

Dragnet

The group returned to Cargo at the beginning of August to record their second album. The producer was Grant Showbiz. Born Grant Cunliffe, he had worked as Steve Hillage's guitar roadie before becoming the sound engineer for Here & Now.[42] Although he had little experience of studio recording at this point, Showbiz had a significant impact on the album. His 'insistence on a near-total absence of reverb and compression,' Paul Hanley felt, 'was the main reason why *Dragnet* sounds so damn different to everything else.' The press release emphasised this rejection of conventional approaches, stating proudly that the album 'isn't a mass of confusion covered by reverb'. Typically, Smith had a more cynical view on the topic: 'Grant was totally useless in a way, but it worked out well. He was always floundering, which brought a lot of good things out... we just bullied him into everything.' The cover art – a stark monochromatic picture of a spider poised to devour a butterfly – was drawn by Tina Prior, who would later

---

[41]Partridge would possibly have had more success as a sleeve note-writer than an A&R man, given that his verdict on Buggles' 'Video Killed The Radio Star' – number one in sixteen countries – was 'won't be a hit'.

[42] He picked up his nickname whilst with Here & Now: 'For our national tour I turned up with a briefcase which was promptly thrown from the tour bus onto the motorway. They called me Showbiz after that. It's a great name for me; it stops me being too serious.'

become Smith's mother-in-law for a brief period in the early 90s. It seems likely that the inspiration for the cover image was the opening credits to *The Haunted Palace* (a 1963 adaptation of H. P. Lovecraft's *The Case of Charles Dexter Ward*), especially given that the film was shown on ITV three months before *Dragnet*'s release.

Dragnet also saw the establishment of what was to become another long-standing feature of The Fall: dubious songwriting credits. Bramah's contributions were expunged. Given that the guitarist had a hand in writing the majority of *Witch Trials* and that several *Dragnet* songs were played live before his departure, it seems highly unlikely that he didn't deserve some recognition. Bramah claimed that he wrote the music for 'A Figure Walks', 'Printhead', 'Put Away' and 'Before The Moon Falls'; he also suggested that he had a hand in the creation of both sides of the 'Rowche Rumble' single and that 'Your Heart Out' was a Tony Friel song.

Psykick Dancehall

Smith's opening call of 'Is there anybody there?' is answered with an emphatic 'Yeah!' from what sounds like everyone else in the studio. The song was inspired by Questors Psychic Disco in Prestwich. Martin Bramah had attended the disco, which was above a psychic centre or spiritualist church that had been set up by Kay Carroll's mother. Smith – who, according to Bramah never visited Questors – claimed the song was based on his own experiences. 'That was based on this Christian Psychic club that I used to go to for a laugh. These psychic women would stop me coming out of the dole and go, "You've got it, come to our meeting." Fascinating stuff. It was like Alcoholics Anonymous for psychics.' (The phrase 'you've got it' presumably points to Smith's alleged 'pre-cog'/psychic talents.)

Musically, it was a fairly radical departure from anything on *Witch Trials*, a sort of mutant punk-disco-funk where the pair of busy guitars provide an effective counterpoint to the solid, unfussy bassline. A spot of bluesy string-bending and a mystery spoken-word sample lurking in the background round the song off nicely. After 12 performances 1979-80, it was revived in 2009 and was played regularly over the following seven years, eventually clocking up 91 appearances in total.

A Figure Walks

The supernatural theme continues in the second track, a mysterious journey through terror and paranoia. H. P. Lovecraft was one of Smith's favourite authors, and his influence is apparent here.[43] Inspired by a walk home where Smith's vision was restricted by his anorak, it's filled with darkly horrific imagery: 'eyes of brown, watery / nails of pointed yellow / hands of black carpet'. 'If you actually listen closely,' Smith explained, 'it's not a human being at all that's following the character, it's actually this monster from outer space. I like to think of it as my big Stephen King outing.' There's particularly effective interplay between the lead and rhythm guitars and the stark cymbal splashes give it more than enough variation to sustain its six minutes. The song's origins (musically, if not lyrically) can be heard in 'My Condition', a track which was played twice in late 1978.[44] 'A Figure Walks' was played 24 times 1979-80 and made a one-off reappearance in 2009.

Printhead

The abrupt three-chord riff is closer to the sound of *Witch Trials* than the two openers, and Leigh's busy drum rolls also echo Burns's approach. One of Smith's many digs at music journalists, it quotes directly from Ian Birch's review of 'It's The New Thing' in *Melody Maker*: 'the band little more than a big crashing beat / instruments collide and we all get drunk'. 'I've met loads of people,' Smith told *Printed Noises* fanzine, 'who were crying their eyes out because they'd just had a bad review from someone that's just learned to write. In my mind, it's just pathetic.' 'Printhead' was another track that received a surprise late-period revival: after 29 outings 1979-81, it was performed twice more in 2011.

---

[43] Howard Phillips Lovecraft (1890-1937) was a writer of supernatural and horror tales. At London's Lyceum on 25th March 1979, Smith's introduction to 'A Figure Walks' was: 'This one's a slow one, dedicated to H.P. Lovecraft. The psychologist said that he thought the shadow was his father. The shad was his dad.'

[44] It can be heard on *The Fall Box Set* (see Appendix 2).

Dice Man

Throughout his career, Smith frequently expressed admiration for Bo Diddley, and 'Dice Man' was the first of several Fall songs to adopt his trademark five-accent hambone rhythm. It clatters along with a ragged verve and sees Smith attempt – fairly successfully – a relatively melodic approach to his vocal. The lyric was inspired by the novel *The Dice Man* by Luke Rhinehart, in which the major decisions of the protagonist are determined by a throw of the dice. It could be argued that the principle of making decisions based on a random variable is one that Smith maintained throughout The Fall's career, although he claimed that 'we don't have a deliberate policy of keeping people guessing – that's just the way I am... I'm dead proud that The Fall aren't just another branch on the tree of showbiz. Basically, rock music isn't very interesting, so it's only people like me who can make it interesting.' It was played live 17 times between 1979 and 1982.

Before The Moon Falls

Here, the album return to the darkly mysterious mood of 'A Figure Walks'. A simple, insistent riff creates a hypnotic backdrop cut through from time to time by a 'Venus In Furs' style clanging guitar. The jarring transitions into and out of the brief uptempo section around the three-minute mark add to the unsettling atmosphere. However, unlike the supernatural tone of 'Dancehall' and the dark horror of 'Figure', there's a more down to earth theme to the lyrics here: 'Up here in the North there are no wage packet jobs for us... while young married couples discuss the poverties of their self-built traps'. Pawlett's departure is also referred to: 'we were six like dice but we're back to five'. It was only played live eight times, the last performance coming in 1981.

Your Heart Out

The lightest moment on the album, and one of the poppiest tunes of the early Fall incarnations. With its jaunty guitar line and ramshackle strum, 'Your Heart Out' seems, in retrospect, like a blueprint for the 'C86' shuffles of Orange Juice, The Brilliant

Corners *et al.* There was often a self-deprecating angle to the C86 janglers, and Smith enters into that spirit here: 'I don't sing, I just shout... all on one note'. There is a darker tone at points, however, the title being given a more literal meaning: 'they take your heart out with a sharp knife... they had no anaesthetic'. There's also a reference to 'Savage Pencil', the pseudonym of music journalist and artist Edwin Pouncey. The song didn't last too long on the setlist, making just 22 appearances 1979–81.

Muzorewi's Daughter

Bishop Abel Tendekayi Muzorewa (Smith mangles both the spelling and the pronunciation of his name) was, for a few months, the Prime Minister of Zimbabwe Rhodesia, an unrecognized state that existed briefly as part of the country's transition from British colony (Southern Rhodesia) to independent state (Zimbabwe) in 1979–80. Because of the repeated references to the 'pot' ('I've been in the pot too long / too hot in the pot too long'), the 'tribal' rhythm conjures the unfortunate air of those 40s–50s animations where cartoon characters end up being scalped or boiled in a large cauldron.[45] This, plus lines like 'I'm too long in the nips / I'm too long in the tits', all feels distinctly uncomfortable from a modern perspective. The lyrics were written by Kay Carroll: 'I hated him. He was so white, but he was black: he was playing Uncle Tom.'[46] The song, and the chorus in particular, feels a little predictable, although it is rescued from mundanity by the unexpected semi-tone drop at 3:24. It was played 23 times 1979–1981, received a surprising revival in 2010, and was played for the 48th and final time in 2013.

Flat Of Angles

Featuring a sliding guitar part that's somewhere between 'Hey Bo Diddley' and 'Little Red Rooster', 'Angles' is an intriguing tale of a murderer who has killed his wife (for 'wasting his life') and is

[45] An example is the 1938 Looney Tunes cartoon *Jungle Jitters*, which was withdrawn by United Artists as early as 1968 because of its racial stereotyping (although it can still be found online).
[46] It should be emphasized strongly that it isn't being implied at all here that Carroll was racist, only that the choice of language seems unfortunate from a 21st-century viewpoint.

hiding out in the aforesaid flat, becoming deranged and paranoid ('the streets are full of mercenary eyes'). It was Mike Leigh's favourite Fall song: 'I'm very proud of the fact that I made up the drum beat at rehearsal one day and very quickly Marc, Steve and Craig joined in with the guitar and bass riffs. Before we knew it, a classic song was born.' It was only played live 18 times, 1979–82.

Choc-Stock

Adapted from one of Hanley and Scanlon's Staff 9 songs (originally called 'Pop-Stock'). There is a certain haphazard charm to the 'Now come on kids...' section, but otherwise it has a distinctly 'cobbled-together-in-a-bedroom-when-we-were-15' air to it. The last of its 21 performances was in early 1981.

Spectre vs Rector

The relentless, aggressive ugliness of 'Spectre' is astonishing. You might think that you've heard nothing as scuzzy as the opening guitar line until the even more grimy bass joins in. And then there's a cacophony of competing, atonal mayhem (0:27–0:48) that threatens to drag the song down into a vortex of fuzzy, tuneless chaos. It's more common for Smith's vocals to be the agents of this chaos whilst the musicians endeavour to anchor the song; here, the opposite is true – Smith's harsh, rhythmic chanting is the only thing clinging to some sense of rationality while the unholy mix of blistered noise bubbles ominously beneath him. All of this only takes you up to around halfway. At 3:50, a crisper, more energetic rhythm kicks in; but only briefly, before we transition to a cleaner, less chaotic version of the first section. A role-reversal sees the group become more focused while Smith loosens up and almost babbles.

The lyric is full of references to Smith's favourite horror/ supernatural writers. M. R. James, a medievalist scholar best known for his early 20th-century ghost stories, is name-checked in the first line. Lovecraft also makes an appearance, 'Yog-Sothoth' being one of his 'outer gods'.[47] Smith also mentions

---

[47] 'Yog-Sothoth knows the gate. Yog-Sothoth is the gate. Yog-Sothoth is the key and guardian of the gate.' (*The Dunwich Horror*, 1928.)

actor Ray Milland, who starred in *The Premature Burial*, a 1962 horror film directed by Roger Corman, the French title of which was *L'Enterré Vivant* ('Buried Alive'). In another Corman film, *The Haunted Palace* – the one that inspired *Dragnet*'s cover art – Vincent Price's character uses a Latin incantation that includes the word 'vivat' ('live!') to reanimate a corpse. This has led some to surmise that the opening line of 'Spectre' is 'M. R. James vivant, vivant', although others insist on the more prosaic 'M. R. James be born be born'.[48] Whatever the first line actually is, it seems likely that *Burial* and *Palace* provided the source material for much of 'Spectre', as both films were shown on British television only a couple of months before the song made its live debut.

As for the story, the Rector (from Hampshire) attempts an exorcism of a spirit who is from 'Chorazina'.[49] He is possessed by the spectre but is then rescued by a hero (whose identity is unclear). Afterwards, however, the hero returns to the mountains whilst the rector is left 'dead on the floor'. Considering that it was only played live on 11 occasions (1979–82), the song was well represented on The Fall's live albums, with three of those performances appearing on official releases.[50] 'Spectre' is a thing of mad, unhinged wonder; not just pushing the limits, not even ignoring them, just bloody-mindedly refusing to acknowledge that they even exist.

Put Away

Its light, jaunty tone and the fact that it was tucked away at the end of the album after the epic 'Spectre' has led to 'Put Away' being a little unjustly overlooked. The rhythm guitar is notably out of tune, which retains the album's distinctive abrasiveness despite the

[48] An example of Fall fans' capacity to create endless arguments out of seemingly trivial detail, the 'be born' / 'vivant' debate has provoked acrimonious exchanges on both *The Annotated Fall* and *Fall Online Forum*.

[49] 'Woe to you, Chorazin! Woe to you, Bethsaida! For if the mighty works which were done in you had been done in Tyre and Sidon, they would have repented long ago in sackcloth and ashes.' Matthew 11:21.

[50] The song's third live outing features on *Live From The Vaults – Los Angeles 1979*, the fourth appeared on *Totale's Turns* and the sixth is on *The Legendary Chaos Tape/Live In London 1980*. 'Spectre' also appeared (in both live and studio form) on half a dozen compilation albums.

song's catchy hook. Smith would later claim that the album was 'purposefully out of tune', but this is disputed by Paul Hanley: 'The fact that The Fall stopped sounding like that immediately after Will Sergeant from Echo & the Bunnymen introduced them to the electronic guitar tuner is probably all you need to know.' 'Put Away' also underlines the different approach of the *Witch Trials* and *Dragnet* line-ups. The Peel version, recorded eight months earlier, is very different in tone even though the structure of the song is largely the same; the spacious sound, with Pawlett's plinky keyboard to the forefront, is anchored by a robust 4/4 beat from Karl Burns. The keyboard-less version on *Dragnet* is dominated by the guitars and Leigh switches to a swing beat, giving the song a looser, murky feel. Furthermore, although guitar solos in Fall songs are not entirely unheard of, they're a rare phenomenon, so it's unusual to hear the track featuring such prominent bluesy slide soloing. 'Put Away' also features the first appearance of the kazoo on a Fall record.

The narrator seems curiously cheerful about being sent to prison ('all metal walls now I'm sent down'; 'no sex or records for a year and a day'), focusing optimistically on the fact that he'll 'be back someday'. Smith's sleeve notes on the expanded reissue – 'PUT AWAY (MES) … In The Rack Under "F" – a sort of sequel to "Angles"' – suggest that the protagonist is the murderer from 'Flat Of Angles', in which case a year and a day seems an optimistic estimate of the sentence. The voice saying 'that'll be right then' at the end is that of Mike Leigh. It was only played live nine times, 1978-81.

Reviews and Reissues

In the *NME*, Paul Du Noyer regretted the loss of Burns's 'distinctive' drumming but was impressed by the 'invention and freshness' of the two new guitarists. Overall, however, he felt that Smith was 'not… any sort of genius; nor do The Fall represent some magical chemistry of talent'. In *Melody Maker*, Paolo Hewitt found it 'inaccessible, sometimes ugly'; whilst he could 'admire the spirit behind it', he was 'not inspired to let The Fall influence my life in any way'. Allan Jones felt that *Dragnet* meant that the group should be 'taken seriously as an important voice' but had reservations about its 'self-righteousness'. It didn't trouble the charts (the independent chart was still not yet established) but was rated as the 35th best album of the year in the *NME*.[51]

Dragnet didn't receive a CD release until 1990. A 2002 reissue added the tracks from the 'Rowche Rumble' and 'Fiery Jack' (see Chapter 3) singles. A further reissue in 2004 included a rather unnecessary selection of outtakes of 'Rumble' and 'In My Area'. In 2019, Cherry Red released a 3CD edition that added the *Retford* and *Los Angeles* live albums recorded in late 1979 (see Chapter 3).

Evaluation

Discussion regarding *Dragnet* often focuses, not surprisingly, on its production. The replacement of Pawlett's keyboards – which had added an extra dimension to the punkish *Witch Trials* – with a second guitar was already pushing the group towards a thicker, more compressed approach. Grant Showbiz exacerbated this by creating a murky, muddy sound that David Quantick memorably described as sounding 'like the whole thing was recorded on a home cassette recorder in a multi-storey car park'. Smith claimed that the studio were so disconcerted by the album's production that they asked to be removed from the credits: 'Later we found out that Cargo... didn't want to let it out... they were nervous about releasing it because of its sound.'[52] In fact the production issue gives the album a more difficult reputation than the songs themselves warrant, deflecting from how conventional many of them actually are. That said, *Dragnet* is not exactly full of three-minute pop tunes: 'A Figure Walks' and 'Before The Moon Falls' are stealthy, eerie slow-burners; 'Spectre vs Rector' takes the group into a whole new territory of discordant bedlam.

The recruitment of Hanley and Scanlon was a pivotal moment, but neither quite make their mark here. This is not a criticism – they'd only been in the line-up for five minutes, after all – but

[51] Ranked between Popol Vuh's *Brüder Des Schattens, Söhne Des Lichts* and The Only Ones' *Even Serpents Shine*.
[52] Blogger hippriestess (also known as drone musician Caroline McKenzie) suggests that Smith and Showbiz 'accidentally invented "lo-fi" several years before anyone really wanted it'.

Dragnet doesn't contain any of the remarkable moments that the two of them would go on to create. Both the drums and the vocals undergo a particularly significant shift in comparison to the group's debut. Smith's declaration that he didn't sing but only shouted 'all on one note' is a little disingenuous. Whilst he never had more than a tentative grip on traditional melody, *Dragnet* sees MES follow a basic melodic structure more often than is the case on many other Fall albums. He is starting to consolidate his unique vocal style; he's not there quite yet (*Grotesque* would see a much greater leap in the originality of his delivery), but the occasional Lydon-isms of *Witch Trials* have faded out of view here. Burns's drumming on the first album, whilst technically impressive, was arguably over-fussy and distracting, although this was more a fault of the production than his performance. On *Dragnet*, there's a sense that the pendulum has swung a little too far the other way. Leigh is a solid drummer, but his contributions here occasionally feel a little pedestrian.

In *A User's Guide To The Fall*, Dave Thompson describes the album as a 'dead end'. This is unduly harsh, but there was a sense that this was as far as this incarnation of The Fall could go. However, the growing confidence of Steve Hanley and Craig Scanlon, plus the appointment of a new drummer would see The Fall go on to scale unprecedented heights as they moved into a new decade.

Grotesque (After The Gramme)
Recorded: Rochdale & London, mid-1980
Released: 17th November 1980

Personnel:
Mark E Smith – vocals
Marc Riley – guitar, vocals
Craig Scanlon – guitar
Steve Hanley – bass
Paul Hanley – drums

Chapter 3: Grotesque (After The Gramme)

'Contains very few choruses but a lot of beat.'

In September 1979, shortly before embarking on a UK tour to promote *Dragnet*, The Fall travelled to Foel Studio in mid-Wales to record their next single, 'Fiery Jack'. Smith had recently been 'dabbling in rockabilly' and had asked Riley and Scanlon to come up with something along those lines. As a result, the new song was, as Steve Hanley put it, 'a little more rhythmic than usual'. Production was provided by Mayo Thompson of avant-garde rock band Red Krayola, and Geoff Travis, founder of the Rough Trade record shop and label.

The 21-date *Dragnet* tour in October and November included a night at Bircoats Leisure Centre, Doncaster (six songs from which would make up the first side of their first live album, *Totale's Turns*) and a date at Middlesbrough's Rock Garden where they faced a rain of bottles and ashtrays from Teesside skinheads. *Live From The Vaults – Retford 1979*, released in 2005, was recorded on this tour. It's a spiky, vigorous performance, although the sound quality is rough. At the end of November, The Fall embarked on their first trip to the USA.[53] Arranged by Miles Copeland's distribution company IRS, the tour saw The Fall play a mix of small clubs as headliners and support slots at larger venues. Their first date was at Emerald City in New Jersey on 28th November, supporting Buzzcocks, who gave out pizza to the audience in the middle of the set.[54] Guy Ewald, writing for punk/new wave magazine *New York Rocker*, was impressed by The Fall's performance at New York's Palladium Theatre on 1st December:

---

[53] MES confided to Steve Hanley that he'd never been on a plane before; this was not the case with the bassist, who had, albeit very briefly, flown a plane whilst an air cadet.
[54] Pizza also played a role in The Fall's 3rd December appearance in Cambridge, Massachusetts, if fall.org contributor Tobin is to be believed: 'Mark E. Smith ate an entire large pizza while performing. Thus, much of his singing was unintelligible and during "Fiery Jack" pizza shot out of his mouth with furious velocity.'

The second-billed Fall saved the show for me. What an attitude on these guys – they acted like the audience wasn't even there. Lead singer Mark E. Smith casually paced the stage, one hand in his pocket, as he sang, screamed, screeched and preached over the band's pumping, menacing drone. Without traditional R&R dynamics, the Fall constructed an impressive wall of sound; the set ended with the guitarists crouched over their small amplifiers, wrestling the last sounds from their instruments. A few heads bobbed, a few mouths booed, but as Smith would later tell the NYR, the Fall are 'not about rock'n'roll', but ideas. An intriguing and highly original band.

Other notable dates included a gig at the infamous CBGB club (where they played with the U.K. Subs) and a performance at the Catamaran Hotel in San Diego supporting Iggy Pop. Unfortunately, Iggy's audience were not overly impressed by The Fall and continually threw drinks at them, although at least – unlike Middlesbrough's skinheads – the Californian crowd hung on to their glasses. The group's date at Madame Wong's West in Santa Monica on 6th December was a fraught one. Headliners The Nu Kats, a new wave outfit fronted by the then husband of Demi Moore, played in between the other two acts (apparently the usual policy of the venue) which meant that the crowd thinned out dramatically whilst The Fall played. Post-gig analysis took the form of an extended rant by Kay Carroll which culminated in her throwing her beer over Steve Hanley. The final date of the tour (one that Marc Riley described as one of his two favourite Fall gigs[55]) can be heard on the 2005 release, *Live From The Vaults – Los Angeles 1979*. In places, the sound quality is even worse than the *Retford* album, but it includes an impressively sprawling 11-minute version of 'Spectre vs. Rector', which features a feedback-drenched 'Sister Ray'-esque section around the five minute mark. Although Smith was not impressed with IRS's organisation of the tour, he found it to be a valuable experience. In particular, the trip provided much lyrical inspiration: 'I got a lot of songs out of it. It's a very evil place.'

[55] The other was the Hammersmith Palais on 25th March 1982 (supported by The Birthday Party).

The Fall opened the new decade with the release of the 'Fiery Jack' single. The sound was crisp and clean, especially in comparison to *Dragnet*, and the 'dabbling in rockabilly' led to Leigh providing a steady shuffle in the style of 'Ring Of Fire' (Smith occasionally included a few lines from Cash's 1963 hit in live performances). Smith's sister Suzanne provided the sleeve art, portraying Jack as a drunken tramp who casts a demonic shadow. Smith described the character ('I just drink drink drink... I live on pies... my face is slack') as representing a certain type of Manchester character: 'hard livers with hard livers; faces like unmade beds'. He also described the song as 'an attempt to get back at the ageism thing, where people are supposed to be screwed after they're 29'. The new direction was well received: *Sounds* made it single of the week and 'Jack' reached number four in the newly created independent singles chart. The song enjoyed a relatively long stay on the setlist – its final performance in 1990 was its 63rd.

B-side '2nd Dark Age' features the trademark tinny Snoopy keyboard, cascading drums and prominent backing vocals from Riley. The lyrics pack a lot into the song's two minutes: references to ABBA ('Miss Fjord and Benny'); the recent Islamic revolution in Iran ('death of the USA'); anarcho-punks Crass ('the commune crapheads sit and whine') and Jean Paul Sartre ('a mediocre anti-Jew'[56]). It also saw Smith introduce his newly created alter-ego: 'I am Roman Totale XVII, the bastard offspring of Charles I and the Great God Pan'.[57] The back cover of 'Fiery Jack' contained a statement from Roman Totale:

> This 'master-tape' is the result of experiments which took place in the remote Welsh hills one autumn... I have not long left now but I urge the finder of this 'master-tape' never to unleash it on humanity! – Ah! already the evil Deit-y Ri-Kol is clawing at my brain! – If it is unleashed – The Fall is here, the ectoplasm exorcised and Humanity Can Either Eat That Grenade Or Face The Second Dark Age!

[56] In his 1948 book, *Anti-Semite and Jew*, Sartre stated that 'the anti-Semite... considers himself an average man, modestly average, basically mediocre'.
[57] *The Great God Pan* is an 1890 horror/fantasy novella by one of Smith's favourite authors, Arthur Machen.

The other B-side was an alternative version of *Dragnet*'s opener entitled 'Psykick Dancehall #2'. Cleaner production aside, it's not vastly different, apart from containing (at 2:24) a brief monologue about Scottish psychic Helen Duncan.[58]

In March 1980, The Fall embarked on a ten-date UK tour to promote 'Fiery Jack', accompanied by The Cramps. Although Steve Hanley was impressed with them ('they're a treat to watch, rockabilly at its most extreme'), the tour was a fractious affair, with predictable disputes about who was headlining each night. On the drive back from the date in Dumfries, Mike Leigh resigned. In his previous band, he had been used to gigging regularly and having a steady income, but was finding the lifestyle change that came with being in The Fall challenging. 'I love doing the tours and making the records. It's the spaces in between I can't stand. When I was in The Velvet Collars we were playing every night. Now there's three weeks at a time when I've got nothing to do.' Paul Hanley, however, points out that in just over a year in The Fall, Leigh played 90 gigs, including an American tour. Smith suggested that the drummer's distaste for the group's drug use was a key factor in his departure. Whatever the reason, Leigh was keen to complete the last two dates of the tour, but Kay Carroll, angered by his disloyalty, was determined to find a replacement as soon as possible. As a result, at Birmingham University on March 18th, he made his final appearance for The Fall.

The last date of the tour, on 21st March at London's Electric Ballroom, saw Steve Hanley's younger brother Paul behind the drum kit. He hadn't been able to do the Birmingham date because he had his Maths mock O-level exam that day, and he turned up for his first performance still wearing his school uniform. Given that his live experience consisted of one gig in a local Catholic club, he had only owned a kit for six months, and there was no full band rehearsal before the performance, he coped amazingly well. This was despite a technical difficulty which involved the

---

[58] Duncan claimed to summon the spirits of the deceased by emitting ectoplasm from her mouth. In 1931, she was revealed as a fraud, her 'ectoplasm' being a mixture of cheesecloth, egg white and toilet paper. She was the last person to be imprisoned under the 1735 Witchcraft Act.

electricity cutting out if he hit the snare too hard. Paul's reward for this remarkable achievement was a tenner from Kay Carroll and the promise of an audition for the permanent role. Having passed this hurdle, he played a further eight gigs with the group before they headed off for a tour of The Netherlands in June. Paul had to stay at home for his exams, so Steve Davies of Hawaiian shirt and congas fame stepped in for the Dutch dates, even though he had never actually owned a drum kit and had to borrow one.

Working with Geoff Travis on the recording of 'Fiery Jack' was to lead to a label change for The Fall. Travis had opened his first Rough Trade shop on London's Kensington Park Road in 1976, specialising in reggae and punk. A record label under the same name was established the following year, its first release being 'Paris Maquis' by French punk band Métal Urbain. Smith saw signing to Rough Trade primarily as an opportunity for increased financial reward:

> They went out to sign us and in the end we were that bloody desperate we had to for money, like. They were good in that they always gave you your royalties. Not like our first label, Step-Forward, for whom we did those first singles and first two albums but we never saw a penny. That's a fact, we were bloody starving to death. 'It's A New Thing' [sic] was single of the year and we had no fuckin' money in our pockets.

The Fall's first release on Rough Trade was *Totale's Turns (It's Now Or Never)*, the group's first official live album. Released on 5th May 1980, it wasn't a traditional live LP as it also included studio/demo tracks, an approach that the group would revisit on several occasions thereafter. The first half came from their performance at Bircoats Leisure Centre in Doncaster on 27th October 1979. The intro (a variation on 'Crap Rap') finds Smith in playful and provocative mood: 'The difference between you and us is that we have brains.' Another memorable comment comes in the introduction to 'Choc-Stock': 'Are you doing what you did two years ago? Yeah? Well, don't make a career out of it.' Side two is a bit of a mishmash. There are a couple of tracks recorded in Bradford in February 1980, 'That Man' (an outtake from the 'Fiery Jack' session in which the group impersonate The Beatles c.1963) and a lengthy live version of 'No Xmas For John Quays' (possibly from Preston on 22nd November 1979) where MES castigates the group for perceived self-indulgence: 'Will you fuckin' get it together instead of showing off!' The strangest moment is the lo-fi home/demo recording of 'New Puritan', an interestingly scratchy fragment of what would be become one of the group's finest songs. Smith claimed that it was recorded 'at home during which said home was attacked by a drunk, which accounts for the tension on that track'.

The first Fall single on Rough Trade – and also the first recorded appearance for the double-Hanley line-up – was released in July. 'How I Wrote "Elastic Man"' revisits the rockabilly approach of 'Fiery Jack' but is fuller-bodied and more forceful; it also features another reappearance for the Snoopy keyboard. The song deals with how celebrity interferes with the artistic process, or as Smith put it, 'how the public kill off their heroes' creativity', giving Jimmy Greaves and George Best as examples.[59] As is often the case with Smith's lyrics, the narration switches from the third to the first-person mid-song. From either perspective, the protagonist seems depressed: 'taken apart' by journalists, he hasn't written 'for 90 days' and is 'resigned to bed'; a situation exacerbated by the fact that people can't even get the title of his book right, MES singing 'plastic man' rather than 'elastic man' throughout. The B-side was the joyfully angular 'City Hobgoblins', which contains the memorable line 'Queen Victoria is a large black slug in Piccadilly, Manchester'. Despite a negative review from *Sounds*' Garry Bushell – 'punk with the stuffing knocked out of it, embellished by the worst singing voice in the world (sort of Max Bygraves crossed with a donkey with hiccups)'[60] – the single reached number two on the independent singles chart, only kept from the top spot by Joy Division's 'Love Will Tear Us Apart'.

---

[59] He also described it as being 'about a guy who wrote a book called "Elastic Man" and everybody gets on his back about it, he's a celebrity and it fucks up his art.'
[60] Notorious right-wing nationalist Bushell's single of the week was 'Last Night Another Soldier' by Angelic Upstarts.

The next single, 'Totally Wired', emerged in September. As Simon Ford rightly comments, 'Paul Hanley's drumming is by now much more assured and the full potential of his brother's bass playing is finally realised. Add to this Smith's most compelling vocal performance to date, with its twist of northern sour, plus lyrics that added new life to a perennial rock'n'roll tale of drugged excess, and you have a decade-defining single.' It was, unsurprisingly, a live stalwart for several years, clocking up 83 appearances between 1980-89 before making a one-off comeback in 2008. Like its predecessor, it reached number two on the independent singles chart. The B-side was the oddity 'Putta Block': nearly a minute and a half of a live recording of 'The N.W.R.A.' is abruptly interrupted by an original song (which alternates between the frantic and contemplative) that sees Smith repeatedly state that he 'put a block on the words'. It finishes with clumsily edited live clips of 'Rowche Rumble' and 'Cary Grant's Wedding'.

Peel session number three, recorded and broadcast in September, was Craig Scanlon and both Hanley brothers' first visit to Maida Vale. To Steve, compared to the likes of Cargo it was 'like being rescued from a poxy wooden raft by an elegant ocean-going liner'. Working with veteran BBC producer John Sparrow was an interesting experience. 'We recorded the first track,' Riley recalled, 'made a right old racket, as we did, went in to start listening back to it, make sure we were happy with it, and I turned round to look at the producer, and his pipe had gone out. This is the truth, his pipe had gone out, and he was asleep.' Whilst the first two sessions had impressed, the third saw The Fall make a remarkable leap in quality and originality. It was a paradigm shift: everything had somehow just clicked into place, forging a unique, almost indefinable Fall sound. It wasn't the case that the group had simply found a signature style and locked onto it, there's huge variety here: the rickety rockabilly of 'Container Drivers'; the wonky shuffle of 'New Face In Hell'; the dark, complex narrative 'Jawbone And The Air-Rifle'. The performance of 'Jawbone' – not, as both Hanley brothers attested, the easiest song to play – is put into context by Steve's revelation that before the session they had 'never played [it] all the way through without messing it up'.

Most astonishing, however, is 'New Puritan'. Paul Hanley's formidable drumming and in particular Scanlon's lacerating chords provide the perfect foil for Smith's 'righteous maelstrom'. The words and ideas simply pour out of MES. Like 'Elastic Man', there's a shifting narrative perspective; it's not always clear whether Smith is criticising puritanism, hailing the new puritan or speaking *as* him ('all hard-core fiends will die by me, and all decadent sins will reap discipline'). His voice spits with furious scorn as he derides a plethora of targets: 'grotesque peasants'; music industry corruption ('ask your local record dealer how many bribes he took today'); British pubs ('the scream of electric pumps in a renovated pub / your stomach swells up before you get drunk') and over-earnest musos ('curse the self-copulation of your lousy record collection… coffee table LPs never breathe'). John Peel wondered if even he was a target: '[I've] always thought they were having a go at me in that you know, all that sending tapes to famous apes'. (In typically self-deprecating fashion, however, Peel immediately dismissed his own thought as 'vanity'.) It was played live half a dozen times in 1980 and then once more, in 1982. Disappointingly, it never enjoyed a 'proper' studio recording.[61]

Grotesque (After The Gramme)

The Fall's third album was recorded at Cargo in Rochdale and Street-Level Studios in London in mid-1980. The striking development of the group's sound was suitably reflected in *Grotesque*'s cover: after the stark, monochromatic *Witch Trials* and *Dragnet* sleeves, their new album saw them burst into vibrant colour. The hideous yet comical figures (perhaps the 'grotesque peasants') created by Smith's sister Suzanne are the perfect representation of the mix of horror and dark humour prevalent in many of the songs. The colour sleeve took up most of the album's tiny budget.[62] Production was provided by Grant Showbiz, Mayo Thompson and Geoff Travis, who between them found a perfect

---

[61] *The Annotated Fall*'s bzfgt considers the song to be the foundation of what 'makes the Fall what they are; everything else they have done before and since seems to me to emanate from this like spokes from the hub of a wheel'.
[62] According to Simon Ford, it was rumoured to have been as little as £300.

middle ground between the prickly murk of *Dragnet* and 'Fiery Jack's slender crispness. The press release stated that the album 'contains very few choruses but a lot of beat'; it also observed that 'most people who like The Fall don't like other groups anyway'. The back cover announced proudly the emergence of a new genre, Country and Northern: 'C 'n' N Music is born!'

Pay Your Rates

The opener is an effective mix of in-your-face punkabilly and abstract down-tempo dissonance that generates excitement and tension by sounding as if it's only just about hanging together. One of Smith's occasional forays into guitar playing adds to the sense of chaos. The vocal is precise and curt, even though Smith comes close to descending into giggles (1:46) whilst warning of the perils of debt. It was played live 40 times 1980–88.

English Scheme

The second track further explores the theme of working-class struggle: 'the lower-class, want brass / bad chests, scrounge fags / the clever ones tend to emigrate'; 'sixty-hour weeks, and stone toilet back-gardens'. Smith made a recording of chirping birds and an ice cream van, considered it to be 'the sound of the lower-class English summer' and ordered the group to build a song around it. Riley designed a keyboard line based on the ice cream van tune and the group created 'an ironically jolly little gem'. Smith was largely delighted, but had reservations about the keyboard part, but for once the group (in particular Riley) prevailed and it stayed. Played 45 times 1980–83.

New Face In Hell

An irresistible and infectious groove with a clear debt to The Velvet Underground's 'What Goes On'. The two-chord pattern provides a loose, scruffy funk that propels the song with a momentum that's somehow both intense and languid. The second half is surprisingly loose and free form, especially considering Smith's general aversion to musicians 'showing off'. The use of kazoo is prominent – an instrument that would reappear sporadically throughout the group's career.[63] The song is also notable for its compelling barrage of deftly delivered complex lyricism. Paul Hanley summarises it neatly: 'The wireless enthusiast hears an illicit broadcast, nips next door, spots his friend's body and gets arrested. Roll titles. But the fact that the government agent poisons the neighbour and frames the wireless enthusiast rather than simply killing *him* opens up a host of narrative possibilities, none of which Mark sees any need to explore – which inevitably forces listeners to fill in the rest of the story's detail for themselves.' Surprisingly, it only had an 18-month shelf-life as far as gigs were concerned, the 31st and final performance coming in October 1981.

C'n'C-S Mithering

A new level of minimalism. The monotonous two-note motif – accompanied by the first glimpse of an acoustic guitar on a Fall record and backed by a sparse snare rhythm – meanders along for nearly two minutes before Smith appears. His delivery is initially calm and measured but intensifies considerably as the group pick up the pace around the four-and-a-half-minute mark. At this point he launches into a typical tirade about the shallowness and hypocrisy of the music industry. This is a particularly incisive version of his trademark rant, dripping with sarcasm and vitriol: 'make joke records, hang out with Garry Bushell / go on Roundtable: "I like your single" / "Yeah, great!" / A circle of low IQ's'.[64] Smith never captured his irritation with life in general better than with the expression 'the things that drain you off and drive you off the hinge'. In addition, the repeated refrain of 'see ya mate; yeah, see ya mate' is one of the most fondly regarded moments of humour in the Fall canon. The second half of the song sees Smith launch into an outpouring of words where it seems that he can barely keep up with his own thoughts; a multitude of ideas and opinions tumbling out with wild invention. As The

[63] *The Annotated Fall* suggests that the kazoo part was an attempt to recreate the theme from *P.J.*, a 1968 crime mystery film starring George Peppard. That the film was released in the UK as *New Face in Hell*, the vague similarity between the melodies of the two pieces of music and the fact that this sounds just like the sort of thing Smith would attempt makes this a far from implausible idea.

[64] It's hard to capture the sheer, withering sarcasm of 'yeah, great' in writing. It's at 5:47.

Fall expanded their fanbase overseas (unlike *Dragnet*, *Grotesque* was released in the US, Australia and New Zealand), non-UK fans must have been increasingly bewildered by Smith's distinctly northern English reference points. This track is a case in point: not only is the title indecipherable to foreign eyes (*The Annotated Fall* translates C'n'C, i.e. cash and carry, as 'wholesale warehouse' and mithering as 'make a fuss or moan or complain') but who knows what 1980s American and Antipodean fans might have made of 'Kwik Save' and 'surplus johnnies'.

Like several other tracks in later years, 'Cash and Carry' (as it's referred to by most group members from the time) started life as a relatively sketchy idea that was used as a set-opener and was little more than backing for Smith's inimitable 'Good evening, we are The Fall' introduction.[65] Between 1980 and 1982 it was played 39 times, either as a standalone song or as a segue into other tracks.

The Container Drivers

A joyful, exuberant, rickety blast of deranged rockabilly and a fine example of the new 'C'n'N' approach. Paul Hanley – who provides extravagant drum fills throughout – points out that the song was an example of Smith 'assimilating a deeply unfashionable musical genre, which he genuinely enjoyed, in order to unsettle, shake up, and hopefully educate the more closed-eared followers'. He also comments that the song 'could have also been described as following a 12-bar blues structure had anyone in the band been able to consistently count to twelve'. The description of the life of the long-distance lorry driver whose work sees him bedevilled by 'bad indigestion, bad bowel retention' and 'grey ports with customs bastards' is grimly hilarious. After being played throughout the early 80s, it was revived in 1997 and again in 2012; its last performance, in 2016, was its 74th.

Impression Of J. Temperance

A curious, disturbing tale of a dog breeder's grotesque experiments:

---

[65] On its first appearance, at Birmingham University on 18th March 1980, this went 'Good evening, we are The Fall. We are not as the poster indicates. It's a change of turn, a different turn on, at first.'

'the newborn thing, hard to describe / like a rat that's been trapped inside a warehouse base, near a city tide / brown sockets, purple eyes / and fed with rubbish from disposal barges'. The twisted tale is well matched by the sinister, oppressive atmosphere the group create via the steady but relentless snare, the stabs of discordant freakshow organ and the shrieking guitar. Where these elements collide, the effect is as creepy as any horror film soundtrack. The press release states that it was written 'in a bed and breakfast in Retford miles from anywhere when the locals got suspiciously friendly and there was a huge man-sized one-eyed teddy bear on the landing'. Played live 33 times, 1980-82.

In The Park

Sex was not a subject Smith regularly dwelt upon, so it's rather startling to discover that 'In The Park' is basically a paean to dogging: 'I take you to the park up the road... rain makes policemen no threat / turns cars into little specks / muffles the shouts of your neighbour and we will have sex here'. Musically, it's a nice mix of Bo Diddley-esque shuffle and Beefheart-ish discordance. Absolute filth, and lots of fun. It only got four live outings, all in 1980.

W.M.C. – Blob 59

The second of what was to become a long line of – depending on one's point of view – either sonic experimentation or self-indulgent filler. Graham Lock was firmly in the latter camp, calling it 'instantly disposable trash' in his *NME* review. The press release described it as a 'very funny track. It's a pity you can't hear what's going on.' Whilst you could debate the comic value of the track, you can't argue with the second half of that statement. It's a jagged mix of distorted noises and a muffled recording of Kay Carroll 'singing' over percussion apparently played on Tupperware. Steve Hanley thought it sounded like Smith had 'recorded it in his shoe'. On its own, it's rather inconsequential, but it sits quite nicely on *Grotesque*, forming a nicely odd interlude between the sprightly 'In The Park' and the slow, snaking blues of the following track. A loose variation on the song, just called 'Blob

59', formed a shambling, tuneless introduction to both 'Lie Dream Of A Casino Soul' and 'Prole Art Threat' at five gigs in 1981.[66]

Gramme Friday

Like 'Totally Wired', 'Friday' was a drug song, 'gramme' being a term Smith often used to refer to speed, by now his stimulant of choice. 'Dr. Morell' is Theodor Morell, Hitler's physician, who is believed to have given Adolf (a notoriously late riser) a spot of methamphetamine to perk him up. The line 'I am Robinson Speedo and this is my Gramme Friday' suggests a link to *Robinson Crusoe*, and implies that Smith is characterising the drug as his own trusty sidekick. Musically, it's a mix of swaggering 12-bar blues and loose, atonal sections featuring the type of off-key chords later deployed by Sonic Youth.[67] Played live 25 times 1980-82.

The N.W.R.A.

The first third of 'N.W.R.A.' has a swing-beat rhythm, providing a jaunty atmosphere that makes an effective contrast to the discordant tone of everything else that's going on. Smith's exclamation of 'shift!' at 3:10 denotes exactly that: Paul Hanley introduces a fuller-bodied floor-tom pattern; the churning metallic guitars become more forceful; Steve Hanley gets a bit more creative and assertive (there's a particularly lovely little fill at 8:09). The kazoo appears again, but is used more sparingly. Over all this, Smith provides a heady mix of off-tune crooning, acidic declamation and idiosyncratic timing ('security guards hung from moving escalators' at 6:24 is a particularly good example). Narrated by Joe Totale, Roman's 'yet unborn son', 'N.W.R.A.' begins with a relatively comprehensible account of a Northern insurrection led by R. Totale that is corrupted by opportunist

[66] *Very* loose, Smith's atonal vocals bearing only a passing resemblance to the singing on the album version. It can be heard on *Live From The Vaults – Glasgow 1981* (see Chapter 4) preceding 'Prole Art Threat'; it also appeared with 'Lie Dream' on the DVD *Northern Cream: Fall DVD That Fights Back!* Released in 2009, the DVD featured footage from Bar 2 in Sheffield, 28th February 1981.

[67] New York's avant-garde noise merchants were admirers of the group; they recorded a Peel session in 1988 wholly comprised of Fall tracks.

capitalist Tony (possibly a reference to Factory Records co-founder Tony Wilson). However, the lyric – as Paul Hanley puts it – 'breaks free of the shackles of narrative cohesion before it's even halfway through'. Blogger and cultural theorist Mark Fisher considered the song to be a 'masterpiece':

> The story is told episodically, from multiple points of views, using a heteroglossic riot of styles and tones (comic, journalistic, satirical, novelistic): like 'Call of Cthulhu' re-written by the Joyce of *Ulysses* and compressed into ten minutes.

Smith felt that many misinterpreted the song: 'Here we go again – Smith talking about flat caps and all that clichéd rubbish. Actually, the message in it is that if the north did rise again, they would fuck it up.' Which is indeed exactly what the song does say: 'the North has rose again / but it will turn out wrong'.

'The N.W.R.A.' is one of several Fall songs that those who believe in such things point to as evidence for Smith's 'pre-cog' abilities. Around six months after *Grotesque*'s release, the first of the 1981 English riots took place in Brixton, to be followed in the summer by further outbreaks in Birmingham, Liverpool, Leeds and Manchester. The Specials' 'Ghost Town', which spent three weeks at number one that summer, captured evocatively the atmosphere of urban decay, resentment and anger prevalent at the time. 'N.W.R.A.' is, however, rather different. Whilst it has an undoubtedly brooding, oppressive tone, it's as much fantasy as social commentary, notwithstanding the references to Teesside docks and kids chucking bricks through windows – 'science fiction stuff', as Smith himself said. It was played live 34 times, 1980-1981.

Reviews and Reissues
Sounds' Johnny Waller gave the album an enthusiastic five-star review, calling it 'an aggressive, cohesive, strong bonded album – the most complete to date and the most diverse'. In the *NME*, however, Graham Lock was surprisingly lukewarm, accusing the

group of being in a rut: 'throwing up fewer surprises these days…
[the] scenarios… are typical Fall terrain'. Despite the *NME*'s
reservations, *Grotesque* topped the UK independent album chart;
it also reached number 38 in New Zealand.

The album was reissued six times between 1993 and 2004. The
1998 Castle reissue added 'Elastic Man', 'Hobgoblins', 'Wired' and
'Putta Block';[68] the 2004 Sanctuary version also included 'Mark
E Smith Self-Interview 1980'. This was recorded in 1980 for
Tapezine – introduced as a 'remarkable self-interview' by a 'rather
out of it Mark Smith', it finds Smith denouncing *Melody Maker* for
'becoming a threat to the proletariat', pronouncing 'Idi Amin' in
a bizarre fashion ('eye-dee ah-min') and expressing outrage that
one of The Vapors is 'a fucking lawyer'.[69]

Evaluation

Grotesque built on the impressive trajectory seen in the group's
third Peel session. The musicians exhibit a remarkable increase
in confidence, invention and harmony, creating a diverse series
of ragged, angular and hypnotically relentless riffs and grooves
that would come to define the classic Fall sound. There's a
shift in balance too: a much greater proportion of the group's
uniqueness originates from the four musicians than from Smith's
lyrics and vocal style. This, of course, does not in any way serve
to underestimate Smith's contribution. He too is transformed
here and sounds utterly in control of his own unique style. There
are many intriguing and well-constructed lines and turns of
phrase on the first two albums, but only 'Spectre' comes close
to the dense, complex poeticism of 'New Face In Hell', 'The
N.W.R.A.' or 'C'n'C-S Mithering'. Now, as Brian Edge put it,
Smith 'executed his ideas without hesitation, as if he had suddenly
come to understand the power of his own words'.

---

[68] The Castle version put the four bonus tracks at the beginning of the album, apparently
believing that a chronological approach was the best one. The later Sanctuary reissue
more sensibly places the extra songs at the end.

[69] MES claims that he was told about The Vapors by his mother; he even sings a brief
snatch of the band's only hit, 'Turning Japanese'. The *Tapezine* recording was presumably
a fanzine flexi-disc, but information is scarce.

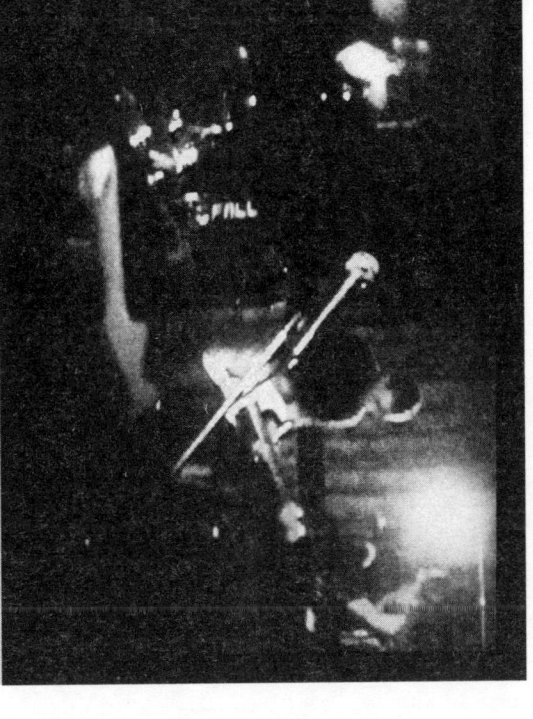

'SLATES'
by:
THE
FALL

incl:
MID-MASS
LOVER ETEC.
PROLE THREAT
WORKING.YEAH
SLAGS.,SLATES.,ETSET.
CAP.!HET!
cost:
TWO POUNDS ONLY
v skinny rats

Slates
Recorded: Berry Street Studio, Clerkenwell, London, February 1981
Released: 24th April 1981

Personnel:
Mark E Smith – vocals
Marc Riley – guitar, vocals
Craig Scanlon – guitar
Steve Hanley – bass
Paul Hanley – drums

With:
Dave Tucker – clarinet, vocals
Kay Carroll – vocals, kazoo

Chapter 4: Slates

'TWO POUNDS ONLY u skinny rats'

By the time *Grotesque* was released, The Fall were in the middle of a UK tour that would see them play 32 dates between September 1980 and February 1981. The tour included occasional appearances by clarinettist Dave Tucker. Tucker was a Prestwich resident who had been in bands such as The Dirty Shirts and Mellotron, the latter of which briefly featured Karl Burns on drums. He met Smith in The Foresters pub in October 1980, and following a conversation about H. P. Lovecraft and Ornette Coleman found himself on stage with the group at Manchester Poly on 1st November. Tucker describes the gigs of this period as 'tense, edgy affairs with a mixture of appreciation and hostility between band and audience – a charged atmosphere in which Smith thrived'.[70]

Although the tour was ostensibly to promote *Grotesque*, new material featured prominently in the set and all six songs that would appear on *Slates* were debuted before the end of the year. The group played two dates at London's Acklam Hall on 11th and 12th December. A recording of the first night, *Live in London 1980*, was released on cassette (semi-officially, limited to 4000 copies) on the Chaos Tapes label in March 1982.[71] It sold out quickly and reached number seven on the independent chart. The Fall tended to develop songs on the stage as much as (if not more than) in the rehearsal room, new numbers often being tried out in gigs in various forms before emerging on a studio release. This was clearly becoming obvious to Fall fans, who, according to Smith, didn't

---

[70] According to Ian, a contributor to thefall.org gigography, this hostility was certainly apparent at Dave Tucker's debut gig: 'Someone in the crowd lobbed a beer can up and hit MES with it. MES didn't blink and carried on the song without pausing. At the end of the song he went over to Hanley and Scanlon who pointed out somebody in the crowd about half way back. MES shouts you fucking ugly twat and walks off stage reappearing a minute later in the crowd striding over to the can lobber and smacking him one in the face.'

[71] *Live in London 1980* received an official release in 1996, retitled as *The Legendary Chaos Tape*.

take long 'to realise they can tape a gig and put them out before the album's released'. The aim of this release, as Smith saw it, was 'to break the back of all these twats who tape our new numbers at gigs'. *Live in London 1980* is not exactly crystal clear sound-wise, but it captures the group at a high point in terms of invention and confidence. 'Middle Mass', for example, is remarkably tight and coherent given that it was only the song's second outing. It includes some interesting variations in the lyrics: 'the son of Mike Parkinson, made from coal… we lost one of our lads today… he was from Lancashire'. 'Spectre vs. Rector' is actually well suited by the variable sound quality: the thinness of the guitar sound gives it a spidery quality that adds to the creepy atmosphere. In what was to become yet another long-standing Fall tradition, the titles provided on the cover are rather hit and miss. 'Middle Mass' is entitled 'Crap Rap'; 'Slates, Slags etc.' is 'Male Slags'; 'Prole Art Threat' is 'Gramme Friday'; 'An Older Lover etc.' is just '?'

Another official release recorded on this tour was *Live From The Vaults – Glasgow 1981*. Released in 2005, it was recorded at the Plaza on 23rd February. The performance sounds excellent in places – 'Slates, Slags, Etc.' is an especially intense barrage, and 'Printhead' (the only relatively old song) gets an enthusiastic workout – but is let down by ropy sound quality. At only 36 minutes (it contains only nine of the fifteen songs played that night), it's not exactly good value for money either. Smith is clearly unhappy about the sound at the beginning of the set: 'It would be a good idea if you turned the PA on!'; 'Can you turn the monitors ON please?' Grant Showbiz is also ordered in no uncertain terms to 'sort out the sound on stage' at the end of 'Totally Wired'.

After recording *Slates* in February, The Fall returned to the BBC for their fourth Peel session. As well as 'Middlemass' (one word at this point) and 'Lie Dream Of A Casino Soul' (which would be their next single) they revisited 'C'n'C-S Mithering', this time bolting on an amusing adaptation of Coast To Coast's version of the old rock'n'roll number 'The Hucklebuck', which was in the charts at the time.[72] The session also saw the first

[72] It's worth reading *The Annotated Fall* entry on the song, if only for bzfgt's startling vehemence regarding Coast To Coast's bit of nostalgic chart fluff.

recorded appearance of 'Hip Priest', which had been played for the first time a week earlier at Leeds University. It's impressive, but a little haphazard and overstretched in comparison to the later album version. Steve Hanley was beginning to realise how devoted Peel was becoming to the group that he dubbed 'The Mighty Fall':

> 'Hip Priest' has developed enough to require nine minutes of recording... It brings our total session time to five minutes more than the usual fifteen-minute allocation. But nothing's edited, Peel plays the lot and loves it. I get the feeling that if we played a twenty-minute song he'd broadcast that.[73]

Slates

Slates was recorded at Berry Street Studio in Clerkenwell. Grant Showbiz produced again, with some assistance from Rough Trade's Geoff Travis and Adrian Sherwood of On-U Sound fame. The cover, an MES creation, is perhaps the archetypal Fall anti-design sleeve, the grainy, indistinct on-stage photo accompanied by random text ('CAP.! HET!' and two alternative spellings of 'etc.').[74] The back cover contained typically cryptic descriptions of each track. The original intention had been to record only two songs for a new single, but the almost boundless creativity of the group at the time led to the lengthier release, as explained on *Slates & Dates*, the press release that accompanied the group's US tour later that year. 'The time was mid-February, The Fall, ORIGINALLY intending to cut 2 tracks ended up with many more. As crumbs of nightmare filtered through they decided to release the lot, as ALL TRAKS ARE RELATED.'

How one should categorise *Slates* format-wise is a surprisingly controversial issue. *Slates & Dates* described it as a '10" 33rpm single release'. The *NME*'s Andy Gill called it 'either a small elpee or a big single'. According to Simon Ford, the 'ten-inch

---

[73] At 20:21, the session was relatively lengthy, but the group would go on to record four that were longer (see Appendix 1).

[74] The layout – in particular the yellow column on the left-hand side – bears a close resemblance to *Under Heavy Manners*, a 1977 LP by Prince Far I. Paul Hanley has suggested that this was deliberate on Smith's part.

record resided unhappily somewhere between a maxi-single and mini-album'. It might seem bizarre to anyone not immersed in Fall culture, but whether or not *Slates* is an album rouses remarkably strong feelings amongst the group's fanbase. On the *Fall Online Forum*, discussion threads that merely touch on *Slates* are frequently diverted into lengthy discourse regarding its status. One argument is that it is a substantial piece of work and its relatively brief duration (23:47) is irrelevant, as other releases that are generally regarded as albums – for example Dylan's *Nashville Skyline* (27:41) and The Byrds' *The Notorious Byrd Brothers* (28:28) – are not much longer. The non-LP contingent point out that it is hardly fair to compare *Slates* to 'full-length' albums of 40+ minutes' duration where engaging the audience's attention is more of a challenge. There are many other sub-arguments that lie somewhere between these positions. Perhaps the most important thing about this issue is that it highlights the passion, attention to detail and stubborn crankiness that is the hallmark of the Fall community.

The unusual format, whatever it actually is, was a typical piece of Fall perversity and, in an era when chart performance was still a crucial issue, was a barrier to the release attaining any sort of commercial success. According to the BPI, to qualify as a single, a release could have no more than four tracks; an album (at the time) had to retail at £2.49 or more.[75] With six songs, and priced – as stated on the cover – at 'TWO POUNDS ONLY' (five dollars on the US version), *Slates* basically did not exist commercially. Smith, however, felt that the format was innovative and was aggrieved that Rough Trade had, in his eyes, failed to promote it effectively. He despaired of what he perceived as the label's bourgeois hippiedom: 'I'd had enough of them and they're all middle class. They don't know what The Fall was about.'

---

[75] The BPI is the British Phonographic Industry, the record industry's trade association, founded in 1973. Worldwide, there is a myriad of different sets of rules on this issue. The Recording Industry Association of America, for example, defines an EP as containing three to five songs or under 30 minutes. The Grammy Awards considers anything with five or more songs and a running time over 15 minutes as an album.

Middle Mass
U are what you call-but it's better than becoming the New Swiss.
A HOLY Characterisation.[76]

The title itself may be a play on the German word 'Mittelmaß', meaning average or mediocre, contempt for middle-class orthodoxy being a theme that Smith would return to on several occasions. MES himself suggested that 'Middle Mass' was about football hooliganism (the reference to 'summer close season' seemingly tying in with this interpretation). Marc Riley, however, was convinced that the lyric (especially 'a quiet dope and cider man' and 'this boy is like a tape loop / and he has soft mitts') was a dig at him but Smith 'didn't have the balls to admit it'. Steve Hanley described Riley's reaction on hearing the vocal for the first time in the studio: 'This is not the calm Marc I've known all my life, I've not seen him look so upset since his sister popped his space hopper.' Whatever Smith's intentions, this incident marked the beginning of a conflict between him and his guitarist that would deepen significantly over the next couple of years.

The main section of the song, framed by an ascending/descending bassline, has a just-off-the-beat, lurching rhythm that gives it an edgy, unpredictable feel, emphasised by the unusual chord progression. The last 80 seconds see a sudden turn into an ostensibly 'lighter' passage, but whilst it has a comparatively gentle lilt, there's still something strange and spiky about it, even if the aggression is a little more veiled. Although it had a long break between 1984 and 2003, 'Middle Mass' was a long-standing setlist favourite, making over 100 appearances altogether.

An Older Lover etc.
real Bert Finn stuff
The back cover comment refers to Albert Finney, one of whose most famous roles was in the 1960 kitchen sink drama film adaptation of Alan Sillitoe's *Saturday Night and Sunday Morning*, in which his character, Arthur Seaton, has an affair with an older, married woman. Beyond this, there's not actually that much in

---

[76] The description from the record's back cover is included with each song title.

the lyric to link it directly to this potential source, but there's certainly a cynical and sordid tone: 'old divorces / children's faces'; 'her love was like your mother's / with added attractions'; 'you'll soon get tired of her / she'll shag you out on the table'. An obvious and frequently reached conclusion is that the song is about Kay Carroll, although she was only eight years older than Smith. There's nothing specific in the lyric that supports this, although Dave Tucker thought that this was the case – 'you should have seen Kay's face when he sang it'. The identity of 'Doctor Annabel' remains a mystery. Paul Hanley's percussion is understated and subtle, the intertwined guitars are hypnotic, and Steve Hanley has sufficient space to enhance his throbbing bassline with frequent flourishes. Although 'Lover' made regular appearances in late 1980 / early 1981 gigs, it wasn't a long-standing feature: its 32nd and final appearance came at the group's last 1981 performance in London in December.

Prole Art Threat
starring 'gent' and 'man' in Asda mix-up spy thriller:
'Prole' leaps belligerently from the speakers from the outset, grabs you by the throat and never relinquishes its grip. Paul Hanley's manic snare sets a tone of galloping fury; his brother's leaping bassline locks horns with the one-chord guitar grind; the whole thing is a reckless, unhinged two-fingered salute at any notion of traditional structure. Smith's frantic yet focused babble fits the song perfectly, despite being utterly divorced from any conventional sense of rhythm or timing. Described in *Slates & Dates* as 'a spy media story found in an abandoned file cabinet', Smith explained that it was about a commuter who 'flips out on leftism and gets caught up with MI5 and all that'. The sheer ferocity and pace of the delivery makes more specific interpretation difficult, but you can't help but enjoy lines like 'hang this crummy blitz trad. by its neck' and 'um-brrrptzzap the subject'. 'Prole' had a longer live shelf-life than some of the other *Slates* tracks: 82 performances, the last of which was in November 1986.

Fit And Working Again

Religion costs much–but irreligion costs more:

The profound rear cover comment (taken from early 20th-century clergyman, Rev. George Lee) seems slightly at odds with what is actually the lightest moment on *Slates* ('a fun piece', according to *Slates & Dates*). 'Fit' is a sprightly, acoustic-guitar driven shuffle accompanied by tinkling piano and almost comic backing vocals. The lyrics start off matching the breezy tone ('walk down the road in the sun') but soon take a darker turn ('my lungs encrusted in blood'; 'sat opposite a freak on a train / warts on his head and chin'). Boxer Alan Minter would not be the last celebrity to be dropped into a MES lyric with apparent randomness. Like 'Rowche Rumble', there's a drug reference ('I just ate eight sheets of blotting paper') and Paul Hanley identifies a further link between the two songs, describing 'Fit' as 'one of Mark's "Underground Medecin" songs, a strange theory about using your body to its full potential, also referenced in "Rowche Rumble".'[77] Smith seems to have tired of the song relatively quickly as it was only played 16 times, the last performance coming in March 1982.

Slates, Slags etc.

Full bias content guaranteed. Plagarism infests the land. Academic thingys ream off names of books and bands

'Here's the definitive rant,' Smith declares, and he isn't kidding. An unforgiving two-chord riff underpinned by squalling feedback sees the group lock on to a serrated Velvet Underground groove once again. Riley's deadpan backing vocals, the distorted double-tracking of Smith's voice and the ghostly subterranean wailing from Kay Carroll all contribute to the unremitting cacophony. Both 'slag' and 'slate' have a variety of differing meanings, and this makes for an ambiguous lyric. 'RT VII', a contributor to *The Annotated Fall*, offers a convincing summary of the lyric's intent: '"Slates" is a term MES used to describe people who were grey, uniform and mundane, people without any inspiration or shred of individuality in their lives. Those who just accepted the status

---

[77] 'The full use of your body isn't it?'

quo. Just like slate tiles, all grey and all the same.' The line 'where they cast off the weights' is possibly a reference to Kurt Vonnegut's short story *Harrison Bergeron*.[78] 'Slates' was one of the growing number of bones of contention between Smith and Rough Trade: the song 'was totally un-PC for Rough Trade. They didn't like the phrase "male slags". A lot of so-called hipsters are very conservative like that.' Although it was a stalwart in the live set throughout 1981, it only made a couple of appearances thereafter and bowed out in August 1982 after its 33rd outing.

Leave The Capitol
Any capital. Polite no-manners plus barman of the year claimants = quick exit.

Despite the back cover's claim that the song refers to 'any capital', there's a clear sense of Smith's oft-repeated disdain for London. As *Fall Online Forum* contributor MartinM puts it, the lyric can be read 'as both anti-London and anti-logic or anti-habit: get out of the confines of metropolitan thought imposed by our barren time modelled on Roman ideals (straight roads, worship of armed force), and return to older, instinctive ways of thought and imagination'. Arthur Machen was another of Smith's favourite horror writers, and his most famous work, *The Great God Pan*, is mentioned here. In addition, 'I live with cancer death wife' possibly refers to Machen's first wife, Amy Hogg. Although relatively traditional in structure, the song's off-kilter arpeggios and choppy chords, plus its bleak production, give it a haunting air. This is offset nicely by occasional snatches of kazoo and harmonica. The track can also be seen as the blueprint for Pavement's entire career.[79] After making its debut in November 1980, 'Capitol' was a virtually permanent feature in the setlist for the next 12 months, clocking up 43 appearances. The performance in Plymouth on 1st November 1981, however, was its final outing.

---

[78] Published in 1961, *Harrison Bergeron* is a dystopian tale set in 2081 where nobody is allowed to be smarter, better-looking, or more physically able than anyone else. As a result, for example, dancers are weighed down to counteract their gracefulness.
[79] In a 1993 interview for *Melody Maker*, MES claimed that when he heard Pavement for the first time he thought it might be a Fall live tape from 1987. He wasn't wrong about The Fall's influence on Stephen Malkmus & co., but he was six years out.

Reviews and Reissues

Album or not, *Slates* was well-received in the music press. Andy Gill, despite lamenting the absence of 'Northern rockabilly', identified that the group had 'come a long way... without sacrificing their essential grating harshness', and enjoyed *Slates*' 'mini-operas... rough-hewn, sore and scabby blocks of narrative, comment, invective... scrambled up and spat out in gobs'. One review came from a particularly unlikely source, *Titbits* pronouncing *Slates* to be 'raw and uncompromising... cynical, witty and often devious'. The magazine – not known for covering pop music, let alone post-punk – even weighed in on the 'LP or EP' debate, describing the release as an 'odd-sized record' before deciding that 'maxi-single or a mini album, it's still good value'.[80]

Slates was reissued in 1992 and 1998, on both occasions being twinned with live LP *A Part Of America Therein, 1981* (see Chapter 5). A further reissue in 2004 added the fourth Peel session and both sides of the 'Lie Dream Of A Casino Soul' single (released five months after *Slates*). It also included the outtake 'Medical Acceptance Gate', which sees Smith deliver a strange narrative about meeting a 'tall and twisted' man who 'was made up of liquid pitch' and 'reeked of bleach and hospitals' over a stark, seemingly improvised backing.

Evaluation

However much enjoyment Fall fans wring out of the perpetual 'format' debate, whether *Slates* is an album, EP, maxi-single, mini-album or whatever is ultimately irrelevant. It's a coherent and inventive piece of work that sees the group take on a variety of styles with consistent confidence. Whilst it doesn't represent the significant shift in sound of 1980, it does see the group settle into and develop the style they had established with *Grotesque*. There's a sense of poise and balance about it – it's beautifully sequenced, something that can't be said about several other Fall releases – and it sees the group working with a unity of purpose that they would rarely better.

[80] *Titbits* was a human interest / lifestyle / gossip magazine that became a common feature of dentists' waiting rooms in the 70s and 80s (although it was founded in 1881).

(1hr)   (1hr)   (1hr)

HEX ENDUCTION HOUR
BY THE FALL

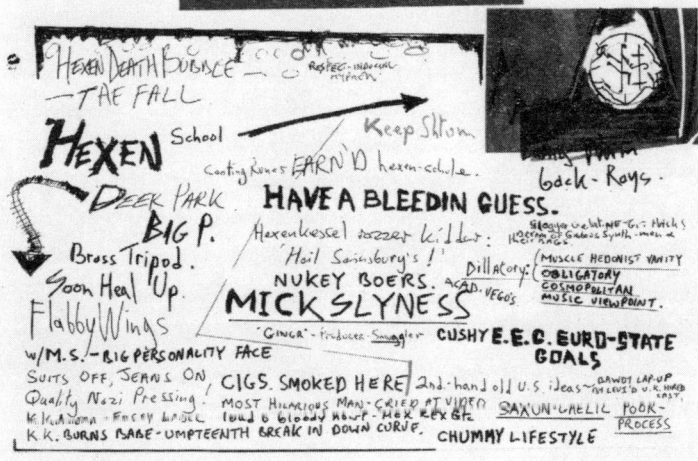

Hex Enduction Hour

Recorded: Hljóðriti studio, Reykjavík, September 1981; Regal Cinema, Hitchin, December 1981 / January 1982[81]

Released: 8th March 1982

Personnel:
Mark E Smith – vocals
Marc Riley – guitar, keyboards
Craig Scanlon – guitar, vocals, keyboards
Steve Hanley – bass, vocals
Paul Hanley – drums, guitar
Karl Burns – drums, vocals, tapes

With:
Kay Carroll – vocals, percussion

[81] There's some debate as to whether the recording began in December or January. Even Paul Hanley was unable to unravel it completely for *Have A Bleedin Guess.*

Chapter 5: Hex Enduction Hour

'Something to do with witchcraft.'

Being signed to Rough Trade had meant that, unlike the first two albums, both *Grotesque* and *Slates* had enjoyed a simultaneous release in the US. As the group hadn't played in America for two years, it seemed commercially advisable for them to return. As the label began to plan the tour, one obstacle became clear: Paul Hanley, still 17, was unlikely to be awarded a work visa to play in America's largely 21+ venues. Smith's solution was to re-engage the services of Karl Burns. Before setting off for the States, The Fall played around a dozen dates in Germany, Belgium and The Netherlands in May 1981. To ease Burns's return to the line-up, he and Paul Hanley played alternate nights for the first few dates. Some of these performances can be heard on the 2005 LP, *Live From The Vaults – Alter Bahnhof, Hof, Germany*, which contained ten tracks from the 22nd May date at Hof in Northern Bavaria plus five more from the following night's performance in Berlin. Although the sound quality is not great, it contains interesting early versions of several *Hex* songs, the first performance of 'Session Musician' and also sees 'Fortress' paired up with 'Totally Wired' (as it was for most of its 1981 performances). One notable moment takes place during Smith's intro to 'N.W.R.A.'. He asks for the lights to be dimmed because 'we've lost enough weight as it is', to which an English voice from the audience (probably Kay Carroll) responds aggressively, 'Well stop over-indulging, you wanker!'

The US tour was an extensive one, the group playing around 30 gigs in just over six weeks. One of them, in New York on 9th June, saw The Fall support The Clash on one night of their 17-gig residency at Times Square club Bond's. Steve Hanley described the tour experience in some detail in *The Big Midweek*: the distances ('we've got *two* weeks to cover three and a half thousand miles?'), the tour bus music ('Frank Zappa, that's what you lot should be listening to. You might learn something'), the drugs ('aided by a pair of invisible bellows stuck up his arse, [Burns] proceeds to finish all several remaining centimetres of the joint in one almighty suck') and the boredom of travel ('massive roads that go through nothing but desert for miles and miles'). The tour was captured on the group's third live album, *A Part Of America Therein, 1981*. Released in America in May 1982, it featured recordings from five different performances. The opening pair of songs, 'The N.W.R.A.' and 'Hip Priest', come from the group's final American date at Tuts in Chicago on 16th July, and sees them get a somewhat portentous introduction ('From the riot-torn streets of Manchester, England…') The absence of keyboards on 'N.W.R.A.' (they've 'broke down', Smith explains) brings the interplay between the two guitar parts into sharp focus. 'You're getting something unique,' Smith remarks at the end, 'anyone who wants a fifty cents refund send an airmail letter to the Outer Hebrides.' 'Hip Priest' (still unreleased, but already making its 25th live appearance) sees Burns demonstrate masterful control of mood and tempo. 'Totally Wired' fizzes with energy and features some interesting extemporisation: 'you don't have to be a dye-haired, punk-fuck-shit-pop-fuck-shut-tick-tock-pad… you don't have to be strange to be strangled'. The second half of the album, however, suffers from inferior sound quality and feels a little sluggish in comparison. *Therein* didn't appear in the UK until 1992, when it was included as part of the CD re-issue of *Slates*; it didn't get a separate UK release until 2004. Despite this, it reached number 9 on the UK Independent Albums Chart in 1983. The original back cover commemorated a personal highlight for Smith and Carroll: a visit to Graceland.

The key question on the group's return to the UK concerned the permanent occupant of the drum stool. Paul Hanley was understandably nervous about the situation, as his brother describes: 'six weeks is a long time to be out of the loop, especially when you know there's a very competent and original drummer taking your place on the other side of the Atlantic'. Nevertheless, the group's fifth Peel session, recorded on 26th August and broadcast on 15th September, saw Paul Hanley back behind the kit. Much to Steve Hanley's excitement, the session producer was

Dale Griffin, ex-drummer of Mott The Hoople. A remorseless 'Deer Park' falls only slightly short of the breathtaking ferocity of the album version. 'Winter' is mesmerising, if slightly hesitant in places. 'It was clear that the band had evolved while I wasn't there,' Paul Hanley explains, 'and Mark was a bit frustrated with my version of "Winter" in particular. I played it how I remembered it, which was quite loose and behind the beat. With Karl it'd become harder and more nailed on.' Despite having several songs that had been thoroughly road-tested in America, The Fall elected to include two brand new songs in the session. 'Who Makes The Nazis?' was virtually made up on the spot, based around a 'daft riff' that Smith had composed on a plastic toy guitar.[82] It is, unsurprisingly, more primitive and basic than the album version, and moves at a much faster tempo. It featured Steve Hanley on backing vocals. 'I'm handed a sheet of paper with some bizarre backing vocals... The lyrics are the usual obscure poetics, so I've no idea if I'm being set up. I have to say some weird stuff about hate, love, soap and enemies.' 'Look, Know' had been worked on during soundchecks on the US tour, but wouldn't be played live until September. Despite having only been briefly rehearsed the day before the session, it hangs together well, although Steve Hanley makes an uncharacteristic error at 3:17.

Paul Hanley was still in the line-up when the group headed to Iceland in September. The visit was organised by 19-year-old Einar Örn (later of Sugarcubes fame) and involved three gigs – supported by Örn's band Purrkur Pillnikk – plus a session in a studio carved out of volcanic rock where the group recorded 'Look, Know', 'Hip Priest' and 'Iceland'. Articles about *Hex* sometimes suggest that the studio was some sort of dank, damp cave, but it was actually much more upmarket than the group were used to, Craig Scanlon describing it as 'plush, beautiful'. Journalist Colin Irwin accompanied the group on the trip and wrote a lengthy piece about it in *Melody Maker*. Irwin found Kay Carroll less than impressed with the country: 'No beer, no trees,

---

[82] According to Paul Hanley, this was 'a Selco "New Beat" toy Beatles guitar, manufactured in 1964 and given to Mark by Kay.' This was the same instrument on which Smith wrote the riff for 'No Xmas For John Quays'.

no telly on Thursdays or in the whole of July, no cigarettes and blokes walking round with toilet rolls in their ears' (a reference to overzealous officials monitoring the group's sound levels). There was no beer because, although prohibition in Iceland had ended in 1935, the sale of beer remained illegal until 1989 (the 1st of March is still celebrated as 'Beer Day'). The spirits-only regime took its toll on the young Paul Hanley in particular, but even Smith suffered: 'You could only drink shit like pints of peach schnapps... I thought my legs had been stolen.' Although a few other British bands such as The Kinks and Led Zeppelin[83] had previously visited Iceland, The Fall's arrival was a rare enough occurrence to make the front pages of a national newspaper and saw large, diverse crowds attend their three performances.

The drummer issue was settled on the group's return to the UK, Burns re-joining The Fall as part of a dual-drummer line-up. Having two drummers wasn't unheard of (The Glitter Band, of whom MES was an admirer and whose distinctive sound would influence a few later Fall songs, were a prominent example) but it was still unusual. It was a move that would play a significant role in defining the Fall sound over the next couple of years.

In what was a significant sign of the group's growing popularity and importance, Smith graced the cover of the *NME* for the first time on 14th November. (It's hard to imagine, in these days of bewildering diverse online media, how big a deal it was back then to be on the cover of the *NME*.) The somewhat breathless article opens with a quotation from Derrida and goes on to describe Smith as 'the only really important writer and singer in the vast, myth-saturated culture of Pop' who has addressed 'questions of art, culture, politics that Pop has only too conveniently ignored for too long... with a severe and violent humour and a vision of incomparable breadth'. The article also discussed the group's new single, released the day before. 'Lie Dream Of A Casino Soul' came out on the Kamera label. Smith had signed to Kamera having tired of Rough Trade's 'hippies' who would 'only send review copies

[83] 'Immigrant Song', from *Led Zeppelin III* ('We come from the land of the ice and snow / From the midnight sun, where the hot springs flow'), was inspired by and written during the band's 1970 visit to Reykjavík.

to left-wing magazines instead of the daily papers'. He described Kamera as an 'old rockers' label' (earlier in 1981 they had put out Freddie Starr's *Spirit of Elvis*) but was uncharacteristically positive about them: 'I have few good words to say about record companies, but [Kamera] were very good; a world away from the limp stuffiness of Rough Trade.' The single was recorded at The Workhouse Studios on London's Old Kent Road. The studio was the choice of producer Richard Mazda,[84] who also played sax on the lead song (although his contribution was far less prominent than Dave Tucker's clarinet on the Peel version). The sleeve art was designed by 'Savage Pencil', aka music journalist Edwin Pouncey, who Smith had mentioned back in 1979 on 'Your Heart Out'.

The single was a significant release in terms of the group's sound, as it was the first recorded output of the dual drummer line-up, although 'Lie Dream' actually saw only Burns behind the kit with Hanley adding extra percussion. Nonetheless, there's still a notable robustness to the rhythm section that gives this serrated stomp what Simon Ford described as 'the weight and momentum of an articulated lorry'. The song paints a grim picture of northern life, the protagonist – who lives in a 'slum canyon' – describing down and outs 'sleeping in outside bogs'. He's clearly had a big weekend: nothing to eat, 'no nerves left Monday morning' and considering cutting his 'dick off / the trouble it got me in'.[85] He later dreams that he's in a department store with 'cameras in the clothes dummies', a scenario possibly inspired by a March 1981 article in *Titbits* about an in-store surveillance mannequin called 'Bionica'.[86] Smith felt that his tribute to Wigan Casino and the Northern Soul scene was misunderstood:

> That song actually did create quite a bit of resentment in
> the North because people thought it was being snobby and

[84] Mazda was singer and guitarist with Tours, whose 1979 single 'Language School' was played regularly by John Peel.

[85] Smith told Paul Hanley that this was 'a more-or-less verbatim quote from someone he knew who was a Wigan Casino regular'. Hanley goes on to say that 'my dick off' was rendered as 'Mein Dyckhoff' on the sleeve so that it wouldn't be banned from the radio.

[86] Bionica 'looks like any other attractive store dummy. But under the latest fashions she hides a TV camera and a microphone that can pick up a shoplifter's whisper at a quarter of a mile.' How far this article actually influenced Smith's lyric is tricky to unravel – see *The Annotated Fall* for more detail.

horrible about the old soul boys, which it was never about anyway. Because I was brought up with people that were into Northern Soul five years before anybody down here [in London] had even heard about it. But they've all grown out of it, which is what the song is about, but it wasn't putting them down at all. If anything, it was glorifying them, but not in the format of, where are those soul boys that used to be here?

'Lie Dream' made an impressive 136 appearances live; after an 11-year hiatus, it returned for regular appearances in 1997-98. It's a mark of the group's productivity at this time that a song as strong as 'Fantastic Life' was used as a B-side. The infectious guitar hook and thumping percussion – both drummers are on full kit here – provide an exuberant backdrop as Smith ruminates on truth and lies ('fantastic' as in 'fantasy'; the lyric alternates between 'life' and 'lie'). According to Dave Tucker, the line about not believing the 'crap' of a 'friend called David [who] said he had a barney on Corporation Street' with a policeman is about him. It's a little more difficult to unpick the beautifully obscure 'the Siberian mushroom Santa was in fact Rasputin's brother'. It was played live 31 times, its last outing being in April 1983.

The Fall's next single, released a month after *Hex*, was 'Look, Know'. Recorded, along with the bulk of *Hex*, at Regal Studios in Hitchin (the Iceland version never saw the light of day), it was a snipe at people overly concerned with fashion and appearances ('our bodies weren't made for times like these / I always have a wash and that's enough'). The music, described by *The Track Record* as 'mildly funky', was largely written by Steve Hanley (although Riley pinched the closing frantic guitar line from The Fire Engines' 1981 single 'Candyskin') but it didn't quite turn out as the 'Dexys-type soul with a brass section' that he'd envisaged. B-side 'I'm Into CB' addressed the contemporary craze for citizens band radio.[87] Smith captures the mundanity and ridiculousness of early 80s teenage

[87] Like, I imagine, many others of the same vintage, I nagged my parents (successfully) for a CB radio in the early 80s and spent many hours basically asking other users – all pretty much within a 5-mile radius – where they lived, how old they were and how strong my signal was. You could have gained much more social interaction by simply riding your bike down to the park.

British life perfectly: using a CB without owning a car or ever having 'been near a lorry'; YTS schemes; your sister reading *Smash Hits* and listening to rubbish chart music; getting hammered in the park on Martini (or whatever you could get your hands on). Like many of Smith's lyrics from the early 80s, there's a strong essence of Englishness about the song and it's easy to imagine non-UK listeners being baffled by it. It's also interesting, in light of Smith's disapproval of attitudes to 'modern' fatherhood, to note how (relatively) affectionate his portrayal of the father figure is here: he may rarely talk to the protagonist, but he did provide the 'wires and bits' and is 'not bad really'. Musically, it's simplicity itself: a two-chord guitar chime, a snare drum and a cowbell, and Steve Hanley largely sticking to one note. The drums pick up pace towards the end, developing into an almost Bo Diddley-esque shuffle, and the guitar gets a little more adventurous, but other than that, it's classic early 80s Fall repetition. Debuted in September 1981, 'CB' was performed 43 times over the next couple of years.

Hex Enduction Hour

The majority of *Hex* was recorded at The Regal in Hitchin, Hertfordshire. The Regal Theatre had opened in 1939 and closed as a cinema in 1977.[88] It was converted to a studio and concert hall (hosting Spandau Ballet, the Thompson Twins and UB40) before being demolished and replaced by an office block in 1986. As Paul Hanley points out, a mythology has grown up around the album's recording that suggests that 'the group broke into a derelict building... in order to ensure that [their] rejection of studio artifice was created with sufficient vérité'. Smith has frequently contributed to this impression: 'I thought we should go to an old cinema and get a bit of a live feel to it.' In fact, The Regal was at the time an active venue with a 16-track recording studio upstairs from the performance space. The choice of studio was once again down to Richard Mazda, who was attracted by its capacity to record the group in an on-stage setting. Around half of the Regal recordings ('The Classical', 'And This Day',

---

[88] It featured Cary Grant in *Gunga Din* on its first night; its last showing was the dubious-sounding *Secrets of a Super Stud*.

'Fortress/Deer Park' and 'Mere Pseud Mag. Ed.') took place on the downstairs stage. The musicians were arranged in a circle, with the two drummers facing each other; Smith recorded his vocals in the upstairs studio. The remaining songs were better suited by a more traditional studio environment; the freezing weather (there was no heating in the stage area) was also a factor in the group moving upstairs.

The album's title was, according to Smith, 'something to do with witchcraft... "enduction" I just made up'. The cover ('just me with a felt tip') was full of typical Smithisms: 'Hexen Death Bubble'; 'Cigs. Smoked Here'; 'Hexenkessel rozzer kidder: "Hail Sainsbury's!"'; 'Flabby Wings'; 'Muscle Hedonist Vanity'. Smith describes himself as 'Big Personality Face'; Karl Burns becomes 'Burns Babe – Umpteenth Break In Down Curve'. The press release described the 'official new Fall product' as 'their most concentrated work to date', and concludes with a contact address, accompanied by the message 'please do not expect a reply, as The Fall are not a condescending French resistance type group nor do they have warehouses packed with info kits on themselves'. The cover and the title both emphasised one of the album's striking features – its hour-long duration. No UK pressing plant would entertain the idea, so the album had to be manufactured at Telefunken in Hamburg, a pressing plant that was experienced in producing lengthy classical recordings.

The Classical

The double drummers have an immediate impact, providing a clattering intensity that is integral to the whole sound. As Paul Hanley quite rightly points out, it is 'one of the best examples of a Fall song where two drummers are central and it doesn't really work with only one'. The breadth of the percussion gives Steve Hanley freedom to add plenty of melodic touches to his muscular bassline. Whilst the song is unerringly focused, there's a palpable air of dissonance and potential chaos. This is at least partly explained by its unusual musical structure, as explained by Stuart Estell: '[It's] bitonal – in two keys at once... the bass part is in a mode of A, while Scanlon's scratchy guitar part is in something like C#. That's why the sound of the thing changes so much when it gets to "I've never felt better…" – at that point Scanlon's chords start following the bass part and suddenly everyone's playing in the same key.'

The lyric opens with the proud philistinism of 'no culture is my brag' and also includes the playful ('I just left the Hotel Amnesia… where it is I can't remember'), the enigmatic ('there are twelve people in the world / the rest are paste'), the wry ('made with the highest British attention / to the wrong detail') and the hilariously abusive ('Hey there fuckface!') Smith commented that 'when we recorded that album we were sick of the music industry, the record was meant to be against that. It was our way of saying "fuck off!" to those people. "The Classical" is the song that sums it all up, it's the anthem of the record.'

The most controversial aspect of the song is, of course, the line 'where are the obligatory n★★★★★s?' The easiest, most comfortable option is to see it as a swipe at tokenism in the media. Moreover, Smith's lyrical abstrusity often made it difficult to disentangle his own thoughts from the words of the characters who populated his songs. It's also undoubtedly true that the use of the word would have been less shocking in 1982 than in the current climate. That said, it's hard to believe that Smith would have been ignorant of the potential impact of his choice of words. It becomes harder to excuse in light of his interview for *Allied Propaganda* fanzine in 1983, where he says that the offending phrase has 'come true, and every programme you see about young people has now got a black boy in it'. He goes on 'no black man's going to come over to me and say "You are the fuckin' oppressor", because I've never oppressed him, and as far as I'm concerned he's oppressing me, because I have to watch his music on TV'. Although these comments make for uncomfortable reading, there's no evidence that Smith held racist beliefs.[89] It's worth noting, however, that when the song returned to the set in 2002 (after a 17 year absence), that particular line was omitted. 'Perhaps…' muses Paul Hanley, 'even Mark E. Smith could grow tired of defending the

[89] *The Quietus*' John Doran published an excellent, thoughtful piece on the issue in November 2019, 'No Obligatory Excuse: Is "The Classical" By The Fall Racist?'.

indefensible.' After being a stalwart in 1982–85 setlists, a 2002 revival saw 'The Classical' clock up a further nine performances, bringing its total to 72.

Jawbone And The Air-Rifle

By the time of *Hex*'s release, 'Jawbone' had already been performed live 40 times. Early recordings show that it was fully formed from very early on. This is reflected in how tautly aggressive it sounds: the grinding riff launches itself at you from the first second, and the group sound utterly in synch. The riff (which Scanlon described as 'clunky') was based – at Smith's instigation – on 'Run Rabbit Run'.[90] The drumming is not as elaborate as on 'The Classical', and for much of the song Steve Hanley takes a more rhythmic role than on the opener; however, in the chorus he follows the melody of Smith's vocal, leaving the guitars to provide the foundation.

The slower sections bring out the dark, gothic tone of Smith's lyrics, which see him follow a relatively linear narrative. The 'rabbit killer' goes out hunting late at night, finding himself in a graveyard. His misplaced shot 'smashed a chip off a valued tomb' and incurs the ire of the grave-keeper ('out on his rounds') who demands that the hunter step into the 'light of the moon' and explain himself; the hunter's explanation is that he thought that he was a rabbit or a 'sex criminal' on the run. The grave-keeper then presents the hunter with a 'jawbone caked in muck' which is some sort of cursed relic from a Scottish 'pentacle church'. Whilst he tells the hunter that it will make him 'a bit of a man', it seems that this curse has devastating effects: the rabbit killer can't eat, has 'mangled teeth', loses his 'bottle' and seems to have a series of disturbing visions. It all gets very *Wicker Man* towards the end, with villagers dancing around prefabs and 'suck[ing] on marrowbones and energy from the mainland'. It's one of Smith's greatest lyrics, full of ominous imagery and gnarled and twisted turns of phrase. You can hear the influence of many of his

---

[90] Written for the 1939 show, *The Little Dog Laughed*, and performed by Flanagan and Allen. The duo enhanced the song's popularity by often changing the words to 'Run Adolf, run Adolf, run, run, run'.

favourite writers, such as Machen, M. R. James and Lovecraft. It also may be one of the Fall songs – alongside 'Theme From Sparta FC' – that is most familiar with those who have never knowingly heard one of the group's records, having been the theme tune to Frank Skinner's chat show in the 90s.[91] Despite being played regularly in 1981, 'Jawbone' was only played four more times after *Hex*'s release, getting 45 outings in total.

Hip Priest

Perhaps the most frequently referenced song in Smith's obituaries, partly due to its appearance in *The Silence of the Lambs*, but more likely because the notion of an alter-ego gave journalists something to hang their pieces on. It's always challenging to assess whether Smith's lyrics are being delivered with a first or third person meaning, and here the perspective swings between the two: 'he' is not appreciated; 'I' can teach. It is, of course, not difficult to imagine Smith feeling unappreciated – a sentiment that over the years he frequently expressed in relation to his musicians and the music press in particular. Several phrases are intriguingly ambiguous. 'White collar' usually suggests non-manual work, but here could just as easily refer to a clerical dog collar. 'Purple psychology' is obscure: purple is often worn by priests, but perhaps the word is used here with the same meaning as in 'purple prose'. The 'last clean dirty shirt' line is easier to pin down, being similar to Johnny Cash's (Kris Kristofferson-penned) 'Sunday Mornin' Comin' Down' ('I fumbled in my closet through my clothes / and found my cleanest dirty shirt'). *The Annotated Fall* makes a case for the 'long draught'-drinking Dan being Danny Baker, as an article he wrote about the group in 1978 contained the words 'appreciated' and 'hip'. Paul Hanley indicates that 'hip' also alludes to 'hypnotic induction process', a phrase that's also used in 'Just Step S'ways'. Smith himself provided a less than helpful explanation in a 1982 radio interview: 'It was a bit of a joke on the group cos they're all like Catholics... it's

---

[91] Skinner – as he explained on his 2010 *Desert Island Discs* appearance – was a late convert to the group but soon became somewhat obsessed. He was tempted to choose eight Fall tracks for his fictional exile but plumped for just 'Rowche Rumble' in the end.

meant to be a bit of a funny song... I have an image of Johnny Cash or somebody, I don't know why... or South America.' He was rather more revealing a year earlier in an interview with J Neo Marvin. When asked if the Hip Priest was, like Roman Totale, 'another one of those figureheads that speak for you', he replied: 'It could well be, yeah. That gets a bit personal at times. Maybe a bit too personal...'

The song originated at a soundcheck in March 1981, described here by Steve Hanley:

> Paul begins with a slow drumbeat, which captures all our attention. He's using just the rim of his snare instead of the skin, and fusing it together with the cymbals and the bass drum. One by one, compelled by the rhythm, we begin to improvise around it, quickly realising something's growing. We're nurturing it with our tempered anguish until a hollow atmosphere begins to fill the empty hall. It continues to build but then, with a sudden unanimous exchange of certain eye contact, a dramatic drop is triggered. Intuition takes over as we induce the pressure again, knowing we've got the bare bones of something different. Absorbing the music, Mark Smith appears from the wings, locks on and, riffling through his mental portfolio, extracts an alter ego, intoning his Hip Priest into existence.

The song is perhaps most striking for the group's control of dynamics. With many artists, the use of the quiet/loud approach is an exciting if not always subtle experience. 'Hip Priest' is far shrewder and all the more effective for it. The quiet passages are so sparse as to be almost falling away from you, and when the group do explode (for example at 3:42) it's not achieved with effects pedals (none were used on *Hex*) – it's organic, physical; achieved by attitude as much as by volume. 'Hip Priest' lasted longer on the setlist than many *Hex* songs, its 108th and final appearance coming in 1998.

After a Casio keyboard preset,[92] a disturbing moan and Smith's TV-presenter style introduction to 'the vitamin B glandular show', Scanlon throws himself into an ebullient, slashing riff. The 'two hours' spent 'with four left-wing kids' refers to Smith's experience of taking part in a round table discussion for Radio 1 show *Talkabout*. The seemingly random streams of numbers and letters ('room C-H-1-0-C-H-11') is actually MES expressing frustration at the arbitrary room numbering system in the BBC building.[93] Although the transition into 'Deer Park' is one of the most thrillingly perfect moments in the group's entire back catalogue, this segue only took place on stage half a dozen times. 'Fortress' was often played as a stand-alone song[94] or was twinned with 'Totally Wired'. On one occasion (New Jersey, 4th June 1981) the sequence was reversed.

'Deer Park' is a sonic onslaught; a wave of hypnotically jagged noise and fury. Smith's snarling vehemence is complemented perfectly by the unrelenting two-chord loop of Riley's keyboards and the grimy Stooges/Velvets guitar fuzz. Like 'The Classical' it was recorded on the Regal's stage with the two drummers facing each other, but on this occasion Burns and Paul Hanley go for enhanced power rather than contrasting complexity. This gives the song a remarkable potency ('Karl and I not only spurred each other to greater heights, but the rest of the group were similarly galvanised by the thumping groove behind them') which results in perhaps the best example of the group capturing the very essence of the '3 Rs'.

The title came from Norman Mailer's 1955 novel of the same name, which Smith had previously cited as an influence. He

---

[92] The same one used by German synth-pop act Trio on 'Da Da Da', a number two hit the month after *Hex*'s release. The Fall would revisit it on 1983's 'The Man Whose Head Expanded'.

[93] The Langham Hotel, a building owned by the BBC 1965-86. MES referred directly to it ('Much discussion in Langham House fortress') when performing the song in Chicago in July 1981. At Hammersmith Town Hall on 7th March 1985, he sang 'I spent time in BBC fortress'.

[94] At the last of the three 1981 Iceland gigs, a lengthier (three minute) version included the lines 'You can wander about Oslo, but we are told that outside of England the rest of the world is a smelly road, with holes for latrines, for urinals.'

equates viewing wildlife in a nature reserve to Northern tourists goggling at the baffling eccentricities of bohemian London. His ire is directed at London's crowds of 'European punks', 'oiks' who hold him up at the off-licence by scraping together their change to buy a couple of cans of lager, 'fat Captain Beefheart imitators with zits' (which possibly refers to Pere Ubu) and Rough Trade ('the sleeping promo dept. – they haven't had an idea in two years'). He also refers to Colin Wilson's 1960 novel, *Ritual in the Dark* and 'sus laws' (the right of the police to 'stop and search'), the use of which were a key factor in provoking the 1981 race riots in Brixton, Toxteth and Handsworth.[95] The most frequently debated line in the song is 'Who is the king shag corpse?' For no apparent reason other than the fact that he was at that time recently deceased, the phrase has often been linked to Ian Curtis. Paul Hanley offers a much more prosaic and convincing explanation: it refers to Karl Burns and/or Grant Showbiz, the only ones who were 'getting some' at the time. It was played 47 times 1981-82, but was never revived after that.

Mere Pseud Mag. Ed.

Another guitar-led onslaught, pushing belligerently at the boundaries of atonality. The riff (a loose adaptation of 'Baby Sitters' by Stupid Babies[96]) has real heft, particularly in the cacophonous increase in tempo just before the two-minute mark. It's a withering character assassination of the 'Mag. Ed.' ('his brain was in his arse'; 'real ale, curry as well – sophisticate'), although it's not clear whether it's aimed at one particular journalist or the profession in general.[97] The vocal is one of the best examples of Smith's wilful disregard for traditional notions of timing, and also one of many occasions where he stubbornly crams a line (here, 'mere pseud mag editor's father') into a space where it plainly doesn't fit. It was one of the longest-serving songs on the

<hr>

[95] Whilst Smith's use of the phrase 'young blackies' is regrettable from a 21st-century perspective, the tone of the comments is, to be fair, obviously sympathetic: they 'get screwed up the worst' by 'the English system they implicitly trust'.

[96] The song was recorded by Adam Tinley (who would achieve fame as Adamski in the early 90s) when he was 11, and featured his 5-year-old brother Dominic on vocals.

[97] At Southampton University, 1st May 1982, MES introduced the song with 'This one is for Mark Ellen and his stinking breed.' At the time, Mark Ellen was features editor for pop magazine *Smash Hits*.

setlist (perhaps because Smith's disdain for music journalists never faded), clocking up 158 appearances between 1982-2005.

Winter (Hostel-Maxi) / Winter 2

A masterclass in minimalism, oddly split between the end of side one and the beginning of side two, 'Winter' is mainly comprised of a metronomic bassline and a single harshly jangling chord (played by Paul Hanley) which yet again recalls The Velvet Underground's 'Venus In Furs'. Riley adds keyboard texture and Scanlon contributes some spindly solo work. Again, the song sees Smith playing around with the very notion of timing; not in his vocal delivery this time, but in his decision to make Burns and Steve Hanley re-record their parts. As there was no click-track, the two of them just had to do their best to keep up. Consequently, just after the halfway point of 'Winter 2' the rhythm section, as Paul Hanley describes, 'slips its moorings and lurches drunkenly away from the rest of the band till it's impossible to work out who's playing along with who... Everyone except Mark thought it was a terrible idea, but the timeslip brilliantly mirrors his lyric's blatant disregard for the conventions of linear time.'

'Winter', according to the press release, 'is a tale concerning an insane child who is taken over by a spirit from the mind of a cooped-up alcoholic, and his ravaged viewpoints and theories'. The 'mad kid' tries to grab the lead of his mother's dog, and at some point wears 'a black cardboard Archbishop's hat with a green fuzz skull and crossbones'. Whilst the song is in vaguely narrative form, it's chronologically confusing. Manny (presumably the 'cooped-up alcoholic') is in the library, hungover at half past three, but then MES talks about 'get[ting] the spleen at 3:15 / but it's 3:13'. There's also an intriguing reference in the press release to 'an earlier version [which] went into the "Clang" process of speech', which is explained as being where 'the sufferer during speech makes sentences containing similar sounding words'.[98] The song was a regular feature in Fall sets throughout 1981, appearing 22

[98] 'In psychology and psychiatry, clanging refers to a mode of speech characterized by association of words based upon sound rather than concepts and is often associated with bipolar disorder and schizophrenia.' (*Wikipedia*)

times. However, after its 25th outing in Liverpool in April 1982, 'Winter' was never played again.

Just Step S'ways

The closest thing to a pop song on *Hex*, 'Step' provides some light relief after the intensity of the first half of the album. The music is framed around Marc Riley's irresistible, driving riff and the same is true of the vocals; Smith, unusually, tailors his lyric to the rhythm of Riley's melody. He also uses double-tracking of his voice to good effect, adding both a bit of a sinister edge to an otherwise relatively poppy track, and some light-hearted 'mouth trumpet' in the intro. The lyric – which decries the modern world ('this grubby place') and disparages nostalgia ('who wants to be in a Hovis advert anyway?') – is a challenge to pin down,[99] but it's possible that the sleeve notes ('"Lie Dream" 80% of 10% OR 6% over no less than 1/4 = ??????') could refer to a deal offered by Rough Trade that was part of the reason why The Fall stepped 's'ways' to Kamera. 'Futurist world' probably references artistic and social movement *Futurismo*.[100] Played 27 times in 1981-82, 'Just Step S'ways' made a surprise one-off reappearance in 2007.

Who Makes The Nazis?

The album version of 'Nazis' has a darker, more serious tone than its Peel session counterpart due to its slower tempo and the absence of toy guitar. It's primitivism, emphasised by the tribal drums and guttural groans, give it a mesmeric quality, and the snatches of distorted background noise (a favourite MES technique, here operated by Burns) add to the unearthly atmosphere. 'Benny's cobweb eyes!' is almost certainly a reference to the character of the same name from UK soap *Crossroads*, who in one episode was blinded and exclaimed 'I can't see nothing, doctor... only cobwebs!' 'Remember when I used to follow you home from

[99] Paul Hanley: 'If you've figured out the lyrical arc of this particular number, you know more than me.'

[100] Futurism, which emerged in early 20th-century Italy, celebrated technology, speed and youth. It had much in common with the modernist Vorticism art movement founded by Wyndham Lewis, of whom MES was a great admirer. Paul Hanley discusses Lewis's influence on Smith in some depth in *Have A Bleedin Guess*.

school babe? Before I got picked up for paedophilia' may refer to Big Star's 'Thirteen', written by Alex Chilton.[101] The repeated references to 'longhorns' may have an indirect link to Nazism via the breeding experiments of the Heck brothers.[102]

Although not generally considered as problematic as the introduction to 'The Classical', 'Nazis' also features language that feels uncomfortable from a modern perspective: 'balding smug faggots'. Suede (who supported The Fall in 1992) released a song called 'Implement Yeah!' that included the line 'The boy Smith's called Saul a Scotch homo'. It's plausible that this refers to Kamera's Saul Galpern, who went on to found Nude records, on which Suede released their first four albums. 'Nazis' was a regular feature on 1981-82 setlists, but its 33rd performance in New Zealand in August 1982 was its last.

Iceland

The final track to be recorded at Hljóðriti in September, 'Iceland' was to a large extent improvised from scratch in the studio, although Colin Irwin recognised some 'abstract tinkering they'd done earlier'. Smith, brandishing a tape recorder, instructed the group to play something 'Dylanish'. Steve Hanley:

> Craig... start[s] throwing two notes back and forth... Mark Smith responds by thrusting the cassette player at his mike and pressing Play to release a barren howl around the studio. Marc Riley abandons his keyboards to address a stray banjo leaning against a wall...

Steve Hanley added a delicate, tentative bassline; his brother 'recreated the relentless pounding in my head that Iceland's ridiculous licensing laws had helpfully provided'. Smith's lyrics,

[101] The song contains the line 'Won't you let me walk you home from school?' According to Simon Ford, Smith met Chilton on The Fall's 1981 US tour.

[102] Heinz and Lutz Heck's 'Heck cattle' were an attempt to breed back aurochs, an extinct species that is the ancestor of all domestic cattle. Although their experiments, which began in the 1920s, pre-dated Nazi government, they certainly fit with the ideology of recreating a 'super race'. Modern accounts of the breed often reference their Nazi associations, for example 'Devon farmer forced to offload aggressive Nazi-bred "super cows"', Steven Morris, *The Guardian*, 5th January 2015.

retrieved from his customary carrier bag and scrawled on hotel notepaper, describe an incident from earlier in the trip that he had related to Colin Irwin: 'Mark decided to go for a coffee in the cafe across the road. He tripped and tumbled across a pile of tables. Nobody laughed. Nobody got upset. Nobody blinked. They thought he was a drunk. It happens all the time in Iceland.' It also references cult Icelandic performer Megas ('hear about Megas Jonsson'[103]), a 'green goblin', legendary sea monster the Kraken and cassette manufacturer Memorex. As Paul Hanley points out, 'It's difficult to imagine many writers who could combine an anecdote about slipping on their arse in a café with a quasi-Norse saga of godmen walking amongst us.'

'Iceland' is a frail, hesitant piece, in many ways a welcome contrast to the uncompromising belligerence of much of the rest of the album. There's a palpable sense of the group getting to grips with their improvised creation from around the halfway mark, although it loses its way over the last minute or so, 'struggling', as Steve Hanley describes, 'to find a natural end'. At their last gig in Iceland in September 1981, the group made an ill-fated and rapidly truncated attempt at performing the song live. Lasting only 55 seconds, it was a bit of a car crash. Wobbly bass, skittering guitar, jaunty drums – none of which seem to have anything much to do with the recently-recorded song or indeed each other.

And This Day

The sleeve notes strike a tongue-in-cheek, self-deprecating tone: 'desperate attempt to make bouncy good of 2 drum kit line-up'. 'Bouncy' is not the best adjective, 'punishing' or 'remorseless' being more appropriate. The dense barrage of noise, the lumbering rhythm and in particular Riley's spooky organ give the song a

---

[103] Colin Irwin: 'Our hosts play us tapes of a man with a cracked voice and a Dylanish air and describe him as "the father of Icelandic rock'n'roll". And they tell us the story of Megas, who ridiculed the sacred Sagas of the land, wrote scathing, surreal lyrics, got heavily into booze and drugs, was barred from radio and shunned by society. In 1979 he released a double album called *Plans For Suicide*, announced his retirement, and hasn't performed in public since he's now a dock worker. Mark Smith is entranced by the story, and rivetted by the music. The following day Megas, a pale, gaunt figure, turns up at The Fall's concert at the Austurboejarbio and shakes him by the hand. Mark will return to England clutching a parcel of Megas records under his arm.'

warped, circus-like atmosphere, one that conjures images of a travelling freakshow or carny from a Tom Waits song or Cormac McCarthy novel. More than ever, Smith appears to be venting his frustration in a myriad of random, unrelated directions: 'no matter what and never who fills baskets or who's just there'; 'the surroundings are screaming on the roads'. The original recording was edited down from 25 minutes to 10 to fulfil the title's promise of an 'hour'. As a result, there's a jarring edit at 5:46 and another at 8:13. The 15-minute version (recorded at Hammersmith Palais on 25th March 1982) that features on *Hip Priest And Kamerads* is impressive, but feels a little slight compared to the album version. 'And This Day' was performed 25 times, 1982–83. It received a one-off revival in 1997.

Reviews and Reissues

The *NME*'s Richard Cook described *Hex* as a 'masterpiece… sixty minutes of The Fall with all their previous incarnations toughened to a bitterly frightening degree'. In *Melody Maker*, Colin Irwin considered it 'incredibly exciting and utterly compelling'. *Sounds'* verdict was that 'into this record's one hour is crammed a selection of songs that are both compelling and astonishing, deeply scored compositions that shine with inventive playing. *Hex Enduction Hour* is the furthest adventure The Fall have ever embarked upon, one that absorbs and holds the listener in a grip of iron.' One dissenting voice was that of Mark Storace of Swiss metal band Krokus. *Flexipop* magazine ran a feature where artists reviewed each other's albums; Storace, paired with MES, considered *Hex* 'mindless' and thought it sounded like it was 'being played by zombies'.[104] *Hex* was the first Fall album to dent the mainstream charts, peaking at number 71. It also reached number two on the independent chart, kept from the top spot by Pigbag's *Dr Heckle and Mr Jive*.

Hex was reissued in 2002 on Castle/Sanctuary, adding the two songs from the 'Look, Know' single. However, when it received a double-CD reissue in 2005, Smith requested that both versions

---

[104] Smith's review of Krokus' *One Vice At A Time* was complimentary in comparison: 'UK hairies could learn much from this l.p.'

of 'Look, Know' plus the Peel recording of 'Winter' be omitted, possibly because of the prominence of Marc Riley's vocals in the former case, and almost certainly due to his dissatisfaction with Paul Hanley's performance in the latter.[105] It included several live tracks. The 'Stars on 45' version of 'I'm Into CB' (from Manchester, 30th September 1981) sees Smith sing a bastardised version of the 'CB' lyrics over an uptempo medley that includes 'Psykick Dancehall', 'Fiery Jack' and 'Leave The Capitol'. There are two live and relatively brief versions of 'And This Day'. The first (from a soundcheck in New Zealand) has Smith's vocals in a very prominent position, which just emphasises that they aren't necessarily the song's main attraction. It does, however, give you a good chance to listen to Riley's frankly bonkers prog-psych keyboard work. The other – its one-off 1997 revival – is of poor sound quality and is mainly notable for being dominated by waves of slide guitar. 'Session Musician' (the version here is from New Orleans on 23rd June 1981) was never recorded in the studio and was only performed 17 times. A diatribe on one of Smith's favourite topics ('all they'll talk about is equipment… they'll play for anybody'), it's an extensive almost prog-like piece. It was also the first of five Fall songs to mention wolverines. 'Jazzed Up Punk Shit' was only played live three times (the version here is its second outing, from Manchester on 15th May 1982). It is, inevitably, neither 'jazzed-up' nor 'punk'. It opens with sustained organ chords, then strikes up a rather menacing prowl involving some gentle hi-hat, rhythmic bass and meandering guitar. Lyrically it references both 'Solicitor In Studio' and 'Who Makes The Nazis?' ('stick with Memorex'), but musically it's more closely related to 'Detective Instinct' from the group's next album, *Room To Live*. The highlight of the bonus tracks is the lengthy version of 'Deer Park' recorded in Auckland on 20th August 1982, an astonishingly intense experience driven by sublime, feedback-drenched guitar.

---

[105] In *Renegade*, Smith spoke very positively of this release: 'I'm pleased with the way Sanctuary re-issued it. They did us proud there. I know for a fact that a lot of kids have got into it as a result.'

Evaluation

Smith described the album as 'probably the first time I'd got to a point where I knew I was alone with my ideas. And you can go in one of two ways: either you curb your thinking, rein yourself in and buy what they're telling you, or you follow your own path, regardless.' Nobody could deny that he pursued the latter path relentlessly for the next 35 years, but it's intriguing to consider that this might have been, if Smith is to be believed, The Fall's last album – 'his commercial last chance', as expressed in 'Just Step S'ways'. 'I went into it thinking that it was the last thing we'd ever do. I thought it was my last LP. Because we were getting nowhere.' Smith's comments were almost certainly disingenuous: Craig Scanlon described them as 'a drama queen moment'; Steve Hanley's view was Smith 'only ever said it in interviews afterwards. I think he was rewriting history'; Marc Riley asked 'what would he have done? What he did was amazing, but he needed a band.' Whilst it's doubtful that Smith ever actually thought that *Hex* would be the group's swansong, there's a palpable feeling of historical significance, of the group stretching themselves and reaching for – if not harmony (The Fall never really did harmonious) – some sort of coalescence of what it actually *meant* to be The Fall.

The first side of the album is simply astonishing, an unyielding torrent of taut, focused tracks full of innovation and carefully judged aggression. It could be argued that the pace of the second half is uneven in comparison to the first, and that the sequencing could have been improved. However, there's such a strong sense of ethos and vision that runs through the album's veins that it feels that these decisions were immutable and inevitable. As Stewart Lee said:

> Unlike other singers, Mark E. Smith did not promise to mend my broken heart. *Hex* offered only an incomprehensible alienation and anger that nascent adolescence recognised. I responded to *Hex* on a primal level. It bypassed sense, understanding and conditioning.

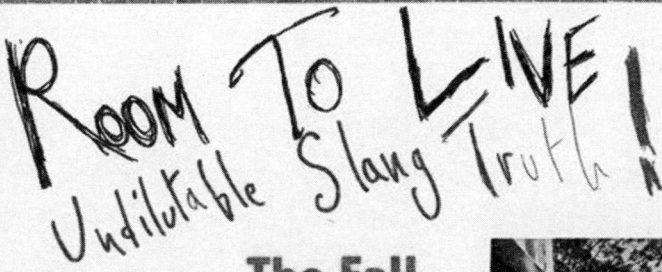

The Fall

ROOM TO LIVE ... MARQUIS CHA - CHA ... UNDILUTABLE SLANG TRUTH ... LOATHSOME TRAITOR

Location - local
Bar song two - here a drifting young man is infected by
The russo-roman scourge due to a combination of keep fit
dances and education at the hands of state lecturers
- their scum influence resulting in a rewind, their influence
Seeping over oceans and into his 'Abroad' mind.
OR An instance of soul-sap on us white folks by this bossa-nova
crap.
Vignette number three shows the harsh results of technology
in yokel hang outs. Horrid truth behind all that romanticised
green grass.

'Anyway, there was no reasoning with this one - knew three
languages but none. and talking of "in particular" a joke
to this person clammed up her his venal reptile observe of
others-but the persona was not slime ridden. Group even
wore support suit ventilated gusset jeans took in too far,
et shirt with small collar for recording. But it was to no
avail. Things had overstepped them. The whining spawn of that
Tent Moon ruled roost for moment. The visage was retard, A :

- ⊙ Joker Hysterical Face   4'35
- ⊛ Marquis Cha Cha   4'15
- ⊙ Hard Life in Country   6'12
- ⊚ Room To Live   4'29

33 R.P.M.

Paul Hanley drums
Karl Burns bass, drums
         guitar
Steve Hanley bass
Marc Riley guitar keyboards
Mark E. Smith vocals violin
Craig Scanlon guitar
Also: Arthur CADMAN
         Guitar
     Adrian NIMAN
         Saxophone
Cargo Studios
John Brierley

Room To Live
Recorded: Cargo Studios, Rochdale, June–July 1982
Released: 27th September 1982

Personnel:
Mark E Smith – vocals, violin
Marc Riley – guitar, keyboards
Craig Scanlon – guitar
Steve Hanley – bass
Paul Hanley – drums
Karl Burns – drums, bass, guitar

With:
Arthur Kadman – guitar
Adrian Niman – saxophone

Chapter 6: Room To Live

'I suppose I'm a contrary bastard – I like to do the opposite of what I've just done.'

Most groups, following the type of critical acclaim that *Hex* received, would have toured the album to death and then tried somehow to recreate its success. Inevitably, The Fall did nothing of the sort. The 29 gigs they played between March and May 1982 saw *Hex* songs already disappearing from the set and eight new songs debuted. Only two of the eight would feature on *Room To Live*, most of the rest appearing on *Perverted By Language* and its related singles the following year. There were two exceptions. 'Surrogate Mirage' was only ever played once, at Leicester Poly on 24th March 1982. A slow, gentle rhythm based around a simple four-note bassline gives it a melancholy air although periodically the group breaks out into a more uptempo section. The lyrics – as far as they can be made out – are intriguing: 'he put his head in the basin / he writes letters to his parents / says they talk to him'. The oddest thing about 'Surrogate Mirage' is how fully realized it sounds. One might expect a one-appearance-only song to be a rough, underdeveloped idea, but although it sounds a little under-rehearsed (especially a couple of minutes from the end) it doesn't feel a million miles away from being a 'complete' song. 'Why it was so unceremoniously ditched,' Paul Hanley pondered, 'is anyone's guess.' 'Backdrop' was debuted in Rotterdam on 13th April. A relentless, sprawling powerhouse of a tune, generally around ten to twelve minutes long, it saw Smith go on a meandering, colourful rant that encompassed a drugged-up Youth Opportunities Programme instructor, stolen racehorses, a 'semite man' with a home 'full of sperm' and 'yellow pills in the Gordon's gin'. It would be played a further 46 times over the following 19 months, but would never receive a studio recording.

The Fall returned to Rochdale's Cargo Studios in June.[106] The aim was to record a new single, 'Marquis Cha-Cha', but as was the case with *Slates*, the sessions ended up producing something more substantial. Unlike *Slates*, where the recording process — Marc Riley's indignation regarding the lyrics of 'Middle Mass' notwithstanding — had been a relatively harmonious process, the sessions that resulted in *Room To Live* were a strained and unpleasant experience for most of those involved. This tense atmosphere was to carry over into the group's Antipodean tour that summer.

The first few dates had to be played with only one drummer, as Karl Burns's departure had been delayed because he had to apply for a new passport, his previous one having been eaten by a dog (one 'with a squint', according to Smith). The tour opened at the Musician's Club, Sydney on 22nd July. Suffering from jet lag after a 36-hour flight, exacerbated by copious alcohol consumption, the group turned in a sub-par (or as Smith put it, 'shit') performance where they struggled to stay awake. Riley, Scanlon and the Hanleys' choice of post-gig recreation led to one of the more infamous incidents in the group's history.

The four of them headed to a club called The Manzil Room. Their body clocks still awry from jet lag, they suddenly found themselves wide awake and decided to hit the dance floor, 'throwing shapes' to The Clash's 'Rock The Casbah'. When Smith arrived, he was enraged by the scene — 'you're not too tired to dance... [but] you were too fucking tired to play a decent gig!' — and proceeded to slap Scanlon and both Hanleys across the face.[107] When his attention turned to Riley, however, the guitarist showed no sign of the 'soft mitts' he'd been accused of having and floored him with a punch to the face. Inevitably, Smith's version of events is very different: the group were in a 'heavy metal disco' whereupon he tried in vain to preserve their dignity by discouraging them from dancing to 'Smoke On The

---

[106] In *Renegade*, Smith suggests that *Room To Live* was recorded after the Antipodean tour in the summer. Although this is echoed in Dave Thompson's *User's Guide*, it seems more likely that the recording sessions took place before the group headed off to Australia at the end of July as suggested in *The Big Midweek*.

[107] 'Was that supposed to hurt? Is he joking or what? Since when did grown men go around slapping their colleagues? It's like we're flies he's swatting.'

Water'; unprovoked, Riley started hitting him.[108] The two of them took part in an awkward, stilted television interview the next day; Smith's black eye can be seen clearly despite the TV make-up. Tension between them had been brewing even before the recording of *Slates*, largely (although not entirely) focused on Riley's perception that he was getting a raw deal as far as song-writing credits were concerned. Now Riley had demonstrated a level of what Smith doubtless considered rank insubordination to his list of misdemeanours. From this point on, the guitarist's days were numbered; over the next few months Smith and Carroll would systematically organise his removal.

Riley wasn't the only Fall musician to stand up to Smith during the tour. Messing around with his musicians' amp settings would become an MES trademark; it was a habit he began at West Town Hall, Geelong on 29th July 1982. Steve Hanley was infuriated by Smith 'indiscriminately twisting all the knobs' of his amp during 'Tempo House' and confronted him after the gig: 'What's the point of me spending hours soundchecking if you're going to fucking ruin it? I'm telling you, don't EVER touch my controls again.' Four days later, the group's performance at the Prince of Wales in Melbourne was broadcast on radio. In May 1998 a cassette recording of the broadcast was released as *Live To Air In Melbourne '82*. Despite the obvious tensions in the group, the awful 'GCSE Art collage' cover, the dodgy track listing ('Hexen Strife', 'Knot Deer Park', 'Totally Twisted') and the less than perfect sound balance, it's one of the best Fall live albums. 'Hard Life In Country' isn't nearly as thin and bleak as its album version; here it's equally doleful, but the thick, distorted guitar sound makes it muscular and brooding. 'Marquis Cha Cha' is a bit ragged around the edges, but is jaunty and energetic, Smith even contributing some enthusiastic if rather odd scat/mouth-trumpet accompaniment. The highlight is 'Room To Live', here an exuberant stomping hoedown and featuring a delightful country/blues guitar lick that was sadly missing from the studio take.[109]

---

[108] One of the biggest flaws in Smith's account is that surely nobody has ever actually *danced* to 'Smoke On The Water'.

[109] Riley resurrected it on his post-Fall band The Creepers' 1983 song 'Cure By Choice'.

There are also some interesting vocal amendments. 'Papal Visit' is referenced in 'Hip Priest' (6:10) and the 'Jew on a motorbike' line from 1983's 'Garden' gets an early try-out in 'Tempo House' (6:56). Smith goes off at an interesting tangent in 'The Classical':

> Welcome to your new XL model / made with the finest technique / with elephant odour inside upholstery / the axles are heat resistant / made in nice units... the bumpers, they're alright / and the tyres, you get them from us, especially.

There are also several (by Fall standards) rather flamboyant bits of musicianship, especially Riley's keyboards on 'Deer Park' and 'Hip Priest' (for example the little solo around the four-minute mark in the latter). Smith expressed his disapproval of this sort of thing at the soundcheck in Geelong: 'None of that showing-off rock shit you keep adding in! Just play the fucking song in time and properly.'

In mid-August, the group travelled to New Zealand, where both 'Totally Wired' and 'Lie Dream' had made the charts (reaching 25 and 17 respectively). The final date, at Mainstreet Cabaret in Auckland on 21st August, was recorded by local musician Chris Knox and released as *Fall In A Hole* in December 1983 on the Flying Nun label. The album was only released in New Zealand, but UK imports quickly became much sought after.[110] Flying Nun founder Roger Shepherd soon found himself the subject of Smith's displeasure: '[He] was not amused... my first contact with the overseas music business was an angry, demanding one. Desist from export, press no more copies, and give us all the income from all of the sales.' The original release consisted of an 11-track album (from the mixing desk) plus a 5-track 12" (from an audience-recorded cassette). The fury of 'Prole Art Threat' is captured well, the introductory kazoo solo on 'Marquis' is hilarious and 'Room To Live' is even more lively than the *Live To Air* version. The album also provides a fascinating snapshot of the deteriorating Smith-Riley relationship. In 'Hard Life', an exasperated Smith

---

[110] At the time of writing, the original vinyl LP will set you back at least £100.

snaps 'Turn it down Marc'; introducing one of the songs from the forthcoming album, he sneers, 'If you look pretty close, Marc Riley has a joker hysterical face. He's happy, cos he's good.' This was probably a reference to the picture of Riley that had graced the front page of the *Christchurch Press* three days earlier, captioned 'Happy Fall Guitarist'. The photo (used on the cover of *In A Hole*) showed Riley arriving at Christchurch Airport, a beaming grin on his face. Smith was disdainful of what he saw as Riley revelling in his minor celebrity status: 'He's parading himself like a chief swan to all these imaginary fans... It wasn't exactly The Beatles in America.'[111] A 2003 CD reissue (*In A Hole* +) contained six bonus tracks from other New Zealand dates, including the group's second and final performance of their unlikely segue from 'C'n'C' into Deep Purple's 'Black Night'.

Room To Live

In his review of *Hex*, the *NME*'s Richard Cook had suggested that the 'dilemma would seem to be where Smith can take them next'. Smith's solution to this dilemma was to make *Hex*'s follow-up its diametric opposite. As Paul Hanley put it, 'It was short where *Hex* was long; it was un-premeditated and deliberately un-prepared where *Hex* was planned and coherent.' Trying to determine Smith's thinking and motivation is a tricky business, but it does seem that he found the group's growing popularity unsettling – perhaps even distasteful or alarming – and was determined to confound expectations. He decided that a radically different approach should be taken, one that involved different combinations of the group – and some newcomers – performing on each track; songs would be developed from scratch in the studio, rather than having been worked out live or in rehearsal. He extolled the merits of this new approach in a 1982 interview:

> I wanted to do something instantaneous... to get back to
> the old Fall way of recording songs straight off the top of
> our heads! I thought we were getting a bit restricted by
> *Hex*, it was so 'thought out', planned, and like, intensive.

[111] In *Renegade*, Smith disingenuously claims 'that's why I chose that picture for the front cover' even though it obviously had nothing to do with him.

That's why I've shuffled round with the band, I didn't want the same sound reproduced twice... I excluded some of the band from certain tracks, shuffled them round a bit, and used some outside musicians. All of The Fall are on the record, but not all of them on every track... The band weren't even familiar with some of the songs, we just went in and did them which is how we always operated in the good old days! ... and I think it's served to stir them up a bit! I suppose I'm a contrary bastard – I like to do the opposite of what I've just done.

This bold new approach was not exactly welcomed by the musicians, who found the experience tense and stressful. Paul Hanley thought it 'a fucking nightmare. You'd turn up and find Smith had only invited half the band, or brought in other musicians without telling anyone!'

One way in which the album did follow *Hex*'s approach was the cover, which was covered in similarly enigmatic text. Emblazoned with the legend 'Undilutable Slang Truth!' it also contained such enlightening phrases as, 'The whining spawn of that Tent Moon ruled roost for moment. The visage was retard.' Smith asserted that the dog in the picture on the front cover was the same squint-eyed one that had eaten Karl Burns's passport.

Joker Hysterical Face

Propelled by a loose, loping guitar riff, 'Joker' is one of only two songs from the album that Steve Hanley considered to be of any merit. It's also the only track to feature the full line-up with both drummers behind the kit. Smith's explanation of the lyric had an unfortunately misogynist tone: 'It's about a couple who live sort of downstairs from us, where we were living, and they used to play ABBA and all that stuff, they always used to have it on full blast. She was a divorcee. I used to know women like her, and it's not very far from the feminist movement. Like the man is the main thing to blame.' It's not clear what Ted Rogers (TV gameshow host of *3-2-1* fame) has to do with all of this ('Ted Rogers's brains burn in hell'). 'Joker' was played 28 times in 1982, but then only made one further appearance, in 1984.

Marquis Cha-Cha

The unstructured nature of the recording process is clearly reflected in the disjointed, spontaneous sound of 'Marquis'. Its slightly crazed energy and punning title makes it sound as if the group are having fun recording it, although this clearly wasn't the case: Steve Hanley, with a tone of weary frustration, recalls working with Smith and Burns 'trying to create some semblance of structure' to the song. Although they didn't entirely succeed in this aim, it's still full of ramshackle charm and there's something endearing about how the awkward shifts in tempo give a sense that the song is in constant danger of imploding. 'Marquis' updates the Lord Haw Haw story[112] to contemporary Argentina. Smith cited the Falklands War as his reason for leaving the Labour Party:

> I left because of the Falklands War. This was 1983, and local members were dead set against the war. I would go in the club and be told the war was a waste of money. We should just give the islands to Argentina. I was arguing, 'Hang on. We're talking about a military dictatorship, in a country that's made a career out of hiding Nazi war criminals. You want to give in to that lot?' No one agreed with me, so I left.

Neither Marc Riley nor Craig Scanlon played on the recording. It was played live 41 times between 1982 and 1985.

Hard Life In Country

'Hard Life' was a particularly good example of how Smith's unorthodox new methods disconcerted the musicians. The Hanleys found themselves recording it with just Smith and a 'long-fringed sap' on guitar, this scenario causing Riley and Scanlon some consternation when they arrived later. The 'sap' in question was Arthur Kadmon (credited as Cadman on the sleeve), a Manchester musician who had played in Manchester post-punk band Ludus. It seems unlikely that Smith actually considered formally adding him to the group, although Kadmon may have

---

[112] 'Lord Haw-Haw' was a nickname applied to the US-born Briton William Joyce, who broadcast Nazi propaganda to the UK from Germany during the Second World War.

been under the impression that this was the case. Mick Middles describes Kadmon's contribution:

> [He was] told to go and tune up and play a few test samples, which indeed he did: four chords, a tune-up and a finger loosening solo. It took just sixteen seconds.
> 'Thanks Arthur. That's superb. That's just what we wanted. You can go home now.'
> 'What? That's it?'
> 'Yeah, thanks cocker.'

'Hard Life' deals with a theme that Smith returned to on several occasions: the urbanite's distrust of the countryside, or as the sleeve notes have it, 'the harsh results of technology in yokel hang outs. Horrid truth behind all that romanticized green grass.' It's not an easy listen. Unremittingly bleak, it strains at the leash throughout to break out into something more expansive and distorted. The mesmeric, trebly guitar scratches away like it's trying desperately to escape from something malevolent, reflecting the oppressive, claustrophobic intensity of village life. It all gets a bit *Straw Dogs*[113] towards the end: 'the villagers are surrounding the house / the locals have come for their due'. Steve Hanley disparaged it as 'shite... there's nothing on it that anybody couldn't do'. The 'John' referred to in Smith's spoken intro is presumably John Brierley, the founder of Cargo Studios, although this isn't the song where he gets his sole production credit (Smith and Carroll having decided that they could handle that responsibility themselves on all but the title track). Although it was a fairly regular feature during the Australian tour, it made only 18 appearances in total, the last one at York University in November 1983.

Room To Live

Disappointingly, the snappy country-blues guitar motif present on the *Live To Air* and *In A Hole* versions is absent here. There's still plenty of good stuff going on, however: nifty solo guitar work

---

[113] Controversial 1971 Sam Peckinpah film starring Dustin Hoffman and Susan George, featuring savage yokels and a disturbing rape scene.

from Arthur Kadmon (even if it's a little buried in the mix) and another guest, Adrian Niman, adds some understated honking sax (Niman was paid the grand total of £26 for his work). The title could be taken as a reference to *Lebensraum*,[114] although other than references to 'foreigners' and a 'murder squad' there's not a great deal to support this link. There are some pleasingly random Smithisms though: 'a D.H.S.S.S. Volvo estate… with a Moody Blues cassette on the dashboard'; 'some men want reporters with no wig'. It was played live 39 times, 1982-83.

Detective Instinct

'Detective' has an air of suspicion and malevolence, created by the pulsing bass and understated guitar fills, which sound as though they might have come from the soundtrack of a 60s spy/mystery/detective TV show. The percussion is also interestingly effective on this; pared down and minimal, almost disappearing in places, adding to the uncertainty. There are several intriguing little details. At various points, both a mandolin and a harpsichord seem to be drifting about in the background, and there's also an occasional electronic 'plink' in the style of an early-80s video game. The very subtle bit of feedback around the four-and-a-half-minute mark is a nice touch too; the sudden swell in volume at 5:14 is not so subtle, however. Working out the line-up on the different songs on this album is obviously problematic, but there do appear to be three guitar parts on this, so presumably Karl Burns contributed one of them. The most striking line of the generally impenetrable lyric is 'he was a blubbering heap / he should have served himself up / preferably in a restaurant with meat'. Only made five live appearances, all in 1982-83.

Solicitor In Studio

The other song (alongside 'Joker') that Steve Hanley considered to be of any merit, and one of only two to feature the full line-up. The main bassline tirelessly stomps up and down the scale; the knotty riff that sits above it is provided by Karl Burns on a

---

[114] Literally 'living space', Hitler's justification for German expansion in the 1930s.

second bass. Craig Scanlon flails vigorously at his two chords, providing an unobtrusive but crucial backdrop; Riley dips into the second half with some splashes of keyboard colour. The feedback that echoes Smith's line about 'high-pitched whines' at 2:11 is another neat touch. The lyric references both Magnus Pyke and Sir Anthony Michael Beaumont-Dark.[115] It's another that disappeared from the setlist after 1983, but not before it clocked up 51 appearances.

Papal Visit

John Paul II's 1982 visit to the UK was the first by a reigning pope, and it saw over two million people attend five large open-air Masses in London, Coventry, Manchester, Glasgow, and Cardiff. The Manchester mass took place in Heaton Park, right on Smith's doorstep, or as the album's press statement had it, 'PAPAL VISIT was mostly recorded less than one quarter a mile away from same visit to Manchester during it'.[116] Often derided as self-indulgent and unlistenable nonsense ('pushing avant-garde to the threshold of dross', as Steve Hanley put it), it sees Smith scrape away painfully at a violin, intone a few lines about helicopters stripping the land and then throws in a couple of samples of the pontiff's speeches while Karl Burns thumps aimlessly on the floor toms.

Reviews and Reissues

Steve Hanley was one of the album's biggest critics. 'Most of the tracks are one riff, if that; they're not arranged properly and they've not been thought out... we could [have done] with taking time to turn these ideas into proper songs.' Although Smith thought it a 'very underrated album', the music press sided with his bassist. In the *NME*, Amrik Rai described *Room To Live* as 'frustratingly sketchy' and 'scarcely more substantial than a tawdry collection of scantily clad doodles'; side two in particular was an 'indulgent hash of ill-researched experimentation'. *Sounds'* Dave

---

[115] Pyke was an enthusiastic scientist who was a staple of British TV in the 70s and 80s; Beaumont-Dark a tiresome rent-a-quote 1980s Tory MP.
[116] In *Renegade*, MES describes how he 'could see all these Jesuits in the gardens below, rooting through the trees for bombs and things'.

McCullough thought it lacked 'bounce and zap'. Looking back, Brian Edge described it as 'misconceived and flawed'; it 'could have been a passable EP, but... sounded like a flabby, overcrowded 12-inch single'.

A 1993 reissue added both sides of the 'Lie Dream' single. The 1998 Voiceprint version came with a bonus CD featuring four live tracks from April 1982. The 2005 Sanctuary reissue contains a different set of six live recordings from 1982-83, one of which was 'Town Called Crappy' (aka 'Don't Like Maggie'). Only ever performed twice, it's no more than a 'Crap Rap'-style intro: 'Got to get out of that city called Crappy / Now I don't like Maggie / All the money I made out of mods has made me feel guilty / A town called Crappy'.

Evaluation

The album's lukewarm reception was perhaps unsurprising. After *Hex*'s focused relentlessness, it was inevitable that the loose, deliberately unstructured approach of *Room To Live* would lead to unfavourable comparisons with its illustrious predecessor. It is frustratingly patchy, and it's hard to dispute Steve Hanley's verdict that it could have been so much different with more time spent on the songs. That said, the musicians' negative experiences of recording the album has clearly (and understandably) coloured their view. In fact, *Room To Live*'s spontaneous, improvisational approach actually works well in many places, giving it a fresh, inventive quality. Smith's bloody-minded determination to avoid recording anything like what people expected often leads to positive results: 'Joker' and 'Solicitor' have a joyful, engaging exuberance; 'Hard Life' has a brittle astringency that might have been lost in different circumstances. It's far from the group's most complete and satisfying work, but there's still much to love about its contrary nature.

Perverted By Language
Recorded: Pluto Studios, Manchester, mid-1983
Released: 5th December 1983

Personnel:
Mark E Smith – vocals
Craig Scanlon – guitar, vocals
Steve Hanley – bass
Paul Hanley – drums, keyboards
Karl Burns – drums, bass
Brix Smith – guitar, vocals ('Eat Y'self Fitter', 'Hotel Blöedel')

Chapter 7: Perverted By Language

'Mark's getting his violin out. Now we're in trouble.'

The second half of 1982 saw the continuing deterioration of the Smith-Riley relationship and the culmination of MES and Carroll's plan to remove him. A new point of contention was Riley inviting his girlfriend to attend gigs on the December 1982 UK tour. Smith criticised him for lacking concentration because of 'fussing round your girlfriend all night' and took to crossing her name off the guest list. Riley's last gig with The Fall was at Manchester's Lesser Free Trade Hall on 22nd December, during which Kay Carroll can be heard on two occasions yelling 'Turn it down Marc!' As ever, accounts vary as to how he came to be fired. Smith's version was that he rang the guitarist on his wedding day and said, 'Congratulations mate, and by the way you're sacked.' However, what actually seems to have happened was that Smith spoke to Riley on the phone during Steve Hanley's wedding in January 1983 (Riley had already married on Christmas Eve 1982 and hadn't told Smith) and arranged a meeting with him the following day. At the meeting, Riley was informed that he would not be travelling to Europe with the group the following month. Although this was ostensibly a 'trial' arrangement, it was the end of Riley's involvement with The Fall. Though he was only part of the line-up for a relatively small proportion of The Fall's lifespan, Riley's contribution to the group should never be underestimated. His bass playing on *Witch Trials* was solid rather than spectacular, but still remarkably assured for a 17-year-old. But it was in the last three of his five-year stint where he made his biggest impact, especially in terms of his songwriting. Considering that he was still only 21 when he departed, he has a writing credit on an impressive number of the group's classic songs.

Smith's feelings regarding his former guitarist had not mellowed by the time he came to write his autobiography 25 years later. 'If it had been left up to him... *Grotesque* and *Hex* would have sounded like mediocre Buzzcocks LPs… he was getting out of hand: wanting to do "Totally Wired" twice a night, playing "Container Drivers" with his cowboy hat on and all that kind of thing.'[117] Smith did strike a more sympathetic tone when discussing Riley's later success as a BBC DJ with Mick Middles. 'How weird do you think it was for me when, during one of The Fall's lower spells [I was] confronted by a giant poster of Marc Riley. That did freak me out for a while, I can't deny. It was such a strange thing to have happened. Not, of course, that I have ever actually heard him on the radio. But I am sure he is very good.'[118]

1983 was a busy year, gig-wise, seeing the group play 80 shows. After a couple of UK dates in January, they set off on a 12-date tour of Switzerland, Belgium and The Netherlands. Despite rueing the 'Marc-shaped hole in the band', Steve Hanley had to admit that MES seemed rejuvenated on stage, focusing more on the 'intricate inner poetics' of his ad-libs rather than constantly castigating the musicians in front of the audience. 'I'm beginning to see,' he ruminated, 'how things are going to shape up without Marc in the band: looser and more weird.'

Peel session six, recorded on 21st March 1983 and broadcast two days later, saw the Maida Vale debut of the dual-drummer line-up. They recorded four *Perverted By Language* songs. The Burns-Hanley duo don't have quite the impact that they would on the final version of 'Smile'; whilst it brims with aggression and Scanlon attacks the song with zest, both Smith and Steve Hanley are rather buried in the mix. The two drummers are deployed to much greater effect on 'Eat Y'self Fitter', which is jagged and raucous; it's just a shame that the backing vocals – a key component of the song – sound as if they have been recorded from a neighbouring building. The lengthy take on 'Hexen Definitive / Strife Knot' is smoulderingly impressive, but the similarly extensive 'Garden' was the highlight of the session.[119]

[117] In comparison, Riley's take was, 'If you're going to work with someone like that you're just going to have to put up with it, he's made more good decisions than bad ones and more great records than not so great ones.'

[118] And indeed he is, of course, his evening show on BBC Radio 6 Music having been one of the best things on British radio for several years.

[119] This was the longest of all the Peel sessions, clocking in at an extravagant 31:29 (see Appendix 1).

The day after the Peel session, The Fall embarked on a 15-date month-long tour of North America. Two significant events occurred on the tour. Firstly, after an incident following the Boston gig on the 17th April, Kay Carroll severed her links with the group. She was refused service in a bar; angered by the group's disinclination to find another one, she took the tour money from the van and left. Reflecting on her time with Smith and The Fall 25 years later, she suggested that her main regret was 'that I didn't hit him more', but also commented that, 'some weeks I wouldn't go near it, some weeks I wish I'd never left, others I'd go back in a heartbeat'. Kay Carroll died in June 2020. Whilst she didn't have the musical influence on the group of some of Smith's later partners, she played a crucial role in defining the attitude and means of operation of the group. It is worth remembering how rare it was in the 70s and 80s for a woman to manage a band, a role that she carried out with consistently impressive aggression and fortitude. As Marc Riley put it, 'She was one of those people that you could rarely win an argument with, even if she was probably wrong she'd just keep going.' In *Renegade*, MES said that her contributions were too often 'overlooked' and described her as 'a financial wizard'. Simon Ford summed up her importance succinctly:

> It's difficult to say that anyone, apart from Smith, was indispensable to The Fall, but Carroll came mighty close. When others floundered or became hesitant she pushed through with a driving force, energetically hectoring the band to maintain its uncompromising attitude.

The second significant event of the 1983 US tour took place at Chicago's Cabaret Metro on 23rd April, when 20-year-old Laura Elisse Salenger – aka Brix (she took her name from The Clash song 'Guns of Brixton') – walked into the lives of Smith and The Fall. Born in Los Angeles, she had played bass in a band called Banda Dratsing whilst at college.[120] She and bandmate Lisa Feder

---

[120] Banda Dratsing is nadsat (the language used in *A Clockwork Orange*) for 'fighting band'. The line-up featured Claus Castenskiold, who also played in Khmer Rouge with future Fall keyboardist Marcia Schofield (see Chapter 11).

had bought *Slates* only a couple of weeks before the Chicago gig and became obsessed with it. Her first impression of the group was that 'they were five normal-looking English blokes. These guys were the antithesis of rock stars. There were no gimmicks or contrivances. This band were a law unto themselves: mighty and brutal, unforgiving, honest and utterly brilliant.' As for Smith himself, she detected 'something a little scary about him... he seemed angry, as if a simmering rage lay just below the surface'. A post-gig drink led to a whirlwind romance, with Brix and Smith spending much of the rest of the tour in each other's company. She came to England in May, and they were married on 19th July.[121] Smith described the proposal (which took place in Chicago) to *Smash Hits*. 'It was on the corner of Lincoln and Clerk where the St. Valentine's Massacre was. It was just where the van was picking us up. I just said "we'd make a good married couple" and she just said "Yeah, it'd be really cool".' The rest of the group were bemused rather than hostile about her sudden appearance in their lives. Steve Hanley was impressed by her knowledge of Joy Division lyrics and in particular by the positive impact she had on Smith's conduct: 'We then undergo what is probably the most good-natured soundcheck I've ever experienced. It's all "Steve, would you mind turning your amp down a little? Could I have just a tad more vocals in the monitors? Thank you."'

The Fall returned to Iceland at the beginning of May for a one-off gig in Reykjavik, which was released in 2001 as *Austurbæjarbíó*. A very clean soundboard recording, it has an oddly empty, hollow feel. Throughout, Smith sounds strangely divorced from all that's happening around him and the guitar sound is thin and brittle. 'The Classical' is possibly the limpest version of the song that you'll hear. The most notable feature is Smith's bizarre 'scat/dial-tone' vocal on 'Eat Y'self Fitter'.

As well as being a year of significant personal and personnel changes, 1983 saw the release of two classic Fall singles. 'The Man Whose Head Expanded' was, thanks to Kamera's financial

---

[121] There is a detailed account of their early relationship in Brix's autobiography *The Rise, The Fall, and The Rise*. Particularly entertaining is her description of Smith's flat (with food kept on the window ledge owing to the broken fridge) and the cooked breakfast he made her: 'I couldn't even put [the black pudding] near my mouth... It smelled like death.'

collapse, released on Rough Trade.[122] The single opens with the sound of Paul Hanley's new Casio keyboard, with which he was 'always fiddling away... programming it to make all sorts of annoying noises'. This leads into a dark yet strangely funny tale of paranoia and plagiarism. The eponymous 'man' is some sort of author who becomes convinced that a 'soap opera writer' is stealing his 'jewels' for prime-time TV. Steve Hanley provides a vibrant but ominous bassline that's fleshed out with some flamboyant excursions away from the main rhythm. After Smith's stuttering, hilarious order to 'turn that bloody blimey Space Invader off!', Scanlon proffers some languorous, distorted chords at first; as the tempo picks up he throws in a little bit of frenetic thrash, but then he withdraws his guitar for a minute or so before providing some jerky, angular work over the last 30 seconds. 'Expanded' was played 73 times between 1982 and 1985 and made a surprise one-off return in 2007. B-side 'Ludd Gang' is a spirited, melodic stomp and features some inexplicable aggression directed at Shakin' Stevens[123] as well as a dig at the Gang of Four: 'I'll stick with the gang of one'.[124] It was played live 68 times, 1982-84. The single reached number three in the UK independent singles chart and also managed number 35 in New Zealand.

September saw the release of one of The Fall's most iconic singles. 'Kicker Conspiracy' was a football song, but one a million miles away from what the record-buying public had come to associate with music related to the sport. It's a withering demolition of what Simon Ford described as 'the early signs of the corruption and greed that would almost destroy the national sport in the coming years', nearly 20 years before Roy Keane derided

---

[122] Leaving Kamera to go back to Rough Trade was a wrench for Smith: 'We had to leave Kamera because we knew it was going down... It broke my heart. Only label I was upset to leave.'

[123] Smith's threat to 'land one on' the bland but inoffensive Elvis copyist for his 'massacre' of 'Blue Christmas' is somewhat ironic given Smith's own mangling of the song in 2011 (see Chapter 30).

[124] Late 70s/early 80s post-punk band from Leeds, best known for their 1979 debut album *Entertainment!* In a 1981 interview, Smith expressed disdain for their overt politicism: 'They went to university and belong to the privileged class. The problem is that they pretend to know what the working class wants. But they haven't got a clue... The English working class (including myself) find [their] music... offensive, insulting, hurtful.'

the 'prawn sandwich brigade'.[125] Smith sticks the boot in (pardon the pun) to some well-known and controversial figures – Jimmy Hill ('J. Hill's satanic reign'), Bert Millichip – whilst lamenting how characters like George Best are punished for their flair. Its rickety, rockabilly blast captures Paul Hanley at his furious finest. The title refrain sounds like nothing else on earth; a collision of rhythms where Smith has no right to fit in those six syllables in the time available. It was played 89 times, the last performance coming on Christmas Eve 1996 after a nine-year gap. 'Kicker' was released as a double 7", the second disc including 'Container Drivers' and 'New Puritan' from the third Peel session. 'Wings', which had been played live throughout 1983, backed the lead song. A convoluted story about time travel, its grinding riff is one of The Fall's finest.[126] A long-standing setlist choice, it racked up 134 appearances: 88 between 1982 and 1985 before being resurrected in 2007-09. 'Kicker' was the first Fall single to be accompanied by a promotional video. Filmed at Turf Moor, home of Burnley FC, it saw Smith miming into a beer can.[127]

Perverted By Language
The album was recorded at Manchester's Pluto Studios. Owned by former Herman's Hermits guitarists Keith Hopwood and Derek Leckenby, Pluto originally opened in 1968 in Stockport and moved to Manchester city centre in 1977.[128] Despite the studio's notable history (The Clash recorded 'Bank Robber' there in 1980), Steve Hanley was less than impressed with its appearance, which he described as 'decor-wise... on its arse'. The

---

[125] A phrase first coined by the Manchester United player in 2000 to describe those supporters who enjoyed the corporate hospitality more than the game itself. It's easy to forget how divorced from the rest of popular culture football was back in the early 80s. These days, any career-minded landfill indie combo takes care to express their devotion to both the national team and a club side. But when 'Kicker Conspiracy' came out (seven years before Gazza wept before the nation), liking football – if you aspired to be taken seriously regarding music, politics, art or literature – was a dirty secret.

[126] The famous riff was absent in the song's first 13 outings, in which it had a very different structure.

[127] There's an incredibly detailed dissection of the video on *The Fall Online Forum* in a thread called 'Kicker Conspiracy Video Frame by Frame'.

[128] The studio is still operated by Keith Hopwood but has moved out of Manchester and these days mainly produces music for children's TV.

cover design was a departure: after the scrawled slogan–dominated covers of recent albums, *Perverted* featured a nightmarish painting of disturbingly grotesque figures by Claus Castenskiold, an old school friend of Brix and the drummer in Banda Dratsing.

More importantly, as Steve Hanley had noted earlier in the year, there was shift in the group's post-Riley sound. Smith explained:

> There's a lot more beauty on this new LP. Some of the new songs aim straight at the heart. It's still aggressive in a way though. *Room To Live* was aiming somewhere else. It wasn't about emotion as such, but it was supposed to be looser in form than anything we had done before. *Perverted By Language* is a lot funnier as well. We craft everything much better these days. Seriousness and humour are blended together more now.

When Brix had joined the group on tour in the second half of 1983 (acting as an unofficial roadie and helping out with the lighting), the rest of the group started a sweepstake as to when she would join them on stage. However, it wasn't until the recording of *Perverted* that she began, tentatively, to establish herself as part of the group, adding vocals to 'Eat Y'self Fitter' and contributing vocals, guitar and a songwriting credit to 'Hotel Blöedel'. 'So we were all wrong,' Steve Hanley reflected, 'her way in is through the studio rather than the stage.'

Eat Y'self Fitter
Backed by an uncompromisingly repetitive and staccato rhythm, Smith's barked vocal takes in being refused entry to nightclubs, bafflement with technology ('where's the cursor?'; 'what's a computer?'), Soft Machine's Kevin Ayers and the use of VCRs ('and your bottom rack is full of vids of programmes you will nay look at'). There's also a disturbingly guttural backing vocal from Burns. Steve Hanley described the song's origins: 'Mark told us, "I've got a new song. I want der-de-der-de-de-der-de." Once we made it aggressive enough for him, he started singing a line out of a cornflake advert.'[129] The engineer struggled

[129] The line was actually from an All-Bran advert.

to find a height for the microphone that would suit both the diminutive Brix and the rest of the group. 'We might be taller but she's definitely louder than the rest of us put together,' Steve Hanley recalled, 'we're doing our usual football-chant drone, but she's layering psychedelic inflection all over it.' 'Fitter' was famously one of John Peel's choices when he appeared on *Desert Island Discs*:

> Over the past decade there's been one band whose music has pleased me I think probably more than anyone else's, and that's been The Fall from Manchester. And they're still around – I suppose they're about the only band which actually does, sort of, last from one end of the decade to the other. Almost any of their records would give me great pleasure but 'Eat Y'self Fitter' is a particular favourite.

After being played consistently throughout 1983, the song's 47th and final performance was in April 1984.

Neighbourhood of Infinity
The album's second track is a strangely fractured swirl of disembodied sound. Although Steve Hanley anchors everything with a weighty bassline, the rest of the elements – Scanlon's grinding guitar, the tentative keyboards, the heavily clobbered drums – circle each other warily until they settle into a tetchy groove in the song's second half. There's something wonderfully fragmentary and mysterious about it, heightened by the layers of indistinct vocals and snippets of jarring noise lurking in the background. Intriguing as it is, its abrupt disappearance well before the three-minute mark gives 'Neighbourhood' a slightly unfinished feel. The lyric plays its part in creating an enigmatic atmosphere – 'and visitor esoteric Jackanapes says analyser' – but also contains two increasingly familiar Fall tropes: self-references ('man whose head'; 'kicker'; 'we are The Fall') and musician/ celebrity mentions (here it's Jim Davidson and Smith favourite Link Wray). The song was dropped from the live set after only a dozen outings. Its final appearance – which was recorded in

Munich in April 1984 and features on the *Palace Of Swords Reversed* compilation – is thrillingly dark and intense and sees Smith ranting about giant moths.

Garden

An intense, hypnotic triumph, 'Garden' showcases perfectly the group's compelling use of controlled repetition, framed around Steve Hanley's distinctive bassline and Scanlon's chiming guitar. Smith is on peerless form, painting a rich, mysterious and evocative picture: 'a three-legged black-grey hog'; 'small, small location on huge continent, sodomised by presumption'; 'less stylish porch, we have the second god's influence'. The mention of 'brown baize', according to Paul Hanley, refers to Pluto's dated decor. One of the song's most memorable lines is 'a Jew on a motorbike'. Brix suggested that it was about Sol Seaberg, singer in a band called FC Domestos who also worked as a driver for The Fall.[130] In a 1984 interview with *Melody Maker*, MES explained further:

> That song's like a skit on the 'prophet syndrome'. Derives partly from those talks I'd have with a driver of ours who was Jewish, long talks about Judaism. I'd say to him, 'Now there's one thing you'll never see, a Jewish person on a motorbike.' Then one day I was going through Golders Green on the way to a London gig and suddenly the street was full of Jewish people on motorbikes.

Unusually, the song's lyrics were included on the album's inner sleeve. By the time *Perverted By Language* was recorded, 'Garden' had already enjoyed 20 live outings; it stayed in the set until September 1984, making 62 appearances altogether.

Hotel Blöedel

In June 1983, when touring Germany, the group's van broke down just outside Dachau and they ended up staying in the Hotel Blöedel. The hotel had a rancid odour ('a reasonable smell of death') and was disturbing enough to give Smith nightmares.

130 Seaberg also co-wrote 'The Man Whose Head Expanded'.

In the morning, he and Brix witnessed what appeared to be a member of staff carrying 'a large, clear plastic bag of blood' – it transpired that the hotel was next door to an abattoir. The song (which was never played live) is notable for being Brix's first major contribution to a Fall recording; also for being the first time that anyone other than Smith sang a lead vocal. The song is based on one of Brix's old Banda Dratsing tunes, 'One More Time For The Record'. During the album's recording, Brix largely retired to a separate room and beavered away with her guitar. However, with Smith's encouragement and some support from Steve Hanley, she sat down and ran through the song a few times, the take on the album being what she thought was just a rehearsal. Smith added some lines about the hotel experience as well as some trademark tuneless violin scrapes. 'Mark's getting his violin out,' Steve Hanley noted, 'now we're in trouble.'

Smile

A ferociously powerful track, 'Smile' sees the most effective use of the dual drummers since *Hex*, Burns and Hanley alternating between complementary variations à la 'The Classical' and 'Deer Park' style doubled–up brute force. Smith is just as focused and belligerent as his musicians, spitting out finely-turned phrases like 'lick-spittle southerner' and 'special vexation process'. He claimed that the song was aimed at the growing cocktail bar culture of the early 80s, although the description of the 'chicken run to the toilet' evokes the kind of grotty nightclub that was already well established across the country. Paul Hanley suggests that the song is at least partly 'a semi–affectionate pen portrait of Karl Burns's indiscreet personality and dress sense', opening line 'tight faded male arse' referring to the threadbare jeans that were the only trousers he took with him on tour. 'Smile' was played live frequently at the time, clocking up 66 outings between 1983 and 1985. It was also the first song The Fall performed on national television. Appearing on Channel 4's *The Tube*, the group were introduced by John Peel: 'They've never been on national TV, which seemed to me to be shocking, so I quite wanted to go down in history as the man who put them on TV.'

I Feel Voxish

More accessible and conventional in structure than many of the other songs on the album, 'Voxish' is driven by a high-register bassline and an almost off-hand descending guitar riff that had originally been concocted by Steve Hanley on the previous year's Australian tour. Karl Burns also plays bass, contributing a deep, reverberating backing that lumbers into view at 1:30 and 2:11. There are some random and tuneless keyboard splashes (e.g. at 2:37) that may well have been Smith's work. He turns out another selection of intriguing phrases ('a pillbox crisp / that French git / the spikes he left in the bathroom'; 'caught my life mould, give me silenced lectures') that receive a number of possible interpretations on *The Annotated Fall*, although MES himself described the lyric as 'just a sound experiment'. Like 'Smile' it was a regular feature on early 80s setlists (60 performances) before being dropped in 1985.

Tempo House

The best Fall is often based around simplicity and repetition, and 'Tempo House' is a prime example: not much more than a languid, shuffling drumbeat and a simple four-note bass pattern. Hanley squeezes everything he can from such a basic riff whilst Smith rambles about Richard Burton's 'chubby round jowls', 'the pedantic Welsh' and Winston Churchill's speech impediment. It doesn't sound like much on paper, but it's a captivating joy. Whilst the version on the album (live from the Haçienda, Manchester on 27th July 1983) is a perfectly decent recording, it's slightly frustrating that a proper studio take was never released. According to Paul Hanley, the reason for this was that the bass sound on the album was 'a little disappointing at times', and since 'the bassline was most of the song' they went with a live version. Almost ever-present in 1982-83 setlists, 'Tempo House' racked up 69 appearances altogether but wasn't played beyond December 1983.

Hexen Definitive / Strife Knot

A lengthy, lugubrious drawl based around Scanlon's meandering, chorus pedal-heavy riff. The two songs – which merge seamlessly here via a beautifully melancholy chord change – were not always played together live, 'Hexen' being played over 30 times before 'Strife Knot' appeared. Smith's voice is curiously distant and muffled (Simon Ford suggests that it sounds as if he's singing into a bucket), but this rather suits the track's inscrutable air, as do the cryptic lyrics: 'kickback art thou that thick?'; 'Greenpeace looked like saffron on the realm'; 'Louis Armstrong tapes waft down the aisles'. A perfect choice for an album closer. Played over 100 times in its various combinations 1982-85.

Reviews and Reissues

Reviews were surprisingly negative. The *NME*'s Jim Shelley described the album as 'slovenly' and 'self-satisfied… it's The Fall plodding on, going nowhere, MAKING DO'. Dave McCullough, writing in *Sounds*, was no more positive, giving the album 2.5 stars and calling it 'a pale zeroxing [sic] of [the] former Fall… laborious and very dull indeed'.[131] Despite the critics' negativity, *Perverted* gave the group their first independent chart number one since *Grotesque*.

A 1998 reissue included the two 1983 singles and their B-sides, as well as studio outtake 'Pilsner Trail'.[132] Most of the track is taken up with an unremarkable two-chord lope, although there's a brief, interesting (and sadly underused) section towards the beginning which is far more dynamic, featuring Smith declaiming in classic megaphone style 'republic grim truth' and 'hot blood erupts'. The 2005 Sanctuary reissue included a bonus CD which added the tracks from the fifth Peel session plus a variety of live recordings. One of these was 'Perverted By Language'. Only played live four times, it features a drum barrage that fades out suddenly just as it's starting to get interesting.

To promote the album, the group produced their first commercial video, *Perverted By Language Bis*. The project was

---

[131] McCullough's review inspired Chris Southon to pen a response, printed in the *Sounds* letters page, which had a dig at the paper's support for the burgeoning Smiths-led scene: 'One can only assume that… the sheer force and humour of the record as a whole are beyond a man who seems happy enough with the weedy, wet, pretty boy pop of the preposterous "handsome movement".'
[132] A live version of the track, entitled 'Plaster On The Hands' appears on the *Backdrop* compilation (see Appendix 2).

driven mainly by Brix's enthusiasm; Rough Trade were less excited about the idea, contributing only £500 towards the costs. It contains various live performances, an MES interview plus promo videos for 'Kicker Conspiracy' and 'Wings'. The latter finds Smith and a glamorous looking Brix sitting in an alcove in the Red Lion on Bury New Road in Prestwich. There's also an entertainingly odd take on 'Fitter', featuring, amongst several other random things, the group sitting around a table (very messily) mixing cocktails and some startling disco-dancing from Smith.

Evaluation

The previous year's criticism of *Room To Live* was perhaps understandable, even though in retrospect it feels overly harsh. The notion expressed in the contemporary music press that *Perverted By Language* saw The Fall lazily treading water, however, is much less comprehensible. It's an album of considerable innovation and contrasting textures and moods. It's almost flawlessly sequenced and in 'Garden' and 'Smile' contains two of their greatest ever songs (an opinion shared by both Hanley brothers). Smith's lyrical inventiveness continued to delight and astonish – obscure poeticism balanced skilfully with playful humour.

Perverted By Language is one of several transitional Fall albums. Both Riley's departure and Brix's arrival play a part in the shift in sound, but although her appearance tends to attract more attention, it should be remembered that she only appears on two tracks – the absence of the 'happy Fall guitarist' has much greater impact. The lack of a second guitarist means that Scanlon has to work doubly hard – a challenge that he undoubtedly rises to – and this gives the album a sparse feel, especially when compared to the monolithic *Hex*. This is by no means a negative feature – it gives 'Voxish' a lithe energy, for example. Also, in places, the double-drummer sound becomes even more effective because the contrast between what the two are playing can be discerned more easily.

It's not flawless: 'Fitter', excellent as it is when considered in isolation, sits slightly oddly as an opener; 'Neighbourhood', frustratingly, feels a little underdeveloped; 'Hotel' is a little pedestrian compared to the rest of the album; it would have been great to have a proper studio version of 'Tempo House'. But these are very minor quibbles. *Perverted By Language* strikes a near perfect balance between the relentless onslaught of *Hex* and the ragged improvisation of *Room To Live*.

The Wonderful And Frightening World Of...
Recorded: Focus Studios, London, mid-1984
Released: 12th October 1984

Personnel:
Mark E Smith – vocals
Brix Smith – guitar, vocals
Craig Scanlon – guitar
Steve Hanley – bass
Paul Hanley – drums, keyboards
Karl Burns – drums, bass

With:
Gavin Friday – vocals ('Copped It', 'Stephen Song')

Chapter 8: The Wonderful And Frightening World Of...

'I decided to pop it up a little and alter the rhythms.'

The Fall's reconciliation with Rough Trade proved to be short-lived. Smith's unhappiness regarding what he saw as the cheapskate recording of *Perverted By Language* was exacerbated by his perception that the label was prioritising the promotion of The Smiths. Another bone of contention was that Grant Showbiz had been 'poache   do The Smiths' sound. It seemed to MES that Rough Trade liked the idea of having a cult band on their books but were unwilling to put the necessary money and effort into helping them achieve wider success – a pressing issue as Smith was facing significant tax bills. He spent much of the group's autumn 1983 tour negotiating with other labels. New label Creation were said to be interested, as, supposedly, were Motown. The Motown story is a well-known tale: they offered the group a £46,000 advance, but hurriedly withdrew the offer when they listened to *Hex* and heard the 'obligatory n★★★★★s' line, saying that they saw 'no commercial potential in this band whatsoever'. This version of the story is rather fanciful. The label was, as Mick Middles points out, 'Motown UK, little more than a holding company for its American owner and The Fall interest lay rather more in the fact that it was manned by drifters from the British A&R brat pack – all of whom were big Fall fans – rather than some heartfelt desire on the part of Motown boss Berry Gordy to sign the band.' In the end, the group signed with Beggars Banquet, who had recently enjoyed chart success with Tubeway Army and Gary Numan. This was, according to Dave Thompson, 'The Fall's acknowledgement that it was finally time they started selling records.' Or, as Smith put it: 'I like it because they're straights... Beggars just want to have hit singles.'

In December, Brix made her first trip to Maida Vale when the group recorded their seventh Peel session, broadcast on 3rd January 1984. The new recruit made her presence felt with prominent backing vocals on 'Pat-Trip Dispenser', 'C.R.E.E.P.' and '2 x 4'. The highlight of the session, however, was 'Words Of Expectation'. A lengthy, repetitive beast in the vein of 'Garden' and 'Winter', it feels completely divorced from the rest of the session tracks. Burns and the Hanleys provide a deep undulating groove whilst Smith expounds on a range of typically random thoughts: 'the roof of my mouth sticks to the tip of my tongue'; 'if we carry on like this we're gonna end up like King Crimson'. It was played live 30 times between 1983 and 1986. Bizarrely, given the quality of the song, it never received another studio recording.[133] A mark of the group's gradual shift into more mainstream circles was the fact that they also recorded three sessions for radio programmes other than Peel's between March and September – David 'Kid' Jensen's and Janice Long's shows, and *Saturday Live* (see Appendix 1).

The Fall played ten dates in The Netherlands and Germany in March and April. At the first two (in Amsterdam and Eindhoven) they opened with a new song called 'He Talks'. A mildly interesting stomp, it's most notable for its strong resemblance to Judas Priest's 'Living After Midnight'. It never appeared on the setlist again or received a studio recording. The first gig that the group played on their return to the UK, at London's Heaven nightclub on 11th June, saw the debut of 'Hey! Marc Riley'. It's another 'Hey Bo Diddley' rewrite, in which Smith calls Riley a 'pillock' and mocks his alleged desire to keep playing old material ('Grotesque here and a Dragnet there').[134]

The first Fall song to appear on Beggars Banquet was 'Oh! Brother', released as a single in June 1984. Back in 1977, the song was a driving, aggressive if tuneless offering; now, with a light and airy production, it was transformed into a piece of quirky pop. It was a significant transformation from the *Perverted* material, the layers of backing vocals in particular giving it a light and sugary

---

[133] It appeared on the 1993 Peel session compilation *Kimble*, but, with typical Fall perversity, not on the 2003 Peel sessions compilation that bears its name.

[134] A live version of the song (from Azusa, California, 23rd May 1985) was included in *The Fall Box Set*; a demo version ('Ma Riley') featured on the 'omnibus' reissue of *This Nation's Saving Grace*. The song is possibly a riposte to Marc Riley's 1983 single 'Jumper Clown': 'Dare to dance on an Aussie floor / Bloody nose, bloody bore'.

feel. An obvious attempt at a more commercial approach, it didn't exactly storm the charts, reaching only number 93. It was retired from the set in 1985 after 35 performances. B-side 'God-Box', like 'Hotel Blöedel', was based on one of Brix's old Banda Dratsing songs, 'Can't Stop The Flooding'.[135] It was played live 44 times 1984-86. 'Oh! Brother' was the first Fall single to be released on 12". It featured a slightly longer version of the title track ('O! Brother'), which, as was often the way at the time, just extended the drum and guitar parts by several bars to no discernible benefit.

The group's next attempt on the charts, two months later, was 'c.r.e.e.p.'. It was an idea rescued by Brix, who found a demo tape of it behind Smith's sofa. Undoubtedly tuneful, but rather lightweight and occasionally shrill, it isn't entirely devoid of highlights. Brix's spoken intro ('Your ears prick up / we call you Hitler / and then kick you around like homogenized milk') is intriguing, and Smith's Elvis impersonation at 1:28 is fun. The 12" bonus track ('C.R.E.E.P.') does that typically pointless 80s remix thing again. Many thought that the song was about Marc Riley; others suggested that the subject might be Morrissey. Smith denied that either was the case: 'It's bits of things. A lot of people think it's about them.' Brix suggested that it was about a tour manager called Scumech, hence the line 'he is a scum-egg, a horrid trendy wretch'. The B-side on both versions, 'Pat-Trip Dispenser', was a more satisfying proposition. Written about tour manager Pat Clark, who allegedly used to pass off powdered caffeine as speed ('thought he could fool The Fall with his imitation speed'), a photo of whom appears on the back cover of the single, it's a carefully textured track. The guitar parts – a central choppy rhythm, a simple Cure-like line that broadly follows Hanley's bass in the left channel and a slightly distorted tinny strum in the right – are especially well interwoven. Commercially, 'c.r.e.e.p.' fared little better than its predecessor, reaching only 91 on the UK charts. It was a popular set choice at the time, racking up 71 performances 1983-87; 'Pat-Trip Dispenser' was played live 30 times 1983-85, and received a one-off revival in 2009.

[135] The vocal melody of 'God-Box' also sounds rather like The Ramones' 'Go Mental' from their 1978 album *Road To Ruin*.

The album was recorded in mid-1984 at Focus Studios in London. A crucial factor in the shaping of its sound was the choice of producer. John Leckie had been employed at Abbey Road studios in the 70s, working with John Lennon and Syd Barrett, and had produced albums for Magazine and XTC. Despite his hippyish background ('He had recently walked off an ashram,' Brix described, 'where everyone had to wear the colours of the rising sun and was encouraged to have group sex') Leckie quickly established a productive working relationship with The Fall. 'I want to capture the energy of the band playing live, but with a cleaner sound than you're used to,' Steve Hanley recalls Leckie saying. 'John makes suggestions about the arrangements themselves in such an unobtrusive manner it's impossible not to engage with his ideas... our music begins to develop another layer.' The cover once again featured a disturbing Claus Castenskiold image, the garishly grotesque figure being perfectly matched to the darkly deranged spirit of many of the songs.

Lay Of The Land

The first track is certainly one that's a fit for the cover art, particularly in its disturbingly arresting introduction. There's a distinct 'folk horror' flavour to the creepy chanting that opens the song, reminiscent of stone circles and pagan rituals. Lovecraft is referenced ('eldritch house'), but the inspiration comes mostly from *Quatermass*.[136] The fact that 'lay' and 'ley' (as in ley lines) are homophones is not a coincidence, according to Brix: '[It] was about ley lines running through the country. Mark was... into spiritualism and haunting and energy and stuff like that.' The main body of the song clatters along like a demented train, much of its pulverising energy supplied by a two-bass onslaught from Burns and Hanley. Smith puts on his best scornful snarl ('my son') and his a cappella refrain at 4:30, followed by Burns's hyperactive

---

[136] Eldritch, meaning 'weird and sinister or ghostly', was a favourite adjective of Lovecraft. The 'lay, lay' chant used here comes from the 1979 ITV series starring John Mills as Professor Bernard Quatermass, a character (created by Nigel Kneale) who first appeared in 1953's *The Quatermass Experiment*. It can be heard on a YouTube video entitled 'Ringstone Round (Huffity, Puffity)'.

bass solo, is a choice moment. It was played almost constantly in 1984 and reached a total of 72 appearances by 1986. In one of their most memorable TV appearances, The Fall performed 'Lay' on *The Old Grey Whistle Test* in November 1984, accompanied by Michael Clark's company. Clark was a talented dancer who had trained at the Royal Ballet School. A Fall fan who had used the group's music in much of his early work, he first came to Smith's attention via a local news programme: 'He was in a tea-time TV show, where he was dancing through a Manchester supermarket in a dress. Everyone was going, "He looks a right idiot," but I thought, "He looks pretty cool to me".' The two became unlikely but life-long friends. On the *Whistle Test*, he and his dancers wore buttock-displaying tights, and the performance ended with a pantomime cow being force-fed cartons of milk. Presenter Mark Ellen was rendered temporarily speechless.[137]

2 x 4

Opening with an aggressive, staccato bass riff, '2 × 4' revisits the punkabilly approach of 'Fiery Jack'. Like 'Lay', it clatters along exuberantly, but unlike its predecessor's dark tone, there's an almost cartoonish atmosphere due to the repeated 'hit 'em on the head with a 2 by 4' line. Brix explained that the 'mental reference point was an American cartoon like Road Runner, where he would take a 2 x 4 which was a plank and whack 'em on the head. Tom and Jerry with the frying pan.' It's also one of those tracks where Brix's vocals are a perfect foil for Smith's. One of the group's most played songs, it clocked up an impressive 134 performances 1983–88.

Copped It

Like 'Oh! Brother', a song that dated back at least to 1977; a reference to 'Copped' by The Outsiders (the choice of name before the group decided on The Fall) in a letter from MES to Tony Friel in September 1976 suggests that it might be even older

---

[137] Smith's mother Irene described to Mick Middles how she invited several friends and neighbours around to watch the performance on TV: 'It was very exciting because it was the first time many of them had seen The Fall... and then it came on and Michael Clark was dancing with no bottom in his trouser... [I] didn't know where to look... It was a bit embarrassing.'

than that. The guitar grind is unrelenting, and Smith makes good use of his trusty megaphone, ably supported by the sinister croon of Gavin Friday from Irish band the Virgin Prunes. Over the last minute, Craig Scanlon chucks in some swirly, aquatic guitar work, and the oddly dispassionate doo-wop backing vocals are an incongruous treat. The lyric throws together 'immovable frogs', Elvis Costello ('Costello, ideas trenchant borrows') and a reference to Bananarama ('it ain't what you do it's the way that you do it' – a hit for the trio two years earlier[138]). It seems to be about plagiarism, although it's hard to decide if that's plagiarism by or of The Fall (or possibly both) – as *The Annotated Fall* puts it, 'MES's conception of plagiarism is very complex.' 'Copped It' is another track that had a decent shelf-life live, making its 67th and final appearance in 1987.

Elves

Speaking of plagiarism… The Fall's recorded history is littered with 'borrowings', some more obvious than others. 'Elves' is definitely at the 'shameless steal' end of the spectrum, its riff being lifted wholesale from The Stooges' 'I Wanna Be Your Dog'. Brix – who did the lifting – claimed that it was a deliberate homage, meant to be a 'witty commentary, a send-up of punk'. Steve Hanley suggests that his brother pointed out the similarity and Brix's response was that she'd never heard the song. Although derivative, 'Elves' is much more than a simple rip-off. Whilst the Stooges' riff is prominent throughout, the group add to it an unearthly and malevolent atmosphere; the simple descending guitar figure, accompanied by the shrill, swirling organ, gives you a sense of spiralling, falling out of control. The chanting, menacing vocals contribute to a dark folk horror atmosphere similar to 'Lay Of The Land', emphasised by the lyric: 'tin-can rattle on the path / the bestial greed is on the attack / the cat black runs round the tree'. The strange vocal explosion at 2:04 perhaps marks the best use of a sneeze in modern music. Live, it had a relatively short shelf-life: 36 performances 1984-85.

[138] According to Gavin Friday, 'We were consciously parodying The Carpenters and Bananarama.'

Slang King

Smith was a big fan of *The Twilight Zone* (Brix described him as 'obsessed' with it) and several Fall songs were inspired by the programme. Created by Rod Serling, it originally ran on CBS for five series between 1959 and 1964.[139] An amalgamation of science fiction, suspense, horror, fantasy, black comedy and psychological thriller, its distinguishing feature was its plot-twist conclusions that often had a moral message. 'A single episode,' Smith noted in *Renegade*, 'has more ideas in it than a full year of modern TV.' 'Wickwire', the first word in the lyrics of 'Slang King', is a character from the 1960 episode *Elegy*, in which 22nd-century astronauts discover an Earth-like planet populated by people frozen in time. The line 'it's no longer a journey down the road for him / it is now escape route' is very similar to dialogue from another episode from the same year, *The Hitch-Hiker*.[140] Not all of the lyric pertains *Twilight Zone* plots, however – 'three little girls with only 50 pence... had to put the Curly Wurly back', was inspired by a real-life scene witnessed by Smith and Brix in their local corner shop.

'Slang King' had an even shorter stay on the setlist than 'Elves', notching up only 29 appearances before being dropped after October 1986. It's a relatively accessible song, featuring a pretty keyboard figure, but there's also a strange, swampish quality to it. The heavily phased/chorused guitar line squats toad-like over the song; an incongruous trilling organ ripples in occasionally; high-pitched, breathy backing vocals drift around. As the song says, 'all here is ace'.

Bug Day

One of those experimental moments, albeit one more fully developed than many others. It's comprised of a gently undulating bassline and various atonal guitar clippings over which Smith rambles about insects ('green moths shivered / cockroaches mouldered in the ground'). Its lethargic oddness is appealing, although it's hard to argue with Steve Hanley's verdict of 'a bit of a filler'. Never played live, unsurprisingly.

---

[139] It was revived in the 80s and subsequently broadcast in several other incarnations.

[140] 'Now it isn't even a trip, it's flight. Route 80 isn't a highway anymore, it's an escape route.'

Stephen Song

An upbeat and joyful song with an infectious marching rhythm, the agile percussion and tumbling chords capturing a spirit of playfulness. The slightly creepy gothic tone of Gavin Friday's vocals cut across the tweeness of Brix's voice to great effect, and it's broken up nicely by the discord at 1:13 and 2:25. Smith described it as being 'about competitiveness, people getting at you, imitating you and your habits', although he also said 'I just made it up as I went along'. The lyric contained the phrase 'adult net', which Brix would go on to use as the name of her side project.[141] Perhaps because Friday's contribution was an integral part of the song, it was only ever played live six times.

Craigness

Like 'Joker Hysterical Face', 'Craigness' is about odd neighbours, this time ones with 'one eye' and 'maroon flares'. The main lyrical refrain is taken from dialogue in the 1982 slasher film *Alone in the Dark*.[142] It's melancholy and understated until Smith's unearthly screech at 2:28 launches a spot of wig-out craziness. Like 'Stephen', it only got half a dozen live outings.

Disney's Dream Debased

Another piece of ramshackle minor-chord jangle, albeit one with a sinister air. The song deals with Smith and Brix's experience of visiting Disneyland on the day that a woman died on one of the rides.[143] It is one often cited as evidence of Smith's 'pre-cog' abilities, as he told Brix repeatedly that the Matterhorn rollercoaster was 'evil' shortly before the accident occurred. The vocal is one of Smith's most mellow and melodic. It received 25 live outings 1984-86.

[141] The Adult Net released a handful of wispy, jangly singles in the late 80s, plus one album – 1989's *The Honey Tangle* (featuring Clem Burke of Blondie on drums and The Smiths' second guitarist Craig Gannon).

[142] Donald Pleasence plays Dr. Leo Bain, a psychiatrist terrorised by four escaped patients. Smith repeats one of his speeches almost verbatim: 'Mind moving fast is crazy. Mind slow is saint. Mind stopped... is God.'

[143] According to *Wikipedia*: 'On January 3, 1984, a 48-year-old woman from Fremont, California was killed and decapitated when she was thrown from a Matterhorn bobsled car and struck by the next oncoming bobsled. The spot where she was killed is now called "Dolly's Drop" by cast members. An investigation found that her seat belt was not buckled. It is unclear whether the victim deliberately unfastened her belt or if the seat belt malfunctioned.'

Reviews and Reissues

In the *NME*, Richard Cook described *Wonderful...* as 'particularly sharp and still terrifically crowded'; any worries that John Leckie 'was persuading them into good taste are vapourised by this clogged, boiling sound'. *Sounds'* Andy Hurt decided that The Fall could indeed 'survive the culture shock of sophisticated recording techniques and find true happiness... rough edges are still very much an integral part of the "new" sound'. The album reached number 62 in the UK Albums Chart.

An EP entitled *Call For Escape Route* (a reference to the *Twilight Zone* quotation in 'Slang King') was released on the same day as *Wonderful And Frightening*. It was a three-track 12" that came with a bonus 7". 'Draygo's Guilt',[144] a poppy, Bo Diddley-ish number (with a passing resemblance to Lou Reed's 'Vicious'), dated back to 1980 and had already had 25 of its 33 eventual live outings by the time of its release. The line 'blow his nose on last pound note' had previously appeared on the live version of 'And This Day' included on *Hip Priest And Kamerads*. 'Clear Off!' was the third track recorded with Gavin Friday. It's a curious mixture of The Cure (the mournful, chorus-drenched lead guitar), C86-indie (the thin, choppy rhythm guitar) and 80s synth-pop (the hesitant, plinky keyboard line). It got 30 live outings 1983 85. The nearly eight-minute 'No Bulbs' has a catchy melody, contains some nice Velvets-style guitar work and features an unusually literal lyric about the 'trash mount' of a flat that MES and Brix shared where neither light bulbs or a belt for Smith's trousers were available. It lasted in the set until 1986 and was played 33 times. The version on the 7" ('No Bulbs 3') is just an edit; 'Slang King 2' (on the other side) isn't radically different from the album version aside from a little voice-over intro.

For the first time, your experience of a Fall album depended significantly on which format you bought. The majority of contemporary purchasers got a nine-track LP. Those who went for the cassette got a whopping seven bonus tracks (taken from the two singles and the *Escape Route* EP), which nearly doubled the album's

---

[144] Infamous conga player Steve Davies was in a band called Victor Draygo in the early 80s.

length.[145] In 2010, Beggars Banquet released a comprehensive four-CD omnibus addition, containing singles, rough mixes, radio sessions and a recording of the group's performance from 22nd September 1984 at the Pandora's Music Box Festival in Rotterdam.[146] The Rotterdam recording is of excellent quality, sound-wise, and is a solid performance. 'Kicker Conspiracy' is an especially intriguing listen: it features a new backing vocal from Brix and has a distinctly spacious sound, allowing you to hear Hanley's bassline much more clearly than is often the case. 'No Bulbs' is spirited and energetic, although it's marred by the fact that both Brix and Scanlon's guitars are distinctly out of tune.

Evaluation

A commonly held view is that Brix, after having dipped her toes in the recording process with *Perverted*, exerted her pop-sensibility influence on *Wonderful* and made it an altogether more accessible and commercially viable prospect. However, although her contributions are undoubtedly a key feature of the album's sound, it was Leckie who had by far the biggest influence on this process, using his years of production experience to find a precision, clarity and spaciousness to the sound that opened up a multitude of possibilities without detracting from the group's intrinsic character. Smith himself also claimed some credit for this transformation, of course: 'I thought we needed to steer it in another direction. It all got a bit monotonous… plain monotony can get fucking tedious… That's why I decided to pop it up a little and alter the rhythms.'

The preceding single and B-sides did signal an increasingly accessible approach. However, if you concentrate on the 'original' nine-song album, the notion that *Wonderful* is a polished, chart-friendly record is hard to support. Despite 'Slang King's pretty keyboard melody and 'Stephen's jauntiness, there's still plenty of challenging Fall noise here: the 'frightening' was just as apposite as the 'wonderful'.

[145] The cassette was entitled *Escape Route From Aie Wonderful And Frightening World Of…* Oddly, the cover boasted of '5 extra tracks!' rather than seven.
[146] The programme (which can be seen on thefall.org gigography), suggests that the group didn't go on stage until 3.15am.

This Nation's Saving Grace
Recorded: The Music Works and The Workhouse, London, June–July 1985
Released: 23rd September 1985

Personnel:
Mark E Smith – vocals
Brix Smith – guitar, vocals
Craig Scanlon – guitar
Steve Hanley – bass
Simon Rogers – keyboards, guitar, bass
Karl Burns – drums, vocals

Chapter 9: This Nation's Saving Grace

'Oh, to be thirteen and have this be the first record one heard.'

Up to the release of *The Wonderful And Frightening World Of...*, The Fall's line-up – notwithstanding the addition of Brix – had been relatively stable for several years. This was to change significantly towards the end of 1984.

The autumn–winter tour to promote *Wonderful And Frightening* saw the group play in Europe and Ireland before returning to the UK in October. On 1st November they played Cardiff's New Ocean Club. Finding the hotel car park chained shut after the gig, the group left their van parked in the street. Come the morning, everything but Steve Hanley's bass amp had been stolen. Smith was 'on a different plane of angry', but arrangements were made for the group to play with borrowed equipment at the next night's gig in Brighton. However, on the tour bus after that performance, Smith launched into a tirade at the musicians, brandishing a stick with which he whacked the headrests of their seats. 'You fuckers! What were you thinking? Who the fuck would be stupid enough to leave a fucking van outside the hotel *with all the fucking gear in it!!*' This was the straw that broke the camel's back for the Hanley brothers, who both quit.

For Steve, the pressure of having recently become a father was undoubtedly a factor in his decision. Eventually, it was agreed (after a surprise visit to his home by Smith and Brix where he received £1000 to tide him over) that he would take a few months off from The Fall as paternity leave. According to Brix, Smith was 'chastened for probably the only time I had ever seen'. For Paul, however, the departure was final (although he was persuaded to play for the infamous *Old Grey Whistle Test* performance later that month and a couple of occasions in 1986). He formed a new band, Shout Bamalam (they were originally going to be called Kiss The Blade, until they discovered there was already a band with that name) who released an EP called *Ambition, The Groover*

And Greed in 1988. Shortly afterwards, he left the music industry to work in IT.[147]

Musically, the solution to Paul's departure was obvious. Finding a new bassist, albeit temporarily, would be more problematic. The answer came via Smith's friendship with Michael Clark. Simon Rogers had worked with Clark at Ballet Rambert. Dave Simpson described him as 'the least likely musician ever to end up in The Fall' – Rogers was a 'proper' musician, who had attended the Royal College of Music, composed ballets and even appeared in the charts as a member of Incantation, who had a top 20 hit with 'Cacharpaya' in 1982.[148] According to Steve Hanley, he could 'play every instrument on the planet'. Rogers's stint with The Fall began in December with a handful of European dates, then continued with four UK shows the following March. Later that month, the group flew to America for a 12-date tour. On the second day of the tour, the group made an in-store appearance at Texas Records in Santa Monica, California. A recording of them playing 'Lay Of The Land', interspersed with an interview with MES and Brix, was broadcast on MTV show *The Cutting Edge*.[149]

Steve Hanley found life on the sidelines tough. Bumping into Karl Burns led to him being regaled with tales of the luxurious studio in which The Fall were currently recording.[150] Unable to resist turning up at the second of the group's UK dates in March (in Blackburn, 20 minutes from his home), he ended up drunkenly joining in on keyboards. Being replaced, albeit temporarily, by a classically trained, highly-skilled musician led to him feeling understandably threatened, especially when Burns played him some of the new material such as 'Cruiser's

[147] In recent years, he has turned – very successfully – to writing. As well as *Have A Bleedin Guess*, he published *Leave The Capital: A History of Manchester Music in 13 Recordings* in 2017. He can also now be found playing in Brix & The Extricated alongside his brother.
[148] A South American pan pipe number that will undoubtedly remind those of a certain age of *The Fast Show*.
[149] The interview (which curiously features Smith sitting about six feet behind Brix throughout) sees MES extol his wife's guitar skills, suggest that there's 'a strong sense of comedy to The Fall', admit that being in the group 'is not a bed of roses all the time' and express a liking for 'the lads in the group' because of how they cheer him up.
[150] Chapel Lane, a live-in studio in Hampton Bishop, a small village just outside Hereford. MES thought it 'too comfy'.

Creek' that had been recorded without him. Consequently, when the bassist was detailed to pick Rogers up from Piccadilly station after the US tour, he approached the task with some trepidation. However, he was surprised and slightly impressed by Rogers's conversion from 'clean-cut, ethnically-dressed kids' TV presenter type' to a 'straggly-haired man in leather trousers and in desperate need of a shave and a good night's kip', and the two of them bonded over an afternoon in the Hanleys' living room going over the new songs.

The Fall recorded their eighth Peel session in May, with Hanley back on bass and Rogers on guitar and keyboards. It included a thumpingly robust version of 'Cruiser's Creek', although it's perhaps a minute or so longer than it needs to be. 'Couldn't Get Ahead' fizzes with energy and is superior to the version that appeared on the single. 'Spoilt Victorian Child' and 'Gut Of The Quantifier' are both raw and assertive, although lacking the depth of the album versions. In June, the group released a double A-side single that had been recorded with the temporarily Hanley-free line-up. 'Couldn't Get Ahead', a bouncy number with an infectious chorus, is a more successful attempt at capturing an accessible-yet-still-The-Fall sound than the previous year's singles. 'Rollin' Dany', a Gene Vincent cover, is a spirited piece of rock'n'roll, featuring a nifty solo from Scanlon. 'Couldn't Get Ahead' was a popular setlist choice 1985-86, making 53 appearances. 'Rollin' Dany' only got five outings, all in autumn 1985. The 12" version of the single added 'Petty (Thief) Lout', in which Smith reminisced about his teenage years hanging around with petty criminals. The main body of the song is an unremarkable Smiths/R.E.M. jangle, but the quiet interludes are more interesting, featuring an understated, bluesy slide guitar. It made 24 appearances in 1985 and was resurrected twice in 1990. The single made no more of a dent in the UK charts than the 1984 releases, only reaching number 90.

The Fall returned to Maida Vale to record their ninth Peel session in September. At just over four months, this would remain the smallest gap between any of their visits to the BBC; it was also the first time that the group had recorded two consecutive Peel sessions with the same line-up. 'L.A.' and 'What You Need' both have a sharper and brighter sound than their album equivalents. The former benefits from the hilariously bizarre introduction, 'Lloyd Cole's brain and face is made out of cow pat; we all know that.' It's unclear why the group decided to revisit a two-year-old single, but the version of 'The Man Whose Head Expanded' is admirably fast and furious. It includes some fine megaphone work from Smith, but doesn't quite have the subtlety and texture of the single version. 'Faust Banana', which would eventually appear in 1986 as 'Dktr. Faustus', saw the unlikely introduction of a xylophone into the Fall sound.

The group's next single, released in October 1985, was 'Cruiser's Creek'. The title was inspired by the Smiths' experiences of holidaying with Brix's family:

> You've never seen anything weirder than Mark E Smith on a fucking luxury cruise. He can't swim, and was panicked just being on the boat. He hates the sun. He will not sit in the sun, never mind sunbathe. The library on the boat was called 'Cruiser's Creek'.

The song's irresistible surf-rock twang is one of the group's best efforts at capturing a Fall-pop sound. It was played 51 times 1985–87. 'Vixen', the bonus song on the 12", is another of Brix's surf-rock numbers but is rather slight. It was never played live. Once again, the single only reached the lower end of the charts – 96 this time.

This Nation's Saving Grace

The album was recorded at London's The Music Works and The Workhouse studios, with John Leckie once again handling production. Smith remained impressed with his work. 'It's not effects that are involved... it's just what's there, bringing out what's always there.' The cover was another Claus Castenskiold piece, this time created in collaboration with photographer Michael Pollard. MES's instructions to Pollard were, 'I want it to look like you are on a train and you are arriving in a city at nightfall, so you're coming through the backstreets.'[151] Castenskiold and Pollard worked completely separately, their contributions then being blended in the Beggars Banquet art department. Although Pollard was concerned that 'the two styles didn't blend at all', the cover is still a strikingly handsome concoction: the detailed rendering of the gritty Manchester skyline, the floating lettering and the mythical horse and chariot in the sky is a perfectly apt mix of the mundane, fantastical and abstract. It was the first Fall album to feature a gatefold sleeve.

Mansion

The album starts with Brix back in magpie mode, as 'Mansion's riff is a clear lift from 'Billy The Monster' by The Deviants.[152] It makes for an effective opener, with its spooky, sci-fi atmosphere – designed 'to evoke the creepy theme song to the Haunted House at Disneyland' – setting the scene nicely for the aural barrage of the next track. How many times it was played live is a tricky issue. It was only used as an intro tape at the time and didn't make its way into the set until 2002 (in which year it was played 25 times). However, whether these performances were of 'Mansion' or its companion piece 'To Nkroachment: Yarbles' isn't entirely clear. Musically, the live versions were closer to the instrumental album track, but they generally contained vocals (although they rarely resembled the lyrics from 'Yarbles'). To add to the confusion, DVD releases from that year call it 'Yarbles' whilst the 2002 setlists call it 'Mansion'.

Bombast

Steve Hanley, not surprisingly, felt a little out of sync with the rest of the group when the album was recorded, several songs

[151] In the booklet accompanying the *TNSG* omnibus edition, Pollard described how he got his shot: 'We drove around in various locations around Ancoats – nothing was working, we were too low-down. I realised we would need to get higher, so we went up Cheetham Hill Road, and you get a much better vantage point of the whole city. We went up there and couldn't see a damn thing: we started wandering round some side streets. There was this brick wall and if you look over it, that's the view you get. I plonked the camera on the brick wall and took a number of different exposures, with slightly different framings. I knew that was the shot I wanted. Most noticeably they got rid of the Arndale Centre on the final album. The CIS centre is nearest to you. The Town Hall is centre right.'
[152] Late 60s psych-rock band, some of whom went on to form The Pink Fairies.

having been written in his absence: 'I'm like a builder who's been off sick, returning to find most of the wall has been built and all that's left for me to do is the snagging.'[153] However, his contribution here (he wrote the riff during his paternity leave) kicks the album into gear in wonderfully boisterous fashion. Smith gets his megaphone out for the striking introduction. It doesn't make much sense grammatically ('whose main entitle is themselves'[154]) but the message is clear: don't give me any of your bullshit, or you'll know about it. (*The Annotated Fall* suggests the somewhat wordier 'all those who are entitled in their own minds, and whose only source of entitlement is themselves, are in for an overdose of vitriol'.) What follows is an absolute marvel. It's like Steve Hanley came up with three great riffs and then thought, what the hell, let's weld them all together and see what happens. It clashes, it grinds, it thrashes; it almost feels as if the song itself is threatening to punch you in the face. There's no real *song* as such here, but it's a glorious slab of noise. It got an impressive 105 live outings over the next five years.

Barmy

Another borrowed riff, this time from The Monkees' 1968 single 'Valleri'. A playful, tuneful verse contrasts with a dissonant and gloomy chorus/middle eight, the latter featuring swampish wah-wah. There's even a bit of sprightly rock'n'roll piano sprinkled over the second half. The lyric contains some interesting wordplay (England's 'creamery' where you might have expected 'greenery') and seems to have some historical context, perhaps pertaining to the Napoleonic Wars ('May 1803' was when the conflict started). The only mild criticism you might level at 'Barmy' is that it very slightly outstays its welcome: it might have finished more satisfyingly at 4:05. It was played 47 times 1985-86.

---

[153] For the benefit of those who, like me, have not the faintest clue about the building trade, 'snagging' is the process of checking a new building for minor faults that need to be rectified.

[154] On the performance for *The Tube*, and a couple of bootleg recordings, MES actually says 'end title'.

What You Need

Inspired by a couple of *Twilight Zone* episodes: one actually called *What You Need*, the other being *The Four of Us Are Dying*. The latter told the story of a con man who can change his face to make it look like anyone he chooses. Smith admitted that he got the two episodes confused.[155] 'The main theme of the song,' he went on, 'is that there are a lot of people in Britain, and a lot of people in America, too, telling people what they need. And in America, especially. I find this really scary.' This is proper '3 Rs' stuff, uncompromising in its adherence to the Fall principle of bludgeoning and beguiling you with relentless repetition. Scanlon's snaking lead line and the sparse, choppy rhythm guitar are simple but devastatingly effective; the vocal is almost devoid of melody, simply declaiming in classic megaphone style a series of intriguing phrases ('been bleeding some itch', 'your verbose kitchen', 'slippery shoes for your horrible feet'). It also eschews anything as namby-pamby as a chorus or middle eight, although the 'spooky carnival' keyboards do add a bit of colour and variety, as does the intermittent appearance of a cowbell. 'What You Need', which was played live 27 times in 1985-86, is perhaps the very definition of the Fall sound. It represents the core of what it is to be a Fall song: the chalkface; the grinding out of what needs to be said and should be heard; the essence of the group's work ethic.

Spoilt Victorian Child

A lyric of which Smith had written an early draft back in the late 70s but had never found suitably 'daft English music' for it until Simon Rogers provided a stuttering riff (in 6/4 time) that fitted the bill.[156] Brix found the guitar part challenging to play and 'felt like Eddie Van Halen' once she'd mastered it. The jerky, awkward guitar contrasts nicely with the solidity of the drums, but the most pleasing aspect is the way that Smith seems to be in a constant battle to keep up with the music, which gives the

---

[155] His confusion probably arose because the two episodes were shown as a double bill in 1983.

[156] It bears a slight resemblance to The Groundhog's 'Earth Is Not Room Enough' from their 1972 album *Who Will Save The World?*

song a dynamic urgency. The Victorian theme is consistent if not entirely coherent overall: pop-up books, 'disfigured poxes' and aqueducts; the reference to 'fairies are flying' may be about the 'Cottingley Fairies'.[157] It was played 34 times in 1985-86, and was resurrected for seven performances in 2004.

L.A.

Famously John Peel's least favourite Fall track, but also Brix's 'most favourite song that I ever wrote'. The oscillating synth and overlapping, sinewy guitar lines give this a dark, sinister edge which is supported well by Smith's understated and minimal contributions. It's one of those songs that exemplifies his wonderfully idiosyncratic timing, particularly in the way that he moves from 'L, L, L, L' to 'A, A, A, A', never quite at the point where you expect it. The breakdown at 3:14 provides a lovely snatch of casual dissonance. According to Brix, the group were aiming for 'the sound of a helicopter… looking for escaped prisoners'. She also suggests that 'white snow, scum-ball' was inspired by US cop show *T. J .Hooker* and 'this is my happening and it freaks me out' was taken from *Beyond The Valley of the Dolls*.[158] 'L.A.' was a long-standing feature on the setlist, racking up 117 appearances between 1985 and 1996.

Gut Of The Quantifier

Yet another appropriated riff, this time from The Doors' 'The Changeling'.[159] A muscular and confrontational tune, all angles and elbows, it's beautifully paced, the crescendos being deployed deftly throughout. The double-tracked vocals create a sense of oppressive intensity, but it's not without humour: the 'Kane Gang' line might be a little lost in history now, but it still raises

---

[157] In 1917 (so actually 16 years after Victoria's death) two young girls, Elsie Wright and Frances Griffiths, gained notoriety for a series of photographs purporting to show them posing with fairies in their garden. Their fame was enhanced when Sir Arthur Conan Doyle wrote an article declaring the pictures to be real. It wasn't until 1983 that Wright and Griffiths admitted that the photos were faked.

[158] A 1970 Russ Meyer film; the character who delivers the line, Ronnie 'Z-Man' Barzell, was loosely based on Phil Spector.

[159] From 1970's *L.A. Woman*, which in turn Jim Morrison pinched from 'Shotgun' by Jr. Walker & The All-Stars.

a smile, as does the manic cackle at 0:48. Not only is it an archetypal Fall title, it's a conglomeration of many 1980s Fall tropes: the relentless, angular rhythm, the astringent guitar, Smith's phraseology ('half-wit philanthropist, cosy charity gig'), the shrieks and 'hup's. 'Quantifier' represents a blend of much that made the frightening world wonderful: 'The entire group moving as a single unit; every element absolutely locked into each other.' It was played 69 times in 1985–88 and was resurrected for a couple of performances in 1995.

My New House

As disorientating as it is to listen to a Fall song that's about a specific, clearly understood subject, 'My New House' is about... the Smiths' new house. The dwelling in question was a semi-detached in Sedgley Park, just around the corner from MES's parents.[160] It was credited to Smith alone, but the riff was probably Craig Scanlon's. One of the few Fall songs to feature a prominent acoustic guitar, it follows the same '3Rs' approach as 'What You Need'. It has a long list of features to treasure: Smith's gleeful whoops on the exclamations of 'seeee my new house'; the oddly timed cymbals in the 'chorus'; the grinding Beefheartesque guitar lurking in the background; the unmistakeably MES lyric 'I bought it off the Baptists / I get their bills / And I get miffed'. It was only ever played live 20 times, all in 1986.

Paintwork

A thing of true wonder. The circular acoustic riff and gently descending organ motif float over an understated drum track and the occasional diversion into a scuffed guitar riff. Smith throws in both a set of enigmatic phrases ('I read Paula Yates on Vision mopeds',[161] 'them continentals are little monkeys', 'as if I hadn't done 10 months service in the USA on the big yachts') and a

---

[160] In July 2021, the news that the house had been put on the market caused a bit of overwrought social media kerfuffle, particularly regarding the shots of the rather dilapidated interior. (See 'Second House Now', Chapter 33.)

[161] In the motoring section of the *Daily Express* of 27th May 1985, p 26, an article headlined 'Paula's pleased by a vision of the future' included a picture of the TV presenter astride a Honda Vision moped (another fact unearthed by dannyno).

madly catchy hook 'Hey Mark! You're spoiling all the paintwork' (a phrase used by one of the decorators of the Smiths' 'new house'). But what elevates the song into unequivocally classic status is one of those pieces of accidental genius that resulted from Smith's haphazard recording habits. Listening back to the track on a Dictaphone whilst watching television, he managed to sit on the device and record part of the programme he was listening to over it. (The dialogue – 'formation of Beryllium 8. Main sequence stars were no good for making carbon in this way. Red Giant stars…' – comes from an Open University programme.[162]) The way that this is spliced into the main recording is a sublime piece of audio collage. 'Paintwork' was only played five times in 1985-86, but got 16 further outings in 2000-04. The group at the very height of their creativity; as Smith said, 'You can't contrive something like that.'

I Am Damo Suzuki

It's possible that many people, on first playing this song, checked to see whether their record player was working correctly, as there were apparently two different songs playing simultaneously. The introduction is itself somewhat askew – the simple, haunting guitar line already sounding somewhat out of sync with Smith's sinister, breathy vocal – but the entrance of the drums at 0:43 provides an exhilaratingly jarring experience. The way that the two rhythms clash, resolve, then draw apart again is masterfully deranged. It's hard to believe that what you're hearing is real or intentional; it challenges virtually everything you'd ever assumed about rhythm or melody. It's worth quoting in full John Leckie's account:

> We did two takes and Mark liked the band on one tape but he liked his vocal better on the other. Now, on a computer you'd be able to edit that and stretch it to make it all work, so I said, 'Well, all we can do is to take the vocal off here and put it on to a piece of tape.' The two takes had

---

[162] *How do red giants make carbon?*, part of the OU *Matter in the Universe* course which ran from 1985-1992. Yet another example of the indefatigable dannyno's research for *The Annotated Fall*.

different arrangements, like the verse and chorus came in at different times, so the whole thing gives the impression of being completely random, but the reason being that the first take was eight bars of verse, four bars of chorus, eight bars of verse and the second take is twelve bars of verse, six bars of chorus, a different arrangement. Also Mark's standing next to Karl, so the drums are coming through the vocal mix and every time the drums stop on the first take you can hear these ambient drums going on from the vocal mix on the second take and I thought it was fantastic and so did everyone else, but a totally unconventional way of doing it.

Musically, the song is clearly indebted to Can's 'Oh Yeah'.[163] As if the complex and challenging music wasn't enough, it's also packed densely with lyrical intrigue: references to Karlheinz Stockhausen and Fritz Lieber; further nods to Can's work ('Soundtracks');[164] and a wealth of lovingly crafted but mysterious phrases ('drums to shock, into brass evil... recipe for fear gas, amount of salt ash... the rock that was an egg, is in wrong cradle'). Despite its unusual construction 'I Am Damo Suzuki' was one of the group's most frequently played songs: 118 performances in total, although it had a 13-year gap between its 48th and 49th outings. It often took the form of an extended workout live, sometimes stretching beyond eight minutes.

To Nkroachment: Yarbles

Like Banda Dratsing, 'yarbles' is nadsat – it means 'testicles'. The companion piece to 'Mansion' has a softer and gentler tone. The vocal melody is indebted to 'Every Day I Have to Cry', written by Arthur Alexander and covered by many artists, including Dusty Springfield. There's a doleful, strangely touching ennui to Smith's vocal ('All the good times are past and gone').

[163] From their 1971 album *Tago Mago*. The lyrics also reference 'Vitamin C', from 1972's *Ege Bamyasi*.
[164] Stockhausen was an influential 20th-century composer, known for his ground-breaking work in experimental, electronic music; Fritz Leiber was an American writer of fantasy, horror, and science fiction; *Soundtracks* was a 1970 compilation of music that Can had recorded for a variety of films.

Reviews and Reissues

In the *NME*, David Quantick declared that 'The Fall have made one of their most accessible LPs yet; at the same time, they have made a record that's infinitely more peculiar then almost anything else released this year.' In *Sounds*, Chris Roberts was even more effusive: 'Oh, to be thirteen and have this be the first record one heard. Life and what you needed would never be the same again.' The *NME* ranked it at number six in their albums of the year and it reached number 54 in the UK album chart, outperforming both *Wonderful* and *Hex*.

At the time of release, the cassette version included 'Vixen' and 'Couldn't Get Ahead' tacked onto the end of side one and had 'Petty (Thief) Lout' closing the second side. When the album was issued on CD in 1988, 'Rollin' Dany' and an edited version of 'Cruiser's Creek' appeared at the end. In 2011, Beggars Banquet released a 3-CD 'deluxe' version, featuring a 48-page booklet. CD2 included a variety of rough mixes, which are interesting if not exactly essential. The third disc rounded up singles, B-sides and the Peel sessions from the time.

Evaluation

It is a mark of the album's quality that the sole, minor criticism is that one song could possibly be about a minute shorter. *This Nation's Saving Grace* is the perfect marriage of The Fall's increasing accessibility and their more challenging qualities. It contains a flawless balance of everything the group did exceptionally well: aural barrage and grinding repetition, off-kilter pop hooks, sonic experimentation and audacious weirdness. Throughout, the group sound perfectly attuned with one another, and Smith puts in a performance that – whilst not quite matching the manic invention of the early 80s – utilises his command of timing and phrasing exceptionally well.

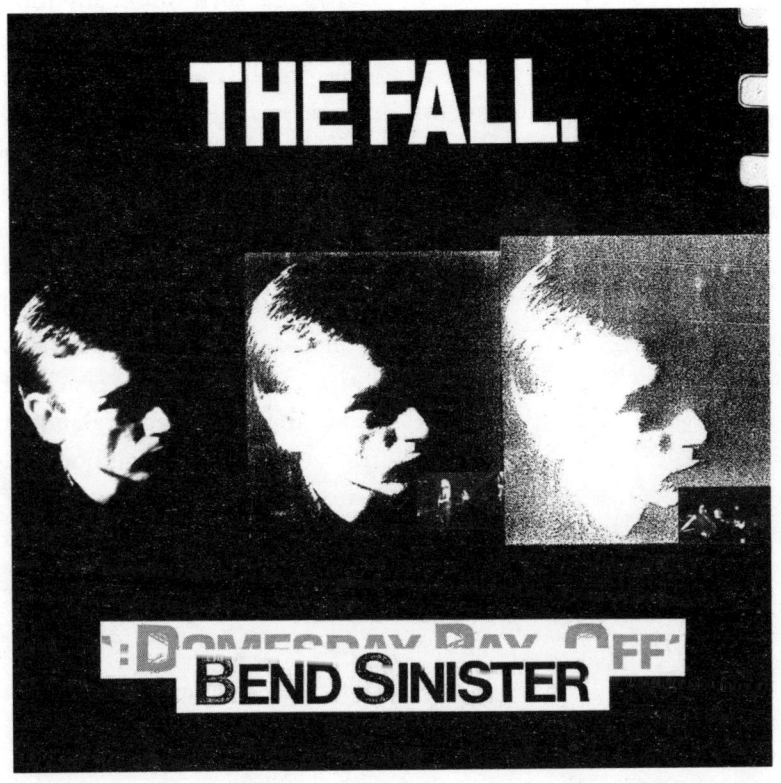

Bend Sinister
Recorded: Yellow 2, Stockport; Abbey Road, London; Square One, Bury, mid-1986
Released: 29th September 1986

Personnel:
Mark E Smith – vocals
Brix Smith – guitar, keyboards, vocals
Craig Scanlon – guitar
Steve Hanley – bass, guitar
Simon Rogers – keyboards, guitar
Simon Wolstencroft – drums, percussion
Paul Hanley – drums ('Dktr. Faustus')

Chapter 10: Bend Sinister

'He sounds like he's been having yodelling lessons.'

The Fall hit the road in the autumn of 1985 to promote *This Nation's Saving Grace*, playing 22 UK dates in October and November. On 8th November they appeared on Channel 4's *The Tube*. Smith and Brix were interviewed by Muriel Gray before the group (with Smith in a long, black leather trench coat and quite noticeable mascara) performed 'Cruiser's Creek' and 'Bombast'. A further seven UK dates followed in February 1986. On the 6th in Woolwich, Karl Burns failed to show up and Paul Hanley was persuaded by his brother to fill in. Despite finding himself unable to master 'Dktr. Faustus', he agreed to stand in again at the next gig two days later, a benefit gig for striking Liverpool Council workers at the Royal Court Theatre alongside The Smiths, New Order and John Cooper Clarke. Steve Davies (of Hawaiian shirt fame) turned up on the off chance of getting a gig; so, eventually, did Burns, but by the time he did Paul Hanley was firmly ensconced behind the kit.[165] The drummer was unmoved by Smith's attempts to entice him back to the group (the Liverpool show would be his final appearance for The Fall), so Burns was back in place for the last few UK shows, which were followed by a 20-date North American tour. The American shows saw the group regularly open the set with 'Countdown', a hectic, bubbly instrumental that was soon dropped and never recorded.[166]

The group had just released a critically acclaimed album that had seen their best chart performance yet, coming within a stone's throw of the top 40. Live recordings from late 1985 and early 1986 find them on excellent form; a ferocious, tight live

---

[165] Burns and Davies did get a chance to perform, when Derek Hatton suggested all three acts get on stage at the end of the evening to play Dylan's 'Maggie's Farm'. 'That was a bit too weird for us, a bit too Live Aid,' Steve Hanley recalled, 'but the only opportunity our extra drummers had to get in the limelight... they all got bottled off by Smiths fans who only wanted to hear more Smiths.'

[166] According to *The Track Record*, Hanley and Burns's post-Fall outfit Ark revived it.

unit. Signed to a label sympathetic to their independent spirit but with the necessary resources to promote the group effectively, all seemed well in the wonderful and frightening world. As ever though, when things were going well, The Fall changed the line-up. In April, Karl Burns left the group for the second time, sacked at least partly because Smith disapproved of the drummer's new girlfriend, Carrie Lawson. There were undoubtedly other factors at play, however. Burns's unreliability and excessive on-tour behaviour exasperated Brix in particular. His refusal to be intimidated by Smith and accept his dictatorial tendencies was also a source of tension.

The new drummer was Simon Wolstencroft. Wolstencroft had played in early incarnations of both The Stone Roses (The Patrol, with Ian Brown and John Squire) and The Smiths (Freak Party, with Johnny Marr and Andy Rourke). Christened 'Funky Si' by Johnny Marr, his band The Weeds supported The Fall in early 1986. After one of these gigs (The Mean Fiddler on 11th February), Smith approached Wolstencroft and asked him if he wanted to join the group after the forthcoming North American tour. The next week, Wolstencroft visited Smith's house, and over tea, whisky, speed and a Link Wray album, his recruitment to the group was confirmed. 'I fitted Mark's criteria at the time,' Wolstencroft explained, 'in that I wasn't really a Fall fan and kept the drumming simple. Beyond that, it was maybe just a case of being in the right place at the right time.'

The new recruit's first Fall gig was in Folkestone on 5th June; by the end of the month he found himself at Maida Vale recording the group's tenth Peel session, which was broadcast on 9th July. The dark and brooding 'Gross Chapel-GB Grenadiers' – which had been played live for the first time three weeks earlier – is not vastly different from the album version. This is also true of 'R.O.D.' and 'U.S. 80's - 90's' (although the latter gains a slightly irritating crashing percussion effect in places). 'Hot Aftershave Bop' had been debuted four months earlier and had already been played live 17 times by this point.

A couple of days before the Peel session went out, the group released their first single of 1986, 'Living Too Late'. Smith's tale of middle-aged regret and ennui ('sometimes life is like a new bar: plastic seats, beer below par, food with no taste, music grates...') is a touching, depressing masterpiece. The loping bass, stolid drumbeat, ghostly violin and gently echoing guitar create a melancholy atmosphere ideally suited to the embittered, wistful lyrics. The relentless, marching rhythm is a perfect companion to the image of a life stuck in a rut. The 'chorus' is a discordant kaleidoscope over which Smith contributes a preposterous falsetto that's at once laughable and oddly moving. The bouncing staccato bass that Steve Hanley uses to bring us back into the main body of the song (for example at 1:21) is one the most memorable and joyous moments in the whole back catalogue. Glamour model Samantha Fox, acting as a guest reviewer for *Smash Hits*, was less than keen: 'I didn't like this at all – it's really crappy... he sounds like he's been having yodelling lessons. It seems to be the fashion at the moment to like The Smiths and these sorts of groups, and to me the lyrics are really depressing.' 'Living Too Late' was played 53 times 1986-87.

'Living Too Long' (the lengthier version on the 12") places a nervy, skittering guitar front and centre, adds steam-locomotive percussion and has the vocals floating around more subtly in a tinny, megaphone style. B-side 'Hot Aftershave Bop' featured one of Steve Hanley's most memorably chunky basslines as well as a nice blend of guitars (Brix's chords and arpeggios in the left; Scanlon letting loose with some blues-rock string-bending in the right). It's amongst the group's best B-sides, although the crisper Peel version is slightly superior. It was played 46 times 1986-88. The 'Living Too Late' sleeve credited the mysterious 'Fredrica Federation' as guest guitarist (probably some form of in-joke pseudonym for Brix). A promotional 7" came with a miniature bottle of 'Hot Aftershave Bop aftershave'. The single – unsurprisingly, given its resolutely uncommercial character – reached only number 97 in the charts.

The next single, released two months later, fared a little better commercially, reaching number 75. 'Mr. Pharmacist' was a cover of late-60s Californian garage-rock band The Other Half's 1966 single, which featured on one of the *Nuggets* compilations. It

177

would go on to be The Fall's most-played live track by some distance, notching up over 400 appearances over the next 31 years. The B-side, 'Lucifer Over Lancashire', is an engaging piece of rickety rockabilly racket which sees Smith getting all high-pitched and 'yee-haw' while the band rattle along like a train. It was played 70 times 1986-89. Tucked away on the 12" was an overlooked little gem, 'Auto Tech Pilot'. The gloomy descending bassline, echoing piano and fuzzy, understated guitar create an eerie ambience. The wealth of transitions and tempo changes feel like the group are somehow simultaneously trying to hold the song together and throw each other off their stride. It's a fascinating and complex song.[167] It was never played live.

Bend Sinister

The album was recorded at Abbey Road in London, Yellow 2 in Stockport and Square One in Bury. For the third and final time, John Leckie acted as producer. However, unlike on *Wonderful And Frightening* (where he had subtly and successfully made changes to the group's usual approaches) and *This Nation's Saving Grace* (where even Smith had to admit he captured the Fall sound perfectly) the Smith-Leckie relationship had now become fraught and volatile. Perhaps it was due to Smith's well-documented desire to throw a spanner in the works whenever he felt things were getting too comfortable at the expense of creative tension; maybe it was due to a combination of his heavy drinking and the early signs of marital problems. Either way, the deterioration in the MES-Leckie relationship had a negative influence on the album's sound, Smith stubbornly insisting that some tracks be mastered directly from his bog-standard C90. Leckie, as a result, decided that this would be his last album with The Fall: Smith's 'idiosyncrasies had become too much to bear'. Brix described the whole experience as 'miserable'.

The recording of *Bend Sinister* provided one of the most hotly disputed topics in Fall fandom history, perhaps only exceeded by the 'is *Slates* an album?' controversy. Some maintain that the

---

[167] There is an oft-repeated rumour that Miles Davis heard the track and expressed an interest in working with The Fall. Sadly, there's no reliable evidence to support this.

whole album was mastered from Smith's ropy cassette version and that it ran 1% too slowly; others are adamant that this was only the case with one song (arguments vary as to which one it was); some are convinced that a 1% speed increase would make no difference anyway; there's also an array of arcane sub-arguments. One thread on the *Fall Online Forum* (there are several devoted to the topic) has 547 posts on the issue. Like the *Slates* debate, this feels like an especially Fall type of issue: a seemingly trivial matter blown out of all proportion by enthusiasm, commitment and obsession.[168]

A 'bend' is a heraldic term that denotes a diagonal stripe that usually runs from the top left to the bottom right – a 'bend dexter'; a 'bend sinister' is the mirror image of this.[169] The album title may well have been inspired by Nabokov's 1947 novel of the same name, in which the hero is persecuted by the totalitarian government of the 'Party of the Average Man'. Simon Ford suggests that 'this theme of antipathy to middle-class conformity recurs throughout Smith's career, from "Middle Mass"... to [2001 track] "Bourgeoise Town".' Smith touched on this topic in more than one interview. 'What really annoys me is that people can't really get it into their head that there really isn't any threat from the left or the right. The threat is some kind of standardised horrible society'; 'People forget that the SS weren't skinhead thugs, they were doctors and lawyers, guys with a grudge.' The (uncredited) cover design matches closely the mood and atmosphere of the music, the smudged, ghostly monochrome images being emblematic of the album's starkly cold sound.

R.O.D.

The opening track (also known as 'Realm Of Dusk') sees one of Brix's sprightly surf-guitar riffs sitting atop a song full of brooding malevolence: 'I added the California beach to the dark dimension,' as she put it. Smith's opening lines are startlingly

---

[168] For what it's worth, I have used Audacity to speed the songs up by 1%, and it makes very little difference to these ears. As for MES's Maxell C90, according to the sleeve notes of the 2019 *Bend Sinister* reissue only 'Riddler' and 'Terry Waite Sez' were mastered from a cassette.

[169] 'Sinister' means 'left' in Latin. It came to take on connotations of unluckiness or evil, in contrast to the 'right hand of God'. In heraldry, a bend sinister is often believed to denote bastardry, although this wasn't actually the case.

menacing: 'It's approaching / 600 pounds gas and flesh / rotten, tainted / it's approaching, lips and tongue abhorrent / flickering lexicon or a stray dog pack leader'. He described the lyric as being 'about approaching the mediocre'. There are several candidates for the title's origins: 'Realm of Dusk' is the title of a collection of poems by Romanian writer Mihail Crama; it's also the title of a 1985 track by Bill Nelson. However, given the track's dark tone, it may simply be a tribute to *Twilight Zone* creator Rod Serling. It was played live 40 times.

Dktr. Faustus

To the casual Fall listener generally familiar with the group's most commercially successful period, 'Faustus' is probably as close to an archetypal Fall song as you get, with a twangy, repetitive guitar riff and a notable (and very effective) contrast between Smith's 'megaphone' vocals and Brix's American drawl. The three most famous versions of the Faust legend, in which the protagonist sells his soul to the devil in return for unlimited knowledge and worldly pleasures, are Goethe's play *Faust* (published 1808), Thomas Mann's 1947 novel *Doctor Faustus* and Christopher Marlowe's *The Tragical History of Doctor Faustus*, published c. 1604. Smith, however, claimed that he had 'read it in a fairy tale book'.[170] Brix (who was called upon to yell 'Banana! Apple! Plum!') disliked the song: 'I cringe when I hear it. I hated having to say those stupid lyrics.' It was played live 51 times 1985–87.

Shoulder Pads 1#

A lightweight track most notable for its cheesy keyboard line, which bears a passing resemblance to the theme tune of 70s sitcom *Are You Being Served?* The line about not being able to 'tell Lou Reed from Doug Yule' refers to an anecdote about David Bowie.[171] It's difficult to fathom how this – let alone two versions

---

[170] Inevitably, dannyno unearthed the likely candidate: *Folk Tales and Legends*, retold by Michaela Tvrdíková and translated by Vera Gissing with illustrations by Vojt ch Kubašta, Cathay Books, 1981.

[171] Bowie, whilst in America in 1971, saw The Velvet Underground in New York and asked to meet Lou Reed backstage after the gig. He ended up chatting to Doug Yule (Reed had left the band the year before) but didn't realise his mistake until the next day.

of it – got the nod over 'Auto Tech Pilot' or 'Hot Aftershave Bop'. Played live 51 times.

Mr. Pharmacist
The bare-bones bouncing riff and mosh-friendly uptempo sections make it easy to see why this was such a live favourite, although the dozens of bootleg recordings see performances range from the thrillingly energetic to the tired and sloppy.

Gross Chapel-British Grenadiers
A masterclass in the subtle creation of mood and tension. Steve Hanley rumbles ominously; one guitar picks out a dark yet delicate and brittle melody line while the other scratches out oblique chords; the drums are at once forceful yet carefully restrained. There's a sense throughout that each element shifts slightly, moves to a different beat, which creates an unnerving, dislocated feeling. Smith's vocals are almost buried, providing texture as much as being a focal point. The whole thing sounds like it's going to erupt at any time, but (as with 'Hip Priest') the group avoids crescendo clichés. As the song beds down around the six-minute mark, you almost want it to burst free and thrash it out; the fact that it doesn't is testament to the group's disregard for rock tropes and their innate understanding of effective dynamics. Around the five-minute mark the words are adapted from the traditional marching song, 'British Grenadiers'. 'Gross Chapel' only had a nine-month stint on the setlist, its 31st and final performance occurring in February 1987.

U.S. 80's - 90's
The opening drums, both in terms of sound and pattern, root this track firmly in the 80s. It's an unusual hybrid, containing electro/hip-hop influences as well as having a space-rock flavour, especially in the skittering synth effects – as if Run DMC had teamed up with Hawkwind rather than Aerosmith. The song was inspired by the group's on-tour experiences at American customs ('had a run-in with Boston immigration'), where they were questioned about some sleeping pills that Brix's mother had

given them ('we practically had stickers on our foreheads saying "search me"'). It's one of those tracks that the group didn't quite capture at its best in the studio; several live versions knock it out of the park.[172] It enjoyed a long stint on the setlist: 160 appearances 1986-97.

Terry Waite Sez

Another of Brix's lively, twangy riffs. Smith claimed on more than one occasion that the song was not about the Church of England envoy who was held captive in the Lebanon – in fact, Waite wasn't kidnapped until four months after *Bend Sinister*'s release – but was simply about a bloke he met down the pub. Despite this, Brix inevitably saw the lyric as evidence of Smith's 'pre-cog' abilities. 'We record the song. He ends up getting kidnapped. The song is released. Then his family call Beggars Banquet record company. They believe there might be clues in the lyrics as to where he's being held.' Played 54 times 1986-87.

Bournemouth Runner

You could never accuse Smith of having a limited scope in terms of lyrical subject matter, but the anecdote related here is not exactly a rich seam of insight. At the group's performance at Bournemouth Town Hall on 23rd October 1985, fan Terry Stoate jumped on stage and stole the backdrop. And that's about it. It begins with a slow, doom-laden bassline and echoing vocals that strive to create a dark and mysterious atmosphere. It's not entirely successful though, as the group's timing is curiously hesitant. Once it gets properly underway it's spirited enough but feels a bit forced and unconvincing, and the 'Rock Lobster' style keyboards are somewhat incongruous. It only got 18 outings 1986-87.

Riddler!

A curious little number, built around a simple guitar line that periodically bursts into energetic rocking out. Despite the rather obvious slow-fast dynamic, it sustains its six minutes without

---

[172] For example: *Live At The Phoenix Festival*, *Various Years*, *The Idiot Joy Show* and (especially) *Cheetham Hill* (see Appendix 3).

issue, perhaps because of the range of intriguingly ominous noises lurking in the background. The phrase 'Riddler!' was from Smith's childhood. 'I always remember we used to shout "Riddler" when we were kids in Salford, but I can't remember what for, it's still a sort of mystery.' It only had an eight month stay on the setlist, its 32nd and final performance coming in February 1987.

Shoulder Pads 2#
A brief and rather pointless reprise, despite Scanlon and Steve Hanley endeavouring to inject some extra energy into the track.

Reviews and Reissues

Reviews were less positive than had been the case with the last couple of albums. In the *NME*, Dave Haslam regretted the lack of 'eyeball-to-eyeball social comment, now replaced by more occasional contributions; pithy, scratchy phrases delivered in so clotted a vocal style that they undermine any potential accessibility in the music'. He still felt that the group sounded 'a good deal better than the rest', but also that 'you don't feel the hard edges, the bite and the snarl you would have felt from their early releases' According to *Melody Maker*'s Simon Reynolds, 'while The Fall's music has grown steadily more vivacious and approachable, Smith's writing has folded in on itself in an ever denser scrawl, beyond decipherment, let alone understanding'. Despite the mixed feelings of the music press, *Bend Sinister* achieved a far higher chart placing than all of the previous albums, reaching number 36.

'Living Too Late' and 'Auto Tech Pilot' were included on the cassette and CD versions, as was a live recording of 'City Hobgoblins' from the Town And Country Club, London on 12th July 1986 (renamed 'Town And Country Hobgoblins'). In the US, the album was released as *The 'Domesday Pay-Off' Triad-Plus!* and featured a different cover and tracklisting.[173] In 2019, the album got a double LP/CD reissue – *Bend Sinister / The*

---

[173] 'Dktr. Faustus' and 'Bournemouth Runner' were replaced with 'There's A Ghost In My House', 'Hey! Luciani' and 'Haf Found Bormann' and the whole thing was in a completely different order.

'*Domesday Pay-Off* Triad-Plus!* (the packaging takes a variety of approaches to the punctuation and capitalisation of the title) – which included a remastered version of the album plus singles and B-sides. The remastered versions are, almost without exception, a great improvement, adding an exciting sharpness and brightness.

Evaluation

Bend Sinister has its undoubted moments of greatness but is uneven in comparison to its two predecessors. There's a lack of coherence compared to *Wonderful* and *Nation*; it's not that there was a specific 'sound' that defined either of those albums, but there was a sense of direction, a joyful discovery of successful approaches. Here, it feels like the group are starting to, if not exactly flounder, to have much less certainty about what they're trying to achieve. Smith's engagement with Leckie on the previous two albums had yielded enormously positive outcomes; *Bend Sinister* saw his control-freakery impinge negatively on the finished product, resulting in a disappointingly flat and cold sound. The 2019 remaster addresses this to a huge extent: listening to it is a breath of fresh air compared to the original.

The Frenz Experiment
Recorded: Abbey Road, London; Brixton and Manchester, mid-late 1987
Released: 29th February 1988

Personnel:
Mark E Smith – vocals
Brix Smith – guitar, vocals
Craig Scanlon – guitar, vocals
Steve Hanley – bass, vocals
Marcia Schofield – keyboards, vocals
Simon Wolstencroft – drums, vocals

With:
Simon Rogers – guitar, saxophone, keyboards

Chapter 11: The Frenz Experiment

'Intro verse, bass solo, chorus, verse, bass solo, chorus, rant with megaphone solo to fade.'

The autumn of 1986 found The Fall in need of a new keyboard player. Although Simon Rogers would continue to contribute to the group's work in various ways over the next few years, he declared himself unavailable for a four-date tour of Austria in October. His replacement was Marcia Schofield, a New Yorker whose band Khmer Rouge had supported The Fall on several occasions. She was thrown into the deep end, performing with the group for the first time at a rehearsal gig in Ipswich a few days before the tour. She was lent a copy of *Bend Sinister* for preparation and arrived at the gig with some hastily scribbled notes on scraps of paper (Steve Hanley recalls one of them reading, 'U.S. 80s 90's Intro verse, bass solo, chorus, verse, bass solo, chorus, rant with megaphone solo to fade'). The group also played two encore songs that she'd never heard before. Brix welcomed having a female ally in the group. 'All the men would drool over her. She was a goddess, the physical opposite to me. I was petite and blonde; she was a dark Amazonian voluptuous woman.'

The group's next single – recorded before Schofield joined – was 'Hey! Luciani', a track which had marked Simon Wolstencroft's first appearance on a Fall record (although he explained that 'all I did was hit this floor tom for eight bars'). Originally written for *Bend Sinister*, it was held back when Smith (inspired by David Yallop's book *In God's Name*) decided to write a play about the suspicious death of Albino Luciani, who was Pope John Paul I for just 33 days. He wrote most of the play during the group's October tour of America and continued writing until only days before the first performance. In a TV interview with Jools Holland, Smith admitted that he 'didn't do a lot of research for it' and that 'I haven't really been very factual'. The final version was 'written on beer mats and delivered to its director in a shoe box'. The play ran for two weeks in December 1986 at Riverside Studios in Hammersmith. It featured, amongst many other things, Brix and Marcia Schofield 'in full army camouflage [with] massive sub-machine guns strapped across our chests – two fierce Jewesses hunting Martin Bormann'. Steve Hanley played John Paul II; Simon Wolstencroft was a cardinal. According to Brix, it was 'non-linear and nobody understood anything about the play. It made no sense whatsoever.'[174] Although Roy Wilkinson in *Sounds* described it as a 'very watchable, incident-packed treatment of this fascinating piece of recent history', Adam Sweeting in *The Guardian* declared that 'the completeness, the thoroughness of Smith's failure must be accounted his only achievement'. The *Melody Maker* review criticised the 'dismally poor acting' and called for 'an immediate and bloody end to Arts Council funding'. In the *NME*, Len Brown was more succinct: 'a heap of shite'.

As for the 'Hey! Luciani' single itself, which was released during the play's run, it's a solid enough bit of commercial Fall; a coherent song in terms of melody and structure, with a memorable poppy hook. It's all a bit polished, though, and Brix's backing vocals are rather akin to pouring treacle onto honey – the song perhaps needed a bit more grit, not more sweetness. 'Luciani' reached number 59 on the singles chart. Including the play performances, it made 98 live appearances between 1986 and 1988 before getting a one-off revival in 2002. The B-side was 'Entitled', a pleasant but inconsequential bit of melancholy C86-style indie-jangle. Those who bought the 12" were treated to a supremely unnecessary five-minute version of 'Shoulder Pads'.

After starting 1987 with a tour of Belgium, Germany and The Netherlands, the group released a new single in April – one that saw them reach the hallowed heights of the UK top 30 for the first time. 'There's A Ghost In My House', a Holland-Dozier-Holland song originally recorded by R. Dean Taylor, was suggested to the group as a cover by Beggars Banquet press officer Karen Ehlers. As part of the promotion, Beggars paid for a sleeve that featured a ghostly hologram (Steve Hanley joked that it cost so much that

[174] There's a full transcript of the play at http://thefall.org/news/luciani.html

any profits were 'purely ethereal'). The single's chart placing of 30 – the highest the group would ever achieve – suggested an appearance on *Top of the Pops*, but despite Brix's excitement at the prospect ('me and Marcia were going, "what will we wear, what will we wear?"'), the call never came. It's a very straight cover and is most notable for one of Smith's biggest efforts to sing 'properly'. The accompanying video was filmed at The Woodthorpe, one of Smith's favourite Prestwich pubs, and saw him sporting an unusual green sports jacket and gold lamé shirt combo. 'Ghost' was played live 39 times between 1987-89, then got another run of 14 outings 2002-03. The B-side was 'Haf Found Bormann', one of the songs from the play. It has a slow, loose-limbed rhythm that brings The Orb to mind; Steve Hanley gets quite free-form jazz in places and a lot of unidentifiable noises float around in the background. After the play's run, it stayed in the setlist for much of 1987, racking up 35 appearances overall.

The Fall's back catalogue is littered with lesser-known gems that were hidden away on B-sides, various artists compilations and other nooks and crannies, and there were two notable examples (both taken from the 'Hey! Luciani' play) on the 12" version of 'There's A Ghost In My House'. 'Sleep Debt Snatches' starts with an uptempo, circular little guitar riff. A sprightly sounding MES joins in for 30 seconds or so with a couple of verses about sleep deprivation before things turn a little strange. The brash drum pattern that enters abruptly at 1:03 sounds alarmingly like it's veering off into 'Addicted To Love', but then everything goes all Test Dept. / Nine Inch Nails – a sort of sludgy, industrial march, backed with an assortment of random clicking, tapping, scraping and other odd noises. Throughout all of this, Hanley maintains a solid, unflappable foundation, Scanlon adds a funky, fluid riff and Smith pops in now and again to add a sinister whisper. Aside from parts of it appearing in the play, it was never performed live. 'Mark'll Sink Us', on the other hand, did stay in the setlist for a little while after the play's run, being performed a further 21 times, the last being in May 1988. It contains elements of jazz, prog and blues: the *Aladdin Sane*-esque piano provides jazzy overtones, and the staccato part that backs the title refrain could easily come from early 70s Yes or Genesis (especially when the moog-ish synth joins in during the coda). Smith's vocal has an air of resigned melancholy that's touching and emotional: 'I am desolate. I live the black and blue of the night'.

The day after the release of 'Ghost', the group recorded their 11th Peel session, which was broadcast on 11th May. Simon Rogers played keyboards rather than Marcia, so for only the second time the line-up was the same as the previous session. In general, the songs are not vastly different to later versions, although 'Athlete Cured' and 'Guest Informant' benefit from a fuller, clearer sound. 'Twister' is the pick of the bunch, adding an impressive level of demented mania to the song.

The group played up and down the UK throughout May, and one performance – their May 19th date at Nottingham Rock City – was broadcast on Radio 1 and released in 1993 as *BBC Radio 1 'Live In Concert'*. It has crystal-clear sound but is a curiously soulless recording (it also only contains seven of the twelve songs played). In July, The Fall acted as an unlikely last-minute support act for U2 at Elland Road. Craig Scanlon ended up with a black eye and a badly-bruised arm after being dragged down a staircase by U2's security; he and Steve Hanley had tried to get backstage to procure autographs for the bassist's Irish relatives. The following month, The Fall shared a bill with Nick Cave, Swans and Butthole Surfers in Hamburg. Tickets for the gig were oversold and a riot ensued.

The follow-up to 'Ghost' arrived in October. 'Hit The North' was the group's first single to be released on picture disc. The genesis of the song's lyric was Smith's dislike of Norwich – complaining on the way back from a gig there that he couldn't wait until they 'hit the north'. Musically, it originated from Simon Rogers playing around with a new sampler.

> I'd just got this 440 and literally the first thing I put into it was a bass and a snare just on two pads, a little tiny Indian bell which I've still got, and a sax note and a bass note from a Gentle Giant record. Mark came round to my bedroom studio and I said, 'Oh, here's the new sampler, have a look at it,' and just pressed play and out comes the

basis of 'Hit The North'. He said, 'What's that music?' And I said, 'Well, it's the first thing I put in.' He said, 'I'll have that, just do me a tape.'

'Hit The North' has a charming exuberance and energy, and the cowboy-style whoops give it a joyful party atmosphere. You won't find a more 80s keyboard sound than its parping riff, and the sequencer, drum pattern and vocal treatments also place the song very firmly in that decade. It feels, however, like a knowing, light-hearted sideways glance at contemporary styles rather than an attempt to ape them. The five remixes that appeared on the various versions of the single are all fun enough, although you probably wouldn't wish to listen to them all at once. The song has an entertaining promo video, too, featuring some funky dancing (and even funkier shirt) from Smith and bemused but enthusiastic participation from the patrons of a Blackpool working men's club. It was made 'Single of the Week' in the *NME*. However, despite the video and picture disc and all the remixes, 'Hit The North' didn't replicate its predecessor's chart success, peaking at only number 57. It was a popular setlist choice though, clocking up 138 appearances 1987-2005. One of the 12" versions featured two further B-sides. 'Australians In Europe' (the opening of which features dialogue between Smith and Trevor Stuart, who played the lead in *Hey! Luciani*) is a driving, fast-paced number that features some Lydon-esque sustained notes from Smith. It was played 25 times 1987-1988. 'Northerns In Europ' consists of what sounds like the group having a chat whilst listening to the same song on a badly tuned AM radio.

The group had by now been going long enough to get the rights back for some of their earlier work. This inspired Smith to set up his own record label, Cog Sinister. The idea was to support releases by obscure and interesting artists, financed by profits from re-releasing The Fall's old material. The name came from Smith's belief that his 'pre-cog' abilities would enable him to spot new talent and neglected geniuses.[175] Brix claimed that

[175] Little ever came of this part of the plan other than a handful of singles and a 1988 compilation called *The Disparate Cogscienti* which featured tracks by The Hamsters, The Lowthers, Andrew Berry and The Next Step.

she came up with the name: 'I remember suggesting the name. It was an amalgamation of Cogswell Cogs – the name of the company George Jetson worked for on the postmodern American cartoon *The Jetsons* – and *Bend Sinister*, our recent album.' The first output from the label was *In: Palace Of Swords Reversed*, a compilation of album, single and live Fall tracks from the early 80s (see Appendix 2).

For their next single, released in January 1988, the group went with another cover, this time a 1969 Kinks song, 'Victoria'. This yielded similar success to 'Ghost', reaching number 35 in the charts. Inevitably, given the prevailing attitudes of the 80s indie scene, The Fall were accused by some of 'selling out'. In *Melody Maker*, David Stubbs 'looked on in sadness as The Fall appeared to have gone hard and soft in all the wrong places'. There were three B-sides on the various formats of the single. 'Tuff Life Booogie' enjoyed a relatively long shelf-life in terms of live appearances, being played 65 times, including 15 in 2015-16. Whilst the choppy rhythm and slide guitar are engaging enough, Smith's yelping of the title refrain tries the patience a little. 'Twister' is much more effective. It opens with a slow, snaky, twangy dual guitar line which is joined by galloping drums, double-tracked MES vocals and even some prog-like organ, before ascending into a crazy whirl featuring some eerie Brix contributions, thumping toms and manic keyboards. It was only ever played live once. The full-length version of 'Guest Informant' appeared on the 12" and cassette.

Around the same time that *Frenz* was being recorded, The Fall contributed a cover of The Beatles' 'A Day In The Life' for *Sgt. Pepper Knew My Father*, an *NME*-sponsored various artists charity album in aid of Childline. It's not one of the group's finest moments, a somewhat lifeless rendition that rather cruelly exposes Smith's vocal limitations.

The Frenz Experiment

The album was originally to be called 'Gene Crime Experience', and the first side of the LP retained the title 'Crime Gene' (the second was named 'Experience').[176] Some of it was recorded at Abbey Road, where recording was briefly interrupted by Duran Duran taking a studio tour (Steve Hanley: 'in they float on a cloud of sweet fragrance and wealthy confidence'). *Frenz*'s cover art was radically different to what had gone before: the first to be constructed primarily around a group photo, it was also The Fall's first misstep in this area. The fault lies not so much in the photograph itself, but in the way the lettering is arranged, obscuring most of the musicians. Scanlon, although he is at least partially visible, is blurred and brutally cropped; Wolstencroft and Hanley, whilst in the foreground, are obliterated by the text; Brix has a capital F sitting right on her face; Marcia fares a little better, elevated above the title, doing her best to smoulder. Smith, of course, suffers no such indignity, remaining sharply in focus, scowling bleakly over their heads – as Brix noted, 'grousing in full view above us, lording it over us'.

It wasn't just the cover design that saw Smith asserting his dominance over the group. Even by Fall standards, the allocation of songwriting credits on *Frenz* raises an eyebrow. While Smith was undoubtedly capable of musical invention, the fact that half of the songs give him a sole credit seems at best unlikely. Brix felt that 'every single one of those songs was a collaboration. It seemed to me that the deterioration of our relationship was reflected in my dwindling songwriting credits.'

Frenz

The opener finds Smith in melancholy mood, the tone of his vocal conjuring both sadness and defiance. The repeated refrain of 'my friends don't add up to one hand' is touching (if grammatically dubious) and the Smiths' vocals complement each other well. The instrumentation is surprisingly delicate, and overall it's almost

---

[176] Several sources suggest that Smith abandoned the original title when he realized that 'GCE' was also the abbreviation for 'General Certificate of Education', the exams (O- and A-levels) that British pupils sat at 16 and 18. Simon Ford, for example, indicates that MES said this in a 1988 interview for Piccadilly Radio. Why this connection (which surely very few would have made) bothered him so much is a bit of a mystery.

startlingly fragile. This is the track where the album's clean, crisp production is at its most effective. It was played live frequently at the time (73 appearances) but disappeared after 1988.

Carry Bag Man

'Carry Bag Man' is a beefy rocker, one that was generally delivered live with some gusto. The Stooges-like blues-rock riff is a little predictable, however, and despite Wolstencroft's energetic contribution it starts to run out of steam towards the end. The fact that Smith carried his lyrics around in carrier bags was an interesting idiosyncrasy, but he doesn't really do enough with it to sustain the lyric. 'Kneel on the croft when the mariah comes round' is a moderately intriguing line, but too much of the rest ('I still need armchairs round my home to put carrier bags on') is somewhat prosaic. It made 75 appearances 1988-1990 before being revived for four performances in 2008-2009.

Get A Hotel

Like 'Frenz', 'Hotel' is slow and measured. Steve Hanley makes the best of a simple bassline, and the drums are crisp and precise. But there's little emotion here: nobody sounds like they have much invested in the track and it feels like a rough sketch rather than a fully-formed song. The slowing of the tempo over the final 30 seconds or so just makes it feel like the group have lost interest. It was played 44 times 1987-1988.

Victoria

Despite Smith's assertion that the group's approach to the track was to 'cut it to bits... to do something extreme to it', it's actually a pretty straight cover by Fall standards. A lively, spirited update of the tune, it injects a bit of well-needed vigour into the album. Played live 57 times 1987-1990, with a one-off comeback in 2002.

Athlete Cured

Lyrically, this is an odd tale even by Smith's standards, relating the story of an East German athlete suffering from the effects of his brother's careless parking arrangements ('an odour resembling hot-dogs permeated the whole bedroom'). The alarming opening scream makes it sound as though the group are about to burst into 'Wipe Out', but the most striking aspect is the brazen copying of the riff from 'Tonight I'm Gonna Rock You Tonight' by Spinal Tap. *This Is Spinal Tap*, Rob Reiner's 1984 mockumentary, was one of only three films that Smith permitted on the tour bus during this period (the others being *The Producers* and *Zulu*[177]). Steve Hanley's repeated exposure to the song on the tour bus led him to be 'doodling it' in a soundcheck, whereupon Smith walked in and declared 'we'll use that'. Despite Simon Rogers's protestations ('it's a total rip-off!') the group ended up using the riff, 'note-for-note, exactly the same, not altered in the slightest by key changes, time changes, chord changes or any other sort of disguise'. It was played live seven times in 1988; it was revisited briefly at the infamous 1996 Motherwell gig (see Chapter 20).

In These Times

Introduced by Steve Hanley's deep, heavily flanged bass, 'In These Times' is another track that finds Smith and Brix complementing each other well. Understated but purposeful, the moody floor-tom-led interludes and fuzzy guitar solo lurking in the background around the two-minute mark are both nice touches; the keyboard stabs towards the end sound rather dated, however. Smith declares that his 'gossamer-thin gate will keep out the trash in which my psychic streets emerge' and his 'Aqua-cat is where it's at, new to mammal range'. More easily explained is the reference to the group's support slot for U2: 'Diluted Jesuits pour out of mutual walkmans from Elland Road to Venice Pensions and down the Autobahns'. Smith commented on the song's origins in an interview with Dave Haslam:

> 'In These Times' was written at a time last year when things were pretty shocking and tasteless. There's a bit in the song relating to when I went to Italy for the first time in four years for a holiday with Brix. I thought at least I'd get away from cars and U2. And the first thing I heard were these two street-theatre people doing U2 songs on acoustic guitars, mixed with Beatles' songs. It was a nightmare.

[177] MES claimed that one of his ancestors fought at Rorke's Drift.

It was only performed live a dozen times, all in 1988.

The Steak Place

A gentle acoustic strum, a bit of finger-clicking and… not much else, really. A potentially interesting scenario (tacky American restaurant full of shady mafia types) fails to generate much interest owing to mundane observations like 'cheap carpet lines the way… things are brought forward and eaten'. A song that Brix not entirely unreasonably dismissed as 'boring'. Never played live.

Bremen Nacht

Like 'Frenz' the clean, clinical production really suits this one, the crisp sound adding to its aggressive punch. A pugnacious, unforgiving slab of oompah-krautrock, Simon Wolstencroft described it as 'always great to play live – you'd see some of the crowd almost going into a trance'. It opens with the line, 'Something happened in Bremen, I know'. Smith elaborated on this in a *Sounds* interview:

> I'd been to Bremen twice before on tours. The first time I just puked my ring up all day spewing up this black liquid. When I went back there this time I just went crazy. The gig had a really low steel roof – it was this German polytechnic with steel everywhere, metal shutters on the windows which made it real claustrophobic. The dressing-room was like a fucking gas chamber, man… In the morning I had all these handprints on my leg, bruises from the inside that looked like a child's handprints.

He returned to this story in 2016:

> My whole body felt like it went up, like it'd been burnt and bruised. It's not a nice experience at all. At the time I thought I'd been pushing myself a bit too hard, hadn't been eating properly, drinking too much… But then we found out six months later that the building we had played in had been firebombed by the Royal Air Force. A bit fucking weird!

As ever, Smith's attempts at German are linguistically dubious. If you bought the CD or cassette, you were treated to three different edits, the pick of which is the hypnotically punishing nine minutes of 'Bremen Nacht Alternative'. A live favourite at the time, played 111 times (out of 151 gigs), 1987-90.

Guest Informant Excerpt

Infuriatingly (if you purchased the album on vinyl), one of the best songs of the era gets a muted, instrumental 40-second run-out – which feels distinctly perverse given the inclusion of 'Steak Place' and 'Hotel'. The 'proper' version, made available to CD/cassette purchasers, is a classic pop-industrial rockabilly hybrid. Brix's memorable chant has been the source of much debate. She has provided differing versions over the years: 'Baghdad, space-cog, analyst'; 'Baghdad, stay-cog, analyst'; and 'Baghdad state cog analyst'.[178] In addition, 'the stool pigeons, cha-cha-cha-cha' seems to reference Kid Creole and the Coconuts' 1982 single. The 'guest informant' was Simon Wolstencroft: he avoided having to pay for the duvet that was thrown out of the window of his Hamburg hotel room by telling the receptionist who was really responsible – MES and Nick Cave.[179] Another popular live choice at the time, it was played 72 times 1986-89.

Oswald Defence Lawyer

A sluggish, lumbering beast, with only Smith's occasional falsetto 'lawyer!' and a couple of interesting phrases ('embraces the scruffed corpse of Mark Twain'; 'in cloudless sky enhancing theory of zig-zag bulletline') to lighten the mood. It seems much longer than its six minutes. Brix hated it. 'The most annoying song I ever had to play on… it was interminable, and when we played it I watched the audience switch off.' This may well be why it was only performed 20 times.

---

[178] *The Annotated Fall* settles on 'Bahzhdad State Cog Analyst'.
[179] According to Steve Hanley, the inebriated pair had planned to live out a rock'n'roll cliché and throw a TV from the window, but finding the set bolted down, had to resort to the hapless drummer's bedclothes instead.

Reviews and Reissues

The album was, in commercial terms, by far the group's most successful so far, reaching number 19 in the charts. This was no doubt helped by promotional events such as the group's in-store appearance at Oxford Street's HMV three days after the album's release. An additional promotional tactic saw initial copies of the album come with a free 7" single, which included 'Bremen Nacht Run Out' (an alternative version of the album track) and 'Mark'll Sink Us'. All of the Beggars albums had featured, as was becoming common practice, bonus tracks on the CD and cassette versions. *Frenz* saw seven extra songs included – 'Ghost', 'Hit The North Part 1', the 'Victoria' B-sides and two alternate versions of 'Bremen Nacht' (one being the 7" freebie track) – almost doubling the length of the album. As was the case with *Wonderful And Frightening*, *Frenz* was a very different experience depending on your choice of format. Critical response was lukewarm. Andy Gill of *Q* felt that *Frenz* represented a 'tentative move towards the mainstream, without sacrificing the peculiarities that keep them underground'. The *NME*'s Danny Kelly was less impressed, declaring that it wasn't 'fit to share the same planet as *This Nation's Saving Grace*'.

The album wasn't reissued until October 2020.[180] The vinyl double LP rounded up the B-sides from the time; the double CD version also included 'A Day In The Life' and the previously unreleased Janice Long session recorded and broadcast in May 1987 (see Appendix 1).

Evaluation

Frenz is not without its highlights – even if too many were denied to the vinyl-purchasing majority at the time – but overall it was a disappointment. The production is a major factor: although it suits the fragile melancholy of 'Frenz' and adds punch to 'Bremen Nacht', there's an over-sanitised sheen that fails to bring out the group's angular dissonance well enough. The greatest problem, however, is with the songwriting: too many tracks consist of thin, sketchy, underdeveloped ideas. It's telling that it was the last of the Beggars albums to be reissued.

[180] Although it was remastered and released as part of the 2013 5 CD box set, *5 Albums*.

I Am Kurious Oranj
Recorded: Suite 16, Rochdale; The King's Theatre, Edinburgh, mid-late 1988
Released: 24th October 1988

Personnel:
Mark E Smith – vocals
Brix Smith – guitar, vocals
Craig Scanlon – guitar
Steve Hanley – bass
Marcia Schofield – keyboards
Simon Wolstencroft – drums

Chapter 12: I Am Kurious Oranj

'For once we're being disciplined by outside influences.'

The Fall played 11 UK dates in the month following the release of *Frenz*, the last of which was released in 2000 as *Live In Cambridge 1988*. Despite the fact that the debut of 'Athlete Cured' is missing (as is the first half of 'Mr. Pharmacist') this is a rewarding live album. There's a fast-paced 'L.A.' and an impressive version of 'U.S. 80's - 90's' featuring an extended instrumental coda. Of particular interest is 'Pay Your Rates', the sole oldie, getting its sixth run-out after a seven-year absence from the setlist. It works well, even if it does sound odd to hear it with 80s-style drums and twinkly keyboard flourishes.

Early 1988 also saw the group working once again with Michael Clark, who had been asked by the organisers of the Holland Festival (the biggest and oldest arts festival in The Netherlands, which takes place in Amsterdam every June) to produce a ballet to celebrate the 300th anniversary of the Glorious Revolution. He turned to Smith as his musical and historical advisor despite the fact that Smith confessed to knowing 'sod all' about the period. As a result, he took a similar approach to that which he had adopted with *Luciani* – very little research and a lot of guessing. The ballet was entitled *I Am Curious, Orange*, the title of which was inspired by the 1967 Swedish erotic drama *I Am Curious (Yellow)*. It gave Smith an opportunity to build further on the literary and artistic ambitions he had revealed with *Luciani*. Notwithstanding the lack of proper research, he took the opportunity seriously, for once forgoing his dictatorial style and partaking in a genuine collaboration with Clark. The composition of the piece involved a significant change in approach for the musicians in terms of writing, rehearsing and recording. As the group played 46 gigs in just over three months between the release of *Frenz* and *Orange*'s first performance, much of the writing had to take place on the road. This put the group in an unfamiliar situation, as Brix described:

It was a completely different way of writing, because we were under pressure. We weren't just bringing whatever we had made up when inspired and presenting it to the group. We had a deadline, and there was a theme. We would frantically write in our hotel rooms, put it on a cassette and send it to Michael.

This approach proved, unsurprisingly, to be a bit of a challenge for the group. The Fall's style had always been to let songs evolve and develop each time they were played, but this was obviously not possible here. 'The music has to fit the dancing,' Steve Hanley explained, 'it has to be exactly the same every night, to the nanosecond, so as not to throw off the dancers... for once we're being disciplined by outside influences.' After the festival appearance in Amsterdam on 11th-13th June, the piece was performed six times at the Edinburgh Festival in August and then had a run of 19 performances at London's Sadler's Wells Theatre in September and October. The ballet featured an 'Old Firm' derby, a giant carton of McDonald's fries that was tipped over the stage and, most famously, Brix playing guitar sat atop a burger whilst being spun round by dancer Leigh Bowery dressed as a tin of Heinz baked beans. Simon Wolstencroft was probably not alone in finding it 'hard to fathom what the hell was going on most of the time'. Reviewers from a dance background were not impressed, especially by The Fall's contribution − *The Observer*'s Jann Parry objected to the 'head-banging repetitiveness' of the music. The rock music press was more positive, the *NME*'s Sean O'Hagan enthusing that it represented 'The Fall in a new context − innovatory, exciting, iconoclastic'.

A recording of the 17th August show in Edinburgh was released in 2000 as *I Am As Pure As Oranj*. In general, the songs don't differ vastly from the final studio versions, although there are some alternate titles ('Dog Is Life' becomes 'Dog Like' and 'Cab It Up' becomes 'Cabbing It Up Town', for example). The main difference is that many of the guitar parts are more pronounced: 'Wrong Place' features a grungy riff which suits the song well and there's a jangly line on 'Yes, O Yes' that's virtually buried on the studio album. The latter features an extensive spoken coda from MES concerning Michael Clark's 'corrective school of soccer coaching'.[181] One of the highlights is 'Dead Beat Descendant', which is a tightly frenetic slice of garage pop-punk featuring one of Brix's most memorable twangy surf-pop riffs.

The group's 12th Peel session was recorded in October 1988, shortly after the end of *I Am Curious, Orange*'s run at Sadler's Wells. Neither 'Deadbeat Descendant' (given a two word title on this occasion) nor 'Kurious Oranj' are huge departures from other studio versions, although the latter is blighted by a distractingly shrill keyboard. 'Squid Lord' is a little faster and brasher than its later re-named incarnation (see Chapter 13). The highlight of the set is 'Cab It Up', which finds Scanlon on particularly fine form, especially during the thrilling finale.

I Am Kurious Oranj

The studio album based on the music from the ballet was released as *I Am Kurious Oranj* a couple of weeks after the final performance at Sadler's Wells. It was produced by Ian Broudie of Lightning Seeds fame and recorded at Suite 16 in Rochdale (as Cargo had been renamed when it was bought by Peter Hook and Chris Hewitt). The cover photo was taken by veteran *NME* photographer Kevin Cummins; it's an interesting portrait of Smith, capturing him in pensive mood, looking simultaneously defiant and vulnerable. The blurred background image of Michael Clark provides an intriguing hint of the colourful mayhem of the show, more of which could be seen in Richard Haughton's pictures in the group's second gatefold sleeve.

New Big Prinz[182]

The album begins with one of the group's classic moments, a track that's somehow simultaneously jaunty and sinister. At its heart is

---

[181] 'Three centuries ago, enraged and stifled with torment, he threw his right arm to the north and his left arm to the south. Enraged and stifled in torment, he threw his left arm to the north and his right arm to the south, and then in swift diseases and torments, the inhabitants of those cities, their marrow rotten, their bones weakened from grindings and throbbings, the senses inward rushed, shrinking beneath the dark net of infection.'
[182] The label on the original vinyl LP entitles it 'New Big Prize'.

one of Steve Hanley's greatest basslines, a bubbly, determined riff that's simple but devastatingly effective. Wolstencroft provides a thumping glam stomp that owes a little something to The Glitter Band's 'Rock And Roll Part 2'. An extension of, or elaboration on, 'Hip Priest' ('drink the long draught for big priest' who is still 'not appreciated'), it was a long-standing feature in the setlist from 1987 to 2007, clocking up an almost unprecedented 231 performances. Live, there was often a lot of swearing involved ('he is *fucking* not appreciated') and frequently featured Smith handing the microphone over to the audience.

Overture From 'I Am Curious, Orange'

A bit of an oddity, not least in the fact that despite its title it didn't actually appear in the ballet. Its minimalist lyric consists entirely of titles of other Fall songs (plus a reference to Dr. Annabel Lies from 'An Older Lover Etc.'), yet perversely this is one of the Fall tracks that sounds least like The Fall. Its chorus-laden arpeggio jangle (especially if you remove Brix's strangled vocal) sounds very much like mid-80s R.E.M. It was never played live.

Dog Is Life / Jerusalem

The opening section, 'Dog Is Life', is an unaccompanied anti-canine diatribe. It's not a theme that Smith ever really returned to, but he displays some seriously unbridled hostility towards man's best friend here: 'Dog shit and baby bit ass-lick dog mirror / dead tiger shot and checked out by dog / big tea-chest-fucker dog'. 'Jerusalem' itself finds the perfect balance between repetition and variety. The 'rant' section around the five-minute mark is matchless: the intensity of the music gradually building as the narrator rails furiously against an uncaring government that is denying him compensation ('I was very let down... I was expecting a one million quid handout'). The song is a reimagining of William Blake's classic hymn. Smith was an admirer of Blake[183] and Simon Ford saw parallels between the two:

---

[183] The closing monologue of the ballet version of 'Yes, O Yes' closely follows a passage from Blake's *The Book of Urizen*.

Blake, like Smith, was single-minded and eclectic, an autodidact with idiosyncratic spelling and a keen interest in occult and esoteric systems of knowledge. Both found it difficult to establish long-term relationships because of their erratic behaviour and short tempers and both were resolutely anti-commercial.

'Jerusalem' was played 84 times 1988-1990 and got a one-off reprisal in September 2002.

Kurious Oranj

Simon Wolstencroft enjoyed this incongruous but charmingly awkward foray into a new style: 'I got to do a reggae beat for the first time... which I enjoyed as it was very rare I could deviate from the basic rock beats Mark wanted.' It's infectiously good-humoured, although possibly a minute or so longer than it really needs to be. Smith extracts the maximum effect from the melody and lyrics through, for example, the alternating phrasing of *or*-ange and or-*ange* and the babbling 'ba-ba-ba-ba-ba's. Moreover, it takes a certain kind of genius to rhyme 'deranged' with 'orange'.[184] It only made a handful of appearances after the theatrical performances (all in December 1988) before being retired for good – 39 appearances altogether.

Wrong Place, Right Time

'One of my best songs,' asserted Smith, 'I wrote every note and every word of it.' The accuracy of Fall writing credits is dubious at the best of times, especially when MES is designated as sole songwriter. However, the song's simplicity (like 'Just Step S'ways', the vocals, bass and guitar all follow the same melody) make this claim a little more credible than most. This simplicity doesn't detract from the song's effectiveness, the jointly played/sung riff (indebted to Creedence Clearwater Revival's 'Gloomy') giving it a pounding garage punk directness. There's an incongruously smooth middle eight that prevents the track

---

[184] 'The Curious Orange' was immortalized as a character on Lee and Herring's 1989-99 series *This Morning with Richard Not Judy*, which can be viewed on Lee's website: https://www.stewartlee.co.uk/video-lee-herring/

from being too one-paced. It's easy to see why it made it onto the setlist 159 times over nearly 20 years (although it was rested between 1993 and 2004).

Win Fall C.D. 2080 / C.D. Win Fall 2088 AD[185]

Some of the tracks on *I Am Kurious Oranj* undoubtedly suffer a little from a lack of context when listened to as part of a 'regular' album. This one is a case in point: it perhaps made perfect sense as part of the ballet, but in isolation it appears not much more than a selection of rather clumsily edited vocal samples (mainly from 'New Big Prinz') over a somewhat dated house-style rhythm track. Never played live.

Yes, O Yes

Another that possibly loses something when taken out of context. MES makes enigmatic interjections ('an ordure from this planet that could not be extinguished') over what could be a soundtrack to a 60s spy film. There's a tense and mysterious tone to it, although in isolation it feels more like an interlude than a fully developed song. It was played 18 times before the ballet was performed and got another five outings afterwards, making 48 performances in total.

Van Plague?

Smith was inspired to write about the origins of AIDS by a story he read about William of Orange bringing VD to England.[186] Despite the rather gauche title, there are some gently poetic lines concerning the spread of the disease: 'all around is pure tension / beliefs and tears now and again / from where has this great sadness came?' 'A body's waste 'neath a gibbous moon' saw Smith deploy an adjective that he had picked up from H. P. Lovecraft.[187] There's

---

[185] The track was titled slightly differently on the LP and CD versions.

[186] 'I heard or read about the theory that William of Orange brought VD to England. Ridiculous of course, probably originating from mad Catholics, but it inspired me to writing a song about the question where AIDS originates from. There are several theories. For the tune I wanted an Amsterdammish melody, a dock melody.'

[187] Gibbous means 'marked by convexity or swelling; of the moon or a planet: seen with more than half but not all of the apparent disk illuminated'. Lovecraft uses the word twice in his 1919 story, 'Dagon'.

a calm, melancholy tone to 'Van Plague?' The gently discordant downtempo sections have a flavour of early 80s Sonic Youth. To conclude, Craig Scanlon adds a restrained but emotive little solo that brings the song home gracefully. It disappeared from the setlist after a few further airings in December 1988, making 34 appearances altogether.

Bad News Girl

The lumbering, ponderous lament that makes up the first two-thirds of the song would have been right at home on *Bend Sinister*; the jaunty final third emerges a little incongruously but is punchy and full of verve. 'It was clearly about me,' Brix stated with confidence, 'this wasn't some kind of riddle, he was putting our problems to the forefront. I knew it.' Whether or not this was the case (and it's hard not to think it was), it's a notably bitter song: 'jaded lust and tiresomeness are not what I want to look at... wet sex'll keep you anaesthetised... goodbye my dear'. It's another that only got a handful of outings after the ballet and never made it beyond 1988: 38 appearances in total.

Cab It Up!

A spirited, uptempo romp, driven by an insistent (virtually) two-note bassline and frantically choppy guitar work. It has an unmistakeably Fall sound, but does display a few contemporary influences in both the keyboards (OMD, early Depeche Mode) and the second guitar line that emerges in the second half (New Order, The Cure). Smith's performance matches the fizz provided by his musicians, deploying the megaphone and a few shrieks to great effect. The lyric conjures a taxi ride through a busy urban scene – 'cabbing it uptown... main strips! main strips! / people going, people going / moving it uptown' – which is well attuned to the track's energy. Michael Clark makes an appearance ('jump in Michael!') as, possibly, does 'Hip Priest's long draught-drinker – 'you know the best, Dan'. 'Cab' got 71 outings 1988-89, before receiving a one-off revival in 2012.

Reviews and Reissues

After *Frenz* reaching the giddy heights of the top 20, *Oranj*'s peak of number 54 (the same as *This Nation's Saving Grace*) may have seemed a disappointment, although it should be remembered that this was the group's second album to come out in eight months. It was well received at the time: in the *NME*, for example, Len Brown welcomed that the group had 'retained the power to surprise, to provoke and occasionally outrage'. Retrospective reviews tend to be more guardedly positive: '[It] may not have been The Fall's greatest album, but it did speak volumes for their ability and willingness to change'; 'Not The Fall's most cohesive album... *IAKO* is nevertheless a dramatic reminder of one of the most audacious moves made by any band of the era'. The musicians themselves rated it far more highly than its predecessor. 'An overlooked gem,' was Brix's judgement, '[the songs are] leagues ahead of anything on *Frenz*.'

The CD and cassette versions contained three bonus tracks. The sinister 'Guide Me Soft' comprises little more than two scratchy chords (from what sound like an unamplified electric guitar), an indistinct bass rumble and a skeletal glockenspiel. The modest lyric – delivered in a wilfully tuneless croon – appears to be William's prayer for divine support of his revolution. 'Last Nacht' is a garish, over-fussy remix of 'Bremen Nacht'.[188] 'Big New Priest' is simply an alternative version of 'New Big Prinz'.

Two singles were released from *Oranj*. 'Jerusalem/Big New Prinz'[189] came out a fortnight after the album as a double 7" single and as a double CD in the exciting new 3" format. Both included 'Acid Priest 2088' (a truncated version of 'Win Fall C.D. 2080') and 'Wrong Place, Right Time No. 2' (not noticeably different from No. 1). 'Cab It Up' (by now having lost its exclamation mark) came out seven months later. The B-side was 'Dead Beat Descendant', which was curiously omitted from the LP even though it had been part of the ballet. Despite this, it was a live

---

[188] Outtake/alternative versions of 'Last Nacht' would be used to ill effect on *Mark's Personal Holiday Tony Tapes*, arguably the worst ever Fall release (see Appendix 3).
[189] From this point onward, the titles 'New Big Prinz' and 'Big New Prinz' seem to become interchangeable on live albums, compilations and bootlegs, with the latter being used more frequently.

favourite at the time, notching up 146 appearances 1988-92. The 12" version of 'Cab It Up' added live versions of 'Kurious Oranj' and 'Hit The North'.

Evaluation

After *Frenz*, *Oranj* is a bit of a relief. It feels more like a 'proper' Fall album, full of surprises, odd turns, things that don't quite work and moments of sublime glory. In 'Prinz' and 'Jerusalem', it contains two of the group's finest, most iconic moments. Production-wise, it lacks the overly clean, sharp edges that rendered *Frenz* rather sterile, although it does feel a little cluttered and muddy in places. It may be that some of it made more sense when paired with the visual elements it was designed to accompany, but even on its own it's far more satisfying than its predecessor. Partly this is because of the better-quality songwriting – perhaps stimulated by the new disciplined approach – but more importantly it sounds like the group trying (although not always succeeding) to stretch their ambition rather than retreating into themselves.

THE FALL /

/ EXTRICATE

Extricate
Recorded: Southern Studios, London; Swanyard Studios, London; The Manor, Oxfordshire; The Wool Hall, Somerset, mid-late 1989
Released: 19th February 1990

Personnel:
Mark E Smith – vocals
Martin Bramah – guitar, vocals
Craig Scanlon – guitar
Steve Hanley – bass
Marcia Schofield – keyboards, percussion
Simon Wolstencroft – drums

With:
Charlotte Bill – flute, oboe
Kenny Brady – fiddle
Craig Leon – vocals, organ
Cassell Webb – vocals
Mike Edwards – guitar

Chapter 13: Extricate

'We didn't look baggy. We didn't sound baggy. We were The Fall.'

At the end of 1988, The Fall seemed to be at a commercial and creative peak. As Simon Ford points out:

> Everything should have been more wonderful than frightening in the world of The Fall. The group had just helped attract sell-out audiences to... one of the most prestigious theatres in the world, and was supported by a record company capable of releasing and promoting two well-received albums in a year... Smith had collected together a team of musicians at their creative prime... What could go wrong?

Ford answers his own question with 'just about everything'. Whilst in many ways this is rather an exaggeration as far as the group as a whole were concerned (just over a year later they would release one of their most commercially successfully albums), 1989 was a difficult year for Smith himself. The marital problems hinted at in 'Bad News Girl' came to head in the new year, and on 4th January, MES left Brix and moved to Edinburgh, driven to his new home by Simon Wolstencroft. In February, the group headed off to Munich for a gig that was broadcast on German TV. Steve Hanley remembers there was 'an empty seat on the plane, the last call for Brix Smith going unanswered'.[190] The Munich date was the only gig The Fall played in the first half of 1989, MES spending most of his time in self-imposed exile in Edinburgh. His difficult year was made even worse in May when his father died suddenly of a heart attack at the age of just 59. Smith did, however, find time to venture into the role of guest vocalist for the first time.[191] '(I'm) In Deep' featured on Coldcut's *What's*

---

[190] The second guitarist who can be seen on the Munich recording was Phil Ames, Brix's guitar technician.

[191] Although he had contributed backing vocals to 'Naughty Or Nice', the B-side to the third single by The Adult Net, 'White Night (Stars Say Go)' in 1986.

That Noise? album; it's an unremarkable piece of techno-pop, but one that demonstrated the potential for Smith's vocals to work effectively with a dance/electronic backing.

Change was also afoot with the record label. In December 1988, Smith announced that the group were parting company with Beggars Banquet, saying that 'it was time to move on... I think it will be good for us to have a change'. Steve Hanley's take on the situation was, 'Far from adhering to the age-old adage, "If it's not broken don't fix it", with Mark it's more a case of "If it doesn't need fixing, break it".' This was no *Room To Live* 'mess with the recording process to shake the band up a bit' scenario though. Smith was a realist who recognised that The Fall was a business, and like any business there were overheads such as studio costs and musicians' wages that wouldn't magically pay themselves. As Simon Ford puts it, 'Smith felt Beggars had taken The Fall as far as it could; it was time for a bigger label to have a go.' Before The Fall could enter into any sort of new deal, however, the fact remained that the group owed Beggars Banquet one more album.

Seminal Live, released in June, was the very definition of a 'contractual obligation' album. Like *Totale's Turns*, the album was a mix of studio and live recordings. The first side consisted of five tracks recorded in Rochdale and Edinburgh in early 1989. 'Pinball Machine' was a cover of a 1960 country song by Lonnie Irving. Smith was fond of country truckin' songs, and here he gives full vent to his enthusiasm for the genre. He makes a seemingly genuine attempt to sing it in a proper, unironic country style, and despite his melodic limitations he just about pulls it off. The group deliver a spirited, if ragged backing, with Steve Hanley adding some rather lovely just-about-in-tune banjo. It was only played live three times. 'H.O.W.' – 'History Of The World' – has a rich, complex narrative, seemingly told from the viewpoint of a malevolent presence who manipulates evidence to thwart humanity's attempts to unravel the mysteries of the world: 'I place minute dust in your microchip vessels / for daring to think all science is immortal'. Despite the fascinating lyric, 'H.O.W.' is a frustrating song. The tag-team approach of the bass and drums give it an interesting stop-start rhythm, but it sounds rushed and under-rehearsed; the keyboards are in a different key, the guitar doesn't sound properly tuned and the timing is off on several occasions. It was never played live. 'Squid Law' sits somewhere between glam and garage rock, nicely balancing staccato strings and scuzzy guitar. The Peel session version, 'Squid Lord', had brighter, cleaner production, but the scruffy sound here suits the song better. The squid image has Lovecraftian connotations (the monstrous Cthulhu is generally portrayed with tentacles) but the image that inspired the song directly was that of the group's soundman Eddie emerging from the Pacific Ocean covered in seaweed during the May 1988 US tour. 'Mollusc In Tyrol' consists of Smith mumbling and grunting over a jagged, industrial sound collage.[192] An instrumental version was used on tape at several gigs during this period. In that context, it made sense; here it feels like padding, and begins to pall before its five minutes are up.

The second side of *Seminal Live* comprises a selection of live tracks (supposedly) recorded in 1988 and 1989. '2 x 4' and 'L.A.' are decent but unremarkable. The latter features a brief 'Papal Visit'-style intro called 'Elf Prefix' that appears to be studio-recorded. 'Victoria' is thin and melodically dubious.[193] 'Pay Your Rates', like the version on *Live In Cambridge* (recorded on the same tour), is a likeably fresh update of an old tune. 'Cruiser's Creek' is introduced by a clearly inebriated Bill Grundy: 'I have never seen five-thousand yobbos in my life... a bit later, I'm going to tell you about how I made the fortune of punk rock.'[194] The CD and cassette versions added live versions of 'Kurious Oranj', 'Hit

---

[192] The music comes from Craig Leon's 'Donkeys Bearing Cups' from his 1981 album *Nommos*. The original has a far fuller, less astringent sound and is much more pleasing on the ear.

[193] It's not clear where it was actually recorded. The sleeve says that the second side was 'recorded in Vienna and Manchester 1988'. 'Victoria' was played in both cities in that year; *Reformation* suggests that this version is from Manchester (where it was played at the Ritz on the 8th March), and *The Fall Online* (by not including it in the list of tracks from Vienna) seems to support this. However, if you watch the video of that gig, the version of 'Victoria' doesn't appear to be the same one as that on *Seminal Live*. In particular, at the end of the song (52:20 on the video), MES turns to Wolstencroft and clearly says 'Simon!' – which is not present on the *Seminal Live* version.

[194] TV presenter best known for his infamous interview with the Sex Pistols in December 1976. Although the sleeve notes say that the live tracks were recorded in Manchester and Vienna 1988, 'Cruiser's Creek' wasn't played in 1988 at all. This recording actually comes from The Festival of the Tenth Summer, Manchester G-Mex, in July 1986.

The North', 'Frenz' and 'In These Times'. The first two are the same versions that appeared on the recent 'Cab It Up' single. It's a mystery as to where or when this version of 'Kurious Oranj' was recorded. It wasn't ever played in Vienna, and the only performance in Manchester was sixth months after *Seminal Live*'s release. 'Frenz' doesn't even seem to be a concert recording, sounding more like it was played live in a studio.

The music press was surprisingly forgiving about *Seminal Live*, if not exactly glowing with praise. *Record Mirror* described the album as 'merely plundering The Fall's back catalogue, conveniently fulfilling the band's contractual obligations with Beggars Banquet as they move on to greater things'. Richard Cook saw it as 'a valediction – part celebration, part clear-up'. Andrew Collins was optimistic for the group's future and (rather generously) felt 'the very fact it's not crap is remarkable enough'. However, he also described the album as 'a parody of a thrown-together clause-filler' and worried that this was a sign of them 'cruising'. Marcia Schofield was less forgiving: 'The worst piece of shit I'd worked on in my life. No songs, no ideas. Done quickly and cheaply in a terrible studio that sounded awful. I thought, "What are we doing? This is really crap."'

Having fulfilled the Beggars Banquet contract, Smith signed a deal with Fontana, a subsidiary label of the Phonogram group.[195] This contracted The Fall to produce five albums over the next five years using the Cog Sinister imprint. The deal 'saw Smith cast off the last remnants of indiedom', as Simon Ford points out. 'He was now label-mates with Elton John, Dire Straits and Status Quo.' The group also gained a new manager. Trevor Long, who had been acting as tour manager, took on the task, as Steve Hanley put it, of 'gelling [The Fall] into a more businesslike unit'.

The changes didn't stop there. The saga of The Fall's ever-changing membership took a surprising twist in July when a gig at Cambridge Corn Exchange saw Martin Bramah rejoin the line-up after a ten-year absence. Bramah had achieved some critical acclaim and modest commercial success with The Blue Orchids in

---

[195] Phonogram had already signed The Adult Net, releasing three singles and an album by them on Fontana in 1989. Poor sales led to them dropping the group in 1990.

the early 80s and had also briefly formed a band called Thirst with Karl Burns in 1987. As is so often the case with The Fall, accounts vary as to how this reappointment took place: Bramah claimed that he offered his services to Smith directly; Steve Hanley suggested that it was initiated by him and Craig Scanlon. Whichever was the case, Bramah seems to have made a relatively smooth transition back into the group. Marcia Schofield was initially sceptical ('Who's that? Oh no! He's one of Mark's friends from down the pub') but was soon won over by the songs that he'd brought with him – 'fucking hell, this guy can actually write'.

After performing at the Tucano Artes Festival in Rio de Janeiro on the 18th and 19th July,[196] the new line-up played at John Peel's surprise 50th birthday party at London's Subterrania in August, alongside The House of Love and The Wedding Present. They resurrected Peel favourite 'Mere Pseud Mag. Ed.' and also played a cover of Gene Vincent's 'Race With The Devil' ('we learned this especially for John's birthday'). The 13th Peel session followed in December. The first for six years not to feature Brix, it saw Kenny Brady playing violin in the first of his pair of session appearances.[197] Three of the songs they performed – 'Hilary', 'Chicago, Now!' and 'Black Monk Theme' – had recently been recorded for the soon to be released *Extricate*, so it's not surprising that they are very similar in structure to the album versions. They do contain some minor flaws – 'Chicago, Now!'s Art of Noise-style synth stabs detract a little from its sinister menace, and the keyboards on 'Black Monk Theme' seem to have been recorded in the same neighbouring building as the Peel 'Eat Y'self Fitter's backing vocals – but overall all three are far more punchy and satisfying than their album counterparts. 'Black Monk Theme' is especially good: the vocals have bite, Brady's fiddle is expansive and expressive and Wolstencroft adds an infectious rumble. The final track 'Whizz Bang' wasn't broadcast because it contained a profanity ('shiny cunt',

[196] Other acts appearing at the festival included Philip Glass and Laurie Anderson. In 2019, Simon Wolstencroft posted a picture on social media of Steve Hanley and Craig Scanlon relaxing on Copacabana Beach in the summer sunshine, both wearing black jeans. 'Mark banned the wearing of shorts,' Wolstencroft explained, 'never mind Speedos.'

[197] Scotsman Brady became friends with Smith in early 1989 – he lived just down the road from him in Edinburgh.

at 1:23). Later reworked as 'Butterflies 4 Brains', the version here is more aggressive, more varied in tempo and features a prominent violin part from Brady that gives it a bit of extra edge.

The single 'Telephone Thing', the group's first release on Fontana, came out in January 1990. It was produced by Matt Black and Jonathan More of Coldcut, with whom MES had collaborated the previous year; the duo also wrote the music. From the second the squelchy wah-wah kicks in, their influence is immediately apparent – The Fall had never sounded so funky. Not surprisingly, 'Funky Si' sounds right at home. The B-side was 'British People In Hot Weather'. Smith's take on Noel Coward's 'Mad Dogs And Englishmen' is a mocking depiction of how the British behave on the rare occasions that the sun comes out: 'beached whale in Wapping / his armpit hairs are sprouting'. Smith's mixture of disdainful sneer and levity (he occasionally sounds on the verge of laughter) works well, but the song is dated by its over-reverbed drum sound and tacky keyboard stabs. 'Weather' was played live throughout much of 1990 and then made a handful of appearances in 1991 and 1994, appearing 36 times altogether. The 12" of 'Telephone Thing' also contained two distinctly inessential alternative versions of the lead song. It made it to number 58 in the charts.

Extricate

The greatly increased resources provided by the move to Phonogram/Fontana saw the recording of *Extricate* take place in a variety of well-appointed and reputable studios. This included The Manor in Oxford, owned by Richard Branson, which had seen the recording of *Tubular Bells*, Tangerine Dream's *Phaedra*, and *Metal Box* and *The Flowers of Romance* by Public Image Ltd. The Wool Hall in Somerset was a 16th-century building converted to a studio by Tears For Fears where their *Songs from the Big Chair* had been recorded, as well as The Smiths' *Strangeways, Here We Come*.[198] This made the creation of *Extricate* a far more

---

[198] The other studios were Southern Studios in London (where all Crass' albums were recorded) and Swanyard Studios, also in London. In his memoir, Simon Wolstencroft states that the group also used Jimmy Page's old studio The Mill (also known as Sol Studios), but this isn't credited on the sleeve of *Extricate*.

pleasurable and relaxed experience than the musicians were used to. Steve Hanley was enthusiastic about the positive impact that this comparative luxury had on the music itself:

> It was the biggest recording project [we'd] ever undertaken. Much more time went into the arrangements and songwriting than in the past, and it shows. It was The Fall as it should be, everyone moving in the same direction.

Production duties were largely shared between Adrian Sherwood (who had last worked with the group on *Slates*) and American producer Craig Leon, whose track record included helping to launch the careers of The Ramones, Suicide, Talking Heads and Blondie. Leon and his wife Cassell Webb also contributed backing vocals and keyboards.[199] Kenny Brady added violin and Charlotte Bill, who had previously played with Blue Orchids, contributed flute and oboe. The cover, a beautifully balanced combination of vibrant shades and bold titles, was by Anthony Frost, who also designed the covers for the two singles released from the album. Frost had written to MES after hearing *Dragnet*; Smith replied that 'it was really nice to get a letter talking about the music in an intellectual way'. He described Frost's work as 'by far the best stuff I've ever been submitted'.

Sing! Harpy

The opening, dominated by Brady's piercing violin, provides a foreboding introduction to a lurching blues swagger borrowed from The Stooges' 'Little Doll' (Smith's 'uh-huh' refrain). Although he would later claim that he never wrote songs about Brix after their separation, MES's cynical drawl is clearly aimed at his ex-wife: 'she gripped me like a hawk / her talons were quite famished'. Given that Brix was at the time dating Nigel Kennedy, the prominent violin seems unlikely to be a complete coincidence. Brix wasn't too offended: referring to the lyric 'thin white skeleton / just too good in bed', she said, 'It's a complete

---

[199] Both had also played with Brix in The Adult Net.

diss track, but I love the song, and at least he calls me skinny and a good lay.' The song also contains one of Smith's habitual endearingly perverse enunciations ('can-*nab*-is'). It was one of two songs credited to 'Smith/Beddington' – Beddington being Bramah's official surname. 'Harpy' was a regular feature in the setlist throughout the first half of 1990, but its 43rd performance in July of that year was its last.

I'm Frank

Smith's sped-up dialogue right at the end says 'that was Craig's tribute to Frank Zappa. Now we can all laugh about this, but that was his attempt to be Frank therefore I've entitled it "I'm Frank".'[200] The strikingly fuzzy guitar contrasts nicely with Charlotte Bill's cute flute line, although there's no obvious similarity to Zappa. The lyric, which consists largely of 'gimme gimme gimme it slowly/gently baby' does little to make the connection either. It was performed 67 times, lasting on the setlist until 1994.

Bill Is Dead

Many assumed that this was about the death of Smith's father ('Bill' was actually one of John Edward Smith's friends); some, inevitably, suggested that it was about Brix. MES provided a different interpretation:

> It's not a love song – it's about the Manchester scene a year ago, before it got fucked up. I don't go to the Haçienda any more. I used to go once a month but it's like mainstream now. It's full of A&R men, students and people from Surrey.

Scanlon's gentle, melancholy tune is backed by a surprisingly melodic and sensitive vocal. The 'came twice / you thrice' line is a little hard to stomach though. It stayed in the setlist as far as 1995, making 61 appearances altogether.

---

[200] The dialogue is taken from Smith's introduction to the song when The Fall played it on *The Late Show* in 1990. The performance features a rare glimpse of MES (sort of) playing the guitar.

Black Monk Theme Part I

Monks were an unhinged 60s garage rock band who had previously gone under the unlikely moniker of The Torquays. 'Black Monk Theme' is a cover of 'I Hate You', a song from their 1966 album *Black Monk Time*. The Fall's version has a loping, lethargic groove that is supported effectively by Brady's keening violin and the cheesy organ breaks. Smith's stuttering vocals – although relatively calm in comparison to Gary Burger's manic performance on the original – tread carefully between daft and intense. It was played regularly throughout late 1989 and 1990, before bowing out in May 1991 after its 55th performance.

Popcorn Double Feature

A pretty straight rendition of The Searchers' 1967 single, with guitar contributions from Jesus Jones' Mike Edwards. The original isn't an especially inspiring song, and The Fall's take doesn't add much to it. Smith's contribution is particularly half-hearted; Simon Wolstencroft described his vocal as 'terrible'. Generally regarded poorly by Fall fans, it made 33 live appearances, all in 1990.

Telephone Thing

Coldcut's Black and More had released their original version of the track, 'My Telephone', in 1989, with Lisa Stansfield on vocals. Smith 'thought the vocals and all the rest of the stuff we did on it were shit', More explained, 'but he really liked the guitar, bass and drums, and he gave the cassette to his band to learn those parts'. By replacing the artificial elements with traditional instruments, The Fall transform the synthetic pop number into a shuffling funk workout that Steve Hanley and (unsurprisingly) Simon Wolstencroft take to with enthusiasm. What completes the transformation, of course, is the MES megaphone snarl. The repeated references to 'listening in' and being 'tapped' suggest paranoia on Smith's part. He claimed that this was based on real life experience: 'I dialled a number and I could hear people munching sandwiches and talking about my last phone call... what they do is tap into lines that they think are gonna be interesting.'

Martin Bramah suggested that Smith was influenced by reading *Spycatcher*.[201] 'He thought the secret service was listening in to his calls, because he had opinions.' The song also features one of Smith's most memorable lines: 'How dare you assume I want to parlez-vous with you, Gretchen Franklin nosey matron thing!' Smith made the unlikely claim that he didn't know that Gretchen Franklin was the actress who played Ethel in *Eastenders*.[202] Played regularly between 1989 and 1992, it was revived ten years later, making its 91st and final appearance in 2004.

Hilary

Whilst Smith's phoned-in vocals made 'Popcorn' much worse than it needed to be, here he elevates a pleasant but unremarkable jangle. It's not so much the lyrical content – a not exactly savage swipe at the pretentious Hilary's new Audi and liking for 'daft African pop' – but his playful delivery. He throws in two of his trademarks: amusingly puzzling enunciation (Audi becomes 'Ardee') and eccentric timing (squeezing 'bull's blood' into a space it has no right to inhabit). That said, his breathless grunts – as well as Marcia's saccharine backing vocals – become a little much after a while. It was played 36 times 1989-91.

Although some sources suggest that the Hilary in question was Tony Wilson's ex-wife, it seems more likely that the subject of the song is Hilary Moss, a mature student at Salford College of Technology who was, according to Julia Nagle, 'a heavy smoker with a wicked tongue'. The track is credited to Smith alone. Many presumed that this was another example of one of the musicians – most likely Bramah – being deprived of a writing credit. However, in a 2016 interview, Bramah asserted that while he did provide Smith with the melody, he had lifted it from America's 'Horse With No Name'. 'I didn't get a writing credit for the tune, but that's fair, because the whole thing is basically ripped off America!'

[201] *Spycatcher: The Candid Autobiography of a Senior Intelligence Officer* was a 1987 book by former MI5 officer Peter Wright, which gained notoriety when Margaret Thatcher's government attempted to ban it.
[202] Ethel (along with her beloved pug Willy) appeared in the very first episode of *Eastenders* in 1985 and remained part of the regular cast until 1997, before returning briefly in 2000. Gretchen Franklin died in 2005, aged 94.

Chicago, Now!
A darkly atmospheric track with sinister guitar and basslines, creepy keyboard flourishes and a haunting oboe from Charlotte Bill, 'Chicago' evokes a late-night urban scene from a film noir (complete with Marcia's simulated traffic noise). Smith's measured vocal matches the tense atmosphere well. Although the transitions into the uptempo sections are a trifle awkward, 'Chicago' comfortably sustains its six-minute length. It may be relevant that Chicago is where MES and Brix first met, although the lyric gives little away. Played only 13 times, all in 1990.

The Littlest Rebel
The song is named after a 1935 film starring Shirley Temple,[203] who is referenced in the lyric ('hips like Shirley Temple'). It's another track that invited inevitable speculation that it was about Brix. The insistent drumbeat and harmonica blasts give it a flavour of American railroads, and there's an interesting 60s psychedelia vibe going on in the chorus. There's a touch of 'rhyming dictionary' about the lyrics, and Smith's odd emphasis ('little-EST reb-ELL') feels a little forced this time. Played live 33 times, the last time being in December 1990.

And Therein...
Bramah's riff provides a sprightly, skiffle-ish rhythm that contrasts neatly with Smith's dolorous vocals. Smith was fond of the song:

> Martin Bramah wrote a good tune and it conjured up the Salvation Army to me. It was quasi-religious and country-and-western, which I'd always wanted to do. I love the way they give a message over, these stories. Get to the beat of it, that's what I wanted to do. Great guitars and a bit of sixth-form poetry cobbled together.

As a result of Smith's fondness for it (also possibly because it was a relatively easy one for new musicians to learn) it had a long shelf-life, being performed live 158 times 1989-2003.

---

[203] The movie glorifies the Confederacy and suggests that many blacks did not wish to be emancipated (although Shirley, aged only seven at the time, can hardly be blamed for this).

Reviews and Reissues

After their lukewarm reviews of *Seminal Live*, the music press breathed a sigh of relief at being able to get back to showering The Fall with praise. In *Melody Maker*, Jon Wilde extolled their 'extraordinary... regenerative energies... they seem to possess this enormous power of renewal... another magnificent Fall LP. Possibly their finest yet.' In the *NME*, James Brown awarded it full marks. Declaring its diversity to be its main strength, he proclaimed it to be 'a fine album glittering with brilliance. Mark E Smith may have been resting on his reputation and experimenting with tutus for a while but once again his music and not his conversation has delivered the strongest statement possible.' *Extricate* saw the group achieve their second highest UK chart placing so far, the album peaking at number 31.

The original CD and cassette contained four bonus tracks. 'British People In Hot Weather' had appeared on the 'Telephone Thing' single. 'Extricate' was, like 'Perverted By Language', a title track that never made it onto its own album. Featuring some rather rocky guitar soloing over a squelchy synth loop, it's engaging enough, although its unfinished feel is emphasised by Smith merely repeating the title and throwing in the odd off-hand 'la la la'. It was never performed live. Pick of the bunch was 'Arms Control Poseur', a lurching, swampy slab of gloriously ramshackle yet controlled noise, everything from the startling blast of harmonica to the raw, distorted soloing guitar to the depth-charge keyboard effects meshing together perfectly. The title seems to have come from a *New York Times* article ('Foreign Policy Fake, Arms Control Poseur') from October 1988, which criticised George Bush for his cavalier attitude to the prospect of nuclear conflict. The lyric, although it contains the usual mix of enigmatic phrases ('I made a calendar that wasn't there / to find whether it was the first of December or not') and well-crafted language ('parliament connives a diseased access company') doesn't appear to have a great deal to say about American foreign policy. A Fall fan club newsletter from early 1991 implied that the lyric had predicted the Gulf War, presumably based on the line 'I feel the inevitable battle creep nearer and nearer'. It's nigh on impossible to identify any time in the 20th century when war didn't seem to be a distinct possibility somewhere in the world, so this is scarcely hard evidence of Smith's alleged 'pre-cog' gifts. Although 'Poseur' was one of the Bramah tunes that had won over Marcia Schofield, the guitarist didn't get a writing credit. Debuted live in August 1989, it was played 10 times in less than a fortnight in December 1990, but only managed 18 appearances overall. It is arguably the strongest the group ever relegated to B-side/bonus status. The remaining *Extricate* bonus track 'Black Monk Theme Pt. II' sees the group give the Monks' 'Oh, How To Do Now' a hi-NRG/Eurovision treatment, complete with manic Casio keyboard handclap effects and startling key changes.

Two months after *Extricate*'s release, 'Popcorn Double Feature' was the unlikely choice for the follow-up single to 'Telephone Thing'. 'What a waste,' was Simon Wolstencroft's despairing verdict, 'we had the backing of a major label, Madchester was at its peak, and this was what we gave them as a single.' It reached only number 84 in the charts. As was the prevailing trend, the single was released in multiple formats. Among the four B-sides, there were two new songs. 'Butterflies 4 Brains' has less bite than 'Whizz Bang' (its earlier Peel session incarnation), but its dreamy psychedelia is equally appealing. It was only played live six times, all in 1990. 'Zandra' – which was never played live – also has a bit of a 60s psychedelia feel but is more at the garage-rock end of things. It's let down a little by Smith's contribution, which is both indifferent and buried in the mix.

Extricate was reissued in 2007. The re-release included all of the associated B-sides, plus 'Theme From Error-Orrori'. This obscure gem originally appeared on a 1990 compilation called *Home* and wasn't even credited as The Fall – it was listed as being by 'Mark Smith, M. Beddington, S. Hanley, S. Wolstencroft'. Dominated by a heavy, ponderous bass and drums pattern, with Bramah contributing the occasional bit of understated bluesy soloing, its heavy, doomy shuffle is reminiscent of Slint or Fugazi. It was played live 21 times.

Evaluation

It's easy to understand the critics' enthusiasm for *Extricate*. In comparison to the intermittently interesting but slapdash *Seminal Live*, the album is consistent, focused and concise. Much credit should go to Martin Bramah, whose under-recognised contributions clearly enhanced the quality of the songwriting. The relatively luxurious recording conditions afforded by the new label also played a part in the album's sleek confidence. Although one can understand Steve Hanley's enthusiasm for being able to work in a pleasant environment for once, you can't help feeling that the time and money lavished on *Extricate* saw The Fall lose a little sharpness. It's notable that the three album tracks recorded for John Peel – a process where time and money are in much shorter supply – were all superior. How much one loves *Extricate* is, in the end, dependent on the relative value you place on solid, good-quality songwriting as opposed to reckless ingenuity that comes at the expense of unevenness.

One thing that is to the album's credit is its refusal to be sucked into prevailing trends. The dawn of the 20th century's final decade saw the British music industry and press obsessed with 'Madchester' and all things 'baggy'. Phonogram may well have thought that The Fall's Manchester background ('from Salford, Mark would say to any journalist trying to lump us into Madchester') would enable them to cash in on the The Fall's north-west credentials. However, although Simon Wolstencroft hoped that the group might reap some commercial reward from being 'swept along on Madchester's coat tails', he realised that The Fall would never be part of that scene. 'We weren't ever going to be baggy,' the drummer remarked, 'we didn't look baggy. We didn't sound baggy. We were The Fall. And Mark was right in seeing Madchester as a fleeting fad.'

Shift-Work
Recorded: FON Studios, Sheffield, late 1990 / early 1991
Released: 15th April 1991

Personnel:
Mark E Smith – vocals
Craig Scanlon – guitar
Steve Hanley – bass
Simon Wolstencroft – drums, keyboards
Kenny Brady – vocals, fiddle

With:
Cassell Webb – vocals
Dave Bush – machines
Craig Leon – organ, guitar
Martin Bramah – guitar ('Rose')
Marcia Schofield – flute ('Rose')

Chapter 14: Shift-Work

'His tongue is dirty. And his musical ideas, very clear.'

Shortly after *Extricate*'s release in February 1990, Smith moved away from Edinburgh. He found it a painful experience: 'I was nearly in tears and I went to this pub round the corner carrying all these plastic bags full of me clothes and stuff.' He spent a great deal of the following 12 months on the road, as The Fall clocked up over 70 gigs in a year for the last time in their career. They played 40 dates in March and April alone, including visits to Zagreb, Belgrade, Prague and Vienna. The Zagreb gig was released in 2001 as *Live In Zagreb*. It's a fairly clean soundboard recording, although it suffers from the vocals and drums being overly prominent at the expense of the bass and guitar (in inimitable Fall live LP fashion, this recording may not even be from Zagreb – see Appendix 3). After a couple of US dates in May, the group headed out for a 12-date tour of Australia, New Zealand and Japan.

During the tour, Bramah and Schofield became an item, Wolstencroft noting that 'once we were off stage we didn't see them'. Not for the first time, group members' relationships – either within or outside the group – proved to be an anathema to Smith; he was, Steve Hanley said, 'unable to handle being around a couple on tour that he's not a part of himself'. Wolstencroft even suggested that the parsimonious Smith was also irritated by a paid-for hotel room going to waste. In fact, Smith's relationship with Schofield had been under strain for some time: as she put it, it had been 'all "I quit/you're fired/I quit/you're fired" for a few months'. The principal point of conflict had regarded her working with other musicians, which Smith – somewhat hypocritically, given his recent collaboration with Coldcut – declared to be unacceptable. She had decided to leave but was persuaded to return for the tour by Trevor Long. However, it was Long who informed her and Bramah in the small hours of 15th July (just before the group set off for the Japanese leg of the tour) that they were booked on the next flight home. As ever, Smith had his own explanation for their departure:

> Martin was always a fill-in, really, and Marcia is a brilliant keyboards player, great image and all that. But I wanted to change the sound, make it even more sparse than it is already. I think the two of them were really out of sync with us, so I sent 'em home.

Despite Smith's desire for a stripped-down sound, it was clear, given the nature of most of the songs in the current set, that someone was going to have to fill in on keyboards. Saffron Prior (at the time the group's office manager but also Smith's new partner) attempted to take on the role but was unable to master even the five-note riff to 'Hit The North'. In the end, at Steve Hanley's suggestion, roadie Kevin 'Skids' Riddles ('eighteen stone of hairy-arsed Motörhead roadie', who had previously played in metal bands Tytan and Angel Witch), stepped in to play keyboards on the Japanese gigs as well as that summer's Reading Festival.[204]

The group's next single, released in August, had been recorded before Bramah and Schofield's departure. 'White Lightning' was a rockabilly number first recorded by The Big Bopper in 1958 and covered by George Jones in 1959. The Fall's take is entertaining enough, but it verges on end-of-a-long-night karaoke and feels a little lazy and obvious. It was the group's third most frequently played song, clocking up 261 performances, often as an encore. It improved a little on 'Popcorn's chart performance, reaching number 56. B-side 'Blood Outta Stone' is more interesting, a 60s-style psychedelic jangle with all manner of odd background sound effects that got 31 live outings 1990-92. A promo 7" of the single came with a miniature bottle of White Lightning tequila. The limited edition 12" and CD (entitled *The Dredger EP*) featured a variety of extra tracks. 'Zagreb' (originally entitled 'Zagreb Daylight') is driven by a forceful delay/wah-wah string-bending guitar line and a techno-flavoured sequencer. It was played live

---

[204] The Fall were second on the bill on the Sunday night, which was headlined by Pixies.

24 times, including a one-off revival in 1999. The longer version, 'Zagreb (Movements I+II+III)', morphs into 'The Funeral Mix' (one of the other extra tracks) towards its conclusion. 'Funeral' itself is an unremarkable slab of instrumental indie-dance crossover that was never played live. 'Life Just Bounces' would go on to appear in different guises on several other releases, including 1995's *Cerebral Caustic* (see Chapter 18). Its first incarnation – which many Fall fans consider to be the superior one – is played at a noticeably slower tempo than later versions.

Autumn 1990 saw the group play in Tel Aviv, Athens and Barcelona. The last of these was as part of 'Il Festival de Tardor' (The Autumn Festival), which lasted for two months and featured hundreds of artists (including, like the previous year's Tucano Artes Festival, Philip Glass and Laurie Anderson) as well as dance, street music and theatre. A review in *La Vanguardia* provided an unusual if evocative description of MES on stage. 'Smith doesn't sing, but rather he goads, bellows, vomits and corrupts. His tongue is dirty. And his musical ideas, very clear.' The most significant aspect of the gig was that it saw the start of Dave Bush's association with the group, at this stage working on backline sound. Bush was an experienced sound engineer who had worked with The Clash and Echo & the Bunnymen. He was not initially a fan of the group ('I always thought The Fall was shit... Les Dawson playing piano') but would come to play a key role in defining the group's sound over the next few years.

In December, the group released their fourth single of the year, 'High Tension Line'. Both its title and the 'step down' refrain may have been inspired by 'The Second Dream Of The High-Tension Line Stepdown Transformer', a 1962 piece by La Monte Young.[205] However, it's hard to see much of a connection between Young's minimalist piece and the accessible and melodic indie-jangle of 'High Tension Line'. The single is a strong enough tune and a solid entry in the group's back catalogue, if not especially ground-breaking. In *Sounds*, Andy Peart rather overstated the case with his description of 'a raw, rough thunderbolt built on hypnotic

---

[205] American avant-garde composer, a pioneer of drone who collaborated with John Cale and Terry Riley.

231

repetition, deadpan aggression and melancholy'. In the same issue, Andy Stout veered the other way, rather harshly describing it as 'innocuous, inoffensive and ultimately as bland and tasteless as a microwave chicken tikka'. Perhaps due to it being the group's fourth single release of the year, it sold relatively poorly, its peak of number 97 in the charts being the group's lowest performance since 'Living Too Late' four years earlier. Talking to Peart, Smith dismissed such matters: 'I don't care about the Top 40 but I have to pretend I do. Anybody who goes on *Top of the Pops* is a ponce.' The video for the single featured Smith in an SS uniform, albeit with the insignia covered up. Smith explained: 'I made everyone cover up the SS symbols and swastikas. I'm very anti-Nazi, actually. What they did was criminal. They put German art back about one hundred years.'

The B-side saw The Fall having a crack at a Christmas song. 'Xmas With Simon', featuring jaunty keyboards courtesy of Wolstencroft and some startlingly delicate and plaintive backing vocals ('Jesus… it's Christmas') is at once terrible, hilarious and delightful. One can't help but wonder what committed Christians make of the notion that the messiah's birth surrounded by animals led to 'no set amount to the number of diseases' or his death at 33 being 'as good a time as any'. It was never performed live. The bonus track on the 12" was 'Don't Take The Pizza'. Oddly, Simon Rogers received a writing credit for the song, despite not having worked with the group for three years (he didn't even remember the track). Featuring a bouncy bassline reminiscent of 'Oh! Brother', it's not exactly indispensable but does contain one of Smith's best put-downs: 'you dopey randy acid clone'. It was played only six times, all towards the end of 1990.

Shortly before *Shift-Work*'s release, the group – at this point a slimmed-down four-piece, augmented once again by Kenny Brady's violin – recorded their 14th Peel session. All four songs would appear on the next album, but only 'Idiot Joy Showland' had been played live at this point. Of the four, 'The Mixer' differs the most from the album version, owing to the absence of Dave Bush's electronics; 'Showland' and 'The War Against Intelligence' have only minor differences, the latter having more prominent backing vocals for example. 'A Lot Of Wind', despite Hanley and Brady's best efforts to keep things lively, is overstretched at nearly five and a half minutes.

Shift-Work

The majority of the album was recorded at FON studios in Sheffield,[206] with production provided by Craig Leon, Grant Showbiz and Robert Gordon (co-founder of influential electronic label Warp). By the end of the year, the group had completed only four songs and by January still only had a few rough ideas for the other tracks. Smith was determined to do without the songs composed by Bramah before his departure, and so much of the new material was written fairly rapidly just before the later recording sessions. Consequently, unlike previous albums, the majority of songs on Shift-Work were not repeatedly road-tested on stage before their release: only 'Idiot Joy Showland', 'You Haven't Found It Yet' and 'Pittsville Direkt' were performed before the album went on sale.

Side one of the LP was subtitled 'Earth's Impossible Day' (a reference to a 1962 edition of the DC comic Hawkman); side two was 'Notebooks Out Plagiarists', a line from the song 'The War Against Intelligence'. The cover art was provided by Pascal Le Gras, a French artist who went on to have a long association with the group. A Fall fan from the moment he heard the group on radio ('I was stupefied and immediately ran to the record shop'), he approached Smith after the group's Paris gig in April 1990 to offer his services. Smith described him as 'a sublime genius', even though he could 'hardly understand a word [he was] saying'. Although Dave Bush only got a 'with' credit on Shift-Work (for 'machines'), Smith seems to have taken a shine to him, and Hanley observed that during the recording that Bush was 'starting to feel like... more band than crew'. Once Bush had become a Fall enthusiast, he became determined to drag the group into the 90s. 'When I hear you guys play, I'm hearing extra sounds in my

---

[206] FON (which stood for 'Fuck off Nazis') was built in 1985 by Mark Brydon of Sheffield industrial funk outfit Chakk. Brydon would go on to enjoy commercial success with Moloko.

head that I can produce alongside... you [Steve] and Craig make a good noise together. But it'd sound banging with loops and beats and sequences and sub-bass.'

So What About It?

The album's opener announces the group's new direction with defiance. Smith's megaphone cry of 'Fall advice' occasionally morphs into 'Fall advance'; fitting, given the track's venture into sequenced electronica. The combination of Scanlon's crunchy power chords and the hard-edged synth gives it an almost anthemic tone. Hanley is too low in the mix though, making the song a less forceful statement of intent than it might have been. 'Year of Bomb / TV wars 24 hours' references the recent Gulf War; 'the work's down the drain' echoes Bowie's 'Suffragette City'. The song was never performed live.

Idiot Joy Showland

Perversely – perhaps with intentional irony – the opening track's musical nod to the contemporary fashion for indie/dance crossover is followed immediately by Smith's famously withering put-down of the whole Madchester scene. Smith stated that he was 'very glad now that I stated at the beginning of the year that The Fall want no part of the Manchester scene', expressing derision for the likes of Shaun Ryder and co. 'The Happy Mondays upset me very much... they practise their north Manchester accents.' 'Showland' nails the shallow, bandwagon-jumping nature of said scene with deadly precision: 'the shapeless kecks flapping up a storm'; 'your mystic jumpsuits cannot hide your competitive plagiarism'. Smith also finds time for a dig at Paul Gascoigne and his Italia '90 tears – 'your sportsmen's tears are laudanum' – revisiting the distaste for the middle-class/mainstream takeover of football that he first expressed a decade earlier in 'Kicker Conspiracy'. The lyric also reflects the derision he felt for non-musicians such as sportsmen getting involved in the music industry: 'I seriously object to boxers and footballers releasing records,' he complained to Andy Peart of *Sounds*, 'because it's too easy.' Although he rather skirts around the melody, Smith takes his singing fairly seriously.

'Showland' was the only song from the album with a lengthy setlist life, being played 97 times, 1990-97.

Edinburgh Man

Originally conceived as a light-hearted pastiche of The Smiths, Scanlon's melancholy composition moved MES to compose a poignant paean to his briefly adopted home: 'I don't mind being by myself / don't wanna be anywhere else / just wanna be in Edinburgh'. It's saved from being too maudlin by a little dig at the city's most famous cultural event ('keep me away from the festival') and the little chuckle at 3:12 ('cobble stones'). There's a melodic similarity to 'Silver Dream Machine' by David Essex. It was played live 39 times.

Pittsville Direkt

Although it has its positive features, in particular Scanlon's languid slide guitar and the contrast between Smith's lazy drawl and Cassell Webb's icy backing vocals, 'Pittsville' falls a little short of the brooding intensity it's clearly aiming for. Played 28 times 1991-92.

The Book Of Lies

Possibly inspired by the Aleister Crowley book of the same name, although the lyric does little more than repeat the title. Smith and Kenny Brady trade equally off-key vocals over a somewhat forgettable 60s pop backing. Only played live five times, all in 1991.

The War Against Intelligence

According to Simon Ford, 'The War Against Intelligence' was 'the original title for the album until the Gulf War started and Smith decided to change the title to something less controversial'. At first glance, this seems a little fanciful, MES generally being less than averse to causing controversy. However, it should be remembered that a bizarrely wide range of songs were banned from radio broadcast at the time, including Cutting Crew's '(I Just) Died in Your Arms', 'Love Is a Battlefield' by Pat Benatar and even Phil Collins' 'In The Air Tonight'. 'Intelligence' has a strong, lively melody, and contains one of Smith's better insults ('you think your haircut is distinguished / when it's a blot on the English landscape'). It was played live only 16 times, 1991-92.

Shift-Work

The title track is a measured shuffle expertly curated by Wolstencroft's expressive drumming. It's a sad tale of a couple falling apart because of incompatible work patterns ('she's ten to five / but I'm shift work'). It's rather touching, although it generally sounded much more direct and powerful in its 19 live performances, 1991-93.

You Haven't Found It Yet

Although it opens with a bracing burst of MES on megaphone ('Where are you going? This work has not yet reached cessation!') 'You Haven't Found It Yet' sees the melancholy theme continue. It finds Smith filled with ennui as he undertakes an aimless drive around 'flashy Camden Town'. There are some odd turns of phrase, such as 'mental saw-down of your head', which even Smith himself seemed a bit perplexed by: 'I got the record out to check the lyrics and I couldn't fucking work them out.' Although the song is largely made up of a circling chorus searching in vain for a verse, the gentle melody and Scanlon's delicate guitar line make for a warmly rewarding experience. After being used as the (instrumental) opening to the group's 1990 Reading Festival set, the song was only played four more times, all in 1991.

The Mixer

Kenny Brady's insistent violin melody is an integral part of the song, and there's a plaintive melody that MES delivers with a weary tenderness; the megaphone is also wheeled out to give a nice bit of texture. However, it's Dave Bush who has the clearest influence here, throwing in delay-heavy dance synths, handclaps and castanet effects. Played live 46 times, 1991-97.

A Lot Of Wind

As a recently-divorced musician, it is perhaps not surprising that Smith had been watching a lot of daytime TV. 'Wind' describes how, 'desperate for entertainment', he switches on the television and is appalled by the banal nonsense that those involved are spouting. Unfortunately, the lyric itself is not much more inspiring than its subject matter: 'you see them selling carpets / you see them in the shops / you see them on the kids' programmes / and they talk a lot of wind'. Kenny Brady does his best to inject some vitality, but 'Wind' feels like rather a thin idea and runs out of steam well before the end. The main point of interest is that Fred Talbot (the 'weatherman... [who] used to teach all our friends') was a teacher at Altrincham Grammar School for Boys which Simon Wolstencroft attended.[207] Only played live seven times, 1991-92.

Rose

The gentle and melancholy theme of side two continues with 'Rose', the only track to feature Bramah and Schofield. The two-chord jangle (a sort of C86 update of 'Flat Of Angles') is pleasingly plaintive and Smith mumbles along mournfully in seemingly heartfelt style. However, it's let down a little by the clumsy wah-wah and rather twee flute. Played live only once, in Sydney, July 1990.

Sinister Waltz

A spooky music box/carnival atmosphere is rendered even more peculiar by Smith's mysterious 'he must come down' mantra, apparently delivered down a crackly telephone line. Weird but strangely lovely, it makes for a great album closer.

Reviews and Reissues

Smith was nervous about how the album would be received, but his fears proved to be groundless as the music press queued up to

---

[207] In 2013 Talbot was arrested and charged with sexual offences against some of his former pupils. In his 2015 trial, Ian Brown gave evidence. Talbot was sentenced to five years in prison and was released in 2019.

lavish the group with praise. In the *NME*, Stephen Dalton gave the album full marks, describing it as a 'no-contest knockout' whose songs came 'thundering out of the trenches with all barrels blazing'. *Melody Maker*'s Jon Wilde thought it represented The Fall at their 'awkward, bloody-minded, self-respecting best'. The public seemed to agree: *Shift-Work* reached number 17 in the album chart, their highest placing yet.

The original cassette and CD versions included 'High Tension Line' and 'White Lightning'. A 2002 reissue added 'Blood Outta Stone' and 'Xmas With Simon'. The album was also released as a double CD package with *Code: Selfish* in 2003. In 2007, it was reissued as a double CD, disc 2 containing 18 bonus tracks. This included all the tracks from 'White Lightning'/*The Dredger* and the 'High Tension Line' singles, plus the March 1991 Peel session, three rather pointless techno remixes of 'So What About It?' and an equally unremarkable remix of 'The Mixer' (called, inspiringly, 'The Re-Mixer'). Two further tracks were included. Outtake 'Cloud Of Black' is a monotonous affair, based around a dreary three-note riff and a vocal that Smith delivers whilst apparently struggling to stay awake. 'Arid Al's Dream', however, is another of those overlooked little gems. Originally entitled 'Simon's Dream' (Funky Si gets a mention in the demo version), it's the second Fall song to mention wolverines. *The Annotated Fall* describes it as 'a sci-fi tale, seemingly about a dream encounter with an alien intelligence'. Perversely thrown out on an obscure 1992 various artists compilation,[208] its spindly, atmospheric guitar line, clattering 'chorus' with frantic violin and thundering drums and energetic, engaging vocals leave you scratching your head as to why it wasn't selected for the album.

Evaluation

The fact that the *Shift-Work* material was largely composed in a hurry without being tried out on the road in customary Fall fashion is obvious in places – especially in underdeveloped ideas such as 'A Lot Of Wind' or 'Book Of Lies'. It's also noteworthy

[208] *Volume Four*, released on the Volume label in September 1992. It also included tracks from Suede, Throwing Muses and Stereolab.

that most *Shift-Work* songs had (even by The Fall's standards) only a brief shelf-life on the setlist. Only 'Idiot Joy Showland' racked up a significant number of appearances; several others didn't make it into double figures and 'So What About It?' and 'Sinister Waltz' were never performed live at all. In addition, there were no late period revivals for these songs – the performance of 'Idiot' in December 1997 at Bristol was the very last outing for any of the dozen songs on the original LP.

There's also a nagging sense that the group don't quite have a clear sense of direction. There's plenty to treasure, such as the hypnotic lope of 'You Haven't Found It Yet', the touching melancholy of 'Edinburgh Man' and the malevolent carnival of 'Sinister Waltz'. But although Bush is starting to nudge the group towards a contemporary, electronic-edged version of The Fall, the shift is as yet tentative; the group are still only scratching at the surface of what 'machines' might bring to the Fall sound. *Shift-Work* was by no means the first or last Fall LP to catch the group at a transitional moment, but here the transition feels hesitant, not wholly realised.

Code: Selfish
Recorded: CaVa Studios, Glasgow; AIR Studios, London, late 1991
Released: 23rd March 1992

Personnel:
Mark E Smith – vocals, tapes
Craig Scanlon – guitar
Steve Hanley – bass
Simon Wolstencroft – drums, keyboards
Dave Bush – keyboards, machines

With:
Cassell Webb – vocals
Craig Leon – keyboards
Simon Rogers – keyboards

Chapter 15: Code: Selfish

'That's why I formed the bloody group in the first place,
so I could hear something I like.'

For Smith, the key date of 1991 was a personal one: on 27th November he married Saffron Prior. For The Fall, however, the most significant event was the promotion of Dave Bush to full band member. He made his full debut at the Cities in the Park festival in Manchester, a two-day open-air show held in Heaton Park on the weekend of 3rd-4th August, which also featured The Wonder Stuff, The Beautiful South, OMD and Buzzcocks. The Fall acted as a last-minute replacement for The Soup Dragons.[209] Bush's influence on the next album was to be even greater than it had been on *Shift-Work*, Simon Wolstencroft noting that he 'had started to shape The Fall's sound in a big way'.

During 1991, Smith became increasingly convinced that Trevor Long had his hand in The Fall's till. During the recording of 'High Tension Line', for example, Smith became highly suspicious when the manager arrived at the studio in a newly-purchased (although not actually new) Audi. Much of Smith's animosity was simply about someone having too much control of his money. As Hanley warned Long, 'We all know what happens if Mark thinks he's losing control of anything.' Smith's suspicions led him to dismiss Long and later take him to court (see Chapter 18).

The Fall made their second consecutive appearance at the Reading Festival in August 1991. Smith sported a striking gold lamé shirt and deployed a headmaster-style lectern for his lyric sheets. In November, the group headed north, where they found themselves in the luxurious surroundings of CaVa Studios in Glasgow. It was a converted church that still contained a pulpit,

---

[209] In the videos of the festival available online, The Fall seem to have been airbrushed from the event. However, a bootleg of the performance captures the first outing – albeit a highly truncated one – of 'Two Face!' which is played at a cracking tempo (about 50% faster than the studio version). There's also a sound failure during 'Pittsville', leaving Wolstencroft, Hanley and Smith to perform an almost dub version of the song.

mahogany panelling and crimson velvet cushioning that cost, as Steve Hanley put it, 'silly money'. The four musicians had spent much of the autumn in Dave Bush's home studio, but the only song they took into CaVa was 'Free Range'. The comfortable surroundings don't seem to have been overly conducive to productivity: despite spending a month in Glasgow, they didn't come up with a great deal of new, satisfactorily completed material, and only five of *Code*'s twelve tracks come from these sessions. After Smith declared himself dissatisfied with the results of their Scottish residency, the group headed to AIR Studios in London, where, showing a slightly more *Witch Trials* pace to their work, they finished it off in five days.

They concluded 1991 with five UK dates in December, where 'Gentlemen's Agreement', 'Return', 'Birmingham School Of Business School' and 'Dangerous' were given their first outings. The new year saw Dave Bush make his first trip to Maida Vale for the recording of the 15th Peel session, which was broadcast on 15th February 1992. The new member's influence can certainly be heard in a robust 'Free Range', even if it doesn't quite match the ferocity of the album version. 'Immortality' and 'Return' are better than their *Code: Selfish* counterparts, Steve Hanley commenting that 'the music sound[ed] much more like it's supposed to'. The former has a beefier bass sound that gives it more body; the latter benefits from livelier, less fussy percussion and a more engaged performance from Smith. The remaining track was 'Kimble', a (loose) cover of a Trojan reggae tune by Lee Perry, released in 1968 under the name The Creators. The Fall's version features a snippet of 'Sinister Waltz' (plus what sounds like someone clearing away last night's wine glasses) before ambling into four minutes of entertaining if aimless reggae.[210]

'Free Range' was released as a single in March 1992. The B-sides were all songs that would appear on the album: 'Everything

---

[210] The group wouldn't play it live until five years later, when it got two outings at their 13th-14th May 1997 gigs at Jilly's Rockworld in Manchester. 'The band,' according to *The Track Record*, 'resurrect an extremely spartan version of "Kimble" which is either a piece of genius or complete rubbish depending on what sort of frame of mind the listener may or may not be in. Somehow reference to "Why Are People Grudgeful?" is made and attempts at dub are made somewhat incoherently.'

Hurtz', 'Dangerous' (without, at this stage, the 'So-Called' in its title) and 'Return'. All three – plus 'Free Range' – were slightly different edits/mixes, although you'd be hard-pressed to spot much difference. The single reached number 40 in the charts, which proved to be the highest ever placing for an original Fall song. It was also the last time any of the group's singles would grace the top 40. The follow up single, released three months after the album (on 12" and CD only – a sign of the times), didn't trouble the charts at all. 'Ed's Babe' is a pleasant if unremarkable slice of breezy pop, most notable for its catchy 'D.I.Y.' backing vocals. Featuring lyrics written by Craig Scanlon, it only made 15 live appearances, the last being in January 1994. There were three B-sides. 'Free Ranger' is, unsurprisingly, a remix of 'Free Range', one which whomps up the drum track and turns up the reverb: this actually takes a little edge off the song, making it distractingly busy and sound somewhat hollow in comparison to the original. 'Pumpkin Head Xscapes' is uptempo and funky (thanks to Hanley's fluid bassline) with a catchy hook: 'we're coming, we're coming, Leo'.[211] Simon Wolstencroft asserts that it's about Scanlon's missing cat. 'The Knight, The Devil And Death'[212] is one of that small group of Fall tracks that doesn't sound at all like The Fall. This is mostly because of Smith's absence (although that could be some of his trademark violin work around the one-minute mark), the vocals being provided by Cassell Webb. It's an atmospheric piece, full of texture (for example the two contrasting guitar parts, one chorus-heavy, one fuzzily distorted), and has a marvellously overblown finale. Neither 'Knight' nor 'Pumpkin' were ever played live.

Code: Selfish

Code: Selfish featured another bold, distinctive cover design by Pascal Le Gras. Craig Leon once again produced, this time joined by Simon Rogers, his first involvement with The Fall since

[211] A song with a similar melody and refrain appears in the 1951 Kirk Douglas film *Ace in the Hole* (the scene in question is at 1:17:13).

[212] The title was probably inspired by *The Knight, Death, and the Devil*, a novelization of the life of Hermann Göring written by Ella Leffland and published in 1990. Whilst this might sound like typical MES reading material, according to Steve Hanley it was Craig Scanlon who came up with the title.

Frenz; both also contributed keyboards. Dave Bush wasn't the only one trying to pull The Fall away from a traditional guitar/bass/drums sound. Smith, always sceptical about the whole 'Madchester' craze, was increasingly derisive of the contemporary tendency to hark back to the mainstream guitar rock of the 70s. He complained that there were 'too many bloody guitar bands' and 'cheap Sonic Youth imitators' – 'all that crap' that he'd been trying to 'go against' in 1979.

> That's why I keep The Fall at arm's length, on the other side of town. I've seen all this shit before. It's not just because I'm old, it's because it's no good. I'm into having a bit of taste, I've got taste, The Fall have got taste. That's why I formed the bloody group in the first place, so I could hear something I like.

The Birmingham School Of Business School

After a disconcertingly dark opening reminiscent of the eponymous Black Sabbath track, there's a brief burst of wonky techno before the group lurch into a rattling assault. It's an expansive, ambitious opener. The vocals are menacing and Wolstencroft and Hanley lay down a formidably solid rhythm track, but it's Craig Scanlon that's the star here. As well as the cascading harmonics that populate the rhythm throughout, he forges a meandering yet focused bluesy solo guitar that complements the song deftly. It treads the fine line between considered restraint and abandoned wig-out with careful balance, and is, as Stewart Lee observes, a guitar solo 'that sounds contemptuous of the very idea of guitar solos'. The lyric is largely aimed at Trevor Long's management practices ('the theft of its concealment') and at the end includes an answerphone message to him. It also finds time to have a dig at Birmingham's view of itself as Britain's second city – 'Olympic bidding again and again' referring to the city's bid for the 1992 Olympics. It was played 28 times, all in 1991 and 1992.

Free Range

It's easy to see why this was chosen as the lead single. 'Free Range' merged electronics with a more traditional guitar-driven approach in a similar vein to 'So What About It?' but here the group achieved a far more hard-edged and aggressive sound that resulted in their best single of the 90s. As Dave Thompson put it:

> One of The Fall's most ferocious... releases, war torn guitars and keyboards cut through with muttered samples, as Smith's chilling vision of a pan-European society regulated according to the Nazi/Nietzsche-ian ideal was borne out by the near-simultaneous eruption of the war in the Balkans.

No song of this period better captures the potential of harnessing Bush's crisp, layered sequences with the trusted Scanlon/Hanley/Wolstencroft axis and Smith's drawling sneer. Unsurprisingly a popular choice live, it clocked up 115 appearances 1991-98, plus a one-off revival in 2002.

Return

Following two such strong openers is a tough task, and 'Return' struggles to rise to the challenge. Hanley gives it some muscular momentum, but the guitar and keyboard churn away aimlessly and Smith sounds disengaged at times. Whilst it contains a few memorable lines ('Is that a hair extension? It's soaked in hair lotion – how can you smell your own head?') the repeated refrain of 'Baby baby baby... come back to me' eventually becomes tiresome.[213] It had more setlist longevity than much of the album, however, being played 39 times 1991-96.

Time Enough At Last

A gentle melancholy strum with a conventional structure and a plaintive if melodically wobbly vocal. It's another song where Smith took inspiration from *The Twilight Zone*, in this case a 1959 episode with the same title. In it, Burgess Meredith plays a man who loves reading – but never has the time – who survives

---

[213] This may well, of course, be the point. In the booklet accompanying the 2007 reissue, Daryl Easlea suggests that the line 'at once parodies and exaggerates the craft of a rock lyric writer'. 'Cynical masterpiece over a violent chug' feels like an exaggeration though.

a nuclear war and finds himself surrounded by books in the ruins of a public library.[214] It was played live 28 times in 1991-92.

Everything Hurtz
Given Smith's recreational habits, it's perhaps surprising that there aren't more hangover-related Fall songs. Whilst it isn't his most insightful lyric, 'pursuing the fuel' is a pleasing euphemism for a heavy night and he captures the morning-after feeling well: painful ('big fat pain in my chest bone'), skint ('got a big fat no no in my chequebook'), sensitive to noise ('got the disease tinnitus') and struggling to speak properly ('speakin' like I've got Tourette's'). It's not the group's most musically inventive moment, being a fairly standard indie-rock chug driven by a fuzzy yet restrained guitar riff, but there's just about enough 'Fall-ness' to the sound to stop it being snared in the early-90s indie-dance-crossover trap. It was played 30 times 1992-96.

Immortality
Described in somewhat exaggerated fashion by the *NME* as 'techno being shagged by The Fall's steamrolling rock machine', 'Immortality' grinds away dutifully but suffers from lethargy, especially in comparison to the more spirited Peel version. Smith's on-stage comments suggest that he quickly bored of the song (see Chapter 16), which may explain why it only got four live outings, all in March 1992. Possibly inspired by Milan Kundera's 1990 novel of the same name, but more likely meant, as Steve Hanley suggests, as a 'tribute to how our music will live on'.

Two-Face!
After a snippet of Dave Bush indie/techno crossover, 'Two-Face!' abruptly lurches into action, lolloping along with bouncy funk. Wolstencroft is on fine form here, certainly living up to his 'Funky Si' moniker. The *NME*, rather bafflingly, described it as 'like sprinkled sandpaper'. Blogger hippriestess has a much more secure grasp of the song's merits:

[214] As he picks up the first book, he drops and smashes his glasses, leaving him unable to read. The final lines are 'That's not fair. That's not fair at all. There was time now. There was – was all the time I needed…! It's not fair! It's not fair!'

Scanlon and Hanley are enjoying themselves for sure, weaving around Wolstencroft and each other with aplomb, Scanlon in particular firing inventive chords into the heart of the beast in all the right wrong places. They are soon joined by Bush's buzzing descending synth line which is approximately the size of Finland and, of course, by MES. This is one of those songs where Smith functions as a fifth instrument, his delivery a rhythmic device but as sonically unruly as one would expect.

The song's title may refer to the Batman villain of the same name, the line 'left side, horrible' describing how the character had the left side of his face disfigured by an acid attack. It was only played live eight times, all in 1992.

Just Waiting

The obligatory cover version – this time of a 1953 Hank Williams tune – is one of the better ones. Unusually, Smith actually *adds* melody to the song: Williams's version is delivered as spoken word, whereas MES conjures up a wry, lop-sided tune. He also amends the lyrics in his inimitable fashion: 'the cretin is waiting for U2 to come on MTV again / but the producer is waiting for the blonde bird'. It mostly swings along with a joyfully deadpan swagger, although the middle eight is a little stilted. When the metronomic drums see the song start to stray into monotony halfway through, Craig Scanlon rescues it with some nicely understated country-blues guitar work. Played live only twice.

So-Called Dangerous

A decent enough if unremarkable piece of indie-dance-rock. In a 2014 *Guardian* article journalist Peter Kimpton explained how he might have inspired the lyric 'same again, sir? / how can you have the same again?' by asking Smith in a Manchester pub whether he wanted a pint of 'the same again'. It was played twice in December 1991, and eight more times the following year.

Gentlemen's Agreement

Framed around a sequence of almost funereal piano chords, the song has a slightly lethargic feel, but is elevated by Scanlon's refined guitar and Smith's genuinely tender vocal. Simon Ford suggests that it's another song about Trevor Long; Simon Wolstencroft that it was about sexual etiquette whilst on tour. However MES, speaking to Q magazine in 1991, said that it was about 'short concentration span. Which connects with sex.' He went on:

> It took me fucking ages to write, really pissed off because the band had written this great tune and I just couldn't get the lyric. It came bit by bit through the two months we were in the studio. I go in to record with a big box of lyrics and the band have their tunes ready, but we'd be in there forever if we stuck to trying to fit one to the other. So in the end I lock the box and start writing on spec. Don't force it, that's the secret.

MES returned to the song in a 1993 interview with *Melody Maker*, calling it 'one of the best things we've ever written... You write a song like that, and expect people to be really impressed, and it just washes over them. They just think it's The Fall A Bit Slower. People always tend to underrate us a bit.' 'Gentlemen's Agreement' was played 17 times 1991-92.

Married, 2 Kids

The swinging rhythm, slide guitar and rock'n'roll piano give 'Married' a barroom blues feel – you could almost imagine the Stones playing it. Smith's laid-back delivery suits both the musical feel of the song and the lyrical content. His vignette of married life is cynical and depressing, as you might expect, but also laced with dark, wry humour: 'aftershave like mustard'; 'peculiar goatish smell'.[215] In a 1992 interview, Smith indicated that this was another song about Trevor Long, suggesting that the group's manager had 'only started conning him once he'd had two kids'.

---

[215] *The Annotated Fall* points out an interesting connection: the Thomas Harris novel *The Silence of the Lambs* (the film version of which featured 'Hip Priest') contains these lines: 'Can you smell his sweat? That peculiar goatish odour is trans-3-methyl-2 hexenoic acid. Remember it, it's the smell of schizophrenia.'

'Married' was only played live 11 times, all in 1992. For those who purchased the LP or cassette, the track's engagingly bleary-eyed swagger rounded the album off nicely...

Crew Filth

...of course, it now being 1992, a substantial proportion of Fall fans would have bought *Code: Selfish* on CD. Unfortunately for them, their version of the album concluded with 'Crew Filth'. Of the dozens of piss-take/experimental/filler tracks that pepper the group's back catalogue, this is a low point.[216] Recorded on the tour bus as the group returned from their 3rd December gig in Blackpool, it's basically the sound of a few pissed-up blokes mucking around. At best self-indulgent and tedious, at worst it flirts with offensiveness (the line about 'we kept our backs to the walls' has not aged at all well). Skulking at the end of the CD, this may well be The Fall song with the smallest ownership-to-listens ratio.

Reviews and Reissues

The album sold well, reaching number 21 in the charts, just four places short of *Shift-Work*. Reviews were again positive. The *NME*'s Dele Fadele described it as a 'triumph', a 'bouquet of barbed wire, emblazoned "F- You", that even the uninitiated will find hard to ignore'. Several reviewers singled out the lyrics for praise in particular. Fadele called them 'some of the best... in the English language'; Mathew Hyland was similarly impressed:

> There's more wit and intellectual rigour here than in 90 per cent of English novels, or in a lifetime of what TV companies call 'quality British drama'. There are far too few rock lyrics in the world featuring the words 'prurience', 'abject' and 'vermin' and Smith is on a one-man mission to right the balance.

Select's David Cavanagh was one of the few dissenting voices, declaring *Code* to be a 'disappointment' and 'the worst Fall album in years'.

[216] It came second in a poll to find the worst ever Fall track on the *Fall Online Forum* in 2017.

A 2002 CD reissue included 'Ed's Babe' and 'Free Ranger'. Like *Extricate* and *Shift-Work*, *Code: Selfish* received a double CD reissue from Fontana in 2007. The bonus CD rounded up all the B-sides plus the 1992 Peel session; it also added two further tracks. 'Legend Of Xanadu', a cover of Dave Dee, Dozy, Beaky, Mick and Tich's 1968 number one, was The Fall's contribution to the 1992 *NME* 40th anniversary charity album, *Ruby Trax*.[217] 'Xanadu' is a more successful charity contribution than 'A Day In The Life', although it does feel a little carelessly tossed off, and while you don't go to The Fall for melodic crooning, Smith is woefully tuneless. It was never played live. 'Noel's Chemical Effluence', a studio outtake, also featured on 1995's semi-live *The "Twenty-Seven Points"* (see Chapter 19).

Evaluation

Whereas *Shift-Work* flirted with contemporary indie-dance crossover approaches, *Code: Selfish* embraced them fully. Although 'So What About It?' and 'The Mixer' made clear use of Dave Bush's 'machines', they were generally traditionally structured songs that were flavoured with a spot of electronics. Several songs on *Code*, however, are clearly constructed via the 'programming in Dave's home studio' approach. When this comes off – most notably with 'Free Range' – it gives the group an impressive contemporary bite. At other times, however, it falls into shapeless grooves like 'Dangerous'. That said, overall *Code: Selfish* was a clear improvement on its predecessor: the songs were more carefully constructed and there's a much greater sense of invention and vitality.

---

[217] On which the group found themselves nestled between the unlikely pairing of Cud's version of Status Quo's 'Down Down' and Sinéad O'Connor's take on Doris Day's 'Secret Love'.

THE FALL:

THE INFOTAINMENT SCAN

The Infotainment Scan
Recorded: Suite 16, Rochdale, late 1992 / early 1993
Released: 26th April 1993

Personnel:
Mark E Smith – vocals
Craig Scanlon – guitar
Steve Hanley – bass
Simon Wolstencroft – drums
Dave Bush – keyboards

Chapter 16: The Infotainment Scan

'Balti and Vimto and Spangles were always crap.'

The Fall played 13 gigs in March 1992 to promote *Code: Selfish*. The support act was Levitation, the band formed by guitarist Terry Bickers following his departure from The House of Love. They didn't last long, leaving the tour after only three dates, alleging that it was 'impossible to work under Smith's oppressive regime'. MES countered that the band had taken up to an hour and a half soundchecking and were using too much dry ice. One of the replacement acts on the rest of the tour was the as-yet unsigned Suede. The second date, at Nottingham Polytechnic on 15th March, was released in 1998 as *Nottingham '92*. A crystal-clear soundboard recording with just a few moments of imbalance, it captures the group in top form. There are several highlights and moments of interest: 'It's a bit like James' (Smith's introduction to 'Free Range'); the vivacious rendition of 'Married, 2 Kids' (its first performance); Smith's weary disparagement of 'Immortality' ('I'm already fed up with this, it sounds like Italian disco, let's wrap it up'); plus a stomping version of 'New Big Prinz', joyful, fresh and forceful, despite this being its 64th performance in four years. After 15 European dates in May and June, The Fall made their first Glastonbury festival appearance, where they played an impressively tight 12-song set. Smith introduced final song 'Birmingham' with, 'We're supporting the Levellers. Marvellous, in't it?' (although The Levellers actually played the day before).

Towards the end of the year, the group headed to old haunt Suite 16 to record the follow up to *Code: Selfish*. By now, the down-at-heel Cargo had been transformed into a clean, modern and well-appointed studio courtesy of owner Peter Hook. Early sessions found Smith in tetchy mood. This was at least partly explained by the fact that Phonogram, worried about the commercial viability of its artists in the uncertain financial climate,[218] had demanded to hear regular demos with which to monitor the group's progress with the new album.

> I was fuckin' haywire, me... How dare you fuckin'... The A&R guy on fuckin' holiday in fuckin' India or summat. So I rang that jerk and I go, 'We've given you three fuckin' Top 30 LPs in three fuckin' years, and this fuckin' kid who's fuckin' just come out of fuckin' business school wants fuckin' demo tapes of The Fall!' And he goes, 'Man, it's the recession, mate...'

In November, Phonogram announced abruptly that they were terminating their relationship with The Fall: 'Both parties felt the relationship had gone as far as it could, but we wish them every success in the future.' MES broke the news to the rest of the group in the pub during a lunchtime break from recording, as Steve Hanley recalled: '"We don't need them," he says, clearly relieved to be sharing all this. "We can finish recording this ourselves."' As the label had reneged on its commitment to release the group's records in America, a substantial settlement was negotiated.[219] Despite the benefits of being signed to a major label, there was always a sense that Phonogram didn't really 'get' The Fall ('that awkward Northern band', as Steve Hanley put it). Smith had increasingly felt uncomfortable with his loss of control over the group's affairs. The break with Phonogram won him back that control, put money in the bank, and – to judge by the recording session that followed the lunchtime announcement – rejuvenated him in the studio:

> 'I've got a new one,' says Mark. 'Operation mindfuck. Craig. That guitar. Do it backwards and stalk across it. It's a curse...' And he's back.

Smith's next move was to sign a deal with Permanent Records – a small label, but one that had a distribution deal with BMG,

---

[218] Factory Records, for example, declared bankruptcy in November 1992.
[219] It was never officially released, but sources put it anywhere between £20,000 and £120,000.

one of the world's largest music companies. In addition, it was run by John Lennard, a promoter whose relationship with the group dated back to 1985.[220] The first product of this deal was the 'Why Are People Grudgeful?' single, released on 5th April 1993. It was a cover (of sorts), based on two different songs – 'People Grudgeful' by Joe Gibbs and 'People Funny Boy' by Lee Perry – although it also sounds a little like a recycling of the riff from 'Kurious Oranj'. It was played live 39 times, its last performance coming in January 1994. The B-sides on the various versions included 'Lost In Music' and 'Glam-Racket' (like other recent singles, alternative versions of album tracks with only minor differences) and 'The Re-Mixer'. 'Grudgeful' improved on the disappointing sales of 'Ed's Babe', reaching a respectable number 43 in the charts.

In February 1993, the group recorded their 16th Peel session. For only the third time, it featured the same line-up as the previous one. Three of the four songs recorded had been debuted on stage towards the end of 1992, although they only had 11 appearances between them. 'Service' wouldn't be played until May, and only stayed on the setlist for a brief period. The version here is distinctly soporific. 'Strychnine' (a cover of a 1965 track by The Sonics) is more successful, a heads-down, no-nonsense slice of garage-punk. The group played it live 148 times over the next 20 years, but never made another studio recording of the song. 'Paranoia Man's intense urgency is no less effective than the album version, but the pick of the bunch is the 'scuffed-up' version of 'Ladybird (Green Grass)'.

The Infotainment Scan

The majority of production duties at Suite 16 were undertaken by Rex Sargeant, assisted by Simon Rogers and Smith himself. Sargeant was the studio engineer and was somewhat surprised to be promoted to producer. He was quick to identify a pattern to The Fall's recording routine: turn up at lunchtime, go to the pub five minutes later, return after a couple of hours and then 'they'd... set everything up properly and start on a piece of music,

[220] As well as promoting some Fall gigs and providing management advice, he acted as Brix's personal manager in the late 80s.

write a really good tune, then Mark'd come in, get his spanner out, throw it in the works, then a bit of fire in the studio, a bit of hostility, a bit of war... and then they'd come out with a killer tune'.

The album's title referred to Smith's distaste for the media's obsession with turning everything into a form of entertainment: 'cheap thrills masquerading as hard news or information'. It was his disdain for nostalgia, however, that formed the central theme of the LP. Pascal Le Gras once again provided the artwork, which has a pugnacious, vivid feel that sits well with an album that finds the group on such coherent and forceful form.

Ladybird (Green Grass)
A punchy opener, driven by a crunchy Scanlon riff. The lyrics were at least partly inspired by that ubiquitous rock'n'roll topic, the Thirty Years' War. The German version of the 'ladybird, ladybird fly away home' nursery rhyme referred to in the song is thought to be about the 17th-century conflict. Fought between 1618 and 1648, the war saw the deaths of around half of the population of Pomerania ('Pomerania is burning down'). The song opens with a potent drum/bass combination, the guitar not joining in until Smith does. This was also the case when it was played live:

> During live gigs around this period, Craig did the same thing – i.e. didn't start playing until MES's vocals started – perhaps he was ordered to do it this way. This led to comical occurrences when MES was in full-on 'do anything but sing' mode, and on more than one occasion, Craig would have to stand patiently for a couple of minutes waiting to start playing whilst MES wrestled with microphone stands, rifled through lyric sheets, looked for missing microphones, wandered off for a ciggy, etc.

'Ladybird' was a frequent feature of setlists at the time, being played 69 times in just over two years.

Lost In Music

When the group were asked to contribute to the *NME*'s charity compilation *Ruby Trax*, this was the other song that was in the running before they decided on 'Legend Of Xanadu'. Possibly the ultimate Fall 'crossover' song, it has probably been included on thousands of mixtapes/compilation CDs by Fall fans trying to gently introduce non-believers into the wonderful and frightening world. The collision of Rodgers and Edwards's slinky funk and The Fall's angular dissonance makes for an intriguing mix, and whilst it does sound a little dated now, there's something enduringly charming about it. It reprises Smith's use of 'ten-to-five' from 'Shift-Work'. A popular live choice 1993-94, with 48 outings, but no later revivals.

Glam-Racket

Among the most aptly named of all Fall songs. Like 'New Big Prinz' it sees the group adopt a Glitter Band-style stomp, and the whole thing bustles along with strident energy. Whilst the main structure of the song is made up of a fairly traditional four-chord sequence, Smith counters this with a largely melody-free series of declamations. There's an amusingly disparaging tone throughout. 'You post out sixty-page computer printouts on the end of forests' is about Sting: 'What made me laugh was Sting's concept album,' Smith explained, 'it had a book in it about how hard it was for him to write the LP, and how concerned he was about the rainforest on 20 pages of this expensive quality paper made out of loads of trees.' The lines 'you are bequeathed in suede / you are entrenched in suede' led some to believe that this was a reference to Brett Anderson and co. (given that they had supported The Fall in 1992 and demonstrated distinctly glam influences). Smith dismissed this notion in typically withering fashion: 'If you've got a job in the media, say in videos, you wear suede shoes and a suede jacket. They all do. The song has got fuck all to do with the group Suede, and they shouldn't flatter themselves to think it is.' Steve Hanley felt that at least some of the words were about him, including the opening line, 'Stop eating all that chocolate; eat salad instead',[221] which was possibly inspired by Smith giving the bassist a bar of Dairy Milk in the studio. 'How is it even possible,' Hanley asked incredulously, 'to take health tips from a man who, in all the years I've known him, I've never once seen eat a vegetable, unless you count pickled onions?' It's a joyful tune; one that pulls together a whole heap of influences and squeezes them into a bouncing, effervescent yet cynical tour de force. Not surprisingly, it had a long live shelf-life – 86 outings 1992-97.

I'm Going To Spain

Steve Bent was an actor who appeared on a variety of British soaps, including *Crossroads*, *Coronation Street* and *Eastenders*. In 1976, he entered *New Faces*,[222] performing 'I'm Going To Spain', which described his desire to emigrate and escape from his boring factory job. The song (which included such memorable lines as, 'the factory floor presented me with some tapes of Elton John / they wrapped me up some sandwiches / and I hate them, yes I hate the cheese and pickle') would later appear on the Kenny Everett-compiled *The World's Worst Record Show*.[223] Steve Hanley commented that Smith 'always had a good knack for finding obscure tracks to cover'. The Fall's version comes close to achieving the touching fragility they seem to be aiming for, although Smith's groping for the already vapid melody is not for the faint-hearted. Perhaps surprisingly, it was played live 51 times. Most of its performances were in 1992-97, but it also reappeared three times in 2000, once in 2003 (see Chapter 24) before getting a final outing in 2010.

It's A Curse

Taut and focused, the guitar sound is full and heavy on the

---

[221] This phrase echoes a line in Roald Dahl's *George's Marvellous Medicine*: 'And stop eating chocolate. Eat cabbage instead.'

[222] 1970s ITV talent show, a precursor to *X-Factor* and *Britain's Got Talent*. Famous winners included Lenny Henry, Victoria Wood and *Catchphrase*'s Roy Walker.

[223] Other songs on the 1978 compilation included Tub Thumper's novelty glam cover of 'Kick Out The Jams', Ferlin Husky's 1954 single 'The Drunken Driver' ('Get out of the road yer little fools!') and the insane screamo-skiffle of 'Paralyzed' by the Legendary Stardust Cowboy (an inspiration for Ziggy Stardust).

distortion, but the choppy style makes it distinct and powerful; there's a nice contrast with the ghostly keyboards echoing in the background. Smith is at his scornful best, channelling his contempt towards 'look back bores' who get a hammering for their 'long egg breath', 'cheap shaving lotion' and 'froglike chins'. It's the first of three songs on the album to use Spangles (a brand of boiled sweets manufactured by Mars from the 50s–80s and staple of TV nostalgia shows) as shorthand for this kind of lazy sentimentality. The venomous enunciation of 'mindfuck' is a treat, and Smith delivered few lines better than 'I do not like your tone, it has ephemeral whinging aspects'. 'Trying to get over' is lifted from Curtis Mayfield's 'Superfly'. 'Curse' was only played live seven times, all in 1993.

Paranoia Man In Cheap Sh*t Room
A depiction of the desperation of the male mid-life crisis ('when girls pass, puts head down, in the street') with an oppressive and anxious atmosphere created by Wolstencroft's clattering drums, and Scanlon's fizzing, looping guitar – both of which blend seamlessly with Bush's array of electronics (which includes a reprise for the Tardis-like noise that introduces 'Lost In Music'). Smith's clipped, dispassionate delivery forms an ideal counterpoint to the frenetic music behind him. Lyrically, he may well have been inspired once again by an episode of *The Twilight Zone*: *Nervous Man in a 4 Dollar Room* (originally broadcast in 1960) concerned a small-time crook who gets embroiled in an argument with his own reflection in a hotel mirror. Spangles get another mention. 'Paranoia' was played 19 times, 1992–95.

Service
After two urgent and intense numbers, 'Service' drops the tempo, deploying a languid house-style piano motif that bears a passing resemblance to The Smiths' 'Oscillate Wildly'. MES adopts a rather conversational style, and there's a vague sense of melancholy and regret in lines like 'they sit rotting, the leaves / kick the brown branches' and 'one who laughs at nothing / and I'm just in between' – although the lyric is harder to interpret than

most of the others here. Repeated refrain 'this day's portion' was likely inspired by a line from Arthur Machen's autobiography[224] although it could also be a biblical reference. It's also the third Fall song to mention wolverines. 'Service' was only played 11 times, all in 1993.

The League Of Bald-Headed Men

Driven by an insistent guitar riff that resembles Led Zeppelin's 'Misty Mountain Hop', 'League' sees Smith focusing on the ageing nature of the group's fanbase: 'All he'd see was bald heads in the crowd,' Ben Pritchard[225] commented, 'That was the thing, you know – he got a bit sick and tired of it.' The title may have been inspired by Conan Doyle's *The Adventure of the Red-Headed League*, which, in Japanese, was translated as *The Bald-Headed League*. It was played 35 times 1992-94.

A Past Gone Mad

Containing yet another reference to Spangles, 'Past' is a further dig at nostalgia. In an interview with *Select*, Smith expanded on his contempt for 'look back bores' –

> There's a lot of fellas in this country who won't grow up... 'A Past Gone Mad' is like, you turn on the telly or listen to the radio and it's all '60s music or '70s music. And they go, It's because they don't make the tunes the same anymore... people in charge want to wallow in their past... really good groups just got an LP out get three lines, and then you get three pages on who Yes' drummers were.

This challenge to complacent nostalgia strikes its target with force. The contrast between the frantic electronica and drum and bass rhythm and the sweepingly epic guitar line is carefully balanced; MES's lethargic, cynical drawl sits on top of it all with casual indifference. It includes the striking line 'If I ever end up

---

[224] 'I lounged on the stile and waited, and when the postman came I would give him my packet – the day's portion of "copy" of that Heptameron translation that I was then making and sending to the publisher in York Street, Covent Garden.'
[225] Fall guitarist 2001-6. See Chapter 22.

like Ian McShane slit my throat with a kitchen tool'.[226] Played 54 times, 1993-2000.

Light/Fireworks
The inevitable experimental / piss-take / filler track is on this occasion deployed as the closer (on the vinyl version anyway). It gives the impression of being the off-cuts from five or six different abandoned songs casually stitched together, including a concluding section taken from 'Legend Of Xanadu'.

Reviews and Reissues
Few of the reviews, as Simon Ford notes, 'picked up on the album's intended social critique. The overriding response was one of surprise at the music's new accessibility.' *Melody Maker's* Dave Jennings in particular seemed to miss the point: '*The Infotainment Scan* is the most light-hearted Fall album ever, the concentrated vitriol of the past replaced by good-humoured piss-taking.' Stephen Dalton of the *NME* thought that 'musically, this album sees The Fall wound up a notch or ten beyond *Code: Selfish...* itchy techno beats and incidental burble underpin most tracks, and a palpable sense of bullish disquiet... pervades the finest moments here'. *The Independent's* Ben Thompson described it as 'a record that even those who've never liked them would be hard pressed not to fall for...'

Despite the move to a smaller label, *Infotainment* achieved the group's highest ever chart placement, reaching the heady heights of number nine – a position they would never come close to attaining again. Smith felt vindicated by his decision to leave Phonogram: 'I think that it's the clearest thing we've done. You can hear everything, you know? I was pleased because we walked out of Phonogram and I thought, "Sod it. I'll do it myself, pay for it myself."'

The CD version contained two bonus tracks, 'Why Are People Grudgeful?' and 'League Moon Monkey Mix', the latter

[226] At the group's Doncaster gig in March 2000, Smith amended the lyric to target Stewart Lee, who had recently compiled and written the liner notes for the compilation album *A Past Gone Mad*: 'If I ever end up like an alternative comedian cut my throat with a garden tool.'

being a quirky but forgettable electro-remix of 'The League Of Bald-Headed Men'. Like the previous few albums, *Infotainment* received a double CD reissue, this one coming in 2006. The bonus disc contained contemporary radio sessions plus the tracks from the 'Grudgeful' single. It also featured an assortment of outtakes, demos and alternative versions, most of which are vaguely interesting if far from essential. The shambolic, folky 'Instrumental Outtake' is an interesting little curiosity, but there's no real need for three more versions of 'Lost In Music', although 'Mix 14' is enjoyably woozy and spacey.

Evaluation

The reassertion of the group's autonomy brought about by the departure from Phonogram is reflected strongly throughout *Infotainment*. There's a palpable sense of renewed strength, the group wrestling back control of its destiny and its essence. The album contains more consistent songwriting, more considered and inventive arrangements and more clearly expressed and thought-provoking sentiments than at any time since the 80s. In particular, Smith seems to have a lot more to say (and many interesting ways of saying it) than he had done for a while. His view of nostalgia and 'look-back-bore'-ism finds its voice with clarity and coherence. It's not the complex lyricism of *Hex* or *Grotesque* – it doesn't have the younger man's vitriol and relentless energy – but it's certainly from the same gene pool.

THE FALL

MIDDLE CLASS
REVOLT

Middle Class Revolt
Recorded: The Windings Studio, Wrexham; Suite 16, Rochdale, late 1993 / early 1994
Released: 3rd May 1994

Personnel:
Mark E Smith – vocals
Craig Scanlon – guitar, spoken vocal on 'Symbol Of Mordgan'
Steve Hanley – bass
Simon Wolstencroft – drums
Dave Bush – keyboards
Karl Burns – drums, guitar, vocals, kazoo

With:
John Peel, vocal on 'Symbol Of Mordgan'

Chapter 17: Middle Class Revolt

'We just went in and made it up in the studio.'

The Fall's May 1993 UK tour saw Karl Burns make his third return to The Fall, albeit to provide 'percussion' rather than as an extra drummer. Unsurprisingly, Simon Wolstencroft was not impressed ('I didn't like the sound of this at all'), echoing Paul Hanley's concerns back in 1981. Steve Hanley was not entirely enthusiastic about his old comrade's return either: 'What do we need a percussionist for when Si's our drummer and Dave's got enough effects to make it sound like a hundred people are playing percussion?' Hanley was also sceptical about the circumstances leading to Burns's re-recruitment (which MES had claimed resulted from a chance encounter in Prestwich), the bassist feeling that Smith's motivation was more about having an ally in the group. If Burns really had only been hired for extra percussion, Wolstencroft was determined to keep it that way. 'It is very difficult for two people to drive the band without being telepathic. We weren't, and I wanted to drive.' Burns was relegated to playing an electronic percussion device called an Octopad, which he described as 'a fucking Dalek's handbag'. Hanley was not convinced that this added a great deal to the group's sound, describing the new percussionist's contributions as 'a range of electronic drum sounds a clockwork monkey could produce'. Burns was determined to secure a more substantial role, gradually increasing the amount of kit he had with him on stage. He was successful, at least in the short term: 'Come July, Karl is infiltrating our cosy songwriting sessions,' noted Hanley, 'by August, he's coming to America.'

The American tour in the summer of 1993 was a gruelling one, involving greater distances than any of the group's previous excursions to the States – 20 dates in a month, and in excess of 9000 miles travelled. The funding for the tour was provided by Matador records, who had released *The Infotainment Scan* in the USA. Matador, who had recently gone into partnership with Atlantic, had only been set up in 1989, but had a big hit in 1992 with Pavement's heavily Fall-influenced debut *Slanted And Enchanted*. Smith was famously disparaging of the band: 'They say imitation is the sincerest form of flattery, but I don't hold with that. I feel sorry for them, actually. I don't get mad, I just can't see the point of forming a group if you're imitating someone else, it's like, get a life, man. Get a real job!' By now, Burns had got his wish, and there were two full drum kits on stage. This double-drummer line-up was not entirely successful in recapturing the magic of the early 80s: 'More competition than complement,' described Hanley, 'they're not gelling, they're working against each other.' This problem was soon resolved, at least temporarily. After the Chicago gig on 28th August, Burns trashed his hotel room, leaving Smith to foot the bill. A furious MES gave the drummer his marching orders.[227]

After their gig at the Hollywood Roxy on 7th September, The Fall received a visit from Kurt Cobain. Accompanied by Courtney Love, Cobain asked to join the group on their tour bus but was denied entry. It's not clear who turned them away: Hanley says it was him, Wolstencroft says it was Smith. Cobain was possibly intending to offer The Fall some support slots on Nirvana's planned 1994 European tour. Given Smith's thoughts on the tour-bus incident and the American grunge scene in general, it seems unlikely he would have accepted:

> ...all those American bands, Pearl Jam and Nirvana are dead into The Fall. Nirvana tried to get into our bus, Courtney whatshername, the actress, tried it and we pushed her off... they're nothing more than glorified longhair guitar salesmen, y'know. Fucking idiots playing pub rock. Aye, pub rock, that's what it is. If they were English you wouldn't put up with it.

[227] Simon Wolstencroft suggests that Burns was actually sacked after an argument with MES about wages, but both Steve Hanley and Simon Ford support the hotel room version. Hanley also says that Smith told the troublesome drummer that he was sacked 'from the tour' rather than from the group.

As the group played their way across the UK, America and Europe during the latter half of 1993, the main talking point about the group was becoming not the line-up or the music, but Smith's increasingly erratic and difficult behaviour. Not that this represented an overnight personality change, but the unpredictability seemed to have increased substantially, as had the frequency of the incidents both on and off stage. During the 28th August gig in Chicago, he smashed up Dave Bush's keyboards – apparently not feeling it was at all hypocritical to then dismiss Burns for his misdemeanours later that same night. A tour manager walked out after Smith threw a pint glass at his head; Bush had hot tea thrown over him as he slept; Wolstencroft was hit in the back of the head by a beer bottle thrown by the irate singer. As the drummer noted, 'Mark's disdain for people was becoming worse. He drank more and charmed less.' Smith's behaviour wasn't just alienating many of the people he worked with – it was starting to have a noticeable effect on the quality of the music. His on-stage antics, such as stopping and starting songs, frequently wandering off stage and berating the band mid-set led Hanley to comment that 'each night involves struggle in some form or other'. This had not gone unnoticed by the music press. Chris Roberts's review of the group's 7th May Manchester performance in *Melody Maker* noted that Smith spoiled their rendition of 'Lost In Music' because he didn't 'even bother to recite the words, just sort of mumbles whatever here and there if anywhere, and deliberately neutralises the song's dance dynamic... because of this wilful perversity, this Fall show isn't as inspiring as it should be'. He went on to describe Smith's behaviour as 'dated, dreary and undignified'. After a London gig in October, *NME*'s Johnny Cigarettes described Smith as a man who had 'started to believe his own press' and accused the group of having 'settled into a terminally workmanlike R&B rumble, with the dynamics and spark removed'. A few months later, he observed Smith shoving an *NME* photographer and tipping a bag of expensive equipment over his head. 'The gig that follows is a rambling, disinterested splatter through the set. Mark is obviously rat-arsed far beyond the call of duty.'

The Fall closed 1993 with a Peel session and a new single. Unprecedentedly, as Burns's temporary dismissal meant that he wasn't present, the 17th session was the third successive one by the same line-up. They recorded four tracks from the forthcoming *Middle Class Revolt*: 'Behind The Counter' and 'M5' both have more vitality than their album counterparts; 'Hey! Student' is also lively, and contains the startling line 'masturbating with your Shaun Ryder face'; 'Reckoning', however, is disappointingly flat and listless.

The 'Behind The Counter' single was released on four different formats (two CD singles and two 12"s) over two weeks in December. Of the five different songs that appeared on the various versions, three (the lead song, 'War' and 'M5') would appear on *Middle Class Revolt*, albeit – as was now becoming customary – in the form of slightly different edits/mixes. 'Cab Driver' was reworked as 'City Dweller' on the LP. This earlier version is much looser in structure than the album take. The vocals, such as they are, mainly consist of multi-tracked samples of Smith and others muttering unintelligibly a fair way back in the mix. All that's easily distinguishable is the rather disturbing growling whisper: 'He's in there now, man: he's listening right to us, I know he is.' 'Happy Holiday' is the only song that's unique to these singles. A disconcertingly jolly piece, it's saved from being too bland by some gently discordant sections and a mixture of unusual spoken contributions, including a Scottish-accented voice (probably Burns) extolling the virtues of lamb, chicken and feta cheese. The Greek dialogue at the beginning is a translation of the opening lines of 'English Scheme'; 'Hanley... it's not right' is a sample from *The Twilight Zone*.[228] 'Holiday' was played live seven times in 1993-94, although one was an instrumental and another lasted less than a minute. Despite all the promotional efforts, 'Behind The Counter' only reached number 75 in the singles chart.

A couple of months before *Middle Class Revolt*'s release, Smith made his one and only appearance on *Top of the Pops*; not with The Fall, but with Inspiral Carpets. 'I Want You' peaked at number

[228] 'The Brain Center at Whipple's' (1964) concerns a factory owner obsessed by replacing workers with machines. Hanley is the factory manager.

18 in the charts in March 1994. Arguably the Oldham band's best single, it's a thrilling blast of Madchester-flavoured 60s garage punk, well suited by Smith's inimitable distorted contributions. The band, all Fall fans, had contacted Smith, fully expecting to be rejected; however, his response was 'get me a bottle of Pils and I'll be there in a minute'. Smith was at pains to explain to *Melody Maker* that 'he wouldn't normally do this kind of thing' (four years earlier, of course, he had declared that anyone who appeared on the programme was a 'ponce'), rather hypocritically stating that he was 'very down on working with other people', considering it to be 'fucking phoney'. He then went on to list a series of famous names that he claimed had requested his services, including David Bowie, Lou Reed, Boy George, John Cale, Dinosaur Jr. and – most incongruously – 80s pop-soul outfit The Blow Monkeys. The *TOTP* performance was sandwiched between a Michael Bolton video and Morrissey's 'The More You Ignore Me The Closer I Get'. Smith, clad in black leather, doesn't look entirely comfortable to begin with, almost as if he doesn't know where to place himself, unused to sharing the stage with another front man. He soon warms up though, even performing a little dance (of sorts) at one point. Inspiral's singer Tom Hingley keeps his eyes glued to the front, seemingly having to concentrate hard in order not to be put off by Smith's melodic waywardness when they sustain the final note in the title refrain together. Not for the first or last time, MES avails himself of a written reminder of the lyrics, just as he had done in the official video. Entertainingly, he was later to be castigated for this by the young viewers of Saturday morning's *Live And Kicking*.

The second single taken from *Middle Class Revolt* was released a few weeks before the album. As was the case with previous singles, '15 Ways' was a (very slightly) different edit from the album version. The two B-sides, 'Hey! Student' and 'The $500 Bottle Of Wine' would both appear on the LP. The promotional device this time was a 10" version on clear vinyl. Once again, this made little impact, '15 Ways' only managing ten places higher than 'Behind The Counter'.

Middle Class Revolt

The recording sessions for The Fall's next album began in late 1993 at The Windings Studio in Wrexham. This was news to Simon Wolstencroft, who, having just returned from holiday, discovered via Steve Hanley's wife Heather that the group had gone into the studio without him. The drummer's mood was not improved when he arrived in Wrexham to discover Karl Burns playing on his kit, although by this stage the group had only recorded one song ('Hey! Student'). The album was finished off at Suite 16. Rex Sargeant once again supplied the production. *Middle Class Revolt* (subtitled 'aka The Vapourisation of Reality') was the fourth consecutive album to feature the artwork of Pascal Le Gras.

15 Ways

The opening serves as a misleading tease, giving us 20 or so seconds of Dave Bush-style lo-fi indie-techno crossover that suggests continuity from the dancier elements of the previous three albums. When the actual song arrives, however, it turns out to be a straightforward mid-tempo indie-jangle-strum with a conventional verse–chorus structure with echoes of R.E.M. and (whisper it) Pavement. Smith's vocal is fairly straight too, an earnest if slurred attempt to follow a recognisable melody. Lyrically, its reference points are twofold: as well as those superficial 'analyse your life/relationship' quizzes in *Cosmopolitan* et al, it also parodies Paul Simon's '50 Ways To Leave Your Lover'. Its weary ennui may also reflect the beginnings of the deterioration in Smith and Saffron Prior's relationship. It was played live 44 times 1993-97 and got ten further revivals – half a dozen on the 2004 US tour and the rest in 2013.

The Reckoning

First played as part of the December 1993 Peel session, the track had gained a definite article by the time it appeared on the album. The opening line, 'I phoned you up from Dallas' ('I followed you from Dallas' on the Peel session) may have been inspired by the country standard, 'My Elusive Dreams'. The 'wandering' tone of the lyric ('I'm left alone in Europe, consulting an atlas') certainly seems to echo the sentiments of the C&W standard.[229] Brix claimed that two of the songs on the album were about her, and so it's possible that the character being addressed is her. This, however, would mean that the 'hippy half-wit, who thinks he's Mr Mark Smith'[230] with whom she's sleeping is Nigel Kennedy, and it's a bit of a stretch to imagine the spiky-haired violinist as a hippy. An alternative explanation is that the song resulted from Smith's relationship with Lori Kramer of US bands The Pendulum Floors and Paper Squares. 'On one of his records he wrote a song for me,' Kramer said, 'he talked about our thing. And I wrote a song back, on our record, called "Dallas". We were in Dallas together.'

Introduced by a plaintive Scanlon arpeggio, 'The Reckoning' is gently bittersweet. Smith's vocals are laid-back, almost lazy, but have a certain understated bite to them. His oddly off-beat timing and phrasing give the whole thing a woozy, fuzzy tone which suits the whole 'sat at the end of the bar after closing time' vibe. Scanlon also contributes some nicely restrained layers of distorted fuzz that give the song a mellow, reflective feel. It was played 27 times, all in 1993-94.

Behind The Counter

Debuted in May 1993, 'Behind The Counter' has a swaggering, loose-limbed energy, reinforced by the regular staccato sections that make it buzz with momentum. The lyric might be written from the point of view of a poor shop worker ('I'm getting thin / From waiting on'), but it's hard to be sure. Smith's aside towards the end – 'chill it, boy' – is a little moment worth treasuring. One of the most long-standing songs in terms of live performances, it was played 126 times between 1993 and 2003.

---

[229] 'You had my child in Memphis, then I heard of work in Nashville / But we didn't find it there so we moved on to a small farm in Nebraska, to a gold mine in Alaska / We didn't find it there so we moved on'. The song was recorded by, amongst others, Tammy Wynette, The Everly Brothers and Nancy Sinatra/Lee Hazlewood.

[230] '*Mrs* Mark Smith' on the Peel version.

M5#1

Like 'Reckoning', this track underwent a slight title change between its single and album appearance, gaining a '#1'. The contrast between urban and rural life ('it's an evil roundabout that leads to the haywain / and you'll never see good trains again') finds Smith equating 'crusty brown bread' with life out in the sticks. The song, Mick Middles felt, was 'carved direct from tedium... from the tedium of being trapped, on tour, surging down another godforsaken motorway or... standing in hideous coned gridlock'. A driving, forceful track, it is let down a little by the messy production. It was a popular live choice at the time, played 90 times 1993-97.

Surmount All Obstacles

Like several other tracks on *Middle Class Revolt*, 'Surmount All Obstacles' has a dense, muddy sound, but in this case it suits the oppressive nature of the track. There's not much of an actual *song*; it's really just a groove over which Smith growls enigmatically ('you must retreat into mysticism to find an origination'). There's a certain unrehearsed and undeveloped feel to the track, but its belligerent strangeness helps it to get away with it. It was only played live 11 times, all in 1994; it was also used as an intro tape in 1998.

Middle Class Revolt!

The title track has many of the right ingredients: the combination of Wolstencroft's busy clatter, Bush's hypnotic sequencer and Scanlon's hyperactive guitar ought to produce one of those thrilling rock/electronic hybrids like 'Free Range' or 'Paranoia Man'. Two factors prevent it from doing so. Firstly, the production reduces the dense layers of guitar, keyboard and percussion into an indistinct sludge; secondly, Smith's apathetic delivery gives the song a weary, jaded tone. As a result, his potentially interesting attempt to pick apart the pretensions of the middle class ('exhumes the cooked pigeon / his words indignant because it was cooked wrong') is lost amongst the murk. Simon Wolstencroft hated it, bemoaning the fact that the group 'hadn't learned it properly' but were instructed by Smith to 'just get on with it'. Bootleg recordings of its 22 performances show that, like *Shift-Work*'s title track, it was a much more satisfying proposition live.

War

A cover version of a Henry Cow / Slapp Happy song that was constructed from Smith's memory because nobody could find the original at the time.[231] As a result, it bears little resemblance to the original, but it's still a strident, aggressive piece, featuring some disturbing chanting, underlying distortion and a guitar line that's distinctly reminiscent of Martha and the Muffins' 'Echo Beach'. One of the more successful covers. Played live 48 times, all in 1993-94.

You're Not Up To Much

A simple, looping guitar figure played with the album's signature lightly distorted jangle guitar sound gives 'Up To Much' a determined feel. There's something both uplifting and melancholy about the chord changes (e.g. at 0:33) where Smith strains to get to grips with the melody. It's a gently bitter lyric, and the fashion references – 'too much Warehouse shop / too many fancy hats / clothes imitation' – suggest that it could be the other song that Brix thought was about her. It was only played live 11 times, all in 1994.

Symbol Of Mordgan

The inevitable experimental moment starts off interestingly enough, with some flicking through radio frequencies in the style of Pink Floyd's 'Wish You Were Here'. Thereafter, the majority of the track consists of a faint, tinny surf-rock instrumental[232] overlaid with a football-related conversation between Craig Scanlon and John Peel. A few other odds and sods are thrown in: some random cuts and reverse-play sections, unidentified incidental film/TV music, Scanlon discussing the existence of

---

[231] Henry Cow was an early-70s experimental outfit formed by Fred Frith and Tim Hodgkinson; Slapp Happy were an Anglo-German avant-garde group fronted by Dagmar Krause; the two groups merged briefly in the mid-70s. 'War' is from the 1975 album *In Praise of Learning*.
[232] It has been suggested that this is Ohio Express' 1968 US hit 'Yummy Yummy Yummy', but I can't hear it myself.

God on an American radio phone-in[233] and what sounds like a snippet of Lou Reed's *Metal Machine Music*. Despite all of this, it's one of the group's duller experimental tracks, and doesn't warrant its three minutes' length. It was never played live.

Hey! Student

Smith occasionally identified some soft targets (cf 'A Lot Of Wind') and this is a case in point. Castigating students for having long hair and wearing 'sneakers' (an oddly jarring Americanism) verges on the petulant. Smith expanded on his views regarding students in a December 1993 *NME* interview:

> It's just the rate of their proliferation that scares me. Have you seen how many people have gone back to school now? Dead weird, innit? It just keeps the unemployment figures down and produces millions of half-educated old coots. I've got nothing against students as such, it's just when you get old mates using words like 'constructively' and 'comprehensively'... It's all a fiddle to make us think they've cracked unemployment, the stupid bastards. There's nothing worse than a half-educated man. Never forget that.

Like 'Copped It' and 'Oh! Brother' nine years earlier, 'Student' saw the group resurrecting an old – *very* old by Fall standards – song, one that appeared on the *Live 1977* album (as 'Hey! Fascist'). Unlike the other two, however, 'Student' had not undergone any notable development over the intervening 17 years. Although it has a certain rickety energy, it still feels like that rare thing: The Fall looking to the past. It's hard to disagree with Simon Wolstencroft's verdict: 'a step backward, musically'. It was played live 28 times 1994-97, and was revisited eight times in 2000.

Junk Man

The album's second cover version, a take on The Groundhogs' track 'Junkman' from their 1971 album *Split*. There's a lurching

---

[233] The same clip was used at the beginning of 'Lucifer Over Lancashire': 'What I'm saying to you really, is that the training that you must have in discussion at your own level regarding the existence of God is far greater than everybody that's ringing you tonight.'

swagger to it, but the constant kazoo and Karl Burns's caveman backing vocals may be too much for some. It was never played live.

The $500 Bottle Of Wine

Like 'I'm Going To Spain', there's at least as much interest to be had from the back story (or, in this case, stories) as from the song itself. According to Steve Hanley, he met three goths after one of the gigs on the 1993 US tour, who explained that their dream was to be told to fuck off by The Fall; Hanley duly obliged. When the group arrived in Dallas, they found that the goths had sent them a bottle of red wine worth $500, which – lacking a corkscrew – they had to open with a drumstick. Brix's version involves her being given an expensive bottle of 1982 Pétrus by Craig Leon which Smith drank whilst she was away and declared it 'tasted shit'. Given that the group's tour bus repeatedly broke down on the way to Dallas, requiring them to push it for part of the way, the lyric itself ('drive through the desert in 36 hours / but when we get the ending we took / the 500 dollar bottle of wine') makes Hanley's account the more likely. The bassist works hard to provide funky vigour, and Smith's Elvis-like slur, 'get down the fucking liquor store boy' makes for an amusing conclusion. However, overall it's a slightly lazy piece of barroom blues with monotonous backing vocals. Another that was never performed live.

City Dweller

An update of 'Cab Driver' from the 'Behind The Counter' single. Based around a sweeping synth riff and underpinned by a simple, forceful bassline, it's sharper and more focused than its predecessor whilst retaining much of its trance-like qualities. Like 'M5#1', it reflects Smith's thoughts on urban life, perhaps even a sense of civic pride ('get out of my city you mediocre pseud') although there is also some scorn directed at Manchester's Olympic ambitions.[234] 'City Dweller' / 'Cab Driver' was only played live three times, all in December 1993.

[234] The city made unsuccessful bids to host the Olympic Games in 1992, 1996 and 2000.

Shut Up!
Whilst one might question the need for a third cover, the group's take on Monks' 1966 track is at least an interesting one. They transform the sparse and creepy original by packing it with layers of choppy guitar, swooping keyboards and wobbly, stuttering vocals; everything zooms randomly between channels which gives it an air of joyfully abandoned chaos. Smith in particular sounds like he's enjoying himself. Not exactly essential, but still fun. It's another that never made it onto a setlist.

Reviews and Reissues
Several members of the group did not rate the album highly. In his autobiography, Steve Hanley devotes only a single, non-committal sentence to it. Simon Wolstencroft thought it 'a botched job'. Reflecting on Smith's *Top of the Pops* performance, he said: 'Typical, I thought, we had this shit album and Mark was lending his hand to a more commercial sound for another band.' Brix called it 'tepid' and 'the nadir of the canon'. Dave Bush wasn't keen either: 'I wasn't happy with *Middle Class Revolt* because I had a smaller role and I never really listen to it now. We recorded the album in a week and we'd done no prior writing for it. We just went in and made it up in the studio. That was amazing really, even though it was a shit album.'

The music press received *Middle Class Revolt* in sympathetic if lukewarm fashion. In the *NME*, Ian McCann awarded it 7/10, although he qualified this by saying that this was 'by The Fall's standards', and that it would be 8/10 'by everyone else's'. He noted that there were 'signs that The Fall are pulling away from the techno-influenced looping of their two most recent albums', which would doubtless have had Dave Bush nodding ruefully. Overall, McCann thought *Middle Class Revolt* 'nothing special: we've been here before'. *The Boston Globe* enjoyed the album's 'caustic barbs and wry witticisms' and its 'expansive spread of crazy sound – grinding guitars, floating keys, relentless rhythms, giddy pop hooks, pounding percussion'. *The Washington Post*, however, felt that although 'Behind The Counter' and 'Junk Man' did 'achieve the band's characteristic clanking shuffle', it was 'counterproductive to polish up The Fall's rant'n'roll with clean keyboard riffs and a mild-mannered mix'. After the top ten placing of its predecessor, *Middle Class Revolt* only managed a mediocre number 48 in the album charts, the group's lowest placing since *I Am Kurious Oranj* six years earlier. It was, however, an achievement that was only to be bettered by four of their remaining fifteen albums.

Like *Infotainment Scan*, *Middle Class Revolt* received a 2-CD reissue in 2006. The bonus CD contained the December 1993 Peel session and the tracks from the 'Behind The Counter' and '15 Ways' singles. There was also a clutch of unenlightening remixes, including three versions of the album's title track. The 'Rex Sargeant mix' is a Mogadon-infused slouch and the other two are unremarkable Ibiza-trance retreads that haven't aged well.

Evaluation

At the time, *Middle Class Revolt* received a generally negative reaction from the group's fanbase because of its lack of new, original material. Apart from 'The Reckoning', 'Surmount All Obstacles', 'Middle Class Revolt', 'You're Not Up Too Much' and the throwaway 'Symbol Of Mordgan' (tracks which made up less than half of the album), everything else was either a cover version or previously released. This, alongside the messy production, gave the impression of inertia and a lack of inspiration.

Looking at the album retrospectively, however, it has probably suffered a little unjustly due to its circumstances. There are plenty of strong tracks here: 'Behind The Counter' is an energetic cracker; 'You're Not Up Too Much', 'City Dweller' and 'The Reckoning' all have mesmeric charm; 'Surmount All Obstacles' is admirably difficult and strange; 'M5#1' has a driven, sneering energy. Two of the three cover versions are inventive reimaginings too.

That said, the hurried, 'this'll do' approach to its recording is reflected by its muddy sound. There are several songs (the title track being a prime example) that sound as though they could have been a lot better with more time spent on them. It has fewer low points than the previous few albums, but also fewer high points. It's not a *bad* album by any means, but it feels flat and lacking in variety compared to many others. Not for the first (or last) time, the awarding of songwriting credits was both somewhat dubious and a signpost for the ever-shifting status of the musicians within the group. Neither Wolstencroft nor Bush got a single credit, which is unlikely to have been a completely fair reflection of the album's composition. In his autobiography, Wolstencroft notes that he and Smith were socialising less by this stage. Despite this, the drummer continued to be well regarded by MES and his role in the group seemed safe for the time being. Dave Bush, on the on the other hand, seemed to be falling out of favour, and his position looked increasingly insecure.

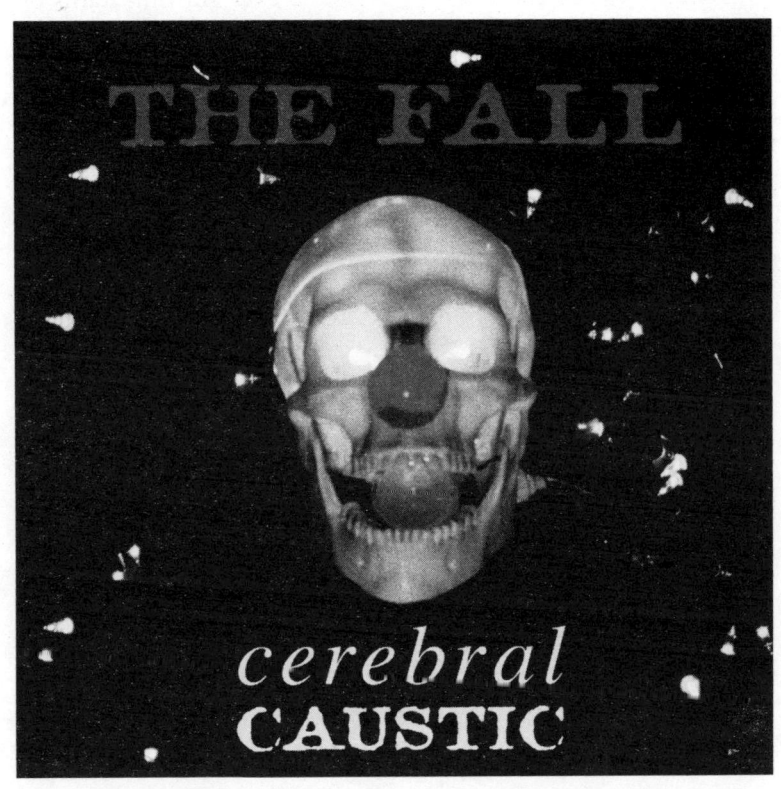

Cerebral Caustic
Recorded: The Pavilion, London, late 1994
Released: 27th February 1995

Personnel:
Mark E Smith – vocals
Brix Smith – guitar, vocals
Craig Scanlon – guitar
Steve Hanley – bass
Simon Wolstencroft – drums
Dave Bush – keyboards
Karl Burns – drums, guitar, vocals

With:
Lucy Rimmer – vocals ('Pearl City')

Chapter 18: Cerebral Caustic

'I think the possibilities are getting endless again.'

If Karl Burns's reappearance in the line-up the previous year had been a surprise, it seemed minor news in comparison to the sudden and unexpected return of Brix in 1994. In the first few years following her departure from the group, Brix had shunned writing or playing music altogether. She had become as well known for her relationship with celebrity violinist Nigel Kennedy as for her connection to The Fall. She had made a tentative return to the music world, playing with Susanna Hoffs of The Bangles and auditioning (unsuccessfully) for the bassist role in Courtney Love's band, Hole. Regarding her return to The Fall, Brix suggested in her book that Smith initiated the contact, but in a 1995 interview both his ('she called me up out of the blue') and her versions have it the other way round. It's hard to imagine the exact phrase that she ascribes to her ex-husband in her book ('please come back. We need you back in the band to kick ass.') actually coming out of Smith's mouth, but it does largely capture the spirit of his feelings:

> At the time, I was looking for a guitarist and arranger. I wanted either a really young kid or an old producer – someone to put some bite back into The Fall, to kick them all up the arse. When I told Brix, she immediately said she'd do it and got on a plane. I'd rather take a chance with someone I know than some smart-arsed kid who wants to be in Oasis.

Brix was shocked by the change in Smith's appearance ('he had aged decades'). Moreover, whilst she was pleased to be reunited with her old band mates (even Karl Burns) and took an immediate liking to Dave Bush, she soon identified that not all was well in the Fall camp. Craig Scanlon, in particular, she felt had 'lost his passion', an impression shared by Steve Hanley, who thought that his old friend was 'losing interest in playing the guitar'. Brix soon discovered that Smith's on-tour behaviour had not improved over the last five years. At the second gig after her return, in Edinburgh on 15th August, he punched both Karl Burns and a sound engineer (the latter for the crime of eating a sandwich at the mixing desk) and walked off stage so many times that many punters demanded their money back.[235]

In September, the group undertook a 15-date tour of North America. Brix described it as 'absolute misery'. Smith – having parked himself in a suite at the Gramercy Hotel – insisted on the group repeatedly travelling back to New York after gigs, despite the distances involved. In Rhode Island, he dragged the group off-stage after 20 minutes and threw a bottle at Dave Bush. He repeated the walk-off in Washington, although this time the group stayed where they were. Smith also alienated the road crew to such an extent (for example by having a gaffer tape boundary drawn out between the 'group' and 'crew' sections of the tour bus) that they flew home in disgust. These were the early days of mass use of the internet, and over the next few years the development of message boards, fan forums and file-sharing sites began to have a significant impact on the relationship between artists, fans and the media. During the 1994 US tour, the ramifications of this cultural shift were becoming apparent to Steve Hanley, who noted that fans sharing stories of Smith's 'nail-chewing, fag-smoking, obvious indifference' seemed to have a negative impact on ticket sales. The tour wasn't an entirely negative experience. Smith and Wolstencroft attended Barry White's fiftieth birthday party in a New York club where they encountered Lisa Stansfield, an old acquaintance of Smith who, the drummer recalls, 'stuck her tongue down [Smith's] throat'. The group also met the up-and-coming Oasis towards the end of the tour, Noel Gallagher apparently offering Wolstencroft a job – adding Oasis to the impressive list of bands that 'Funky Si' was *almost* in.

1994 also saw Smith's case against Trevor Long come to court. The hearing didn't start well for Smith when his designated

[235] The performance was cut short because the group had to vacate the stage by 10.30pm to make way for hypnotist Peter Powers.

taxi driver (Wolstencroft) was late picking him up due to being hungover from a Primal Scream gig the night before. Smith, possibly unwisely, represented himself.

> The judge threw the whole thing out of court on account of Mr Smith being unable to remember the evidence he had given in the morning and therefore contradicting it in the afternoon. 'Your life is a mess, Mr Smith!' declared the judge.

Inevitably, the MES version differs from other sources. According to him, his evidence wasn't heard properly in court (literally) because the microphone in front of him wasn't working, and the main reason that Long was acquitted was that Smith had 'quoted a figure of £1200 when the actual figure was £1215'.

The 18th Peel session saw Brix's first appearance at Maida Vale since 1988, and the return of a two-drummer line-up – last seen on the seventh session in 1983. It was also one of the briefest sessions, falling just short of the 11-minute mark. Recorded on 20th November and broadcast on 17th December, it found The Fall in festive mood, recording two Christmas-related songs. Sadly, neither of the Yuletide-related tunes are especially successful. Their version of 'Jingle Bell Rock', a 1957 hit for Bobby Helms, is a shambles, although at least, at 70 seconds, it doesn't outstay its welcome. Steve Hanley's account of the recording explains why it sounds as it does:

> It's my job to go into town and hunt down a copy of the original vinyl for us to work from, but I can only find a Chet Atkins version. When it's played in the studio, we realise I've gone and bought an instrumental. There's no lyrics at all except for the chorus, which is why Mark ends up singing that three times in a row. Somehow he manages to lace it with different nuances of meaning every time, until the last ten seconds when he can take no more and is forced into improvising lyrics about Brussels sprouts and green carrier bags on Oxford Street. Class. Just over a minute we manage to stretch it out to.

'Hark The Herald Angels Sing' starts off promisingly, with a laid-back R.E.M./Teenage Fanclub strum and Smith's entertainingly terse delivery. However, the chorus (sung by Lucy Rimmer in deliberately over-the-top operatic style), although hilarious the first couple of times you hear it, is enough to set anyone's teeth on edge after a short while. Thankfully, the other two tracks are much better. In one of the rare occasions where the group revisited an old song (although in this case it was less than two years old) they recorded an exuberant romp through 'Glam-Racket', which on this occasion included Brix's 'Star' section. The extra lyrics on this version, which had appeared in the group's shows since Brix's return, are a not-even-thinly-disguised swipe at Smith's egotism (possibly her retaliation for 'Bad News Girl'):

> You say that you're a star but I don't give a fuck
> I watch your head expanding as you're running out of luck.

Whether Smith didn't realise or didn't care is unclear. What is certain, though, is that Brix's vehement vocals (although, not unreasonably, she ducks out of saying 'fuck' at 2:06) make for an excellent version. 'Numb At The Lodge' (the original title of 'Feeling Numb') is a spirited, poppy thrash, its ragged energy making it preferable to the album version.

The Fall rounded off 1994 with five UK dates in November and December. After taking a couple of months off, they played London's Forum (March 10th), and then four nights (19th-22nd) at the Roadhouse in Manchester. The 20th-22nd performances are compiled on the 1997 live album, *In The City...* It's an often-overlooked entry in the overcrowded Fall live canon, but is one of the better ones. The sound quality is excellent, and the group are tight and energised. Brix provides some strong and effective vocals, especially on 'Middle Class Revolt', which puts the album version to shame. An uptempo version of 'Gut Of The Quantifier' is another highlight, but the best moment is a nine-minute 'Life Just Bounces' that thrashes the hell out of the tune in a blissfully abandoned fashion.

Cerebral Caustic

Cerebral Caustic was recorded in late Autumn 1994 at The Pavilion Studios in London (which both MES and Hanley describe as a 'disco studio'). Smith co-produced alongside Mike Bennett. In a 1995 interview, Smith claimed that Bennett had worked with glam-rockers Sweet: 'He's really good 'cos he sort of used to do The Sweet when he was about 17, y'know, so he knew what I wanted, he could get the drum sounds.'[236] It was recorded quickly: Simon Wolstencroft suggests 12 days; Steve Hanley a week. The sessions were riven with tension. It didn't help that the studio was a tight fit for the seven-piece, two-drummer line-up, although this problem was eased by Karl Burns once again being given his marching orders for hotel-related mayhem – this time for detonating fireworks out of his window. Another factor contributing to the tense atmosphere was the fact that Smith was clearly distancing himself from Dave Bush's influence. In a May 1995 interview, Smith discussed the departure in the group's sound that made *Cerebral Caustic* a very different proposition from the previous four albums. He described the almost complete abandonment of the technology that had characterised much of the group's early 90s output as a 'very conscious' decision:

> It was getting a bit sludgy, with the process we were using and that. As you probably know, it's all computers in studios now, and they're always losing the plot really. You can't get people like Craig and Steve and myself to play to drum machines, so if I hadn't got Brix and Karl back, I think it probably would have ground to a halt.

Steve Hanley could see that Bush's days were numbered. 'Dave's giving it rock-sounding beats instead of effects, but there's only so many beats that can go in. Every time he tries to do an effect, it is wiped out and we can all feel the chamber revolving.' Whilst Bush was disappearing from the group's sound, a new

[236] Bennett's own website (www.mikebennettproducer.com), however, suggests that his only involvement with The Sweet was to create a 1996 remix album called *Solid Gold Action: 15 Alternative Mixes*. According to *allmusic.com*, this was 'a collection of '90s industrial/dance remixes of 70s party hearty glitter rock'. Thankfully, it doesn't appear to be available online.

name appeared on the album sleeve. Lucy Rimmer – credited with (barely audible) backing vocals on 'Pearl City' – was Smith's current girlfriend.[237] Like Saffron before her, she was organising the group's fan club, reinforcing Steve Hanley's comment that, 'Every one of Mark's girlfriends was involved in some way. His personal life was always mixed up with the band.'

Pascal Le Gras supplied the artwork for the fifth album in a row, and it was a marked departure from the bold, colourful, semi-abstract designs of the previous covers. Brix considered the stark, gaudy skull image to be the group's worst ever cover. 'The skull clown is Mark. It's prophetic. He looks like a fucking skull, and he acts like a fucking clown.' Even more curious was the back-cover image of Smith adorned with a crudely drawn set of angel wings. Smith described the album as 'very diary-ish... it wasn't a nice time for me personally. I'm OK now but I thought it would be nice to get it down really fast.' He reiterated his aversion to nostalgia: 'A lot of musicians would gladly do "Totally Wired" every night. You just can't have it.' He also expressed a sense of optimism: 'I feel a lot better than I have for a couple of years about the group actually... I think the possibilities are getting endless again. We've got a bit more jump to it.'

The Joke
The album's return to a techno-free back-to-basics garage rock approach is flagged up clearly on its opener. It's not the most innovative riff, but for not the first or last time the group squeeze maximum energy from a few obvious chords. The interplay between Brix and Scanlon's guitars (one in either channel) makes the track a satisfying headphones experience. The two aren't playing anything radically different, but the subtle variations give a seemingly straightforward song surprising levels of texture and depth. For example, if you listen from where the group kick in at 0:15, over the next few seconds you get a choppy thrash on the right but a more sustained lead guitar on the left. At 0:51–0:54, you get a similar lead/rhythm effect, where the left pulls a bluesy string-bend while the right hammers away on one chord. They

[237] Smith and Saffron Prior had divorced in February 1995.

work like this all the way through, circling around and colliding with each other, producing a gloriously ragged and layered fuzzed-up thrash. Dave Bush is notable by his absence for much of the album, although there are still traces of his work here: an underlying drum & bass-style rhythm that's relatively unobtrusive (you might not even pick it up until it's exposed right at the end of the song) but subtly adds a bit of momentum.

Smith's vocal fights its way belligerently through the layers, sounding acerbic and casually aggressive. The 'five years in a PC camp' line might suggest a diatribe against political correctness, but the lyric is mainly characterised by mysterious asides such as 'violent food' and 'multicoloured sweets in bottom of white sweet pack'. Milan Kundera's novel of the same title may have been a reference point.[238] The song was a particular live favourite, clocking up 134 appearances between 1994-2004, and featuring on no less than 11 of the group's live albums.

Don't Call Me Darling

The second track takes a similarly garage-punk approach, but the vocals are the most striking aspect. Back in the mid-80s, Brix's vocal contributions tended to work best where she offered a tuneful sweetness as a contrast to Smith's rough acerbity. Here, there's a role-reversal: Smith croons his way through the song while Brix is in full-on rasping shouty punk mode (her vocal chords, she said, would be 'thrashed' after singing the song). Smith was keen to point out that the song was not actually about Brix. 'There are no songs on the LP about Brix, not even "Don't Call Me Darling". I write about ex-girlfriends, readies, the milkman... but never Brix. It's funny, you'd think I would, but I don't feel the need to.' He claimed that the song was about 'being assaulted... being beaten up'. The lyric is full of well-crafted but obscure phrases such as 'the long black hair of wretched bluebottle darting all over to no avail' and 'they smell of oak panelling / voices thick with Bouncing Jackson'. It was played live 20 times 1994-96.

[238] *The Joke* was Czech writer Kundera's first novel, published in 1967. It describes how a student's private joke leads to him being expelled from university and the Communist Party and then forced to work in a labour camp.

Rainmaster

A spartan track, based around a simple, descending twangy guitar line and a solid, unobtrusive rhythm track. There's something fragile, vulnerable yet defiant about it; it captures a certain rawness that emphasises how the group are often at their best when they just throw around a basic idea and let Smith loose on it. And of course what MES does is to throw in some fascinatingly inscrutable imagery: 'curserer of blights once too often / in the ridiculous muggy envelope stained'; 'Rainmaster in Basingstoke's portaphone traffic'. Despite his gradual side-lining, Dave Bush once again manages to just about elbow his way into the margins of the song. A few squiggles and effects float about here and there, and a brief spot of drum programming peeks over the parapet right at the end. According to Brix, the musicians loved the song, which led Smith to bloody-mindedly turn against it being included on the setlist. However, although Brix and several other sources assert that it was only ever played live once – at The Phoenix Festival on 14th July 1995 – there are at least two other live recordings of the track.[239]

Feeling Numb

Like 'Darling', this is a robust, largely uncomplicated rocker that once again has the MES–Brix vocal interplay as its point of focus. Here though, the roles are more traditional, Brix chirping away just on the right side of twee in contrast to Smith's off-hand sneer. And whilst it's not exactly Simon and Garfunkel, the moments when they come together to deliver the same melody are actually quite touching, albeit in a haphazard way. It's not as straightforward a song as it first appears; there's a rather odd stuttering guitar part lurking in the background during the verses that adds an angular unpredictability. The lyric references Prozac, known for its numbing qualities. It was played live 29 times between 1994 and 1997.

---

[239] For unknown reasons, the Phoenix Festival performance of the song was omitted from the *Live At The Phoenix Festival* album (see Chapter 19). The version included on the *Oxymoron* compilation (see Appendix 2) is definitely a different performance, as is the version online that purports to be from Manchester Roadhouse on 22nd March 1995.

Pearl City

The title refers to a Manchester Chinese restaurant that was one of Smith's favourites, although the establishment itself is probably not the focus of the lyric – 'cappuccino and a slice of quiche' not being the standard fare of a Chinese eatery. The song seems to be a dig at yuppie pretensions. This is reinforced by the rather sixth-form poetry of 'no one cares / about your world of stocks and shares'. Smith discussed the song in a local radio interview in May 1995:

> I'm very pleased with it. It was like a two and a half minute riff that Karl and me wrote at my house. When I came to develop it, I didn't really know what to do with it. I just wrote about eight sheets of lines about Manchester over it and when I sort of randomly chopped it together it all came together really well.

There's a nice contrast between the choppy rhythm guitar and Hanley's solid foundation; in addition, there's an interesting guitar part lurking in the background, pulling some subtle blues-rock moves. It made 42 live appearances 1994-98.

Life Just Bounces

By now rather a relatively old song, having been played live since 1990 and first appearing on the 'White Lightning' single / *Dredger EP*, this version injects the song with a welcome dose of adrenalin, although many fans prefer the slower-paced original. The most aptly-named Fall song since 'Glam-Racket', it's framed around a simple but effective up-and-down-the-scale guitar line that's more than ably supported by Wolstencroft's thunderous drumming and Hanley's agile bass. Smith's distorted vocals are a treat too: 'rock group' at 2:41; the '...and!' at 3:50. The way that the volume is suddenly cranked up at the end is an odd but nice touch too. Played live 36 times, 1990-2000.

I'm Not Satisfied

A cover of a Frank Zappa song from The Mothers of Invention's 1966 debut album *Freak Out!* It lacks the ghostly grandeur of the original, but there's something strangely appealing about its bleak, clipped tone. Only played live three times, 1994-95.

The Aphid

'The Aphid' sees the group return to full-throttle ragged garage-punk. Lyrically, it may have been inspired by Philip K. Dick's *A Scanner Darkly*, in which the main character imagines himself covered in aphids. There's something intriguing lurking right back in the mix that might be a descant recorder (you can hear it best around 0:46-0:48). Like 'The Joke', it's a good example of The Fall doing a simple thing very effectively. Surprisingly, it only got half a dozen live outings (all in 1994-95) – two of which were instrumental versions.

Bonkers In Phoenix

A Brix song called 'Shiny Things' that Smith mangled and embellished with a wide range of outlandishly garish sound effects that were apparently intended to capture the experience of attending a music festival. You can hear the original version on the 2006 reissue of the album, which confirms that it was – as Brix herself admitted – rather 'girly and sickly'. The notion of slathering a kaleidoscope of sonic effects over the song to capture the atmosphere of a festival is a potentially interesting idea, but it palls a long time before its six minutes are up. It was played live twice, both performances coming in March 1995.

One Day

A heads-down frenetic rocker. The prime force behind the song is a lively surf-rock guitar line, which powers along in the right channel of the stereo. On the left, there's all sorts of stuff going on: a choppy, scratchy, almost skiffle-ish (acoustic?) guitar mainly, but also a selection of weird and wonderful random noises that scrape, screech and squawk away merrily. There's also a very dodgy edit at 2:20. Smith's blaring vocals are a strong feature of the song, and his enunciation of 'vacuum breath' and 'transparent or not' are both moments to relish. Oddly, it was never played live.

North West Fashion Show
The obligatory novelty/piss-take/filler. There's a potentially decent riff lurking in there somewhere, but whilst it's not as banal and pointless as 'Crew Filth', it does have a similar level of self-indulgence and laddish 'humour' (for example in its references to 'sheep-shaggers'). Never performed live.

Pine Leaves
A strangely fragile and wistful track. The references to concentration camps, Smith's slurred, whispering (often double-tracked) delivery and the indistinct dialogue sample lurking in the background give it a dark, enigmatic air. Tommy Mackay rightly identifies that the lyric is 'packed with impenetrable... imagery revolving around death and annihilation during occupation and wartime'. It starts in a relatively straightforward fashion – 'they gave their lives during the occupation / arranged at the end of Japan... annihilation / a million dead here' – but then evolves into evocative but obscure imagery: 'the corpor of this leaden leaf / folding out with ghost / censure / still in the tub of side for bone shakes'. It's another that benefits from listening on headphones. The section from 1:15-1:26 is especially affecting, Smith's whispered vocal in the left channel contrasting with his almost delicate, breathy 'ahhh' in the right. The 'reversed' section just after the two-minute mark adds to the melancholy strangeness. There's all manner of interesting guitar detail too, such as the gentle, repeated figure that appears at 2:26. It's just full of fascinating, interwoven layers, and is unutterably haunting. Another that was never played live.

Reviews and Reissues
Despite Smith's positive outlook, reviews were once again mixed, and overall were the most negative the group had received since *Seminal Live*. Although American magazine *Trouser Press* heard 'prime-slice Fall in all its caustic, cerebral glory', John Harris's 4/10 evaluation in the *NME* was more typical. Harris complained that the album was 'worryingly generic', full of 'predictable, drone-laden rumble' and that several tracks had the 'uninspired

aura of recycled goods'. Commercially, it fell short even of its predecessor's mediocre performance, reaching only number 67 in the album charts – the group's worst placing for 11 years. *Cerebral Caustic* was The Fall's third consecutive album to be released on the Permanent label. Unlike the last two, however, it didn't get a US release at the time, not coming out in the States until 2006. After all the concerted promotional efforts of recent years, there wasn't even one single released to support the album.

The 2006 Sanctuary reissue of *Cerebral Caustic* did not represent the same good value as the other reissues of the early 90s albums that emerged at the time. After the contemporary Peel session tracks, the next ten songs are 'pre-release rough mixes' of all the album bar 'Fashion Show' and 'Pine Leaves'. It had been rumoured that a vastly different (possibly superior) version of the album existed that included more of Bush's contributions, but these tracks would seem to disprove this, sounding like little more than, as the names suggest, rough demos. The last three tracks on the bonus CD are a little more interesting. The 'alternate' mix of 'Bonkers' provides some relevant context for the track. The 'promo interview' gives some valuable insight. By far the most intriguing, however, is the Rex Sargeant mix of 'One Day'. For much of its duration it bears virtually no resemblance to the album track, stripping away most of the traditional instrumentation in favour of synths and sequencers; it's only in the last minute or so that it starts to resemble the final version. It is perhaps the only real clue as to what the album might have sounded like had Bush not fallen out of favour.

Evaluation

Cerebral Caustic is often criticised for being rushed, simplistic, retrograde and generally shoddy. It is undoubtedly all of those things to some extent, but, in many ways, these factors are what make the album. There's a clear sense of reinvention, a desire to pursue a radically different direction; it also recaptures (as *Infotainment* had to some extent) the group's independence and disassociation from everything around them. There is an argument, of course, that The Fall were still in some way following the general musical trend. 'Alternative' music at the time had moved on from Jesus Jones to Oasis: less sequencers, more guitar-based anthems. However, the bands in the emerging Britpop scene were plundering their parents' Beatles, Kinks and The Who albums, not referencing The Stooges and *Nuggets*.

Brix's role in the group and on the album was different here. She was now more forceful, more independent and more inclined to stand up to Smith's nonsense. This is reflected clearly in songs like 'Numb' and 'Darling', as well as in the group's live performances at the time, where she frequently stepped up to cover for Smith's drunken, self-indulgent stage absences. She has less influence on the group's overall image and public perception, but her effect on the group's actual sound is much more striking.

Cerebral Caustic is almost wilfully inconsistent. 'Bonkers' (whatever you might think of the concept) is excessively long for the sake of it; 'Fashion Show' is one of the group's less inspired 'novelty' tracks; 'Satisfied' and 'Pearl City' might have been a lot better if not so casually tossed off. But three-quarters of the album is highly effective, full of dark, edgy intent that was clearly inspired by the intense, difficult and claustrophobic circumstances of its creation.

The Light User Syndrome
Recorded: The Dairy, Brixton, London, early 1996
Released: 10th June 1996

Personnel:
Mark E Smith – vocals
Brix Smith – guitar, vocals
Steve Hanley – bass
Julia Nagle – keyboards, guitar
Simon Wolstencroft – drums, programming
Karl Burns – drums, guitar, vocals

With:
Lucy Rimmer – vocals
Mike Bennett – vocals

Chapter 19: The Light User Syndrome

'The ingredients are pretty much the same as ever.'

Dave Bush's departure had seemed inevitable for some time, and he was sacked by letter at the start of 1995. Bush, although only a member of The Fall for four years, made a substantial impact on the group; arguably, nobody else would have such an effect on the Fall sound in such a short period of time. His demise coincided with Julia Nagle's emergence into The Fall circle. Nagle was an ex-pupil of St Winifred's, Stockport, whose choir became famous in 1980 with 'There's No One Quite Like Grandma'.[240] After playing in a couple of punk bands, she had trained as a sound engineer and worked with renowned producer Martin Hannett. In late 1994, she sent her CV to Cog Sinister, and after an interview with Smith became the group's keyboard player. In due course, she also became his girlfriend. Nagle denied stealing Bush's job, but Bush saw it differently: 'She fucked it up for me in the end. She kept telling Mark that I wasn't happy, and I was, but eventually I got kicked out. She was his girlfriend and there was a campaign going on.' This version of events is supported by Steve Hanley: 'Since our keyboard player wasn't happy, she [Nagle] could always step in if required, was the gist of CV-accompanied letters she immediately began to send in.'

The Fall spent a large proportion of 1995 recording their next single, 'The Chiselers'. It was not a happy experience for the seven-piece line-up; despite all the difficult times he'd been through, Steve Hanley went as far as to say that 'it has never felt so awkward being in this band'. Craig Scanlon was feeling the strain in particular. Both Brix and Hanley had noted the guitarist's growing disillusionment with playing the guitar and songwriting; it can't have helped that both Nagle and Burns were now showing an increasing interest in playing the guitar in the studio. To add to the woes of all the musicians, Smith had a seemingly infinite

[240] Nagle sang with the choir but wasn't involved in their most famous moment.

number of ideas about how 'The Chiselers' might be constructed and recorded and seemed hell bent on trying out every single one. As the recording sessions dragged on and on, Scanlon – perhaps to distract from the frustrating tedium – brought in a clarinet he'd bought in a junk shop. Grant Showbiz's account of MES's attitude to this development is illustrative of what the group were having to put up with:

> Craig Scanlon had gotten a clarinet and we tried very hard to make it work, to get a good sound. Then Mark heard it and said, 'What the fuck is there a clarinet on this song for?' He told us to wipe it off the track. We played the mix again and Mark was like, 'This is shit. Where is the clarinet? That was the best thing on the track.'

The group did at least manage to get another record out in 1995, The "Twenty-Seven Points" being released in August. Like Seminal Live, it was a live-studio hybrid. However, it was a more complicated proposition in comparison to Seminal's studio side/ live side approach, weaving studio outtakes, home recordings, intro tapes and live performances together in an inventive if not always entirely successful manner. Regarding the derivation of its title, Smith's explanation was that 'the 27 points are what the Nazis brought in to take away everybody's freedom in Germany. And they're all contradictory points as well. Very similar to our government now. You can drive, but you can't own a car. Things like that. You can read books, but we're going to burn them all.'[241]

The credits on the album are sketchy, to say the least; establishing when and where the recordings were made is a nigh on impossible task. For a start, the phrases used on the cover, 'Live '92 – '95' and 'Prague – Tel Aviv – London – Glasgow – N.Y.C. – M/cr' are both contradicted by the sleeve itself, which identifies 'Mr. Pharmacist' as originating from a 1991 gig in Prague and 'Life Just Bounces' from Leeds. Furthermore, the group only ever

---

[241] This seems to be an example of Smith mis-remembering his history, as the plan drawn up by Hitler and Anton Drexler in 1920 had 25 points. Other suggestions for the tile's origins have included T. E. Lawrence's guidelines on military leadership, 27 Articles (the Spanish Falangist 1934 fascist manifesto) and the 27 'depravities' outlined in Don DeLillo's 1982 novel The Names.

300

played in Tel Aviv three times, two of which took place many years after the album's release (2011 and 2016). This means that any tracks that did come from Israel are from the performance in October 1990. Even if one accepts that the recordings are, unless otherwise stated, from the locations named on the cover, the origins are still difficult to unearth. The group played 29 dates in the named cities in the 1992-95 timeframe; some of the songs featured very regularly in those sets – 'Free Range', for example, was played at over 20 of them – and there are no known setlists or bootlegs for several of the dates. The dates and venues are not the only misleading aspects. The personnel credits are more of a reflection of Smith's attitude at the time than a true record of who actually played on what. In particular, Dave Bush's fall from favour is illustrated clearly by the nonsensical claim that he only contributed keyboards to three tracks. Conversely, Julia Nagle, who had only joined the line-up five months earlier and is unlikely to have played on more than half a dozen of the songs here, gets a full band credit.

As for the music, it's a mixed bag, but not without its highlights. The pacey version of 'Return' is one of its most successful outings. 'Idiot Joy Showland' sets off at a similarly frantic pace, but it proves to be a false start, Smith ordering the group off stage less than a minute in, tersely warning Rex Sargeant that he'd 'better get this sorted out'. (When the group return for a spirited romp through the song, the sound has indeed improved.) 'Intro – Roadhouse' is basically 90 seconds worth of the theme from *Zulu*. '95: Glam-Racket/Star' features a jarring edit (2:24) between two different recordings of the song. 'Prague '91' is an engaging bit of country-folk led by Kenny Brady's fiddle, backed with a few squiggles of Bush electronica that segues into an energetic if by now rather predictable blast through 'Mr. Pharmacist'. An energetic version of 'Middle Class Revolt' (subtitled 'Simon, Dave & John') sees Brix dominate the vocals.

The "Twenty-Seven Points" is a flawed but interesting release, the spoken-word interjections giving it the feel of an experimental mixtape. The most compelling reason for owning it, however, is 'Noel's Chemical Effluence'. An outtake from *Code: Selfish*, it's the very definition of both a hidden gem and an outlier: intense, murky, psychedelia driven by a jagged and increasingly frantically strummed 3–chord guitar part. There's a long tradition of rock songs about the tour bus, life on the road, etc., but few others have taken the chemical toilet as their main subject, let alone discussed the 'red–purple vomit stream'. The shambolic ending seems to catch Craig Scanlon by surprise.

1995 was a quiet year for Fall gigs, only 17 being played. The first, on 10th March at The Forum in London, was Nagle's first performance with the group. 'The Chiselers' debuted on 28th April at Rennes, but further material from the forthcoming album didn't make its way into the set until the autumn. The group opened their 8th October Glasgow gig (as they would do on three subsequent occasions) with 'Tunnel', an instrumental that would eventually morph into the introductory section of 'Interlude/Chilinism'. 'Stay Away (Old White Train)' was played for the first time on October 24th in Cambridge, Craig Scanlon's last performance with the group.

Although Bush's exit had been an important one, Scanlon's departure was even more significant. For 16 years he had coped stoically with all of Smith's foibles and mind games and abuse; he had always just kept his head down and ploughed on with playing the guitar and writing songs. But it seemed that Brix and Hanley had both been correct in identifying that by 1994 he had lost his enthusiasm – not just for the group, but for playing the guitar in general. Like Bush, he was sacked by letter, allegedly because of 'failure to maintain equipment'. 'He reached a point where Mark finally broke him,' Brix concluded, 'his passion for music and spirit were broken.' Despite his reserved nature, Scanlon's contribution to the first half of The Fall's existence should never be underestimated. He played a key role in the writing of many of their classic songs, his often-unusual choice of chords frequently being one of their key distinguishing features. His importance can be measured by the fact that, amongst all of Smith's sackings, his is the only one that he ever publicly regretted, later admitting that it was 'a bad decision… I do miss him'. (Scanlon later claimed that Smith had actually asked him to return in 2000.) After leaving The Fall, he largely abandoned the music business and has kept himself out of the public eye. It would be over ten years before he gave an interview about his time in the group (for *The Guardian*'s Dave Simpson) and even then only consented to answer questions via email. Subsequently, he maintained his silence until he agreed to contribute to *Have A Bleedin Guess* in 2019. '[Craig's] perspective on things is absent from most previous attempts to tell the story of The Fall,' Paul Hanley observed, 'and is sorely missed.'

The Fall's 19th Peel session – the first in 17 years not to feature Scanlon – was recorded on 7th December and broadcast on the 22nd. 'Tunnel' is used as the introduction to 'He Pep!'; 'Oleano' is a little hesitant at first, but builds in intensity over its second half thanks to a churning, distorted loop and Brix's startling scream. 'Chilinist' eschews the complexities and nuances of its other incarnations (see below), leading to a refreshingly straightforward rendition of the song. It's hard to imagine what motivated the group to cover Nancy Sinatra's saccharine piece of 60s kitsch, 'The City Never Sleeps'. Smith doesn't appear, leaving the vocal to Lucy Rimmer. Despite her best efforts, the group make no improvement on the rather limp original.

'The Chiselers' was finally released in February 1996, a mere eight months after recording had begun. The group's first single for nearly two years, it was released on Jet Records (best known for their association with ELO), Smith having walked away from Permanent over their perceived lack of support for the group's new material. The musicians had not enjoyed the process of making the single and they were scarcely more impressed with the outcome. 'What we eventually emerge with,' Steve Hanley commented, 'is an over-processed, convoluted, over-extended version... It's a self-indulgent montage of disjointed styles, none of which have any real connection with one another... There's the bones of a decent song in there, buried by Mark and a producer with too much time on their hands.' Smith himself even tired of it, describing the single as 'a pain in the arse, it took eight bloody months to do 'cos it's got nine parts, 12 different speeds and eight different vocal arrangements'. The record-buying public seemed to concur, the single peaking at number 60. It's undoubtedly true that a single, more focused recording would have helped. However, there is much reward to be had from listening to all three versions. The skittering drums, grinding guitar and the contrast between MES and Brix's vocals are a strength in all of them, but there's also a spirit of invention to be found in, for example, the spacey, spooky 'Interlude' (previously 'Tunnel') and the plaintive double-tracked vocals towards the end of 'Chilinist'. In addition, in 'The Chiselers', the abrupt shout of 'Chiseler!' followed by that raw, grinding riff (at 2:39) is a moment to be treasured.

Around the same time that he left Permanent and signed with Jet, Smith also made a deal with Receiver Records, a subsidiary label of Trojan Records. Receiver would subsequently release a seemingly endless series of Fall compilations, produced and compiled by Mike Bennett. These albums were characterised by poor quality sleeve notes, inaccurate track-listings, spelling mistakes and erroneous, misleading or missing information about the songs' origins. Three were released in the first four months of 1996 alone – *Sinister Waltz*, *Fiend With A Violin* and *Oswald Defence Lawyer* – a trio of CDs that, as Simon Ford rightly states, had 'just enough interesting and new material for one album' (see Appendix 2).

Despite his long-standing objection to Fall musicians working with other artists, Smith made another guest appearance in March 1996, this time on a single by D.O.S.E. called 'Plug Myself In'. An example of the burgeoning big beat genre, there were even more versions of the single than there had been of 'The Chiselers' – seven in total. It managed ten places higher in the singles chart too. The label it was released on, Coliseum, was part of Pete Waterman's PWL group, home of Kylie, Jason and 2 Unlimited. Smith expressed admiration for Waterman – 'he's not about the "rock" world, he's about the real world' – and even declared himself a fan of The Reynolds Girls' 'I'd Rather Jack' ('a bloody great song').

The group were not more active on the live front in 1996 than they had been the previous year, not playing until the end of May and once more clocking up only 17 performances in total. In 2003, two official live albums were released which feature performances from the summer of 1996. *Live At The Phoenix Festival* (a BBC radio recording) finds Smith a little off-hand and disengaged, occasionally struggling to keep up with his musicians. There's a thumping version of 'Glam-Racket', with Brix giving the 'Star' section real gusto, and an entertaining '15 Ways' that's played at a hundred miles an hour. However, 'He Pep!' is lethargic, and 'Powder Keg' sounds under-rehearsed. *The Idiot Joy Show* (a double CD compiled by Mike Bennett) features ten tracks from Cambridge, 24th October 1995, plus a further ten from the Roskilde Festival in Denmark in June 1996. It also includes two (inferior) recordings of songs from the 1995 Phoenix Festival that are also on *Live At The Phoenix Festival*, which it incorrectly identifies as being from 1996 (the track-listing is riddled with errors). Whilst the sound quality isn't terrible, imbalanced levels occasionally distract from the performances. It isn't without interest, however: 'Chiselers' sees the song in the early stages of its development; 'The Coliseum' is an intriguingly ugly, fragmented and sprawling mess; the 'Intro' to the second disc sees the group playing around (at least partly via the studio) with the drum and bass pattern that would go on to be 'Ten Houses Of Eve'. It's also mildly interesting to hear what 'The Mixer' sounds like without Dave Bush, even if the answer is hectic but thin.

The Light User Syndrome

The album was recorded at The Dairy in Brixton, with Mike Bennett once again co-producing – and this time also contributing vocals. Like its predecessor, *Light User* was recorded very quickly (in about two weeks) and in a tense atmosphere. Creativity wasn't the issue: Steve Hanley described how the 'competition for songwriting dominance between Si, Karl and Julia [that was] raging' was starting 'to translate into a new kind of energy'. The issue was with Smith. He didn't even appear for the first week of recording and, as Brix explained, just 'couldn't get it together. He had a sore throat, he couldn't get up, he was depressed.' Smith recorded most (possibly all) of the vocals on the last day of recording.

The album's cover was the first to feature a group shot since *The Frenz Experiment*. At Jet's request, the abstract designs of Pascal Le Gras were ditched in favour of moody, sepia group portraits by Peter Cronin on both front and back covers. 'From the front the group look out apprehensively over Smith's shoulder,' Simon Ford observed, 'while on the reverse they line up behind him like soldiers about to be inspected by a particularly short-tempered corporal.' Smith wasn't happy with the images: 'I look fucking terrible… I wasn't eating my greens, and my mouth was wearing whisky perfume.'

D.I.Y. Meat

The album hits the ground running with a trademark piece of jagged garage rock. The guitar's sharp, bright distortion is a highlight, as is the unusual percussion, which sounds in places like someone is taking a drumstick to a dustbin. The theremin-like keyboard part adds a bit of cosmic variety. The hurried way in which the vocals were recorded isn't a negative here, Smith's slurred cackling suiting the song perfectly. Potential subject material includes Ian McEwan's *The Cement Garden* and serial killer Fred West; either way, there's something darkly unsettling about the lyric ('what you doing round that grave?') that complements the troubling title. Surprisingly, it was only played live eight times.

Das Vulture Ans Ein Nutter-Wain

Steve Hanley carves out a ludicrously flatulent, driving bassline that is the main focus of the whole track; Julia Nagle flings in a random series of atonal keyboard frills; either Wolstencroft or Burns (probably the latter) cuts through the whole thing with a recurring series of outrageously loud cymbal crashes reminiscent of 'Smile'. Its lurching menace brings The Birthday Party to mind. Smith might have thought (or at least pretended) that he could speak German, but he really couldn't (Brix suggested he tried to learn it from Nazi war movies) and the title doesn't actually mean anything even vaguely coherent in German.[242] It was played live 14 times, twice in the same gig on one occasion and as an instrumental in one other.

---

[242] *The Annotated Fall* suggests 'The vulture and another one', or even 'The vulture lands on the nut-wagon'.

He Pep!

'D.I.Y.' suggested a continuation of *Cerebral Caustic*'s back-to-basics approach, but 'He Pep!'s barrage of programmed percussion and twisted synth oscillations almost make it feel as though Dave Bush had never left. Brix's vocal (which she described as 'cheerleader backup') is a perfect foil for Smith, who barks his way through the song with desperate, ill-tempered intensity. 'Smith's obvious poor health and frustration,' Simon Ford comments, 'actually help the track.' Brix summarised the song as 'another one of Mark's odes to speed mixed with a rant about record companies'. The line 'I wrote a song about it / conceptually à la Bowie' made 'He Pep!' the third Fall song to contain a reference to him. It was played 76 times 1996-2001.

Hostile

A weighty and ominous track, driven by rolling, tribal drumming and layers of scorched guitar. The lightness of Brix's vocal again provides an excellent contrast to Smith, who declaims the darkly enigmatic words ('we are the elite gangsters of the damned, criminals of the damp') like some sort of bitter, world-weary Mancunian preacher. The lyrics reference obscure Catholic organisation the Neocatechumenal Way.[243] As one online reviewer put it, 'The atmosphere... is quite unlike anything else encountered anywhere within the group's immense back catalogue. It's equal parts paranoia, tension, suspense and shadow.' It was never played live.

Stay Away (Old White Train)

The inevitable cover arrives five tracks in, and it's a throwaway affair. Based on Johnny Paycheck's 1979 single '(Stay Away From) The Cocaine Train',[244] Burns's Friday night pub karaoke vocal places it firmly in 'possibly forgivable as a B-side' territory. Smith lurks in the background, adding the odd haphazard slur. Played live only twice.

---

[243] See *The Annotated Fall* page for details of dannyno's determined research.
[244] Paycheck (real name Donald Eugene Lytle) was a country singer best known for his 1977 single 'Take This Job and Shove It'.

Spinetrak

Thankfully, the album gets back on track straight away with a spiky bit of catchy punk-pop. It takes a similar approach to 'Feeling Numb' and 'Don't Call Me Darling', laying Smith's acerbic style over Brix's melodic surf-rock-riff. In common with several other *Cerebral Caustic* tracks, there's also effective use made of contrasting guitars in either channel. Whilst the Brix/MES vocal combination once again works well here, there's a hesitancy about his muffled contributions that emphasise the hurried way in which his vocals were recorded. Even *The Annotated Fall* struggles to identify what a 'spinetrak' might be, making only a tentative link to a mountain trail in the Quantocks. Both Brix and Wolstencroft rated it as one of the best tracks on the album. It was played live 26 times 1996-97.

Interlude / Chilinism

The version of what Simon Ford called 'The Fall's "Bohemian Rhapsody"' that made it onto the album was, perhaps, inevitably, the longest and most difficult one. The array of interlinked sequences give the track a prog-rock flavour, but although the various permutations of rolling snare, heavily reverbed loops, quietly ominous passages and scuzzy riffing show great invention, the song treads a fine line between abandoned creativity and messy incoherence. Mike Bennett's vocals, whilst offering a bit of variation from the familiar Brix-MES combination, are best described as an acquired taste. The lyric has an unusual fascination with shortness, the description being applied to 'The Stones', 'Mr. Grumbly' (with his white Ferrari), and Pink Floyd. There are also several references to money, including the entertainingly nonsensical 'ninth richest country in the world bar none'. The message printed on the back cover of the 7" single states that the 'song is relevant to the recent experiences of Halifax town football club'.[245] It was played 24 times 1995-98, before receiving a one-off revival in 2002.

---

[245] Halifax were relegated to the Football Conference in 1993.

Powder Keg

The description of Manchester city centre as a 'powder keg', the reference to Enniskillen[246] and the fact that an IRA bombing took place in Manchester a few days after the album's release has inevitably led to this track being cited as evidence of Smith's 'pre-cog' abilities. Smith himself said that the song was inspired by his sister getting caught up in a 1992 Manchester bombing by the IRA. It's a solid if unspectacular track, based around a straightforward riff and a rather obvious keyboard line. It has a stilted, underdeveloped feel, probably a result of the album's hurried recording. The existence of the 'Powderkex' remix by D.O.S.E. suggests that it might have been planned as a second single from the album. It was played live 29 times 1996-98.

Oleano

Melodramatic and urgent, 'Oleano' is driven by a trio of complementary guitars (an insistent, alarm-like chime, a choppy low-end rhythm and some fuzzy power chords), some melodic synth work and a weighty bass throb. The way that the group suddenly ramp things up a 2:13 is a particularly effective moment. It verges on the one-dimensional – you feel like you're waiting for a chorus that never arrives – but its relentlessness is matched well to Smith's clipped interjections. Lyrically, it's 'a sketchy and obscure story of a nautical disaster' but even the intrepid researchers of *The Annotated Fall* can't find any link to a real vessel. It was played live 31 times, 1996-98.

Cheetham Hill

A tawdry tale of kerb-crawling and soliciting ('only way you stop is for passion at the station / why you cruising? / to be unfaithful') which features a somewhat lumbering pun on Cheetham/cheat 'em. Mike Bennett performs it as a duet with Smith (who frequently used to leave Bennett to sing nearly all of it himself on stage) and once again the combination offers some variety on an album which relies quite heavily on the familiar

---

[246] The IRA detonated a bomb at a Remembrance Day ceremony in the town in 1987.

MES/Brix contrast. Although his falsetto interjections are a bit of a bugbear to some, Smith's wry, nicely timed delivery is a strength, particularly his enunciation of 'mission of passion' and 'Manchester'. The line 'don't scratch my nice blue Merc' refers to the day that Frank Lea of Jet records arrived at Smith's house to sign the group's new contract. It got 24 live outings between 1996 and 1998.

The Coliseum

The album's lengthiest track finds the group sounding a little behind the times, its clunky indie-dance rhythm sounding like an awkward and forced attempt to capture the baggy groove of The Happy Mondays or 'Fool's Gold'-era Stone Roses. Some of The Fall's longer songs ('Garden', 'Tempo House') pass by in the blink of an eye; 'Coliseum' starts to drag around halfway through its eight minutes. The single grinding guitar chord that runs all the way through adds to the monotony. It's hard to fathom why it was allowed to run to such a length, as it's not as if the album was short on run-time. It's a shame, because there's a germ of a good idea here, but things are not helped by Smith's distinctly half-arsed delivery. It was only played live four (possibly five) times, all in 1995-96.

Last Chance To Turn Around

At 15 tracks and an hour in length, the album hardly needed a second cover. A cover of a 1965 Gene Pitney single,[247] it has a bit more oomph than the original, but the cheesy 80s brass section-effect keyboards are a little toe-curling. In addition, Smith is very much in just-got-back-from-the-pub-which-song-is-this-again? mode. Never played live.

The Ballard Of J. Drummer

'Ballard' (it's not clear if there's any significance to the misspelling) relates the tale of Johnny Drummer, a stranger in town who extols the use of real drumming as opposed to everyone else's 'computer

---

[247] It's often erroneously reported that Pitney's original was entitled 'Last Exit To Brooklyn'.

tricks'. There appears to be some sort of showdown in a bar at the end. 'Don't ever follow the path of being hard and tough when your heart is soft' might possibly refer to Karl Burns. There are a few ponderous notes from Steve Hanley and some ominous mellotron-ish keyboards floating in the background, but overall the song is almost completely dominated by the militaristic snare drum. You can hear the group grasping for some sort of epic spaghetti western-style atmosphere ('Johnny Drummer came to the outskirts of town' conjures up Clint Eastwood in a poncho chewing a cheroot), but they fall short of realising the concept. An interesting but clumsily executed idea, it's a song that Brix hated (she refused to play on it), an opinion shared by the majority of Fall fans. It was never played live.

Oxymoron
You could view Oxymoron as a 'He Pep!' remix; there's certainly overlap, not least in Brix's 'cheerleader backup'. However, there's definitely enough invention about it to warrant its place on the album. It's focused around a pounding, overloaded drum track that seems to be a Wolstencroft/programming mix, plus a chugging blues guitar. There's a pleasingly random 'cut and paste' feel to the whole thing, Smith's vocals and the various electronics being thrown into the crowded mix with carefree abandon. This produces an atmosphere that's an intriguing mix of playful and ominous. The lyrics seem nonsensical – 'Mr. Moody's scruffed up... Oh yeah! Mr. Moody's lair, You pep!' – but this suits the overall haphazard and chaotically creative tone of the song. It certainly strengthens the generally weak final third of the album: *The Annotated Fall* calls it 'the scraggly cactus in the mini-desert at the end'. Another that was never played live.

Secession Man
Someone presses the 'disco rock' button on a Casio, then experiments with the 'Phil Collins horn section' sound. Smith sounds particularly lackadaisical, as if it's some sort of ironic joke to which he's forgotten the punchline. It trundles on for a seemingly endless nearly five minutes. Like 'Ballard', Brix refused

to play on it, describing both songs as 'heinous'. It was only ever performed live once, at Sheffield Leadmill on 29th June 1996.

Reviews and Reissues

John Mulvey's *NME* review was respectful but gently disparaging: 'the ingredients are pretty much the same as ever: pinballing rockabilly riffs; awesomely sludgy, chundering basslines... another Fall album to gather dust in a pile of several dozen not-entirely-dissimilar ones'. Smith himself called *Light User* 'a whisky-rash of an album'. He discussed (albeit reluctantly) his alcohol issues in February 1996:

> I've had me problems. (Nods to beer) Skulk 'em down. Whisky. (Even bigger pause.) I don't think this sort of stuff should be talked about because it's... excuses. I hate all that... being self-obsessed and thinking about your diet and what you drink.

Chart-wise, *Light User* did a little better that *Cerebral Caustic*, but fell short of *Middle Class Revolt*, reaching number 54. The album was reissued in 1999 and 2002, both versions adding the other two versions of 'The Chiselers' from the single.

Evaluation

The Light User Syndrome is a frustrating album. Roughly speaking, half of it is excellent; a quarter is flawed if potentially interesting; a quarter is weak. It also suffers from the curse of recently established CD age, being overlong, which gives it a bloated and indulgent feel. In the brave new mid-90s world of brash, patriotic and nostalgic Britpop, The Fall were becoming even more of a square peg in a round hole. They may have been admired vaguely by some of the current crop of guitar-driven 60s influenced rock-pop bands that were starting to dominate the British music scene, but the group – and Smith himself in particular – seemed to be descending into anachronism. They offered neither the stadium-friendly sing-along guitar anthems nor the dancefloor-friendly big beat rhythms that were currently garnering column inches and sales.

Where the album really works, it combines the best elements of the early 90s indie-dance approach with the back-to-basics garage punk of *Cerebral Caustic*. Another strong feature is the MES/Brix vocal combinations, which often see them complement each other as effectively as they ever did in the 80s. The problem with the album lies in the tense recording process and muddled production. Whilst spontaneity was often a positive feature of The Fall's work, there's a feeling throughout *Light User* – even on the best tracks – that it would have benefited enormously from more time being spent on it. Smith was clearly at a low ebb at this point, and his hurriedly delivered performances find him struggling to do himself and the material justice. On some occasions, this approach works well – the energetic bark on 'D.I.Y. Meat', or the random interjections on 'Oxymoron' – but in many places it feels like he's floundering, only just managing to squeeze out some kind of coherent contribution.

Levitate
Recorded: West Heath Studios, London; Beethoven Street Studios, London;
PWL Studios, Manchester, mid-1997
Released: 29th September 1997

Personnel:
Mark E Smith – vocals, keyboards
Steve Hanley – bass
Julia Nagle – keyboards, guitar, programming
Simon Wolstencroft – drums
Karl Burns – drums
Tommy Crooks – guitar
Andy Hackett – guitar

Chapter 20: Levitate

'Either the best or worst record you've ever heard.'

The Fall were booked to play at Denmark's Roskilde Festival in the summer of 1996. On the way to the festival from the airport, not wishing to share transport with UK hip-hop group The Brotherhood, Smith used the unfortunate phrase 'get off the bus, boy'. Brix and Wolstencroft defended Smith against charges of being a racist, but both were clearly shocked by the incident. Both also report that Smith received 'a hiding' for his troubles. The troubles didn't end there: on their return from Denmark, Smith revealed to Wolstencroft and Hanley that the group had been presented with a £32,000 VAT bill, for which the three of them were jointly liable. They avoided bankruptcy by agreeing to pay the debt out of future earnings, but money was becoming a serious issue for the group, Wolstencroft even turning to driving a taxi to supplement his income. Declining sales – since *Infotainment Scan*'s impressive number nine chart placing, the group had failed to dent the top 40 of the album chart, and they hadn't had a top 40 single for four years – meant that revenue from gigs was more important than ever. This income, however, was limited by the fact that the group only played live 17 times in both 1995 and 1996 (compared to 56 in 1993 and 43 in 1994).

Smith's continuing alcohol-related issues and their on-stage impact no doubt weighed heavily on the minds of potential promoters. At London's Astoria in June 1996, for example, he walked off stage three times. This performance was released in August 1997 as *15 Ways To Leave Your Man* (although only about half of the tracks are actually from the Astoria gig). It's an interesting recording in that it documents the group at a very difficult point in their history, but it's not an easy listen. The vocals are way too loud throughout, the music buzzes away thinly in the background and the often tuneless backing vocals are distractingly obtrusive. There's a certain tense energy about it, but the overall impression is of a group only just about holding it together; 'The Mixer', for example, sounds like they only learned the track half an hour before the gig.

At the end of June, the group headed to Maida Vale to record their 20th Peel session. Even this familiar haven couldn't disguise the group's ongoing issues though, and it was a disjointed and underwhelming set. 'D.I.Y. Meat' is thin and hesitant. 'Spinetrak' is spirited enough, but Brix's panting is uncomfortably high in the mix. The cover of Beefheart's 'Beatle Bones 'N' Smokin' Stones' has some unhinged charm, but overall is an off the cuff, self-indulgent mess. 'Spencer' at this point is little more than a half-formed idea with a comically flatulent synth.

Spanish newspaper *La Vanguardia*, reviewing the group's performance at September's Barcelona Acció Musical festival, painted an increasingly familiar picture:

> It seems that The Fall arrived at a time of big internal tensions and this was obvious on stage. A wrinkled and stubborn Mark E Smith constantly kept leaving the stage during a gig which lasted under an hour and which was summarily interrupted by him during the encore.

Smith had declared himself tired of touring the same old rock venues, so the itinerary for the group's autumn 1996 tour included small, provincial council-run venues such as Worthing Assembly Rooms, South Shields Arts Theatre and the Prince of Wales Centre in Cannock. Karl Burns had fallen into Smith's bad books once again, so the group were back to a single-drummer line-up; Steve Hanley was appointed as tour manager. Brix was nervous enough about the tour to insist on being paid in advance (and in cash) for each date. Her apprehensiveness was well-founded. Not only did she fail to get her cash in advance (apart from the first night), but her ex-husband's behaviour was starting to spiral out of control. The Cheltenham gig on 4th October (where Smith temporarily sacked half of the group during the set) was an especially tetchy one, as one Fall Online contributor described: 'Mark was constantly messing around with Brix's guitar amp, turning the dials, changing the sound, altering the volume, much to her annoyance. Loads of tension.' Things got even worse at Motherwell the next day. Smith threw a mike stand at an unfortunate soundman during the soundcheck, leading to a huge row with Brix during which she threatened to hit him with her guitar. Angry and shaken, she headed for Glasgow airport and flew back to London. Another Fall Online review paints a sorry picture of the gig:

> [Brix] never appeared on stage. Mark, unfortunately, did, and peering at the audience shook his head at the fifty-plus crowd and immediately tried to pull the band offstage. Hanley refused... The gig was a farce... numerous walk-offs... After forty-five minutes Mark E grabs a guitar and hides behind a speaker, strumming and grinning with no teeth. What a disaster.[248]

The group's insane tour itinerary (Cheltenham – Motherwell – South Shields – Worthing) saw them arrive on 6th October for a performance at the opening weekend of the new South Shields Arts Theatre. It never took place. The theatre manager insisted on the group performing at the prescribed time; Smith felt unable to oblige and things descended into chaos. The disgruntled crowd ripped up seats, attacked the group's tour bus and six police cars arrived. Two nights later, the group played Worthing Assembly Rooms, a gig that some consider to be The Fall's worst ever performance; Simon Ford describes the tour at this point as an 'increasingly macabre pantomime'. Smith sang very little and just gave the mike to the crowd; he exited then reappeared bare-chested beneath a jacket (possibly Nagle's). Finally, he fell flat on his back after someone at the front of the crowd tied his shoelaces together. Worthing Council were so appalled that they refused to pay the group's fee.

Smith's problems had gone far beyond poor, inebriated performances. Brix described how once, in a hotel room, he turned all the paintings to face the wall because they 'were

---

[248] The bootleg recording of the Motherwell gig is actually not the car crash you might expect it to be. It's messy, certainly, but the most notable thing is how well – given the circumstances – the musicians (Wolstencroft and Hanley in particular, yet again) hold things together.

speaking to him and spirits were coming out of them'. She, Wolstencroft and Hanley all noted Smith's growing obsession with washing his hands, '...claiming he'd caught a skin disease after shaking hands with a young girl in a wheelchair. He had welts on his arms, trying to bite away the sores.' Brix also suggests that he was having seizures at the time: 'Often he would turn up to a gig with a blackened tongue or a bruised face, from where he's smacked it while thrashing and writhing on the ground.'

Brix was persuaded to return for one last gig – the group's penultimate 1996 performance at London's Forum on 11th October. At the end, she said 'goodbye' rather than her customary 'good night'. Steve Hanley's summary of the tour was 'total tour wreckage: five mike stands, seven bus lights, several theatre seats, three cordless mikes, two amps and one lead guitarist'.

A new guitarist, Adrian Flanagan (Smith's sister Caroline's boyfriend) joined the group for their final gig of the year in Berlin on Christmas Eve, and would play with them four more times. Fans were divided on the value of his contributions, views ranging from 'Flanagan adds different nuances and the odd unique angle on the material' to 'inappropriate guitar soloing... why the guitarist just can't play the chords instead of doing little twiddles/ noodles is a little odd'. His last gig was at London's Astoria in February 1997, a tribute gig to music journalist Leo Finlay. The group played 'And This Day' (Finlay's favourite song) for the first time in 14 years, the track's final outing.

Despite his issues, Smith managed to squeeze in another guest appearance, this time on Edwyn Collins's 'Seventies Night'. Steve Hanley was less than impressed ('the hypocrisy is sickening'), but Smith enjoyed the experience and asked Collins to produce The Fall's next album. Collins declined, but did offer the use of his Hampstead studio; his guitarist Andy Hackett also played on *Levitate*. After Flanagan's departure, the guitarist role was filled by Tommy Crooks. Crooks, who had contributed some (uncredited) artwork to The *"Twenty-Seven Points"*, had written to Smith offering his services when he heard about Craig Scanlon leaving the group. He was appointed to the role after a chance meeting with Smith in Edinburgh. In time-honoured tradition, he was given a long list of songs to learn and then discovered that none of them were to be played at his debut gig on 13th May at Jilly's Rockworld, Manchester. The two gigs that the group played at Jilly's also featured Simon Spencer of D.O.S.E. (with whom Smith had collaborated the previous year) on keyboards. The other half of D.O.S.E., Jason Barron, engineered parts of *Levitate*. Kier Stewart, Spencer's partner in another duo, Inch, had made a one-off appearance for The Fall at the Leo Finlay tribute gig on 26th February. He and Spencer were asked to produce the group's next album.

Levitate

Work began on the album in July 1997. It was partly recorded at Pete Waterman's studios in Manchester, Smith once again expressing admiration for the PWL boss: 'He's been really good to me... At PWL they just have PWL artists working there, but he did it as a favour to me... [he] says, "Let Mark do what he wants, all right? He knows what he's doing."' The group then relocated to Edwyn Collins's West Heath Studios, where Smith's working relationship with his new producers did not go so well. Spencer and Stewart found Smith's behaviour in the studio ('staggering around, kicking things over and shouting stuff down the drum mikes') impossible to work with. MES dismissed them, disparaging their overly 'rock' approach.

> I had to fire them... Working with them was great, but the mistake I made there was asking them to work on *Levitate*. They went dead rocky. I felt like a real corrupter. They obviously read a book on how to be a rock producer, or how to behave.

Steve Hanley was sceptical about the duo ('two zeitgeist blaggers who are desperate to work with us') and suggested that remuneration issues were their greatest concern. He also doubted their competence:

> They set about miking up the drums, seeming for all the world like they've been doing this for years. But it was

321

only last week that they were procuring a crash course from the demo-studio technician.

Hanley's account of Smith at work does give some credence to Spencer and Stewart's complaints: 'It's impossible getting him to sing at all today... instead he starts to mess around with a stylophone and spends the entire day working his way around the plethora of antique studio equipment.'

Most of the material recorded with Spencer and Stewart seems to have been wiped. However, the duo did retain a track called 'Inch' (the basis for '4 1/2 Inch'). Adding a secretly-recorded piece of MES dialogue (where he describes to Stewart how the bass and drums should sound in an absurdly comical human beatbox fashion), they sent it out to John Peel and several record companies with the message, 'Hey guys, check out the sound of my new album. This is the brand new Fall sound and I think you'll agree – it rocks!' It was released by Spencer and Stewart in 1999 under the name Inch.

Levitate proved to be Simon Wolstencroft's last contribution to The Fall, the drummer packing up and leaving only three days into the album's recording. One of the reasons for his departure was an ongoing argument with Smith regarding 'Everybody But Myself', which Wolstencroft had co-written and had anticipated being a poppy, commercial single. The drummer's need to resign from the partnership that he and Hanley had signed up to in order to avoid the crippling VAT bill was undoubtedly also a factor. Wolstencroft sums it up best himself: 'I was out of money and patience.' And so, the group said goodbye to one of its most stalwart contributors. Eleven years in The Fall is a remarkable achievement in itself, but 'Funky Si' should also be commemorated for his huge contribution to the Fall sound, both through dozens of writing credits and well over 400 live performances.[249] Karl Burns was reinstated for the umpteenth time to complete the album.

[249] After leaving The Fall, Wolstencroft drummed for Ian Brown in the late 90s and has subsequently played with a variety of Manchester acts. As well as his entertaining memoir, *You Can Drum But You Can't Hide*, he has produced a highly-recommended series of podcasts about his life and career, *Funky Si's A-Z of Manchester*.

Levitate was released on Artful Records, a new label set up by John Lennard after Permanent had folded in 1996. The distinctive, abstract cover was designed by Tommy Crooks.

Ten Houses Of Eve

The album's opener is a blatant lift from The Seeds' 'Evil Hoodoo'. Here, the original's fuzzy psychedelia is largely replaced with a squelchy synth line and a crisp drum & bass rhythm track (that develops into something more grinding and industrial over the last third) although the surf-rock guitar echoes the song's 60s origins. It also throws in a soft-rock ballad curve-ball of an interlude, with tinkling piano and MES intoning earnestly about 'your blue green and grey heart / bedecked in lace'.[250] The contrast of Smith's languid, off-hand tone with the frantic rhythm is a strong feature. It was performed 88 times 1996-2000.

Masquerade

A piece of danceable indie-techno-pop, 'Masquerade' is a decent enough tune, although perhaps not quite good enough to justify its multitude of subsequent remixes. Once again, Smith's languid contributions contrast nicely with the sharp rhythm. A money-related theme runs through the lyric, with references to accounts, debt, 'fifty percent interest' and 'you rich pig'. It was played 34 times 1996-98.

Hurricane Edward

An abrasive cacophony that sounds like the rough ideas for several different songs tossed into a blender: spoken word segments (the opening lines are spoken by Sebastian Lewsley, one of the West Heath studio engineers), live snippets, Sonic Youth style guitar torturing, electronic squiggles, cut-up drum machine samples and fuzzy drone noise. The 'farm hand' character (it's not clear whether this is 'Edward' or not – the name isn't mentioned in the lyric) seems to be narrating the song from beyond the grave, having died in a hurricane. It was played live 39 times 1996-99.

[250] Another line from the interlude, 'Identity art / if only the shards would relocate back in place', formed part of a mosaic portrait of MES at Affleck's Palace in Manchester created by artist Mary Goodwin in 2018.

I'm A Mummy
One of the group's more successful covers. Two versions of novelty single 'The Mummy' were released in 1959, one by Bob McFadden & Dor, the other by 'Bubi & Bob'.[251] Both are entertainingly bizarre and manage the remarkable feat of making The Fall's version sound quite straight in comparison. Despite the difficult circumstances of the album's creation, the group sound like they're having a whale of a time on this one, and it buzzes with enthusiasm. The scratchy, trebly lead guitar is a bracing treat, all sorts of entertainingly random noises pop up throughout, and there's a deadpan hilarity about Smith's delivery. It was played live 17 times in 1997-98.

The Quartet Of Doc Shanley
Hanley contributes an absolute beast of a bassline, a piece of deranged, mutant funk distorted to the point of lunacy. It was inspired (according to 'Shanley' himself) by The Osmonds' acid-glam boogie 'Crazy Horses'. There's almost no mixing to speak of – everything is just *loud*; you can imagine Smith brushing the engineer aside and just sweeping an arm across the desk. The multitude of layers fall slightly out of synch just after the three-minute mark. There's little sense of coherence to the cut-and-paste lyric ('iadomine penternine', 'dentist November', 'pseudo hark') although it's plausible, given Smith's previous interest in the practice, that 'pentangle nine' might be a tarot reference.[252] The repeated use of 'complete and utter pranny' adds incongruous humour to an otherwise intense track. It was only played live twice, both times in 1997.[253]

---

[251] McFadden was an impressionist and voice-over artist who voiced several US cartoons in the 60s and was also the voice of Snarf in *ThunderCats*. 'Dor' was a pseudonym of poet and songwriter Rod McKuen. Nobody seems to know who Bubi & Bob were.
[252] On *The Annotated Fall*, 'antisyzygy' points out the nine of pentacles card, when reversed, indicates lack of stability and financial hardship, which seems to be a fair representation of the group in the late 90s.
[253] The second of these, from Bristol on 9th December bears little resemblance to the album version, sounding more like the Red Hot Chili Peppers covering AC/DC.

Jap Kid

A sudden change of pace, 'Jap Kid' is sparsely delicate and played at a funereal tempo. Julia Nagle's simple piano figure is pretty, although the track's inclusion in addition to the version with lyrics later on is rather puzzling. It was used as a backing tape at five gigs in 1997-98.

4 1/2 Inch

We immediately get back to something abrasive and challenging. Part of the short-lived Spencer/Stewart sessions, it may well be that Smith is the only member of The Fall that actually appears on this track, although Hanley claims that it contains samples of both him and Wolstencroft. Simon Ford suggests – although it seems rather too neat to be true – that the title came from Smith's perception that the song 'half-reminded [him] of industrial rockers Nine Inch Nails'.

It's an insanely glorious mess: the sound of several genres being battered relentlessly against a wall until they're bloodied and semi-conscious then being crushed and crammed forcibly into the mixing desk. The drums crash, blare and distort; a heavy, twangy funk-rock riff muscles its way in periodically, trying in vain to assert its dominance; a shrill, atonal sci-fi synth darts in periodically, surveys the chaos, shrugs its shoulders and wanders out again; somewhere, lurking in the shadows, a frightened little harpsichord-effect keyboard tinkles shyly. Over all this, the multiple layers of cut-and-paste MES swarm like enraged wasps; it's like being surrounded by a crowd of furious drunks in a Wetherspoons closing-time brawl. The words are angrily garbled and challenging to make out: 'the house is falling in / ecstatic midges / cloud coverage'. It is, *The Annotated Fall* suggests, 'a good example of MES letting the language take over... a pile of verbal imagery that somehow achieves sublimity without being mediated through the discipline of poetry'. 'Inch' captures perfectly the overall spirit of *Levitate*: bleak, chaotic, punishing and yet exhilarating. It was played live only once, in New York on 30th March 1998 – 'with some venom' according to *The Track Record*.

Spencer Must Die

Co-written with Simon Spencer, 'Spencer Must Die' is another song that has contributed to the MES 'pre-cog' mythology following Spencer's death at the Glastonbury festival in 2003 – although Smith does little more here than mumble about sunflowers and raspberries. Hanley provides a fluid, oscillating rhythm that unobtrusively underpins everything (notwithstanding the little misstep at 1:19). There are lots of details to love: the descending synth line that adds a splash of colour; the snippets of understated guitar twang; the placid strum that appears in the second half. It also features a fade-out that's abrupt even by The Fall's standards. Like 'Inch', there's an air of confident disregard about the notion of what constitutes a 'proper' song that's refreshing. Debuted the week before *Levitate*'s release, it had a decent run on the setlist – 38 performances over the next two years – and was often more guitar-heavy on stage.

Jungle Rock

The original (by Hank Mizell) was a pretty standard 50s rockabilly/ novelty tune that, for no easily explained reason, became a UK top ten hit in 1976. The original had a light-hearted, tongue-in-cheek tone; The Fall transform this into something much harsher and abrasive. The synth blares like a distress signal, the guitars are like buzzsaws and Smith drawls his way through the ridiculous lyrics with impassive disdain. There's something slightly discomforting about the way it teeters between strangely compelling and just plain silly. Hanley didn't think it worked: 'We were really trying to do a jungle version… and it really didn't come off.' It was played live 16 times, 1997-98.

Ol' Gang

Framed around a hammering, off-key piano motif, 'Ol' Gang' is hypnotically bleak and relentless. Smith's vocals are aggressively distorted and right at the front of the mix, sometimes uncomfortably so. The 'walking down the street' line was one of Smith's favourites: it had already appeared in 'Jerusalem' and 'Hey! Student/Fascist' and would remerge in several later songs.

The pause before 'fist fight' is reminiscent of 'Sunglasses After Dark' by the Cramps (where it's 'knife fight') with whom The Fall toured in 1980. It was a popular setlist choice at the time, racking up 54 performances 1997-2000.

Tragic Days

Ninety seconds of lo-fi pissing about. It was recorded in Martin Bramah's flat in 1990, hence his songwriting credit, although the guitarist remembers it actually being a rough idea of Craig Scanlon's. Typically perverse and pointless, it therefore sits entirely comfortably in the middle of such a wilfully challenging album. In 2017, it was voted the worst Fall song of all time in a poll on the *Fall Online Forum*, beating 'Crew Filth' in the final by a Brexit-mirroring 52%-48%. Unsurprisingly never played live.

I Come And Stand At Your Door

The somewhat ponderous 'Jap Kid' is given life by Smith's touchingly hesitant and vulnerable vocals. The melancholy lyric ('death came and turned my bones to dust') is based on a poem by the Turkish writer Nâzım Hikmet Ran called 'The Little Girl', told from the perspective of a dead child who perished at Hiroshima. Although credited on *Levitate* to 'Anon / J Nagle', the poem was originally set to music in 1961 by Pete Seeger and was originally called 'I Come And Stand At Every Door' (the song was also covered by The Byrds). Another that was never played live.

Levitate

The most conventional original song on the album. It's a soothing and pleasant tune, and Smith tries uncharacteristically hard to work within the boundaries of melodic convention. The production is less conventional: the treble is turned up ludicrously high and the bottom end is almost non-existent, giving it a feeling of frailty and brittleness. There's a vague sense of some sort of narrative developing in the first part of the lyric, the narrator, perhaps in hospital, listening to the person in the adjacent bed talk 'about his house in the Lake District'. 'Had to levitate from a grey map pate' suggests a desire to escape from mundanity. The second half retreats into the playful manipulation of language: 'the snazzy japes of a Basingstoke shot / basing in stocks under the green frock'. It was played 37 times, 1997-2000.

Everybody But Myself
The final track opens with a mournful harmonica-effect keyboard that segues into a roughly recorded live take that features raucous audience interaction and house-style piano chords. After a jarringly clumsy transition into the studio recording, the song settles into a lively groove driven by Nagle's shrill, insistent keyboards and Wolstencroft's lithely funky drumming. Smith's double-tracked vocals contrast weary ennui with playful falsetto. Clearly a long way from the chart-friendly pop song that Wolstencroft envisaged, it was only played live nine times, the live section used here being from Jilly's Rockworld on 14th May 1997.

Reviews and Reissues
Despite *Levitate*'s reputation as a difficult and flawed album, reviews at the time were generally positive. In the *NME*, Steven Wells invited his readers to 'Imagine pop without perimeters. Imagine rock without rules. Imagine art without the wank.' He described it as 'either the best or worst record you've ever heard'. In *Select*, Ian Harrison said that the group's 'grudging, scrambled avant-rock has been a weeping sore on music for 20 years now... This is a band as far away from the mainstream as ever with the confounding ability to come back sounding vital just when you least expect it.' Steve Hanley's summary was 'weird, but respectable enough. Like a shanty town almost completely destroyed by natural disaster, against the odds, a meticulous rebuild has left us with a finished product belying the traumas which underlie its creation.' Despite the positivity, *Levitate* only reached 117 on the UK album charts, the worst performance by a Fall album for 14 years.

A limited-edition version of the album was released at the time which included a 5-track bonus CD. 'Powderkex' is a mildly interesting drum and bass-inflected remix of 'Powder Keg'; 'Christmastide' is a rather pointless reworking of 'Xmas

With Simon'; 'Recipe For Fascism' is a brief, fractured piece of spoken word. 'Pilsner Trail' was a *Perverted By Language*-era tune (originally entitled 'Plaster On The Hands') – the rather thin live recording here is from a March 1983 London gig. The live version of 'Everybody But Myself' is the full version of the second Jilly's Rockworld performance that was used on the studio take.

'Masquerade' was released as a single in February 1998. There were three versions – two CDs and a 10". All of them included the 'single mix' of the lead song, which contains a spoken contribution by Julia Nagle's son Basil. The vinyl version featured two further versions of the song: the 'Mr Natural Mix' is a ham-fisted and overlong funk/techno take; the 'PWL mix' just sounds like the album track with the bass turned up a little. The assorted B-sides on the two CD versions included a curious live version of 'Spencer Must Die' that splices together two different recordings in a way that makes you feel like you've suddenly switched from FM to AM radio, a remix of 'Ten Houses Of Eve' (which doesn't add a great deal to the original beyond boosting the bottom end and turning up the reverb) and performance of 'Ol' Gang' from 9th December 1997 at the Bristol Bierkeller where the nagging one-note piano of the original is replaced by a less than subtle power-chord guitar.

There were also three studio-recorded B-sides. 'Scareball' is an agreeable, straightforward rocker that was played live nine times, all in 1998. The other two are further examples of those obscure little gems that are dotted around the group's back catalogue. The languid 'Ivanhoe's Two Pence' is closely related to *Levitate*'s title track in terms of melody and structure; it features a spoken sample taken from the 1971 film *Ivanhoe, the Norman Swordsman* that intertwines effectively with Smith's vocal. A cute little high-pitched keyboard line, a bit of basic one-fingered piano and a squeaky recorder make brief appearances too. It was played live once, in New York on 30th March 1998. 'Calendar' is even better. The collaboration with Damon Gough (aka Badly Drawn Boy) came about following a famous incident when Smith mistook Gough for a taxi driver and left his dentures in his car. The encounter led to Gough persuading MES – by giving him his copy of *Pet Sounds* – to record a song of his, at that point entitled

'Tumbleweed'. Gough described the recording session as 'quite uncomfortable. He was having a go at the rest of the band, telling them I was the boss 'cause I'd written the tune... the way he was treating his band members was a bit unnerving. I just came away thinking, "How the hell did The Fall ever record anything?"' Given the perverse nature of most things to do with Smith and The Fall, the last thing that you might expect from a Fall/Gough collaboration is that it would actually sound like Smith singing a Badly Drawn Boy song. Surprisingly, that's exactly what it does sound like. The combination of the intricate, precise guitar line juxtaposed with the indolent smear of Smith's voice is simply lovely. One of Smith's long-running bugbears was how long it took record companies to get albums released: 'October gives way to Christmas... January... calendar... what gets in the way?' possibly sees him returning to this theme. 'Calendar' was played live 18 times 1998-99.

For a long time, *Levitate* was out of print and very hard to obtain. In 2018, however, Cherry Red reissued the album in triple vinyl and double CD formats. Both contain the five original bonus CD tracks, plus all nine songs from the various versions of 'Masquerade'.

Evaluation

Steven Wells's description of the album as 'either the best or worst record you've ever heard' might seem at first glance to be a typical piece of throwaway soundbite journalism, but there is some substance to what he says. The album is one of the most divisive amongst Fall fans, a majority considering it substantially flawed and a fair few considering it to be one of their weakest moments; it also has a small but passionate coterie of admirers.[254] Both sonically and lyrically, *Levitate* captures, possibly better than any other Fall album, the emotions and dynamics of the group at the time of recording. An atmosphere of bleak, chaotic desperation runs through it: the abrasive bedlam of 'Inch'; the keening pathos of 'Everybody But Myself'; the anti-song aggression of 'Hurricane'. This reflects with brutal accuracy the dysfunctional

[254] dannyno is one of them: it's his favourite Fall album.

and disintegrating environment that the group's world had become by 1997. Smith's alcoholic paranoia, Hanley's stoic but simmering frustration, Wolstencroft's nervous impecunity – plus the resentful, regretful ghost of Brix's promising but unfulfilled second coming – are etched clearly into every groove.

Levitate epitomised catastrophe and triumph in equal measure. It saw the group sinking into obscurity: 117 in the charts; gig attendance sometimes only in double figures. Its promotional tour, as will be seen in the next chapter, led to utter turmoil and bitter implosion. But it also represented triumph amidst adversity: there cannot be many other artists who would ever even have got any sort of album recorded and released under the circumstances, let alone one that mixes the sublime and the ridiculous, the beautiful and the ugly and the desolate and the ecstatic to create such a bewildering, fascinating and exhilarating experience.

THE Fall // The Marshall Suite

The Marshall Suite
Recorded: Battery Studios, London, late 1998 / early 1999
Released: 19th April 1999

Personnel:
Mark E Smith – vocals, keyboards, guitar
Julia Nagle – keyboards, guitar, programming
Tom Head – drums
Neville Wilding – guitar, vocals
Karen Leatham – bass
Adam Helal – bass

With:
Steve Hitchcock – string arrangements

Chapter 21: The Marshall Suite

'I'm never getting on stage with you again.'

'WHAT A CORK-UP!: TOUR FALLS APART' read the *NME* headline of 15th November 1997. The three-gig trip to Ireland had started innocuously enough, with the first two dates, in Cork and Dublin, passing without incident. Things went pear-shaped in Belfast, however. Smith 'walked off the tour bus, straight onto the stage, and started kicking stuff about', recounted Mark Erskine, the venue's stage manager, 'he sacked the band and they went away'. Erskine went on to describe Smith smashing a ketchup bottle against a backstage door. Hanley saw it more as a strike than a sacking, the musicians responding to the singer's behaviour by returning to the tour bus and refusing to move. Smith, inevitably, gave a very different account to the *NME*'s John Robinson:

> You give musicians space, and trust them, then you come back and everything's in complete bloody chaos... That's what happened in Belfast. Someone kicked a guitar stand over at rehearsal, and it was like .. open rebellion!

Smith considered going ahead with the gig, playing with Nagle alone; Robinson (and the *Belfast Telegraph*) even suggested that he proposed playing an a cappella set of Beach Boys covers with the assistance of Terri Hooley, an old friend of his who had promoted some of The Fall's early gigs in Ireland. The Robinson interview gave rise to one of the most infamous quotations about the group: 'If it's me and your granny on bongos, then it's a Fall gig.' The quip is nearly always misquoted as '...it's The Fall', including on the back cover of *The Fallen*. However, it's unclear whether Smith himself even said it. According to Robinson, the phrase was reported to him by a PR called Bernard.[255] In 2019, Dave Bush suggested that *he* was the origin of the phrase:

---

[255] This may well have been Bernard MacMahon, who was credited as associate producer on *The Marshall Suite*.

[I] told Mark I could do some programming for them and make them sound brilliant. He asked me what I knew about the group and I said, 'If it's you and your granny on bongos, it's The Fall.' He laughed so much he used that line himself.

A group meeting shortly after the Belfast debacle did, in the short term at least, resolve the issues. The remaining 1997 dates were not without incident though. At Oxford, the venue's management pulled the plug when the group played past the 10pm curfew; they carried on regardless with an improvised version of 'I'm A Mummy'.[256] An increasingly disillusioned Hanley decided that if Smith could get away without contributing to large portions of their performances, so could he. 'For the duration of "Hip Priest" I sat on the monitor stack, bass in the stand next to me, not playing a single note. Nobody on stage took any notice, they just carried on regardless.'[257] In addition to his dissatisfaction with life on stage, Hanley was also feeling financial pressure. Just as Simon Wolstencroft had taken to taxi-driving to supplement his income, the bassist accepted a position as a school caretaker in early 1998.

January 1998 saw Smith being presented with the title of 'Godlike Genius' at the NME 'Brat Awards'. The award was presented by Eddie Izzard, who launched into a eulogy about Smith's work that was interrupted by the recipient himself striding onto the stage in the middle of his speech. Smith thanked a few people, including John Lennard, Steve Hanley and Julia Nagle, before wandering off stage, leaving the trophy on the podium. The post-award interview – in which Smith described the award for Marc Riley's radio show as 'hilarious' – saw the usually calm Jo Whiley express distinct irritation with his vague answers.

The Fall's 21st Peel session was recorded on 3rd February and broadcast a month later. Tommy Crooks, for unexplained reasons, did not play on it. It was not one of their finest. 'Calendar' lacks

---

[256] 'Karl and Mark just keep it going, while Julia and Steve mime sarcastically – and silently – Tommy joins in enthusiastically with b/vocs; altogether absolutely bloody hilarious.' (David Williams, quoted on Fall News, 3rd December 1997.)
[257] The gig was The Junction in Cambridge, 7th December 1997. Some online reviews suggest that he actually sat out 'Masquerade', which does make more sense.

the subtlety of the original. 'Masquerade' meanders on for much longer than it needs to and has a clumsy edit at 2:27. 'Jungle Rock' is also unnecessarily lengthy, a shrill and piercing synth making it a trying listen; Julia Nagle at times appears to be dismantling her guitar rather than playing it. Only one track from the forthcoming new album was recorded, a sloppy, under-rehearsed 'Touch Sensitive' which featured backing vocals from John Rolleson, the group's tour manager at the time.

The Belfast incident was only a warning sign, an indication that the entrenched issues within The Fall were bubbling closer and closer to the surface. It was nothing in comparison to the disastrous events of the US tour – their first for four years – that the group embarked upon in March. The first two dates were at Coney Island High in New York, where Smith appeared on stage sporting a black eye, apparently caused by 'an altercation between him, Nagle and a telephone receiver'. Nonetheless, apart from an impromptu 10-minute break on the first night, the first two dates went reasonably well.[258] The next gig, in New Jersey, was a tense one, involving walk-offs and near fisticuffs. The 3rd April performance in Cambridge, Massachusetts went more smoothly (it featured the first live outing of 'Touch Sensitive' and the unusual sight of MES in a t-shirt), but things took another downturn the next night in Philadelphia, where Smith made only sporadic, slurred appearances and the whole performance was an incoherent mess.[259] Hanley was starting to lose his patience with Smith:

> During the gig he tries to push me aside so he can fuck with my amp. It is the first time he has laid a finger on it in years… I push him out of the way with the end of my bass and turn my back… I finish the song and walk off, to be joined shortly after by Tommy and Karl, leaving him with nothing else to do but to sing 'Everybody But Myself' all by himself.

[258] A bootleg of the second night sees the group in solid form, MES giving a relatively coherent performance. Crooks's limited technique is exposed on occasion, however, most notably on 'Hip Priest'.
[259] The bootleg recording is one of the very poorest, both in terms of sound quality and performance.

To add to the group's woes, their tour van was broken into that night and several pieces of equipment, including Nagle's keyboard and guitar, were stolen. Although the stolen items were recovered a couple of days later, this meant that the group had to borrow equipment for the next night's gig at the Black Cat in Washington, D.C.. Nagle, frustrated by the unfamiliar keyboard, walked off after a couple of songs. With all the seething tension and bad feeling, it was only a matter of time before things reached breaking point. That time was 7th April, at Brownies in Manhattan, New York.

The night started cordially enough, with Hanley and Smith having a pre-gig drink in the bar next to the group's hotel. Whilst the rest of the group walked to the venue, Smith got a taxi and somehow managed to get into an altercation with the driver (the argument seems to have started when Smith opened a can of beer in the cab), who he claimed pulled a gun on him. It's not clear what occurred backstage just before the performance, but conflict was in the air: after the opening song Smith, clearly the worse for wear, remarked (in a peculiar mock-American accent) that the group were going to 'beat me up like the big men they are'. For the next few songs, the musicians ploughed on – the Hanley-Burns rhythm section as tight as ever – whilst Smith spent much of his time crouched, back to the audience, in front of the drum riser, barking out the occasional lyric. After a horrendous 'Hip Priest' (Smith handed the mic over to the audience, Crooks threw in some tuneless thrash, Hanley kept himself awake by fashioning a few jazzy bass solos) the group launched into a ragged 'Free Range'. A couple of minutes in, Smith decided to amuse himself by chucking Burns's spare drumsticks across the stage. At this point, even Burns – a veteran of Smith's antics – had had enough. He leapt out from behind his kit and wrestled MES across the stage into Nagle's keyboard. Hanley ordered Burns back behind his kit, but shortly afterwards Smith tried to grab Crooks's guitar; Crooks promptly gave the singer a firm kick up the arse. At the end of the song, Smith launched into a slurred rant:

What we've got here is a Scottish man, a fucking animal
on drums and a fucking idiot. I've been assaulted in public
here, by two people, or three people; you be witness to
this; bear witness laddies. They're very big. I'll tell you
what – these three... I got a taxi, and some fucker pulled
a gun out on me, from fucking Pakistan or someone [sic]
... These three were cowering in the fucking dressing
room – as usual. They're nowhere to be seen. They're
very hard, when they're together.

It was a sad spectacle. During Smith's outburst, Burns
repeatedly shouted 'cock!' from behind his kit while Hanley did
a mocking 'sad violin' mime with his bass. Remarkably, the group
ploughed on, performing a Smith-less 'Levitate' that bristled
with frustration and anger. He rejoined them for a disjointed
'Lie Dream'. An equally messy 'Behind The Counter' ('Get the
fucking song going, you fucking cunts! Can you manage it?') was
followed by a chaotic, desultory 'He Pep!' At this point, Hanley,
Burns and Crooks had had enough and walked off. The last few
minutes are painful: Smith and Nagle attempted 'Powder Keg',
his incoherent ramblings accompanied by her occasional vague
prods at the keyboard. Smith picked up Hanley's bass and tossed
it casually across the stage – a depressingly symbolic moment.
    Steve Hanley's version of post-gig events describes Burns
wrapping a guitar lead around Smith's neck. 'A line's being
crossed. Any remaining respect from either side is being lost. Him
trashing the gear is him trashing the band, and the three of us
have finally lost interest.' Back at the hotel, Smith and Nagle had
a quarrel that resulted in him being charged with third-degree
assault and harassment. Smith's version of events, recounted in
Renegade, was: 'So, back in my room, I'm having a cigarette, and
I just put it out on her trainer and went to sleep. Next, I've been
reported by them and her, and handcuffed and put in jail.' The
account that Julia Nagle gave Dave Simpson doesn't clarify matters
completely. She says that 'the incident was distorted, and made out
to be about Mark and myself, but there was a lot more to it... he
was lashing out angrily in all directions and it was unfortunate
[that I] was in the way'. After post-gig drinks with Burns in a bar

near the venue, Hanley witnessed Smith being arrested. 'There's Mark outside the hotel, whiter than ever, handcuffed in the back of a police car.' Although he did contact a lawyer to ask him to help Smith out, Hanley refused to accompany Smith to the police station. The bassist made his position clear: 'I'm never getting on stage with you again,' and he was true to his word. On the 8th April 1998, Steve Hanley boarded a plane back to the UK. The final sentence of *The Big Midweek* reads: 'As the plane heads up over New York, one thing's certain: I'm never going to play bass with The Fall again.'

If Wolstencroft's departure had been significant, Hanley's was seismic. Not only had he been in the group for a record-breaking 19 years, he had defined the Fall sound more than anyone other than Smith himself. 'Garden', 'Tempo House', 'Bombast', 'The Classical', 'New Big Prinz'... so many of The Fall's very best songs would have been critically diminished without his contribution. Always solid, deep and resonant; never unnecessarily showy, but sparingly flamboyant. Fifteen years earlier, Smith had admitted that 'the most original aspect of The Fall is Steve on the bass. I've never heard a bass player like him in my life. I don't have to tell him what to play, he just knows. He is the Fall sound.' Hanley's role was not only musical: his organisational skills and ability to mediate between irate group members and the irascible Smith were all that kept the group from disintegrating on many occasions. Even more than Craig Scanlon, he was Smith's greatest loss.

The aftermath of the Brownies gig saw Tommy Crooks leave the group too, but also, more notably, the final departure of Karl Burns. Whilst he did not have quite as consistent a level of influence on the group's sound as Steve Hanley, his distinctive, flamboyant drumming – particularly in tandem with Paul Hanley in the early part of his second stint – had a sizeable influence on much of the group's work over three decades. Enigmatically, Smith remarked that 'In the end he became his own audience. He wasn't sure of his role,' before remarking sourly, 'I don't miss him.' Despite Dave Simpson's best efforts, Burns's current whereabouts remain a mystery. Paul Hanley renewed the attempt to track him down when writing *Have A Bleedin Guess*, but to no avail. 'It was an absolute honour,' he wrote, 'if sometimes a white-knuckle ride, to have been in a two-drummer line-up with him.' Burns's sheer tenacity – a handful of musicians have at various times rejoined The Fall, but who else could have managed to do so so many times? – makes him in some ways a symbolic group member, representing the stubborn refusal to quit and the capacity to launch a surprise comeback that runs deeply through the history of The Fall.

A week after the Brownies meltdown, Smith appeared in court and was ordered to undergo an alcohol treatment programme and anger-management counselling. His most pressing concern, however, was the remaining April gigs – two at Camden Dingwalls and one in Reading. Remarkably, the group fulfilled their commitments and just about got away with it. Smith and Nagle were joined by Kate Themen, drummer with Polythene (she presumably had one of those infamous crash courses in the group's back catalogue) and, aided considerably by backing tapes, stumbled through the three performances. Jonathan Romney described the first of the Camden gigs:

> What the partly-enraptured, partly aggrieved audience got was a subsistence-level Fall – Smith with Julia Nagle on keyboards, guitar and stacks of rough-and-ready pre-programmes, and a terrified-looking woman on drums. Sometimes it sounded like Suicide's pared-down electronica, sometimes it harked back to the Xerox scrappiness of The Fall's very early days on the Manchester punk scene. It was possibly in honour of those days that Smith revived their antique number Industrial Estate... a prospect as likely as David Bowie encoring with The Laughing Gnome. The makeshift feel was part of the fun, but it's doubtful any other band would have got away with it.

Over the next few months, Smith set about rebuilding the group. On bass, he recruited Karen Leatham, an acquaintance of Nagle's who had played in a band called Wonky Alice. Tom Head became the new drummer. Born Thomas Murphy, Head was the younger brother of Smith's friend Steve Evets and a part-time actor who had appeared in *Emmerdale, Coronation Street* and *The League of Gentlemen*. Smith enthused about his new recruit to *The Wire*: 'I'm lucky to get him, he's brilliant... he can play anything; I mean, really play it... He can get what you want like [he clicks his fingers].' The Smith / Nagle / Leatham / Head line-up played only two gigs, at Manchester University and London's Astoria on 11th and 12th August. By the time they played St. Bernadette's Catholic Social Club in Whitefield on 21st October, the line-up had been augmented by guitarist Neville Wilding, formerly of Rockin Gomez, a psychobilly outfit from Rhyl. The rapidly shifting line-up and subsequent impact on rehearsal opportunities led some fans to think the unthinkable – that The Fall might be beyond rescue.

> The Fall arrived on stage at around 10.30pm. Same line-up as before, didn't look like they'd practised since the LA gig. No new material whatsoever – virtually the same set as the Astoria, including F-olding Money and This Perfect Day (encore). The version of Pharmacist 'improvised' at the end of the main set was so appalling it was almost funny. Almost. Can't see any future for this band at present.

Even though the group seemed to be on the verge of disintegration, 1998 saw five 'new' Fall albums released. Two of them, *Northern Attitude* and *Smile... It's The Best Of*, were further entries in the growing list of pointless and shoddy compilations resulting from Smith's deal with Receiver (see Appendix 2). The other three were live albums: *Live To Air In Melbourne '82, Live Various Years* and *Nottingham '92*. These were the result of a deal Smith signed in 1997 with Rob Ayling of Voiceprint (a label that had previously specialised in re-releasing prog-rock albums) which allowed Ayling to release live Fall recordings using the Cog Sinister imprint. A plethora of Voiceprint live albums would be released sporadically from this point on, varying widely in terms of both recording quality and tracklisting accuracy (see Appendix 3). To be fair, *Melbourne '82* and *Nottingham '92* are two of the best Fall live albums. *Live Various Years*, released in September 1998, was patchier. It contains a mix of recordings from 1988, 1993 and 1997. The first half a dozen are, according to the credits, from New York and Munich in Autumn 1993, but whilst the group did play in Germany at the time, there was no Munich gig. 'Hip Priest' is clumsily spliced in two for no apparent reason and several songs are inaccurately labelled. However, *Live Various Years* is not without its interesting moments. 'Spinetrak', despite Smith and the group's best efforts, feels distinctly empty without Brix; 'Hip Priest' (here revived after a nine-year absence) sees Nagle add some interesting if incongruous keyboard work. The most entertaining moment comes when MES, apparently irritated by Bush's sluggish intro to 'Strychnine', tries to gee up the group by calling them 'fucking pot heads'.

The 22nd Peel session was recorded on 18th October and broadcast on 4th November. Elspeth ('Speth') Hughes, a studio engineer who produced some audio collages that the group used as intro tapes for gigs at the time, contributed 'special effects'. Given the line-up's very limited experience of playing together, plus the fact that the material was very new (only 'This Perfect Day' had been played live by this point, and that only twice), it would be only reasonable to expect the session to be on the rough and ready side. But it's more than that: it's a shambolic mess. 'Bound Soul One', which features some *Aladdin Sane*-style free-jazz piano from Leatham, sounds both like the group only learned the song that afternoon and that none of them can hear each other. 'Antidotes' verges on the unlistenable, Head toiling away at his John Bonham impression whilst Smith seemingly attempts to swallow the microphone whole. 'This Perfect Day' is a little more effective, but still sounds distinctly under-rehearsed. 'Shake-Off' (which wouldn't be debuted live for another couple of months) also sounds very much like a work in progress.

Karen Leatham quit the group after bottles were thrown onstage at the 14th December Bristol gig. She was replaced by Adam Helal (original surname Bromley), a friend of Wilding. Despite the continual upheavals, Smith somehow found time to record and release a spoken-word album. *The Post Nearly Man*, recorded at Pete Waterman's PWL Studios, is a determinedly inaccessible and fractured mix of Smith's musings and snippets of Fall songs. 'I got this commission to write six episodes of what was going to be like an *X-Files* thing,' he explained, 'I said I'll do six 25-minute stories. So I spent all this time doing it... and they said "Oh, we've changed our minds".'[260] The *NME*'s Johnny Cigarettes was less than impressed. Awarding it 2/10, he declared that 'you can count the substantial ideas here on the fingers of a Kit-Kat'.

The Smith / Nagle / Wilding / Helal / Head line-up brought some relative stability to the group, staying in place for nearly two years (although Nagle was absent for several gigs during this period). They began to debut new material in early 1999, 'On My Own', 'Inevitable', 'Birthday Song' and 'Mad.Men-Eng.Dog' all appearing for the first time during a three-night residency at The Witchwood in Ashton. On 15th April, the group played an afternoon gig sponsored by XFM Radio at Sound Republic in London where they first played their less than distinguished cover of the New York Dolls' 'Jet Boy'. The first recorded product from this new incarnation of The Fall was the March 1999 single, 'Touch Sensitive' – one of the most recognisable Fall songs to those generally unfamiliar with the group's work owing to its deployment in an advert for the Vauxhall Corsa. Almost inevitably, there was a pointless seven-minute 'dance remix' on the B-side, as well as 'Antidote', an alternative version of '(Jung Nev's) Antidotes' from the forthcoming LP. Despite the catchy riff and chorus, 'Touch Sensitive' only crawled to number 90 in the singles chart. The next single, released in August 1999, was 'F-'oldin' Money'. It fared even worse than its predecessor, only managing a chart placing of 93. Released as two different CD singles, the B-sides included four more alternative versions of tracks from *The Marshall Suite*, one of which saw MES sing 'Perfect Day' in a strangely wavering falsetto.

The Marshall Suite

The album was recorded at Battery Studios in Willesden in north-west London. It had once been part of Morgan Studios, which

---

[260] Smith mentioned *X-Files* creator Chris Carter in 'The Quartet of Doc Shanley'.

in the 60s and 70s was used by the likes of Paul McCartney, Led Zeppelin, Pink Floyd and Paul Simon. Early recording sessions featured only Smith, Nagle and Head, but as time went on Leatham, Helal and Wilding also contributed. The album, once again on Artful Records, was released on vinyl as a three-sided affair, the fourth remaining blank. Smith explained that he'd had this idea in mind from the very beginning:

> I had the concept in my head, you know, the three sides. That was from the offset really... I'd always wanted to. And you couldn't do it with the old group, you know. I wanted a straightforward side, a second side that was opening up and a third side that was like really off the wall.

Smith suggested to *The Wire*'s Tony Herrington that it was a form of concept album, the 'Marshall' being 'a figure, to link it together... I thought it would be good to do it as the story of his life, a themed LP, with a thread running through it'. He went on to express dissatisfaction with the work of producer Steve Hitchcock: 'I'm still very mad that some of the mixes on the new record were pissed about with by the producer while I was away... It's only one or two tracks, no one else will notice it, but I'm furious. I won't talk to him.' He also dismissed the notion that the 'Marshall' character was, as some suggested, based on Thomas Hardy's *The Mayor of Casterbridge*. The blame for this misunderstanding is also placed on Hitchcock: 'That got out because I was trying to explain the concept to the so-called producer, a loony, who'd get everything wrong anyway.'

Touch Sensitive
The album kicks off with a lively slice of rock'n'roll. Head's thumping drums, Wilding's crafty little riff (which owes more than a little to Iggy Pop's 'Girls') and the catchy 'hey hey hey hey' backing vocals combine to give the opener an infectious vitality. The strings (courtesy of Hitchcock) add welcome breadth and texture.[261] Smith's performance seems to show him bearing

[261] They would eventually lead to a legal dispute – see Chapter 32.

few scars from the previous year's trauma. There's real bite to his delivery, the lyrics are sharp and funny and his off-kilter timing is impeccable, especially in the way he phrases 'and a Star Wars police vehicle pulls up / I say gimme a taxi!' The phrase 'vanity and presumption' references both the Bible (Ecclesiastes 6:9) and Thomas Paine's *Rights of Man*. Regarding the song's use on a car advert, Smith remarked drily, 'I didn't have full control over that. And at the time I needed the money. Sometimes that's the sad case. We're not all Elton John.' It was a setlist favourite: 160 outings 1998-2006.

F-'oldin' Money

The album maintains its opening momentum with a spirited cover of Tommy Blake's obscure 1959 rockabilly tune. It was another long-standing live favourite, being played 142 times 1998-2006.

Shake-Off

A song which, according to fanzine *Pseud Mag*, 'begs to be played at excessive volume'. It opens with floating synths and reverb-heavy proclamations of a portentous but obscure nature – 'Give me the teachers who said if you deny the strong pot or ecstatic imbibed within you will be end up in eyeball-injecting' – before a gloriously brash and jagged drum and bass rhythm kicks in. The combination of taut, angular rhythms and layers of Smith's shouting and crooning is sublime. 'Shake-Off' encapsulates the defiant attitude of the whole album. It was played live 33 times 1998-2002.

Bound

A cover of a Northern Soul instrumental by obscure 70s act The Audio Arts Strings called 'Love Bound', with additional lyrics from Smith. It's a little slight and predictable, although Wilding does try to add some interesting variations on the chord progression as the song develops. It was played 20 times, all in 1999.

This Perfect Day

Another cover, this time of Australia's The Saints.[262] The Fall's version is appealingly distorted but feels a tad flat compared to the original. It was played 38 times, 1998-2000. On the vinyl version of the album, 'This Perfect Day' closed side one.[263]

(Jung Nev's) Antidotes

The album steps up a gear with a bombastic, sweeping wave of noise, featuring multiple layers of heavy feedback, reverb and distortion. There are echoes of Led Zeppelin's 'Kashmir' (especially in the hefty drum track), as well as U2's 'Bullet The Blue Sky'. It's another that begs for high volume. Smith delves into the first half of the 20th century for his lyrical inspiration: 'if chewing gum is chewed / the chewer is pursued' is from the Marx Brothers' 1933 film *Duck Soup*; he also references 'Mairzy Doats', a popular novelty song from 1943. Moving on a couple of decades, he also seems to allude to the *Carry On...* film franchise ('carry on sir').[264] Elsewhere, mentions of secondary moderns, sports teachers and the inner-city suggest some thoughts about working-class education; at a stretch, it could be argued that 'those who vote' and 'liberty is screwed' hint at the effect of the education system on working-class political engagement. However, it's just as plausible that, as was often his wont, Smith was simply riffing on a word that he liked the sound of. It was played live 84 times, 1998-2002.

Inevitable

A delicate, plaintive song based around a simple two-chord guitar part, hesitant piano and a melancholy oboe-effect keyboard line. Smith's vocals are understated to the point of indistinction,

---

[262] Punk act formed in 1973. Their debut single, '(I'm) Stranded' was released in September 1976, beating The Clash and the Sex Pistols into the record shops. MES had previously discussed his admiration for the band in a 1981 *NME* interview: 'Did you ever see them on *Top of the Pops*? They looked, y'know, just slightly wrong! They had all these pullovers on, and they were really, like, dirty, and really over the top, and the singer stood at this strange angle, I think he had a pint in his hand... fuckin' great!'

[263] Or, as Smith had planned, the 'straightforward side' – a description that could legitimately apply to four of the five tracks, but 'Shake-Off' hardly qualifies.

[264] Although there wasn't a *Carry On Sir*, there was a *Carry On Teacher*.

and we don't learn much about the narrator other than he likes dancing on Saturdays and has some sort of interest in Burma. It was only played 11 times (three as an instrumental), all in 1999.

Anecdotes + Antidotes In B#

A companion song to '(Jung Nev's) Antidotes' that recycles many of the same lyrics. It's much lighter in tone, Wilding's wah-wah giving it a slightly funky feel. During a performance of the song in Los Angeles in 2001, Smith's amended lyric seems to confirm the *Carry On...* reference in the 'Nev' version: 'and so secondary modern British Carry On film, Carry On, Sir, Carry On, Sir.' It was played 25 times, 1998-99.

Early Life Of Crying Marshal

An inconsequential but not unpleasant interlude: 51 seconds of classical strings and tape collage. On the vinyl version, this opened the last of the three sides.[265]

The Crying Marshal

The song came about as a collaboration with The Filthy 3, a project of Jason Barron of D.O.S.E. ('they had a song and they didn't have any lyrics for it; that song came from that; throwing things around'.) Here, the group revisit the brutal, industrial sound of '(Jung Nev's) Antidotes'. It throws the kitchen sink at you: overloaded big beat drums, snaking, grizzly guitar lines and strings, synths and liberal doses of distortion applied across the board. Smith doesn't tell us much about the title character who supposedly linked the album together other than 'he left town over 60 times, mainly for the fashion exhibition'. He claimed the version that appeared on the album was a remix, and that a Hitchcock error led to the original version being omitted. It was never played live.

Birthday Song

An ethereal composition by Julia Nagle (originally composed for her sister's birthday) accompanied by an uncharacteristically

---

[265] The second side had concluded with 'Finale: Tom Raggazzi', which did not appear on the CD or cassette versions.

romantic MES: 'in dreams I stumble towards you... I am in the next room with you always'. The use of samples of his own voice as backing vocals is a nice touch. If MES had really intended the third side of the record to be the 'really off the wall one', 'Birthday Song' seems a strange track to have selected for it. It was played live 21 times, 1999-2000.

Mad.Men-Eng.Dog

The second of the two 'interludes' is radically different from the first. This experimental piece finds Smith rambling about 'platonic air corps staff' over layers of dark, murky noise. Perhaps surprisingly, it was played live – 18 times, all in 1999. In Leeds on 4th May it was quite similar to the album version, although briefer and with few lyrics; the next night in Birmingham it was reduced mainly to a drum beat that Smith ranted over; by September (in Brussels) it generally consists of Wilding apparently attacking his guitar with a screwdriver.

On My Own

A rather unnecessary reworking of *Levitate*'s 'Everybody But Myself', which smooths most of the original's edges with a predictable house chug. Gives the distinct impression of having been tacked on to the end to bring the album up to a respectable running time (just shy of 40 minutes). It was performed 25 times in 1999, then was played once more the following year.

Reviews and Reissues

Smith was defiantly proud of the album, describing it as his 'glorious return'. '[It] must have annoyed certain people when it was released, because the general consensus was I'd had it; no more comebacks for Mad Mark.' The critical response was guardedly warm. In *The Guardian*, Caroline Sullivan felt that the album's 'itchy garage rock and irascible shouting' demonstrated that the turmoil of 1998 had 'sparked a creative renaissance of sorts' and there was 'a sense of purpose that has long been missing'. *Select* took a similar view: 'the upheaval has clearly spooked him into making a renewed effort... A varied and strange album, expected Fall requirements of tangential freakishness and nagging pop lucidity are at their highest levels for some time.' *The Times'* Mike Pattenden was more cautious, giving the album 6/10, although he acknowledged that the group could 'still nail-down a groove with that same blend of ruthless precision and perverse amateurishness'. *Uncut's* Simon Goddard gave the album five stars and declared that 'The Fall have pulled it off again... *The Marshall Suite* sees Smith in his finest form in aeons'. The positive words did not translate into sales: whilst *The Marshall Suite* sold a little better than *Levitate*, it still only made number 84 in the album chart.

Cherry Red reissued the album in 2011 as a 3 CD set. CD1 contained the bonus track from the original three-side vinyl version, 'Tom Raggazzi', a half-arsed bit of reggae in which Smith seems to have little interest. CD2 contains Peel sessions 21 and 22, plus the B-sides from the 'Touch Sensitive' and 'F-'oldin' Money' singles. One of these is 'The REAL Life Of The Crying Marshall (New Version)'; it may be that this version, which features a prominent rock-guitar riff, is the missing original that Smith claimed had been omitted from the album. CD3 consists of the eight tracks recorded at the afternoon gig sponsored by XFM Radio in April 1999. It's raw, unbalanced and generally all over the place; Smith's vocals are slathered with gratuitous amounts of reverb.

Evaluation

Considering where the group were in Spring 1998, it's incredible that they put out any sort of album at all – let alone one this good – only a year later. It's undoubtedly uneven, but it still contains some blistering and exciting moments, and there's an indefatigable, resilient spirit that runs through the whole thing.

After the back-to-basics *Cerebral Caustic*, the best moments on *Light User Syndrome* and *Levitate* saw the group find an effective blend of garage rock and dance-infused electronics. The highlights of *The Marshall Suite* see the group strengthen and harden this sound. '(Jung Nev's) Antidotes', 'The Crying Marshal' and 'Shake-Off', for example, see them add a grinding, industrial tone that broadens their palette with occasionally thrilling results.

Often, the best Fall albums capture the ever-changing group at a specific moment in their evolution, and this is precisely what *Marshall* does. In 1998, it seemed that The Fall might die; this album shouted boldly (if not always coherently) 'long live The Fall'.

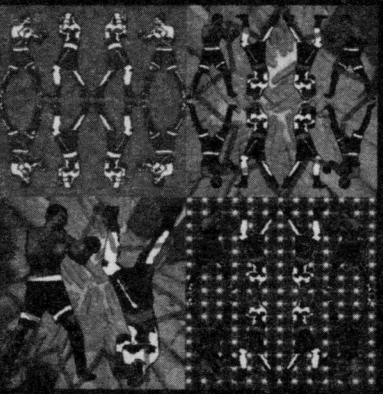

THE FALL

The Unutterable

The Unutterable
Recorded: Testa-Rossa Studios, Manchester; Street-Level 2 Studio, London;
Sonic Surgery, Manchester, mid-2000
Released: 6th November 2000

Personnel:
Mark E Smith – vocals, SFX
Julia Nagle – keyboards, guitar, vocals, programming
Tom Head – drums, percussion
Neville Wilding – guitar, vocals
Adam Helal – bass, pro tools, vocals

With:
Steve Evets – vocals
Kazuko Hohki – vocals ('Cyber Insekt')
Ben Pritchard – guitar ('Dr. Bucks' Letter')
Grant Cunliffe – vocals

Chapter 22: The Unutterable

'Smith's scattergun muse has certainly been refreshed by something.'

Mid-1999 saw Smith involved in several of his increasingly frequent collaborations, both on record and on screen. He revisited his connection with Inspiral Carpets, appearing on stage in Camden with The Clint Boon Experience (the band that Boon had formed following the Carpets' demise), providing vocals for their cover of 'I Wanna Be Your Dog'. This haphazard gallop through the classic Stooges number was the B-side of their August 1999 single 'You Can't Keep A Good Man Down'. Smith also worked with Dave Bush, now a member of Elastica, contributing to two tracks on their *6 Track EP* – 'How He Wrote Elastica Man' and 'KB'. Justine Frischmann of Elastica described the experience:

> We were in the studio and [MES] was in a pub around the corner. Dave bumped into him and invited him to come down. He was up for doing some stuff so we did. I was initially too scared to come out of the control room but when I did he was charming. I think he probably can be quite scary but he chose to be the perfect gentleman when he was working with us. He was actually very inspiring to be around – really cool. We'd had that track for a while and we didn't know what to do with it and he walked into the studio room and plugged his mic into an amp, turned it up until it was all feeding back and started shouting 'E!-L!-A!' doing his cheerleader bit which was quite bizarre.

Two of the songs on *The Unutterable* were linked to Smith's late-90s flirtations with the world of acting. He had made a brief appearance in a Jerry Sadowitz sketch show called *The Pall Bearer's Revue* in 1992, but his first proper screen role was in *Diary of a Madman*, a bewildering ten-minute piece that appeared on BBC2 in 1997. Based on a 19th-century Russian short story and starring Smith's friend Steve Evets, Smith's appearance lasts around 30 seconds and largely consists of him repeating the word 'name'. The following year, he appeared in Mark Aerial Waller's short film *Glow Boys*, playing 'The Caterer'. In 1999, he appeared in another Waller film: *Midwatch* was set in the galley of a ship returning from Operation Mosaic, a series of nuclear tests conducted by Britain in 1956. It was described by the director as:

> ...an intensely claustrophobic scenario shot in infrared that depicts the plight of two individuals trapped in the galley of a ship returning from the first British nuclear test... the characters, played by Steve Evets and Mark E Smith of the band The Fall, act out their frustrations with each other in a comic rambling exchange.

The new line-up and positive critical reception for *The Marshall Suite* saw the group invigorated on the live front, playing 32 dates in 1999, including a run of 12 consecutive gigs between 3rd-14th May. It's a period that is especially well represented by bootleg recordings, and they offer an intriguing picture of the line-up's development and their capacity for producing highly variable performances. At Leeds on 4th May, for example, the group sound stilted and uncertain. Like many recordings from this period, Smith's vocals are smothered in excessive layers of reverb. 'Spencer' sounds like early-period Mogwai and 'Ol' Gang' has more than a touch of Status Quo about it. The 13th May date in Luton was a particularly unusual one: exceptionally concise (21 songs in under an hour), it opened with an intriguing version of 'Birthday Song' that's radically different from the album. Wilding sang most of 'Ten Houses Of Eve'; 'The Joke' was played twice for no apparent reason (as was 'Ketamine Sun'); 'Shake-Off' made reference to a 'Simple Minds reunion'. Although the May tour passed off without major incident, their Reading Festival appearance that summer saw The Fall revisit the previous year's violent chaos. A bust-up with Tom Head resulted in Smith sacking the drummer. Wilding persuaded Nick Dewey (ex-member of shoegaze band Revolver and at the time part of The Chemical Brothers' management) to perform with them, even though he hadn't played drums for several years.

Dewey found himself being led on to a tour bus with blacked-out windows. Mark E Smith was on one of the tour bus benches, shirt off, passed out... Wilding tried to wake Smith and couldn't rouse him, so punched him in the face. After two or three blows, Smith finally woke up to be informed by Wilding, 'Mark, this is Nick. He's going to be playing drums for us.'

By the time Smith appeared on stage, he was covered in blood, apparently as a result of being 'at it with knuckle-dusters' with Wilding backstage. The bootleg of the gig reveals that Dewey performed heroically. The drums are (understandably) generally plodding and generic, but taking into account that he had only a couple of hours to prepare for a set of unfamiliar songs, it's incredible how well he keeps it together. Smith sounds thoroughly inebriated, particularly on 'Birthday Song', where he launches into a drunken ramble: 'Backstage, the chitter-chatter of the Reading backstage camp is louder than the music of the group.' Head was reinstated in time for the next day's performance in Leeds.

Half a dozen gigs in the Low Countries followed in September. The performance in Brussels on the 18th was full of extemporaneous lyrics: 'Cos I'm living in a pawn shop lately. Princess, Dapple, pony' ('Touch Sensitive'); 'We had a mixer called Deaf Pete. He couldn't make it today. He lost the ticket to the ferry... Unlucky for him, he was on free enterprise 101. Then he met John Lennon' ('Ketamine Sun'); 'If only the shards could reconnect in a Pink Floyd and Led Zeppelin type of style... If only it can be done in a rap sort of style, like Ice T. Like Ice T.' ('Ten Houses Of Eve'). The last date of the tour, at Leiden in The Netherlands on the 19th, was an unmitigated disaster. Wilding wasn't present, Smith appeared only sporadically, they played a particularly horrible version of 'Shake-Off' and the whole sorry affair was over in only 38 minutes.

New material emerged gradually from October 1999, including 'Hands Up Billy' and 'Cyber Insekt', the latter at this stage a heads-down garage-rockabilly number bereft of the distinctive backing vocals that would appear on the album. In early 2000, 'Two Librans' and 'Way Round' were debuted. A few days before the group's 24th March date in Leeds, Smith bumped into Craig Scanlon at a pub in Prestwich and allegedly invited him to play, but he didn't turn up. The 24th May gig at London's Astoria 2 saw a particularly interesting debut, that of 'Dr. Bucks' Letter'. The distinctive, treated drum loop appeared briefly at the outset, but thereafter the riff was played by live bass and guitar. The lyric at this stage mainly consisted of Smith reading out a magazine interview with Pete Tong that outlined the DJ's favourite books, magazines and TV shows.

The Unutterable

The Unutterable was recorded – in just a month – at Grant Showbiz's Street-Level 2 in Ladbrook Grove,[266] Helal and Wilding's Sonic Surgery studio, and Testa-Rossa in Longsight. Grant Showbiz returned to produce, his first studio production credit since *Shift-Work*. The album was released on the Eagle label.[267] Pascal Le Gras supplied the cover art, his last design for a Fall studio album, although his work was used on several subsequent live releases. The contrast of the kaleidoscopic variations on the 'boxers' image with the brutal simplicity of the monochrome titles is an apt reflection of the album's combination of garage rock and electronica.

Cyber Insekt

The album opens with a piece of lively sci-fi skiffle that has a curiously wobbly guitar line and is broken up with a couple of spacey, Gong-like interludes. Kazuko Hohki (Grant Showbiz's wife) of Frank Chickens contributed the deadpan, robotic vocals without ever meeting any of the group. According to Julia Nagle, such lines as 'book of film', 'film of book' and 'film of book with soundtrack' refer to the 1998 Brownies gig: 'We said the whole incident had been incredulous [sic], and we should write a book about it. And being in America, we then laughed about making

---

[266] Grant Showbiz had set up the studio in 1979 with Kif Kif, drummer in Here & Now.
[267] Eagle was part of the Eagle Rock Entertainment group, which was co-founded by Terry Shand. In 1983, Shand had been one of the founders of Castle Communications, which released a handful of Fall compilations in the late 90s.

the "film of the book, of the film" etc, which in turn became the lyrics.' 'Book on station rack' also suggests that a paperback on display in a railway station might have caught Smith's eye.[268] The song was played live 74 times, 1999-2002.

Two Librans

After the comparatively light and breezy 'Insekt', 'Two Librans' bursts in with a garage-rock attitude reminiscent of *Cerebral Caustic*. But there's something new here: the grizzly bassline strikes a different note to the Steve Hanley years; a coiled, fuzzy, menacing tone that the group would return to regularly. The verse's understated, circumspect guitar line circles the vocals, waiting to pounce when they reach the chorus, at which point the fuzzed-up chords crash in. Smith finds a perfect balance between disdainful slur and aggressive bark. On several occasions, he throws in a growling, gargling enunciation of the song's title, another style that would be adopted with increasing frequency over the rest of the group's career.

It's a typically opaque lyric, but the line about Oprah Winfrey studying bees always raises a smile. In another example of The Fall community's ability to conjure up a heated argument over the most obscure and trivial issues, one contributor to *The Annotated Fall*'s page on the song made around 20 posts insisting with increasing exasperation and irascibility that the word 'bees' doesn't appear at all, claiming it's 'peace' and 'being'. This debate spilled over into the *Fall Online Forum*, where a poll was set up to decide the issue which generated over 100 posts.[269] 'Two Librans' was played live 72 times, 2000-2002.

W.B

The title refers to William Blake ('you've heard about mad Blake'), from whom Smith had taken inspiration for 'Jerusalem' 12 years earlier. On this occasion, the specific influence was his

---

[268] On *The Annotated Fall*, Crimm suggests the book may be *The State of the Art* by Iain M. Banks, albeit without any evidence other than the fact that its cover features what does indeed look like a robot insect.
[269] 'Bees' was a clear winner, attracting 82% of the vote.

poem 'A Song Of Liberty'. The swirling synths and looping guitar provide an effective backdrop for Smith's sinuous drawl. Only played ten times, all in 2000.

Sons Of Temperance

As is the case with much of *Unutterable*, 'Temperance' features an exciting mix of electronics and garage rock. It's a tale of two halves (or four quarters, to be more accurate) – a taut, riff-driven onslaught and a floaty, laid-back interlude. The first is sharp, biting and fizzes with energy, especially the staccato bursts; the second is woozy, menacing and psychedelic. The full arsenal of MES techniques is deployed: random growling; a double-tracked chorus refrain; a slightly disturbing and creepy falsetto. The way he enunciates 'temp-or-anzh' is a particular highlight. Mark Aerial Waller suggests that the song is a reference to his 2000 short video *The Sons of Temperance* ('a journey into a dark sphere of information retrieval'). bzfgt of *The Annotated Fall* considers the song to be a companion piece to 'New Puritan', being 'concerned with the tension, and the mutual implication, of discipline and ecstasy'. It was played 19 times, 2000-2001.

Dr. Bucks' Letter

One of the group's finest ever moments, where a disparate array of sounds, words and approaches coalesce into a magnificent whole. The coarse, grainy programmed rhythm track is complemented perfectly by Head's delicate rimshot drums; the simple, melodic guitar line that runs through parts of the song subtly cuts through the fuzz and distortion; the riff that appears on the little break at three minutes is distorted yet tidy, hazy but perfectly contained and controlled. Ben Pritchard, who wouldn't join the group full-time until February 2001, added the guitar riff to Helal's programmed rhythm.

> I came up with just a little riff that ended up being 'Dr. Bucks' Letter'. So we went in the studio and I just started playing this riff, and Mark said, 'Yeah, that's it! That's great! Yeah, do that! Do that!'

The music is sufficiently inventive to support even the most half-hearted of Smith vocals, but here he more than matches the excellence of the music. There are multiple examples of specific words and phrases where the enunciation hits that sweet spot that was his unique talent: 'recompense', 'magazine', 'checklist', 'CDs', 'download it'. There are also several beautifully crafted lines, in particular 'vulgar and arrogant abeyance'. It's a melancholy tale of broken friendship. Having lost his temper with a friend, who he 'mocked' and 'treated… with rudeness', the narrator 'tried to make amends', but is depressed about their estrangement. He hopes that 'one day a door will be ajar… so we can recompense our betrayal of our hard-won friendship'. The punctuation of the title suggests that the title character's name is Doctor Bucks. It's not entirely clear if the doctor and the friend are one and the same or if character in question is a real friend of Smith's, an invention, or from a story that he read. Suggested candidates for a 'real' friend have included Craig Scanlon, Alan Wise and Rob Waite, editor of *The Biggest Library Yet* fanzine.

The 'Pete Tong magazine article' section is the best-known element of the song, and for good reason – Smith's deadpan delivery of DJ Tong's ridiculous 'checklist' ('I was in the realm of the essence of Tong') is arguably the funniest moment in The Fall's entire back catalogue. Tracking down the source for this passage, which took him nearly 20 years, is dannyno's proudest Fall detective moment. It comes from *Hot Line*, 'the complementary magazine for Virgin Trains passengers', no 8, Autumn 1999.[270] The song was played live on 113 occasions.

Hot Runes
A tasty piece of swinging rockabilly twang whose riff resembles a faster-tempo version Howlin' Wolf's 'Spoonful', most famously covered by Cream. Smith references Alan Brazil and Derek Hatton, pronounces 'hyperbole' as 'hyper-bowl' and with typical perversity sings 'hot June' rather than 'hot runes' throughout. Its truncated length is disappointing – things are just getting cracking

270 Dan discussed his remarkable find in this interview: https://soundcloud.com/magculture/episode-14-september-2019

with some added distorted guitar before it fades away. Live versions (there were 20 of them, 2000-01) were generally more frantic.

Way Round

More twanging guitar, but 'Way Round' also has an electronic, sci-fi flavour. Tommy Mackay captures it neatly as 'Iggy Pop meets Doctor Who'. According to Julia Nagle, the lyric (which includes the glorious phrase 'glass disco sweatboxes') is about Smith getting lost in a disco. It got 82 outings, 2000-04.

Octo Realm/Ketamine Sun

The opening minute sees Rob Ayling, Julia Nagle and Grant Showbiz[271] providing 'comedy' introductions ('Hi! I'm Spliffhead I like to lie on the floor!'). Smith's abrupt interjection ('I'm Smith') provides a spot of real humour. The next minute or so sees a diversion into *Post Nearly Man* territory, MES declaiming tinnily over a thin, distant drum track and delivering one of his best put-downs, 'you're a walking tower of Adidas crap'. The main part of the song is one of the group's clearest 'borrows', being heavily indebted to Lou Reed's 'Kill Your Sons'. It's an atypical Fall track; a dark, brooding, hypnotic but actually quite conventional rock tune, one that most bands would probably have chosen as the album closer. Julia Nagle described its recording:

> There was also this joking sort of fatherly thing going on between MES and Nev [Wilding]... I think the song was partly about this 'surrogate paternal' relationship, not sure whose idea it was initially, probably Mark's. When we recorded the vocals at Grant's [Showbiz] in London, Mark did this really stuttering chorus 'k.k.k.ket...a.mine' sounding like a seizure. It wasn't as nice on the ears as another vocal take, but MES and I were really wanting this to be used, as it was reflective of how dangerous drug taking is, but Grant wanted the song to sound nice and when it came to the final mix this vocal take was left out.

The 'Ketamine Sun' section was played 59 times, 1999-2002.

---

[271] Grant Showbiz's contribution gained him an album credit under his real name Cunliffe (though spelled as 'Conliffe' on the album sleeve).

Serum

A dark slab of ominous electronica that one could easily imagine sitting alongside 'Oxymoron' and 'Hostile' on *The Light User Syndrome*. The combination of grainy, twisted drum track, disturbing synth effects and spooky *Twilight Zone*-esque guitar lines creates a richly oppressive and foreboding atmosphere. The most surprising line – given that Smith rarely wrote directly about physical relationships – is 'many have found pleasures in curvaceous women / their undulating curves upper and lower / but what I really need is a glass of cold water'. This echoes a piece of advice from his father that he quoted in *Renegade*: 'If you're feeling too sexy, have a glass of water and a run round the backyard.' It had a brief and chequered live history. It first appeared as an instrumental intro in May 2000, its next appearance was aborted; it got five more outings in 2000, the last of which was another instrumental version.

Unutterable

Dutch music magazine *OOR* summed the song up succinctly: 'No more than a minute of a grumbling Smith while somebody in the background is playing a radiator rhythmically.' Would possibly have sat more comfortably on one of Smith's spoken word albums. His Elvis impersonation is fun though.

Pumpkin Soup And Mashed Potatoes

In which the group have a flippant crack at lounge-jazz, throwing in mellow electric piano, excessively shrill flute and some laid-back brassy keyboard stabs. Never played live.

Hands Up Billy

One of the handful of Fall songs that don't feature Smith as main vocalist, although he does contribute the opening lines and some backing vocals. Neville Wilding's vocals are energetic if not exactly subtle, and it all rattles along entertainingly enough. The lyric was inspired by a screenplay by Jon Tregenna (who had previously played with Wilding in a band called Hangar Straight) set in a used car showroom which was made into an S4C comedy drama in 2006 called *Cowbois ac Injans*.[272] A 'hands up Billy' is, according to *Annotated Fall* contributor IanFraff, 'a hands up punter (Billy Bunter), a derogatory term used by car sales people when someone who's an easy target walks into the showroom'. The song got 17 live outings in 1999–2000.

Midwatch 1953
Presumably inspired by Smith's experience of Waller's film *Midwatch*, the lyric consists largely of variations on the chronologically curious question 'Who could foresee what happened in 1953?' Synth strings, squelchy sequencer, swing drumbeat, strummed acoustic, some sort of plinky 80s video-game sound effect – all at different tempos and apparently taken from different songs – are mangled and merged and shoehorned into five and a half minutes of disorientating mayhem. Nothing fits, nothing is in tune or time, there is no sense of it being within a million miles of what most people would recognise as a proper song; it's also overly long and self-indulgent. All of which is what some (the author included) love about it, although it's a fairly divisive track amongst Fall fans. The eerie whispering in the background is probably what Steve Evets received his vocal credit for. 'Midwatch' was played live only seven times, all in 2001.

Devolute
Given the title and the reference to 'English glasnost', the lyric might well refer to the moves to devolve power to Scotland and Wales that took place in the late 90s. The phrase 'since end of May' possibly references the election of the Blair government that enacted the reforms. In the first half, Smith's vocals are double-tracked to mesmeric effect; in the second, he sounds like he's been locked in a cupboard and left to mumble to himself. Smith's disdainful delivery of 'fat arse' is another amusing moment. Musically, it consists of synth oscillations that resemble a mangled old cassette of an early Tangerine Dream album and odd little

---

[272] *Cowboys and Engines* – the similarity between the Welsh word for 'engine' and the English word 'Indian' providing the pun.

pieces of brittle percussive noise. It was only ever attempted on stage once, without great success.[273]

Das Katerer

A fleshed-out version of 'The Caterer' from *The Post Nearly Man* that in turn recycled the riff from 'Free Range' (giving Simon Wolstencroft a writing credit). It's a pleasant enough if unremarkable bit of electro-pop, but the fact that it's a retread of an already retrodden song make it a bit of a damp squib with which to conclude the album.

Reviews and Reissues

Reviewers and fans alike embraced what was generally seen as a strong return to form: '[It] succeeded,' Simon Ford commented, 'in refreshing many a jaded fan.' In *Mojo*, John Mullen described it as 'The Fall's most musically exciting LP since 1990's *Extricate*. An unutterable pleasure.' *Uncut*'s Simon Goddard thought it 'tight, witty and deliriously catchy'. Piers Martin of the *NME* found the album to be 'as vital and relevant as The Fall have sounded for a considerable length of time'. Dave Simpson's *Guardian* review was especially glowing:

> When Mark E Smith sacked his band in 1998[274] it seemed as though the old curmudgeon had finally tipped the scales from being an institution to entering one. However, it has rejuvenated the group… this is a career peak. Smith's scattergun muse has certainly been refreshed by something, and the old vitriol is increasingly laced with delicious humour.

This critical acclaim did not, sadly, transfer into sales. The album only reached number 136 in the charts, 19 places lower than *Levitate* – the worst commercial performance by a Fall album for 17 years.

[273] It appears on *Live 16th April 2001 – TJs Newport Wales UK* from *Set Of Ten* (see Appendix 3). Played as the first encore, it gets a rather desultory, plodding 90 seconds before it runs out of steam and the group play 'Touch Sensitive' (for the second time that night) instead.

[274] It would, of course, have been far more accurate to have said that the band sacked him.

There was a double CD reissue of the album in 2008. The second CD consisted of the 'Testa Rossa Monitor Mixes' – early, rough versions recorded at the first studio session. They're not especially enlightening, although 'Hot Rune' (singular here) features a later discarded monologue by Julia Nagle that rails against soap operas: 'life is so much better than that... but now these ugly, psychotic, attention-seeking crap actors scare me'.

Evaluation

It's easy to see why *The Unutterable* gained such positive reviews. Whilst there was a feeling of renewal with *The Marshall Suite*, there's a distinct sense of purpose and energy here, things coalescing into a driven, coherent piece of work. The album is laced with inventive electronica that adds texture and contrast and gives the album a more organic feel than *Shift-Work* or *Code: Selfish* without retreating into the garage-rock bunker of *Cerebral Caustic*.

It's not without its flaws, and those shortcomings are not dissimilar to those of *The Light User Syndrome*. It's too long for a start – the curse of the CD age again – and it includes tracks that are clearly B-side material. The fact that there were no singles released at the time is possibly a contributory factor: 'Das Katerer' and 'Pumpkin Soup', for example, may well have been B-sides had a couple of singles been released. The received wisdom is that the album deteriorates towards the end. Whilst this attitude is understandable, bzfgt's comments on *The Annotated Fall* (regarding 'Devolute') are pertinent:

> It is strong evidence, in my view, against the claim sometimes made that the album runs out of steam down the final stretch; there is plenty of steam here, but there is no doubt that the running order of the album is odd, with most of the more conventionally-structured or accessible songs in the rear-view mirror at this point.

Are You Are Missing Winner
Recorded: Noise Box, Manchester, mid-2001
Released: 5th November 2001

Personnel:
Mark E Smith – vocals
Ben Pritchard – guitar
Jim Watts – bass, guitar
Spencer Birtwistle – drums

With:
Brian Fanning – guitar, vocals
Ed Blaney – guitar, vocals
Julia Nagle – keyboards (live excerpt of 'Ibis-Afro Man' only; not credited
on the album)

Chapter 23: Are You Are Missing Winner

'Evidently recorded in a tin filled with seagulls.'

The Fall's first live performance following the release of *The Unutterable* was an in-store appearance at Oxford Street's HMV. The group played drummer-less, the official reason given for Head's non-appearance being his acting commitments. One online reviewer described the performance of 'I'm Going to Spain' as 'the worst I've ever heard... Adam appeared to forget the notes halfway through (or maybe he'd just lost the will to live – it's a possibility that MES includes it in the set purely to piss the musicians off)'. A few days later, it became apparent that Head had gone for good when a new drummer appeared. Spencer Birtwistle had previously been a member of Manchester bands Laugh, The Bodines, and Intastella. In time-honoured tradition, his first rehearsal was at the soundcheck for his debut gig in Nottingham on 21st November. On *The Fall Online*, Ian Leaver described the performance:

> Shambolic, drunken, bad tempered at times, funny at others but not for one second dull. [MES] doesn't look a well man and was pretty pissed... although I've seen him worse. Made Adam go and stand at the front instead of lurking by the amp, pulled Nev over who landed on top of him and continued to play while lying on the floor. Smith himself got up about three songs later.

By the end of the year, Wilding and Helal had followed Head out of the door. Their exit was linked to arguments over royalties from *The Unutterable*, although it's unclear as to whether their dispute was with Smith himself or the record label. As usual, Smith was quick to acquire new recruits. Ben Pritchard was a Prestwich native who he had known since he was a teenager. Jim Watts was from the band Trigger Happy, who had been due to support The Fall in early 2001. The Smith / Nagle / Pritchard / Watts / Birtwistle line-up played throughout the first half of 2001.

Two other notable characters entered the Fall circle during this period: Ed Blaney and Eleni Poulou. Salford-born Blaney had played in Trigger Happy with Jim Watts. He played some guitar on *Are You Are Missing Winner*, contributed backing vocals at several gigs and was for some time the group's manager. A long-standing and close friend of Smith, the two of them would go on to record and perform together on several occasions. His role within The Fall was not always clear, and he dipped in and out of the group's career trajectory. Smith first met Eleni Poulou in 1996.[275] They bumped into each other again in December 2000 when Smith was in Berlin helping out his old collaborator Michael Clark. They were married the following year.

The first gig of 2001 was in Dublin on 24th February. The new line-up was significantly under-rehearsed, even by Fall standards. Ben Pritchard had only practised four songs; Jim Watts had to be cajoled by Smith into even travelling to Ireland and his only rehearsal was no more than a 'short strum'. In the end, Smith just shouted out titles and the band made it up as they went along. The group played three Dutch dates in April, which seem to have been more successful. Shortly afterwards, MES performed a well-received spoken word set in Dublin.[276] Bootlegs of the next few UK gigs showed that the new line-up was gelling successfully. A recording of the 22nd April gig in Oxford finds Pritchard confident enough to add quite a few showy rock'n'roll flourishes of the sort that Smith would probably not have put up with 20 years earlier.

In the summer, Julia Nagle ended her six-year stint in the group. Speaking to Dave Simpson, she explained that she 'deliberately priced herself out of being in The Fall because she needed a break and to spend time with her son'. According to Simon Ford, her other reasons for leaving were 'continuing contract problems (i.e.

[275] Her first name gets a multitude of different spellings, but Eleni is what's on the album sleeves and so I have stuck with that throughout for consistency. Several sources – including Simon Ford – state that the two first met in December 2000, but in a 2009 interview with website *La Bouche Zine*, Eleni confirmed that they'd known each other for five years before they married.

[276] At Trinity College, Dublin, 12th April 2001. Alan McBride (quoted on *Fall News*): 'Tonight Smith was warm, affable, amused, tolerant and didn't seem to hold the audience… or himself in contempt, which made a nice change.'

the lack of one) relating to *The Unutterable* and the mistreatment of Helal and Wilding. She also had little stomach for the hard slog of breaking in another transitional line-up.' In August, the group gained another guitarist. Brian Fanning had previously worked as a guitar technician; he contributed to recordings for the forthcoming album, but only performed in a handful of gigs before leaving owing to the peculiar demands of touring with The Fall: 'What do you do, just get the fuckin' darts out and throw them at a map of Britain?'

The group's first single for two years was released in August 2001. 'Rude (All The Time)', recorded at Ed Blaney's home studio, came out on Flitwick Records, a label that specialised in limited-edition releases (in this case 500 copies). Originally a Trigger Happy song, here it's little more than a half-arsed strum. B-side 'I Wake Up In The City' couldn't be more of a contrast. A companion piece to 'My Ex-Classmates' Kids' – different lyrics, but they share the same primitive three-chord riff – it's a searing piece of scuzzy garage rock. The completely overloaded guitars are a joy, as is Smith's belligerent snarl. He even manages a cough at 1:15 that is simultaneously comical, sneering and menacing. Despite the similarity to 'My Ex-Classmates' Kids', both songs were on the setlist whenever the group played 'I Wake Up In The City' in late 2001; at its final three outings in 2002, the two songs were played as a medley.

Fresh material from the new line-up began to emerge in the autumn of 2001. On 8th October in Leeds, 'Crop-Dust', 'Jim's "The Fall"', 'Kick The Can' and 'My Ex-Classmates' Kids' were debuted; 'Bastardo' followed four days later in Dublin. A recording of the 17th October Bristol gig finds Ben Pritchard in full-on Eric Clapton mode on 'Bourgeois Town' while 'Dr. Bucks' Letter' is performed as a heavy, stoner-rock instrumental.

Are You Are Missing Winner

The album wasn't recorded under the easiest of conditions, as Ben Pritchard describes:

> The studio we were recording it in was still being built, it was damp and dark and we were directly underneath a body builders' gym. We had to keep deleting takes because you could hear the clanging of dumbbell weights being dropped on the recordings!

The cover is regarded by many as one of The Fall's worst: a blurred negative image of Smith and his new wife is surrounded by cheap and nasty lettering and ugly splotches of pink and purple. The first editions of the CD contained typos, incorrect titles and were poorly mastered, with lots of skips and inexplicable gaps. As to the origins of the album's title, Ben Pritchard explains:

> There was an article at the time about the National Lottery, someone had won and didn't come forward to claim the prize. It's as simple as that. Mark took his inspiration for lyrics and titles from anywhere he could find. Are you 'our' missing winner, he just spelt it wrong.[277]

Jim's "The Fall"

A brash, no-nonsense opener that also serves as a defiant statement of intent by the new line-up. It was named after new recruit Watts, who wrote the tune. The meaning is, for once, very clear: 'we are new Fall / not like the old one'. The '799 or one million pounds' line may well reference *Amazon* et al selling CDs at budget prices. It doesn't *quite* break out into the abandoned melee that you might want it to, but it's still a solid starter. Played 18 times, 2001-02.

Bourgeois Town

A cover of blues legend Lead Belly's 'The Bourgeois Blues'. The sleazy riffing is solid rather than spectacular. Smith quoted the

---

[277] This isn't to suggest that MES mis-spelled it out of ignorance. Perhaps he saw the dodgy spelling in a newsagent's window or maybe he simply enjoyed the visual symmetry of 'Are You Are'.

song in performances as far back as 1985, suggesting he'd had it in mind for a while.[278] It got 70 outings, 2001–04.

Crop-Dust

One of the group's most shameless steals, being lifted virtually wholesale from The Trogg's 'I Just Sing'. It's a venomous piece of warped psych-garage-punk, led by snake-charming lead guitar fuzz and bolstered by a galloping, drone-clatter rhythm section. Although not as extreme as 'Ibis-Afro Man' (see below), it is similar in its stitching together of several brutally-edited segments. The transitions between these sections are unsettling and compelling, especially the discordant overlaps at 1:18, 1:42 and 2:30 (the last of which leads into a woozy descent in tempo). Besides the hypnotic lead part, there are fascinating layers of guitar: the cracked, hesitant chords that emerge at 0:07; the wavering feedback that cuts in and out from 0:57; the atonal drone at 1:13; the sharp, tinny fuzz at 4:30.

As for the lyrics, *The Track Record* suggests it's about the gentrification of Manchester; *The Annotated Fall* that it's about post-9/11 terrorist paranoia. The latter interpretation is supported by a *Record Collector* article which says that the song was 'inspired by a dream Smith had about two towers and office executives running from a building'. 'Crop-Dust' was played 21 times in 2001 and got a final performance in Milan in 2002.

My Ex-Classmates' Kids

A scruffy piece of blues-rock that echoes the sentiments and lyrics of 'Married, 2 Kids' ('aftershave like little twigs'). It rocks, but falls slightly short of the crackling energy of 'sister' song, 'I Wake Up In The City'. It was performed 30 times between 2001 and 2003.

Kick The Can

The song opens with a guitar part so heavily flanged and distorted that it sounds like it's being played underwater. Two minutes in it kicks into a clean and taut groove; the tight motorik of this

[278] During 'Gut Of The Quantifier' at the Hammersmith Palais, 11th November 1985.

second half is very Can-like and may partially explain the title. Lyrically, it's a rather minimal effort (live versions often saw Smith just bark out the refrain whilst the group churned out the riff), although it does contain the pleasingly mysterious line 'you are sailing and finish up a bird I guess / you're in the heart of France'. It was played 61 times 2001–03, often as part of a medley with 'F-'oldin Money'.

Gotta See Jane

Having secured their highest ever chart position with one of his songs, the group return to R. Dean Taylor. 'Jane', co-written by Eddie Holland of Holland-Dozier-Holland fame, was a top 20 hit for Taylor in 1968. The original has a keening tone that's emotionally involving; The Fall's take is a bit pedestrian in comparison. It only had three live outings, all in October 2001.

Ibis-Afro Man

One of the most divisive tracks in the group's history: *City Life* magazine called it 'the worst song in The Fall's 25-year-old career'. Loosely based around Iggy Pop's racially dubious 'African Man',[279] 'Ibis' is arguably the most deliberately challenging and obstreperous moment in the whole back catalogue. It's a close relation of 'Hurricane Edward' in that it sounds like several unfinished versions of the same track edited together by chopping the tapes up with blunt scissors and binding them with Sellotape. There's something both ridiculous and exhilarating about the way the different versions of its thumping, primal stomp barge into each other from either side of the stereo. The 'chattering monkey' section is tough territory, no matter how committed you are. Stewart Lee commented that the track was 'evidently recorded in a tin filled with seagulls'. The live section at the end is taken from the 23rd April 2001 gig at The Mean Fiddler and contains some of the lyrics from 'Race With The Devil'. The keyboard squiggles mark Julia Nagle's final contribution to The Fall. Jim Watts defended the song:

[279] 'I live in the bush and I'm going to stomp like a gorilla / Here I beat my chest'. From his 1979 album *New Values*.

The Fall deservedly or not seem to get the laziest criticism around. I don't care about the album but I wrote the music to african man and it was intentionally stupid and juvenile. And it would take me all of 5 seconds to think of a worse song from the back catalogue.

'Ibis' was played 21 times in 2000-01. Live performances were generally a model of coherence compared to the album version.

The Acute

A country-ish toe-tapper built around a predictable chord progression. Smith's vocals teeter precariously between 'idiosyncratic' and 'unlistenably tuneless', a situation that isn't helped by their excessive prominence in the mix. The line regarding 'the motive of this film' may possibly refer to *One Flew Over the Cuckoo's Nest*. Jim Watts suggests that there was an alternative version of the song that included lyrics referring to Frank Skinner. Never played live.

Hollow Mind

Another simplistic tune, based around a straightforward three-chord pattern played on a scratchy acoustic accompanied by a bog-standard root note bassline. The melody is very close to that of 'Jerusalem'. Although it's quite slight, it has a certain ramshackle charm, and the gnarly electric guitar that emerges over the last third peps it up a little. Ed Blaney's almost comically deep backing vocal gives it a bit more body as well. Contains one of MES's less subtle but still entertaining insults, 'you don't know fuck shit'. It was never played live.

Reprise: Jane – Prof Mick – Ey Bastardo

The album's closer revisits a couple of Fall tropes: experimental mucking about (the lengthy 'is there something wrong with my CD player?' gaps) and the roll-call roasting of group members (cf 'North West Fashion Show'). As the title suggests, it's a mix of the loose jam 'Bastardo' that was played a few times in 2001 and a reprise of the cover of 'Gotta See Jane'. Mick Middles is an obvious candidate for 'Prof Mick'. *The Fallen* contains an account of the song's recording based on Brian Fanning's recollections:

> When they were recording... 'Gotta See Jane'... Smith suddenly started shouting at the drummer, Spencer Birtwistle, that the music was all wrong... Smith suggested a ten minute break, during which Birtwistle started playing a different beat. Fanning picked up the bass and played along. Then Smith started rapping over the top – 'Spencer is a bastardo, he needs to go back to Rusholme' – before going on to sing the same song as before over a completely new rhythm.

It's not without its charms – the group sound like they're having a great time (Smith in particular) and Pritchard contributes some nifty guitar work – but its seven-minute length is rather indulgent for a novelty interlude. It was played (albeit in a very different form) five times in autumn 2001.

Reviews and Reissues

Although *Are You Are Missing Winner* was officially released on 5th November, it was available at gigs from 8th October.[280] This may well have had an impact on official sales figures: whilst the previous three LPs had achieved only lowly placings, *AYAMW* didn't trouble the chart at all. It was not received positively, either by fans or by the music press. In *Q*, Ian Harrison described it as sounding like 'wildly variable fragments recorded in Smith's shed' that at their worst were 'bemusingly thin'. He thought it 'strictly for the kind of fans keen to display levels of dutiful devotion last seen at the *Charge Of The Light Brigade*'. Edwin Pouncey, writing in *The Wire*, described it as a 'rockabilly racket which makes no apparent sense at all', although he did recommend playing it 'loud enough to wake the dead'.

A remastered version of the album was reissued in 2006. It included six bonus tracks: both sides of the 'Rude (All The Time)' single, two studio outtakes from 2001, 'New Formation Sermon'

---

[280] It can be heard being promoted in an announcement at the end of the bootleg recording of the Bristol gig on 17th October.

and 'Distilled Mug Art' (see Chapter 24), a live version of 'My Ex-Classmates' Kids' and 'Where's The Fuckin Taxi? Cunt'. 'Taxi' (recorded at the same session as 'Rude') is an appalling piece of self-indulgence; five minutes of Smith, Blaney, et al rambling drunkenly while someone tortures an acoustic guitar. Cherry Red reissued the album once more in 2021. The double vinyl version featured the same tracklisting as the 2006 reissue. The 4xCD package included three live albums, each of which had been released separately in 2007: *Live At The Garage – London – 20 April 2002*, *Live At The Knitting Factory – L.A. – 14 November 2001* and *Live At The ATP Festival – 28 April 2002* (see Appendix 3).

Evaluation

Cerebral Caustic saw Smith attempting to drag The Fall away from its dance/electronica-tinged early 90s incarnation and establish a stripped-down, back-to-basics approach, but it still features a few electronic effects buried amongst the primal garage rock. *Are You Are Missing Winner* represents a much purer take on the guitar-bass-drums ethos. Nagle's departure, which left the group without a keyboard player, means that *Winner* is almost entirely devoid of electronic sounds. This was, according to Smith, deliberate: 'It's straight down the line, this one . . we've got a new line-up. I can do what I want the way I want it. Simple, you know.'

This minimalist approach is not in itself a problem. Where the group demonstrate invention, for example with 'Crop-Dust', it makes sense, even if the results don't always represent easy listening. But overall, the songwriting is not consistently strong enough to sustain the back-to-basics approach. Whilst many of the songs contain some effective guitar work, too many of them ('Acute', 'Hollow') feel a little obvious and uninspired. The covers are adequate but a bit workmanlike. It's not a terrible album by any means, but overall it's just too ragged and disjointed to be consistently and fully satisfying.

The Real New Fall LP Formerly 'Country On The Click'
Recorded: Gracieland Studio, Rochdale, December 2002-January 2003
Released: 27th October 2003

Personnel:
Mark E Smith – vocals
Ben Pritchard – guitar, vocals
Jim Watts – bass, guitar, computers
Dave Milner – drums, vocals, keyboards
Eleni Poulou – keyboards, vocals

With:
Stephen Beswick – keyboards ('Recovery Kit')
'The Plouty'[281] – organ, text ('Proteinprotection')
Simon 'Ding' Archer – bass ('Green Eyed Loco-Man')

[281] MES's pet name for Eleni.

Chapter 24: The Real New Fall LP
Formerly 'Country On The Click'

'They were swearing, throwing newspaper with snotballs...'

Shortly after *Are You Are Missing Winner*'s release, the group played a short, well-received US tour. The night before the first gig, Smith performed one of his spoken sets in Los Angeles.[282] It found him sitting at a table, moodily lit by the retro lamp behind him, with a soundtrack of scraps of noise and snippets of songs in the background. It went down well, although some were disappointed at the brevity of the 25-minute performance. The American dates found Smith in particular on good form. *2G+2*, released in June 2002, was largely comprised of recordings from this mini-tour.[283] The sound quality is excellent and it's full of dynamic performances. As was becoming a regular habit, it featured a few studio tracks as well. 'New Formation Sermon' and 'Distilled Mug Art' had been scheduled to be released as a part of an EP called *The Present* that was shelved. The former has a laid-back hoe down/honky-tonk vibe and features an enigmatic lyric that Smith slurs through engagingly: 'the arms outstretched / fearsome waist / elbows in triangle / the bracing chill of the market is no friend / like pictures of yours from the fifties'. The latter is a folky, swampish blues with a Jew's harp twanging away in the background. Smith seems to be having a rant about the indiscriminate use and manipulation of images for merchandising purposes. His despairing groan at 2:38 has a movingly resigned tone. Neither were ever played live.

Despite the success of the US tour, it concluded with yet another change of personnel; on the last night, Birtwistle quit

---

[282] At the Knitting Factory on 13th November. Gail Ann Dorsey (best known as David Bowie's long-serving bass player) also played.

[283] The four nights used would all eventually receive separate releases: two of them on the *Touch Sensitive... Bootleg Box Set*; the others on the imaginatively titled *Live At The Knitting Factory – L.A. – 14 November 2001* (included in the 2021 *Missing Winner* reissue) and *Live In San Francisco* (see Appendix 3).

after a fight with Ed Blaney. His replacement was Dave Milner, the drummer from Trigger Happy. Par for the course, he had less than an hour of rehearsal time before his first gig, in Manchester on 29th November. The bootleg recording of the gig, despite the poor sound quality, demonstrates that Milner did an admirable job in the circumstances. After a one-off appearance in Athens in January 2002, the group embarked on a 15-date European tour in February-March. After the fractious and chaotic late 90s, The Fall were rebuilding their reputation as a live act, and they were due to build on their recent success by returning to the US for half a dozen further dates in April. Unfortunately, they were cancelled because of visa problems, which led to Blaney resigning as manager. He claimed that the group had been in Europe and hadn't been able to attach their passports to the visa application because they wouldn't have been able to get home otherwise. Blaney rather dramatically announced that 'the fiasco was not his fault and that his long-term friendship with Mark E Smith is now over' (although this seemingly irrevocable separation didn't last long). Eleni took over as manager.

A 20th April gig at The Garage in London was filmed (on an amateur camcorder) and released in 2004 as one half of the double DVD *Access All Areas – Volume One*; the recording was also released as a live album in 2007, *Live At The Garage – London – 20 April 2002*. The performance at All Tomorrow's Parties in Camber Sands eight days later also made its way onto a live LP and DVD; amateur footage made up the second disc of *Access All Areas – Volume Two*. By this stage, it had been around six months since The Fall had debuted any new songs – a substantial gap by their standards. This changed in Copenhagen on 24th May, where the setlist referred to both 'New One' and 'New New One', although it's not clear what these were.[284]

A notable gig took place on 22nd September at King George's Hall, Blackburn. Not only would this performance go on to be released as a DVD and, in varying forms, on no less than three live

---

[284] Jim Watts says one of them was an early version of 'The Past', and that 'New New One' might have been an early 'Mike's Love Xexagon' or 'Contraflow', or 'possibly something else the band had just come up with'.

albums (see Appendix 3), it saw the debut of two new keyboard players. Most significant was Eleni's first appearance as group member, the beginning of a 14-year stint, but in addition Ruth Daniel joined Nick Dewey in the 'in-The-Fall-for-one-day' club. Daniel was invited to play after performing with her band Earl in Manchester.

> At the end of the gig he asked me if I would be interested in playing some keys for The Fall. I said 'I'd love to,' but didn't really think it would go anywhere. I rehearsed with the band (minus Mark) in Sankeys and learnt all the songs in one rehearsal. Then I was rushed out of the building when Mark arrived. This was because his girlfriend was also playing keys for the band and I gather that the manager hadn't told Mark that I was playing. So, I turned up at the gig, still unsure whether I would be playing that night or whether Mark would fire me, before even really hiring me! But it all worked out fine, I played the gig and loved it. It was a top laugh.

The 'he' that Daniel presumed was the manager was, of course, Ed Blaney, who – six months after his resignation and estrangement from MES – was once more involved in the group's affairs.

The Blackburn gig was filmed and released on DVD as *A Touch Sensitive*.[285] Presumably because of the filming, it was a lengthy performance (around two hours) and the group resurrected several oldies.[286] They were in raucous form, but on the older songs they sound a little 'rocky' and one-dimensional. Although they make a decent fist of 'Mere Pseud Mag. Ed.', 'The Classical' lacks subtlety and suffers – despite Milner's best efforts – from not having two drummers. Ruth Daniels acquits herself well in her sporadic appearances. Eleni doesn't appear until 'The

[285] It's not easy to get a hold of the DVD these days (certainly not for a reasonable price), but the whole thing can, at the time of writing, be found on YouTube.
[286] Although the group were in the habit of resurrecting the occasional oldie, this was as close to a 'greatest hits' set as The Fall ever got. 'The Classical' appeared for the first time in 17 years; also returning after a lengthy layoff were 'Free Range' and 'Hey! Luciani' (both 14 years), 'There's A Ghost In My House' (13), 'Jerusalem' (12), 'Telephone Thing' (10) and 'Hit The North' (9).

Classical', to which she adds some jarring keyboards. Steve Evets makes a bizarre appearance during 'Touch Sensitive'. Fag and can of lager in hand, he starts off by yelling 'buy the car' before proceeding to drown Smith out by shouting out random song titles. He does, to be fair, make a more successful contribution to 'Big New Prinz' before Smith ushers him off stage. Ed Blaney also pops up to sing the first part of 'I Wake Up In The City'. Throughout, Smith seems relatively sober, sings with focus and behaves himself, although he spends a lot of time squatting by the drum riser, rifling through his lyric sheets. He also unplugs Pritchard's guitar during 'Free Range'. 'Hit The North' makes for a shambolic finale, featuring both keyboard players performing together plus Blaney and Evets taking a drumstick each to the drum kit as Milner ploughs on determinedly.

In September 2002, Smith released his second spoken word album. *Pander! Panda! Panzer!* adopted a similar approach to *The Post Nearly Man* – lyrical fragments accompanied by snatches of Fall songs – although this album was merged into one 43-minute track. Several passages were recorded live in America. It's more varied than its predecessor, although still perhaps better experienced in snatches.[287]

There were a further seven UK gigs to round off 2002. At the last one, at The Electric Ballroom in Camden on 21st November, 'Susan vs. Youthclub' made its only appearance. The song was released as a single in December, the group's first proper single release for over three years.[288] 'Susan' is an intriguing tale (possibly inspired by an episode of *Neighbours*) that encompasses the famous Badly Drawn Boy/false teeth incident and involves the eponymous Susan travelling back in time and being appalled by her 16-year-old self. *Time Out* commented that 'Smith "sings" as if stricken by chronic toothache in a wind tunnel and the whole lurches along in a twisted disco fashion'. The B-side was 'Janet vs Johnny', a slowed-down, delicate take on 'Janet, Johnny + James'

[287] There's a very detailed review here: http://www.tangents.co.uk/tangents/main/2002/october/mark-e-smith.html
[288] Both the 7" and CD had the title 'The Fall vs 2003' on both the cover and label, suggesting that it was an EP, but given that the 7" had one B-side and the CD only added a remix of the title track, it's best considered a single.

from the forthcoming album. The CD version also throws in a pleasingly crunchy, distorted remix. The single reached number 64 in the UK charts.

The Fall's 23rd Peel session was recorded in February 2003 and broadcast on 13th March. For the first time in several sessions, the group sound like they're actually enjoying themselves. A fierce 'Sparta' is believed by many Fall fans to be the song's best recording. 'Contraflow' – which wouldn't get its live debut for another three months – is impressively tight and focused for a new song. The cover of 'Grooving With Mr Bloe'[289] forms a nifty little introduction to 'Green-Eyed Loco Man'. To finish off, the group make one of their occasional session revisits to an old tune. 'Mere Pseud Mag. Ed.' had returned to the setlist at the Blackburn gig after a five-year absence; the group tackle it successfully enough, although it falls short of the original's jolting angularity.

Yet another line-up change occurred in early 2003. The night before the group's gig in Turkey on 5th March, Jim Watts was sacked.

> Mark came to the pub to meet us. Bought the others a drink and purposefully didn't get me one, then came out with some nonsense saying I was off in London spending The Fall's money... playing with a Heavy Metal band and his contacts at MI5 had intercepted my calls to book rehearsal rooms... [he said] I could play the gig in Turkey then leave the band, and obviously I opted not to go to Turkey and just walked out.

Watts seems not to have taken it too badly, saying that there was no 'blazing row' as he was 'laughing too much'. Steve Evets filled in on bass for one gig and a TV appearance[290] before Simon 'Ding' Archer (the sound engineer on *Pander! Panda! Panzer!*) took over. In the summer, the group returned to America for a 21-date

---

[289] A 1969 instrumental hit for one-hit wonders Wind. The track was actually the B-side, but Radio 1 played the wrong song by accident.
[290] On 27th March, the group played two songs ('Behind The Counter' and 'Green-Eyed Loco Man') for the Granada TV show *Made in the Northwest*. Evets was on bass and Stuart Carswell (a relative of someone involved in the show's production) stood in for the unavailable Dave Milner. In the style of many new Fall members, he learned the songs on the way there in Ben Pritchard's car.

tour. Online fan reviews suggest that this was a successful visit and that Smith was in good spirits. In Minneapolis, he even made a gift of a bottle of whisky to a fan who provided the group with a free breakfast. At Atlanta on 12th July, 'I'm Going To Spain' received an unlikely revival:

> Only MES and the drummer return, and the latter taps the hi-hat as the former subjects us to a bizarre, feedback-laden a cappella-solo version of 'Going To Spain' totally off key – even more so than the original – and marginally heartfelt. All that feedback on the one mic could have been corrected so I suppose it was intentional. Very successful as a performance art piece but musically hopeless.

On 29th September, in Lisbon, the group had their first crack at 'Open The Boxoctosis' (aborted after only a minute or so) and also made a shambolic attempt at the 'Mr Bloe/Loco Man' medley. The most notable thing about this gig, however, was that it inspired the track 'Portugal'. The hired Portuguese road crew walked out on the group, outraged by their behaviour. Smith described the incident to *The Independent*:

> We arrived and they sort of pissed off on the day of the show, saying we behaved really badly and all this. Somebody threw a bit of paper at them, like a plane or something. It was quite funny... if you saw these blokes you'd laugh your head off, because they were four big blokes with long hair and leather jackets.

'Portugal' consists of a glam-metal beat and volleys of rock riffery over which the group, *sans* Smith, simply read out the po-faced email of complaint ('I told him that if this continued I would have to review my position') in a hilariously straight fashion. The 'Snotballs!' moment (1:38) is especially precious. Smith wanted to use the track as a B-side, but was told it might be libellous. It did, however, appear on the US edition of the next album, as well as a 'hidden track' (only playable via computer) on the CD version.

The Real New Fall LP Formerly 'Country On The Click'
The album was recorded at Lisa Stansfield's Gracieland Studio in Rochdale between December 2002 and January 2003. Originally entitled *Country On The Click*, it was due to come out in April, but the release date was pushed back. At some point in the first half of 2003, *Country On The Click* was leaked online, which led to the original release being withdrawn and the album being remixed, re-sequenced and re-titled. On 5th July *Fall News* reported that Amazon were listing a revised date of 4th August. Jim Watt, posting on the *Fall Online Forum*, said that 'the leak[ed] version was pretty much mine and Grant Showbiz's vision. We edited and mixed all the tracks.' He added that he 'worked out exactly who leaked the album in the end. I know they meant well but at the time I was just as annoyed as Mark about the leak.' According to the official Fall website:

> Mark E Smith... remixed and rerecorded large parts of the album, and re-sequenced it, interrupted by a highly successful tour of the USA. The first mix of the album, which had leaked onto the internet under the original title *Country On The Click*, is easily surpassed by the final version. This is *The Real New Fall LP*!

Although this suggests the new version was all Smith's work, it seems likely that Archer and other members of the group contributed significantly to the new version. According to Dave Simpson, Archer's brief was to 'water down' or get rid of Watts's parts on the new recordings. Ben Pritchard felt that this had a positive impact on the final result:

> The internet leak was the best thing that could've happened to COTC because we were all really unhappy with the album especially Sparta and Recovery Kit. Mark gave us some time to go back and remix them. Hence Sparta #2 and a version of Recovery I was really happy with.

Green Eyed Loco-Man

One of the group's strongest album-openers, 'Loco-Man' harks back to the best moments of the *Infotainment Scan* era, a densely layered blend of potent rock and slinky, twisted electronica. The lyrics reference jealousy, vanity and Batman ('riddle me this'); it's hard to tell if the 'Loco-Man' is a crazy guy or a train driver. It was played 85 times, 2003-06.

Mountain Energei

The loping drumbeat sees the group once again (cf 'Big New Prinz' and 'Glam-Racket') taking percussive inspiration from The Glitter Band's 'Rock and Roll Part 2', although this time it's used in a slightly more restrained fashion. Combined with Pritchard's simple, understated guitar, Watts's elastic bass and the haunting keyboard melody, it makes for a fluid, hypnotic track. Smith, accompanied by a variety of subtle vocals effects, produces a sensitive and carefully-timed vocal. The lyric, which addresses money-related woes in a similar manner to 'F-'oldin' Money', features the unlikely juxtaposition of Dolly Parton and Lord Byron. The lines 'Dear dope, if you wanna catch us / you need a rod and a line / signed, the fish' are adapted from the 1950 cartoon *A Fractured Leghorn* (starring loudmouthed Texan rooster Foghorn Leghorn). The origins of the song can be heard in Dave Milner's demo, '8 Clothorn Road'.[291] It was a popular setlist choice, and was played 194 times over the next eight years.

Theme From Sparta F.C.

An even more popular live choice, racking up over 300 appearances, making it The Fall's most played song other than 'Mr. Pharmacist'. 'Sparta' is one of the Fall originals that non-fans are most likely to have heard, due to its use as the theme music to the *Final Score* section of BBC television's Saturday afternoon sports coverage.[292] It's sharp and crisp, the crackling guitar riff contrasting beautifully with Smith's confrontational growl and

[291] https://hippriestess.tumblr.com/post/60830509220/ex-fall-drummer-dave-milner-posted-this-to-his
[292] This led to Smith's hilarious performance when invited to read the results in 2007: 'Tottenham Hotspur postponed; West Ham United one aitch'.

the spirited backing vocals. The song appears to be narrated by a Greek football hooligan, a supporter of Sparta FC. Unlike 'Kicker Conspiracy', 'Sparta' focuses more on crowd violence ('we live on blood') than the gentrification of the game. That said, it does contain a reference to 'ground boutique at match in Chelsea', a dig at Ken Bates's attempts to commercialise and modernise Chelsea in the 80s and 90s.

Contraflow

Twenty years previously, a hard life in [the] country gave Smith a terrible urge to drink. His feelings appear not to have mellowed, 'Contraflow' seeing him express his distaste for all things bucolic ('I hate the countryside so much') over a furiously driving beat and powerful dual guitars. The lyric was inspired by the group having to pick Dave Milner up via Snake Pass, a road that crosses the Pennines near Glossop in Derbyshire. Perhaps slightly reminiscent of 'Please Don't Touch' by Motörhead and Girlschool,[293] it got 67 outings 2003-05.

Last Commands Of Xyralothep Via M.E.S.

A dark and sinister piece, based around a coiling three-note figure that builds in intensity throughout; the emergence of the discordant synth over the last minute adds to the drama. 'Xyralothep' – a reference to Nyarlathotep, one of Lovecraft's 'outer gods' – sees Smith, referring to himself in the third person throughout, take on the role of seer or preacher. He advises his audience to beware of 'characters connected with car adverts' (a grumble about the 'Touch Sensitive' TV royalties), 'cod-science/cod-psychology' and 'fat aggressive men and handsome aggressive men' (potentially a reference to Max Ehrmann's 1927 poem, 'Desiderata'). Concluding line 'the wrath of the drude quarters' is likely a response to criticism from Smith's old friend and self-styled 'arch-drude' Julian Cope.[294] It was only played eight times, all in the summer of 2003.

[293] A cover of Johnny Kidd & the Pirates' 1959 debut single, it was the lead song on the 1981 *St. Valentine's Day Massacre* EP (released under the name Headgirl).
[294] In his review of Boredoms' *Vision Creation New Sun* (2001): 'You hear that new Fall record and it's just more embittered semi-mystical coded fraudulent ramblings about NOTHING nothing NOTHING.'

Open The Boxoctosis #2

A regular live choice 2003-06, making 96 appearances, 'Boxoctosis' is based around a circular riff reminiscent of Iggy Pop's 'The Passenger'. The lyric references Pandora's Box, 50s/60s TV game show *Take Your Pick*[295] ('take the money... open the box!), and an episode of *The Twilight Zone*.[296] A more prosaic interpretation is that it's just about cigarettes, 'I opened the box of imperial stuff / and to my surprise I found twenty-five warriors' referring to Royals cigarettes which came in 25s rather than the customary 20s.

Janet, Johnny + James

The song features another chord progression similar to 'The Passenger', although it may also have been influenced by the fact that Ben Pritchard was developing his finger-picking style by practising 'Classical Gas' at the time.[297] The track is quietly unassuming, and the pairing across the channels of two similar but distinct guitar parts – one with a folky tone, the other with just a dab of distortion – is delicately balanced. Smith's breathy, almost whispered vocal gives the song a secretive, mysterious air. Opening line 'What if the world crashed down' suggests that the titular characters find themselves in some sort of post-apocalyptic scenario, and overall there's a religious tone to the lyric – 'From you, our creator, a startling vision of a future that didn't happen'; 'Dear Lord, help them in their abject search'.[298] It replaced 'Susan vs Youthclub' on the final remixed version of the album and was played live 68 times, 2002-05. PJ Harvey (with Ding on bass) covered the song in 2004.

The Past #2

Brisk, robust and concise, 'Past' is virtually guitar-free; there's only a touch of high-pitched wailing lurking in the background.

---

[295] The first game show broadcast in the UK to offer cash prizes.

[296] *What's In The Box?* (1964). A man's television set displays his past, present, and future, revealing to him that he will kill his wife.

[297] 'Classical Gas' was an instrumental track first released by Mason Williams in 1968 and subsequently covered by dozens of artists. Pritchard played a snippet of it at the Blackburn King George's Hall gig in 2002 (although it didn't make it on to any of the official recordings) and again a few days later at Leeds Irish Centre.

[298] At the Knitting Factory, New York, on 9th April 2004, MES introduced the song as 'a religious number'.

Smith's vocals are very forward in the mix and, as with 'Two Librans', there's some early sight of the gargling growl (for example, 'but I love the justice and falling for the melancholy' at 0:10) that would later become his default setting. The stream-of-consciousness lyric contains the second reference to 'abdominizers' in a Fall song.[299] It was played three times on the European tour of May 2002, and then once more in 2004.

Loop41 'Houston

The 'Loop41' part section – which was used on several occasions as an intro tape – is a 30-second blast of staccato distortion and what sounds like a snippet of Kraftwerk's 'Trans-Europe Express'. It cuts incongruously into a whisky-soaked country ramble, a cover of a Lee Hazlewood song that was also performed by Dean Martin. The leaked version was entitled 'Ho(e)uston', probably to reflect that Smith sounds like he's singing 'Euston' and adds the word 'station' at 1:35 and 2:58.

Smith sings this pretty well. He stays within spitting distance of the actual melody and puts a bit of feeling and verve into it, capturing the song's (admittedly rather cheesy) maudlin world-weariness with no little style. The group's plain and simple backing is just right for the song's sat-in-a-honky-tonk-bar-down on-my-luck atmosphere. Halfway through, Ben Pritchard steps forward, tilts back the brim of his stetson and knocks out a neat little country-style solo. B-side material, really, but it does provide a little light relief in a generally intense album.

Mike's Love Xexagon

Opening with heavily treated drums that resemble an uptempo version of 'Dr. Bucks' Letter', the most striking thing about the song is the backing vocal harmonies, a curious mix of Low and ELO. It has an unworldly sci-fi atmosphere (not unlike 'Last Commands') which is emphasised by the vocal wandering across the stereo channels and the rapid-reverb effect when Smith sings 'good vibrations'. First line 'Studio was a hexagon' may refer to

---

[299] The first being in 'Noel's Chemical Effluence'.

Maida Vale (although Jim Watt insists it doesn't), but the main subject matter seems to be the Beach Boys. Mike Love was a founder member of the group, there's the mention of 'Good Vibrations' and it's plausible that 'BB' is also a reference. It's also possible to hear a bit of Beach Boys in the backing harmonies. More tenuously, *The Annotated Fall* suggests that the 'three bald triplets' might be Love's cousins; Brian, Dennis and Carl Wilson. The Beach Boys were not someone that Smith frequently expressed admiration for, although Damon Gough did claim that he persuaded Smith to record 'Calendar' by giving him his copy of *Pet Sounds*. 'Mike's Love Xexagon' was played 11 times, all in 2004.

Proteinprotection
Taut and full of menace from the word go, the relentless bass/drums intro sliced through by a grainy, slashing guitar.[300] The verse is controlled, malevolent; the chorus breaks out with abandon. The group's control of this shifting dynamic is exemplary, and the heavily phased breakdown at 1:28 is a masterful touch. Smith is on superb form: he sits above everything, aloof and disdainful yet utterly in sync with the group. Highlights include his enunciation of 'abstraction' at 1:02, the simmering anger of 'no protein protection' at 1:50 and above all the 'hey, wuh!' at 1:13. There are several potential specific references in the lyrics (shampoo, doppelgängers, Nietzsche and founder of Scientology L. Ron Hubbard, for example) but no easily discernible overall theme. 'Proteinprotection' was played 19 times 2003-4 and once more (as an instrumental) in 2006.

Recovery Kit
Revolving around a hypnotic bassline and softly insistent sequencer, 'Recovery Kit' has a mesmerising, despondent atmosphere. Heavily treated guitar and harsh electronic noise bookend the song to great effect; Smith demonstrates a shrewd calmness that he would rarely better. The standout feature, however, is Dave

---

[300] The riff is quite similar to that on Afghan Whigs' 1993 track, 'Fountain and Fairfax'.

Milner's drumming: the measured pace, the ebb and flow of the emphasis and the expertly judged rolling snares are reminiscent of Can's Jaki Liebezeit at his best. *The Annotated Fall*'s summary of the song is worth quoting in full:

> 'Recovery Kit' has a somewhat melancholy air, but it's ambiguous whether the dominant emotion is sadness or calm; it's even possible, depending on one's reading of the song, to detect a sense of elation, as the protagonist throws off the constraints of a well-plotted life and finds a sort of vindication or redemption in the form of the 'recovery kit', whatever the latter actually is. The song is remarkable in that it is so subtle and multivalent, as the music perches on a razor edge between these three emotions (sadness, calm and elation) without betraying the lyrics by committing to one or another of them. The ambiguous entwining of all three of these, as well as the ambiguity of their joining, can be captured by the single adjective 'haunting', which is perhaps clichéd but nevertheless seems apt in this case.

Stephen Beswick, credited with keyboards on the track, was a friend of Ben Pritchard. 'Recovery Kit' was used at a few gigs as an intro tape, but was never played live.

Country On The Click

It's difficult to make a truly fair comparison between the final LP and the original *Country On The Click* based on the 'leaked' version, as it is still a rough mix – although that doesn't prevent some fans from declaring some tracks or even the whole thing superior.

A summary of the major differences:

'Loco Man': a little more skewed towards the electronica, lighter on the guitars and features a menacing double tracked MES vocal (as well as jarring, clumsy edits at 2:06 and 2:55).

'Mountain': intriguingly quirky background noises, but rather listless.

'Sparta': more prominent electronics again; somewhat lethargic and flat.

'Contraflow': lacks the crisp, sharp edges of the final version, although Dave Milner's almost 'urban' backing vocals halfway through are an interesting touch.

'Last Commands': not vastly different.

'Boxoctosis': includes a neat little extra guitar line over the chorus, and the comparatively delicate second half (with acoustic guitar flourishes) makes it nearly an equally attractive alternative to the final album take; the shouty backing vocals are a bit of an unwelcome distraction, however.

'Past': a busy, full-band version; energetic, but feels obvious and unsubtle next to the final version.

'Ho(e)uston': missing the opening 'Loop41' section; otherwise much the same.

'Xexagon': another to feature more prominent electronica; the backing vocals 'swoosh' about a little aimlessly and overall it feels hesitant and stilted.

'Protein': varies the least from the finished article.

'Recovery Kit': Largely similar to the final version, although features some solemn synth floating around in the background from around a third of the way in.

'Susan vs. Youthclub' was replaced by 'Janet, Johnny + James' on the final album. It's not hugely different from the single version.

Reviews and Versions
The music press was almost entirely enthusiastic. *The Wire*'s John Mulvey considered it 'one of Mark E Smith's perennial "returns to form".' *Mojo*'s Ian Harrison thought it the group's best since *The Infotainment Scan* – 'this newest payload of hostile cryptic garage rock impacts so immediately with its purpose and strength'. In *The Guardian*, Helen Pidd gave it 4/5 and declared that 'Smith

is on magnificently mad form here... incomprehensible but irresistible'. The *NME*'s Stephen Dalton was a rare voice of dissent, decrying the album's 'workmanlike anonymity'. Despite the critical acclaim, however, the album only reached 156 in the UK album charts. Smith was clearly proud of the album. As with *Extricate* and *Hex*, he felt he had 'proved something':

> It does bring out the best in me when I'm forced into a corner. I don't wilt like other people. I'm used to being up against it.

The US version of the album, released in 2004 on Narnack Records, featured a different cover, different track selection,[301] and different names for many of the songs (such as 'Green Eyed', 'Mountain' and 'Xralothep'). The promo CD carried the warning: 'For promotional use only – anyone abusing this will have Mark E Smith to contend with and may God have mercy on your soul!!!'

Evaluation

Smith's pride at having 'proved something' with this album is well-earned. Not for the first time, The Fall at the beginning of the 21st century were being written off by many: an interesting footnote in 'alternative' music history, perhaps; a much-loved institution, certainly – but one that people were glad existed without having any great desire to actually listen to their contemporary material. Following the group, both in terms of buying their music and attending the gigs, was increasingly being seen as the preserve of nostalgic obsessives. Listening to live recordings from 2001-02 provides some explanation of this attitude. Although Smith's repeated walk-offs and onstage bust-ups were in abeyance, the setlist was in danger of becoming samey and predictable; several of the more straightforward tunes ('The Joke', 'Touch Sensitive', 'F-'oldin' Money', 'And Therein') were being wheeled out with increasingly predictable regularity.

The 'return to form' Fall album (complete with 'their best album since...' reviews) has become a cliché for good reason.

[301] It included 'Mod Mock Goth' (see Chapter 25) and 'Recovery Kit #2' (from the Christmas single), the 2004 single version of 'Sparta', plus 'Portugal'.

Throughout their history, Smith and the group repeatedly pulled out something special when most thought that they (or – more to the point – *he*) didn't have it in them/him. Never was this more the case than with *Real New*, the patchy, shambolic *Winner* suggesting that the highly regarded *The Unutterable* might be the last 'renaissance' album of which The Fall were capable.

And yet, somehow, *Real New* was one of the most consistently strong albums of the group's career. Not only was it full of outstanding material, thrillingly well executed, it was almost entirely free of the low points that had marred several previous releases. True, it did contain the obligatory throwaway cover version, but 'Houston' is one of the better examples of its kind. The material is notable for consistency of quality. As well as this consistency, the album offers great variety: the dynamic fury of 'Sparta', 'Contraflow' and 'Proteinprotection'; the surreal sci-fi spaciness of 'Last Commands' and 'Xexagon'; the delicate nuances of 'Mountain Energei', 'Janet' and 'Recovery Kit'. *Real New* is arguably the album that sees the most successful fusion of the group's post-punk/garage and electronica/experimental tendencies.

Fall Heads Roll
Recorded: Gigantic Studios, New York, January 2005; Gracieland Studio, Rochdale, mid-2005
Released: 3rd October 2005

Personnel:
Mark E Smith – vocals
Ben Pritchard – guitar
Steve Trafford – bass, vocals, guitar
Spencer Birtwistle – drums
Eleni Poulou – keyboards, vocals

With:
Simon 'Ding' Archer – banjo ('Clasp Hands'), bass ('Youwanner'), vocals ('Trust In Me')
Billy Pavone / Kenny Cummings / Phil Schuster – vocals ('Trust In Me')

Chapter 25: Fall Heads Roll

'Robert Plant turned up in a bullet-proof limo, The Fall
were transported by Salford Van Hire.'

The Fall's last act of 2003 was to return to the festive approach of their December 1994 Peel session and release a Christmas single. Lead track '(We Wish You) A Protein Christmas' was a reworking of 'Proteinprotection'. Musically more understated than the original, it also contained an amended lyric outlining God's dissatisfaction with the commercialisation of the season and overly early celebrations: 'The feast of man in October / menus for hampers / why did I come back?' The single contains another reworking of an album track, 'Recovery Kit #2'[302] as well two new songs. '(We Are) Mod Mock Goth' was a popular live choice in 2003-04, making 40 live appearances. Devoid of percussion (other than the occasional brief assault on a tambourine), it's driven by two guitar parts: in the right channel, a choppy, brittle three-chord figure; in the left a fuzzy, grungy equivalent that lags just slightly behind. Smith's double-tracked vocal is unnervingly unworldly. All of the instrumentation on '(Birtwistle's) Girl In Shop' was supplied by Spencer Birtwistle, so it was presumably recorded at some point in 2001. It sounds like a novelty 60s dance-craze single that Smith came back from the pub and shouted over randomly, but it has a certain haphazard charm. It was never played live.

Smith began 2004 by fracturing his leg and hip by slipping on an icy pavement after a gig in Newcastle. This led to seven dates being cancelled; when he returned the first few gigs saw him perform in a wheelchair, on crutches or sat at a table. Despite this, 2004 was the busiest year gig-wise since 1990, the group managing 69 performances. On 23rd January, they shared the bill with The Magic Band at London's Royal Festival Hall.[303] Dougie

---

[302] Rob Lally, friend of Smith's (he was best man at his wedding to Eleni) gets a co-writing credit here, although he didn't on the album version.

[303] The Magic Band – minus Don Van Vliet, who had gone off to live in the desert and paint – re-formed in 2003.

James, leader of Dougie James and the Soul Train, and a friend of Smith's, joined the group on stage in February to contribute backing vocals to 'Big New Prinz'.[304] In March, Smith squeezed in a spoken word performance, although poor sound meant that it did not go well.[305]

The Fall headed to America in April with a new bass player. Steve Trafford was invited into the group via a conversation with Ben Pritchard in a Manchester pub toilet: 'The next thing I knew, I was touring America.' He played a couple of UK gigs alongside Simon Archer before Ding was 'loaned out' to PJ Harvey. Although this was supposed to be a temporary arrangement, Archer's future involvement with The Fall was only on the production and engineering side of things, although he did make a few guest appearances in March 2008. The group played 20 gigs in America; there should have been more, but several were cancelled. The dates in Columbia and Oklahoma City didn't take place because Smith had food poisoning. Ten others were called off in May, a note from MES stating that this was because 'The Group / New York Agency + Tour Manager are too lazy to play. 50% refund to all ticket holders.'

Shortly after the group's return from America, Dave Milner decided to leave The Fall. One reason for his departure was a foot problem that interfered with his ability to play; he also expressed frustration with the management style of Ed Blaney. His final gig was at the Primavera Sound Festival in Barcelona on 28th May.[306]

Spencer Birtwistle returned to the fold to replace Milner. Jim

[304] James, who worked with Michael Jackson, Frank Sinatra, Edwin Starr, Bill Haley & His Comets, Norman Wisdom and Tommy Cooper over the course of his long career, was something of a local soul legend in Manchester. His son Ryan Thomas played Jason Grimshaw in *Coronation Street*. James made several appearances at Fall gigs 2004-06.

[305] Manchester's Bridgewater Hall on 6th March. Reviewer Gareth (quoted on *Fall News*) described the event: 'Mark's words were reduced to a series of distorted snarls and grunts... People started walking out almost immediately and many of those who did stay did so only to boo and heckle. After what seemed like an embarrassing eternity, but was probably more like fifteen minutes, the slow hand clapping started and MES beckoned to leave. I can't be sure whether the applause was for him or for the bloke who wheeled him off...'

[306] A gig that nobody seems to know much about. No setlist, no photos and no reviews other than this anonymous comment on a Spanish website: 'The Fall sounded good, though Mark E Smith was a caricature of what he was years ago. Luckily, his vocals are still up to it.'

Watts also re-joined the group (this time on guitar), playing throughout the second half of 2004. On 4th August, the group recorded their 24th and final Peel session, which saw Trafford, Birtwistle and Blaney make their sole appearances on the show. The recording of the session was filmed, excerpts appearing in an excellent BBC documentary, *The Wonderful & Frightening World of Mark E. Smith*. First broadcast in January 2005, it included contributions from several ex-members of the group as well as Paul Morley, Tony Wilson, Stewart Lee and Richard Boon. After an opening scene which sees MES and Eleni arriving at Maida Vale, it cuts to Peel at his turntables, customary glass of red at his side, introducing his 12th August show:

> Time for me to warn you that it is possible that in the course of the next hour and 55 minutes or so you may hear some rough language or be introduced to concepts you find unwholesome. If you fear that this is a possibility, clearly you should be listening to something else. As regular listeners will know there are few words in English finer than 'Tonight, a new session from The Fall'.

The session take of 'Clasp Hands' includes an 'Elves/I Wanna Be Your Dog' interlude that was cut from the album version. The version of 'Blindness' is considered by the majority of Fall fans to be the definitive one. 'What About Us?' is a little less dense than its album equivalent but still forceful and direct. 'Wrong Place, Right Time' belies its age, the group taking it on with vibrant enthusiasm (listen to Smith's exuberant 'shout!' at 1:54). The segue into 'I Can Hear The Grass Grow' is remarkably subtle by Fall standards, featuring a post-rock style spoken-word sample over a bed of feedback. The group recorded a fifth track, 'Job Search', that was pressed as a one-off acetate and presented to John Peel for his 65th birthday at the end of August. It's an odd and incoherent lo-fi ramble, but its strangeness makes for a wholly appropriate conclusion to the group's contributions to Peel's show.

John Peel died on 25th October. His wife Sheila Ravenscroft described the part that Smith and the group played in their lives:

As if further proof were needed of the esteem in which John held The Fall, it should be remembered that he kept all their records separate from the rest of his collection. Tens of thousands of albums are squeezed onto John's shelves. But only The Fall have their own special VIP enclosure, away from the hubbub, like religious artefacts with voodoo properties.

There was simply no other band that excited him quite so much. He once said, in a documentary made by the BBC to mark his sixtieth birthday, that he didn't want to die yet because there would be another Fall album out soon; we even chose that comment to play at John's funeral. What I can't quite come to terms with now is that there will be Fall records that John will never hear.

Two of Peel's best-known statements about the group are, 'always different, always the same' and 'a band by which in our house all others are judged'.[307] However, his feelings about the group are captured best in an interview that he recorded for the 2015 documentary *It's Not Repetition, It's Discipline*[308] – the origin for the title of this book and the original blog upon which it was based.

> People write to me and say, 'I heard The Fall, which record should I get?' And I never have any hesitation in telling them: you must get them all, because it's impossible to pick one. You have to have them all, you do. And you have to have any new record that comes out... *Live in Nova Scotia 1984*... even if the sound quality's terrible, and he was pissed, or he'd just fired half the band or whatever, you still have to have them. You do. So there is no answer to that... and in fact I'll go further. I say: anybody who can tell you the five best Fall LPs, or the five best Fall tracks, has missed the point, really. It's the whole body of the work that is to be applauded.

Smith took part in an interview, alongside Michael Bradley of The Undertones, on a BBC *Newsnight* feature about Peel's death.

[307] See Appendix 1 for the full context of both quotations.
[308] Produced by three Danish Fall fans, the DVD includes contributions from, amongst many others, Henry Rollins, Thurston Moore, David Gedge, Stephen Malkmus, Dee Dee Ramone, Peter Hook, Grant Showbiz, John Cooper Clarke and Damo Suzuki.

Smith was a little acerbic in places ('Am I allowed to speak now?') and some thought he was rather dismissive of his group's greatest champion ('we never were friends or anything like that'), but he was much warmer about Peel than the interview's reputation suggests. MES admitted in retrospect that he 'probably looked mad' but claimed this was because he couldn't hear himself properly. It is true that Smith occasionally expressed indifference about Peel. In *Renegade*, he said 'We never depended on John Peel for our livelihood. I don't put my career down to him.' In fact, he even suggested that being a 'Peel group' was a 'limitation' for The Fall. However, he also said that 'it's a shame that he's not around anymore. He was a one-off.' Sheila Ravenscroft confirmed that the two men were not exactly close friends: 'The strange thing is that John and Mark never exchanged more than a few words over the years. Their friendship involved little more than a mumbled greeting and an occasional punch on the shoulder or squeeze of the arm.'[309] She goes on to say, however, that Smith often wrote to Peel (signing his letters 'Your mate Mark') and that he was 'very kind and considerate' to her when he died.

New songs emerged gradually in 2004. 'Clasp Hands' had been debuted on the last American date, and 'What About Us?' and 'Blindness' followed in July. In Germany on 5th October they played 'Bo Doodack', an early instrumental version of 'Bo Demmick'. One of the most notable gigs of the year took place at Bristol's Bierkeller on 3rd December. Trafford and Birtwistle didn't make the gig owing to being stuck in traffic, so Jim Watts filled in on bass and the support band's drummer, Chris Evans, stepped up to play.[310] The gig was cut short because the venue had a 'heavy metal youth club night' planned for 10.30. MES refers to this in the introduction to 'Mountain Energei': 'Good evening, we are The Fall. We have to be on quickly so the youth club can start...'

In November, The Fall released *Interim*, an album-length

[309] Smith was undoubtedly a difficult man to strike up a friendship with anyway, but it's likely that Peel kept his distance after the chastening experience of his friendship with Marc Bolan, who cut the DJ out of his life once he became a star.
[310] He does a remarkably good job, although he gets a little lost in places during 'Mr. Pharmacist'. In the last few minutes of 'Blindness' he performs a series of extravagant drum rolls that would have led to any permanent Fall drummer being docked a week's wages at least.

mix of, as it says on the cover, 'rehearsals + live'. Originally entitled *Cocked* (a word Smith deploys in the early version of 'What About Us?' included here), it has more in common with *The "Twenty-Seven Points"* than *Seminal Live*; its spliced, scatter-gun randomness has the feel of a home-made mix tape. There are several re-spellings/re-wordings of titles, such as 'Green-Eyed Snorkel', 'Spoilt Victorian Childe' and 'Boxoctosis Alarum' (renamed in light of the smoke alarm that goes off in the studio at 1:24). 'Snorkel' opens with a ropy live recording from York on 12th July before transitioning (with seemingly deliberate awkwardness) into the demo version of 'Green Eyed Loco-Man', 'Iodeo'.[311] 'I'm Ronney The Oney' is a potentially interesting little riff that meanders along for a minute and a half before disappearing abruptly. The highlight of the album is the alternative take of 'Mod Mock Goth', a sharper and more coherent version than that on the 'Protein Christmas' single.

Critics, possibly still startled by the unexpected strength of *Real New*, were surprisingly kind to *Interim*. Stewart Lee called it 'inexplicably cohesive... Smith's fearsomely focused narratives and majestically brutal accompaniment [are] an accurate document of Britain's greatest band at work'. *Vox* felt that 'golden greats such as "Wrong Place, Right Time" and "Mere Pseud Mag. Ed." haven't aged one jot [and] the new tracks are simply breathtaking'. *Pitchfork*, awarding the album 5.8/10, were a little more realistic, calling it 'a haphazard jumble... no one that I know of needs a disc like this... it further muddies The Fall's already confusing and (to a newcomer) somewhat monolithic discography'.

Jim Watts made his final exit from the group in December 2004:

> Well for anyone who is interested I have left The Fall. Again. Not amazingly acrimonious. Usual reasons. Sick of the whole credits/royalties charade. No creative control whatsoever. Finding out that apparently Dave Milner wrote 'Boxoctosis'. And sick of the hassle over the fucking intro CDs.

[311] The complete (radically different) lyrics are here: https://sites.google.com/site/reformationposttpm/the-university-of-fall-ephemera/perverted-by-language/iodeo

The group's first release of 2005 was the limited edition *Rude (All The Time)* EP in February. Oddly, the title song didn't even appear, withdrawn at the last minute at Smith's request. The alternate mixes included are for highly committed Fall completists only. A far more significant release was the 6-CD box set, *The Complete Peel Sessions 1978-2004*, released in April 2005.[312] Several of the group's session recordings had been made available on official releases in the past, but what this box set had going for it was comprehensiveness, and it was greeted with universally enthusiastic reviews. *Pitchfork* gave it 9.3/10, calling it a 'sprawling, amazing release' and 'the definitive look at The Fall's career to date'. *Rolling Stone* described it as 'six CDs of peerless clang and harangue'. In *Uncut*, Simon Goddard waxed lyrical about the release and DJ alike:

> You couldn't ask for a more fitting tribute to the man, or the object of his affection, than this monolithic compendium... it's hard to imagine a more satisfying or comprehensive career overview than this... As for the irreplaceable Peel, these discs say more about the man's broadcasting ethos than a thousand broadsheet obituaries.

Simon Goddard commented that 'when The Fall were on form, Peel caught them at their very best...' It's not that they were always 'on form', of course: the box set captures several low points in amongst all the highs. But that, in many ways, is the beauty of it. What it does do – incredibly well – is capture the undulating, random, inconsistent and complex narrative of the group's history up to this point. Listening to it from start to finish is a rewarding, frustrating, baffling, inspiring and thought-provoking journey through a unique story. The great leap forward of 1980; the ebb and flow of Brix's contributions; the rise and fall of Dave Bush's electronic influence; the descents into intoxicated sloppiness; the proudly disdainful renaissances... all are captured here – and in a way that no book, article or blog can possibly hope to capture fully on their own. Understanding the historical context of

---

[312] See Appendix 1 for the full details.

this 26-year chapter of The Fall's history adds immeasurably to your appreciation, of course, but it's these seven hours of music that does the real, meaningful talking. Outside of the strange and obsessive world of Fall fandom, it is surely their greatest contribution to the music world in general.

Whilst the glowing tributes didn't lead to huge sales, the box set did make a big impact, building on the press attention that the group had garnered in the wake of Peel's death. It seemed that The Fall were flavour of the moment in the liberal media and the music press ('they have never seemed more musically influential' commented *The Guardian*'s Alexis Petridis), even if many of those writing about the group – and about MES in particular – probably liked the *idea* of The Fall as much as (if not more than) listening to the music itself. What remained to be seen was whether the group could deliver an album to build on their renewed profile.

To do so, the musicians headed to New York to begin recording; Smith following later, delayed by bad weather. Whilst there, they played a one-off gig at New York's Knitting Factory on February 10th where 'Pacifying Joint' and 'Ride Away' received their debuts. Returning to the UK, they played a dozen gigs between March and May, where more new songs began to emerge. In March, whilst playing in Milton Keynes, Smith was joined on stage by a mystery dancer:

> A young lady got on stage during Wrong Place and tried rubbing herself up against MES for a while. He gallantly continued, moving around the stage to shake her off until he could do so no more and turned to her to have words (smiling with it). Eventually a security guard escorted her back to the crowd and MES gave him a kiss for his trouble.

May saw The Fall make an unlikely appearance on long-running TV music show *Later... With Jools Holland*.[313] Reputedly, Smith insisted in advance that the host would 'not play fucking boogie-woogie piano over any of his songs'. Sources vary on the

[313] Only three years earlier, MES had disparaged the very notion of appearing on the show when it was suggested to him by Mick Middles: 'Never fuckin' appealed... I wouldn't wish to put the lads through that... all getting together and jamming... Fucking musos... The Fall have never been about that.'

exact wording, but the message was evidently clear, as Holland was nowhere to be seen when The Fall were playing. After a tight medley of 'Pacifying Joint' and 'I Can Hear The Grass Grow' (featuring a surprisingly smooth transition between the two) the group belted out a cracking 'Blindness', Smith sporting a single leather glove. According to pop gossip website *Popbitch*, Smith 'delayed filming several times by wandering in and out of shot, calling Robert Plant cunty and just generally behaving like what he is, The Last Great Englishman... Robert Plant turned up in a bullet-proof limo, The Fall were transported by Salford Van Hire'.

The group played the Feedback Festival at Parc de la Villette in Paris on 10th July. There is video footage of the whole gig available online, shot by Pascal Le Gras. It's a fascinating watch (despite the shaky camera work), which sees Smith in an affable and communicative mood, even handing out bottles of water to the audience. The most intriguing moment comes three minutes in, which captures Smith looking genuinely apprehensive and nervous before his entrance. The group concluded the gig with 'Carry Bag Man', which hadn't been played since 1990. The week before *Fall Heads Roll* came out, 'I Can Hear The Grass Grow' was released as a single. Backed with 'Clasp Hands', it only managed number 104 in the UK charts. The US version of the single contained a 'slow version' of 'Grass Grow' which sounds like the whole group are on Mogadon.

Fall Heads Roll

The bulk of the album was recorded at Gigantic Studios in New York. MES was delayed by heavy snowfall, so the group had over a week to record, as Ben Pritchard put it, 'maybe 10 tracks – absolutely perfectly, averaging recording a 4-track [song] every day'. On his arrival, Smith demanded they re-record virtually all of it. In addition, whereas the musicians had been laying each track down an instrument at a time, he insisted on them recording the songs together.[314] *Fall Heads Roll* was finished off at Gracieland (only 'Blindness' was recorded in its entirety there). It

---

[314] Ben Pritchard: 'There has been some keyboard overdubs and there's been [some] doubling up on the guitar tracks, but 90 percent of those songs are all a live take.'

was produced by Simon Archer, Tim 'Gracielands' Baxter – who had also engineered *Real New Fall LP* – and Smith. The designer of the sparse and simplistic cover (which bears a resemblance to Van Der Graaf Generator's 1975 LP *Godbluff*) is unknown.

The album was released on Slogan records, a subsidiary of Sanctuary; the US release came out on Narnack. The album sleeve contains a photograph of Andy Whyment, the actor who played Kirk Sutherland in *Coronation Street*, presumably because of his resemblance to Ben Pritchard. The American version had a slightly different front cover, and listed the tracks in the wrong order. It also contains portraits of Rwandans taken by New York photographer Robert Palumbo, with the group's names affixed below. Speaking to *Pitchfork* in October 2005, MES suggested that he had only suggested this as a joke.[315] Posting to the *Fall Online Forum*, Palumbo himself (writing in the third person) provided a different version.

> A New York photographer... randomly emailed Narnack... asking about the possibilities of shooting photos of The Fall... Mark E. Smith was standing beside Camille at Narnack as the email came in. Mark said let's have a look at his stuff, and proceeded to check out his website, and was especially impressed by the Rwanda photos. He laughed at the B/W portraits, and tagged several of them by name: that's Ben, that's Steve, that's Eleni, and the poor albino girl is me. At Mark's suggestion, the photos were used in the artwork as he prescribed.
>
> The choice to use the photos as band photos was made by Mark, and Mark and the band loved the result. The photographer assumed that the choice was partially ironic and partially something else... which is hard to pin down, but certainly has something to do with identification, fascination, confusion, nightmares, and beautiful chaos. The photographer struggled with giving Narnack/The Fall permission to use the images, but ultimately had so much respect for The Fall's vision of a haywire world that he couldn't refuse.

[315] 'I was in the Narnack office, and I said, "Wouldn't it be a good laugh [to have the photos there]," and they did it without telling me. I was sort of half serious, and said, "It would be great if you just put the names of the group [below the photos]," and being Americans, they took me literally. I meant it as a joke, like for a poster or something like that.'

There were also differences between the vinyl releases: the UK one was a single disc; in the US (where it also came out on white marbled vinyl) it was a double. The American version contained an alternative recording of 'Blindness'.

Ride Away

Another of those divisive tracks among Fall fans: to some it's a lazy, embarrassing bit of half-arsed nonsense; to others a bouncy bit of fun that sees the group challenging preconceptions with a spot of unpredictable humour. Whatever your opinion, it's clearly not reggae, as many reviews suggested. Everything about it is odd and wonky: the Bontempi organ 2-step drumbeat; the parping oompah bass; the choppy guitar chords; the stylophone-esque keyboard. Smith, obviously enjoying himself, is clearly having a dig at someone: 'you spread lies and discontent, I wish you could see yourself / you think you're a giant you know you're nothing'. Certainly a bold choice to open the album, it's also one of those 'borrows', owing a clear debt to Tami Lynn's 'I'm Gonna Run Away From You'. It was played live 34 times, 2005-06.

Pacifying Joint

Based around a hammering two-chord/note guitar/keyboard assault, it's not among the group's most complex or subtle moments, but it does have a driving muscularity that's well-suited by high volume. The lyrics make a rather obvious play on the various meanings of the word 'joint': 'with carrots and meat / a place where nice people should meet / the kind that puts you to sleep'. It was a popular live choice, being played 146 times 2005-08.

What About Us?

The album continues at thunderous pace with another heavy three-chord riff supported by Eleni's chunky synth line. Her coolly dispassionate backing vocals ('hop hop hop!') make an ideal foil for Smith's slurred but perfectly timed snarl. Much of the lyric (including the infectious chorus) focuses on Harold Shipman, a GP who murdered many of his elderly patients: 'there was a doctor going around / he was dishing out drugs / he was dishing out left and right / to old ladies'.[316] MES had first used the phrase 'What About Us, Shipman' in September 2002 (at the Blackburn gig captured on the *Touch Sensitive* DVD), possibly inspired by an ITV dramatization of the story broadcast two months earlier.[317]

The lyric is more than a throwaway reference to a notorious news story, however. The overall narrative seems to be some sort of allegory concerning the disappointment of immigration – the immigrant 'rabbit from East Germany' being happy to 'frolic... in the green grass' until he is saddened and disillusioned by reading about the Shipman case. On being asked if the song was satire, Smith replied, 'No, a lot of these Eastern European fellas you meet are grossly disappointed. That's why they're plumbers. They're crushed.' Eleni had a stuffed rabbit called Gunther o' Leipzig,[318] but there's also perhaps a more serious side to the cunicular reference: the thousands of rabbits who lived happily in the strip of no man's land on the eastern side of the Berlin Wall for whom the dismantling of the wall had catastrophic effects. Another popular live choice at the time – often stretched out to 7-8 minutes or beyond[319] – 'What About Us?' got 159 outings over the next ten years.

Midnight In Aspen

After the brace of riff-heavy monsters, the album takes a melancholy turn. Pritchard's delicate minor-key arpeggios (written by Steve Trafford) provide a wistful background for Smith's pensive musings about the suicide of Hunter S. Thompson, which took

---

[316] In 2000, Shipman was convicted for the murder of 15 of his patients. The total number of his victims was estimated to be 250, making him the most prolific serial killer in history. He committed suicide in prison in 2004. Other artists to write songs about Shipman include Fat White Family ('Shipman Decides') and Church of Misery ('Doctor Death'). Most bizarre of all is music entrepreneur and convicted paedophile Jonathan King's 'The True Story Of Harold Shipman' which suggests that Shipman was some kind of victim of the media.

[317] Entitled *Harold Shipman: Doctor Death*, it starred James Bolam of *Whatever Happened to the Likely Lads?* fame.

[318] He was thanked in the album's sleeve notes, and made a further appearance in a Fall song 3 years later (see Chapter 27).

[319] The version played in Wigan on 18th January clocks in at an impressive 15:15. The group attempt to finish around the 10-minute mark, but MES is having none of it and counts them back in.

place in February 2005.[320] This, the first half of the song, deals with Thompson's self-inflicted gunshot: 'He aims the highest bestest powered rifle at the stars'. Smith's timing is beautiful ('hyphen' at 0:55, for example) and, unusually, he expresses genuine emotion without ever retreating into cynicism.

Assume

Back to the hefty riffs, this time with a more staccato approach; there's also a bit of discordant guitar that's reminiscent of the group's early 80s work. It has been suggested that the tune is inspired by the theme to *Supercar*, a 60s TV show created by Gerry Anderson of *Thunderbirds* fame. In 2006, Smith 'explained' the lyrics: 'That was a random one, definitely... it's about humans, and air flight, and um, rabbits, and um, things like that.' Played live 45 times, all in 2005 and 2006.

Aspen Reprise

The Fall had last split a song 23 years earlier, but the bisection of 'Aspen' is more considered and meaningful than was the case with 'Winter'. The bullet that, in the first half, Thompson had aimed at the stars (specifically Orion – the hunter, of course) here 'bounces back', destined to return to its source. It 'misses him tonight / but wait till this time next week next midnight...' One of the most genuinely touching songs The Fall ever recorded, 'Aspen' was played (as a singular entity) 37 times in 2005-6.

Blindness

Not surprisingly, many of the album's reviews focused on this song, widely regarded as the towering achievement of the 21st-century Fall.[321] A brief swathe of oscillating distortion leads us

---

[320] Writer, 'gonzo' journalist and renowned drug taker, best known for his 1971 book *Fear and Loathing in Las Vegas*. A lifelong firearm enthusiast, in accordance with his wishes his ashes were fired out of a cannon in a ceremony funded by his friend Johnny Depp.
[321] Although Fall fans are by no means the only ones who have the habit, 'I prefer the Peel version' is a well-established trope amongst the Fall community; nowhere is this more true than with 'Blindness', which the majority would say is the superior version. And it is a magnificent beast, throbbing with bristling aggression and perhaps more focused and relentless than the LP version. It also has its own set of intriguing references, including to actress Jane Seymour and Greek shipping magnate Aristotle Onassis.

into a robust drumbeat which is followed by *that* bassline, thick with distortion and menace. A metallic guitar loiters furtively behind this wall of noise. The bassline is suddenly re-energised by a second version from another recording; less raw distortion, but a thick, reverberating coil of bottomless snarl. The highlights just keep coming; the choppy slashes of guitar (1:41); the bass's brief, surprising diversion into an ascending pattern (2:34); the floor tom-led lull (4:18) that builds and breaks into a crescendo rounded off by a machine-gun blast of the snare (4:56). The final two minutes are simply hypnotic.

The lyric contains several of Smith's most striking and memorable phrases, such as 'the flat is evil', 'cavalry and Calvary' and '99% of non-smokers die' – the last of which he may have picked up from Bill Hicks.[322] 'Living leg-end' – also deployed on 'What About Us?' and scrawled across the cover of *Interim* – and 'I was only on one leg' may refer obliquely to Smith's 2004 accident where he fractured his leg and hip.[323] As for overall meaning, one of *The Annotated Fall*'s potential interpretations links the song to the Oedipus myth, the name Oedipus meaning 'swollen foot' and the story ending with him blinding himself. Smith himself provided a more prosaic explanation:

> It's about the blind politician we've got here in Britain. He wants to set up camps for people, camps for dysfunctional fathers, and camps for dysfunctional kids... And he's blind, as well.

The politician, of course, was David Blunkett, who was Secretary of State for Work and Pensions at the time. 'Do you work hard?' (which echoes 'Chicago Now!') certainly sounds like something a politician in his position might ask rhetorically in a speech, and it's plausible that the 'poster at the top of the street' that caught Smith's eye might have been a party political one.

Vocally, Smith uses a variety of styles – abrupt snatches of

---

[322] 'Non-smokers die every day.' (*Relentless*, 1991).
[323] The 1973 debut album of Henry Cow (whose 'War' The Fall covered in 1994), *The Henry Cow Legend* is sometimes referred to as 'Leg End'. Perhaps making a similar pun, it featured a sock on the cover.

dialogue, a strange, almost tuneless kind of crooning, even (2:28) what sounds like him attempting to play the kazoo whilst having forgotten the kazoo itself – and every bit meshes perfectly with the beast of a riff pounding away behind him. Just listen to his timing at 5:10 as he delivers 'blind man, have mercy on me' – each utterance never quite where you expect it. Even though the whole song centred around Steve Trafford's hypnotic bassline, it was inexplicably credited to Smith/Birtwistle. According to Jim Watts:

> In the car on the way back [from the pub] we heard 'Witness' by Roots Manuva[324] and Spencer got very excited. We were inspired by the groove and I think Spencer started the beat, then Steve came up with the bass and me and Ben came in with our guitar parts.

Despite the fact that MES declared in 2005 that he was already 'sick to death of the song', 'Blindness' was played – apart from in 2011 and 2016 – at least once a year for the rest of The Fall's career, clocking up 189 appearances altogether. Often the closing number, like 'What About Us?' it was frequently extended substantially in live performances, sometimes to ten minutes or more.

I Can Hear The Grass Grow
Having reached track eight, it must be time for the obligatory cover version, and it's a pretty decent one. The Move were Roy Wood's band before he went on to ELO and Wizzard, and are most famous for the psychedelic pop of 'Flowers In The Rain', the first ever song played on BBC Radio 1. Several of the album reviews referred directly to the cover, the general tone being that the group had 'flattened' (Stuart Maconie) or 'laid waste [to]' (Alexis Petridis) the song. In fact, it's a fairly straight rendition. Smith makes a relatively concerted effort to deliver the song conventionally, although this has the usual hit-and-miss results melodically. He even affects a pleasingly Jagger-ish swagger on the

[324] 'Witness (1 Hope)' was a 2001 single by the British rapper; the riff was intended to mimic the theme tune to *Doctor Who*.

'get a hold of yourself...' sections. It's energetic, good fun and sits nicely in the middle ground between the slabs of full-on riffery and occasional gentle touches of the rest of the album. It racked up 126 appearances between 2004 and 2007.

Bo Demmick

Another Fall track that deploys the signature Bo Diddley beat (it was actually called 'Bo Diddley' on its first appearances on the setlist) 'Demmick' has a slight air of soundcheck jam about it without being too formless or indulgent. The lyric is partly lifted from 'The CD In Your Hand' from *The Post Nearly Man* and sees a reprise of Smith's favourite made-up word, 'moderninity'. *The Annotated Fall*'s suggestion of Bo Derek as the identity of the 'he' referred to throughout is one of their more outlandish ones. Played 80 times, 2004–07.

Youwanner

A heads-down no-nonsense guitar assault that Alexis Petridis described as 'a riff that could strip paint'. It charges along with brutal force, threatening occasionally to break into a chorus of some description, but always resisting the temptation. It's a great example of the Fall writing technique, as described by Ben Pritchard:

> We've never got any idea what vocals he's gonna do or what lyrics he's gonna sing. He never tells us; he just turns up and he does it. When he does, that's the first time we hear it. So you have to get into the mentality of writing a song that you can't put a melody or anything over... You just have to write a repetitive riff that just goes 'round and 'round so that he can just come in and do whatever he wants on [it].

In the lyric, Smith once again delves into his spoken-word material, 'it is the outsidedness flavour of it' being a variation on 'the outside flavourness of it' from *Pander! Panda! Panzer!* 'Meandering through the trash pedal weight of investment guest solo' is a reworking of another line from the same piece. *The*

Annotated Fall suggests that song might be a dig at Trafford and Pritchard regarding their romantic relationships.[325] It was played regularly in 2005, but overall had a shorter shelf-life than the other 'heavy' tracks on the album: it was played for the 28th and final time in June 2006.

Clasp Hands

A cheery piece of rickety rockabilly that finds Smith in uncharacteristically positive mood, expressing an enthusiastic esprit de corps regarding a successful Fall performance: 'It was a pleasure... it was one of the best shows ever seen / ludicrous, majestic and exhilarating'. The lyric also refers to the fact that the song, written by Trafford, was originally called 'NYC Steve'. Smith also revisits his inexplicable obsession with wolverines. Simon Archer plays banjo on the track: 'I just got thrown a banjo and got told, play on that.' As with many of these tracks, it was played frequently at the time before being dropped after a couple of years: 66 performances 2004-06.

Early Days Of Channel Führer

Like 'Aspen', 'Early Days' provides light relief from the heavier tracks that dominate elsewhere. It's amongst the most fragile Fall songs in the whole back catalogue; a brittle, tender waltz, to which Pritchard contributes some tender folkish guitar whilst Birtwistle adds delicate brushstrokes. Smith once referred to 'channel führer' – in reference to stations that regularly churn out WW2 documentaries – during a lively discussion about late-night television on Channel 4's *Flipside*.[326] The lyric is sparse and strange ('the snow is all around, like my hat'; 'the man who brushes against me in Heathrow') and sees MES have one of his occasional stabs at German: 'mit mir ist schrecklich' ('with me, it's terrible'). There's a particularly curious moment lurking in the background at 1:19, when Ben Pritchard's apparently helium-infused voice

[325] '[Trafford] started losing it when he met that actress out of *Shameless*, Maxine Peake,' MES wrote in *Renegade*. 'He didn't realize she was only hanging around with him because he was in The Fall.'

[326] Late-night live show presented by Richard Bacon in 2003-04, in which guests would flick through the TV channels and provide 'amusing' commentary.

squeals 'Where's all the choccies gone?' Whilst this might appear a little flippant, *The Annotated Fall* has a serious assessment: 'It conveys the narrator's alienation from his surroundings, as his sad meditation is punctured by cries bespeaking a more trivial and temporary trauma.' It was only ever played live twice, at Middlesbrough and Nottingham in October 2005.

Breaking The Rules
A cover of Frankie Valli and the Four Seasons' 'Walk Like A Man' (which the group had first played in 2003) with amended lyrics by Bec Walker, a 17-year-old aspiring singer who was doing work experience at Gracieland Studio at the time. Whilst it's bouncy and fun, it does feel at this point like the album's starting to be stretched just a little too far. The 'have we finished?' last ten seconds emphasise the throwaway nature of the track. The cover version was played 25 times in 2003-04; it was only performed with the new lyric once, at Wrexham in October 2005.

Trust In Me
A curious closer. The strangest thing about it, obviously, is that it's one of that select band of songs that doesn't feature Smith.[327] The vocals are supplied by Simon Archer, engineer Billy Pavone and Kenny Cummings and Phil Schuster from New York band Shelby, who were present at Gigantic to sign their recording contracts. Cummings and Schuster (like Robert Palumbo, writing in the third person) described their experience:

> Enjoying a break from recording their parts, Mark and Elena were happy to join in the signing ceremony acting as official witnesses. One thing led to another, and before the ink was dry, Kenny and Phil were in the recording studio adding vocals to one of the new Fall tracks. Mark christened the song 'Kenny and Phil and Billy and Ding'… commemorating vocals added by engineer Billy Pavone and producer Dingo. We don't know if the track will make the album, but it was a fun experience.

[327] *The Track Record* suggests that Smith does appear, using an 'old man voice'. I presume they mean the 'trust in me' part at, for example, 1:14, but this seems doubtful.

It's not just the absence of Smith's voice that makes the track unusual – it doesn't sound much like The Fall musically either. Tommy Mackay suggests that it resembles a cross between Wire and Queens of the Stone Age, but the discordant arpeggio/spoken word section at the minute mark is also highly reminiscent of Slint. The identity of 'Dr. Lee'– the dentist who will come around to your house and give you an x-ray for the price of a cup of tea – remains a mystery. 'Trust' was never played live.

Reviews

The death of John Peel raised the group's public profile considerably, as many mainstream media obituaries referred to Peel's love of the group. As a result, the release of *Fall Heads Roll* generated more column inches than had been the case for many years. Even the *Daily Mirror* reviewed it:

> The late John Peel's favourite band are, as ever, masterminded by Mark E Smith who now looks like a scary toothless gargoyle. But the group's ferocious blend of lo-fi intrigue and brain-busting underground rock is as strong as ever. Peel is no doubt smiling down.

In general, reviews were glowing. In the *Sunday Times*, long time fan Stewart Lee said that the album 'balances provocative noise and hypnotic hooks, benefits from an uncharacteristically spatially aware mix, showcases a disciplined, ferocious and finessed Fall, and finds Mark E Smith at his cryptic and quietly hilarious best'. *The Guardian*'s Alexis Petridis gave it the full five stars and described it as being 'of head-turning quality... Nobody else writes like this.' The *NME* gave it 8/10 and challenged readers to 'try and deny this is a band on form'. In *The Wire*, Sam Davies called it 'full-blooded Fall, fired up and amped up by some muscular production and rhythm playing... It's harder than it looks to make simplicity sound this satisfying.' Stuart Maconie felt that:

> The current hirelings play with a vim and vigour that continual harangues from the boss will surely quell, but right now they rock... a sterling addition to a great canon,

someone somewhere is hearing this glorious racket for the first time and their lives will never be the same.

Mick Middles, writing in *Record Collector*, sounded a rare note of caution. Whilst recognising the 'sheer brilliance' of the 'towering' 'Blindness', he felt that 'hints of the formulaic do start to appear before the album's eventual conclusion. In short… it's too long.' The increased media coverage did not, sadly, translate into greatly improved sales. Whilst *Fall Heads Roll* achieved the group's highest chart position for six years, it only peaked at number 115.

Evaluation
Despite the positive press attention, the received wisdom in the Fall community regarding *Fall Heads Roll* is that, whilst it contains some outstanding tracks, it's overlong and lacking in variety; over-reliant on simplistic and unsubtle three-chord bangers. It certainly could have been made more concise. There's no need for both covers, and despite the novelty of the original lyric, 'Breaking The Rules' would have been better-suited as a B-side; this is also true of 'Trust In Me', despite its strangely dark, driving energy. Making 'Channel Führer' the wistful send-off would have brought the album in at a more digestible 49 minutes. This would also have given it a more satisfactory balance, the light-hearted 'Ride Away' and the two melancholy tracks nestling in perfectly amongst the uncompromising rockers.

Fall Heads Roll does not have the same level of unpredictable innovation and layers of nuance that were the hallmark of *Real New Fall LP*. Nonetheless, what it does have is a line-up firing on all cylinders and, for once, working in harmony (as portrayed in 'Clasp Hands'). This can be heard in live shows from the first half of 2005: the group are tight and potent; MES – despite his health issues – sounds more energised than he had for many years, exhorting his musicians to squeeze every ounce of drama out of the lengthier numbers. The live approach to the album's recording that Smith insisted on gives the album a fizzing, speaker-bulging vitality that captures this with great success.

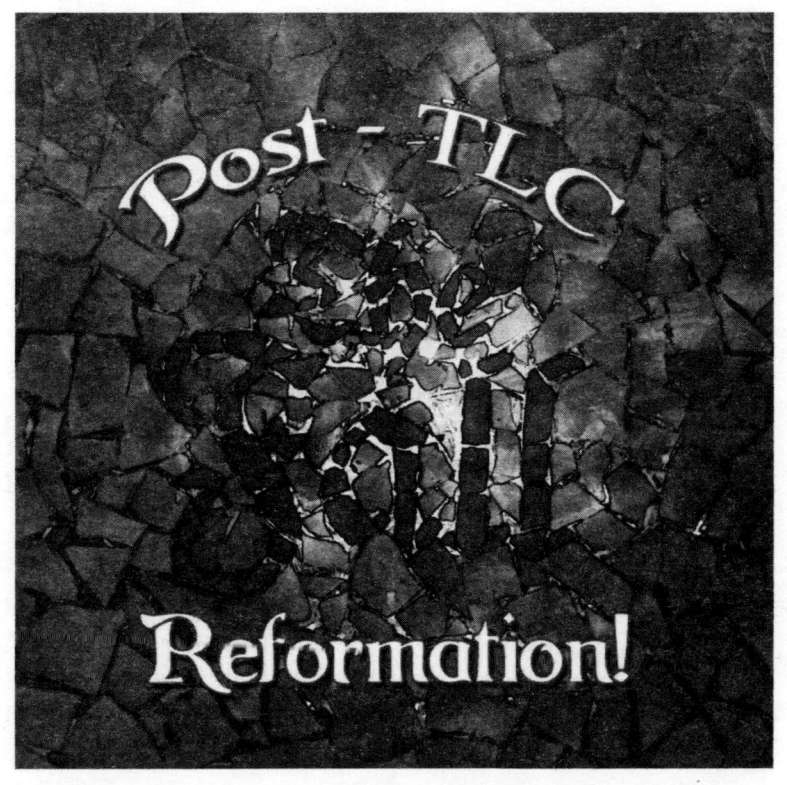

Reformation Post TLC
Recorded: Gracieland Studio, Rochdale, late 2006
Released: 12th February 2007

Personnel:
Mark E Smith – vocals
Rob Barbato – bass
Eleni Poulou – keyboards
Orpheo McCord – drums, vocals
Tim Presley – guitar
Dave Spurr – bass

With:
Pete Greenway, Gary Bennett – guitar

Chapter 26: Reformation Post TLC

'The Fall aren't really a band in the usual sense.'

The Fall performed extensively in the UK during the autumn of 2005, playing 22 gigs in October alone. After having played some of their best-received shows for some time in the first half of the year, the autumn dates saw the group becoming, once again, an unpredictable experience live – as ever, largely dictated by MES's mood and level of alcohol consumption each night. The apparently settled camp that had recorded *Fall Heads Roll* seemed to have lost the esprit de corps of 'Clasp Hands': Ben Pritchard found the tour 'the most stressful ever'; Steve Trafford described 'paranoia and general, unexplainable nastiness', recalling an incident when Smith stole his suitcase and poured water over its contents. Under the circumstances, it was no surprise that some gigs were marred by the re-emergence of familiar flaws, in particular Smith wandering off stage, resulting in meandering instrumental versions and truncated sets. 'If I want to see a bunch of instrumentalists I can listen to buskers at Oxford Circus for nothing,' commented one disgruntled poster on *The Fall Online Forum* after the Islington gig on 2nd November, 'Either MES was totally off his face tonight or completely taking the piss out of us poor punters.' Four days later, however, the group finished off the tour with an excellent 15-song 65-minute set at Sankeys Soap in Manchester. 'He's on his best behaviour in Manchester,' noted one forum member wryly, 'but treats you like shit if you live in a little town like London.' Another notable feature of the autumn tour was the first appearance of support act Safy Sniper. Sniper (real name Assaf Etie, and often referred to as 'Safi') was a Berlin-based Israeli and avant-garde visual artist who specialised in lengthy video collages that chopped up and manipulated clips of Michael Jackson, Elvis, ABBA and others. Despite (or perhaps because of) the generally hostile reaction of most Fall fans, he would go on to be one of the group's longest-serving support acts, making periodic appearances up to 2016.[328]

Despite the growing tension in the Fall camp, the 15 gigs that the group played in the UK and Europe between January and April 2006 generally went well; some blistering sets continued to include lengthy, pulverising versions of 'What About Us?' and 'Blindness'. The only unfamiliar tune to appear in the autumn 2005 tour had been a cover of Monks' 'Higgle-Dy Piggle-Dy',[329] but a steady stream of new material emerged throughout 2006. In Croydon on 15th March a mystery tune was played: largely an instrumental, with Smith only adding 'over four hundred years in Athens' before his traditional 'Good evening, we are The Fall'.[330]

Some of this new material was recorded, with Grant Showbiz producing, in April 2006.[331] Trafford and Pritchard both say that more than an album's worth of material was recorded, which Trafford described as 'amazing'. Smith, as usual, had his own version of events:

> We did a session in Lincolnshire in March. They had eight days in a studio and came back with 10 Eric Clapton-like tunes, and it was just like not good enough. It was flat as a pancake.

---

[328] Whilst a few Fall fans enjoyed Safy's contributions, comments such as 'fucking torture' and 'load of old shit' were representative of the general feeling on the *Fall Online Forum*. Many have suggested that MES deliberately deployed him to build up tension leading to the group's entrance.

[329] This was released as a limited edition 7" single in October 2006, backed by the deranged 'Monk Time' by Alec Empire ft. Gary Burger. It also appeared on a tribute album called *Silver Monk Time*, the sleeve of which suggested the unlikely line-up of: MES – vocals and guitar, Birtwistle – drums, Eleni – synthesizer, organ, bass. The group also recorded it for Radio 3's *Mixing It* in October 2005 (broadcast February 2006 – see Appendix 1). 'Higgle-Dy Piggle-Dy' is an absolute belter, and is the author's favourite Fall cover.

[330] Nobody seems to know what this might have been called. Reviews confirm that it wasn't any other known song, and the setlist (which they didn't keep to anyway) doesn't provide any clues.

[331] Grant Showbiz confirms this, saying that he has a copy of the recording which contains guide vocals on just a couple of tracks. He recalls Smith and Eleni returning to Manchester during the session and never coming back. MES called to give the bizarre explanation that he was 'snowed in and couldn't make it back'. One of the songs recorded was 'The Boss', a sprightly if not hugely original rock'n'roll-style instrumental backing to Smith's habitual variations on 'Good evening, we are The Fall' that the group played 14 times in early 2006. It eventually appeared on *The Fall Box Set* in 2007 (see Appendix 2).

The Fall embarked on a US tour in May.[332] Recent American visits had generally gone well and enhanced the group's reputation; this trip, however, saw them revisit the dark days of the Brownies disaster. Problems began as soon as the group arrived on American soil, as the stage backdrops, which Smith had entrusted to the musicians while he travelled separately, were lost in transit. At the first date in Austin, Smith walked off stage after 40 minutes, cutting the planned set short by a couple of songs and leaving the group to play an instrumental 'Systematic Abuse' (a new tune that had been debuted in March). In Tucson, Smith threatened Birtwistle with a corkscrew backstage. The line-up disintegrated completely following the fourth date, in Phoenix. Steve Trafford maintains that he, Pritchard and Birtwistle had already made their decision to leave before the gig, following an incident where Smith flicked cigarettes at and poured beer over their tour manager whilst he was driving the group between gigs. In *Renegade* – where Smith spends his first seven pages laying into the three of them with vitriol – he admits that he did 'spill some beer over the driver… [and] flick a bit of paper at him; because he was asleep'. The gig itself was a farce. Few had turned up because the venue had recently lost its liquor licence. Justin Williams, singer of tour support The Talk, threw a banana peel at Smith on stage, hitting him in the face, leading Smith to chase him to the car park. Trafford, Pritchard and Birtwistle flew home the next day.

Consequently, Smith found himself with The Fall reduced to a husband-wife duo – and with 13 dates of the tour remaining. Somehow, as ever, the group kept going. The new recruits, organised by Narnack, were guitarist Tim Presley and bassist Rob Barbato from LA band Darker My Love, and drummer Orpheo McCord from The Hill.[333] After his seven-page rant about the old group, Smith spends a couple of pages of *Renegade* extolling the virtues of his 2006 recruits, whom he describes as 'a solid bunch of lads'. McCord is 'a complete professional'; Presley, unlike nearly all guitarists, 'doesn't sulk and think [he's] the centre of

---

[332] Information about parts of the US tour is a little sketchy because the *Fall Online Forum* suffered its 'great server crash' a few months later, which resulted in the disappearance of hundreds of posts reviewing the gigs.
[333] Or 'On The Hill' – sources vary.

the universe'; Barbato's identified quality is that he 'knows how to balance that drink-and-work thing'. Regarding the very fully-bearded Barbato, Smith seemed to have softened his stance on facial hair – Barbato was excused because his was a proper, manly beard whereas previous group members such as the 1982 line-up 'couldn't even grow proper stubble'.[334] 'The Dudes', as they came to be known, were understandably under-rehearsed at their first gig in San Diego on 9th May.

> The new backing band hardly had any knowledge of how the songs were played and mostly jammed out playing whatever. The pinnacle worst moment of the show came on the second song when Elena and Mark played/sang the rocking 'Pacifying Joint' while the rest of the band strummed on 'Midnight In Aspen'.

They hit their stride rapidly though. At only their sixth performance, they banged out an incredibly powerful ten-minute 'Mountain Energei' like they'd been playing it for years. But whilst this new incarnation of the group churned out excellent performances, their long-term future seemed uncertain. One could hardly imagine Smith relocating to America, and The Fall's finances were unlikely to be able to sustain 'The Dudes' moving full-time to the UK. Sure enough, the logistics of a transatlantic line-up soon caused issues. Although the new line-up did manage a Manchester gig in June and travelled to the Øyafestivalen festival in Norway to deliver a scorching half-hour set a couple of months later, Presley and Barbato were unable to perform at that summer's Reading Festival because of prior commitments with Darker My Love. So, dipping once more into the seemingly endless supply of musicians prepared to join The Fall at short notice, two extras were recruited – both of whom would turn out to be keepers.

Pete Greenway had been guitarist in Das Fringe (aka Pubic Fringe), who had previously supported The Fall. Bassist Dave 'The Eagle' Spurr had been in En-tito and MotherJohn. Although

---

[334] On the 1982 Australian tour, Riley, Scanlon and the Hanleys main act of rebellion against the rule of MES and Kay Carroll was to hold a beard-growing contest (it lasted four days). Ben Pritchard also described Smith insisting on he and Trafford shaving.

both would later become permanent members, during the next few months they acted as a sort of subs' bench, with The Fall operating on a squad rotation basis. Several gigs saw Barbato and Spurr play together in a double-bass line-up. The squad was expanded in October when Keiron Melling (a bandmate of Spurr's in MotherJohn) stood in for McCord in Dublin. He joined the group again as part of a one-off two-drummer line-up the following month for the group's last gig of the year in Manchester.[335]

Reformation Post TLC

The album was recorded towards the end of 2006 at Gracieland. Life in Lancashire was a bit of a culture shock for the American recruits: Smith recalled 'sitting in a pub with Orpheo and all these lumpen Rochdale blokes are in there with dents in their bald skulls, belting down pints. He handled it well, even though they were just staring at him every time he opened his mouth.' Although the booklet accompanying the 2020 reissue of the album states that the group 'took some of the abandoned album's tracks and added a slew of new and often road-tested material' Smith was always keen to play down how much of the Grant Showbiz recording remained on *Reformation*. He was particularly disparaging of Trafford and Pritchard's notion that there was some sort of 'great lost album':

> Ben talks about how they recorded all these great tracks in Lincolnshire, just before the tour. They recorded shit – a few lame incarnations of what they thought The Fall should sound like. It was like a Sunday-before-work, been-drinking-all-weekend, karaoke take on *Fall Heads Roll*. It had no zip to it. I'm amazed he has the audacity to even mention it... The great lost album. What a load of shit!

There's a certain amount of mystery about many of The Fall's album titles. There's not much of that here. Smith was clearly portraying what he saw – or what he wanted others to see – as

[335] The group played 50 gigs in 2006 – the last time that they would reach this annual figure.

the complete rebirth of the group. As for the 'TLC' part, Smith was typically ambiguous:

> It's Reformation Post Treacherous Lying Cunts. You follow me? Heh heh heh. No, not really – that's what somebody said to me, though, and I think it sounded pretty good. No – TLC. It's Tender Loving Care, isn't it?

Steve Trafford had no doubt which it was: 'That's us,' he says, referring to himself, Pritchard and Birtwistle. 'Thieving Lying Cunts!'

Reformation's Roman mosaic / medieval stained-glass window cover was designed by Manchester artist Mark Kennedy. The US version – a rather stiffly posed group shot – came in for criticism from Smith:

> The cover looks like a poxy school picture, or a prison Polaroid taken for the family back at home by the screws who have loosened up a bit after a couple of Christmas cans.[336]

Gary Bennett, credited on the sleeve for guesting on rhythm guitar, is a bit of a mystery. All that's known about him is that he was a friend of Tim 'Gracielands' Baxter. 'St. Etiel' (aka Safy Sniper) was mentioned on the UK sleeve; on the US version he was credited with 'presence' and also appeared in the cover photo.

Over! Over!

The album opens with an impressively demonic cackle from Smith before the group settle down to a fuzzy blues-rock groove. It's borrowed from 'Coming Down', a 1968 song by The United States of America.[337] Like much of the album, there's a strange disassociation between Smith's vocals and the music; his voice floats around the group, only occasionally connecting with

---

[336] The photograph was taken by Bob Gruen, a veteran music photographer who had worked with Elton John, Led Zeppelin, The Clash and the Sex Pistols. His reputation did not impress MES. 'He's done everybody. Sadly, they're all dead or nearly dead... I mean they're good pictures and everything, but his eye has obviously had its day.'
[337] LA-based psychedelic band, who split up after their eponymous 1968 debut album.

what they're playing. It gives the song a spacious but strangely hollow feel. There's a deep, gruff, slightly comical backing vocal lurking in the background, the sort of thing that Karl Burns used to provide; here it's supplied by Orpheo McCord. It's a strange song: somehow aggressive yet muted; exuberant yet reserved. It was played 82 times, right up to the group's final performance. A looped, instrumental version of the riff was used as a tape intro on some 2006 gigs.

Reformation!

A metronomic heavy bass riff dominates, over which Smith barks phrases such as 'Black River', 'Fall Motel' and 'Cheese State'. Random as this might seem, there actually is a Falls Motel in Black River Falls, Wisconsin – which is the state that produces about a quarter of the cheese consumed in the US. It's easy to see how it became one of the few Fall songs to be played live over 100 times (it clocked up 135 appearances) – its simplistic structure frees the group to lock onto the mammoth groove and leave Smith to contribute as, when and how he sees fit. Bootleg recordings vary widely in both length and Smith's engagement.

Fall Sound

The album is rather oddly sequenced. 'Fall Sound' is undoubtedly a strong tune – a snarling, defiant manifesto – but it feels very much like a variation on the preceding track, and you have to wonder at the motivation for putting the two together. That said, there's an admirably driving fury about it, the group homing in tightly on another fuzzy riff, giving Smith scope to declaim about '80s reprobates' and 'laptop wankers'. It also contains one of his most notably bizarre put-downs: 'I've seen POWs less hysterical than you'. Another popular live choice, it was performed 105 times and, like 'Over!', featured in the last Fall gig.

White Line Fever

After three pieces of intense, confrontational aggression, the obligatory cover version makes an early, abrupt and somewhat dissatisfying entrance. The Merle Haggard original is a little predictable and workmanlike, but it still has more spark than this offering, a piece of slurred, post-pub karaoke. *The Guardian's* Alex Petridis liked it though, commenting that 'there's something weirdly moving about [Smith's] dissolute croon'. It got only seven live outings in early 2006 before the group tired of it.

Insult Song

An angular, funky Beefheart-esque jam in the spirit of 70s comedy 'roasts' – not a phrase that you could imagine being applied to many other artists. The group play around with the loose-limbed rhythm while Smith's improvises a monologue that mentions Amon Düül and Captain Beefheart, Eleni ('the mad Greek woman, The Hydra'), McCord ('Orpheo, the ancient name from Greece') and Dave Spurr ('put a stocking over his head, and you couldn't tell the difference'). Although not without musical interest or humour, it's rather self-indulgent and falls short of justifying its nearly six-minute length. It received four live outings, all in March 2007.

My Door Is Never

At this point, the album returns to the tone set by the opening three songs. The bassline reverberates thickly and menacingly throughout and there's some nifty distorted string-bending – but, by this stage, you can't help feeling that they've covered this ground already. Having four such similar songs and front-loading them over the first six tracks seems a little perverse. Performed live 74 times 2006-16, 'My Door' generally had much more vigour on stage than was the case with the album version. Here, it's a little sluggish, despite Presley's best efforts. The blame rests mostly with Smith, who seems to lose interest after the first few lines.

Coach And Horses

A track with a distinctly 60s vibe, but its bluesy soft-rock is more like The Doors' *Soft Parade* than the group's customary garage-punk approach. It's a peculiar little thing, swirling around in a diffident haze before exiting hastily and almost apologetically before it even reaches the two-minute mark.[338] Smith is once again rather off-hand in his delivery, although this rather suits the song's torpid groove. The lyrics vaguely suggest a time travel narrative ('I looked through the 1860s window pane'); Tim Cumming suggested that the song was one part of the 'long history of occult references in Smith's work. The mid-Victorian atmospherics of "Coach And Horses" is another pull on that long-running esoteric thread. "...coaches and horses moving round in the slashing rain", he slurs, one of the lyrics that haunts the rest of the album in the same kind of way that restless spirits haunt the work of MR James and Arthur Machen.' It was only performed live once (and with completely different lyrics), in September 2006.

The Usher

A rather rambling interlude. The 'Dr. Bucks' Letter'-style list is amusing and the typical MES perversity of making a list run from A-F and then go to six is a neat touch. On a stronger album, it might have made for a perfectly enjoyable little intermission; here, it sits amongst too many other examples of unfinished ideas. It was never played live.

The Wright Stuff

The tight little bass-heavy riff underpins the verse well enough, and the swirling organ adds a bit of colour. The light-hearted tone of the lyric ('eccentric lad / he keeps false, plastic women's bosoms under his TV desk and dressing room') contrasts nicely with Eleni's deadpan delivery. *The Wright Stuff* was a TV chat show hosted by tabloid journalist Matthew Wright, but it's also possible that there's a football theme here, related to England and Arsenal striker Ian Wright (although of course Paul Gascoigne has a stronger link with plastic breasts). The mention of 'fake' or 'mock' cameras might refer to *Spy TV*, a short-lived BBC1 *Candid*

---

[338] *The Annotated Fall*: 'It is typical of the wonderful but confounding *Reformation Post TLC* that one of the chordally most thought out, tightest (both instrumentally and compositionally), and most accessible songs on the album seems to be almost a throwaway, in terms of how short it is and how little interest MES seems to have in adding any other sections or allowing the band to explore, whereas the longest songs all consist of repetitions of a single hastily composed riff.'

Camera-style show that Wright hosted in 2004. Reality show *I'm A Celebrity* is referenced directly (Smith was allegedly invited to replace John Lydon after he walked off the programme in 2004[339]). The football connection is reinforced by the fact that the song is a clear borrow from Don Fardon's 'Belfast Boy', a tribute to George Best.[340] Like several of the songs on *Reformation*, live versions – of which there were 23 in 2006-07 – tended to pack a much greater punch than the studio take.

Scenario

A variation on 'Over! Over!' that takes a looser approach but still derives from 'Coming Down'; it also borrows, equally clearly, from Beefheart's 'Veteran's Day Poppy'. It finds Smith in melancholy and introspective mood, reflecting on his 'childhood days'. Presley contributes nicely understated bluesy meanderings over the chunky bassline, and whilst once again there's an odd disconnect between voice and music, this rather suits the sad, empty mood. The song contains several mentions of wearing poppies on TV, which might refer to the growing concerns regarding 'poppy fascism' at the time.[341] There are also historical references, both to the 1920s 'parlour' song 'Pal Of My Cradle Days' and the 'Chindits', special operations units that fought in Burma during WW2. Smith said that the lyric had partly been inspired by a friend giving him some poems written by his father, who had served in one of the units. It was played live ten times in 2006, eight more in 2009-10 and made a one-off return in 2012.

Das Boat

'It just got out of hand, that track... That's me and Elena. I was going to take it off, but people love it.' Whatever Smith might

---

[339] Speaking to Rich Pelley of *The Guardian* about the invitation in 2012, MES said 'I could have handled it then. I couldn't handle it now. I was tempted because I was absolutely broke. Thing is, you cross that line, you never go back. People look at you different.'

[340] Fardon's 1970 single 'Belfast Boy' was re-released in 2006 following Best's death. His biggest hit was 'Indian Reservation', which reached number three in 1968.

[341] 'Poppy fascism' is the notion that there is a disproportionate, almost fanatical pressure on people (especially public figures) to wear a poppy at all times around Remembrance Day. The term was coined by *Channel 4 News* presenter Jon Snow in 2006.

say, you won't easily find many Fall fans who will defend this ten-minute slab of noodling electronics. For the first and only time in their career, the group sound like Pink Floyd; not only that, they manage to sound like two different eras of Pink Floyd. The portentous opening pulses with oscillating synth and delay/reverb-heavy rock guitar hero soloing that would be right at home on the Floyd's multi-million selling mid-70s LPs. The rest of the track features quirky noises and childish voices that recall the whimsicalities of the Syd Barrett era. Although not without the odd moment of interest, it's still a piece of overlong self-indulgence. Unsurprisingly, never attempted on stage.

The Bad Stuff

The first minute of 'Bad Stuff' – more Dave Gilmour-style guitar and meandering synth, this time backed with some studio chatter – would have been a perfectly acceptable interlude had we not just had ten minutes of similar stuff. Thankfully, things pick up in the second half, which features a tidy little new wave riff. Nonetheless, the album by this stage feels like a series of incomplete ideas with the odd fully formed song thrown in. 'Bad Stuff' was played twice in 2007, both times as a coda to 'Insult Song'.

Systematic Abuse

Whereas 'Bad Stuff' crams several ideas into its two and a half minutes, 'Systematic Abuse' takes the opposite approach, stretching just one to nearly the same length as 'Boat'. It certainly meets the '3 Rs' criteria, pounding along with impressive determination and little variation. Smith's vocal is more closely anchored to the music than it is on many of the other tracks; he doesn't have a great deal to say, but he does revisit his inexplicable aversion to roundabouts.[342] Barbato, Presley and McCord's writing credits are a bit of an anomaly: 'Systematic Abuse' was debuted live two months before they even joined the group and a recording from Croydon on 14th March shows that the song was already fully

[342] 'It's an evil roundabout' ('M5#1'); 'I don't need no roundabout stop' ('Pearl City'); roundabouts also get a mention in 'Birmingham School Of Business School' and 'Way Round'.

formed at that point. It would go on to have a relatively long shelf–life: 50 performances 2006–2015.

Outro

A single note repeated in batches of three for 36 seconds. In the strange and mysterious world of Fall credits, this required the songwriting skills of five people.

Reviews and Reissues

In general, contemporary reviews expressed admiration for the group's persistence in the face of adversity and were far more positive about the album's contents than has been the case with most retrospective evaluations. *The Guardian* saw cause for optimism: 'It doesn't really sound like anything The Fall have recorded before, which bodes well for the future.' *Uncut* identified an 'abundantly confident Fall'; *Mojo* felt that the group had 'forge[d] on with standards maintained' and had 'high hopes that more music of the same potency will follow'. The *Pitchfork* review (4/10) was harsh but perhaps more realistic:

> The first thing to realize is that The Fall aren't really a band in the usual sense. It's MES & Musicians Currently in His Favour... With only a few exceptions, the album is a mess, and not a very memorable one at that.

The album reached number 78 on the UK album chart, the group's best showing for 11 years.

Two tracks from the album were released as singles in 2007. 'Fall Sound' was an iTunes download that came out in February. Two months later, the album's title track was released on CD and 12" It was backed by 'rough mixes' of 'Over Over'[343] and 'My Door Is Never'. The former makes Presley more prominent and trebly; the latter gains an extra layer of fuzzy guitar. 'Reformation!' did not trouble the charts at all – this would be the case with all of The Fall's remaining singles. The US CD version of the album omitted 'The Usher' but included four live video recordings.

[343] With typical punctuation inconsistency, the song lost its exclamation marks on this release.

A 4-CD reissue of the album was released by Cherry Red in April 2020. Disc 2 contains a variety of alternative versions of tracks from the original album, including those from the 'Reformation!' single. The disc is only moderately interesting; in most cases the sound is a bit sharper, but there are only minor differences otherwise. 'Fall Sound' is the main exception, benefitting from Smith's more coherent and committed vocal performance. It's doubtful whether even the most diehard fans were clamouring for two new versions of 'Das Boat'. That said, the shorter take (here entitled 'Onto Insanity') suggests that cut down to a little over two minutes it might have worked perfectly well as a short interlude. A shame, perhaps, that it 'got out of hand'.

Disc 3 is entitled *Early Rough Mixes 2006* and is a bit more worthwhile. It's not clear which line-up is playing on each track, but 'Over! Over!' is definitely pre-Dudes, as this is the version used as an intro tape as far back as March. On the other hand, two different American voices can be heard at the end of '60s Wack', making it unlikely that this is from the Grant Showbiz sessions. In addition, 'Scenario' appears to be a different mix of the same performance used on the album. It therefore seems probable that the disc is a mixture of the April 2006 recordings and The Dudes' first studio demos. 'Blonde' is a harder-edged early take of 'Coach And Horses'. 'Song 2/3 With Tape Of Tour Manager' is an alternative mix of what became the second half of 'The Bad Stuff'. 'Wed 2' is a guitar-heavy version of 'The Wright Stuff'. Confusingly, 'The Boss' here is a completely different tune to 'The Boss' that was played live in early 2006; 'The Vine' contains a section of the live 'Boss's riff, but has lost the rock'n'roll guitar part. The fourth disc is *Live At Hammersmith Palais April 1 2007* which was released on CD and DVD in 2009 (see Chapter 27).[344]

---

[344] At the time of writing, confusion awaits anyone accessing the reissue via download or streaming, as several of the titles on discs 2 and 3 are mixed up: 'Reformation (Edit)', for example is actually 'My Door Is Never (Rough Mix)'. The early rough mix of 'The Wright Stuff' isn't even credited to The Fall, being labelled as 'The Summer Rain' by an artist called 'Shoes'!

Evaluation

It's hard not to see *Reformation Post TLC* as a disappointment. *The Real New Fall LP* and *Fall Heads Roll* had signalled a renaissance in the group's fortunes; not the commercial success of the late 80s/early 90s perhaps, but the first few years of the 21st century had seen the group back on the radar of people who cared about 'alternative' music. This had been strengthened by the acclaim for the *Complete Peel Sessions* box set. *Reformation*, unfortunately, feels like a step backwards; a retreat into the inconsistency and wilfully perverse decisions that bedevilled some of their work in the 90s. Once again, the album is unnecessarily long, clearly not having enough strong material to justify its length. The stronger songs are undermined by overlap and overuse: 'Over!', 'Fall Sound', 'Reformation!' and 'My Door' are great tunes, but there's a distinct air of recycling about them that's emphasised by them being grouped together. A surfeit of underdeveloped sketches adds to the sense of incoherence.

As is the case with every Fall album, it's not without high points. However, even if one has to admire Smith's tenacity at once again getting another album out despite the obstacles, in general the album sounds rushed, self-indulgent and simply not properly thought through. The production doesn't help. It has a curious sound, somehow feeling simultaneously flat and thin but over-produced and glossy. Ultimately, the most frustrating thing about *Reformation Post TLC* is that a great live line-up never got the chance to record a studio album that did them justice.

THE FALL

Imperial Wax Solvent

Imperial Wax Solvent
Recorded: St. Martin Tonstudio, Düsseldorf, May-June 2007; Gracieland
Studio, Rochdale, late 2007.
Released: 28th April 2008

Personnel:
Mark E Smith – vocals
Peter Greenway – guitar
David Spurr – bass
Keiron Melling – drums
Eleni Poulou – keyboards, vocals

Chapter 27: Imperial Wax Solvent

'Just when you think The Fall must finally fail its MOT, he tinkers around beneath the bonnet, slams it shut with a shower of rust, and off it trundles again.'

Smith celebrated turning 50 by performing at Bilston in the West Midlands. The group finished the set with a new song, named on the setlist as 'Wolve Kidult Man'. However, it was actually an early incarnation of '50 Year Old Man', written specially for the occasion by Rob Barbato. (In true Fall tradition, the bassist never received a writing credit for the song.)

It's a great shame that the American line-up never got to record a studio album that did them justice, but there is, thankfully, a release which captures them at their peak. *Last Night At The Palais*, released in 2009 on CD and DVD, includes the whole set from The Fall's 1st April performance at London's Hammersmith Palais.[345] Supplemented by both Spurr and Greenway on this occasion, the three Americans demonstrate throughout how they were such a valuable – if all too brief – addition to the Fall sound. Presley and Greenway complement each other perfectly, as do Barbato and Spurr. McCord's drumming, delivered with grinning exuberance throughout, is also outstanding. Eleni makes a substantial contribution to the performance through both her keyboard work and vocals. Occasionally, she presented a slightly icy persona on stage, but here she's full of smiles and seemingly brimming with confidence. Her delivery of 'The Wright Stuff' puts the album version to shame, which sounds flat and uninspiring in comparison. Smith also rises to the occasion. Focused and dynamic throughout, he does indulge in the odd bit of knob-twiddling, but it's good-natured mischief rather than nasty antagonism. Like the rest of the group, he seems to

---

[345] Despite the album title, the *actual* last concert at the Palais was by Groove Armada on 3rd May; the gig by Damon Albarn and Paul Simonon's 'supergroup' The Good, the Bad & the Queen (the night before The Fall's) was also billed as the venue's final performance.

be having a genuinely good time. The version of 'Blindness' is a particularly excellent one, and there are several golden moments in the video: Eleni hanging her handbag under her keyboard as the song starts; Smith's surprisingly affectionate little pat on the cheek for Rob Barbato; the way, after handing over the mic to the audience, he surveys the crowd, impassive and inscrutable; and the best bit of all, around four minutes in, where Smith 'conducts' the band with impeccable timing. The gig wasn't without its controversial moments. Before the encore, a tired and emotional audience member climbed on stage to castigate Smith for not making some sort of tribute to the venue (he clearly didn't know much about MES if he really expected this). Several reports also suggest that the security were rather heavy-handed with stage invaders during the encore, although you can only catch glimpses of this in the DVD. Smith's parting remark was 'Thank you for allowing us in your security area... we're off to civilisation.'

Smith had first worked with German electronica duo Mouse On Mars back in 2004, resulting in the tracks 'Sound City' and 'Cut The Gain' that appeared on their EP *Wipe That Sound*. Further recording sessions in 2006 led to full-length album, *Tromatic Reflexxions*, released under the name Von Südenfed shortly after the Palais performance. The album was very positively received, and is generally regarded as Smith's most successful collaboration. The *NME* enjoyed the 'claustrophobic dance music that frightens and fascinates in equal measure, but never bores'. *The Guardian*'s Dorian Lynskey found the duo's abrasive beats and Smith's role as 'surreal and belligerent master of ceremonies' to be a 'snug fit' and 'more satisfyingly adventurous than recent Fall albums'.

The Fall's performance at the Primavera Festival in Barcelona on 1st June 2007 marked the last appearance of The Dudes, the rest of the year's gigs featuring the Smith / Poulou / Greenway / Spurr / Melling line-up. The first Dude-less Fall gig took place at The Ritz Manchester on 1st July. It was part of the Manchester International Festival and served as a launch party for a recently published book of short stories inspired by Fall songs, *Perverted By*

Language. It included readings by Stewart Lee amongst others.[346] The audience soon ran out of patience with the spoken word elements,[347] as Lee describes:

> On the night, 3 or 4 writers had agreed to read from the book, as part of the Festival, before The Fall's set. Alan Wise the manager came back stage and hung around wheezing and snuffling and told us all how Mark hated the book, which freaked the other writers out and made some of them nervous... I read a bit of my story then split for the pit. All the other writers went on too long and the standing audience got restless... The Fall came on and MES tore the book up on stage, which was a struggle for him as it was sturdier than he had imagined. I don't know if MES hated the book or not. Some of the pieces (not mine) were very good, some weren't. It made sense for 'the character of MES' to hate the book, whether he did himself or not.

The second half of 2007 saw debuts for many of the *Imperial Wax Solvent* songs, including 'Tommy Shooter' (which had the working title 'I Am Me, Mark'). 'Exploding Chimney', 'Latch Key Kid' and 'Is This New' followed in March 2008. During this period, the group continued their habit of occasionally dropping random oldies into the set. 'The Man Whose Head Expanded' received a one-off revival, the first time it had been played for 22 years; 'Wings' reappeared after a similarly lengthy absence; 'Totally Wired', which hadn't been heard at a Fall gig for 19 years, received its final outing in March. Many of the 2008 shows began with a roadie called Nikki/Nicky reading out some text written by MES. It varied slightly as the tour went on, but this version, from Leeds University, 20th March, is typical:

> Hideous, hideous, evil album. You will try and remember songs and you can't. You strain. Then an inside flash, they come in one-third seconds that will not set your mind

[346] Stewart Lee secured a hand-written note from MES checking he was okay with the book before writing his piece, 'The Aphid'. Lee says that the note is lost, 'tucked in a record somewhere, along with a postcard from Berlin from Steve Hanley, answering fan mail, in 1982'.
[347] The crowd's malcontent was probably exacerbated by the fact that the venue rigorously enforced the national indoor smoking ban that had been introduced that day.

free. I can turn on the TV to see something moving down, down into the long days of your self-semi-educated childhood. I can turn on the TV to see something moving down into the giving green sun. Etcetera! Etcetera! Etcetera! Extra! Extra! Extra! This is your worst, terrifying gig. Gig! I am the impresario of The Fall and the so-called compère grand. I, Wise Alan!

Smith's autobiography *Renegade* was published in April. Written in collaboration with Austin Collings, it's an entertaining and often hilarious read. However, anyone hoping for an in-depth discussion of the lyrics or a detailed account of how The Fall's best-known songs were written and recorded is (a) going to be disappointed and (b) clearly hasn't followed Smith's career very closely up to this point. At its best, the book is acerbically funny, touching and insightful; at its worst it descends into bitter axe-grinding (particularly regarding ex-members such as Riley, Pritchard and Trafford). A frustrating mix of brilliance and nonsense, it's exactly what any Fall fan would have expected of him. John Doran described it as 'one of the funniest books written about music. Despite the self-aggrandising and incomplete nature of Smith's tale, it makes for a genuinely brilliant snapshot of one of the last English eccentrics in public life.'[348]

Shortly before *Imperial Wax Solvent*'s release, Smith was involved in a controversy that was peculiar even by Fall standards. After an interview in which he claimed to have killed two red squirrels because they were eating his garden fence, it was reported that the RSPCA were considering investigating his comments and having him charged under the Wildlife and Countryside Act. Several newspapers carried the story, including the *Daily Mail*, whose headline reflected the paper's usual level-headed approach: 'Veteran rocker Mark E Smith faces RSPCA probe for chopping up rare red squirrels with hedge-clippers'. The rest of the article had a similar tone, describing Smith as a 'short-tempered punk rocker' and opening with the memorable statement, 'Ever since

[348] At the time of writing, the book has a very respectable average rating of 4.5 stars on Amazon. There are only a very small number of dissenting voices, one of whom comments, 'If you've ever relished the prospect of being cornered in a lift by a gobby drunk, this is the book for you.'

Ozzy Osbourne bit the head off a bat, hard-core rockers have had much to live up to in the depravity stakes.' Interviewed backstage at the *Mojo* awards (where he received the 'Maverick' award) Smith laughed off the story: 'There's no fuckin' red squirrels in Salford!'

Imperial Wax Solvent

The album was recorded at Mouse On Mars' Düsseldorf studio, Britannia Row in London and Gracieland in Rochdale. Unusually, most of the album was mixed in mono – only 'Wolf Kidult Man', 'Can Can Summer', 'Tommy Shooter' and the first part of 'Senior Twilight Stock Replacer' were in stereo. An alternative version of the album – which had circulated unofficially amongst Fall fans for several years under the name 'The Grant Showbiz Mix' – eventually appeared in 2020 as the 'Britannia Row Recordings' (see Reviews and Reissues below). The 'Dudes' were due to play on the album, but Presley and Barbato's Darker My Love commitments made this impossible.

According to Pete Greenway, most of his guitar parts 'were recorded on the last day, probably within an hour, in a blind panic'. This involved him at one point sitting on a fire escape to record an acoustic guitar track because Smith 'liked how it sounded there'. 'I remember being surprised at how cohesive the final LP sounded considering the chaotic environment that it was recorded,' Greenway recalled. 'I later learned that Mark would thrive in these situations and use the chaos to his advantage, taking control of the project and steering it his way.'

The bold, abstract cover was provided by long-time fan Anthony Frost, and is similar in approach to his design for *Extricate*. The album attracted some mainstream press attention when it was released, owing to an error at the pressing plant that saw it issued accidentally as teenage *Britain's Got Talent* entrant Faryl Smith's eponymous debut. *The Sun* reported that 'a cock-up in production meant that instead of delicate balladry in the honeyed tones of their recently signed youngster, what actually ended up on discs bearing her artwork and info were the grumblings of Mark and his fellow Manc veterans' 2008 album *Imperial Wax Solvent*'.

Alton Towers

A true outlier in the group's back catalogue. 'Alton Towers' is a wonky, unusual delight; a squelchy, spacious jazz–tinged groove that even has a touch of Gong about it. The lyrics reference Lauren Laverne (with whom Smith had an uncomfortable encounter in 2007[349]) and James Brown, ex–editor of *Loaded*, for which MES undertook a famously well–oiled and antagonistic interview.[350] It also contains the intriguing line 'the crows are not reflecting any form of quality'. It was only played live seven times, all in 2007 and 2008.

Wolf Kidult Man

A burst of lupine howling, strident drums, reverberating bass and a wonderfully scuzzy, snaking fuzz–guitar riff – all within the first ten seconds – propel you into a raucous piece of garage thrash. The voices at the end come from a *Twilight Zone* episode called 'Printer's Devil'.[351] 'Wolf' was played live 139 times and was the opening song of The Fall's final gig.

50 Year Old Man

The opening four minutes are an unforgiving onslaught of fury, noise and distortion. The pounding combination of drums, bass and guitar bludgeon you into submission whilst Smith extols the priapic and excessive virtues of reaching half a century ('I got a three–foot rock hard on, but I'm too busy to use it'). A shift to shrill keyboards and loping, hoedown banjo is followed by a more down–tempo (but no less intense) version of the first section. Around the eight–minute mark, things get distinctly weird and proggy before returning to a pared–down, relatively restrained reprisal of the main riff. It concludes – all too quickly, despite its

[349] On the TV show *Transmission* (broadcast 30th March 2007) Laverne asked a rather odd question: 'Your missus is still in there, and she was in the last lot, right? Did you ever think about, sort of, maybe replacing her and then think, oh, I can't go that far?' MES, deadpan, replied, 'Don't get funny now.'

[350] According to the transcript published on *Drowned in Sound*, he called interviewer John Perry 'a cunt', tried to stub a cigarette out in his face, described John Peel as 'a bastard' and abused Tim Wheeler of Ash, who happened to be in the pub in which the interview took place.

[351] First broadcast in 1963, it starred Burgess Meredith (who also played the lead role in *Time Enough At Last* – see Chapter 15).

extravagant length – with a late uptempo rally, Smith ordering the group to 'fade out'. A startlingly forceful barrage of defiance, in which Smith strikes a perfect balance between pathos, aggression and humour, it was played live 55 times, 2007-09.

I've Been Duped

Described by *The Track Record* as a 'fairly conventional punky tune', 'Duped' (with Eleni on lead vocals) sounds like Nico covering The Rezillos. There are several of the by now familiar clunky edits towards the end. Bizarrely, the lyric makes direct reference to *Edwardians in Colour*, a BBC documentary about Albert Kahn.[352] One can only guess, however, as to the identity of the 'two hairy men digging up Scotland'. Like 'The Wright Stuff', it worked a lot better live: bootleg versions find Eleni's vocal a great deal more urgent than the slightly stilted diffidence of the studio take. This may explain its setlist longevity: 161 outings 2007-15.

Strangetown

Five tracks in, and to nobody's surprise it's obligatory 60s/70s cover version time. Here, the group dip into The Groundhogs' back catalogue for the second time. 'Strange Town' originally appeared on The Groundhogs' 1970 album *Thank Christ For The Bomb*; the slower sections of the Fall's cover are adapted from 'Garden', from the same album, giving 'Strangetown' the unique status of being a borrow within a cover. On first impression, it feels like just another bog-standard garage rock trundle, but there are a few elements that prevent it from being too mundane. Firstly, there's the 'Wish You Were Here'-style radio tune-in intro followed Smith's creepy mumble, 'I like your plants, they are nice'. There is also a series of 'skips' that make it sound as though it's a taped copy of a scratched LP, plus a range of curious background noises. The moment halfway through where Smith seems to lose the plot and has to count himself back in is an endearing touch. It was played live 24 times, 2007-10.

[352] French banker and philanthropist, responsible for *The Archives of the Planet*, a collection of 72,000 colour photographs.

Taurig

Eleni throws in a bit of abrasive electronica, the whispered backing vocals – it's unclear whose they are, but it doesn't sound like Smith – adding a touch of menace. Used as an intro tape on a few occasions, but never played live.

Can Can Summer

A scratchy piece of funk-rock that has a distinct air of Can, presumably the origin of the title. Like 'Duped', there are several awkward edits which give it a nervy urgency. The layers of Smith and Eleni's vocals work well, as there's a pleasing merger of the guitar-based and the electronic. The 'my boss, he has the imagination of a gnat' interlude adds a spot of levity. It was only played live 13 times, between 2007 and 2011.

Tommy Shooter

A calm, understated groove, shaped by Greenway's ascending guitar pattern and Eleni's simple synth line. Although what sounds like a mellotron begins to lurk in the shadows during the second half, the backing is relatively static, making Smith the focal point. He certainly rises to the occasion, hitting a particularly rich vein of imaginative expression: 'I got news for you my friend / to which you will have to attend'; 'sit on your shoulder bone'; 'the locals are in the realm of humiliation'. He's completely in tune with the ebb and flow of the music around him, but also pulls off that trick where he's just off the beat but still hits that perfect yet unexpected moment. Played 30 times in 2007–08, Smith often handing vocal duties over to Nikki/Nicky the roadie.

Latch Key Kid

The grizzly bassline from Spurr, overlaid by a double-tracked growl from Smith about tobacco, sugar and Gunther o' Leipzig' (Eleni's stuffed rabbit of 'What About Us?' fame) is followed by yet another ham-fisted edit (0:38). The group are impressively solid and the interplay between the various vocal tracks works well, although it starts to wander a little aimlessly towards the end. It was played live 43 times. The best performance of the song is the muscular version the group played in December 2008 for *From The Basement*, a web TV series created by Radiohead producer Nigel Godrich.[353]

Is This New

Crisp and concise – only just passing the two-minute mark – 'Is This New' features a slinky riff broken up with urgent, staccato interludes. The curious narrative, which involves Jeremy Kyle and Jeffrey Archer (and, possibly, Dot from *Eastenders* as well as Judy of *Richard & Judy* fame), becomes increasingly surreal. At first it seems to be Archer that's being pursued (possibly by the 'time blenders'), but the result of the search finds 'them' tracked down to 'a dancing high school... his goddamn rock school, featuring an Egyptian... and a trombone musician'. It was played 24 times in 2008 – each time as the opening song following Nikki/Nicky's introductory speech – before getting two more outings, in 2011 and 2012. The 2008 performances rarely contained many of the album version's lyrics, instead serving as the vehicle for one of Smith's traditional introductions, such as this one from Inverness, 27th March 2008:

> Good evening, we are The Fall. I have emerged from the lake experience and the waters of Lake (Pálava) to come to you from the valleys of Cheshire Cheese. We are The Fall, good evening. Hit it! Sanctioned and latch key kid.

Senior Twilight Stock Replacer

A well-established part of the live set before *Imperial Wax Solvent* was released, having already been played 23 times. The unremitting riff was written by Spurr, who also came up with the archetypal Fall title. Inspired by a friend who jazzed up the sound of being a kitchen porter by calling himself a 'Sub Aqua Ceramics Operative', the bassist described his job working nights at a hardware superstore as 'Senior Twilight Stock Replenishing Technician', which was shortened to fit the riff. Although there's

[353] They also played 'Wolf Kidult Man', 'Is This New' and '50 Year Old Man'. At the time of writing, it's widely available online (it has been taken down in the past) and is one of the best Fall performances you'll see on video.

much to admire about its bass-driven muscle, the repetitive chant-along backing vocals, plus the fact that the lyrics contain little more than the title and Smith's habitual use of random numbers ('zero seven seven fifty-eight') and mystery abbreviations ('S.N.I.P.') give it a rather one-dimensional feel. The song switches from stereo to mono at 1:07. Its last live appearance came three months before the album was released.

Exploding Chimney
Smith's reference to 'herpes, scabies and AIDS' around a minute in shed a bit of unsavoury light on the opening lines, where he describes having 'rat poison' in both his 'workshop' and his 'vicinity'. All of which suggests that the chimney that's undergoing detonation might not be an architectural feature. Disturbing imagery aside, it's a cracking tune, bristling with taut, aggressive energy. Primarily a garage rock number, the use of a mellotron in both the quieter passages and the staccato bursts give it an interesting hint of prog. Greenway's performance is the highlight: the screech of fingers down the frets at 0:38; the strangled chords at 1:24; the shrieking runs at 2:07; the crackling distortion of the finale. Its only fault is that it ends at least a minute too soon. The group attempted 'Chimney' on stage only four times (all between March and July 2008), Nikki/Nicky contributing most of the vocals on two of them.

Reviews and Reissues
The album reached number 35 in the UK albums chart, the group's highest placing since 1993's *Infotainment Scan*. Critical reception was highly positive. Dave Simpson gave it 4/5, identifying the group as 'Britain's most berserk, uncompromising and brilliant band'. Andy Gill commented that 'nothing seems able to halt Smith's progress. Just when you think The Fall must finally fail its MOT, he tinkers around beneath the bonnet, slams it shut with a shower of rust, and off it trundles again.' *The Quietus'* Taylor Parkes described it as 'pure surge and shudder, the heaviest, grimiest, most guttural Fall of all... *IWS* is powerful enough to pin you in the present, bellow in your face until all you understand

is this, here, now – and what the hell are you doing with your life that it doesn't match up to this?'

The infamous 'Grant Showbiz Mix' finally emerged in October 2020, when Cherry Red released a 3xCD / double LP reissue of the album. Disc 2 of both was entitled 'Britannia Row Recordings 21/9/07'. Overall, the production is more gentle and spacious. This suits 'Alton Towers' well, which is delicately trippy. 'Strangetown' is briefer and glitch-free. For many of the songs, the crisp sparseness of the sound brings clarity and precision, although they tend to have less intensity than the final versions. 'Taurig' tones down the electronica and is focused on Smith and Eleni's overlapping, dislocated vocals. '50 Year Old Man' – split into two parts, the second of which is called 'Inferior Product Man' – captures the difference between the two versions most clearly; although admirably tight and focused, it lacks the unhinged abandon of the official version. One of the most interesting moments is 'Ponto', which didn't make it onto the final album at all: a mix of twitchy math-rock and heavy three-chord guitar, it contains the memorable phrase 'ice cream palaver'.

Evaluation

Although *Imperial Wax Solvent* may have been perceived by some as a case of 'another year, another album, yet another line-up', it was more of a transition than a clean break like *Reformation*: Greenway and Spurr had contributed to the previous album and they and Melling had played in various combinations with 'The Dudes' over the preceding months. It was certainly more fully formed than its predecessor. Whereas *Reformation* was a frustratingly incomplete draft of a potentially exciting album – one that fell considerably short of making best use of the line-up at the time – *Imperial Wax Solvent* saw the group moving towards a clear definition of their new incarnation. It wasn't *quite* there yet – as Pete Greenway pointed out, they hadn't fully gelled at this point – but you can feel a new, dynamic sound emerging. Considering how closely it followed on the heels of *Reformation* and the disruption of 2006, it's a remarkably consistent and effective piece of work.

Your Future Our Clutter
Recorded: Chairworks Studios, Castleford; 6dB Studio, Salford; Saddleworth
and London, mid-late 2009.
Released: 26th April 2010

Personnel:
Mark E Smith – vocals
Peter "PP" Greenway – guitar
David "The Eagle" Spurr – bass
Keiron Melling – drums, percussion
Eleni Poulou – keyboards, bass, backing vocals

Chapter 28: Your Future Our Clutter

'The Fall will abide: they have broken out of time, and exist slightly away from the rest of us.'

Although the group continued to gig regularly during the second half of 2008, Smith also found time to promote his autobiography. At a Q&A event in Brighton, hosted by his ghostwriter Austin Collings, Smith answered questions (including one about his attitude to squirrels) with attentiveness and good humour. The positive atmosphere was undoubtedly helped by the fact that he drank water rather than beer throughout. His appearance at the Hay-on-Wye literary festival was less successful:

> The session with Mark E Smith of The Fall and the co-writer of his autobiography, Austin Collings, was what you might call a car crash. The interviewer had a habit of throwing out richly curlicued baroque questions – often answered by Smith with a long, buttock-clenchingly embarrassing pause followed by a growled 'Yeah', 'Sometimes', 'Nah', or even 'Start again?' The audience reacted with nervous titters.

A further book-related event at London's Southbank Centre in July was a similarly unedifying spectacle. This time the 'nervous titters' were complemented by some drunken heckling from the audience.

The first sight of new Fall material came in Dublin in September. 'Chino' (at this point called 'Chino Splashback') was largely an instrumental vehicle for Smith's customary introduction. More new songs emerged throughout autumn: 'Hot Cake' (an instrumental to begin with), 'Bury' and the cover 'Funnel of Love'. The group also debuted a cover of Screaming Lord Sutch's 'Jack The Ripper' that they would revisit only once, four years later.[354]

---

[354] 'Jack The Ripper' was a 1963 novelty single that was banned for 'violent imagery and unbridled horniness'.

September 2008 saw the publication of Dave Simpson's *The Fallen*. A true labour of love, it chronicles Simpson's obsessive attempt to track down every single person who played in the group.[355] Whilst ultimately unsuccessful (spoiler alert: he never manages to track down Karl Burns), it's full of intriguing anecdotes – especially about bit-players like Ruth Daniel and Nick Dewey – and thoughtful reflections on Smith's leadership style.

Smith and Ed Blaney released an album in October, imaginatively called *Smith And Blaney*. It's a patchy affair, although not entirely without the odd moment of interest: 'Ludite' is a sparsely angular take on 'Shake-Off'; 'When We Were Young' is a more traditionally structured version of 'Job Search'. Overall, however, it's about 15 minutes of potentially interesting material stretched over nearly an hour and has a distinct air of 'recorded after we got home from the pub' about it. The duo played a handful of gigs in early 2009 to promote it. In February 2009, a couple of Smith/Blaney dates and a literary festival discussion were cancelled, and Smith played the next two Fall gigs in a wheelchair. The official reason given at the time was that Smith had once again fallen and broke his hip. In reality, however, he had been diagnosed with cancer and had undergone an operation to remove a kidney. The truth did not fully emerge until ten years later, revealed by Eleni in an interview with Q in May 2019: 'He didn't want to tell anybody because he didn't want to be "poor me". He went straight from the hospital and continued recording in a wheelchair.'

The Fall played a 'Mojo Honours' gig in London on 10th June with Buzzcocks and John Cooper Clarke, which saw them perform a few oldies: 'Psykick Dancehall', 'A Figure Walks' and 'Rebellious Jukebox' (all of which hadn't been played for 29 years). 'Pat-Trip Dispenser' was revived in October after a 24-year absence. Further new material also appeared: 'Cowboy George' in April; 'Slippy Floor' (at this point 'Sloppy Floor') in July; from November, several sets opened with a new untitled instrumental, an early version of 'O.F.Y.C. Showcase'. On 16th November,

[355] The quest started life as a January 2006 *Guardian* article, 'Excuse me, weren't you in The Fall?'

452

'Slippy Floor (Mark Mix)' was released as a limited edition 7" and CD single. The version here is not hugely dissimilar to the album track, but is quicker to get to the livelier sections. The single also contains an alternative version of 'Hot Cake' and a live recording of 'Strangetown'. The cover photo featured the Blackburn Junior Hawks Under 16s ice hockey team.[356]

The first Fall gig of 2010 was in Berlin in February, and saw the debut of 'Mexico Wax Solvent', Ed Blaney performing a large proportion of the vocals. The following month saw the release of another Smith collaboration. He contributed vocals to 'Glitter Freeze' by Damon Albarn's Gorillaz; that summer, Smith joined Gorillaz on stage at Glastonbury to perform the track.[357] The week before *Your Future Our Clutter* emerged, 'Bury' was released as a 7" single. It was a limited edition, part of 2010's Record Store Day. Confusingly, the A-side is called 'Bury! #2+4' on the front cover, 'Bury 1 Bury 2' on the back cover and simply 'Bury!' on the label. It's a more concise and crisp version of the album take, and has only a very brief lo-fi introduction. The B-side was 'Cowboy Gregori'. It shares some lyrics with 'Cowboy George', but is very different musically; much lighter in tone, it's driven by a light, nimble Greenway riff. It was played live four times.

Your Future Our Clutter

Most of the album was recorded at Chairworks in Castleford and Simon Archer's 6dB Studio in Salford. It was released (as part of a one-album deal) on Domino records, an independent label responsible for recent high-profile releases such as The Arctic Monkey's *Whatever People Say I Am, That's What I'm Not* and Franz Ferdinand's eponymous debut. The two-year gap between *Imperial Wax Solvent* and *YFOC* (a lengthy intermission by Fall standards) was caused partly by the label being dissatisfied with early versions of the album and sending it back for more work. The press release stated confidently that the album represented

---

[356] It's not entirely clear why, other than the fact that ice hockey players by definition play on a very slippy floor.
[357] At the time of writing, the BBC footage is available online. MES (reading from a lyric sheet) puts in an excellent performance; being a guest doesn't deter him from a spot of amp fiddling.

'The Fall at their most rampant, most forward moving, bone shaking best. With nine tracks that rock like raw fury, we see The Fall heading into their next decade with the same intensity with which they started.' The cover (which bears a passing resemblance to The Jam's 1982 LP *The Gift*) was designed by Manchester artist Mark Kennedy, with assistance from S. Etiel aka Safy Sniper. Gunther o' Leipzig was thanked once again.

In an interview with *The Quietus*, Smith expressed satisfaction with his newly settled line-up:

> It's a good balance and I hope to keep it, touch wood. You've got Pete, that's who Cowboy George is, who is into really weird rockabilly. And then you've got the rhythm section who are really into Motörhead and shit like that and then you've got Eleanor who's into German experimental stuff. It's a nice combination.

O.F.Y.C. Showcase

A strong contender for most striking opening track on a Fall album, 'Showcase' is a forceful statement of confidence and intent – like 'Jim's "The Fall"', only more so. It was played (not surprisingly, generally as a set-opener) 53 times in 2009-11. One of its main strengths is that it's actually constructed from very little: direct, pummelling drums, a simple blues-rock guitar line supported by a throbbing bass and Smith occasionally shouting 'Your future, our clutter'. There's nothing difficult or complicated about it, which enables all the aggression and energy to be channelled into a focused assault on the senses.

After a brief, barely comprehensible bit of MES mumble ('little Baco mongers'), Melling strikes up a no-frills muscular pattern that he batters away at unfailingly throughout. At 0:26, Eleni joins in with an oscillating synth motif; at 1:14 Greenway adds a bit of understated chugging top-string guitar; and then, at 1:25, it all kicks off gloriously. Smith is fantastic on this: he snarls, growls, shouts, and even does some (almost) tuneful singing. His enunciation of 'clutter' (e.g. at 1:34) is perfect. Smith talked about the meaning of the title phrase in a 2010 interview:

The title of the LP came, then that tune came, then I thought I might as well do the title of the LP over this tune. It was good because I couldn't really articulate what the title of the LP meant but it's like, you know – it does fit in with the rest of the songs. What sparked me off was I distinctly remember playing Belfast and coming out and remember saying to the bass player, there were all these posters – it was well before we started recording the LP – all these really massive posters in Belfast and it had like, 'Our Equity is Your Future'. I remember saying to Dave, 'That is really fucking Irish.' Our equity is your future. That is like – you can't say fairer than that, can you?

'What You Need' was the epitome of The Fall's work ethic in the 80s; this is MES much older, not much wiser, but still defiant and hell-bent on grinding out results. It's the sound of a 50+ year old man who doesn't give a flying one what you think but still knows how to make his group conjure magic – even if it's by now a very different kind of magic.

Bury Pts. 1 + 3

After its introduction to the set in January 2009, 'Bury!' quickly became a live favourite and managed an impressive 169 outings over the last eight years of the group's career. It's not difficult to see why: it's a stomping bruiser that must have caused considerable moshpit mayhem. After an almost uncomfortably extended lo-fi opening (which one review described as 'like a muddy footprint being forced through a fax machine'), Spurr and Melling lock onto a tight groove that's complemented by Eleni's oscillating keyboards and Greenway's carefully judged thrash. There are plenty of other sounds lurking beneath to add to the entertainment: laser guns, someone trying to tune in an old AM radio and assorted clammy gurgles. Once again, Smith's vocal is crisp, coherent and perfectly timed and enunciated – 'a French composition on a fluted instrument' and 'then one day a Spanish king with a council of bad knaves, tried to come to Bury' being notable examples.

It's just like… me and the rhythm section actually live in Bury, or we're adjacent to it. I'm actually Salford. But…

for some reason I'm in Bury. It's much more a comment, a Lancashire comment, cos the drummer's from Burnley, and the bass player's from Ramsbottom, and we were laughing about the attitude of Lancashire, you know. It's our 'California Über Alles' [laughter] of Lancashire. One thing we did unite on mentally – 'Bury – fuckin' shit!'

'A new way of recording / a chain round the neck' probably refers to Domino sending the album back for more work. The lyric also revisits the squirrel controversy: 'got rid of vermin like the grey squirrels by reading out Ben Marshall's articles'.[358] In addition, 'Bury' features the fifth and final reference to wolverines in a Fall track.

Mexico Wax Solvent
After two intense openers, the group take things down a notch with a track that still has a firmly determined sound but also features some lighter, contrasting features: the delicate guitar arpeggio that appears at 1:40; the gently lilting, almost jazzy keyboard part that emerges around the four-minute mark. Smith's delivery is more relaxed than in the opening duo, and this suits the song's laid-back atmosphere well. The references to barbiturates might allude to his recent medical treatment, but Smith himself suggested that the song is about English people living in Mexico: 'It's about expats... after Spain, Mexico is the next place for retirement expats. Spain is getting too crowded.' This may explain the reference to Bisto, if not the surprising appearance of Doogie Howser ('12-year-old doctor / a fresh faced physician'[359]). It was only played six times, all in 2010.

Cowboy George
'Cowboy George' opens at a furious gallop, powered by a mix of surf-rock and epic spaghetti-western soundtrack. It owes a debt to both Link Wray's 'Jack The Ripper' and The Seeds' 'Pushin' Too Hard': the former provides the epic yet strangulated chords

---

[358] Marshall's interview with MES for *Uncut* was the first to feature the squirrel story.
[359] An American TV series (1989-93) that dealt with the life of a teenage physician played by Neil Patrick Harris, who would go on to star in the hit sitcom *How I Met Your Mother*.

that bookend the first section of the song; the latter the surging 'stagecoach-racing-across-the-plains' riff. In addition, it features the unlikely scenario of The Fall sampling Daft Punk.[360] Halfway through, we descend into an eerie, experimental coda, filled with mangled delay-pedal guitar and oscillating electronics. Over this, Smith half-mumbles, half-croons a series of thoughts, including a mention of 'Das Boat' and the marvellously incongruous phrase 'Chicory Tip in a shopping centre'.[361] The reference to broken/ brown bottles echoes the words of the 'Hip Priest', but may also relate to Smith's relationship with Brix – 'I had two broken bottles / I had two brown bottles / and a white nose as I entered / five years of confinement' seems to recall their first meeting as she described it in a 2018 interview: 'He had a bottle of beer in each hand and white powder coming out of his nose.'

Regarding the identity of title character, Smith was typically contradictory. He told John Doran that Cowboy George was Pete Greenway, but in an interview with Tim Cumming, he said the musicians had come up with the song's name: 'I don't know why the hell they come up with that. Sometime the group's good at titles.' The 'unseen' motif (applied to knowledge, facts, hills, footage, refinement and extension) is clearly important, not only in the fact that the word appears in the song 15 times, but also in its prominence in the album's artwork. 'Unseen hills' certainly fits well with the spaghetti-western vibe of the music. Smith was asked about this aspect of the song by Tim Cumming in a 2010 interview:

> In 'Cowboy George' there are lyrics about 'unseen knowledge, unseen forces'. Is that about mortality? Death? The other side?
>
> That's, uh, very much sort of the case… I don't even know what I'm saying really, because I'm still on medication

---

[360] The distorted robotic voice that appears nine seconds in is taken from the French electro duo's 2001 single, 'Harder, Better, Faster, Stronger'.

[361] Chicory Tip were an early 70s pop group mainly known for their 1972 number one single, 'Son Of My Father' (the music of which was written by Giorgio Moroder of 'I Feel Love' and 'Together In Electric Dreams' fame). In the 80s 'Father' became better known as a football terrace chant, generally only bestowed on players with two-syllable / three-syllable surnames, such as Frank(ie) Stapleton and Teddy Sheringham.

from the wheelchair... Heavy German medication, you
know. Which I'm not used to. It is a bit mystical, that
one, yeah.

In a 2013 interview with Cumming for *The Independent*, Smith
claimed that his publisher struck a potential deal with the producers
of *Twilight* for The Fall to contribute a song to the soundtrack of
the film version of the hit TV show ('They said they'd give us
$50,000 to come up with a song, So I said, I'll give them some
horror...') Cumming implies, albeit vaguely, that the song in
question was 'No Respects Rev.' (see Chapter 30). According to
Greenway, Spurr and Melling, however, it was 'Cowboy George'
that was offered (and rejected). 'George' was another long-serving
live song: 134 performances from 2009 until almost the very end.

Hot Cake
Spurr starts things off with a hyperactive 12-bar blues; Melling
clatters in exuberantly; Greenway joins in with a snaky rockabilly/
surf twang (it's possible that the track's name is derived from
an effects pedal that he favoured). The song alternates between
reckless thrash and tight rockabilly shuffle, supported by Eleni's
cooing backing vocals. The lyrics make reference to both 'Slippy
Floor' and 'Chino'; fitting, as musically the song sits somewhere
between the manic chaos of the former and the dark, reverberating
atmosphere of the latter. Another popular live choice, the song
made 97 appearances 2008-14.

Y.F.O.C. / Slippy Floor
Kicked off by an impossibly deep double-tracked Spurr riff where
you can virtually hear his calluses scraping over the strings, after
a couple of minutes it ignites into a barrage of pile-driving noise
in which Melling lets loose like Animal from *The Muppets*. Just
after four minutes, a deep, sludgy, scraping noise makes its way
into the mix, lurking menacingly beneath the chaos. Around the
five/six-minute mark, Greenway excels himself with a barrage of
feverish variations on the riff. This whole section is awe-inspiring,
a piece of crazed but controlled garage punk mayhem. There's also

a strange but lovely little coda: a lo-fi snippet of '986 Generator' (see below), followed by a series of haphazard noises, including what sounds like a quick burst of tap-dancing and a snatch of an answerphone message. The telephone number quoted in the message – in keeping with the medical theme of the album – is that of an osteopath based in Salford.[362]

At the time, the hospital references ('all I get is a slippy floor in a hospital') were interpreted as an allusion to the alleged broken hip accident. In interviews at the time, Smith made several references to the recent credit crunch, which may be reflected in the line about 'the land of finance retail'. Much of it is still distinctly cryptic: 'I'm 95% in inside of B Drake'; 'This new approach is on the borders of necessity'. Smith's delivery demonstrates the full range of his techniques: the faultlessly timed 'is on the CIDV, underneath you' (1:10); the oddly touching off-key croon of 'we're gonna get married' (1:29); the guttural growl of 'apartment hall' (3:53); the joyful, exuberant 'hup!' (6:17). It was played live 39 times; on one occasion (the Swiss For Noise Festival on 21st August 2010), the two sections were played the other way round.

Chino

A richly atmospheric and ruminative track. Introduced by a pendulous bass glissando and swooping sci-fi effects, it soon settles into a heavy, ponderous groove, Greenway providing ominous reverb/tremolo guitar. Smith's plaintive refrain 'When do I quit?' is quite jarring; seemingly at odds with his frequent pronouncements about work ethic, and certainly a long way from the sharp and acerbic instruction to 'stop mithering' 30 years earlier. His vocal is measured but unusually fragile; there is a sense that Smith is vulnerable, confronting his own mortality. Two years earlier, he had forcefully pronounced his defiance at turning 50 ('what you gonna do about it?') and displayed certainty about his longevity; here, he's not so sure, and it makes for a touching and melancholy experience. When asked about the

[362] One Dr. Kalman, from whom MES presumably received treatment at the time. I don't know if any obsessive Fall fan has ever attempted to call him (even bzfgt thought that this would be 'going overboard'), but at the time of writing, googling the number still brings up Dr. Kalman's name.

song's repeated references to 'quitting', Smith was ambiguous: 'It's never something that I think about... I've thought about quitting once every two and a half months for the last 25 years.' Like several other tracks on the album, 'Chino' had a long stay on the setlist: 106 performances, 2008-13.

Funnel Of Love

The cover version finally arrives, and it's not at all bad. The original was by Wanda Jackson, who achieved some success in the late 60s and early 70s mixing rockabilly and country. The Fall give the song a more psychedelic-pop feel and add a bit of gusto in the forceful staccato middle eight. It was played live 30 times, 2008-11.

Weather Report 2

The finale opens with a surprisingly jaunty set of guitar harmonics, before settling into an understated, low-tempo rhythm. Despite the slow pace and Smith's cautious delivery, there's still a sense of urgency about it – Greenway's arpeggios around the two-minute mark giving the impression that it's about to break out into something much more expansive. But when the mood does change, it's in the form of an unexpected diversion into deep, throbbing electronica. The remainder of the song is framed around a dark, oscillating sequencer; everything is distorted and overloaded, broken up by sharp, snapping percussion, occasional electronic squiggles and a malevolent keyboard line. Live versions (it was played 51 times, 2010-11) had a very different coda, the ambient electronica being replaced with a rousing, uptempo guitar-based finale.

Smith is once again in reflective and melancholy mood ('you gave me the best years of my life'), delivering his vocals in a movingly hesitant manner. The repeated refrain 'nobody has called me sir in my entire life' is an intriguing one: throughout his career, Smith was frequently at pains to point out that he cared little for the opinions of his peers, and was generally disparaging of those who were obviously influenced by his work. Yet here he seems genuinely regretful that he hasn't been shown a due level of respect, a far cry from the defiant 'he is not appreciated' of 20 years earlier. Smith made the recording of the song sound rather haphazard:

> So it's like you've got to do it very quick. The idea of it was to co-op an acoustic track with a machine track. Then I reversed it. Then Ding said, 'If it's going to work –' I was going to sing bits and bobs over it, just joining it up – and he said, 'You can't do that because we need a vocal level.' So a lot of that is getting levels. They are the lyrics for it, but the middle bits – they've come out very well, and the end bits, I would've chopped them out, but they work out very well.

Reviews and Versions

The vinyl version contained two songs that didn't appear on the CD (which also had a slightly different running order). '986 Generator' is a lengthy, loping murky blues work-out that sounds like a mixture of Gomez, Beefheart and Blind Faith. It's especially effective when it breaks out into a full-on onslaught in the last couple of minutes. 'Get A Summer Song Goin'' is based around a fuzzed, phased and flanged 60s psychedelia guitar riff, and is the fourth and final Fall song to reference David Bowie.[363] '986' was never played live; 'Summer' only once, in May 2010.

The album repeated the respectable chart performance of its predecessor, reaching number 38 in the UK album charts. Both contemporary and retrospective reviews rate the album very highly. Stuart Berman gave the album's 'lean, brute-force rockers' 8/10. Reflecting on Smith's references to his mortality throughout the album, Nick Neyland encouraged listeners to 'cherish him while he's here. We won't see his like again, and future generations will look back with considerable envy that we got to be around when an album that could so effectively eviscerate our expectations of what music is and can be was released by a band entering its fifth decade of existence.' On the BBC website, Kev Kharas, after pointing out that the group had spent years 'looping in and out of critical approval as endlessly

[363] See 'Mere Pseud Mag.Ed.', 'Hard Life In Country' and 'He Pep!'.

as the snarling, nagging guitars that have underpinned [Smith's] scornful non-sequiturs', struck a similarly portentous note:

> Hipsters, slaves to the day, be damned – The Fall will abide: they have broken out of time, and exist slightly away from the rest of us. They are, as Smith proclaims on Mexico Wax Solvent, 'Invincible'.

John Doran was in no doubt regarding the group's continued importance:

> In 2010 it should no longer be our job to explain to people why The Fall are the greatest English rock band of the last 40 years. In fact, I'd politely suggest the onus is now on others to find out for themselves instead of us having to draw them a fucking map.

Evaluation

The first Fall album in 17 years to feature the same line-up as its predecessor,[364] *Your Future Our Clutter* is often described as The Fall's last great album. Whilst there is much to recommend the albums that followed, there is a strong case for it being so. It's certainly one of the group's most consistent efforts. There's not the sense of transformation of, say, *Dragnet* to *Grotesque*, but there's still a sense of a unit bonding and hitting their stride. *Imperial Wax Solvent* demonstrated admirable variety and diversity, but here the new group really get to grips with a sound that's utterly their own.

It's a lyrically complex and intriguing album. There's a thread of fragility and the recognition of mortality running through it that represents a level of introspection (although generally couched in the vaguest possible terms) that's unlike anything we've heard so far. Also, it *rocks*: it's brimful of joyful, abandoned noisiness. All four musicians make crucial contributions: Greenway's variations on a surf-rock garage thrash theme; Spurr's deadly, coiled assault; Melling's mixture of full-on barrage and subtlety; Eleni's deep range of electronic effects and increasingly confident backing

---

[364] *The Infotainment Scan* featured the same Smith / Scanlon / S Hanley / Wolstencroft / Bush line-up as *Code: Selfish*.

vocals. *Clutter* is full of experimentation, for example the extended codas to 'Cowboy George' and 'Weather Report 2'. In the past, the group's experimental tracks often felt like entertaining enough (to a varying extent) interludes that mainly served to break things up a little. Here, they make a much more meaningful and worthwhile contribution, extending and broadening the songs' horizons.

The whole 'comeback' / 'best Fall album since...' trope was by now a very well-established cliché. But it really is true here. The fact that The Fall released such a vital, inventive and powerful album 31 years after their debut is a thing of absolute wonder.

Ersatz GB
Recorded: Metropolis Studios, London; Toe Rag Studios, London, mid-2011.
Released: 14th November 2011

Personnel:
Mark E Smith – vocals
Peter Greenway – guitar (uncredited)
David Spurr – bass
Keiron Melling – drums
Eleni Poulou – keyboards, vocals

Chapter 29: Ersatz GB

'Their 317th studio album, or whatever it is.'

Many publications have brief Q&A features where celebrities are asked a few random questions designed to give a little snapshot into their life and personality. Of course, when MES did this – for *The Guardian* in May 2011 – all readers learnt was that Smith was either pissed or taking the piss (possibly both). Asked 'Which living person do you most admire, and why?' he responded, 'All nurses and television programmers at 4am who "update". But mainly myself, as Napoleon.' His desired superpower was, 'No food necessary. True bats know false powers drag you down.' The only answer that provided any sort of insight into his thoughts was 'fear is something I try not to absorb'. This phrase was later used as part of a 20ft high mural of Smith created by graffiti artist Akse P19 as part of the 2018 Prestwich Arts Festival. It was painted on the wall of a chip shop, coincidentally adjacent to the building that had housed the disco of 'Psykick Dancehall' fame.

The spring tour to promote *Your Future Our Clutter* did not make an auspicious start. At Studio 24 in Edinburgh on 24th April, Smith only managed six songs, leaving the rest of the group to play an instrumental 'Mexico Wax Solvent', 'I've Been Duped' and 'Mr. Pharmacist' (with Eleni singing and Safy on what might generously be called backing vocals).[365] Thankfully, things picked up significantly over the next few nights, with well-received full-length sets in Aberdeen, Dublin and Keele, and in general the rest of the tour seemed to find the group back on an even keel. A couple of new songs ('Greenway' and 'Age Of Chang') had been debuted in August and November 2010 – 'Muzorewi's Daughter' also made a surprise reappearance in November, the first time it had been played in almost 30 years – but fresh material didn't begin to appear in earnest until the summer of 2011, with eight of

---

[365] On the bootleg, one punter can clearly be heard shouting 'We want our money back!' at the end.

Erstaz GB's tracks receiving their debuts in the space of a couple of months. The new songs and the group's performances were greeted with enthusiasm, but things took a negative turn again in the autumn. Two dates planned for October in Brazil were cancelled, apparently because of Smith's ill health. At Cardiff on 22nd October a visibly drunk Smith only managed to perform for around half an hour, before walking off during 'Greenway' and leaving the group once again to play a handful of instrumentals and songs with Eleni on vocals.

November saw Tim Presley return to the live line-up for the remaining dozen 2011 gigs, covering for Pete Greenway who was on paternity leave. The first of these dates, on 2nd November in Leeds, saw the group perform a cover of Warren Zevon's 'Werewolves Of London' for the only time. The gig was another messy one, Smith once again well-oiled, wandering on and off stage and, at one point, being sprayed with beer from the audience. The next night in Edinburgh was even worse: Smith barely appeared on stage, leading to boos and glasses being thrown. Eleni told the crowd that he had 'wounds on his feet'[366] and got into a confrontational exchange with the audience. The gig descended into farce as an audience member took to the stage, delivering an impressively flamboyant improvised lyric to 'Reformation!' before being escorted off-stage by a bouncer. Thereafter, a sheepish-looking Smith re-emerged to finish the song and then launch into a spirited 'Mr. Pharmacist'. Subsequent gigs in Newcastle and York saw him on much improved form, although some fans were starting to look at these inconsistencies with a cynical eye: 'Good that things are back to "normal",' commented one Forum member, 'but it looks like he knew that he wouldn't get away with the same crap 4 gigs on the trot so decided to make the effort.'[367]

[366] MES was apparently still suffering when interviewed by *The Quietus* later that year: 'Smith hands me £20 and sends me over to brave the bar. "Do you want to get another one? Could you please? I've got something on my feet," he says. He's been rubbing them underneath his shoes and it's clear they're causing him some pain.'

[367] One particularly disgruntled contributor even went as far as to say, 'He's taken the piss for 3 nights, then come back and let his fans know that he's taken the piss. The fans seem too dumb to realise. For fuck's sake. The man is a con artist, when are you going to realise?'

Ersatz GB

The album was recorded at Metropolis (a studio created in 1989 in the lower floors of The Power House, a former electricity generating station on Chiswick High Road) and Toe Rag in Hackney (an analogue-only studio equipped with a mixing console originally used in Abbey Road). Simon Archer and MES produced. The deal with Domino had only been for one album, and as soon as *Your Future Our Clutter* was released The Fall had signed to Cherry Red, an independent label founded in 1978 by Iain McNay. McNay first met MES via Adrian Sherwood in 1980, and The Fall had been a target for Cherry Red for decades. 'When Mike Alway joined us as A&R manager in 1981, The Fall were high on a list of acts he wanted to sign,' McNay explained. 'Mike was always persistent, but it wasn't to be. We had to be patient and wait... although I didn't think it would take another 30 years...' The group would stay with the label throughout the rest of their recording career.

Mark Kennedy once again designed the cover, this time with some assistance from Smith himself. A rather lurid cut and paste collage, it included cuttings from *Metro*, 2nd August 2011 and the 3rd August edition of the *Daily Mail*. Prior to the album's release, Cherry Red's website had showed a different album cover, albeit one in a similar style, most of the cuttings coming from a single issue of the *New York Times* (31st July 2011). Speaking to *The Quietus*, Smith described how he was keen to get the album out just before Christmas, despite record companies' general inclination to put out 'Christmas rush Best Hits Of Robbie Williams or whatever'. Not for the first time, he despaired at how slowly labels work:

> 'We need six months to do it. We need six weeks to develop the marketing.' All this shit. 'We need six weeks to do the marketing, six weeks to do the interneting.' Can't you just get the fucking thing out?

Pete Greenway was not credited on the sleeve, although he plainly did play on the album, and has four songwriting credits.

Whether this was Smith having a dig at him for taking paternity leave, a peculiar MES joke or just a cock-up is unclear.

From the outset, Smith's unconventional and innovative use of language was a key part of The Fall's appeal. His most ambitious lyrics ('Garden', 'The N.W.R.A.', 'Winter', 'New Puritan') were undoubtedly dense and complex, but contained themes and ideas that were at least partly perceptible to those prepared to put some thought and graft into their analysis. As time went on, however, Smith's words (and often the group's music as well) became increasingly unmoored from any notion of traditional song structure. *Ersatz GB* represents a tipping point: here, at least half of the tracks leave the listener without any meaningful chance of deriving meaning. In these songs, as *The Annotated Fall* comments, the lyrics are 'about the sound of the words as much as anything else'.

Cosmos 7

The album wastes no time in getting down to business. As one review put it, '"Cosmos 7" races out of the blocks like a greyhound jacked-up on amphetamines; Smith's utterances and curses anchored dead centre amidst a whirling cacophony of rockabilly clatter.' Greenway and Spurr work hard to keep up with Melling's muscular krautrock beat; Eleni throws in splurges of wiggly synth; Smith gibbers manically ('Rat's head!' 'Russian in back!') and makes some distinctly disturbing noises (a deep, malevolent growling just after two minutes, plus an alarming rolling ululation that appears at 1:04). His unhinged incoherence blends well with the cacophony surrounding him. 'Cosmos' was played live 26 times, 2011-12.

Taking Off

Although a little more understated than the opener, 'Taking Off' maintains the album's momentum. After a sliding, spacey intro that zooms across the channels, the group settle into a laid-back psych-rock riff in which Greenway alternates between intricate little guitar runs and heavy, distorted chords. 'Tidy Italian!' MES barks; 'grating three-fold within a thorough lack of paper'; 'forty carat scum at Newquay train station' – it even references gum treatment Bonjela.[368] It's speculated that 'digest, ingest' might be an oblique reference to Beefheart's 'Neon Meate Dream Of A Octafish'. 'Skip', at 2:02, is one of Smith's indefinably splendid enunciations. Played live 22 times, 2011-14.

Nate Will Not Return

Musically, Greenway once again takes centre stage, ploughing an agile krautrock furrow over a tight rhythm. The lyric, unlikely as it might seem, discusses the character of Nate Archibald (from American teen drama *Gossip Girl*) through a series of rhymes with his name: 'sublimate', 'replicate', 'New Jersey State', 'straight', 'crate' and so on. Although 'I might visit the gallery known as Tate' is amusing, the rhyming dictionary approach begins to pall over six minutes. Played live 38 times between 2011 and 2014.

Mask Search

A lively, scampering piece of rockabilly. Smith's vocals are disturbingly high in the mix; on headphones it feels as if he's breathing into your ear. Although it's intriguing as to why MES is on the lookout for 'Esso lubricant', Snow Patrol are a rather lazy target and he doesn't have much of note to say about them. Only played live twice, the first under the working title 'Scaramanga'.

Greenway

Another of the group's more divisive songs, 'Greenway' sees The Fall take an unexpected left-turn into Greek heavy metal. Musically, it's a cover of 'Gameboy' by Athenian comedy-thrash-metallers Anorimoi.[369] The lyrics are mostly Smith's own, although the eyebrow-raising line 'I had to wank off the cat to feed the fucking dog' (and vice-versa) is adapted from Jon Wayne's 'But I've Got Texas'.[370] The group that MES watches on 'Danish rock TV' is probably These New Puritans. Smith's phlegm-ridden

---

[368] You might think that 'Taking Off' would be the only song ever to reference Bonjela, but it's also in the lyrics of 'Pick Up The Mic' by grime MC JME.
[369] Or ανώριμοι, Greek for 'the immature ones'.
[370] 'I've gotta jack off the dog just to feed the god damned cat.' Wayne was the recording alias of David Vaught; 'But I've Got Texas' was the opening track on his 1985 album, *Texas Funeral*.

gargle, a major feature of the album, is particularly conspicuous here. Played live 41 times, 2010-12.

Happi Song
Another divisive one: mentioned frequently in the contemporary reviews, both as the best or worst song on the album. Eleni delivers her vocal with cool detachment, but while there are a couple of mildly interesting phrases ('stofftier', German for stuffed toy, could be a reference to our old friend Gunther o' Leipzig) the refrain ('If I can see and you can see, why can't they see?') is a little banal. The backdrop of chopped-up MES samples does at least give it some wonky charm. Only played live five times.

Monocard
Not content with exploring Greek comedy-thrash-metal, the group turn their attention to sludge/doom-rock. 'Monocard' is an unlikely hybrid of Bardo Pond, Earth, Sonic Youth and early Sabbath. The title may refer to the Korg Monotron mini-synthesizer that was responsible for the electronic effects, or even to a drug used to treat angina. The most notable line (amongst several candidates) is 'I walk into village, fate-infected / trenches in Hounslow / the true chiefs / gorilla's an apprentice of Chiswick'. It has a slow-burning, swampy menace, and whilst some find its sprawling eight minutes a little monotonous, *The Annotated Fall* observes that, 'Like many of the most repetitive Fall songs... the melodic uniformity is offset by subtly shifting textures, rhythmic ecstasy, and a sense of total commitment on the part of the musicians.' Only played live nine times, all in 2011.

Laptop Dog
Despite Melling's unremitting snare, 'Laptop' is relatively restrained, the acoustic strum and stylophone-like keyboards providing welcome variation from the album's generally heavy sound. The off-beat rhythm is reminiscent of mid-period Teenage Fanclub[371] and the chord progression possibly borrows a little from Thin Lizzy's 'Jailbreak'. Smith's vocal is similarly reserved and

[371] See, for example, 'Start Again' from 1997's *Songs From Northern Britain*.

is largely free of the excessive growling and hissing elsewhere. Not for the first time, he disparages the influence of technology, although 'Laptop' doesn't quite have the aggressive, hectoring tone of later songs on the same topic. Smith mocks the 'laptop craze' which leads people to believe that 'all life' is held therein. The internet is personified as 'a big creature' that 'will stalk you, and it will alliterate and proclaim'. Basically, Smith is still saying 'turn that bloody blimey Space Invader off!' 30 years later. It got 17 live outings, all in 2011. It was released as a 33rpm 7" single the week before *Erstaz*, with alternative (although not very different) versions of 'Cosmos 7' and 'Monocard' included.

I've Seen Them Come

After 20 seconds of what sounds like Melling settling himself down for a soundcheck, 'I've Seen Them Come' locks onto a brutal, simplistic three-chord motif and doesn't let go for six minutes. There's something admirable about its sheer bloody-mindedness, but it was one that several reviewers singled out for criticism. Pitchfork declared it 'an idea for an intriguing 20-second passage of a song, stretched out to an unbearable six minutes'; *Soundblab* described it as 'substandard, aimless ramalama thrashing'. To be fair, it's not entirely without variation: at 1:40, there's a brief pause before the group pile back in with gusto; at 4:41 Greenway takes centre stage with the circular riff and Eleni smears some oscillating sci-fi stuff over the top. It doesn't quite sustain its length, but it does flirt with that hypnotic quality that the group often achieved. It's not one of Smith's most thoughtful efforts, much of it being little more than a long list of places, although he also throws in a reference to French erotic drama *Betty Blue* and 'metal mass' (a heavy metal church service popular in Finland[372]). It was performed 13 times, all in 2011.

Age Of Chang

After an abrasive, lo-fi opening that recalls 'Bury', 'Chang' hits a metronomic rhythm akin to its predecessor. It's equally uncompromising, but there's a little more variety and subtle

[372] This is a real thing; have a look on *Wikipedia*.

texture here, a more considered ebb and flow. Smith contributes his strongest vocal on the album: a venomous, fractured diatribe that's full of fury and bile. The language has a strange elegance: 'Into the flower duct, into the lowlands, the flower drum awaits'; 'contractual land and laptop survey, a dam of vast proportions'. Played live 21 times, 2010-12.

Reviews

Smith himself frequently expressed dissatisfaction with the album. He told *The Irish Independent* that it 'could have been a lot better... The problem with that LP is the mix. They pressed the wrong mix.' He did, however, go on to say that 'it's still alright... people have responded well to it'. In fact, *Ersatz GB* received perhaps the most polarised reviews of The Fall's career. In *The Sunday Times*, long-time champion Stewart Lee welcomed the group's metamorphosis into an 'amphetamine-drone rock band... The Fall remain our most vital group'. The *NME*'s Ben Hewitt was similarly impressed, giving the album 8/10:

> ...they continue to lob the occasional hand grenade into the mix and revel in the resulting chaos... there's really only one salient truth about *Ersatz GB* – The Fall, even at nearly 30 albums old, still stand alone and aloft.

John Robb admired its 'total brilliant disdain for tedious "proper songwriting" laws'; Marc Masters was also a fan:

> [Smith's] bilious delivery makes even the goofiest songs on *Ersatz GB* shake with urgency... his bark infects everything around it, giving the music a nervous, vibrant edge and turning potentially slick songs into serrated mantras. Its peaks thrust it toward the upper end of The Fall's daunting discography.

Several reviewers strongly disagreed. Gavin Martin felt that 'the allusion to the decline in the nation's craftsmanship in the title is painfully ironic'. Douglas Wolk thought that the album's 'abrasiveness, inscrutability, and tedium are increasingly tough to take with repeated close listening'; the musicians sounded like an 'anonymous pickup crew' creating an 'almost totally generic hard rock record'. Garry Mulholland struck a similar note:

> The problem with The Fall in 2011 is straightforward, really. The band isn't very good. Or, to put it another way, they are very slick and versatile rock musicians, but they have absolutely no sound of their own. A poor LP that proves that Mark E. Smith alone does not The Fall make.

In *The Guardian*, Rob Fitzpatrick also put the boot in. Describing Smith's vocals as a 'gruesomely liquid growl spooned over the top like a cold, rather unpleasant custard', he went on to accuse the group of predictability: '[Their] 317th studio album, or whatever it is, has absolutely no chance of reaching beyond the people who dutifully queued up for their 316th album: everyone already knows what to expect and, largely, they'd be right.' Neil Gardner was one of the few critics to remain ambivalent: 'A curious mixture of the slapdash and the inspired, The Fall remain as strange, esoteric and infuriating as ever.'

In terms of chart performance, *Ersatz GB* fell short of its two predecessors' decent top 40 placings, reaching number 88 (although this was 27 places higher than *Fall Heads Roll* and 68 better than *Real New Fall LP*).

Evaluation

Although it has its champions, *Ersatz GB* is not a generally well-regarded album, and it's easy to see why. It's messy, unfocused, and often a challenging listen. That said, there are great rewards to be had from repeated plays, even if you do have to work harder to hear them than you do on some other albums. Critics tend to home in on two specific faults: Smith's vocal style (one article, which rates *Ersatz* as the worst ever Fall LP, describes his contributions as 'wet slop') and the musicians' perceived workmanlike mundanity.

Whilst one can sympathise with those who struggle with Smith's vocals on *Ersatz*, the accusation that the unusually settled group line-up are churning out something uninspired and mundane is far less defensible. It doesn't take extensive listening to pick up a wide range of nuanced and intriguing sounds. Pete Greenway displays versatility throughout; Spurr and Melling are solid but still inventive; Eleni adds an array of interesting and intriguing textures.

Ersatz sees Smith's vocals and lyrics fall a long way short of the lucidity and eloquence of past glories like 'New Puritan' or 'Garden'. It's also true that he too often falls back on growls and hisses that sometimes pay scant regard to the music surrounding them. Some of the lyrics, such as 'Nate' and 'Mask', have a tossed-off 'this'll do' feel to them. However, there is still much inventive and entertaining use of language. Moreover, Smith is clearly settling into a vocal style that matches his reduced physical capacity. It doesn't always work, but in some instances, such as 'Age Of Chang', you get a sense of transformation; a redirection and refocusing of his craft. This transition had not manifested itself overnight. You could arguably draw a line from, say, 1994's 'Surmount All Obstacles' through 1997's '4 1/2 Inch', 2000's 'Midwatch 1953' and 2008's 'Alton Towers' to trace Smith's history of disregard for the conventions of narrative construction and externally discernable imagery. *Ersatz* was the third LP that he had recorded with this line-up, so the musicians were by now 'bedded in' and clearly seen as reliable and trustworthy; the considerable age gap between them and Smith created a dynamic where he was something of a father figure. Given his worsening health, and the increased focus on his own mortality seen in the previous LP, plus a band and fanbase that would support him through thick and thin, *Ersatz* sees MES arrive at a place where he simply didn't have to give a toss about anything beyond his personal vision.

The result was undoubtedly flawed and inarguably some way from The Fall's best, but it remains a distinctive and uncompromising piece of work. As Luke Turner of *The Quietus* said, 'To mediocrity, The Fall continue to say "no".'

Re-Mit
Recorded: Konk Studios, London; Blueprint, Manchester, January–February 2013
Released: 13th May 2013

Personnel:
Mark E Smith – vocals
Keiron Melling – drums
Dave Spurr – bass
Peter Greenway – guitar
Eleni Poulou – keyboards

With:
Tim Presley – guitar ('No Respects, 'Kinder of Spine', 'No Respects Rev.')

Chapter 30: Re-Mit

'It's quite horrible. The Fall have had enough and we're coming for you.'

The Fall played half a dozen UK dates to round off 2011, with Tim Presley continuing to cover Pete Greenway's paternity leave. They remained on good form, one reviewer even describing Smith as 'sharp, sober, engaged, relaxed, and really enjoying himself; smiling [and] interacting with the crowd'. The last date of the year saw them play a seasonal cover of 'Blue Christmas' that was catastrophically tuneless and made the anti-Shakin' Stevens sentiment of 'Ludd Gang' seem distinctly hypocritical. 2012 was relatively quiet as far as gigs were concerned, with only 24 being played. The first performance, at Athens on 10th February, saw 'Damflicters' (which would eventually become 'Victrola Time') open the set; it also marked Pete Greenway's return.

In April, the *NME* published a joint interview with MES and Mystery Jets' vocalist Blaine Harrison. The Mystery Jets' recently released album, *Radlands,* referenced The Fall in the song 'Greatest Hits' which dealt with a separating couple's division of their record collection ('no way you're having "This Nation's Saving Grace" you only listen to it when you're pissed / but when you sober up it's always "why the fuck are you still listening to Mark E. Smith?".') The theme of the interview was 'heroes'.

> I'm not big on heroes. I never wanted to be Gene Vincent or Elvis. I didn't want to be Damo Suzuki. I don't want to be anybody else, and I think that's why people respect The Fall... I've never wanted to be anyone else... I don't fucking like anybody – that's why The Fall exist.

A new single was released in April as part of Record Store Day. 'Night Of The Humerons' was a 7" (limited to 1000 copies) that featured 'Victrola Time' on the A-side and a live version of 'Taking Off' on the other. Smith was unhappy with the single's distribution: 'We believed this event was created to promote vinyl and help record shops survive. What Cherry Red didn't tell us was that they were only going to send one copy to each shop and that meant that some customers were misled. I'm just sorry they were inconvenienced.'

The summer saw a surprise return (after a 15-year absence) for 'The Container Drivers', which stayed in the set for much of 2012.[373] The group's capacity to roll out new material regularly remained undiminished. 'Gapa' ('Sir William Wray' – it also went under the working title 'Gray' or 'Grey') and 'Defurbish' ('Loadstones') debuted in July; 'Irish' and 'Hitman' ('Hittite Man') in September;[374] 'Spider' ('Kinder of Spine') in October;[375] 'No Respects' in December. 'Spider' was debuted in Norwich, at an event in celebration of John Peel Day which also featured The Undertones on the bill. A good-humoured Smith, interviewed at the event, recalled Peel's death by saying, 'I knew the minute he died... we're never going to get played on the BBC again, that's for fucking sure.' The group took four months off from touring in early 2013, during which time they recorded *Re-Mit*. Despite Smith's reservations about the previous year's release, Record Store Day 2013 saw The Fall produce another limited edition 7" for the occasion. 'Sir William Wray' was released on 20th April – this time restricted to 1500 copies.[376]

Like the previous year, 2013 was fairly quiet on the gig front, seeing only 25 performances. The first of these, in Clitheroe, was released as a live album in 2017 (once again as part of Record Store Day[377]). *Live In Clitheroe* documents an interesting performance, although the sound is incredibly uneven: Smith's vocals lurch uncomfortably forward in the mix on many occasions, and the impact of his 'on-stage mixing' can be heard clearly – in

---

[373] Bootlegs find it distinctly slower than its earlier incarnations, the frantic rockabilly becoming more of a hoedown; the vocal meanders woozily around the beat in stark comparison to the crisp delivery of MES c.1980. Still great fun though.

[374] For one gig only (Glasgow, 21st November) it was named 'Three Dreams'.

[375] Whilst Smith's deranged vocal was already in place, musically the song was much more conventional at this stage. Framed around a trademark twangy Greenway riff and a (mainly) basic 4/4 beat, it did not yet feature the creeping menace of the studio version.

[376] The cover suggested that the lead track and B-side 'Hittite Man' were 'single mixes', but there's no easily detectable difference from the LP versions.

[377] On orange vinyl. In time-honoured fashion, the tracks on side two were listed incorrectly.

the second half of 'Blindness', for example, Greenway's guitar veers dramatically from inaudible to deafening and back again. An audience member contributes enthusiastic backing vocals throughout 'Fall Sound'. She also provides an excitable commentary over the opening of 'Jetplane's debut: 'Fuckin' hell, it's a new 'un... this is groovy as fuck!' The most unprecedented moment, however, came at the end of 'Hittite Man'. Smith wandered to the front of stage, and, with the opening line 'I embrace you all', proceeded to indulge in what can only be described as a minute or so of good-humoured banter with the front row of the audience.

A few days before *Re-Mit*'s release, Smith appeared on Radcliffe and Maconie's BBC Radio 6 Music afternoon show. He was moderately slurred, but entertaining and genial, and only nearly-swore once (for which he sounded genuinely apologetic). He also demonstrated a genuine warmth towards the current line-up: 'I've got a perfect group at the moment.' He agreed with Radcliffe that the oft-cited 'granny on bongos' attitude did them a disservice:

> They've stuck with me for the last four or five years, and I've been in a wheelchair for about a year and a half of them. They've been pushing me around and that; they didn't have to.

Re-Mit

The album was recorded in January and February 2013 at Konk, a studio located in Crouch End that was founded by The Kinks. It saw Grant Showbiz (as engineer) make his final contribution to a Fall album. Smith offered a typically terse and cryptic explanation of the title: '[It] means I need a glove when I go out.' The cover was designed by Anthony Frost and Smith's sister Suzanne. Her painting of the group is funny and touching: the Cleopatra-esque portrayal of Eleni captures her often imperious on-stage attitude; Smith, replete with flowing locks, reclines extravagantly on a chaise-longue.

No Respects (Intro)

The first instrumental opener since 'Mansion', 'No Respects' is a sharp burst of surf-rock that clatters along energetically for about 40 seconds before morphing into a portentous and proggy fuzzed-up guitar line that then fades (incredibly rapidly – like someone leaned over the mixing desk) almost as soon as it arrives. Co-written by Tim Presley, who also played on it, it was performed live – both as an instrumental and in its longer 'No Respects Rev.' form – 16 times, 2012-15.

Sir William Wray

A gutsy garage-rocker. Smith launches into it from the word go with a warped, manic introduction. The title could be seen as a reference to Link Wray, an artist who Smith greatly admired.[378] However, in his BBC Radio 6 Music interview, Smith described it as 'just a wordplay... I wanted it to be anti-lyric really, anti-music with anti-lyric'. Greenway alternates between surf-rock lead and distorted chords, both of which snake around the meandering synth. It was on the setlist 42 times between 2012 and 2015.

Kinder Of Spine

Another track featuring Tim Presley, 'Kinder' is a crazed piece of 60s-psych-art-garage-punk with a lurching, menacing rhythm, stabs of abrasive, aggressive organ and a pair of guitars – one thrashing out fuzzy chords, one scratching out little bluesy solos that fight to keep their head above water. It may have been inspired by The Monocles' disturbing 1966 single 'The Spider And The Fly'. The vocals are particularly deranged, a weird mixture of broken crooning (the odd little whimper at 1:07-1:08), angry, guttural growling ('so there' at 1:41), demonic cackling (2:07) and plaintive wailing ('Oh judge, judge of the "Persecute Me" talent show' at 1:15). *The Annotated Fall* proposes a link to the 1958 film *The Fly*, which also contains the line, 'Help me! Help me!' It was performed 24 times in 2012-13.

---

[378] He certainly seems a more likely candidate than English politicians Sir William Wray, 1st Baronet of Glentworth (c. 1555–1617) or his namesake the 1st Baronet of Ashby (1625–1669).

Noise

An experimental interlude, featuring a grinding, swirling mix of electronics and an insistent, trebly guitar. Cluster's 'Rote Riki' might have provided some inspiration.[379] Like 'Insult Song', it finds Smith performing a group 'roast': Greenway is 'nasty noise Peter', Spurr is 'David, warrior of the dark forest' and Grant Showbiz becomes 'Emperor Cunliffe'. The studio also gets a mention: 'the altar of Konk'. Unsurprisingly, never played live.

Hittite Man

A sparse and tense piece. Melling's rolling drums and Spurr's deep rumble allow Greenway to take centre stage with one of his trademark spaghetti-western/surf-rock guitar lines – an especially evocative one, conjuring up lonesome desert highways. Eleni's random oscillations add to the song's unearthly atmosphere. There's also an odd rustling/crackling/clinking lurking in the background to add to the intrigue. The Hittites were an ancient race whose empire, covering much of modern-day Turkey, was at its height around 3500 years ago. In a 2013 interview, Smith explained the inspiration behind the song:

> I read daft history books. Sometimes the books I read are a bit crackers or strange. So it sounded interesting. The Hittites didn't believe in debt or insurance. When I first started thinking about it was when I went to Greece, because the Hittites were with the ancient Greeks. And they didn't believe in debt or overdrafts, which sounds crazy, and I thought they didn't believe in wrongful communication, which I believe is the cause of a lot of trouble in the world.

It was a popular live choice at the time, getting 74 outings between 2012 and 2016.

Pre-MDMA Years

Another experimental interlude, one that doesn't overstay its welcome at just over a minute. Smith rambles about ecstasy

---

[379] Cluster were a German krautrock duo consisting of Hans-Joachim Roedelius and Dieter Moebius; 'Rote Riki' was from their 1974 album *Zuckerzeit*.

over some minimal parping synth. Rather inconsequential, but does contain some interesting phrases such as 'the bone seraton unconnected composite years' and 'the orc marrow gone down green jelly mama your kid brother than your years'. Never performed live.

No Respects Rev.

It wouldn't have been entirely unlike The Fall to have thrown away the cracking 'Respects' riff on a minute-long instrumental, but thankfully it returns here with a bit of space to expand and develop. Musically, the opening to the 'full' version is identical to the opener, but the production is a little shinier; there's much less reverb, which gives it a punchier sound. As in the shorter version, Greenway is to the fore, producing an effective mix of scrabbling surf-punk runs, choppy chords and bright, Byrds/early R.E.M.-esque arpeggios. It's also another track where Eleni's interjections provide valuable splashes of texture. A pleasingly manic atmosphere takes hold about halfway through and builds progressively, with Smith's vocal transforming into mad cackling.

Journalist Tim Cumming implied that this was the song that the group put forward (and had rejected) for the *Twilight* film. It seems likely that the song in question was actually 'Cowboy George' (see Chapter 28) even though 'No Respects Rev.' has a more authentically 'horror' feel to it. It also contains a reference to Whitby (3:37), the setting for Bram Stoker's *Dracula* and mecca for goths.

Victrola Time

A Victrola is a wind-up phonograph, one with a concealed horn (unlike that made famous by the HMV logo) that was used as a generic term in the early 1920s for any device that played records. The lyric – which has much in common with those of 'Pre-MDMA Years' – seem more concerned with the taking of ecstasy. Smith's opening vocal salvo is startling: a keening, broken warble that morphs into an aggressive gargling shriek. The track has a powerful yet restrained krautrock beat, although Melling occasionally breaks out from the taut motorik to venture something looser and more flamboyant. Spurr's bassline is fuzzily glutinous, but it's Eleni that takes centre stage with some meandering, doleful synth accented with the occasional curlicue. The chime that can be heard from time to time is Smith striking a glass with a teaspoon; the distorted voice at the end is that of Simon Archer, recorded on Smith's answering machine. It was played live 25 times, 2012-14.

Irish

When Von Südenfed's *Tromatic Reflexxions* was released in 2007, several critics noted a similarity in sound to LCD Soundsystem – in particular their debut single 'Losing My Edge' – suggesting that Smith was perhaps showing their singer James Murphy how such things should be done.[380] (Smith first heard the song on the radio whilst buying groceries: 'This sounds exactly like me,' he told the hapless shop assistant, 'are you taking the piss?) 'Irish' sees Murphy join the long list of artists that have attracted a sardonic glance from Smith, although he admitted that it wasn't his most thoughtful lyrical effort: 'I had to make up some lyrics quick for that one... the tune's better than the lyrics.' That said, 'they show their bollocks when they eat' ranks amongst his most entertaining lines. It may or may not be relevant that the shop assistant in the anecdote above was Irish.

Spurr kicks things off with a gristly riff while Melling clatters along with enthusiastic discipline. It verges on the messy and formless on occasions, but overall there's a well-judged balance between the menacingly restrained verse and the more uninhibited chorus, packed full of Greenway's chunky ascending-descending chords. Only played live 13 times, 2012-14.

Jetplane

Originally titled 'Suddenly, Certainly', 'Jetplane' is similar in structure to its predecessor, featuring once again a balance between a understated verse and a heavy, guitar-driven chorus. It

[380] Murphy is a big fan of the group, even once going as far as to say 'The Fall are my Beatles'. Curiously, although the multitude of artists listed in 'Losing My Edge' includes many MES touchstones – Can, Beefheart, Monks, Lou Reed – The Fall are never mentioned.

has a slightly lighter tone than 'Irish', however, due to the lively snare pattern and Greenway's jaunty guitar melody. It's a curious tale regarding 'Diane Worstock' and 'Dr. Jeffery Henning', who come up with an 'innovative new idea' whilst stuck in a queue at Milan airport. There are few clues as to who these characters might be, although MES did use the line 'Margaret Rutherford first came up with her amazing travel plan' when performing the song in Wakefield in June 2013.

Smith is in conversational, almost chirpy mood; the double-tracking of his vocals with Eleni's works well, giving the track a busy and layered feel and suggesting the kind of hubbub you might experience in an airport.[381] It's also particularly rich with inexplicably perfect MES-enunciated words and phrases, such as 'obliterated', 'the Italians certainly like their Sundays' and 'rock group'. The childishly exuberant 'whooosh' (1:29) is an oddly touching moment. It made 21 setlist appearances in 2013-14.

Jam Song

In which The Fall find themselves in a bar brawl with Led Zeppelin and Orbital. There's something wonderfully perverse about the very notion of The Fall recording a 'jam'. You can almost hear the MES of 30 years earlier berating his future self for such self-indulgence via the opening mumble 'Could do with a fucking chorus, that's the main fucking thing, innit?' It's a fantastically messy collage that sounds like every member of the group is playing a different song in a different time signature and/or key. Melling decides that it's John Bonham tribute day; Greenway flails and screeches away in several different directions, stamping on his effects pedals; Eleni plays the keyboards like she's not on the same planet, let alone in the same key. In amongst all of this, Smith warbles incoherently, plainly having fun (listen to the little chuckle at 3:30). It was never played live, although there is a sprawling, marvellously chaotic nine-minute outtake version to be found online.

---

[381] According to *The Annotated Fall*, the unidentified male voice speaking in French says 'The Milan to London flight has been delayed. Types of rap... tin foil handkerchief.'

Loadstones

An album closer that has a certain affinity with 'Exploding Chimney', featuring similarly heavy, staccato chords. Greenway's exuberant, almost hoe-down-ish guitar line leads the way, supported by Eleni's variety of smooth synth touches that provide a counterpoint to the over-arching blues-rockabilly sound. 'Shoes for the dead' harks back to 'Gut Of The Quantifier'. *The Annotated Fall* can only render the lines at 1:12 as 'sataffopsagaffop / sataffsagopfa'. It's an excellent album closer, full of impish energy. It only got 13 live outings, all in 2012 and 2013.

Reviews

In interviews at the time, Smith expressed both happiness with the new release and dissatisfaction with its predecessor. He told the *Lancashire Telegraph*, 'I didn't like [*Ersatz GB*]. I can say that, can't I? But this one… is what we are all about and I think it will terrify people.' He revisited this theme when talking to *Q*: '*Re-Mit* is going to terrify people. It's quite horrible. The Fall have had enough and we're coming for you.' Reviews were again mixed, although not quite as polarised as had been the case with *Ersatz GB*. Joe Kennedy felt, somewhat unfairly, that the unusually settled line-up was having a detrimental impact:

> Spurr, Greenway and Melling have gone from being great fits for the project to simply being very good musicians from the ponytailed-guy-who-works-in-the-guitar-shop school. No matter what they're playing – and let's face it, that 'what' is largely going to be barrelling Can-rock – there's a lack of expressive wit, giving the impression that they're just tossing this off as a demonstration of competent eclecticism before resuming their Steve Vai or Joe Satriani agendas.

The Guardian and *NME* were both lukewarm. *Pitchfork* were a little more positive, giving the 'dense, unwieldy tangle of rockabilly rhythms, 60s proto-punk petulance, krautrock thrust, musique-concrete spoken-word splatter, and sci-fi synth-tones salvaged from 70s bargain-bin prog' 6.8 out of 10. John Robb, as ever, was an enthusiast, calling it a 'timeless place' and a 'dense and strange world'. J.R. Moores mused on Smith's increasingly tenuous relationship with the English language:

> *Re-Mit* might not be the record on which Smith finally relinquishes language altogether in favour of communicating in only a dry-mouthed hangover gargle, but it's close. At times, not only is it impossible to determine what Smith is saying, it's impossible to determine whether he is even attempting to pronounce any recognisable human words with his reptilian chops.

The most succinct summary came from Ben Ratliff of the *New York Times*: 'Rating among recent Fall albums: Better than *Ersatz GB* (the 29th); far better than *Reformation Post TLC* (26th); not as good as *Your Future Our Clutter* (28th) and a full mile worse than *Imperial Wax Solvent* (27th). Go get it.'

The LP reached a respectable number 40 in the album charts.

Evaluation

Re-Mit is puzzlingly underrated. Not only is it bursting with strong tunes, but the now well-established line-up have locked onto a particularly satisfying blend of their various attributes that brings out the best in them all. In addition, they haven't just settled on a specific 'sound': across the tracks (even within them) there's a sense of each member taking turns to lead. *Ersatz GB* had a largely uniform sound that led some reviewers to question whether the group's unusual stability was breeding mediocrity. *Re-Mit* sees the group disproving this notion with assurance, branching out and offering significant variety: prowling horror ('Hittite'); heads-down garage punk ('William'); driving guitar-jangle ('Respects'); crazed beat-psych ('Kinder'); taut krautrock ('Victrola') – even, God forbid, a spot of good, old-fashioned self-indulgent studio jamming.

There are many instances in the back catalogue where MES offers a little chuckle, or delivers a line in a manner that suggests a twinkle in his eye, but *Re-Mit* may well be the later-period Fall album where he most consistently sounds like he's really enjoying himself. Even when he descends into hissing and growling, there's an enthusiasm and sharpness that was missing from parts of *Ersatz*.

It's not without its flaws. The two experimental tracks are pleasant enough but rather inessential, and in the case of 'Noise', it feels like they could have done much more with a potentially interesting piece of music; sequencing-wise, they're also rather too close together. Furthermore, whilst there are many intriguing lyrics here, *Re-Mit* does not have the emotional depth of *Your Future Our Clutter*. However, there's no tossed-off cover version to shrug your shoulders about, and overall it's an album of remarkable consistency, invention and – believe it or not – fun.

The Remainderer
Recorded: Chairworks Studios, Castleford
Released: 9th December 2013

Personnel:
Mark E Smith – vocals
David Spurr – bass
Keiron Melling – drums
Peter Greenway – guitar
Eleni Poulou – keyboards

With:
Simon 'Ding' Archer and Tamsin Middleton – backing vocals
Daren Garratt – drums ('The Remainderer', 'Amorator!', 'Mister Róde', 'Say
Mama') (uncredited)
Martin Bramah – guitar, Craig Scanlon – guitar, Marcia Schofield – keyboards,
Steve Hanley – bass, Simon Wolstencroft – drums on 'Race With The Devil'
(uncredited)

Chapter 31: The Remainderer

'Vampirism... is a crime at the end of the day.'

Re-Mit was released in the middle of the group's spring 2013 UK tour. Reviewing their gig at Clapham on 17th May, *The Independent*'s Nick Hasted captured the flavour of The Fall's performances at the time:

> The Fall survive by moving forward, and as usual the set is drawn almost entirely from *Re-Mit* and other recent work... Smith is an abrasive, unstable presence, one minute Les Dawson lugubrious, the next puffing his pigeon chest out as he haughtily inspects the crowd.
>
> When Poulou takes over the vocal for 'I've Been Duped', Smith turns his back to her, arms folded, somewhere between a Salford Napoleon and Steptoe. Poulou can hardly contain her grins at a husband who is unusually, playfully happy and singing with proud power over the band's thundering, relentless groove. For the encore 'Theme From Sparta F.C.', Smith holds the mic with his arms flung back like Christ, and prowls the stage with the exaggerated grace of a benign drunk. He clocks off on the stroke of 60 minutes: all business, all pleasure, all Fall.

In the same month, Smith recorded a guest appearance on *Error 500*, an album by Ginger Wildheart's 'supergroup' Mutation.[382] He featured on two tracks, 'Mutations' and 'Relentless Confliction'. A hilarious online video entitled 'Mark E Smith vs The Sound Engineer' captures MES at work in the studio, haranguing the hapless Kevin: 'I'm sorry Kevin, in my headphones it sounds like fuckin'... the Smurfs.' (Unusually, Smith eventually accepts that Kevin, not him, is in the right.)

The Fall played a handful of festival dates over the summer, including Día de la Música in Madrid and All Tomorrow's Parties in

---

[382] David Walls, aka Ginger Wildheart, was a guitarist, singer and songwriter in The Quireboys and The Wildhearts. Mutation featured members of Napalm Death, The Sisters Of Mercy and The Cardiacs.

Iceland. Rob Barbato filled in for Dave Spurr (who was on holiday in Cuba) at two Irish dates in August. In November, at Utrecht, Tim Presley joined the group for the encore. Daren Garratt (who had been in Pubic Fringe with Pete Greenway and had also played with The Nightingales) played drums alongside Keiron Melling at Leeds, and then replaced him at Cologne in December whilst Melling was on paternity leave. In the week that *The Remainderer* was released, Smith made an appearance in the 'What I see in the mirror?' column in *The Guardian*. Although not especially enlightening about his approach to songwriting or performance, it was at least more coherent than his earlier *Q&A* interview:

> I only really look in a mirror before I go on stage, in case I've got anything on my face. I've got a comb. It's good to look a bit straight: a clean shirt and all that. And I've started to wear underpants and I clean my teeth now and again. But that's about it.

An interview with John Doran shortly afterwards had rather more substance. In it, we learn that Smith considers Black Francis a 'dickhead' and that the group were allegedly asked for three songs for *Twilight*. Smith also asserts that vampirism 'is a crime, at the end of the day'. Doran's question, 'Have you been watching the *Great British Bake-Off*?'[383] leads MES into a rambling but entertaining diatribe about cookery programmes, which is then broadened to take in property shows ('should be banned... that's an estate agent's job') and reminiscences about daytime TV shows like *Crown Court*. When Doran asks about Smith's health, in particular his time in a wheelchair in 2009, Smith tries to brush it aside ('it's not *This Morning* programme') and bullishly declares that 'my liver's replenished... my liver's stronger than ever'. They also discuss veteran bands reforming for nostalgia tours — a topic addressed by *The Remainderer*'s title track and 'Rememberance R' — Smith claiming that he has been offered money over the years to play old albums in full. He also expresses a desire to take The Fall in a 'noisier direction', despite the fact that 'even the group don't like it'.

---

[383] Doran described this as 'the riskiest interview gambit I've ever gone with on a whim'.

The Remainderer

The EP was recorded, like *Your Future Our Clutter*, at Chairworks in Castleford, with Simon Archer once more producing alongside MES. It was released as both a CD and a 2x10" with gatefold sleeve. The promo CD contained different versions of the title track and 'Mister Rode' from the official CD, and both were retained for the vinyl version. The cover is not one of the group's most aesthetically pleasing moments, a grim picture of a fag end in the gutter being overlaid with tacky WordArt fonts. The most notable feature is the Fall coin, rather hubristically engraved with 'REX M.E.S.'

The Remainderer

After a plaintive guitar chord and a sawing oscillation, the song fastens onto a lumbering beat, Melling and Garratt's extravagant percussion recalling the Paul Hanley/Burns glory days. It seems a little far-fetched, even given Smith's fondness for daytime TV, but there is an undeniable melodic similarity to the *Baywatch* theme tune.[384] Smith's vocals veer between the surprisingly tuneful and his increasingly familiar reliance on growling and extreme sibilance; the double-tracking of his voice adds to the sense of disarray. The paradoxical 'never forget, rememb(e)rance is worth nothing' suggests one of Smith's favourite themes, the futility of nostalgia. The moment (2:20) where the group drop out and Smith exclaims sardonically that 'it was a good day – whatever that is' provides an exciting change of pace. The coda finds Smith reduced to an asthmatic, Dalek-like gargle. The vinyl/promo version kicks into gear more rapidly and features some interestingly deadpan backing vocals. 'The Remainderer' was played live 30 times, 2013-16.

Amorator!

An urgent, scrabbling piece of frantic psychobilly, full of dramatic ebbs and flows. Although 'never forget your brain is a bubble of water' is the most striking phrase, the most interesting line is 'the frost covers up what the summer men made'. Again,

[384] Pete Greenway confirmed this 'lift' via Twitter.

this seems to hint at nostalgia, or is possibly a reflection on mortality. Played live 17 times between 2013 and 2015, it was the 18th and penultimate Fall song to feature an exclamation mark in the title.

Mister Rode

Opens with what sounds like Mötorhead being played at excessive volume on a broken AM radio before a menacing drum salvo leads into a melodic guitar arpeggio and throbbing bassline. A minute in, it feels like you've had three different songs already. Melling and Garratt, flailing and bludgeoning like their lives depend on it, are the focal point, with Greenway's looping riff providing the foundation. Like 'The Remainderer', effective use is made of extra vocal tracks, but here it's much more than mere double-tracking: multiple, heavily-reverbed layers of Smith's voice create an oppressive, malevolent atmosphere. In the last couple of minutes, swathes of distorted noise (including what sounds like a snippet of 'Crazy Horses' at 6:04) join in the fun to produce a tumultuous, discordant finale. The main body of the promo/vinyl version is slightly shorter, and has a different but no less effective ending.

Smith's main vocal is relatively melodic, revolving around the 'I got a name, I got a say/face' refrain. *Annotated Fall* contributor 'SlightlyDislocated' suggests that the lyrics are 'a meditation on identity and anonymity, from the perspectives of, first, a passenger at a subway or commuter rail station, second, a patient about to be wheeled into surgery in a hospital, and third, a soul boarding an airplane and experiencing its subsequent takeoff'. He also points out that the line 'its summers were all in a day' possibly refers to Ray Bradbury's 1954 short story 'All Summer in a Day'.[385] Perhaps because the dual-drummer assault worked so well on stage (when Garratt was available at least), 'Mister Rode' had a longer shelf-life than anything else on the EP, being played 43 times and staying in the set almost to the end, its last appearance coming in January 2017.

---

[385] Published in 1954, the story is set on Venus, where the sun is visible for only one hour every seven years.

Rememberance R
Nearly 30 years on, the group returned to The Stooges' 'I Wanna Be Your Dog', from which Brix had borrowed back in 1984. Although it's played at a much slower tempo, it's also closer to the spirit of The Stooges' track, having a similarly foreboding atmosphere as opposed to the lighter, psychedelic tone of 'Elves'. Melling (drumming solo here) provides sparse yet expressive percussion that allows Greenway space to emerge gradually with grinding, abrasive chords. It has been suggested that this might be Smith on guitar, but rough sounding as it is, this seems unlikely.

The reference to a 'fire escape' might relate to the recording of 'Alton Towers', but even *The Annotated Fall* is stumped as to what a 'canajetta' might be. The closing monologue (delivered by Archer) revisits the nostalgia theme, a sardonic commentary on bands that reform and trade in on past glories: 'They're just running on remembrance, and reminiscing of encore time at the end of the 90 minutes on the stage.' Smith's belief in the importance of a strong work ethic is emphasised through his dismissal of those artists lacking long-term commitment to a musical career: 'They appear out of nowhere and like expect you to treat them like an equal, while they've been decorating or teaching for like the last 10 years, having a life and a wife and kids.' 'Rememberance R' was only played live once, at the Out.Fest festival in Portugal on 12th October 2013 – it was very different to the studio version, being a fast-paced guitar-heavy thrash.

Say Mama / Race With The Devil
After a minute or so of a lively but predictable Gene Vincent cover (you half-expect someone to shout 'White lightning!' at some point) the track segues awkwardly into another Vincent song, this time recorded at John Peel's 50th birthday party. This was the only time the group performed 'Devil'; 'Mama' was never played live.

Touchy Pad
'Touchy Pad' makes a curiously sudden entrance, like it's an old, scratched vinyl record. Despite the mellow strum and gentle guitar

melody, it's no less strange than the EP's earlier songs, thanks to the lurching, off-kilter rhythm, Eleni's deftly applied synth effects and Tamsin Middleton's contributions.[386] Middleton's intense vocals ('Where's my time machine?!?'; the impressively anguished scream at 0:32) make an effective contrast to Smith's calm delivery.

The title suggests one of Smith's anti-technology rants, although you have to work quite hard to sustain this interpretation. 'Time machine' is a vaguely technological reference; he mentions 'AI' (possibly) at 0:59; 'Asians with weak bones' might have something to do with Japanese tech companies, at a stretch. It's hard, though, to see the anti-tech thread in the 'Welsh kids [whose] slime leaks and mixes' or the Lovecraft reference ('the tentacles of the Old Ones'). Tamsin Middleton identified the behaviour of the UK Border Agency as the inspiration behind the lyrics, presumably referring to the Home Office's controversial 2013 advertising campaign, which involved vans emblazoned with the slogan 'go home or face arrest' being driven around areas with significant immigrant populations. This could conceivably explain the line 'your lousy country stinks anyway'. The abrupt opening and similarly sudden conclusion give 'Touchy Pad' a fragmentary feel, which enhances its ambiguity and mystery. It was never played live.

Reviews

The EP was well received. Niall O'Keeffe, writing in *The Quietus*, saw it as one of the group's frequent transitional moments:

> *The Remainderer* slots into a lineage of interim records that bridge different eras of The Fall, like the sprawling 'Chiselers' single, which telegraphed a darkening of mood in the mid-90s, or the *Fall Versus 2003* EP, which signalled the band's reinvigoration after career-low *Are You Are Missing Winner*. To judge from this record, the future Fall will be chaotic, cryptic and collaborative. Its music will be shape-shifting, fragmented and fierce.

[386] Middleton, along with Archer, was a member of As Able As Kane, who would later play as support for The Fall in 2015. She is credited erroneously on the sleeve as 'Tasmin'.

The Line of Best Fit gave it 7.5/10: 'The best thing about this band is that they are perpetually evolving, and in that respect, *The Remainderer* carries on triumphantly where *Re-Mit* left off... Abrasive but not completely inaccessible, it's The Fall very nearly at their best.' Stuart Berman of *Pitchfork* was similarly positive: 'More than anything, *The Remainderer* is an encouraging sign that stability has yet to ossify into stagnation with this ongoing iteration of the band, who formidably exercise their elasticity over the course of these six wildly divergent tracks.'

Evaluation

When asked if the EP was leftover material from the previous album *Re-Mit*, Smith replied, 'That's why it's called *The Remainder* [sic].' Cherry Red's promotional material also suggested that it was some sort of 'bridging point' between *Re-Mit* and the next album. This view of *The Remainderer* is unconvincing. It certainly doesn't sound like any sort of *Re-Mit* bonus disc, the album's songs being generally much more melodic and traditionally structured than those on the EP. *The Remainderer*, whatever Smith's intentions might have been, stands firmly as an independent and coherent release.

Whilst it's true that some elements of the EP echo *Ersatz GB* and would be revisited on *Sub-Lingual Tablet* – particularly Smith's often uncomfortably phlegmy gargle – there's something almost indefinably *different* about *The Remainderer*. It has a spirit of enthusiasm, experimentation, playfulness and anarchy that sets it apart from the group's other contemporary releases. There are tantalising glimpses into some form of overarching theme regarding music as a career and the role of reflection and revisiting the past, but it's challenging to pin it down. As bzfgt puts it, *The Remainderer* remains 'steadfast in its impenetrability... You will never understand these lyrics, nor will I.'

Its inclusion here as a separate chapter may raise an eyebrow amongst some in the Fall community, but this is no sort of attempt to ignite yet another heated debate (there is a more than sufficient amount of those already) – *The Remainderer* is simply a substantial enough piece of work to warrant it. It sounds very little like *Slates*, musically or vocally, but there's something more than length and number of tracks that bridges the 32-year gap between the two. It's the determination to confound expectations; to redefine the group's sound; to utilise every strength of each musician.

THE FALL

SUB-LINGUAL TABLET

Sub-Lingual Tablet
Recorded: Chairworks Studios, Castleford; 6dB Studio, Manchester
Released: 11th May 2015

Personnel:
Mark E Smith – vocals
Dave Spurr – bass
Peter Greenway – guitar
Keiron Melling – drums
Daren Garratt – drums
Eleni Poulou – synths

With:
Rob Barbato and Tim Presley – all instruments ('Black Roof')

Chapter 32: Sub-Lingual Tablet

'The Fall are anti-social, anti-communal, and best experienced in the flesh, in a room full of strangers. We need it more than ever.'

The group played one final 2013 gig after the release of *The Remainderer*, in Cologne. It saw Daren Garratt as the sole drummer, covering Keiron Melling's paternity leave. 2014 kicked off in Athens on 1st February with Melling and Garratt playing together on two full kits, early 80s-style. Videos of the performance show the pair battering away in jubilant synchronicity, especially on recent material such as 'Mister Rode'. Smith only appeared for the first half, however; vocal duties thereafter were shared between Eleni and Daren.

After three months off, the group returned to the stage in Coventry on 1st May. The gig was notable for two reasons: the first performance of a rather sketchy version of 'Auto Chip 2014-2016' (at this point just called '2014') and, despite his long-standing and well-documented aversion to facial hair, the first sight of Smith sporting a beard. Later that month there were debuts for 'Fibre Book Troll', at this point called 'Facebook' (musically almost fully formed already, although Smith's vocals were still rather improvised) and 'Pledge' (according to Garratt, written in the dressing room just before the gig). In August, at the Beacons Festival in Skipton, the group were temporarily pulled off stage due to high winds after only four songs. The last of these was 'BAM (Student-Village)', an early incarnation of 'First One Today'. They returned to play four more songs, the last being a hectic cover of The Stooges' 'Cock In My Pocket'. Later that month, in York, two more new songs appeared in the setlist, both of which had working titles: 'Bumblebee' ('Dedication Not Medication') and 'Jungle' ('Junger Cloth'). Eleni didn't appear at the gig, the reason given being an allergic reaction to the freshly-painted venue.

Steve Hanley published his memoir of his experiences in The Fall in September. *The Big Midweek: Life Inside The Fall*, co-written by Olivia Piekarski, is especially effective at both demystifying the 'romance' of life on the road and exploring the changing relationship dynamics within the group. It was well-received in both The Fall fan community and the media – Barney Hoskyns in *The Guardian* thought it 'phlegmatic and gently droll'.

New material continued to appear throughout the group's autumn performances, again with working titles: 'Gone To Venice' ('Venice With The Girls') in Brighton; 'Get Off The Phone' ('Quit iPhone') in Brixton. The Brixton performance was reviewed by Digby Warde-Aldam in *The Spectato*r:

> And blimey was this fun. The Fall are rock music as imagined by Brecht. They play, or rather attack their instruments, like five-year-olds with OCD. It's bad – terrible! – but excitingly so. The songs (if they can be so described) were indistinguishable, though one senses such trifling things aren't really the point. Mark E. crowed out every word like a man possessed. Every word was nonsense, granted, but more zealous nonsense you're unlikely to hear anywhere.

After two nights at Lower Kersal Social Club, Salford (27th-28th September), the group played at the Supermassive Festival in Helsinki on 25th October. For undisclosed reasons, Eleni performed in a wheelchair. In October, The Fall – or, as they were credited here for the first time, 'The Fall Group' – released their fortieth official live album, *Live Uurop VIII-XII Places In Sun & Winter, Son*. It contained a selection of recordings from 2008-2012, but doesn't make clear what was from where or when, and even the more obsessive elements of the *Fall Online Forum* struggled to identify the origins of half of the tracks. It contained a couple of alternate studio versions: 'Auto (2014) Chip Replace' is a relatively brief take on the track, more focused on quirky electronic squiggles and random vocal interjections than the driving krautrock of the album version; 'Amorator' (here without its exclamation mark) sees Eleni playing a more prominent role.

Another Fall-related memoir appeared in November. As well as his time in The Fall, Simon Wolstencroft's *You Can Drum But You Can't Hide* (co-written with journalist Stuart Bisson-Foster) detailed how 'Funky Si' was almost in both The Smiths and The Stone Roses, and also dealt frankly but humorously with his drug issues. Like Steve Hanley's book, it provides an intriguing insight into the constantly evolving relationships within The Fall and their recording and touring processes. It was similarly well-received, too: *The Quietus* described it as a 'punchy and addictive memoir [that] proves as endearing and self-effacing as Wolstencroft himself'.

The group's first gig of 2015 was at the Grauzone Festival in Amsterdam; one of those rare occasions where MES sported a t-shirt. John Robb captured the mayhem enthusiastically:

> There is a madness in the area, Mark sings through a plastic cup, shouts without the mic at the audience, stares into space, swops mics around, grins when hit by a plastic glass, tries to get drummer number 2, Daren, to sing the vocals and lurks behind the amps on the stage. There is a lot of humour and deliberate chaos to the proceedings and somehow in the middle of it all the band keep their shape like a giant-killing football team not buckling down in an unlikely FA Cup game.

In February, The Fall appeared at the BBC Radio 6 Music Festival in Gateshead. The performance is impressively powerful and focused, but the standout moment is 'Reformation!', which features MES twiddling knobs, using his mic as percussion, directing both Greenway and Melling to sing, and throwing a crumpled-up lyric sheet into the audience.

A dispute regarding the royalties for 'Touch Sensitive' saw Smith appearing in court in March. Steve Sharples (known as Steve Hitchcock back in 1999) had provided some string arrangements for 'Touch Sensitive'. Although credited 'Smith/ Nagle/Hitchcock', the royalties were split one-third MES, two-thirds Julia Nagle; Sharples claimed that he was entitled to a one-third share. Judge Amanda Michaels – who found Smith 'to be a truthful witness, who was frank about the vagueness of his recollection of some of the events from the relevant period' – concluded that Sharples was entitled to royalties, but only awarded him 20%. The media took great delight in reporting the judge's expressed difficulties with examining the song: 'Mr Smith delivers the lyrics in a manner which at some points makes it hard to hear the words.'

There were four more gigs in April and May before the new album's release (although it was already available for sale at the first of these, in Brixton). Reviewing the Brixton performance, Tim Cumming captured the compelling chaos of the group:

> ...though it's all but impossible to hear a word [MES] says, the way he pulls focus – amp-fiddling, abrupt walk-offs, abrupt returns, three encores (the last when the venue is emptying out) – means he remains compelling, visceral, venomous and a potent, sub-lingual antidote to the beige like-and-share community culture of these times. The Fall are anti-social, anti-communal, and best experienced in the flesh, in a room full of strangers. We need it more than ever.

Shortly after the release of *Sub-Lingual Tablet*, *Vice* published an interview which found Smith on cantankerous and entertaining form. He expressed admiration for Dave Eggers's novel *The Circle* (although he couldn't actually recall the author's name, referring to him as 'some daft cunt'), but most of the interview comprised of a long list of targets for Smith's typically blunt and withering criticism: Northern people, especially Mancunians ('there's something about Manchester musicians that's particularly fucking irritating'), Sheffield ('shit'), London ('was always a shithole'), his once-beloved Edinburgh ('a fucking boring, yuppie place now'), older Fall fans at gigs ('anyone over 43 shouldn't be allowed in'), Bitcoin ('worth like tuppence now') and Frank Skinner ('I mean what does he do now? Adverts for fucking HP Sauce or something?')

Sub-Lingual Tablet

The album was recorded in two familiar studios: Chairworks and Simon Archer's 6dB; 'Ding' also engineered the LP with MES getting sole production credit. As well as the CD version, the album was released as a double vinyl LP, which featured different takes of 'Dedication Not Medication', 'Auto-Chip 2014-2016', 'Pledge' and 'Fibre Book Troll'. The somewhat underwhelming sleeve design was credited to Ken and Charlie Pearson.[387] In his last ever interview for the *NME*, Smith discussed the album's title: 'It was going to be called *Dedication Not Medication* but, you know, it looked a bit like a Barclays advert.'

Venice With The Girls

In the long tradition of garage rock album openers, 'Venice' bursts forth with a crackling energy. It's almost a traditionally structured song, having what feels like a verse and a bridge, albeit a bridge that leads straight back into the verse, eschewing the need for a chorus. There's a choice moment at 3:31 where the band drop out and smash back in again with impeccable timing, made all the more effective by Smith's strangely ghostly and atonal multi-tracked vocals. This layering of his voice is a strong feature throughout; there's the familiar sneering and growling, but there's also an oddly robotic, dispassionate tone. The combination gives the song a broader texture than some of the group's other heads-down rockers.

The lyric seems to have been inspired by an advert for Staysure Insurance, which included the line 'I'm off to Venice with the girls'. The reference to 'mad seniors' suggests that the song is poking fun at middle-aged Britons letting their hair down whilst abroad. The repeated refrain of 'waiting so long' echoes both Bowie's 'Look Back In Anger' and Cream's 'Sunshine Of Your Love'. 'The best thing for you to do is hide' was probably inspired by 'Little Diesel Driving Devil' by Don Bowman, which contains the lyric 'He's the fastest thing alive / when he puts that truck

[387] Information on the pair is hard to come by. The LP's *Discogs* page once suggested that Charlie was a Manchester techno DJ and producer, but given that it also identified Ken as a pianist from Montreal who played organ on Janis Joplin's 1971 album *Pearl*, this may well not have been accurate.

in overdrive / the safest thing for you to do is hide'. In Smith's appearance on *The Adam and Joe Show*'s regular 'Vinyl Justice' feature, 'Devil' was one of the records that was played.[388] 'Venice' was performed live 54 times, 2014-17.

Black Roof

Tim Presley had contributed creative insanity to *Re-Mit* with 'Kinder Of Spine'; here, he and fellow 'Dude' Rob Barbato provide something similarly deranged. The two Americans performed all of the music on 'Black Roof', described by *Mojo* as '...varispeed insanity [with] a thrilling anything may happen edge'. After a brief, sprightly passage featuring a shrill sci-fi keyboard, things slow down and get a little weird. We get a throbbing bass loop beneath Smith in semi-megaphone mode, soon accompanied by a keyboard (or maybe guitar) impersonating the mating call of a seagull. Then (1:18) it's back to the original section, with a little bit of *Doctor Who* sound effects thrown in (1:22), before it all concludes abruptly, still some distance from the two-minute mark. It's a hell of a lot to fit in just over 100 seconds, and sounds like at least 12 unfinished ideas flung together; but somehow, inexplicably, it works.

In places, Smith's vocals on 'Black Roof' are reminiscent of those on 'They're Coming To Take Me Away, Ha-Haaaa!', a 1966 novelty hit for Napoleon XIV, pseudonym of American songwriter and producer Jerrold Samuels. The lyric is aptly surreal: 'You simply cannot prove your fog-accenting notions...

---

[388] Don Bowman (1937-2013) was an American country music singer, songwriter, comedian and radio host who had a novelty hit in 1964 with 'Chet Atkins Make Me A Star'. MES frequently expressed his love of 'trucking' songs. *The Adam and Joe Show*, presented by Adam Buxton and Joe Cornish, ran for four series between 1996 and 2001. The 'Vinyl Justice' section saw the duo 'raid' rock stars' homes and search their record collections for embarrassing albums. In Smith's appearance (filmed at Buxton's flat as MES refused to use his house), he dances (sort of) to 'Little Diesel' with Buxton and Cornish. Speaking to *The Guardian* in 2019, Cornish said: 'The only way you could get in touch with him was to get his manager to pin a message on a board in a working man's club in Salford... To persuade him to cooperate we had to get him a great deal of booze and £200 in cash.' In a 2020 Instagram post, he elaborated further: 'Adam was a big fan of The Fall whereas I knew almost nothing about them. I think Mr. Smith picked up on that and took a dislike to me. He proceeded to put a plastic bag over my head, sit on me and punch me repeatedly in the head while smoking a fag and grinning. Only now, all these years later, do I realise what an honour it all was.'

Easter Island profile and care from old inwardly truck land'. Originally entitled 'Black Door', it retained that title on some digital versions. It was, sadly, never played live.

Dedication Not Medication

The almost-title-track of the album is a wobbly slice of twisted funk and mutant electronica, wrapped in a deceptively calm, metronomic beat. It's quite similar to 'Cold November' by Paradox Obscur, a Greek minimal synth duo formed in 2014. The striking opening line – 'Pierce Brosnan how dare you prescribe / sad grief and bed wet pills?' – would seem to tie in with the ex-Bond actor's role in promoting Indian chewing tobacco Pan Bahar, one of the side effects of which is incontinence. However, what would be a neat connection is rather spoiled (unless you're a believer in MES's 'pre-cog' abilities) by the fact that Brosnan's advert didn't come out until the year after *Sub-Lingual Tablet*. In a 2015 interview for *Q* with Ted Kessler, Smith said that the song was actually about his doctor, who had prescribed him antidepressants.[389] 'I've always thought the most dangerous drugs are prescribed antidepressants… They tried to prescribe me some, for my chest, to stop smoking. That was the final straw. Luckily, I've mates who know about pharmacology, as you can imagine…'

The vinyl version of 'Dedication' is notably different, being much more frenetic and drum-focused; it's also nearly twice as long. In this take, Smith doesn't get to the melody until the last two minutes; much of the vocals are taken up by a curious dialogue between him and Ding which refers to 'Connie and Cookie' – almost certainly a reference to Conway Paton and Stefan Cooke of *The Fall Online*. Given the context, the 'anti-Fall association' seems likely to be Smith's catch-all term for the variety of online sources of information about the group that remained frustratingly beyond his grasp. The group's backdrop on their autumn 2014 gigs was emblazoned with the grammatically dubious slogan, 'Dedication not medication: you decide!' It was

---

[389] In the interview, Smith suggested that his urinary function had been impaired by taking some dodgy 'orange speed'. Kessler noted that 'during a four-pint, one-bottle and six-shot session he does not leave the table for the urinal once'.

a popular setlist choice, played live 70 times from 2014 right up to the last gig in 2017.

First One Today

The jumble of disparate elements – snaking bassline, chiming keyboards, scampering drums and dual guitars (one playing a focused spidery blues, the other doing something much more randomly atonal) – only just about hangs together. The endearingly awkward tempo drop halfway through gives everyone a chance to catch their breath before Greenway's crafty riff leads them back into the last minute of disarray. Against all odds, the group get away with the scattergun construction, although it's perhaps just as well that they stop short of the three-minute mark before the song collapses under the weight of its own haphazardness. The concise lyric contains several interesting reference points. Both the title itself and 'there stands the door' suggest a link to Webb Pierce's 'There Stands A Glass'.[390] 'Behold the man' is both a Michael Moorcock novel and the English translation of the title of Nietzsche's final book.[391] 'Social media psyche' is a theme that Smith would revisit throughout the album. It received 59 live outings, including at the group's final gig.

Junger Cloth

The shuffling Afro-beat drums and choppy guitar find the group revisiting a frequent source of inspiration, Can. Spurr's ballooning bassline is a highlight, but it's Eleni who anchors the song with a serene, sustained keyboard melody. Although Smith begins the song with a calm demeanour, the lyric soon develops a caustic tone: 'inexplicable and disgusting'; 'all that is foul in man and creature'; 'spacious and wasteful'. His distaste is directed at a piece of text, but oddly it appears to be the handwriting that offends him: 'a letter so simple, yet disgusting in a stroke'.

His vocals float, disassociated, above the music. Not, as with *Reformation Post TLC*, in a distractingly artificial way; here,

[390] Webb Pierce was a 1950s honky tonk artist whose biggest hit was 'In The Jailhouse Now'.

[391] *Ecce Homo*, published posthumously in 1908. The phrase was spoken by Pontius Pilate at the trial of Christ.

the separation between the group's spacious sound and the sharp disgust of the vocal creates an unpredictable and prickly atmosphere that resolves beautifully with the final, definitive three chords. It was played live 29 times, all in 2014-15.

Stout Man

'Cock In My Pocket' was a Stooges song, written in around 1973, that never received a proper studio release, although it did appear on the band's infamous *Metallic KO* live album. Performed by The Fall as a cover at the wind-disrupted Beacons Festival, by January 2015 it had become 'Stout Man'. Smith discussed the song at some length in his *Vice* interview. He challenged the rest of the group to learn the relatively obscure track, and when they did so he scornfully accused them of having 'shazammed it' (an interesting choice of verb, given Smith's professed obliviousness to all things internet or technology-related).

> They'd been tricking me, they'd been sneaking back into the studio to keep tightening it up. I couldn't catch them out but in a car on the way down to London I was looking behind the seat and there was this CD, covered in dirt, with the original rough mix of it. I made them use that; they'd been doing about eight or nine different versions of it, it was pathetic. They must have worked more on that song more than any other on the whole album.

All of which throws some intriguing light on his attitude to recording and musicianship. Unfortunately, this is more interesting than the song itself, 'Stout Man' being a disappointingly obvious pub-rock trundle in which Smith veers perilously close to self-parody. The banal lyric ('shut your trap skinny or I'll shit in your brain / ram it up your crack') still manages to squeeze in a nod to the technology theme: 'All my kids are behind Asiatic tech'. Its seventh live performance was the last thing the group would ever play on stage.

Auto Chip 2014-2016

The album's centrepiece is a lengthy, mesmeric tour de force.

511

Whilst the rhythm section nail things down with powerful precision, it's Greenway that makes this special. The way that he takes a simple guitar line and stretches it over ten minutes through subtle variation and nuance – without ever resorting to histrionics – and unwaveringly grips your attention is a masterclass in intelligent guitar playing. The lyric takes a similarly repetitive approach to the music, but finds time to take a swipe at 'English musicians'. 'Chip', of course, was one of Smith's favourite words, and this marked its ninth and final appearance in a Fall lyric.[392] In contemporary and retrospective reviews, 'Auto-Chip' is frequently cited as the album's highlight. Michael Hann described it as 'a tide washing up on the same beach over and over and over again. It's magnificent.' Stuart Berman thought that its '10 exhilarating minutes' saw the group 'for once, casting out with a clear destination in sight, gradually applying pedal pressure on a sun-bound motorik rhythm until it achieves lift-off'. The shorter vinyl version is not vastly different.[393] 'Auto Chip' became a sort of emblem of the group's defiance, resilience and adherence to the '3 Rs' mantra, being played at the overwhelming majority (62 out of 78) of their final gigs.

Pledge

The group did not spend a lot of time writing 'Pledge' and, comparing its early performances with the final version, didn't develop it much further from the original idea. Although Greenway in particular puts in some hard graft trying to elevate the song a little, 'Pledge' is a plodding, unedifying grind, although this is possibly exacerbated by its proximity to the fluid, pacey 'Auto Chip'. The mix is peculiar: the guitar and bass lurk timidly in the background; the drums are thin and insubstantial; Eleni's keyboards and (especially) Smith's vocals are aggressively front and centre.

[392] The others being 'Arms Control Poseur', 'Devolute (Testa Rossa Monitor Mix)', 'Jerusalem', 'Eat Y'self Fitter', 'Enigrammatic Dream', 'Gut Of The Quantifier', 'Jawbone And The Air-Rifle' and 'Medical Acceptance Gate'.
[393] The first 42 seconds and the last 68 of the CD version are missing. Although they sound like the same take, the two versions are at a slightly different tempo; if you align them by the first 'two-oh-one-four!' they end up out of step with each other after a minute or so.

Smith seems to have come across the concept of Pledge and crowdfunding via his involvement with Ginger Wildheart. It didn't leave him with much interesting to say on the subject: 'Went to get money for download, they said "Two Ten Pledge!"' The vinyl version is a considerable improvement. The sound is much better balanced, and the whole thing is more concise and focused. 'Pledge' was played live 24 times, 2014–17

Snazzy

'Snazzy' fades in almost timidly, bops along agreeably for nearly a minute, takes a pleasingly down-tempo turn and then the group strike up a rousing pace that, disappointingly, fades out after only another minute or so. Smith had a cynical, perhaps even resentful attitude towards the various books (and their associated interviews and articles) by ex-Fall members that had emerged in the previous few years: money made out of the group's name that didn't come his way was always an anathema to him. It's conceivable that the lyric here – 'Let me tell ya about the wee lads… I never saw them again and if I ever do, I'm sure it will be in purgatory' – might be an expression of those feelings. That said, his tone is more melancholy than spiteful.

The track has engaging swagger to it, but it's frustrating that it's so abruptly curtailed just as it's getting interesting. 'Snazzy' didn't receive its live debut until after the album's release, being played as the encore in Newcastle on 23rd May; it only got another half a dozen outings thereafter.

Fibre Book Troll

First recorded as far back as December 2013, the song first appeared on a 2014 various artists LP called *Modeselektion Vol. 03*. On the sleeve of this compilation, it was entitled 'Fibre Book Troll', although it appeared on the setlist as 'Facebook' for its live debut in May 2014 and simply 'Troll' for the next couple of outings. To confuse things further, it reverted to 'Facebook Troll' when it reappeared on the *Wise Ol' Man* EP in 2016. It only got 18 live outings.

The song sees the group revisit the motorik approach of 'Auto

Chip', this time framing it around Eleni's malevolent three-note motif. It has a pummelling intensity, but lacks the subtlety and dynamic range of 'Auto Chip'. It's always a pleasure to hear The Fall grasp a basic idea and thrash the living daylights out of it, but 'Troll' is stretched perhaps a minute or so too far. The concluding 45 seconds of whistling are also a tad self-indulgent. Smith's vocal ranges from belligerent to explosively furious as he rants about people impersonating him online. 'I had these fellas saying they were me,' he told Ted Kessler, 'three on Facebook, two on the Twitter... there was one getting 14,000 hits a day.' Mysteriously, Smith went on to claim that he used technology invented by Richard Madeley to deal with the problem.[394]

The *Modeselektion* version has rather more lyrical substance; it's also more subtle, and has a satisfyingly skewed atmosphere. Whilst it still feels a little stretched, the chaotic breakdown over the last minute is more successful at maintaining interest than the whistling. On the vinyl version of the album, 'Fibre Book Troll' is simply bizarre. Long (11½ minutes), resolutely lo-fi (it was apparently recorded on an iPhone) and meandering; it almost gets quite jazzy in places. Smith doesn't just sound furious, he sounds deranged. It's simultaneously horrifying and strangely impressive.

Quit iPhone

Smith continues his anti-technology diatribe in 'Quit iPhone', this time expressing his feelings in a simple and direct fashion: 'Just quit using your phone... I don't want to look in people's home'. He does so over a conventional garage rock riff, one that sounds like a slowed-down take on 'Cock In My Pocket'. The group do their best to inject a bit of vigour into proceedings, but

---

[394] 'Using Richard Madeley's technology, Smith says he called one of his impersonators and left a message for him. 'I said, "I am Mark E Smith and every day I awake weeping over this intrusion. Please stop." Worked, but on the Fall websites everybody was saying what a bastard I was.'" The Twitter account that MES particularly objected to was a spoof one set up by a member of *The Fall Online Forum* (which several journalists took to be real, as well as – if the perpetrator is to be believed – ex-members enquiring about unpaid royalties). After an interview on ITV local news show *Granada Reports*, Smith asked the producer to appeal via Twitter for the account to cease, which it did, signing off with a final tweet, 'I love you Mark.' Richard Madeley was a reporter on *Granada Reports* in the early 80s which may at least partly explain Smith's garbled account.

the absence of any keyboards emphasises its workmanlike nature. Eleni still makes a valuable contribution, her clipped backing vocals providing a welcome contrast to Smith's phlegmy bark. His broken, drunken croon at the end ('my eye muscle is bright as I stare into the morn / and I see the citadel of media city shining bright') is weirdly touching. It was played live 25 times.

Reviews

Reviews were less polarised than was the case with the previous two albums, and were generally lukewarm. In *Dusted*, Jennifer Kelly was relatively upbeat, however, calling it a 'rabid punk deconstruction... Mark E. Smith continues to morph in unpredictable ways'. *The Skinny*'s Chris McCall thought it their best since *Reformation*: 'The sort of sharp garage rock nuggets that Smith is now best suited to.' Whilst admiring 'Venice' and 'Auto-Chip', Michael Hann of *The Guardian* felt that *Sub-Lingual Tablet* 'certainly has its share of Fall-by-numbers'. Devon Fisher was frustrated by the limited scope of the lyrics – 'the most coherent messages one can find throughout the album are that Smith thinks prescription drugs are overprescribed and isn't particularly fond of smartphones'. Some reviewers disagreed with Jennifer Kelly's assertion that the album was 'not evidence of stasis' and felt that the unusually settled line-up was indeed having a negative impact. *Pitchfork*'s Stuart Berman, for example, thought 'the distance between front man and backing band feels more pronounced than ever... the group churning out rehearsal-space warm-up exercises for Smith to spew over'. Luke Turner reiterated this point of view, suggesting that it was 'time for a purge':

> The trouble is, The Fall at the moment are too good. They're capable, muscular, increasingly boring. It's hard not to think of the times when a radical personnel overhaul has resulted in The Fall making some of their best work.

The album reached number 58 in the UK albums chart.

Evaluation

After *Re-Mit*'s playfulness and invention, *Sub-Lingual Tablet* feels a little like a backwards step, revisiting the unevenness and wilfully bloody-minded approach of *Ersatz*. Like *Ersatz*, there's a mix of highlights and underdeveloped or overstretched ideas. Outside of the bonkers 'Black Roof' and the squonky 'Dedication' and 'Junger', the group tend to rely on obvious kraut-garage riffery that they pull off admirably on occasions, but not with consistency.

Lyrically – to some extent at least – the album reverses the 'words-as-sound' trend notable on *Ersatz*, there being far more directly stated messages here. Smith's praise for Dave Eggers's *The Circle* – a dystopian take on the negative potential of social media - is interesting, as there is a clear thread that runs through the album of Smith's mistrust of technology and social media ('the Twitter'). This was, of course, nothing new – 'what's a computer?'; 'turn that bloody blimey Space Invader off!' – but here he occasionally falls back on an obvious and reactionary middle-aged curmudgeonly persona that verges on self-parody. Several reviews reflected on the effects of the group's unusually settled line-up, suggesting that this was encouraging stasis and mediocrity. Whilst this is largely unfair, you can't help feeling that Smith did not get as much out of his talented 'English musicians' here as he might have done.

New Facts Emerge
Recorded: Chairworks Studios, Castleford; 6dB Studio, Manchester; Hilltown
Studios, Colne, Lancashire
Released: 28th July 2017

Personnel:
Mark E Smith – vocals
Peter Greenway – guitar, synth, backing vocals
Dave Spurr – bass, Mellotron, backing vocals
Keiron Melling – drums

Chapter 33: New Facts Emerge

'An uncompromising, belligerent, hideous, beautiful idea... This, you imagine, is what the inside of Smith's fogged head sounds like.'

The group's first performance following *Sub-Lingual Tablet*'s release, in Liverpool on 13th May 2015, saw Daren Garratt back on second-drummer duty. The group played their cover of Captain Beefheart's 'Dropout Boogie' for the first time (although Smith had previously interpolated both the lyrics and melody of the song into 'Dr. Bucks' Letter' in a few 2004 performances). It was played again the next night in Birmingham, but only got one more outing after that. The group were busy over the summer festival season, playing at the Lunar Festival in Warwickshire, the Zanne Festival in Sicily and Green Man in Brecon. In Brecon, Smith was interviewed in front of a live audience by *Mojo* journalist Ben Thompson. MES was on amenable form, teasing Thompson remorselessly: 'Ask me some *Mojo* questions, like "What strings did you use?"'

The highlight of the group's summer was their triumphant performance at Glastonbury. At the time of writing, the whole performance is available on YouTube, and is simply one of the best examples of a full Fall set from the group's final years. A very visible stain on Smith's trousers led some to suggest that he had had an unfortunate pre-gig accident, but it was actually the result of him having champagne thrown over him backstage by a member of Fat White Family. It was a real shame that so many people focused so much on the state of Smith's trousers, as this was a remarkable performance, the passion and commitment of the musicians palpable throughout. Spurr is immense: solid, implacable, thunderous; Greenway is a model of calm amongst the chaos, churning out riffs with fluidity and impeccable timing; Melling is phenomenally tight and dynamic; Garratt's drumming meshes perfectly with his counterpart's, and his impassioned vocals (for example on 'Dedication') give the group's sound a whole new dimension. Eleni's contributions are more subtle, but no less vital, for example the reverberating synth line that runs through 'Hittite Man' and the intro to 'Junger Cloth'. A striking aspect of the performance is how much the group seem to be genuinely enjoying themselves. Smith's random bellow of 'Greenway!' during 'Sparta', for example, provokes beaming grins from both Melling and Greenway himself. There's also a touching interaction between Smith and Eleni during 'Pledge'.

In October, The Fall appeared at the Rockaway Beach Festival in Bognor Regis, where 'Wise Ol' Man' received its first outing.

> It was a bizarre sight to behold: The Fall – about as unwholesome a band as they come –playing in the 'Reds' venue, home to the legendary (and decidedly family-friendly) Butlin's Redcoats. Mark E. Smith snarled, barked and yelped incomprehensibly at a slowly depleting audience (you got the feeling a lot of people had just shown up to see what was on, and they couldn't handle what they found); but the band was tight [and] the fans up front clearly couldn't believe their luck at seeing their hero in such close proximity.

This was Daren Garratt's final gig. His departure was a noteworthy loss; he made a significant contribution to the Fall sound, despite only being in the line-up for just under two years. His partnership with Keiron Melling recaptured much of the spirit of the classic early-80s Burns-Hanley dual-drummer line-up. His vocal contributions – especially on stage – were also excellent.

After a couple more UK dates, the group set off on a seven-date Antipodean tour. At the penultimate performance in Melbourne, 'Tuff Life Booogie' was played for the first time in 25 years. In February 2016, the group released the *Wise Ol' Man* EP. Although often innovative, it wasn't quite the stand-alone piece of work that *The Remainderer* was; only two new songs (two versions of each) plus alternative takes of relatively recent songs and one live performance of a nearly 40-year-old tune. The opening version of the title track is driven by a typically tremolo-heavy three-note Greenway riff, supported strongly by Eleni's cool backing vocals. It's by no means clear who the 'man' in question is, although *The Annotated Fall* suggests a potential link to Manchester music promoter Alan Wise. The 'instrumental' version isn't actually an instrumental – it's a slightly different mix with less prominent vocals. The most striking piece on the EP is 'All Leave Cancelled', where the group recapture and extend the anarchic spirit of *The Remainderer*. Spurr's abrupt, chunky bassline is all that's holding the song together; otherwise, it feels like the whole thing would dissolve and collapse into itself. Grainy swirls of synth and guitar float about malignantly; the tempo stretches and contracts as nauseatingly as a dodgily-maintained fairground ride. Smith sounds on the verge of manic collapse and is even more surreal than usual: 'Who can't be trusted with a one half bucket of whiskey without injecting salad?' It's full of shifting moods, and the transitions in focus (for example the re-emergence of the main theme at 4:22) are thrilling. 'All Leave Cancelled (X)', is a brief, tight and controlled mini-version. The remix of 'Dedication' is pleasingly deranged; 'Venice With The Girls' has a slightly sharper sound than the album version, Eleni's keyboards being more conspicuous. An energetic 'Facebook Troll' merges clumsily into a live version of 'No Xmas For John Quays' recorded in Leeds, November 2014.

PopMatters commented that, 'Newcomers... won't be able to tell if *Wise Ol' Man* is the sound of a band firing on all cylinders or the sound of a band coming apart. Let it be known that The Fall never makes things easy, for neither themselves nor their fans.' *The Line Of Best Fit* described it as 'not entirely pointless, but it's far from an imperative addition to their output... it's quite obvious that their glory days are behind them; but the sporadic glimmers of promise mean that there's always hope for something better next time'.

The Fall's first 2016 gig took place in Tel Aviv in March. Smith delivered many of his vocals from the corner of the stage with his back to the audience. Although her keyboards were set up on stage, Eleni failed to appear at this gig, and did not even travel to Israel. Whilst she had missed gigs before (most recently in August 2014), this time it led to speculation that all was not well between her and Smith. This was largely fuelled by an interview for Israeli newspaper *Ha'aretz* which referred to 'a friend of Mark' called Pam. This was Pamela Vander, who was eventually to be Smith's final partner. Eleni was, however, back in the line-up for the next gig in Berlin 10 days later. The group's third 2016 date found them in Prestatyn, playing at the All Tomorrow's Parties festival curated by Stewart Lee. They opened with 'Unlimited Time Collection', an early version of 'Victoria Train Station Massacre' / 'New Facts Emerge'. Halfway through, Smith took the group off stage for one of his 'team talks'. Daren Garratt was in the audience, apparently having turned up not sure if he was playing or not. Eleni did not appear at the next two performances in Newcastle and Manchester. She reappeared, however, for the four dates that the group played at The Garage in London, 25th–28th April. On the third night, the group played an extravagant 'Auto Chip' that clocked in just short of 20 minutes.

The last of the four nights at The Garage marked Eleni's final appearance with The Fall. Reviews seem to suggest that she bowed out enthusiastically. On the *Fall Online Forum* Chris Goodhead remarked that she 'was just a ball of energy. She was filming the crowd... [and] seemed to be enjoying herself.' Eleni was another sad loss. Her contribution to the Fall sound is far too often overlooked, particularly her keyboard work, which – whilst never exactly virtuosic – frequently added creative layers of texture to the garage rock. Like Brix, her vocals were generally more successful when acting as counterpoint to MES rather than when she took the lead, but the part she played in The Fall's greatest 21st-century moments should not be underestimated.

Another Fall-related autobiography appeared in May, Brix's *The Rise, The Fall, and The Rise*. The middle part of the book that deals with her time in The Fall provides some interesting insights into relationships within the group and their creative processes. In particular, she captures vividly the horror show that was the autumn 1996 tour.

July 2016 saw The Fall return, albeit briefly, to a dual drummer line-up. Paul Bonney was an unlikely choice for the role, given that he was best known for his work with The Australian Pink Floyd Show. Bonney made his second and final appearance at Aberdeen in October. New songs continued to be introduced to the set throughout autumn. 'Fol De Rol' and 'Brillo De Facto' got their first outings at the Glasgow gig (the latter was originally entitled 'Brillo Filo'), and 'Gibbus Gibson' was debuted in Edinburgh on 3rd October. Their final gig of 2016 took place at York Fibbers on 19th November: it began with the first ever (comparatively brief) performance of 'Nine Out Of Ten'. In January 2017, 'Second House Now' was introduced in Liverpool and at Southampton the group played a more expansive version of 'Nine Out Of Ten' as well as debuting 'O! Zztrrk Man' (at this point entitled 'Zaptrack'). At Leamington Spa on 1st February, 'Reece Stick' got the first of its half a dozen outings. The song went down well with audiences, even though it consisted mainly of a lumbering, primitive riff and Smith just shouting the title repetitively. It was never recorded. After the Cardiff gig on 3rd February (where the group played a one-off cover of Eddie Cochran's 'Jeannie Jeannie Jeannie') it became clear that Smith was not in good health. The Newcastle and Leeds gigs scheduled for 23rd-24th February were cancelled owing to him having, according to the official website, 'influenza coupled with a chest infection'. The same happened with the Bristol date planned for 31st March.

On 5th March, Smith turned 60. Dave Haslam, reflecting on the occasion, admired how MES had, 'revolutionised the vocabulary of modern music. Amazing lyrics, tales of disorder, caustic dissections, hallucinations, wordplay.' The BBC celebrated the event by mistakenly reporting his death. In the same month, Keiron Melling was the victim of a vicious assault whilst travelling on a train between Manchester and Blackburn. He had intervened to defend a teenage boy from being harassed by two men, both of whom were jailed for the attack.

The Fall played at Belgrave Music Hall in Leeds on 23rd May where Michael Clapham (a Manchester comedy promoter) made his debut on keyboards, becoming the final new recruit to the group. Pete Greenway sported a new, fully shorn hairstyle, but more notably Smith appeared to be suffering from swelling to his face. *Counterfeit* published a respectful, sympathetic but reluctantly critical review of the gig. It recognised how well the musicians performed ('phenomenal, almost telepathically in sync, bags of energy and charisma, a faultless display'), but reported regretfully that Smith seemed to struggle with his performance:

> Despite visibly seeming uncomfortable and weary, Smith manfully battled through the early part of the set, but then he seemed to reach a point of no return. Repeatedly wondering off stage, taking the microphone with him and performing his vocals away from the glare of his adoring fans.

John Robb was relieved to see Smith 'back prowling the stage' at the group's appearance at Manchester's Transformer Festival on 28th May. Although recognising that Smith looked unwell, Robb thought that 'mentally he seems as acidic and on fire as ever, bellowing down his two mics and stalking the stage like his vision of Fiery Jack finally come to life'.

> The Fall are never meant to be easy but there is an added focus about their mithering tonight, Smith seems focussed in the maelstrom connecting directly with the audience with his baleful stares at the moshpit daring anyone to try and understand the message in his madness. It's impossible to hear a word he says in the reverbing room but somehow it all makes sense. You can feel his genius... as he glowers, cajoles and spits his brittle poetry over the churning backbeat.

The Fall's last gig before *New Facts Emerge*'s release was at London's 100 Club on 27th July, the day before the album came out. MES was visibly ill, his face now notably swollen, and he sang much of the gig from the dressing room. New partner Pamela Vander was prominent on stage, performing a sort of cheerleading role – dancing, prowling the stage, clasping hands with the front row, even climbing into the mosh pit at one point – to distract from Smith's prolonged absences from the stage.

New Facts Emerge

Most of the music was recorded at Chairworks. The vocals were done mainly at 6dB, but some were recorded at Keiron Melling's Hilltown studio in Colne, where the drummer also mixed the album. Pamela Vander provided the cover artwork. The garish, almost childlike simplicity of the design is a good match for the album's brash and enthusiastic contents. As well as the CD, it was released on vinyl as a double 10", this time the tracks being the same versions and in the same order.

There was minor controversy regarding the title of 'Victoria Train Station Massacre'. A couple of months before the album's release, a suicide bomber had killed 23 people and injured 139 at an Ariana Grande concert at Manchester Arena, which is adjacent to the station. A Cherry Red representative stated that this was an 'unfortunate coincidence... The track was recorded and the artwork sent off for manufacture long before the terrible events in Manchester.'

Segue

There's something exceptionally Fall-like about calling an opening track 'Segue', and few other artists have explored the 'inebriated-tramp-hits-a-bottle-with-a-stick' genre. One *Annotated Fall* contributor proposed that the track might actually be a segue between 'All Leave Cancelled (X)' and 'Fol De Rol', although this suggests an unlikely amount of strategic thinking on Smith's part.

Fol De Rol

The first 'proper' song almost immediately launches into one of the unforgiving, bludgeoning riffs that characterise much of the album. Here, the weighty, staccato guitar part is derived from Black Sabbath via Rocket From The Crypt;[395] it's also not a million miles away from that played by Craig Scanlon on 'Fortress'. The precise rigidity of the riff works well in contrast to Smith's layered, off-kilter snarl. Two-thirds of the way through,

---

[395] Sabbath: 'Zero The Hero', from their 1983 album *Born Again*, the only one they recorded with ex-Deep Purple vocalist Ian Gillan. Rocket From The Crypt: 'On A Rope', their 1996 single.

everything is sucked into a chaotic, murky void before bursting forth again with renewed vigour.

The Annotated Fall commented that, 'With every album that goes by, transcribing becomes more difficult.' It's true that, by this stage, trying to interpret Smith's words feels even more futile than it did with *Ersatz GB*; the sound of his voice has become as much an instrument as what the musicians are playing. Here, there are several references to Homer ('kitchens Homeric', 'Homeric metal') as well as puzzling phrases such as 'you block hotel area / with metal wedge potato'. You just have to roll with the gloriously incongruous language: 'Homeric cogs of steel / imaginary / excite plastic wheels'. It was played live 21 times.

Brillo De Facto

Another heavy riff, but although it's just as relentless as 'Fol De Rol', it's more supple and has a slight tinge of both funk and R&B to it. The lithe choppiness of Greenway's guitar is vaguely reminiscent of Wilko Johnson's work on Dr. Feelgood's 'Roxette'. Melling provides a solid, unfussy foundation that still manages to provide some rhythmic complexity. The main section is interspersed with slow, ponderous interludes full of reverb-heavy, ghostly sounds. Over the final third, the group launch into a crescendo that resolves into a wall of feedback.

Again, Smith's voice is deployed as a shifting, textured instrument rather than providing any sort of coherent melodic narrative. In the first 30 seconds, the vocal is relatively straightforward, sitting traditionally in the centre of the mix. At 0:39 it descends into muffled distortion; thereafter its stereo placement, equalisation and level of distortion and reverb all veer wildly across the musical background, differing versions of MES overlapping and clashing. At 1:04, for example, a bright, trebly snarl in one channel is complemented by a disturbingly deep, guttural groan in the other. At 2:18, a double-tracked, almost robotic Smith plays backing vocalist to a lead voice that switches between crisp bark and murky growl.

It's possible that the first word of the title might be some sort of reference to facial hair ('Brillo chin'), especially as this was a topic about which Smith expressed strong feelings several times over the years. Interestingly, given the vague musical nod to Dr. Feelgood, Smith himself suggested a link to their singer Lee Brilleaux: 'It's Lee Brilleaux out of Dr. Feelgood, but this track's better than Dr. Feelgood. Imagine it played by Motörhead, with Pete's guitar.' There's also a reference to James Fennings, a DJ who provided pre-performance music for the group around the turn of the century, and was a long-standing friend of Smith's. However, beyond the occasional recognisable reference, the lyric is beautifully abstract: 'and the asphyxiation of the troll will finally be… all salute at the altar of filo pastry'. 'Brillo' was played live 19 times.

Victoria Train Station Massacre / New Facts Emerge

Although named as two separate songs on the album, 'Victoria' and the title track are basically parts one and two of the same song. The main difference between the two is Greenway's guitar, which, relatively understated in the first section, bursts into life in the second, providing a crunchy, boisterous riff that anchors the rest of the track. Another distinguishing feature is the deployment of reversed vocals from around the minute mark. Anyone wondering whether this might contain some form of subliminal 'Stairway To Heaven'/Judas Priest-style satanic message will be disappointed to learn that it's just the 'I crave drama' refrain from earlier in the song played backwards. As mentioned above, the song's title attracted some minor controversy. Speaking to *Uncut*, Smith elaborated on the subject matter:

> I'm actually very fond of the architecture of Victoria Station, but it's all been trashed to fuck, and that's what the song's about. You know all that beautiful Victorian latticework, like they have at Paddington? They ripped it all off. And you know why? Because the students coming to Manchester wanted to have access to north Manchester [pauses]. We don't want 'em here [laughs]! So they put this big canvas canopy up, and about six months ago it fell on all the passengers in the rush hour.[396]

[396] According to the *Manchester Evening News*, 18th October 2016, 'the plastic panel – part of the station's new "bubble" roof – is believed to have cracked then given way due to the weight of a build-up of rainwater'.

The lyrics focused around the nonsensical if weirdly charming exhortation to 'stop shaking down those frogs'. The indistinct backing vocals (in French) at 0:58 and 1:48 were supplied by studio engineer Christophe Bride; the words are adapted from Jacques Brel's 'Les Bourgeois'.[397] The song is a joyful, spirited stomp. Relentless and intense, like much of the first half of the album, it is nonetheless laced with good humour and carefree abandon. It was played live 22 times.

Couples Vs Jobless Mid 30s

Despite Smith's oft-stated derision for the 'dinosaurs' of the 70s, The Fall wandered into prog territory on several occasions over their career, albeit in their own inimitable fashion. 'Couples' is arguably the most prog of all Fall songs, described by Tom Pinnock of *Uncut* as 'an unhinged multi-part suite that veers from lumbering rock grooves complete with manic laughter to sections of chanting and detuned Mellotron'. It opens with an intense, reverberating refrain that sounds like the Butthole Surfers jamming with Hawkwind. At 1:15, a ponderous, sludge-rock riff lumbers into view, backed by wildly oscillating synths. After a rather clumsy edit at 1:48, Spurr's throbbing bassline backs a random assortment of layered vocals and manic cackling. Following a reprise of the heavy doom-metal riff (interspersed with snatches of pulsing sequencer, off-key operatic vocals, disturbing crooning and further cackling) the song resolves into a taut, thunderous coda. The section from 'waiting...' (6:18) is breathtaking: the way that the group suddenly navigate themselves out of the dense, swampy chaos of the first six minutes into a focused gallop towards the song's conclusion is thrilling.

Keiron Melling and Pete Greenway described the song's conception:

> Melling: We started 'Couples Vs Jobless' in a hotel room and recorded it with the whole band going through a guitar amp, and the vocals on a dictaphone.

[397] The title track of Brel's 1962 album. The original lyrics translate as, 'The bourgeoisie are like pigs, the older they get, the more they become cunts.' (Brel never sang the final 'con' (cunt), although it was implied by the rhyme.)

Greenway: [It] was conceived in a hotel room. Mark came up with the idea to do this long, operatic thing with chanting, and we took him at his word and did it. A very odd song.

Smith's version was inevitably different. According to him, having left the group in Chairworks Studios 'for a week or so', he then created 'Couples' by 'savaging' three or four of the songs they'd come up with. He went on: 'They were trying to do something about Eagles of Death Metal, and about heavy metal groups. I said, "That's not on," because they were the group in Paris, weren't they? So I changed it to all this.' Eagles of Death Metal (a Californian band co-founded by Queens of the Stone Age's Josh Homme) were indeed the 'group in Paris'.[398] A reference to the group remains – you can hear their name in the faux-operatic backing vocals from 3:46.

Smith offered a terse summary of the song's meaning: 'This fucking woman is shouting at her young son who owns a factory.' This presumably refers to the lines, 'his mother spouse / she tortures him in big house'. It's hard to know what to make of 'gargoyle legs are droopy', 'irrelevant to your latent sex and shock your lizard' or the reference to Snow White and the Seven Dwarfs ('Heigh Ho!') – it's advisable to simply revel in the wonderfully abstruse language: 'clotted breath... upwardly B.T. rancid laughter'. 'Couples' was never played live.

Second House Now
The first *NFE* track to emerge publicly (via BBC Radio 6 Music), 'House' opens with a minute or so of indolent, affable rockabilly that's totally at odds with the first half of the album. At 0:49, however, the group kick into a brawny riff that echoes the approach of many of the earlier songs. The music is once again taut and punchy and contrasts effectively with Smith's meandering delivery. However, although his voice is frequently drenched in reverb, it's more centred in the mix than previous songs and

---

[398] On 13th November 2015, a series of co-ordinated terrorist attacks took place in Paris. At Bataclan concert hall, where the Eagles of Death Metal were playing, gunmen killed 89 people.

doesn't have quite as much emphasis on overlapping layers and effects (although there's a nice touch of megaphone-style backing vocals at 3:25). This gives the song a more direct and forceful feel. Spurr and Melling are customarily solid, giving Greenway the opportunity to embellish the song with several flourishes: woozy phasing (for example at 1:13), urgent shrieks (1:26 and 2:24) and overloaded, distorted bursts of J. Mascis-style solo guitar during the last minute or so.

One of Pamela Vander's Instagram posts is possibly relevant to the title and lyric: '[we] found a second home a couple of years back, moved in, set up shop. Total privacy. He loved it there, wrote a lot, walked in the garden...' When it emerged in July 2021 that Smith's old Sedgley Park house had been put on the market, the estate agent's web page containing several pictures of its dilapidated interior, Pam was quick to react to the somewhat overwrought online reaction:

> Mark was long DONE with that house. It was in a total state w/no working kitchen and many other major problems, the place was falling apart and Mark himself named it the 'House of Doom'... that's why we moved out, hence 'Second House Now' on the *New Facts Emerge* album... he passed in peace somewhere clean and warm and where he felt safe & free, with me.

Robert Brokenmouth saw a political message in the song:

> MES often hints at the social origins of Nazism... in his lyrics. The title 'Second House Now' echoes the chant popularised by the Communist Party and their adherents in UK from late 1942, 'Second Front Now'... This ties in with the lyrics to 'Couples Vs Jobless mid-30s' as well, the way in which large chunks of the young population are both disregarded and used as fodder, forcing their ambitions to be selfish and unthreatening to those genuinely in power.

There's a looping, circular quality to the lyrics; certain phrases ('going to big city', 'my image in black and white', 'tearing of muscle years') revolve at differing tempos like orbiting planets, as if Smith is gradually zooming in on some sort of resolution. This resolution never actually arrives, and ultimately the lyric is never fully coherent; but however one might evaluate it intellectually, there's a distinctly visceral effect here. The aggressive yet plaintive repeated exhortation, 'C'mon, c'mon!', incongruous in its adherence to traditional rock'n'roll tropes, is genuinely moving because of the gleeful and apparently non-ironic way Smith delivers it. Knowing that Smith was aware at this point that his days were numbered makes his unfettered joy and enthusiasm all the more poignant. It didn't get quite as many outings as some on the LP, being played live only ten times.

O! Zztrrk Man

Here, Smith's voice is frankly disturbing: sluggish, fractured, disdainful, inebriated and unworldly. The song (which bears more than a passing resemblance to Gary Numan's 'M.E.') is strangely uplifting. It sounds like several Stooges tracks being played simultaneously through a broken transistor radio. It's a celebration of the joy of thrashing the hell out of everything; of the power of three simple but devastating chords; of the unmitigated joy of just... noise for the sake of glorious noise. There is always great pleasure to be had from an impeccably timed chord change, and here, at 0:53, there's a shift that lifts the soul. Throughout, Greenway wrestles a grimy, guttural sound from his guitar that captures the spirit of thousands of teenagers in garages and rehearsal rooms stamping on effects pedals in furrowed-brow expressions of frustration and hope. Played live only five times, all in early 2017, it was the 19th and final Fall song to feature an exclamation mark in the title.

Gibbus Gibson

'Gibbous' is a word that Smith took from H. P. Lovecraft and used in both 'Van Plague?' and 'Hittite Man'. As for the rest of the name, *The Annotated Fall* suggests a link to Gordon Gibson of Action Records. Greenway's clipped, circular riff is complemented well by Smith's wobbly vocal. In the final minute, a chirpy keyboard line crops up that's soon superseded by some incongruous 80s-style synth chords. It was never played live.

Groundsboy

Another track with a light-hearted, sprightly feel. There's a shuffling, railroad-style rhythm that brings Johnny Cash to mind; the backing vocals also give it a 60s comedy-Western soundtrack atmosphere. It has been suggested that the song refers to Steve Hanley's post-Fall career as a school caretaker although there's little in the lyric itself to really support this. It was debuted the night before *New Facts Emerge*'s release, and was then played at the group's two final gigs.

Nine Out Of Ten

It is fitting that the final song on the last Fall LP is such a challenging and perplexing one. Pared down to Greenway's galloping, abrasive guitar (played in the style of Billy Bragg on *Life's A Riot*) and Smith's wilfully tuneless vocal, 'Nine Out Of Ten' sees Smith display what *theartsdesk* described as 'reckless vulnerability'. It was played at seven consecutive gigs around the turn of 2016-17, but didn't appear in the group's final seven performances. John Robb suggested that the song was 'an acidic dark humoured snark attack' on him for having given Ed Blaney's recent album a good review. Whilst it is true that Smith mentioned him in the song's third performance in Southampton on 27th January ('I got a review from John Robb') this doesn't really sound much like an 'attack'; it's possible that he just improvised the line having spotted Robb in the audience.

The vocals on 'Nine Out Of Ten' are more clearly audible and the words much less surreal and abstract than is the case with the rest of the album. This does not make them any easier to interpret, however. It's far from clear who the 'they' that gave him 9/10 are, although 'the company' could plausibly represent the numerous record labels that he dealt with throughout his career. Although 'You don't break rules you don't follow them' doesn't appear – on paper at least – to be especially cryptic, Smith's typically unpredictable phrasing and emphasis make it difficult to unravel.

It's unclear whether Smith is suggesting that he has been unfairly criticised for following (or not following) rules, or whether he is exhorting others to follow (or not follow) said rules.

It's hard to imagine any other artist stopping a song so abruptly halfway through – it's an inelegant edit even by Fall standards – and then letting a lone guitar simply hammer out the riff unaccompanied for a full five minutes. In the first half, there seem to be two guitar parts that are given some stereo separation which alleviates the spartan harshness of the sound at least a little. This is not the case in the coda, however; this is the sound of a solitary, almost desperate guitar with no clear hope of conclusion or resolution. In 2019, Pete Greenway commented on the song's recording:

> We didn't know at the time that it would be the last album and I'm sure Mark didn't. People have drawn conclusions from the last track, 'Nine Out Of Ten', and how it ends [without vocals for the second half]. I'd met Mark for a beer and we ended up at the studio. I was too drunk to play and Mark just spouted lyrics about his life, spontaneously. I was surprised it ended up on the album.

David Cavanagh provides a poignant account of the song's conclusion:

> He was animated as he sang his final vocal for the album... with guitarist Greenway seated beside him. The song came to a natural end. Greenway stopped playing. 'No,' Smith said. 'Play it again.' He got up and walked slowly around the studio, tapping bits of percussion, while Greenway strummed the chords for three, four, then five minutes.
> And that's exactly how we hear it on the record. The track ends. The guitar resumes. But Mark E Smith is now silent.

Reviews
Although *The Guardian*'s Rachel Aroesti was unenthusiastic about the group continuing 'to plough a familiar, fractious furrow', reviews were mostly positive. In *The Quietus*, Harry Sword

described the group as 'a physical place, almost: some sideways dimension where you tap into coded truths, odd anomalies and sinister parallels among the static, phlegm and hard rain'. He felt that The Fall were as necessary as ever: 'This kind of music is needed, right now: untethered, shot through with rough-shod immediacy, anchored by punishing bass weight, grinding repetition and stark pounding rhythm.' In *Mojo*, Ian Harrison awarded the album four stars, praising its 'raw music, stimulating confusion and... monstrous glee'. *Drowned In Sound*'s Marc Burrows described the group's current incarnation as, 'Not just an institution, but an idea. An uncompromising, belligerent, hideous, beautiful idea; where noise pollution and bloody mindedness hover on the edge of art.' The Fall in 2017, he felt, were 'the purest version of the band there has ever been. This, you imagine, is what the inside of Smith's fogged head sounds like.' Regarding Smith's vocals, he went on to say:

> Here Smith finally lets go of the idea of singing at all. You're sure there are fine words here, but more than ever MES is really not bothered if you can make them out or not. His voice has dropped into a guttural, tarry growl, 100% menace and 0% melody.

John Robb, writing for *Louder Than War*, described it as 'one of the five greatest Fall albums ever'. He gave the album 9/10, wryly noting that he did so because of the final track's 'snark attack... otherwise it would have been a ten'.

Evaluation

A common criticism of *New Facts Emerge* is that it finds the group over-reliant on blunt, unsubtle riffs and lacking in intricacy and sophistication. Whilst it does have more than its fair share of bludgeoning riffery (especially in the first half), this view is not entirely fair. For a start, the production on Smith's vocals on, for example, 'Fol De Rol' and 'Brillo' demonstrates fascinating creativity. Moreover, the second half contains substantial variation and light-heartedness. It is true that the sequencing is a little perverse, giving the album a certain lop-sided feel. That said, it seems fitting that the group's final LP should exhibit a trait that was such a long-standing feature of their work.

Despite Smith's career-long aversion to nostalgia and contempt for 'look back bores', some commentators detected a sense of reminiscence about *New Facts Emerge*; a reflective review of his life and career. One contributor to *The Annotated Fall*, for example, suggests that it is 'a bit of a grab-bag Fall album – lots of homages to past career stylings, knowing it was potentially his last record...' The lyrics of 'Groundsboy' could plausibly be interpreted in this way: 'He goes back now... every day on the airstrip' perhaps referring to the group's productivity and work ethic; 'noticed by none' a reinforcement of the underappreciation of the Hip Priest. Certainly much of The Fall's musical past is recalled here: the garage rock of *Are You Are Missing Winner* and *Cerebral Caustic*; the rockabilly shuffle of 'Fiery Jack'; the Stooges-style 'Elves'; the prog subversion seen in several B-sides and obscurities.

It's hard to believe, given the growing intensity of his medical treatment, that it hadn't at least crossed Smith's mind that this record might be his last. Despite the album's sense of finality, however, Greenway, Spurr and Melling have insisted that they did not feel at the time that *New Facts Emerge* was going to be The Fall's last release.

> We'd already booked a studio to make the next record. A big cottage. And we were going to get Grant Showbiz to bring a mobile rig and set-up in this cottage and turn it into a recording studio and take however long it takes to make the album.

New Facts Emerge isn't the intricate, articulate wordplay of *Grotesque*; it isn't the dense, angular aggression of *Hex Enduction Hour*; it isn't the perfect pop/post-punk cocktail of *This Nation's Saving Grace*; it isn't the forward-facing merger of garage punk and electronica of *The Unutterable* or *Real New...* What it is, is the sound of well-deployed resources; a group that knows its strengths and limitations intimately. The sound of musicians that have developed a deep, fundamental understanding of how each other play and have locked on to a forceful expression of that understanding. It is also the sound of a man who has 'let go of the idea of singing' but still understands the power that his voice commands.

Overleaf: Mark E Smith, Queen Margaret Union, Glasgow, 4th November 2017 – The Fall's final performance. (Photo by Phil Lancaster)

Epilogue

'I would have had an utterly different life without The Fall. It's hard to know what will replace that...'

The week after *New Facts Emerge*'s release, Smith was due to appear at an event at the Imperial War Museum North in Manchester, part of an exhibition called *Wyndham Lewis: Life, Art, War.* Smith's contribution was billed as *Responding to a Rebel: Mark E. Smith Agent of Chaos,* 'a performance of speeches, poems and ramblings driven by roaring live percussion, vintage cassette players and large-scale projections from IWM's archive'. The event sounded intriguing, but sadly never happened, cancelled on the day owing to Smith's poor health. Illness also forced him to pull out of a planned appearance in *No End to Enderby,* a film installation project for Manchester International Festival to mark the centenary of novelist Anthony Burgess's birth. Co-director Graham Eatough, commenting on Smith's withdrawal, said that 'a brilliant lost day [with MES] taught us why he couldn't be in it'.[399] The group were also booked to play a five-night residence at Baby's All Right in Brooklyn in September. Demand was such – the Friday and Saturday night dates sold out in ten minutes – that two further performances were added. The Fall were also due to play at the Cropped Out festival in Louisville, Kentucky. Once again, however, Smith's health resulted in cancellations. On 25th August, Pamela Vander – by now acting as the group's manager – announced that:

> It is with great regret to announce that Mark E. Smith & The Fall have had to cancel all upcoming U.S shows... due mostly to terrible timing, reality and a mix of bizarre and rare (true to form) medical issues that Mark is currently

---

[399] *Enderby's Dark Lady, or No End to Enderby* is a 1984 novel by Anthony Burgess. MES expressed admiration for the author on several occasions.

being treated for. Unfortunately it would be a gamble on his health to fly anywhere over the next couple of months. Mark's current problems are connected to his throat, mouth/dental & respiratory system... so throwing all the meds together and continuing with the travel/shows would certainly harm any progress that we have made over the past few weeks.

The group didn't perform again until 20th October, when they played Unity Works in Wakefield. Smith performed in a wheelchair and sang the last third of the gig from off-stage. He delivered a forceful performance of opener 'Wolf Kidult Man', but 'Blindness' was tentative, as if the group weren't entirely sure of how to deliver the song without his prowling and amp-fiddling. There was, inevitably, much discussion regarding Smith's appearance on the *Fall Online Forum*:

It felt a bit like there was a sharp intake of breath. A collective, unspoken sense of shock and perhaps sadness. And a sense of what's going to happen now, am I going to witness something I'd rather not have seen. And once he'd been positioned, it was straight into 'Wolf Kidult Man'. And it was OK. He had two microphones. The audience now seemed to be holding its breath. Willing him on.

Three nights later, the group played at The Boiler Shop in Newcastle, where Smith appeared to be in better shape and managed over 45 minutes on stage before performing the last three songs from the dressing room. He looked as if he was itching to get out of his wheelchair; during 'Blindness' his glance at Greenway (who had been fiddling with his pedals for the previous 15 seconds or so) suggested a strong desire to work his 'magic' on the guitarist's amp.

The Fall's final live performance took place on Saturday 4th November 2017 in Glasgow. The gig had been due to take place at Òran Mór, where the group had played the previous year. On the 25th August, however, it was announced that demand for tickets had been such that it was to be moved to the larger Queen

Margaret Union. Peter Ross, reviewing the gig for *The Telegraph*, described Smith's entrance:

> Smith had begun singing the opener, 'Wolf Kidult Man', from the wings, rising up behind a speaker stack on a wheelchair lift and then wheeled centre-stage to cheers and raised fists. It didn't feel awkward or pitiable, it felt triumphant, a grand entrance...

A YouTube video, 'Final stage entrance by Mark E Smith of The Fall' has, at the time of writing, had well over 70,000 views. There is, however, a longer, better quality one posted by Mike Ritchie, '1DynamicEntrance'. It's hard to imagine anyone who has any interest in The Fall failing to be moved by the crowd's welcome for MES at 1:26. Smith had sufficient energy to wheel himself around the stage and indulge in some of his customary knob-twiddling. Peter Ross described him as 'a compelling presence... He never spoke to the sell-out crowd, acknowledged no applause. Even when the music was at its most furious, he maintained a regal blankness.'

The group were due to play in Portugal a couple of weeks later, but this was cancelled. They were also scheduled to perform in Bristol on 29th November. This was again abandoned, this time moments before showtime. A clearly emotional Dave Spurr announced the news to the crowd; a similarly distraught Pete Greenway couldn't even bring himself to speak. The next day, Pamela Vander announced on Instagram that the 30th November date at London's KOKO would also not go ahead. She included a message from Smith himself. It's a remarkable thing: 100 or so words that display a tenderness, humility and affection almost totally at odds with virtually everything he ever uttered over the previous 40 years.

> A Message to All, to All. From Mark E. Smith/The Fall group. As I, like Pr Rupert leave Bristol with my tail between my legs, I wish to give my great apologies to everybody. This idiotic idea to do both shows was purely my idea, against the advice of Pamela and The Fall group,

agent & promoter. Hope to replace shows within 4 – 6 weeks. In the interim we have eight new songs ready to go and will try and let you hear a few before Christmas. From head patient to you, the patients. I love you all but cannot embrace you all, Mark E. Smith.[400]

On 24th January 2018, it was announced that Smith had died. His struggle with lung and kidney cancer (first diagnosed in 2009, although he enjoyed several years in the clear after his operation that year) was at an end. Marc Riley was broadcasting his Radio 6 Music show when the BBC confirmed the news. Riley, clearly emotional, commented that 'we're just getting to grips with it now' before playing an uninterrupted sequence of Fall songs: 'It's The New Thing', 'Oh! Brother' and 'Edinburgh Man'. The nine o'clock handover between Riley and Gideon Coe was another emotional moment. Coe's show was superb, an eclectic mix of Fall tracks and songs the group covered (for example The Sonics' 'Strychnine' and Sir Gibbs' 'People Grudgeful') interspersed with messages from Fall fans. It was an outstanding piece of impromptu broadcasting.

Some Fall fans sit firmly in the 'early 80s as golden age' camp; some believe the 21st century saw them expand their perimeters and ambitions and create some of their most innovative and remarkable music; most reside in one of the myriad positions in between. But what united all Fall fans following Smith's death was the sense of loss on realising that we would now never hear another new Fall album. No more 'returns to form' or 'best album since...'; no more patchy 'what-could-have-been' LPs; no more 'sudden-change-in-direction-with-a-completely-new-line-up' moments, just... no more.

Smith's sisters published a statement on the official website: 'Mark had a great life and loved and lived it to the full and always by his own rules and we, as his sisters were privileged to be part

---

[400] The 'cannot embrace you all' phrase has been attributed to Napoleon, although it's not entirely clear the exact words he used. It features (at 9:41) in the 1970 film *Waterloo*. Smith had used the line before: 'I LOVE YOU ALL, MEIN COMRADES, But I cannot embrace you all-because, in the main, I have pulled out the lap-top lead to use as a handy throttling device for mediaists, activists, groupies and Alan Wise (show not on ever).' ('A message from Mark E Smith', *The Quietus*, 21st May 2008.)

of it too. Mark is at peace now and pain free, but we, his three sisters have been left heartbroken and will miss our big brother very much.'

Whilst some media tributes smacked of a hurried, 'copy-and-paste-from-Wikipedia' approach (usually misquoting the 'granny with bongos' line), many were thoughtful and heartfelt. In *The Guardian*, Adam Sweeting said that 'Smith's work defied categorisation, combining as it did elements of satire, social commentary, grumbling misanthropy and an abiding enthusiasm for cunning wordplay.' Dave Simpson described him as 'ever the contrarian, but if there was one thing that was predictable about him, it was his commitment to the Fall... Music has lost one of its most distinctive, inimitable characters.' Frank Skinner tweeted: 'I loved him. He was quite simply better than all the rest. I thought he'd live forever. He seemed too belligerent to die. But he has and oh the difference to me.' Long-time devotee Stewart Lee commented, 'I will miss the adventure of being a Fall fan and of being part of this community of people... who had this begrudging loyalty to it. I would have had an utterly different life without The Fall. It's hard to know what will replace that.'

Pamela Vander posted two particularly touching photos on Instagram. One finds MES contemplating the flowers in their garden; the other is especially poignant – Smith is walking down a woodland path, fag in hand, a spring in his step. It is captioned 'So thank you, near and far, for being fans of Mark E. Smith. For loving him and believing in him and his sounds and visions. We have lost a genius. Life, the written word and music will never, ever be the same. But we will feel Mark whenever it rains, and whenever the music plays.'

And so, this was where the music stopped. The simplicity of the message posted on the official website is perhaps the best place to end: 'RIP Chief'.

Appendix 1: The Fall's Peel Sessions
(and other radio broadcasts)

Appendix 1:
The Fall's Peel Sessions (and other radio broadcasts)

*'As for the irreplaceable Peel, these discs say
more about the man's broadcasting ethos than a
thousand broadsheet obituaries.'*

Virtually every obituary of Mark E Smith that appeared in January 2018 made reference to John Peel's love of The Fall. Of course, the quotation that best sums up Peel's feelings about the group is 'you must get them all', but the two that journalists most often went for in these pieces were 'always different, always the same' and 'a band by which in our house all others are judged'. The former phrase was used by Peel several times (in a variety of forms) to describe The Fall, the first occasion probably being on 11th May 1987: after playing 'Twister', he remarked, 'The mighty Fall – always the same and always different; can you ask for anything more?'[401] The latter came from a radio interview in 1998 and the full quotation was: 'But The Fall have given me more pleasure, over a longer period of time, than any other band. And when people ask me why, I always say gnomically, "They're always different, always the same." I'm not sure that that means anything but it sounds reasonably good. They're just The Fall – a band by which, in our house, all the others are judged.'

The Fall recorded 24 Peel sessions, more than any other artist.[402] They also dominated his Festive Fifty, achieving more entries (89) than the next two on the list (The Wedding Present and The Smiths) combined. But the relationship went further than that.

---

[401] On his show of 5th February 1994, he said, 'Always the same, always different, as I've said before.' In fact, Peel was recycling a phrase that he'd used previously in a different context. Speaking to *Melody Maker* in 1983 about the forthcoming 1000th edition of *Top of the Pops*, he remarked that 'All that [*TOTP*] does is present what's popular – the only thing they can vary is the packaging. The content is always the same but always different.'

[402] As The Wedding Present did 13 and his side project Cinerama 11, David Gedge might claim a tie with some justification. The nearest other rivals were Ivor Cutler (22); Loudon Wainwright III (16); Michael Chapman, Half Man Half Biscuit, Fairport Convention, Incredible String Band and Vivian Stanshall (12); Thin Lizzy and Billy Bragg (11).

The Fall were a seemingly constant presence on Peel's show; so much so that someone was able to compile nearly three minutes of Peel just saying 'The Fall'.

The Complete Peel Sessions 1978-2004

The 6-CD box set was released on 25th April 2005 on Castle Music. It was not the first time that The Fall's Peel session tracks had been officially released. 1987's *The Peel Sessions EP* consisted of the second session from December 1978 and the 1993 EP *Kimble* contained (across its three different formats) five tracks selected from 1981-92 Peel appearances. The compilation album *The Peel Sessions* (assembled by Steve Hanley) was released in 1999. The double CD *Words Of Expectation* emerged in 2003, containing sessions 1-5, 19 and 20. In addition, by the time of the box set's release, several reissues of the group's early albums had already included related session tracks.

The Complete Peel Sessions, as its name suggested, included every single one of the 97 tracks that the group recorded for Peel. Whilst it received universally enthusiastic reviews, this didn't lead to huge sales – although it should be remembered that this was a relatively expensive box set. It reached number 139 on its first release; number 97 when it was reissued in 2013.

The box set is an immense, fascinating and inspiring collection. There are few better ways to spend seven hours of your time than to sit and listen to one of the greatest, most complex musical stories ever told.

Peel Session Facts

- The group recorded 97 tracks for Peel, of which 95 were broadcast 'normally' as part of a session. 'Job Search' was played separately 19 days after session #24; 'Whizz Bang' (recorded for session #13) was not broadcast.
- The total duration of The Fall's Peel session tracks was 7 hours, five minutes and 37 seconds. The average length of the sessions (as broadcast) was 17:26.

- The longest sessions were:
    Session #6 (31:29)
    Session #24 (24:08)
    Session #9 (20:51)
- The shortest sessions were:
    Session #1 (10:36)
    Session #18 (10:48)
    Session #13 (12:07)
- The biggest gap between sessions was 4 years, 4 months – between session #22 (18/10/98) and session #23 (19/2/03); the second largest was 1 year, 10 months – between session #2 (27/11/78) and session #3 (16/9/80).
- The smallest gap between sessions was 4 months – between session #8 (14/5/85) and session #9 (29/9/85); the second smallest was 6 months – between session #1 (30/5/78) and session #2 (27/11/78).
- The average gap between sessions was 14 months.
- 30 different people appeared on a Fall Peel session at least once:
    24: Mark E Smith
    19: Steve Hanley
    16: Craig Scanlon
    11: Simon Wolstencroft
    10: Karl Burns
    9: Brix Smith
    5: Paul Hanley
    4: Marc Riley / Dave Bush / Julia Nagle / Simon Rogers
    3: Martin Bramah
    2: Yvonne Pawlett / Marcia Schofield / Kenny Brady / Lucy Rimmer / Ben Pritchard / Jim Watts / Eleni Poulou
    1: Steve Davis / Dave Tucker / John Rolleson / Neville Wilding / Karen Leatham / Tom Head / Speth Hughes / Dave Milner / Steve Trafford / Spencer Birtwistle / Ed Blaney
- Sessions 15-17 were the only ones where the line-up was the same for three consecutive sessions (MES / Scanlon / S. Hanley / Bush / Wolstencroft).

- There were only two other occasions where the line-up remained the same for two sessions in a row: sessions 8-9 (MES / Brix / Scanlon / S. Hanley /Rogers / Burns) and sessions 10-11 (MES / Brix / Scanlon / S. Hanley / Rogers / Wolstencroft).
- Adam Helal and Una Baines were the longest-serving members of the group never to play on a Peel session. Neither Tommy Crooks nor Tony Friel ever made it to Maida Vale either.

The Peel Sessions

Session 1
Recorded: 30th May 1978
Broadcast: 15th June 1978
Mark E Smith – vocals; Martin Bramah – guitar, bass, vocals; Yvonne Pawlett – keyboards; Karl Burns – drums; Steve Davies – congas

Futures And Pasts / Mother-Sister! / Rebellious Jukebox / Industrial Estate

The Fall's Peel debut saw bassist Eric 'The Ferret' McGann quit because of conga player Steve Davies's Hawaiian shirt, leaving Martin Bramah to contribute both bass and guitar. The confident sharpness to the songs belied the group's lack of studio experience at this point.

Session 2
Recorded: 27th November 1978
Broadcast: 6th December 1978
Mark E Smith – vocals; Martin Bramah – guitar, bass, vocals; Yvonne Pawlett – keyboards; Marc Riley – bass; Karl Burns – drums

Put Away / Mess Of My / No Xmas For John Quays / Like To Blow

The impressive 'Mess Of My' was an early example of the group producing a top-notch song for Peel that they never recorded elsewhere.

Session 3

Recorded: 16th September 1980

Broadcast: 24th September 1980

Mark E Smith – vocals; Marc Riley – guitar; Craig Scanlon – guitar; Steve Hanley – bass; Paul Hanley – drums

Container Drivers / Jawbone And The Air-Rifle / New Puritan / New Face In Hell

An awe-inspiring paradigm shift in the group's sound. Like 'Mess Of My', the astonishing 'New Puritan' was never 'properly' recorded other than here.

Session 4

Recorded: 24th March 1981

Broadcast: 31st March 1981

Mark E Smith – vocals; Marc Riley – guitar; Craig Scanlon – guitar; Steve Hanley – bass; Paul Hanley – drums; Dave Tucker – clarinet

Middlemass / Lie Dream Of A Casino Soul / Hip Priest / C'n'C-Hassle Schmuck

Featured the unlikely scenario of The Fall covering rock'n'roll revivalists Coast To Coast. The first appearance of 'Hip Priest', a sprawling, nine-minute version.

Session 5

Recorded: 26th August 1981

Broadcast: 15th September 1981

Mark E Smith – vocals; Marc Riley – guitar; Craig Scanlon – guitar; Steve Hanley – bass, vocals; Paul Hanley – drums

Deer Park / Look, Know / Winter / Who Makes The Nazis?

'Nazis' featured Steve Hanley on plastic toy guitar and somewhat hesitant and embarrassed backing vocals.

Session 6

Recorded: 21st March 1983

Broadcast: 23rd March 1983

Mark E Smith – vocals; Craig Scanlon – guitar; Steve Hanley – bass; Paul Hanley – drums; Karl Burns – drums

Smile / Garden / Hexen Definitive-Strife Knot / Eat Y'self Fitter

The first two-drummer session; features the definitive 'Garden'.

Session 7
Recorded: 12th December 1983
Broadcast: 3rd January 1984
Mark E Smith – vocals; Brix Smith – guitar, vocals; Craig Scanlon – guitar; Steve Hanley – bass; Paul Hanley – drums; Karl Burns – drums

Pat Trip Dispenser / 2 x 4 / Words Of Expectation / C.R.E.E.P.

Brix's first Peel appearance and Paul Hanley's last. The epic 'Words Of Expectation' was never recorded elsewhere, and – with typical perversity – did not appear on the Peel sessions compilation that bore its name.

Session 8
Recorded: 14th May 1985
Broadcast: 3rd June 1985
Mark E Smith – vocals; Brix Smith – guitar, vocals; Craig Scanlon – guitar; Steve Hanley – bass; Simon Rogers – guitar, keyboards; Karl Burns – drums

Cruiser's Creek / Couldn't Get Ahead / Spoilt Victorian Child / Gut Of The Quantifier

Simon Rogers's first Peel session appearance includes arguably the best version of 'Couldn't Get Ahead'.

Session 9
Recorded: 29th September 1985
Broadcast: 7th October 1985
Mark E Smith – vocals; Brix Smith – guitar, vocals; Craig Scanlon – guitar; Steve Hanley – bass; Simon Rogers – guitar, keyboards; Karl Burns – drums

L.A. / The Man Whose Head Expanded / What You Need / Faust Banana

Most notable for Smith's megaphone intro to 'L.A.' – 'Lloyd Cole's brain and face is made out of cow pat – we all know that.'

Session 10
Recorded: 29th June 1986
Broadcast: 9th July 1986
Mark E Smith – vocals; Brix Smith – guitar, vocals; Craig Scanlon – guitar; Steve Hanley – bass; Simon Rogers – guitar, keyboards; Simon Wolstencroft – drums

Hot Aftershave Bop / R.O.D. / Gross Chapel-GB Grenadiers / U.S. 80's - 90's

The first Peel appearance for 'Funky Si'.

Session 11
Recorded: 28th April 1987
Broadcast: 11th May 1987
Mark E Smith – vocals; Brix Smith – guitar, vocals; Craig Scanlon – guitar; Steve Hanley – bass; Simon Rogers – guitar, keyboards; Simon Wolstencroft – drums

Athlete Cured / Australians In Europe / Twister / Guest Informant

Recorded at the peak of the group's commercial success: 'There's A Ghost In My House' (which reached number 30 in the UK singles chart) was released the day before the session was recorded.

Session 12
Recorded: 25th October 1988
Broadcast: 31st October 1988
Mark E Smith – vocals; Brix Smith – guitar, vocals; Craig Scanlon – guitar; Steve Hanley – bass; Marcia Schofield – keyboards, vocals; Simon Wolstencroft – drums

Deadbeat Descendant / Cab It Up / Squid Lord / Kurious Oranj

Recorded a couple of weeks after the conclusion of *I Am Curious, Orange*'s run at Sadler's Wells, the 12th session featured a thrillingly effervescent take of 'Cab It Up'.

Session 13
Recorded: 17th December 1989
Broadcast: 1st January 1990
Mark E Smith – vocals; Martin Bramah – guitar; Craig Scanlon – guitar; Steve Hanley – bass; Marcia Schofield – keyboards, vocals; Simon Wolstencroft – drums; Kenny Brady – violin

Chicago, Now! / Black Monk Theme / Hilary / Whizz Bang

Brix had gone; Bramah (briefly) reappeared; Kenny Brady made the first of his two appearances. 'Whizz Bang' wasn't broadcast because it contained a profanity.

Session 14
Recorded: 5th March 1991
Broadcast: 23rd March 1991
Mark E Smith – vocals; Craig Scanlon – guitar; Steve Hanley – bass; Simon Wolstencroft – drums; Kenny Brady – violin

The War Against Intelligence / Idiot Joy Showland / A Lot Of Wind / The Mixer

The sacking of Bramah and Schofield meant that the group were now a four-piece outfit, although Kenny Brady's violin once again expanded the sound.

Session 15
Recorded: 19th January 1992
Broadcast: 15th February 1992
Mark E Smith – vocals; Craig Scanlon – guitar; Steve Hanley – bass; Dave Bush – keyboards; Simon Wolstencroft – drums

Free Range / Kimble / Immortality / Return

New recruit Dave Bush's influence can be clearly heard on 'Immortality' and 'Free Range'. 'Kimble' was a bit of an oddity, a loose cover of a Lee Perry tune that wouldn't be played live until 1997, when it got two rather undistinguished runouts.

Recorded: 28th February 1993

Broadcast: 13th March 1993

Mark E Smith – vocals; Craig Scanlon – guitar; Steve Hanley – bass; Dave Bush – keyboards; Simon Wolstencroft – drums

Ladybird (Green Grass) / Strychnine / Service / Paranoia Man In Cheap Sh*t Room

The cover of The Sonics' 'Strychnine' was another track that never received another studio recording, although it was performed live an impressive 148 times.

Session 17

Recorded: 8th December 1993

Broadcast: 5th February 1994

Mark E Smith – vocals; Craig Scanlon – guitar; Steve Hanley – bass; Dave Bush – keyboards; Simon Wolstencroft – drums

M5 / Behind The Counter / Reckoning / Hey! Student

The first and only time the same line-up had appeared on three consecutive sessions. In general, these versions were livelier and more effective than their album counterparts, only let down by a somewhat lacklustre 'Reckoning'.

Session 18

Recorded: 20th November 1994

Broadcast: 17th December 1994

Mark E Smith – vocals; Brix Smith – guitar, vocals; Craig Scanlon – guitar; Steve Hanley – bass; Dave Bush – keyboards; Simon Wolstencroft – drums; Karl Burns – drums; Lucy Rimmer – vocals

Glam-Racket-Star / Jingle Bell Rock / Hark The Herald Angels Sing / Numb At The Lodge

Session 18 saw the return of both Brix (who contributes the marvellously vitriolic 'Star' section to 'Glam-Racket') and a two-drummer line-up. It also had a festive theme. The last of Craig Scanlon's 16 session appearances.

Session 19

Recorded: 7th December 1995

Broadcast: 22nd December 1995

Mark E Smith – vocals; Brix Smith – guitar, vocals; Steve Hanley – bass; Julia Nagle – keyboards; Simon Wolstencroft – drums; Karl Burns – drums; Lucy Rimmer – vocals

He Pep! / Oleano / Chilinist / The City Never Sleeps

Recorded during a particularly turbulent and difficult time, session 19 is still intriguing and inventive, although 'The City Never Sleeps' is arguably one of the lowest points in the group's back catalogue.

Session 20

Recorded: 30th June 1996

Broadcast: 18th August 1996

Mark E Smith – vocals; Brix Smith – guitar, vocals; Steve Hanley – bass; Julia Nagle – keyboards; Simon Wolstencroft – drums; Karl Burns – drums

D.I.Y. Meat / Spinetrak / Spencer / Beatle Bones 'N' Smokin' Stones

A disjointed and underwhelming set, recorded just before the group's disastrous autumn tour. Brix's final session appearance.

Session 21

Recorded: 3rd February 1998

Broadcast: 3rd March 1998

Mark E Smith – vocals; Steve Hanley – bass; Julia Nagle – keyboards, guitar; Karl Burns – drums; John Rolleson – vocals.

Calendar / Touch Sensitive / Masquerade / Jungle Rock

Another disappointingly sloppy set. Although he was in the group at this point, Tommy Crooks didn't play on the session.

Session 22

Recorded: 18th October 1998

Broadcast: 4th November 1998

Mark E Smith – vocals; Julia Nagle – keyboards, guitar; Neville Wilding – guitar; Karen Leatham – bass, keyboards; Tom Head – drums; Speth Hughes – special effects

Bound Soul One / Antidotes / Shake-Off / This Perfect Day

Coming only six months after the group's on-stage meltdown in New York, it's not a surprise that the session is a shambolic mess. You can just about hear the outstanding track that 'Shake-Off' would become, but otherwise this is the nadir of The Fall's Peel sessions.

Session 23
Recorded: 19th February 2003
Broadcast: 13th March 2003
Mark E Smith – vocals; Ben Pritchard – guitar, vocals; Jim Watts – bass, vocals; Dave Milner – drums, vocals; Eleni Poulou – keyboards, vocals

Theme From Sparta F.C. / Contraflow / Grooving With Mr Bloe – Green-Eyed Loco Man / Mere Pseud Mag. Ed.

A proper return to form. A completely new line-up and, for the first time in several sessions, the group sound like they are actually enjoying themselves. Includes a surprisingly effective revisit to the 21-year-old 'Mere Pseud Mag. Ed.'.

Session 24
Recorded: 4th August 2004
Broadcast: 12th August 2004 (Job Search broadcast on 31st August 2004)
Mark E Smith – vocals; Ben Pritchard – guitar; Jim Watts – guitar, bass; Steve Trafford – bass; Spencer Birtwistle – drums; Eleni Poulou – keyboards; Ed Blaney – guitar, vocals

Clasp Hands / Blindness / What About Us? / Wrong Place, Right Time – I Can Hear The Grass Grow

Recorded less than three months before Peel's death, the final session includes a magnificent 'Blindness' that a majority of fans consider the definitive version. The group recorded a fifth track, 'Job Search', that was pressed as a one-off acetate and presented to John Peel for his 65th birthday.

Other Radio Sessions / Broadcasts

As well as the 24 Peel sessions, the group recorded several other radio broadcasts. Their commercially successful period in the late 80s / early 90s in particular saw them branch out into sessions for more mainstream Radio 1 shows, such as those of David Jensen, Janice Long and Mark Goodier. Many of these sessions feature on a bootleg, *On the Wireless – The Non Peel Radio Sessions*.

Part of the group's 17th May 1981 performance at Groningen in The Netherlands was broadcast on Dutch radio, and this recording has popped up on bootlegs in various guises. Their August 1982 gig in Melbourne (captured on the 1998 release *Live To Air In Melbourne '82*) was broadcast live on Australian radio. There were several more live radio broadcasts of this type in the 80s and 90s.

David Jensen Session
Recorded 19th February 1984
First broadcast 1st March 1984 on BBC Radio 1
Mark E Smith – vocals; Brix Smith – guitar, vocals; Craig Scanlon – guitar; Steve Hanley – bass; Paul Hanley – drums; Karl Burns – drums

Lay Of The Land / God Box / Oh! Brother / C.R.E.E.P.

The group's first 'mainstream' radio session was for David 'Kid' Jensen. Jensen hosted Radio 1's evening show between 1981 and 1984 and was a close friend of John Peel – the duo presented *Top of the Pops* together on several occasions. The session is quite low-key by The Fall's standards ('Brother' and 'C.R.E.E.P.' are particularly light and poppy; even 'Lay Of The Land' is relatively restrained) but this was still challenging stuff by the standards of early 80s prime time British radio.

Saturday Live Session
Broadcast live to air 29th August 1984 on BBC Radio 1

Mark E Smith – vocals; Brix Smith – guitar, vocals; Craig Scanlon – guitar; Steve Hanley – bass; Paul Hanley – drums; Karl Burns – drums

Copped It / Elves / Fortress – Marquis Cha-Cha

If the group had put on their 'pop' face for Kid Jensen, they were distinctly more aggressive here. There's a grinding version of 'Copped It' and grimy take on 'Elves'. Most interestingly, 'Fortress' segues into a sprightly 'Marquis Cha-Cha'.

Janice Long Session 1
Recorded 9th September 1984
First broadcast 17th September 1984 on BBC Radio 1
Mark E Smith – vocals; Brix Smith – guitar, vocals; Craig Scanlon – guitar; Steve Hanley – bass; Paul Hanley – drums; Karl Burns – drums

Stephen Song / No Bulbs / Draygo's Guilt / Slang King

Janice Long took over the Radio 1 evening slot from David Jensen in 1984. Another Radio 1 DJ who struck up a close friendship with Peel, she was also often to be found presenting *TOTP* with him. The group are relatively restrained in their approach, perhaps because of the early evening audience, but they still produce four taut and focused (if rather 'clean') versions of *Wonderful And Frightening* tracks. Steve Hanley makes 'Slang King' a particularly funky affair.

Steve Barker's 'On The Wire'
Recorded and broadcast 16th June 1985 on BBC Radio Lancashire
Mark E Smith – vocals; Brix Smith – guitar, vocals; Craig Scanlon – guitar; Steve Hanley – bass; Simon Rogers – keyboards, guitar; Karl Burns – drums

2 x 4 / Couldn't Get Ahead / Petty Thief Lout / No Bulbs / Gut Of The Quantifier / Spoilt Victorian Child / Barmy / Stephen Song / Lay Of The Land

Free open-air concert at Clitheroe Castle organized by the station and Ribble Valley Borough Council. The broadcast omitted opener

'Kicker Conspiracy' and encores 'Cruiser's Creek' and 'Oh! Brother'. The recording was released as a live album, *Take It Down To The Wire At Clitheroe Castle*, in December 2020 (see Appendix 3).

Janice Long Session 2
Recorded 13th May 1987
First broadcast 19th May 1987 on BBC Radio 1
Mark E Smith – vocals; Brix Smith – guitar, vocals; Craig Scanlon – guitar; Steve Hanley – bass; Marcia Schofield (?) – keyboards; Simon Wolstencroft – drums

Frenz / Get A Hotel / There's A Ghost In My House / Haf Found Bormann

Three years after their first session for her, the group returned to Janice Long's show. 'Frenz' finds Brix rather overdoing the sugary backing vocals, and there's some rather clunky electronic percussion. The version of 'Get A Hotel', however, is a bit leaner and more energetic than the album version (even if someone's guitar is a little out of tune). There's also a sharp, uptempo take on 'There's A Ghost In My House' that's amongst the group's best performances of the song. 'Haf Found Bormann' is, as ever, a bit mad – it's hard to believe that it was actually broadcast on early evening Radio 1. Some sources suggest that Simon Rogers played keyboards on this session, but it was more likely Marcia Schofield. The session was recorded in the afternoon of 13th May, and the group played the Astoria that night – video footage shows that Schofield was on keyboards that night.

In Concert
Recorded 19th May 1987
First broadcast 25th May 1987 on BBC Radio 1
Mark E Smith – vocals; Brix Smith – guitar, vocals; Craig Scanlon – guitar; Steve Hanley – bass; Marcia Schofield – keyboards; Simon Wolstencroft – drums

Australians In Europe / Shoulder Pads / There's A Ghost In My House / Hey! Luciani / Terry Waite Sez / Fiery Jack / Lucifer Over Lancashire

The recording of The Fall's Nottingham Rock City gig from May 1987 (which was released as a live album in 1993) was broadcast on Radio 1. It's an adequate but rather flat recording. Oddly, the live album's credits state 'Brix E Smith (keyboard)', but it's highly unlikely that Marcia Schofield didn't play keyboards on this recording.

Piccadilly Radio Session
Recording date unknown
First broadcast 25th February 1988
Mark E Smith – vocals; Brix Smith – guitar, vocals; Craig Scanlon – guitar; Steve Hanley – bass; Marcia Schofield – keyboards; Simon Wolstencroft – drums

In These Times / Carry Bag Man / Cab It Up / Oswald Defence Lawyer

Not much is known about this session. It consists of fairly unremarkable versions of three songs from *The Frenz Experiment*, plus a curiously lethargic 'Cab It Up'.

John Peel's 50th Birthday Party
Recorded 29th August 1989
First broadcast 30th August 1989 on BBC Radio 1
Mark E Smith – vocals; Martin Bramah – guitar; Craig Scanlon – guitar; Steve Hanley – bass; Marcia Schofield – keyboards; Simon Wolstencroft – drums

Mere Pseud Mag. Ed. / I'm Frank / Arms Control Poseur / Fiery Jack / Race With The Devil / Carry Bag Man / Mr. Pharmacist

The Fall, along with The Wedding Present and The House Of Love, played at the Subterrania in London as part of Peel's 50th birthday celebrations. The only officially released track for this performance was their Gene Vincent cover 'Race With The Devil', which eventually appeared on *Backdrop* in 2001 and the 2013 EP *The Remainderer*.

Norwich Sound City 92
Broadcast live to air 21st April 1992 on BBC Radio 1

Mark E Smith – vocals; Craig Scanlon – guitar; Steve Hanley – bass; Dave Bush – keyboards; Simon Wolstencroft – drums

And Therein / Blood Outta Stone / Time Enough At Last / Free Range / Idiot Joy Showland / Gentlemen's Agreement / Edinburgh Man

Broadcast as part of Mark Goodier's show.

Sheffield Sound City 1993
Broadcast live to air 7th April 1993 on BBC Radio 1
Mark E Smith – vocals; Craig Scanlon – guitar; Steve Hanley – bass; Dave Bush – keyboards; Simon Wolstencroft – drums

Why Are People Grudgeful / Ladybird (Green Grass) / Glam-Racket / Free Range / I'm Going To Spain / The League Of Bald-Headed Men / Lost In Music

Another live broadcast on Mark Goodier's show. Available as a free download via the Sheffield Tape Archive on Bandcamp (see Appendix 3).

Mark Goodier Session
Recorded 1st May 1993
First broadcast 17th May 1993 on BBC Radio 1
Mark E Smith – vocals; Craig Scanlon – guitar; Steve Hanley – bass; Dave Bush – keyboards; Simon Wolstencroft – drums

Glam-Racket / War / 15 Ways / A Past Gone Mad

Mark Goodier hosted Radio 1's evening show in the early 90s. Unlike Jensen and Long, he didn't have a close relationship with Peel, although he was Goodier's inspiration for becoming a DJ. The session consists of four decent if unremarkable versions of *Infotainment Scan / Middle Class Revolt* tracks. The recording of 'A Past Gone Mad' turned up on the Steve Hanley-curated compilation *The Peel Sessions* in 1999 (see Appendix 2).

Manchester Roadhouse 1993
Recorded 8th December 1993
First broadcast 29th April 1994 on Radio 1

Mark E Smith – vocals; Craig Scanlon – guitar; Steve Hanley – bass; Dave Bush – keyboards; Simon Wolstencroft – drums

M5 / Ladybird (Green Grass) / Behind The Counter / I'm Going To Spain / The League Of Bald-Headed Men / War / I'm Frank / A Past Gone Mad / Glam-Racket / Lost In Music / Strychnine / Cab Driver / Return / Free Range

Broadcast on Peel's show. It features the third and final outing for 'Cab Driver', in which MES does not appear, vocal samples being used instead.

Phoenix Festival 1995
Recorded and broadcast 14th July 1995 on Radio 1
Mark E Smith – vocals; Brix Smith – guitar, vocals; Craig Scanlon – guitar; Steve Hanley – bass; Julia Nagle – keyboards; Simon Wolstencroft – drums; Karl Burns – drums

Pearl City / Behind The Counter / Free Range / Don't Call Me Darling / The Chiselers / Feeling Numb / Idiot Joy Showland / Edinburgh Man / Glam-Racket

The group's set at 1995's Phoenix Festival (or part of it at least) was broadcast on Peel's Radio 1 show on the same day as the group's performance. It wasn't, however, a live-to-air affair: several songs from the setlist were missing, and the group's position on the bill (fifth, between Van Morrison and The Wedding Present) can't have matched with the 10pm start of Peel's Friday show at the time as online footage of the performance clearly shows the group performing in daylight. The performance was released as a live album in 2003.

Roskilde Backstage Danish Radio
Recorded 27th June 1996
Broadcast date unknown
Mark E Smith – vocals; Brix Smith – guitar, vocals; Steve Hanley – bass; Julia Nagle – keyboards, guitar; Simon Wolstencroft – drums; Karl Burns – drums

Spinetrak / U.S. 80's - 90's / 15 Ways / U.S. 80's - 90's (No Fun At All Mix)

The Fall played Denmark's Roskilde festival in the summer of 1996; a not entirely happy visit, as it involved Smith's rather unfortunate encounter with UK hip-hop group, The Brotherhood. This radio recording doesn't actually feature the group's festival set – it was a 'live session performed for Danish Radio in the backstage area of the Roskilde festival'. It's not clear when (or even if) it was broadcast on Danish radio, but a good quality recording emerged a few years later. There's a brisk version of '15 Ways', enlivened by added vocals from Brix. 'Spinetrak' sees the vocals way too high in the mix, the guitar virtually inaudible and MES referencing Kid Creole and the Coconuts' 'Annie, I'm Not Your Daddy'. 'U.S. 80's - 90's' is pleasingly sharp; the 'No Fun At All Mix' (the title possibly inspired by the Sex Pistols' appearance at the festival, which saw them walk off after being bombarded with bottles) just takes the same recording and rather pointlessly throws in a few half-hearted 'swooshing' effects.

Phoenix Festival 1996
Recorded and broadcast 21st July 1996 on Radio 1
Mark E Smith – vocals; Brix Smith – guitar, vocals; Steve Hanley – bass; Julia Nagle – keyboards, guitar; Simon Wolstencroft – drums; Karl Burns – drums

He Pep! / U.S. 80's - 90's / The Chiselers / 15 Ways / Pearl City / Powder Keg / Behind The Counter

The group found themselves on the same bill as the Sex Pistols once more at the 1996 Phoenix Festival. Their set was broadcast on Peel's show on the same day as the performance, but once again wasn't 'live to air', this being only a selection from the group's set. Four songs from the performance were included (alongside nine tracks from the previous year's Phoenix appearance) on the 2003 LP *Live At The Phoenix Festival*.

Robert Elms Session
Broadcast live to air on BBC's GLR, 15th April 1999
Mark E Smith – vocals; Neville Wilding – guitar; Adam Helal –
bass; Tom Head – drums

Antidotes / F-'oldin' Money

Another session about which little is known. On the same day,
the group performed a raucous eight-song set – swathed in reverb
and distortion – at an afternoon gig sponsored by radio station
XFM (see Chapter 21).

Mixing It Session
Recorded 13th October 2005
First broadcast 10th February 2006 on BBC Radio 3
Mark E Smith – vocals; Ben Pritchard – guitar; Steve Trafford
– bass; Eleni Poulou – keyboards; Spencer Birtwistle – drums

Higgle-Dy Piggle-Dy / Assume / Midnight In Aspen / Pacifying
Joint

Six months after the release of _The Complete Peel Sessions_, the group
made its first BBC Radio 3 appearance, on the experimental
music show _Mixing It_. 'Midnight In Aspen' concludes with a brief
Smith monologue: 'Maybe next Saturday when he can shoot /
as he descend into the mall / the frogs never told me this, he said
/ neither did the group.' The session also featured the group's
excellent cover of The Monks' 'Higgle-Dy Piggle-Dy'.

Mike Joyce Coalition Chart Show
Recorded and broadcast 17th June 2010 on East Village Radio
Mark E Smith – vocals; Pete Greenway – guitar; Dave Spurr –
bass; Eleni Poulou – keyboards; Keiron Melling – drums

Mexico Wax Solvent 1 / Over! Over! / Hungry Freaks Daddy /
Mexico Wax Solvent 2

Five years after their penultimate radio session, the group recorded
four songs for ex-Smiths drummer Joyce's show on internet station
East Village Radio. It included two versions of 'Mexico Wax

Solvent': both are sparser than the album version, but 'Part 1' is especially lithe and fleet-footed, featuring some dexterous, funky wah–wah from Greenway.

Appendix 2: Fall Compilation Albums

Appendix 2: Fall Compilation Albums

'It's just daft deals I signed when I shouldn't have done.'

Many artists, like The Fall, have a dauntingly large back catalogue. There are, for example, over 100 Frank Zappa albums (around half of them released posthumously); the same is true of Johnny Cash.[403] It is a challenge to pin down the exact number of Fall albums in existence, not just because of the endless debate regarding the status of *Slates* (which I am going to count), but also due to the fact that new live albums seem to pop up every five minutes. However, my best stab at the correct total (at the time of writing, anyway) is 162: 32 studio albums, 53 compilations and 77 live albums.[404] The compilations make up a sizeable chunk of The Fall's back catalogue, and are wildly variable in terms of quality and value.

In early 1996, Smith signed a deal with Receiver Records that allowed them to put out compilations of previously unreleased Fall material. This led to a slew of Fall compilations emerging in the late 90s. They were compiled and produced by Mike Bennett, who also co-produced *Cerebral Caustic* and *The Light User Syndrome*. This series of releases, although they contained the odd bit of interesting material, are not generally well regarded, as Simon Ford explains:

> Compilation albums obviously have their place, especially for a band of The Fall's longevity, but rather than introduce new listeners to the best of The Fall, or document in detail the band's development, these compilations... merely represented The Fall as inconsistent and exploitative.

---

[403] Other 100+ album artists include Miles Davis, Sun Ra and Tangerine Dream. Masami Akita (best known for his noise project Merzbow) has made around 400.

[404] Given the rate with which Fall live releases appear, it's almost inevitable that this figure will be out of date by the time you read this. For the record, the latest one to be counted in this total was the 12-CD box set, *The Fall Take America*, released in March 2022.

In 2001, Smith did express some regret about the situation. 'It's just daft deals I signed when I shouldn't have done. And I do apologise to my fans for that... but I also look at it the Elvis Presley way: if people can't differentiate between the real stuff and the cash-ins, that's their lookout.'

Fall Compilations 1977–93
Before the onslaught of Receiver releases, there had already been ten Fall compilations.[405]

77 – Early Years – 79 (Step-Forward, September 1981)
Compiles the first four singles and throws 'Dice Man' in for good measure. It was reissued as *Early Fall 77-79* in 2000, adding 'Stepping Out' and 'Last Orders', the group's very first appearances on record, from *Short Circuit – Live At The Electric Circus*. If you're not familiar with the group's late 70s work, then it's a solid enough introduction. However, all these tracks are on the 2004 reissues of *Witch Trials* and *Dragnet*.

Hip Priest And Kamerads (Situation Two, March 1985)
The original vinyl LP included both sides of the 'Lie Dream Of A Casino Soul' and 'Look, Know' singles, a couple of tracks from *Room To Live* and three from *Hex*, plus a live version of 'Mere Pseud Mag. Ed.' The cassette version (and 1988 CD release) added four more live *Hex* tracks, most of which are of good quality (although 'Jawbone' is rather muffled and imbalanced). The version of 'And This Day' from Hammersmith Palais in March 1982 is considered by many to be the best recording of the song. In what was to become a bit of a tradition for Fall compilations, the label on the original vinyl pressing gave the title as *Rip Priest And Kamerads*. Although many of the songs appear elsewhere, for those who got into the group in the late 80s, *Kamerads* provided invaluable access to early tunes that were hard to get a hold of at the time. It also hangs together well as a coherent album.

---

[405] Many Fall compilations contain a substantial amount of live material, just as several of their 'live' albums actually feature studio recordings. Sometimes it can be hard to tell which is which. For simplicity's sake I have gone with the categories identified on *The Fall Online*'s compilation and live album pages.

Nord-West Gas (FünfUndVierzig, 1986)
A German compilation that collects together a dozen easily obtainable tracks from the *Wonderful And Frightening / This Nation's Saving Grace* era. The cover art by Chris Kenny seems to be going for a Lovecraft vibe, lots of flailing tentacles engulfing what looks like a ladder on its side.

The Fall (PVC, 1986)
PVC was a sublabel of New Jersey-based Passport Records, which folded in 1988. This eponymous collection was, in fact, more an expanded version of the 'Rollin' Dany' single than a proper compilation album. On one side it contained the three songs from the 'Dany' 12", plus 'Vixen' and 'Barmy' – and then it repeated them on the other.

In: Palace Of Swords Reversed (Cog Sinister, November 1987)
A collection of album tracks and singles from the early 80s. Like *Kamerads*, it was both a helpful point of entry to material that wasn't always easily accessible at the time and a cracking album in its own right. Features an intriguing live version of 'Neighbourhood Of Infinity' from Munich, April 1984 (see Chapter 7).

Box One / Box Two (Beggars Banquet, June 1990)
Two 4-CD box sets, released in Japan only. *Box One* consisted of *Wonderful And Frightening* (the 16-track version), *This Nation's Saving Grace* (ditto) and *Hip Priest And Kamerads* (split over 2 CDs). *Box Two* contained *Bend Sinister, The Frenz Experiment, I Am Kurious Oranj* and *Seminal Live*. Around £50 each for the true completist.

458489 A Sides (Beggars Banquet, December 1990)
Does what it says on the tin, rounding up the singles from the Brix era. It's a strong choice for introducing a newcomer to the group, although arguably it misses out on several of the most interesting moments from that period.

458489 B Sides (Beggars Banquet, December 1990)
Also just as described. Contains arguably a more varied and satisfying range of songs than the A-sides version. Most are

available on the reissues of the relevant albums, but for someone who has only a casual knowledge of mid-80s Fall, it's potentially a great eye-opener.

The Collection (Castle Communications, April 1993)
Founded in 1983 by Terry Shand (who went on to co-found media company Eagle Rock Entertainment), Castle Communications specialised in mid-price catalogue reissues.[406] These releases were characterised by cheap and nasty covers and a seemingly haphazard approach to plucking songs at random from the artist's back catalogue. This is very much the case here on both counts. The cover very much has the look of something you'd see for sale in a motorway service station.

The Collection is made up of early 80s album and single tracks, plus selections from *In A Hole*, *A Part Of America Therein* and *Totale's Turns*. It also includes the cover of 'A Day In The Life' (from the 1988 *NME* compilation *Sgt. Pepper Knew My Father*) and the previously unreleased 'Medical Acceptance Gate', an outtake from 1983 (see Chapter 4). Despite the naff cover and somewhat overblown sleeve notes ('Bourgeois and proletarian alike can become culturally rich overnight... with this budget-price entry'), *The Collection* is actually a reasonable compilation of the group's early 80s work. In addition, 'A Day In The Life' and 'Medical Acceptance Gate' weren't available elsewhere until 2007 and 2004 respectively and the early 80s live albums were difficult to find at the time.

The Receiver Years 1996-98
Up to this point, the provenance of the songs on the compilations had been generally straightforward to ascertain. The advent of the Receiver compilations made things a great deal more difficult to unravel, as the sleeve notes were, as Simon Ford puts it, 'minimal or inaccurate'. As an overview:

Three Receiver compilations were released in early 1996: *Sinister Waltz*, *Fiend With A Violin* and *Oswald Defence Lawyer*. In

---

[406] For example, Black Sabbath (*Between Heaven And Hell 1970 – 1983*) and Motörhead (*The Best Of Motörhead – All The Aces*).

October, the three of them were collected together as a 3-CD box set, *The Other Side Of...*

In 1997, two further compilations were released which simply recycled a selection of the material from the three 1996 compilations: *Archive Series* (May) and the double-CD *The Less You Look, The More You Find* (July).

In November 1997, Receiver released *Oxymoron* and *Cheetham Hill*, both of which were largely a mixture of 'alternative' versions of *Light User Syndrome* tracks and other live recordings.

In June 1998, *Northern Attitude* featured a selection of tracks taken from the original three 1996 compilations, the two 1997 collections plus the live album *15 Ways To Leave Your Man*.

Sinister Waltz (Receiver Records, January 1996)

It's not clear why *Sinister Waltz* was chosen as the title, given that the song doesn't appear in any of the compilations from this era; presumably, it was considered to be an archetypal Fall title. By the standards of these things, it has a relatively inoffensive cover, featuring a rather pensive-looking MES.

'A Lot Of Wind' appears to be exactly the same as the version on *Shift-Work*, but does contain one minor change: the line 'he's the king of Granadaland' (at 3:17) which was snipped out of the album version is reinstated here.[407] 'Couldn't Get Ahead' is a raw and ragged but entertainingly energetic romp that feels like a live soundboard recording. 'Blood Outta Stone' also has the feel of a live recording from the soundboard, but could possibly be a rough studio demo; either way, it has a hard, frantic edge that elevates it above the 'White Lightning'/*Dredger* version. 'Arid Al's Dream' originally appeared on a 1992 compilation called *Volume 4*, and was later included on the 2007 reissue of *Shift-Work*. Its combination of scrabbling violin, twangy, reverb-heavy guitar and frantic drumming make it well worth a listen.

The instrumental version of 'The Knight, The Devil And Death' is a studio demo that lacks the overdubs and, above all, Cassell Webb's vocal contributions that made it such an

[407] There's some debate as to whether this refers to Fred Talbot or Tony Wilson.

obscure gem. 'Chicago Now!' is the Peel session version from January 1990. 'Birthday' was possibly the album's greatest selling point, as the track had never been released up to this point (and never would be again other than on one of the 'compilations of compilations'). One of the group's typically obscure covers, it was originally performed by The Idle Race (one of Jeff Lynne's early bands). Like 'The City Never Sleeps', Lucy Rimmer provides the lead vocals, with no sight of MES at all. It's all a little bog-standard indie-jangle-rock.

'Pumpkin Head Escapes' seems to be a studio demo, and a distinctly muffled one. The version of 'Wings' also feels like a studio outtake; the vocals are rather buried in a muddy mix. 'Dr. Faustus' (as it's titled here) is a curiously lo-fi version that feels like a tape of a tape of a tape soundboard recording; its origins are unknown. 'Telephone Thing' is a studio outtake; the sound is much denser and murkier than the album version. Steve Hanley's bass has a deeper, more resonant sound and there's an air of chaotic abandon that arguably makes this a little more enjoyable than the original. 'Black Monk Theme (Alternative Mix)' appears to be the Peel session version (presumably not identified as such because Receiver didn't actually have the rights to include it). 'Gut Of The Quantifier' features a range of interestingly squiggly keyboard effects, some rather alarming barks and yelps from MES and some sustained distorted guitar that isn't present on other recordings of the song. There's a little crowd noise right at the beginning that suggests it's a live recording, but from when and where is anyone's guess. Somewhat randomly, 'Edinburgh Man' is just the *Shift-Work* version.

Melody Maker dismissed the album as 'staggeringly OK'. The *NME* was slightly kinder, giving it 7/10 and describing its 'refried schizophrenia' as 'utterly bonkers' – suggesting, not unreasonably, that the album was only 'for the Fall trainspotter zone'.

Fiend With A Violin (Receiver Records, February 1996)
Fiend's garish red cover (featuring lettering apparently constructed by someone only just mastering Microsoft Paint) was largely based

on an illustration by Victorian caricaturist and illustrator George Cruikshank.[408]

The 'alternative' version of 'I Feel Voxish' doesn't appear to be any different to the album take other than in sound quality, having a 'taped off the radio' quality to it. 'The Man Whose Head Expanded' is more interesting. It's a weirdly dark and abrasive industrial version – The Fall meets Einstürzende Neubauten. It's highly unlikely that this was actually from 1983; it's probably Mike Bennett playing around with the song much later on. 'Ed's Babe' is basically an instrumental demo, featuring some mildly interesting synth squiggles and effects. It's hard to tell if 'What You Need' is a dodgy live soundboard recording or a very rough studio outtake; the slight 'boom' on the vocals in places suggests the former. There are also unremarkable takes of 'L.A.' and 'Petty (Thief) Lout', both of which are unidentified live versions, almost certainly from 1985. 'Married, Two Kids' also sounds like a live recording, although it's not clear whether the occasional electronic oscillations lurking in the background were added later.

'Fiend With A Violin' itself is just a rough draft of '2 x 4'. The 'Vox' version of the track is more abstract and a little more interesting, mainly because of the ghostly violin part. It's not clear who the violinist is, but it certainly isn't (as the sleeve notes bizarrely claim) 'Mark. E Smith in the usual role of violin player'. The live recordings of 'Spoilt Victorian Child' and 'Bombast' are both thin and scratchy; 'Haven't Found It Yet' clumsily dubs some crowd noise over the album version. 'Gentlemen's Agreement' is yet another thin and ropy soundboard recording of unknown origin, although it is pretty clear that Craig Scanlon's guitar is not in tune.

Whereas *Sinister Waltz* is patchy but has a few moments of genuine interest, *Fiend* is a pretty weak affair. Besides the unusual (although dubious) version of 'The Man Whose Head Expanded'

---

[408] From the British Museum website: 'The Devil, seated on a podium, playing on a violin and using his tail as a bow, ladies, gentlemen and children watching from the ground, the trees of Hyde Park beyond; illustration to "The Bands in the Park" (1856)'. *The Bands in the Park* was, according to novelist and critic Wilfrid Hugh Chesson (1870–1952), 'a quasi-temperance pamphlet'.

there's really very little here to expand one's understanding or enjoyment of the group.

Oswald Defence Lawyer (Receiver Records, April 1996)
The third Receiver compilation features MES on the cover wearing a cable-knit jumper. The sleeve notes are uninformative and badly written.[409]

'Just Waiting' is a pleasant enough if imbalanced (sound-wise) swagger through the Hank Williams song.[410] 'Oswald Defence Lawyer' possibly comes from the group's performance in Vienna, April 1988; the tinkling piano doesn't add much value. On 'Victoria' (date and venue unknown) the crowd noise has a curiously overdubbed feel – a recurring feature throughout this album. The version of 'Frenz' (again from an unidentified gig) is a particularly sparse and fragile take on the song, and features a chiselling percussive noise that has echoes of Tom Waits.

'2×4', 'Bad News Girl' and 'Get A Hotel' are all acceptable if not especially notable live performances, most likely from 1988, although once again it's not clear from which gigs. 'Guest Informant' is possibly a studio outtake. 'Big New Prinz' is devoid of any crowd noise, but there's an underlying amplifier buzz at the beginning and a few 'drop-outs' in the vocals that suggest a live soundboard recording. 'Bremen Nacht' features an unfortunate mix of muffled instrumentation and 'boomy', overly reverbed vocals and possibly comes from the same 1988 Vienna performance as 'Oswald Defence Lawyer'. 'Carry Bag Man' also features incongruous, overdubbed crowd noise, and has a rather odd opening, with double-tracked ensemble vocals and industrial-style percussion. Thereafter, it seems to be another soundboard recording, probably from 1988 – most likely a snippet of studio outtake grafted onto a live recording. The conclusion is an energetic if rather hollow-sounding version of 'Bombast' – a different one to that on *Fiend With A Violin*.

---

[409] 'This particular compilation is a testament to the groups [sic] sheer raw live energy which when coupled with Mark E. Smith's brilliant lyrics and his ability to evoke imagery with his distinctive delivery proves to be an exciting and electric experience.'
[410] *The Track Record* only lists one known live performance of the song (3rd October 1992 at Manchester Free Trade Hall), but concedes that this version might come from elsewhere.

Overall, *Oswald Defence Lawyer* is a pretty mediocre offering. The performances are generally sound enough, but the overdubbed crowd noises give it a rather cynical flavour. The lack of information about the songs' origins is also a frustration.

Oxymoron (Receiver Records, November 1997)
Oxymoron has a hideous cover, featuring what looks like a crudely drawn illustration from a biology textbook superimposed on a piece of crocodile skin. It's interesting to see which songs are listed on the front cover: presumably 'Italiano' is there to entice the purchaser with the promise of new, unheard material. The sleeve notes, as per previous Receiver releases, are full of dire prose and devoid of relevant information: 'Mark E. Smith delivering his nail bitten wit over a dense thicket of edgy and at times menacing Rock and Roll.'

Things get off to an underwhelming start with 'Oxymoron' itself; not that it isn't a great song, but it's just the album version. 'Powder Keg' is technically an 'alternative' version, in that it has minutely faster tempo than the original, but the only substantive difference is that it features eight seconds of looped bleeps and guitar feedback at the end. 'White Lines' is at least an actual studio outtake. It's pretty awful though, sounding like something that Orbital might have knocked about in the studio before discarding as unfit even for a B-side.

'Pearl City' is a decent, energetic live recording (date and venue unknown); 'Birmingham School Of Business School' is also a live version, presumably from 1992. It's a little thin sound-wise, but features some interesting clattering electronica and Scanlon is on top form. With 'Hostile', we finally get something new and different. It's a slowed-down, spacey take on the song, practically a dub version. Particularly effective use is made of Brix's vocals, which float around ethereally. The live version of 'Glam-Racket' captures the atmosphere of the 1994-95 live performances well: MES wandering off after 25 seconds, leaving Brix ('take it, babe...') to shoulder the rest of the song, which she does with some vehemence, adding a few expletives and delivering the 'Star' part of the song ('your act has lost all its appeal') with real feeling.

'Italiano' is a hamfisted and pointless house-techno mangling of 'Oleano'. 'He Pep!' is an alternative mix, not radically different in terms of musical structure or sound, but there's some cutting and pasting of the vocals, which come in at different points to the original. 'Behind The Counter' and 'Bill Is Dead' are further examples of unidentified, satisfactory but unremarkable live performances. 'E.S.P. Disco' is a mellow, understated version of 'Psykick Dancehall' with most of the rough edges knocked off and a curiously soft and gentle sound. Despite the fact that *The Track Record* lists only one live performance of 'Rainmaster', the version here is definitely not the one with which the group opened their 1995 Phoenix festival set.[411]

According to the sleeve notes, the 'masterpiece Interlude/ Chilinism' is 'heard here for the first time in all it's [sic] glory'. What actually happens is that the original is padded out with a couple of minutes of vague and pointless techno-lite filler. And then things are rounded off with a brutally truncated live version of 'Life Just Bounces'. The album's casual disregard for one of the group's finest songs is indicative of *Oxymoron*'s overall approach; there's a dispiriting sense of 'this'll do' that runs throughout the whole thing.

Cheetham Hill (Receiver Records, November 1997)
Released in the same month as *Oxymoron*, *Cheetham Hill* has a slightly less horrendous cover, although it does look as though it should grace the 1983 debut album of a prog-metal band called something like Darkhammer.[412] The sleeve notes are once again uninformative and poorly written ('The Fall have been an inspiration to many groups both sides of the Atlantic for 20 years with a prolific album and single's [sic] output as well as a rigorous touring schedule.')

The clumsy opening of 'Time Enough At Last' sets the tone, sending you back to the days when you used to rush to hit

[411] There were at least three performances of the song: the *Oxymoron* one, the Phoenix Festival one, and one that can be found on YouTube that's possibly from Manchester Roadhouse on 22nd March 1995 (see Chapter 18).
[412] The cover image is one of Gustave Doré's illustrations for an 1866 edition of *Paradise Lost*.

'record' to tape something off the radio. It's yet another track that could either be a studio demo or a live recording. It's a satisfactory enough ramble through the song, the most notable feature being the 'fuck off' that MES casually throws in at 2:46. Thirty seconds of random sound effects are pointlessly tacked on to the end. The compilation's title track is almost the exact same version as that on *Light User*. The only difference is in the ending: in the original, the main track ends abruptly at 3:25 and we get a few seconds of heavily-reverbed voices; this version concludes instead with a very brief bit of fuzzy guitar and then a faint loop of Smith singing what sounds like either 'I'm a Brix toe' or 'I'm a brick stone'.

'Free Range' is a solid live version. It uses the same taped intro as the version on *Live Various Years* – which was recorded (possibly) in Munich in October 1993 – but despite its similarities it isn't the same version although it presumably comes from this period. 'The Chiselers' is just the shortest version from the single with the intro and outro lopped off. 'U.S. 80's - 90's' is an energetic, chaotic live version from a May 1992 gig in Brussels.

The Track Record states that 'Spine Track' (as it's titled here) is 'a truncated version of the originally released track', but it's actually a live version (of unknown origin) and a rather good one too: it rattles along at an unrelenting pace and sees both MES and Brix on fine form. 'Idiot Joy Showland' is also a live recording, but a rather sketchy one. 'Oleano' is moderately interesting: it's the same as the album version for the first three minutes, but then extends it by a couple more. It doesn't do anything radically different, but it's a strong enough song to warrant the bit of extra play time. 'The Joke' is another okay-ish unidentified live recording, as is 'Ed's Babe', although the latter is inexplicably truncated; 'Hit The North' is also just a brief snippet. There follows a spirited enough romp through 'White Lightning' (date and venue again unknown), but the fact that the sleeve lists it as 'White Lighting' is indicative of the generally shoddy nature of the release.

'Secession Man' is exactly the same as the original album version, other than that it omits the keyboard 'stab' right at the very end. 'Last Exit To Brooklyn (Last Chance To Turn Around)' is just 'Last Chance To Turn Around' with a longer title. A live version of 'The Coliseum' (date and venue yet again unknown) isn't, thankfully, the excessive length of the *Light User* version, but is still an ungainly, awkward mess. Bizarrely, things are rounded off with the first minute and a half of 'Eat Y'self Fitter'. Like *Oxymoron*, there's a handful of worthwhile material here, but there's also a pervading atmosphere of cynicism and poor quality.

The Compilations Of Compilations

The exploitation of the group's back catalogue continued with three further releases in 1997-98. *Archive Series* (April 1997) consisted of a random selection of tracks from the original three Receiver releases. *The Less You Look, The More You Find* (July 1997) did something similar over two discs. *Northern Attitude* (July 1998) also added a few tracks from the live album *15 Ways To Leave Your Man* (see Chapter 20).

Smile… It's The Best Of (Castle Communications, August 1998)
A random selection of songs from *Perverted By Language*, *Slates*, *Totale's Turns*, *The Light User Syndrome*, *A Part Of America Therein* and *Grotesque*.

Fall Compilations 1999-2004

The deluge of Fall compilations that gained momentum in the late 90s – ten in two and a half years – maintained its relentless onslaught around the turn of the century, with 16 being released between January 1999 and May 2004 (an average of one every four months).

The Peel Sessions (Strange Fruit, January 1999)
Compiled by Steve Hanley, who commented that it was 'impossible to pick twelve songs out of a hundred without disappointing someone'. There were in fact 17 tracks, one of which ('A Past Gone Mad') came from the May 1993 Mark Goodier session (see Appendix 1). Peel himself contributed some sleeve notes, which alluded to the Brownies debacle ('This past year has been

especially turbulent, of course, resulting in an all-new Fall') and summarised neatly the trials and tribulations of being a Fall fan: 'There have been times, as with football teams, when the fans have grumbled, feared for the future, left a performance shaking their heads in disbelief.'[413] At the time, this was a valuable release, as most fans would only have had these songs on homemade C90s recorded from Peel's show.

A Past Gone Mad (Artful Records, February 2000)
Sub-titled 'Best Of The Fall 1990-2000' – a collection of previously released material from the 90s albums, selected by Stewart Lee.

Psykick Dance Hall (Eagle Records, October 2000)
A 3xCD set that featured 49 album and single tracks from the first few years of the group's career, all previously released. According to *The Fall Online*, it was 'largely mastered from inferior Voiceprint CD reissues, so the audio quality is not optimal'.

Backdrop (Cog Sinister/Voiceprint, February 2001)
A 1994 bootleg that received an official release seven years later. It contains an interesting variety of obscure B-sides, live recordings and songs from freebies (the alternative version of 'Hey! Luciani', for example, came from a 7" given away with the 28th February 1987 edition of *Sounds*). It also saw the first official release of 'Dresden Dolls'. The album concludes with an entertainingly odd lo-fi recording of Smith interviewing himself, recorded just before the release of 'How I Wrote Elastic Man' in July 1980. In *The Sunday Times*, Stewart Lee described *Backdrop* as 'essential to acolytes'.

A World Bewitched (Artful Records, March 2001)
Similar to *A Past Gone Mad*, this double-CD compilation was subtitled 'Best Of 1990-2000'. However, it was more a rarities compilation in the vein of *Backdrop* rather than a straightforward

---

[413] 'I always cite a night at The Junction, Cambridge, in this last context,' he went on. This was probably the performance on 7th December 1997, about which *The Track Record* has this to say: 'The group members at various stages appear to down tools and the encores include walk outs, non-appearances and other oddness. There is a walk off by the band in the middle of "Lie Dream" – MES says "there's been a revolution". MES "plays" guitar on Hurricane Edward.'

'best of'. The album was compiled by *Q*'s Ian Harrison who described it as 'a vital sieving mechanism for all but the most monomaniacal Fall panhandler'.

It contained numerous hard-to-find gems, such as 'Theme From Error-Orrori', and also rounded up a wide range of MES collaborations, such as those with Badly Drawn Boy, Edwyn Collins, Inspiral Carpets, Elastica and Tackhead. Whilst some of these were fairly well known, others were much more obscure. 'Fistful Of Credits' is an atmospheric piece of slow-tempo techno that was recorded in 2000 with 'Mild Man Jan', aka Spencer Marsden (who co-wrote 'Mad.Men-Eng.Dog'). 'The Heads Of Dead Surfers' was a track by Scottish band Long Fin Killie, released as a single in 1995 (it also appeared on their album *Houdini*). It's an engaging piece of folk/jazz-tinged post-punk skronk, with MES contributing some trademark distorted megaphone backing vocals.

The Rough Trade Singles Box (Castle Music, April 2002)
Box set of the four singles released on Rough Trade ('Elastic', 'Wired', 'Expanded' and 'Kicker'). On the original issue of the set – owing to issues regarding getting clearance from the BBC – 'Container Drivers' and 'New Puritan' were the versions from *Grotesque* and *Totale's Turns* rather than the Peel session performances that had appeared on the double 7" 'Kicker Conspiracy'. After permission had been secured, later pressings did include the two Peel tracks, although there's nothing to visibly distinguish the two. It was released as a single album the following year (see below).

Totally Wired – The Rough Trade Anthology (Castle/Sanctuary, July 2002)
A collection of early 80s songs, all previously released. Great selection of tracks, and at £6-7 (the current going price according to *Discogs*) it would serve as a good intro to someone unfamiliar with the group's work from that period.

High Tension Line (Recall/Snapper Music, September 2002)
Another collection of previously released 90s material. It begs the question as to who, compiling a 24-track 'best of the 90s' would include 'Why Are People Grudgeful?' and 'Cloud Of Black'.

Listening In (Cog Sinister/Voiceprint, November 2002)
Subtitled 'Lost Singles Tracks 1990-92', *Listening In* rounds up (as the title suggests) the various B-sides from the *Extricate* to *Code: Selfish* era. It included three remixes of 'So What About It?' from a white label promo 12" that were otherwise hard to obtain, if not exactly essential listening. It also featured the first appearance of all three sections of 'Zagreb' on an album.

Early Singles (Cog Sinister/Voiceprint, December 2002)
A compilation of the A- and B-sides up to 1982. A useful enough round-up, although quickly made redundant by album reissues over the next few years.

It's The New Thing! The Step Forward Years (Castle Music, March 2003)
A 1978-80 singles/B-sides compilation.

Time Enough At Last (Castle Music, April 2003)
A 3-CD box set of *Oxymoron*, *Cheetham Hill* and *15 Ways To Leave Your Man*.

Words Of Expectation – BBC Sessions (Castle Music, May 2003)
A rather odd compilation, in that it includes all the tracks from the first five Peel sessions (1978-81) and then leaps to sessions 19 and 20 from 1995 and 1996. It also doesn't contain the song from which it derives its title. Full of great moments, but soon superseded by the *Complete Peel Sessions* box set.

The Rough Trade Singles Collection (Earmark, September 2003)
Simply *The Rough Trade Singles Box* (see above) on one vinyl album.

The War Against Intelligence – *The Fontana Years* (Fontana, September 2003)
Yet another compilation of early 90s material. If you'd never heard

The Fall and you picked this up in a charity shop, then it might form a half-decent introduction. Otherwise, it's just the same old dead horse being flogged.

Rebellious Jukebox (Shakedown Records, November 2003)
Even by the shoddy standards of most Fall compilations, this one has a dreadful cover, featuring a disembodied MES Madame Tussauds-style head looming over a catastrophic and disjointed series of fonts. *The Fall Online* describes it as:

> A completely unfathomable compilation – the cover says 'from 3 decades of studio recordings' yet 20 tracks are from 1978-1983, then there are 6 tracks from *Extricate* (1990) and 4 from *Are You Are Missing Winner* (2001).

The final track is a video interview with Mark E Smith conducted by 'Jet' Martin Celmins in 2002.[414] It doesn't rescue this carelessly knocked-out compilation from bargain basement status.

50,000 Fall Fans Can't Be Wrong – 39 Golden Greats (Sanctuary Records, May 2004)
Regarded by many at the time as the best, most comprehensive Fall compilation, *50,000* (the title and cover of which was inspired by an Elvis Presley album[415]) is a 39-track summary of the group's work from 1978-2003. Anyone who loves The Fall could quibble about exactly what is included or omitted, but most would agree that it's a balanced and comprehensive retrospective.

---

[414] The date given for the interview (19th September) would appear to be incorrect. At the beginning of the interview, whilst discussing the appearance of 'Touch Sensitive' in a car advert that Celmins had seen the previous night, MES remarks that the group are going to play the song 'tonight'. The Fall didn't have a gig on the 19th, so it's more likely that it was recorded on Sunday 22nd, when they played 'Touch Sensitive' at King George's Hall, Blackburn (the performance on the *Touch Sensitive* DVD). Given that Blackburn is only a short drive from Manchester, this seems the most plausible explanation.

[415] *50,000,000 Elvis Fans Can't Be Wrong: Elvis' Gold Records, Volume 2*, released in 1959. The original title was simply *Elvis' Gold Records, Vol. 2*; the '50 million' phrase was added to the record's label in 1962, was removed in 1968 and then reappeared when it was released on CD. It came from a 1956 article that criticised Elvis and included the comment 'Fifty million Americans can easily be misled'. The first use of the expression was in 1927, in a song called 'Fifty Million Frenchmen Can't Be Wrong' by Sophie Tucker, and has been used in many articles, books and songs subsequently.

Fall Compilations 2005 – 2019

After the deluge of compilations around the turn of the century, the pace of releases did thankfully slow a little over the remainder of the group's career. There wasn't, however, any noticeable overall improvement in quality.

The Complete Peel Sessions 1978-2004 (Castle Music, 2005)
6-CD box set containing all 97 tracks recorded for Peel's show (see Appendix 1). An essential purchase.

Permanent Years (Paranoia Man In Cheap Sh*t Room) (Fulfill Records, May 2006)
An 18-song compilation of tracks from the mid-90s; all but two were album tracks drawn from *The Infotainment Scan, Middle Class Revolt, Cerebral Caustic* and *The "Twenty-Seven Points"*. The remaining two ('The Remixer' and 'Cab Driver') had appeared earlier in 2006 on the reissues of *Infotainment* and *MCR*, so this release didn't contain anything new. The inclusion of two of Smith's brief spoken-word interludes from *The "Twenty-Seven Points"* seems a little perverse.

The Fall Box Set 1976-2007 (Castle Music, September 2007)
A 5-CD box set (often referred to as 'the red box') compiled by Conway Paton that was a companion release to the *Complete Peel Sessions* box set. 'Career spanning' is a cliché often applied casually to compilations, but it was entirely appropriate here. It's a real treasure trove, bursting at the seams with all sorts of oddities and obscurities, several of which had never appeared on an official UK album before, such as alternate versions of 'Fall Sound' and 'Blindness'. Other highlights include an excerpt from one of the December 1986 performances of *Hey! Luciani* (which almost feels like Smith doing stand-up); the moody shuffle of 'Theme From Error-Orrori'; the excellent Damon Gough (Badly Drawn Boy) collaboration, 'Calendar'; the sharply delirious version of '(We Are) Mod Mock Goth' from the 'Protein Christmas' single; and the unforgettably hilarious 'Portugal'.

There's also plenty of material that – despite shortcomings in song and/or sound quality – are still of historical interest: 'Pop

Stickers';[416] the title track of *Perverted By Language*; the surprising cover of Deep Purple's 'Black Night'; the only twice-played 'He Talks'; quirky mid-80s instrumental 'Countdown'; prototype 'Chiselers' intro 'Tunnel'; and ropy New York Dolls' cover 'Jet Boy'. The only notable omission from such a comprehensive round-up of obscurities is the mysteriously-only-ever-played-once 'Surrogate Mirage' (see Chapter 6). At the time of writing, a second-hand copy will set you back around £40: for 91 tracks and over six hours' worth of the groups' more obscure and intriguing moments (plus a 60-page booklet) this represents great value for money.

I've Never Felt Better In My Life – 1979-1982 (The Great American Music Company, July 2008)
A pointless collection of a dozen already easily available tracks from the group's early career. The cover is a mirror image of 2003's similarly needless *Rebellious Jukebox*.

Rebellious Jukebox Volume Two (Psycho Rockabilly Nightmare) (Secret Records, September 2009)[417]
The cringeworthy title is matched by another horrendous cover, seemingly created using Windows XP-era Microsoft Paint. The 'floating disembodied MES head' image makes another appearance, this time inside the CD booklet and tinted orange. There's nothing previously unreleased: it's a random assortment culled from, for example, *Backdrop*, *Austurbæjarbíó* and *Live Various Years*. In the grand tradition of Fall compilation shoddiness, the live version of 'Hit The North' is attributed to the album *Live in Zagbreb*.

---

[416] 'Pop Stickers (aka Let's)' was a jerky, light-hearted (and almost tuneless) song played only five times, all around the time of *Witch Trials*' release. Verging on pop-punk parody, some of the lyrics were recycled on 'Chock-Stock'. It is one of Marc Riley's favourite Fall songs.

[417] In 1985 Colin Newman (not the one out of Wire) bought Trojan Records. He sold it to Sanctuary in 2001. That same year Newman started 'Trojan Two', which within a few months was renamed Secret Records. Shakedown (who released the first *Rebellious Jukebox* compilation in 2003) was formed the same year; Newman is also a director of that company, and it and Secret are linked. Great American (who used virtually the same cover as *Rebellious Jukebox* for *I've Never Felt Better In My Life*) are licensed to release Secret/Shakedown material.

Totally Wired… Another Fall Best Of (Secret Records, December 2009)
A download only compilation of previously released material from 1979-1990. The use of ellipsis in the title suggests that the missing word is 'yet'.

Rebellious Jukebox Volume Three (Secret Records, May 2010)
Another pointless offering from Secret, featuring live tracks harvested from *Live 1977*, *Live To Air In Melbourne '82*, *In A Hole*, *Live In Cambridge 1988* and *Live In Zagreb*. It was subtitled 'Burn It All Down Live!!', an inexplicable reference to Dexys Midnight Runners.[418] There is stiff competition for the title of 'worst set of sleeve notes on a Fall compilation' but this may well be the winner:

> Abrasive guitar-driven sounds and cryptic lyrics all masterfully presented in glorious technisoundabilly colour! Full force power and this time it's all Live and in your face… Mark E Smith once again at the helm delivering the Fall message to the army of Fall fans around the world. It's a popcorn double disc double feature with a side order of Louie Louie!

13 Killers (Secret Records, May 2013)
Another addition to the Fall compilation horrendous cover hall of fame, this one seems to belong to some sort of late 80s glam-metal band. The 'orange MES head' makes yet another appearance, this time on the back cover. Sleeve notes are this time provided by 'contemporary Pop Artist' Billy Chainsaw (who was also responsible for the front cover artwork): 'In 1976… Smith cragged his sonic angst kicking and screaming into existence'. Another pointless release.

5 Albums (Beggars Banquet, August 2013)
A 5-CD box set round-up of *Frenz*, *Kurious Oranj*, *Seminal Live*, the various mixes of 'Hit The North' and A- and B-sides from the late 80s singles.

---

[418] 'Burn It Down' was the opening track on their 1980 debut album *Searching For The Young Soul Rebels*.

White Lightning (Secret Records, April 2014)
Released as part of 2014's Record Store Day, 'pressed on 180g clear vinyl… with silver printed insert and silver foil cover'. The ten tracks seem to have been chosen with an almost insultingly casual randomness.

The Wonderful And Frightening Escape Route To… (Beggars Banquet June 2015)
Basically a vinyl release for the bonus tracks that appeared on the original cassette version of *The Wonderful And Frightening World*, although it also includes 'Slang King 2' and 'No Bulbs 3'. All of this had already been released as part of the 'omnibus' edition of *Wonderful And Frightening* five years earlier.

Schtick: Yarbles Revisited (Beggars Banquet Jun 2015)
A collection of *This Nation's Saving Grace*-era B-sides and Peel session tracks, all easily available elsewhere.

The Classical (Secret Records April 2016)
Yet another pointless Secret release for Record Store Day. Again, ten songs flung together in a contemptuously random fashion. The lack of serious effort is well illustrated by the fact that 'Sing! Harpy' is labelled as 'Sing Happy'.

The Fontana Years (Fontana Records, Aug 2017)
The three 2007 double-CD reissues of *Extricate*, *Shift-Work* and *Code-Selfish* compiled into a 6-CD box set. If you only had the original three albums then this would be worth buying, given that – at the time of writing – you can do so for under £20.

A-Sides 1978-2016 (Cherry Red, November 2017)
Does what it says on the tin: all the singles on a 3-CD box set.

Singles 1978-2016 (Cherry Red, Nov 2017)
The same as above, this time with added B-sides. If you're just starting out with The Fall, and you have £40 to spend, it's a pretty good place to begin.

58 Golden Greats (Cherry Red, December 2018)
This is *50,000 Fall Fans Can't Be Wrong* expanded to three CDs

rather than two. It's hard (although far from impossible) to argue with the choice of songs that make up the third disc; an admirable attempt at a thankless task.

Medicine For The Masses (BMG, April 2019)
The Record Store Day offering for 2019, a 5 x 7" box set with the same content as *The Rough Trade Singles Box*. Rather pointless unless you're a big fan of badges (four were included).

(1982) (Cherry Red, October 2019)
Hex, Room To Live, In A Hole and *Live To Air In Melbourne '82*, plus assorted session bonus / live / session tracks from the early 80s.

Appendix 3: Fall Live Albums

Appendix 3: Fall Live Albums

'Are you doing what you did two years ago? Yeah? Well, don't make a career out of it.'

There is no aspect of The Fall back catalogue more 'wonderful and frightening' than the frankly bewildering range of live albums. They vary in quality to a huge degree, in terms of both the quality of the recording and the attention to detail and accuracy in the packaging. Most of the official live albums are discussed in the main narrative of the book. This appendix lists them, as far as is possible, in chronological order by date of recording.[419]

Live 1977
Recorded: Stretford Civic Theatre, 23rd December 1977
Released: March 2000 (Cog Sinister via Voiceprint)
The earliest full-length recording of a Fall gig, probably their 23rd. Horrifically lo-fi in places, it's notable for the audience's spitting and beer-chucking, the announcement of Tony Friel's departure, early appearances of 'Copped It' and 'Oh! Brother' and John the Postman's contribution to an almost unlistenable 'Louie Louie' (see Before The Witch Trials).

Rock Against Racism Xmas Party
Recorded: Stretford Civic Theatre, 23rd December 1977
Released: 5th November 2021 (Dandelion)
Rather pointless vinyl version of *Live 1977*.

Live At Deeply Vale
Recorded: People's Free Festival, Deeply Vale, 22nd July 1978
Released: 6th June 2005 (Ozit-Morpheus Records)
Ozit-Morpheus was a label owned by Chris Hewitt, one of the organisers of the Deeply Vale festivals. This recording (of the gig at which the group first met Grant Showbiz) is horribly tinny and

---

[419] This is complicated by the fact that several releases are either a mix of studio and live recordings or include tracks recorded over several years. Where this is the case, albums are listed by the date of the latest live recording.

features a layer of hiss that suggests it's from a second or third-generation tape. The final track is a medley of rehearsal takes of 'Psycho Mafia', 'Dresden Dolls' and 'Industrial Estate'.

Bingo Masters At The Witch Trials
Recorded: People's Free Festival, Deeply Vale, 22nd July 1978
Released: 16th April 2016 (Dandelion/Ozit-Morpheus Records)
Featuring an unspeakably horrible cover, this was a re-release of *Live At Deeply Vale* that omitted the rehearsal medley and added 'Bingo-Master' and 'Brand New Cadillac'.[420]

Live From The Vaults – Oldham 1978
Recorded: Tower Club, Oldham, 21st August 1978.
Released: 15th August 2005 (Hip Priest via Voiceprint)
The pick of the early live recordings, it captures Martin Bramah in top form and features a pleasingly lengthy version of 'Repetition' (see Chapter 1).

Liverpool 78
Recorded: Mr. Pickwick's, Liverpool, 22nd August 1978
Released: 4th June 2001 (Cog Sinister via Voiceprint)
Mastered from a cassette bought at a market stall. The whole album was included as bonus tracks on the 2004 Sanctuary reissue of *Live At The Witch Trials*. Sound quality is not great: the bass is ludicrously prominent, and the drums are non-existent.

Live From The Vaults – Retford 1979
Recorded: The Porterhouse, Retford, 16th November 1979
Released: 15th August 2005 (Hip Priest via Voiceprint)
Recorded a couple of weeks before the group embarked on their first US tour. The sound quality is pretty grim.

Live From The Vaults – Los Angeles 1979
Recorded: Anticlub, Los Angeles, 14th December 1979
Released: 15th August 2005 (Hip Priest via Voiceprint)
One of Marc Riley's favourite Fall gigs. The sound quality is

---

[420] A 1959 song by Vince Taylor, most notably covered by The Clash on *London Calling*. The only other known performance of the song by The Fall was on 1st September 1978 at Manchester's Band On The Wall.

fairly rough, although the lengthy version of 'Spectre vs. Rector' is impressive (see Chapter 3).

Totale's Turns (It's Now Or Never)
Recorded: Bircoats Leisure Centre, Doncaster, 27th October 1979; Palm Cove, Bradford, 29th February 1980; The Warehouse, Preston, 22nd November 1979
Released: 5th May 1980 (Rough Trade)
The first official Fall live album to be released. Notable for a couple of often-quoted MES comments: 'Are you doing what you did two years ago? Yeah? Well, don't make a career out of it' and his castigation of the group, 'Will you fuckin' get it together instead of showing off?' Also features a couple of studio / home-recorded tracks (see Chapter 3).

Live 1980 – Cedar Ballroom Birmingham
Recorded: As title, 20th November 1980
Released: 1st March 2019 (Cog Sinister)
On 14th December 2018, Cog Sinister released a CD box set called *'Set Of Ten' – Ten Previously Unreleased Live Recordings.* Confusingly – but given the history of Fall releases, perhaps not entirely surprisingly – it contained 11 live CDs, all of which became available individually.[421] *Cedar Ballroom* is the earliest, and it's a decent soundboard recording that finds the group on fierce form. 'Underground Medecin' is especially fast and furious.

Live In London 1980
Recorded: Acklam Hall, London, 11th December 1980
Released: March 1982 (Chaos Tapes) (cassette only)
A 'semi-official' cassette release that captured the group at a high point in terms of invention and confidence even if the sound quality is again no better than mediocre. Featured some rather haphazard labelling of the songs (see Chapter 4).

The Legendary Chaos Tape
Recorded: Acklam Hall, London, 11th December 1980

---

[421] A limited edition of 500, *Set Of Ten* was initially available only through Pledge. According to the release's *Discogs* page: 'Originally intended to contain only 10 discs, an 11th disc (Derby 1994) was added by way of an apology after the release was delayed from its original date.'

Released: 1st November 1996 (Scout Releases/Rough Trade)
The official release (14 years later) of *Live In London 1980*.

Live at St. Helens Technical College '81
Recorded: As title, 20th February 1981
Released: 19th February 2021 (Castle Face)
The Castle Face label was founded by John Dwyer of Osees (previously Thee Oh Sees). The release was prompted by Marc Riley:

> I stumbled upon the link to the recording of the St. Helens Technical College gig on Twitter. I started to listen and recognised it as one of the better sound-board recordings I'd ever heard. Knowing John [Dwyer] was into The Fall I sent him the link just for him to enjoy. He got back and said it was one of the best live Fall sets he'd ever heard and asked if we were cool with him releasing it. So I contacted Steve and Paul Hanley... then Paul got in touch with Craig Scanlon – and within the space of a week we'd given Castle Face the 'OK' from four of the five Fall members on the recording. The fifth of course being Mark E Smith who is no longer with us. I believe (from a mate who is armed with a functioning memory and was there on the night) the gig was poorly attended. So much so that the promoter attempted to pull our fee... which resulted in him being pushed to the floor by our manager Kay Carroll. Sounds about right.

50% of the profits from the release were donated to Manchester homeless charity Centrepoint.

Live From The Vaults – Glasgow 1981
Recorded: Plaza, Glasgow, 23rd February 1981
Released: 31st October 2005 (Hip Priest via Voiceprint)
Strong performance, but rather let down by the thin, wobbly sound. There were apparently sound problems on the night too, an exasperated Smith ordering Grant Showbiz to 'sort the sound out' after 'Totally Wired'.

Mark's Personal Holiday Tony Tapes
Recorded: Bar 2, Sheffield, 28th February 1981
Released: 22nd March 2019 (Dandelion/Ozit-Morpheus Records)
An Ozit horror. Billed as 'a mix of live and studio outtakes', this is

neither a proper live album nor any sort of coherent compilation. What it is, is a tawdry, barrel-scraping abomination. The four live tracks that appeared on the *Northern Cream* DVD (see Chapter 5) are interspersed with a variety of ugly, ham-fisted remixes of 'Last Nacht'. The cover – a stock image of donkeys on Blackpool beach with random images grafted on Microsoft Publisher-style – is an atrocity only rivalled for sheer horror by Dandelion/Ozit's earlier offering, *Bingo Masters At The Witch Trials*.

Live From The Vaults – Alter Bahnhof, Hof, Germany
Recorded: As title, 22nd May 1981; SO36, Berlin, 23rd May 1981
Released: 21st November 2005 (Hip Priest via Voiceprint)
Another decent performance let down by poor sound. Contains the first outing for 'Session Musician' and features what sounds like Kay Carroll calling Smith a wanker (see Chapter 5).

Live 23rd June 1981 @ Jimmy's Music Club
Recorded: As title, New Orleans
Released: 13th April 2019 (Cog Sinister)
Disc 11 of the *Set Of Ten* box set. Whilst the sound quality is no better than a B-, it doesn't distract from a blistering performance. 'Leave The Capitol' is especially sharp and taut, and 'Impression of J. Temperance' ('this is a horror story') is impressively intense. The version of 'Session Musician' was included on the UK version of *A Part Of America Therein*. The cover is a shocker, though, featuring a strangely warped image of the group in which Marc Riley resembles Dobby from the *Harry Potter* films. Stephen Hanley is erroneously credited as 'Steven'. Even more bizarrely, a 'Duncan Burndred' appears on the credits – Burndred was the group's driver 1980-81.[422]

A Part Of America Therein, 1981
Recorded: Antenna, Memphis, 20th June 1981; The Island, Houston, 24th June 1981; I-Beam, San Francisco, 13th July 1981; Tut's Chicago, 16th July 1981

---

[422] Paul Hanley: 'When we were at the cut for "Totally Wired" Mark asked him if he could think of something for Porky PC to scratch in the run-out. "Not off hand," he replied, so that's what he scratched.' He is referred to in *Slates & Dates* (the press release for the 1981 US tour – see Chapter 4) on page 3: '"Totally Wired" is not off-hand" – D. Burndread'.

Released: May 1982 (Cottage – US only) / 22nd November 2004 (Castle Music)

One of the best Fall live albums, especially the tracks on the first, 'North' side (see Chapter 5). The 2004 UK release added four bonus tracks also taken from the 1981 US tour: 'Middle Mass' and 'Container Drivers' (The Spit, Boston, 11th June); 'Session Musician' (Jimmy's, New Orleans, 23rd June); 'Your Heart Out' (Keystone, Palo Alto, 8th July).

Live 1982 3rd May Band On The Wall Manchester UK
Recorded: As title
Released: 5th April 2019 (Cog Sinister)

Another of the discs from *Set Of Ten*, recorded at the first of three consecutive dates the group played at the Northern Quarter venue in May 1982. Mediocre sound quality; it's most notable for the version of 'Wings' that featured the much more frantic and less subtle version of the riff that was used in the song's first dozen or so performances.

Live To Air In Melbourne '82
Recorded: Prince of Wales Hotel, Melbourne, 2nd August 1982
Released: 4th May 1998 (Cog Sinister)

Originally broadcast on Australian radio, *Live To* Air is another of the group's best live releases, even if its cover is another poor one.

In A Hole
Recorded: Mainstreet Cabaret, Auckland, New Zealand, 21st August 1982
Released: Late 1983 (Flying Nun – New Zealand only)

This was a rich period for Fall live albums: *In A Hole* is another that's among their best, although the final five tracks (an audience recording) don't quite match up to the first 11. Originally only released in New Zealand, but import copies sold well in the UK, much to Smith's consternation (see Chapter 6). A poorly mastered version got a UK release on Cog Sinister in 1997. A superior version, *In A Hole* + was issued in the UK in 2003 on the same label, this time including six other tracks from the 1982 New Zealand tour.

[Austurbæjarbíó] – Reykjavík Live 1983
Recorded: Reykjavík, Iceland, 6th May 1983
Released: 5th February, 2001 (Cog Sinister)
A soundboard recording that's almost crystal clear but strangely
cold and soulless (see Chapter 7). Reissued as part of Record
Store Day 2020.

Live @ ICC Hannover 11th April 1984
Recorded: As title
Released: 13th December 2019 (Cog Sinister)
At the end of 2019, Cog Sinister released the box set *Another Set
Of Ten* (which once again featured 11 discs, despite the title). They
were, this one included, fairly undistinguished audience recordings.

Take It Down To The Wire At Clitheroe Castle
Recorded: Clitheroe Castle, 16th June 1985
Released: 4th December 2020 (Ozit-Morpheus)
From a free open air concert broadcast on BBC Lancashire (see
Appendix 1).

Sheffield Poly 26-11-1986
Recorded: As title
Released: 24th January 2019 (download only)
One of four Sheffield performances released via the Bandcamp
page of the Sheffield Tape Archive.[423] Ropy sound, but a spirited
performance, including an energetic 'U.S. 80's - 90's'.

BBC Radio 1 Live In Concert
Recorded: Rock City, Nottingham, 19th May 1987
Released: 2nd August 1993 (Windsong International)
Broadcast on BBC Radio 1's *Live in Concert*, 25th May 1987,
although it's not the complete performance. Like *[Austurbæjarbíó]*,
the sound quality is crystal clear, but it has a cold, hollow feel
(see Chapter 11).

Live In Cambridge 1988
Recorded: Corn Exchange, Cambridge, 19th March 1988
Released: October 2000 (Cog Sinister)

---

[423] All four are available on a 'name your price' basis: https://sheffieldtapearchive.
bandcamp.com/

Whilst there's a customary bit of shoddiness about this Cog Sinister release (the spine and disc label spell Cambridge as 'Cambrige', 'Mr. Pharmacist' becomes 'Mr Pharacist', the debut of 'Athlete Cured' is omitted) it's otherwise a top-notch recording of an excellent performance.

Seminal Live
Recorded: G-Mex, Manchester, 19th July 1986; Fritz Club, Vienna, 16th April 1988[424]
Released: 19th June 1989 (Beggars Banquet)
A hit and miss mishmash of live and studio tracks cobbled together in the spirit of contractual obligation (see Chapter 13).

I Am As Pure As Oranj
Recorded: King's Theatre, Edinburgh, 17th August 1988
Released: July 2000 (Burning Airlines)
Recorded on the third of six nights that the group performed *I Am Curious, Orange* in Edinburgh, *Pure* benefits from excellent sound quality and a tight, controlled performance from the group (see Chapter 12).

Sheffield Leadmill 16-12-1989
Recorded: As title
Released: 24th January 2019 (download only)
Another live recording released via the Bandcamp page of the Sheffield Tape Archive. Dreadfully muffled and murky.

Live In Zagreb
Recorded: Dom Sportova, Zagreb, 15th April 1990[425]
Released: 4th June 2001 (Cog Sinister)
A clean soundboard recording, although one that feels a little lifeless; it also sounds as if it might have been mastered at slightly too slow a speed. Not without the odd moment of interest – MES

[424] The origins of the live tracks are far from clear.
[425] There is some doubt as to whether the recording is actually from Zagreb, although Dave Thompson's assertion that it was recorded in Germany in May 1990 (*User's Guide to The Fall*, p116) doesn't hold water as the group didn't play in Germany that month. They did play nine dates there in April, however, and the gig at the Metropol in Berlin on the 9th seems the most likely candidate. Given Cog Sinister's track record, it's not entirely unbelievable that they might title the album so erroneously; something that's reinforced by the fact that 'Tuff Life Boogie' here is actually 'Dead Beat Descendant'.

instructing the group to pick up the pace with 'Hit The North' ('faster, faster!'), for example – but certainly not one of the more essential purchases.

Nottingham '92
Recorded: Trent Polytechnic, Nottingham, 15th March 1992
Released: November 1998 (Cog Sinister)
One of the best ones: generally good sound, the group on top form and peppered with interesting MES asides (see Chapter 16).[426]

Live 1993 at Hallam University, Sheffield
Recorded: As title, 7th April 1993
Released: 7th January 2016 (download only)
Another 'name your price' download from the Sheffield Tape Archive. Originally broadcast live to air on Mark Goodier's Radio 1 show (see Appendix 1), it finds the group in fine fettle, knocking out a concise (it was for a half-hour radio slot) and exuberant run through most of *The Infotainment Scan*. Hanley, Wolstencroft and Scanlon are on excellent form, Dave Bush's electronics squelch and bleep entertainingly throughout and MES adds extra texture through a series of taped snippets of his voice. Very much worth acquiring.

Live 1993 11th October Batschkapp Frankfurt Germany
Recorded: As title
Released: 26th October 2018 (Cog Sinister)
Another from *Set Of Ten*. Reasonable sound quality and a decent performance, including impressively pacey versions of 'Strychnine' and 'Big New Prinz'.

Live At The Assembly Rooms, Derby 1994
Recorded: As title, 5th June 1994
Released: 16th November 2018 (Cog Sinister)
Featuring cover art by Pascal Le Gras that echoes his sleeve for *Middle Class Revolt*, *Derby* is not one of the highlights of the *Set Of Ten* box set. The sound quality is mediocre at best, and the group

---

[426] Good as it is, it isn't *quite* worth the £1,584.30 price tag on Amazon at the time of writing. Free delivery though.

sound strangely lethargic in the first half of the set — relatively long versions of 'Reckoning' and 'Up To Much' in particularly drag on interminably. Things do pick up a little in the second half though, and there's a brutally intense seven and a half minute thrash through 'Hey! Student'.

Live @ Tramps New York 10th September 1994
Recorded: As title
Released: 13th December 2019 (Cog Sinister)
From the *Another Set Of Ten* box set, labelled as 1984 on the spine. Better sound quality than most of the recently-released live albums, although Smith's vocals are rather buried in the mix.

In The City...
Recorded: The Roadhouse, Manchester, 20th-22nd March 1995
Released: 27th January 1997 (Artful Records)
An often-overlooked gem, definitely worth a place in the top ten Fall live albums, not least for the joyous nine-minute romp through 'Life Just Bounces' (see Chapter 18).

The "Twenty-Seven Points"
Recorded: Various dates and venues — 1991-95[427]
Released: 7th August 1995 (Cog Sinister via Permanent)
Six years after *Seminal Live*, the group released another live/ studio hybrid, albeit one with a more complicated approach than just studio-side/live-side. The various interludes give it an intriguing collage-like feel, and there are several highlights, not least the bafflingly obscure gem 'Noel's Chemical Effluence'. It is, however, rather an uneven and sprawling mess (see Chapter 19).

Live At The Astoria 1995
Recorded: Astoria, London, 23rd October, 1995
Released: 16th November 2018 (Cog Sinister)
Many of the *Set Of Ten* discs feature cover art by Pascal Le Gras that's in his usual abstract style and is clearly designed to be a companion piece to the cover of the album that the group were promoting at the time of the performance. Here,

---

[427] The cover says '92-95', but 'Mr. Pharmacist' was recorded in Prague in 1991 — the introduction to the track is even called 'Prague '91'.

inexplicably, he elects to use a photograph of a tartan slipper on fire. The sound quality is fairly good for an audience recording, and it's an interesting if variable set. 'The Coliseum' meanders haphazardly before petering out limply after only 90 seconds; a nicely sparse 'Middle Class Revolt' is the 'Simon, Dave & John' version (see Chapter 19); the nine-minute 'Chiselers' is a bit of a mess, dominated by Burns and Bennett's backing vocals; 'Birthday' is gruesomely tuneless; 'D.I.Y. Meat' (making its debut) is enjoyably chaotic. The highlight is the surprisingly lively version of 'Edinburgh Man'. This was Craig Scanlon's penultimate gig.

15 Ways To Leave Your Man
Recorded: London Astoria, 26th June 1996
Released: May 1997 (Receiver Records)
Another very variable set (see Chapter 20). Only around half of the tracks actually come from the Astoria gig,[428] and closing duo of 'Reckoning' and 'Hey! Student' are actually lo-fi versions of Peel session tracks with audience noises and sound effects cynically dubbed over the top.

The Idiot Joy Show
Recorded: The Junction, Cambridge, 24th October 1995; Roskilde Festival, Denmark, 30th June 1996; Phoenix Festival, 21st July 1996
Released: 14th July 2003 (Alchemy/Burning Airlines)
A double CD compiled by Mike Bennett; the sleeve notes and track-listing are riddled with errors. Worth a listen, however (see Chapter 19).

Pearl City
Recorded: Roskilde Festival, Denmark, 30th June 1996; Phoenix Festival, 21st July 1996
Released: 15th November 2004 (Get Back – Italy)
A single CD released in Italy, comprised of the second disc of *The Idiot Joy Show* for no apparent reason.

---

[428] 'Darling', 'Numb', 'Prinz', 'Mr. Pharmacist', 'Hurtz', 'M5' and 'Return' all come from earlier performances, possibly as far back as 1992.

Live At The Phoenix Festival
Recorded: Phoenix Festival, 14th July 1995 and 21st July 1996
Released: 29th September 2003 (Strange Fruit)
Nine tracks from the group's appearance at the festival in 1995, plus four more from Phoenix 1996. It was released on BBC distributor label Strange Fruit as they were broadcast as part of the John Peel Show (see Appendix 1). Obviously, there's considerable overlap with above two releases.

Live 1996 28th September, Corn Exchange, King's Lynn
Recorded: As title
Released: 22nd February 2019 (Cog Sinister)
From *Set Of Ten*. A fairly poor audience recording of the third date of the group's disastrous autumn 1996 tour (see Chapter 20). 'The Mixer' is played twice consecutively for no obvious reason; 'Chiselers' is a ragged mess; there's an unforgiving nine-minute version of 'U.S. 80's - 90's'. The low point is either the slurred, lumbering shamble through 'Mr. Pharmacist' or MES attempting 'Birthday' on his own. Historically interesting, but not an easy or pleasant listen.

Live @ Motherwell Concert Hall, 5th October 1996
Recorded: As title
Released: 13th December 2019 (Cog Sinister)
From the *Another Set Of Ten* box set. Another audience recording from the autumn 1996 tour. Brix didn't appear and MES only does so sporadically, several songs ending up as instrumentals; there are also a few false starts. During 'New Big Prinz', MES 'plays' guitar. Wolstencroft and Hanley do their best to hold things together, and it's not quite as bad you might expect, given the gig's reputation. Nonetheless, it's still a difficult listen. It also has a predictably terrible cover, featuring what looks like a miniature cardboard cut-out of Smith.

Live Various Years
Recorded: 1988-1997[429]
Released: September 1998 (Cog Sinister)
The first result of Smith's deal with Rob Ayling of Voiceprint that allowed him to release live Fall recordings using the Cog Sinister imprint; also the first of six albums to feature the famous 'MES flicks the Vs' image on its front cover. It set a precedent for poorly constructed and uninformative releases on the label: several of the dates/venues are wrong, and the ending of 'Hip Priest' – an interesting version featuring unusually 'floaty' keyboards – is spliced into another track for no apparent reason (there's a spot of 'Hurricane Edward' at the end too).

Live 1997 30th November Stage Stoke UK
Recorded: As title
Released: 22nd February 2019 (Cog Sinister)
Another from *Set Of Ten*, and another messy performance. It opens with an impressively menacing and aggressive 'Spencer', the recording of which is briefly interrupted by what sounds like an altercation between whoever's recording and the venue's security. 'Jungle Rock' is similarly forceful, but for some reason Burns disappears around the four-minute mark, leaving the song to descend into rhythmless chaos for a couple of minutes before he re-joins for its finale. 'Idiot Joy Showland' is played as an instrumental; 'Masquerade' is awkward and lumbering; 'Container Drivers' (making its first appearance for 13 years) is an incoherent mess (half of the group seemingly mistaking it for 'Fiery Jack'); Crooks's contributions to 'Hip Priest' are ham-fisted and simplistic; 'M5' and 'Ol' Gang' become little more than one-dimensional dirges. A surprisingly tight version of 'Lie Dream', however, morphs into an impressive repetitive thrash. Another release that's of historical interest even though it doesn't exactly catch the group at their best.

---

[429] Roughly. The dates/venues given are almost certainly inaccurate. Four are attributed to Munich, October 1993; the group were in Germany at the time, but did not perform in Munich. 'Deadbeat Descendant' wasn't played in New York on 17th September.

Live 1998 12th August Astoria 2 London
Recorded: As title
Released: 13th April 2019 (Cog Sinister)
The second of only two gigs performed by the post-Brownies slimmed down Smith / Nagle / Leatham / Head line-up (see Chapter 21), it's yet another from *Set Of Ten*. Given the circumstances, it's not surprising that there's a distinctly under-rehearsed and improvised tone to the whole thing ('Plug Myself In' in particular is a complete mess), but it captures a typically defiant and resilient Fall performance.

Live At Doonroosje, Nijmegen 1999
Recorded: As title, 14th September 1999
Released: 5th October 2018 (Cog Sinister)
A *Set Of Ten* release that features a brief set (not much over 50 minutes) that still manages to cram in 15 songs. After the chaos of 1998, this recording – taken from the group's autumn mini-tour of the low countries – sees the Wilding / Nagle / Helal / Head line-up starting to cohere to some extent. However, the performance has its ragged moments: 'Touch Sensitive', despite having been played (occasionally twice) at each of their previous 22 dates, sounds in places like they'd only learnt it that afternoon. An audience recording, it's pretty dodgy sound-wise, and Wilding is plagued by feedback throughout.

Live 16th April 2001 – TJs Newport Wales UK
Recorded: As title
Released: 5th April 2019 (Cog Sinister)
An undistinguished *Set Of Ten* audience recording that features a rare outing for 'Devolute', which is rather spoiled by audience chatter, although it does feature some interesting variations on the lyrics: 'Where is the great bridges built by the Scottish? They are disintegrating now. I've got my passport with me… Sorry, I forgot where I was with that one…in the land of Grolsch… in the land of grubby Grolsch. Where's the torches? In this area, I am used to torches and people singing.' 'Dr. Bucks' Letter' features references to Super Furry Animals and the Stereophonics.

Live @ Edinburgh Liquid Rooms 10th October 2001
Recorded: As title
Released: 13th December 2019 (Cog Sinister)
From the *Another Set Of Ten* box set. Reasonable audience recording, although the audience chatter is occasionally irritating. The highlight is a rather bluesy 'Dr. Bucks' Letter'.

Live At The Knitting Factory – L.A. – 14 November 2001
Recorded: As title
Released: 19th February 2007 (Hip Priest/Voiceprint)
A recording of the first night of the group's mini-tour of the US in November 2001. A rather poor recording, especially in comparison to those on the *Touch Sensitive* set (see below).

Live In San Francisco
Recorded: Great American Music Hall, San Francisco, 19th November 2001
Released: 17th June 2013 (Ozit-Morpheus Records)
Far superior to the L.A. recording, even if Smith's vocals are a tad over-dominant in places. The group are on top form here, MES sounding particularly focused and vehement. 'Bourgeois Town' (played at a cracking pace) gets a whole new lease of life; 'Sons Of Temperance' is also delivered at breakneck speed, but the slower passages also have a delirious wooziness. Even 'And Therein', which by this point was starting to sound like a rather lazy opportunity for a breather, fizzes with gusto.

Touch Sensitive… Bootleg Box Set
Recorded: Patronaat, Haarlem, The Netherlands, 6th April 2001; Melkweg, Amsterdam, The Netherlands, 7th April 2001; Concorde 2, Brighton, 17th April 2001; Crocodile Cafe, Seattle, 20th November 2001; The Knitting Factory, New York, 23rd November 2001
Released: 14th July 2003 (Castle Music/Sanctuary)
A very good value collection of five full gigs from 2001.[430] Sound quality varies from good to very good, and it's full of dynamic, punchy performances. The versions of 'Dr. Bucks' Letter' and

[430] At the time of writing, a second-hand copy will set you back around £30 – not bad for 80 tracks over five and a half hours.

'Ibis–Afro Man' are particularly varied and interesting; the latter is a model of coherence compared to the album version.

2G+2
Recorded: Studio Wentworth, Salford mid-2001 (studio tracks); Crocodile Cafe, Seattle, 20th November 2001; The Knitting Factory, Los Angeles, 15th November 2001; The Knitting Factory, New York, 23rd/25th November 2001
Released: 10th July 2002 (Action Records)
Another studio/live hybrid – arguably the best Fall release of this type. Three intriguing studio outtakes are interspersed among a selection of energetic, dynamic performances from the group's short US tour of November 2001 (see Chapter 24).

Live At The Garage – London – 20 April 2002
Recorded: As title
Released: 29th January 2007 (Hip Priest / Voiceprint)
Middling-quality audience recording of a solid enough but unremarkable performance. It was included as disc two of the 2004 DVD *Access All Areas – Volume One.*[431]

Live At The ATP Festival – 28 April 2002
Recorded: Camber Sands, East Sussex, as title
Released: 19th February 2007 (Hip Priest/Voiceprint)
As above, a middling-quality audience recording of a solid enough but unremarkable performance.

Yarbles
Recorded: King George's Hall, Blackburn, 22nd September 2002.
Released: 17th October 2014 (Secret Records)
A vinyl only selection from the performance recorded for the *A Touch Sensitive* DVD (see below).

Creative Distortion
Recorded: King George's Hall, Blackburn, 22nd September 2002
Released: 5th December 2014 (Secret Records)
Double CD of the performance recorded for the *A Touch Sensitive* DVD: Eleni's debut and Ruth Daniel's sole appearance. An

---

[431] In the grand tradition of Cog Sinister releases, the DVD includes the titles 'More Pseud Mag. Ed.' and 'I Can The Grass Grow'.

energetic and spirited performance, if lacking a little in subtlety in places.

Best Of The Fall & Mark E Smith
Recorded: King George's Hall, Blackburn, 22nd September 2002
Released: 18th May 2018 (Secret Records)
Another vinyl rehash of the 2002 Blackburn gig. Eleven tracks, seven of which were on *Yarbles*.

Live At The Knitting Factory – New York – 9 April 2004
Recorded: As title
Released: 27th January 2007 (Hip Priest/Voiceprint)
Also known as 'Punkcast 2004', this recording was filmed and released as disc one of *Access All Areas – Volume One* (see above). It's of fair sound quality, and contains decent versions of 'Sparta' and 'Mere Pseud Mag. Ed.', plus a nicely understated 'Janet, Johnny + James'.

Interim
Recorded: August – September 2004
Released: 1st November 2004 (Hip Priest/Voiceprint).
Originally entitled 'Cocked', *Interim* was a collection of live and rehearsal recordings in a similar spirit to *The "Twenty-Seven Points"*. It's wildly uneven but full of intriguing curiosities (see Chapter 25).

Sheffield Boardwalk 6-10-2005
Recorded: As title
Released: 24th January 2019 (download only)
From the Sheffield Tape Archive. The group sound on good form, but it's no more than a medium–quality audience recording. Features Smith's mate Dougie James (see Chapter 25) on backing vocals for the encore of 'Boxoctosis'.

The Fall Take America
Recorded: City Gardens, Trenton, New Jersey, 12th June 1981; Al's Bar, Los Angeles, 4th July 1981; Larry's Hideaway, Toronto, 21st April 1983; Traxx, Detroit, 22nd April 1983; Exit Club, Chicago, 4th April 1985; The 9.30 Club, Washington D.C., 4th March 1986; Irvine Meadows, California, 1st November 1986; New Ritz, New York, 18th May 1990; Liberty Lunch, Austin,

11th September 1993; Crocodile Club, Seattle, 20th November 2001; Knitting Factory, Los Angeles, 13th May 2006
Released: 14th March 2022 (Cog Sinister)
A 12-CD box-set that, like *Set Of Ten* and *Another Set Of Ten*, is comprised of generally mediocre quality bootleg recordings that were already widely available. *Live At The Crocodile Club...* was previously released as part of the *Touch Sensitive... Bootleg Box Set*.

Last Night At The Palais
Recorded: Hammersmith Palais, London, 1st April 2007
Released: 24th August 2009 (Sanctuary via Universal)
'The Dudes' were a fabulous live act who sadly never got to record a Fall album that did them justice, so thank God for the existence of the superb *Last Night At The Palais*. Among the very best of The Fall's live albums, it includes a simply monumental version of 'Blindness' (see Chapter 27).

Live @ MOHO, Manchester 11th November 2009
Recorded: As title
Released: 13th December 2019 (Cog Sinister)
From the *Another Set Of Ten* box set. Includes 'Cowboy Gregori's first (rather sketchy) outing and the second for 'O.F.Y.C. Showcase'. Features a rather tasteless cover depicting an empty wheelchair.

Live @ Newcastle Riverside 4th November 2011
Recorded: As title
Released: 13th December 2019 (Cog Sinister)
From the *Another Set Of Ten* box set. Features Tim Presley on guitar, filling in for Pete Greenway's paternity leave. An odd cover, depicting a pistol with a cocktail umbrella sticking out of the barrel. The track listing is full of errors.

Live @ Pavilion Bar Cork 21st July 2012
Recorded: As title
Released: 13th December 2019 (Cog Sinister)
From the *Another Set Of Ten* box set. Only contains six of the fourteen songs played (even though a full bootleg does exist).

Live @ Brudenel Social Club Leeds 30th November 2012
Recorded: As title
Released: 13th December 2019 (Cog Sinister)
From the *Another Set Of Ten* box set. No more than reasonable audience recording, although the group are in fine fettle – 'Hot Cake' and 'Cosmos 7', for example, are pretty lively.

Live Uurop VIII-XII Places In Sun & Winter, Son
Recorded: Europe, 2008-12
Released: 27th October 2014 (Cherry Red)
Contains a selection of live tracks that even the hardened Fall detectives on the online forum have found challenging to identify. It's a mixed bag: 'Cowboy George' seems to have been recorded from the bar of the venue; '50 Year Old Man', although lacking the demented distortion of the album take, is an intriguingly low-key version. The most interesting tracks are the alternative studio recordings of 'Auto-Chip' and 'Amorator'.

Live In Clitheroe
Recorded: The Grand, Clitheroe, 25th April 2013
Released: 22nd April 2017 (Ozit-Morpheus Records)
Interesting performance, uneven sound. The last official live album to be put out in Smith's lifetime.

Live @ Cathedral Quarter Arts Festival Belfast 8th May 2013
Recorded: As title
Released: 13th December 2019 (Cog Sinister).
From the *Another Set Of Ten* box set. Decent quality audience recording.

Live @ The Button Factory Dublin August 17th 2013
Recorded: As title
Released: 13th December 2019 (Cog Sinister)
From the *Another Set Of Ten* box set, this is a pretty poor quality audience recording. Features Rob Barbato (filling in for Dave Spurr) providing vocals on '15 Ways', here revived after a nine-year absence from the setlist. With the usual attention to the wrong detail, the final two songs ('Cowboy George' and 'Fall Sound') are indexed as one and labelled 'Over The Hill (Encore)'.

Out Ferroviarios
Recorded: OUT.FEST Festival, Portugal, 12th October 2013
Released: October 2021 (Cog Sinister)
An official double-CD release for a no better than a middling quality bootleg that had been widely available since 2013.

Live @ the Soy Festival Nantes 31st October 2013
Recorded: As title
Released: 13th December 2019 (Cog Sinister)
From the *Another Set Of Ten* box set. In another perfect example of how shoddily put together these live CDs are, 'Muzorewi's Daughter' is labelled as 'Muzorenis' – presumably because that's how it was written on that night's setlist.

Appendix 4: Who's Who

'Who's the bloke with the long hair?'

If you ask someone with no more than a passing acquaintance with the history of The Fall to tell you something that they know about the group, chances are that the first thing they will mention is the incredible number of members that they had over the years. It is undoubtedly true that a lot of people were in The Fall at one time or another: 'List of the Fall band members' warrants its own separate page on *Wikipedia*, and is over 9000 words in length; in *The Fallen*, Dave Simpson created a whole book based around the phenomenon. The famous (mis)quotation 'If it's me and yer granny on bongos...', to many people, is the very definition of what makes The Fall unique. But whilst it is understandable that the 'granny' quotation has become so ubiquitous, it's also a little unfortunate, because it does a disservice to the dozens of characters who contributed to the group's rich and complex history. It's true that The Fall without Mark E Smith would simply not have been The Fall; but, conversely, MES would have been nothing – or at least a whole lot less – without his ever-changing supporting cast.

Exactly why The Fall got through so many musicians is – like many aspects of the group – challenging to pin down precisely. In the early years, Smith's strategy (aided and abetted by Kay Carroll) was to establish the group as 'his'. As a result, Martin Bramah's departure in April 1979 meant that Smith was already the sole original member. Thereafter, there was never any doubt that MES called the shots. In *The Fallen*, many ex-members identified Smith's aversion to things becoming too comfortable and his desire to maintain 'creative tension' as a key factor in the high turnover. In addition, Smith was often simply bloody difficult to work with, even if he could also be generous and considerate when the mood took him. It's worth noting that – perhaps mellowing with age – he frequently expressed contentment with the settled line-up that took the group through the final quarter of its career.

Simply constructing a list of who was in The Fall is a nigh on impossible task, given that the people involved range from Steve Hanley (19 years' stalwart service) to Ruth Daniel (half a gig on keyboards) to Ed Blaney (occasional manager, guitarist and backing vocalist) to 'Nikki/Nicky' (a roadie who read out some MES text at a few 2008 gigs). Consequently, this list is divided into separate categories, although deciding who should be in which section is often tricky to resolve and will doubtless cause argument on the *Fall Online Forum* and elsewhere – whichever way it's organised.[432]

Group Members

Mark E Smith
Vocals, tapes, violin, guitar, keyboards, amp-twiddling (1976-2018)
Originally planned to be the guitarist, but hampered by a lack of aptitude.

Martin Bramah
Guitar, backing vocals (1976-1979, 1989-1990)
Real name Martin Beddington, he was the last of the original line-up to leave. Probably wrote more Fall songs than he received official credit for. Achieved critical acclaim and modest commercial success with The Blue Orchids in the early 80s before making a surprise return to the group for *Extricate* in 1990. Unceremoniously dismissed along with Marcia Schofield (his then partner) during the 1990 tour of Australia, New Zealand and Japan.

Tony Friel
Bass (1976-1977)
School friend of Martin Bramah. At least partly responsible for the

---

[432] Toying with different criteria led me to the conclusion that it would be impossible to apply any black and white rule successfully. Clearly, just playing a single gig wouldn't be enough to qualify, but setting the bar at 'more than one' would include, for example, Paul Bonney, who I don't think many people would count as a 'proper' member. Any number above that would just be arbitrary. Another thought was 'played at least a full season' i.e. at least one album credit and a tour, but that would have excluded, for example, Una Baines, who clearly was a member of The Fall. In the end, I have simply gone for an unscientific gut feeling approach – the original membership plus (once Martin Bramah had departed) people who seem to have been appointed by MES on the basis that they were going to be part of the group for the foreseeable future. A bit vague, I know, but if you have any complaints they can be sent in via an airmail letter to the Outer Hebrides.

group's name and also organised their first gig. The announcement of his departure can be heard on the *Live 1977* album.

Una Baines
Keyboards (1976-1978)
Founder member and radical feminist who first met MES in 1973. Originally designated as The Fall's drummer, she later switched to keyboards but had to sit out The Fall's first gig as she didn't have an instrument to play. She left the group after a breakdown related to drug use and her torrid relationship with bassist Jonnie Brown. Tensions relating to her subsequent relationship with Bramah led at least partly to the guitarist leaving the group as well. She played in The Blue Orchids with Bramah; they married and had a child but later separated.

Karl Burns
Drums, guitar, bass, keyboards, vocals (1977-1978, 1981-1986, 1993-1996, 1997-1998)
Renowned for his on-tour carousing, lack of personal hygiene and ability to vanish from public sight over the last 20 years, despite the best efforts of Dave Simpson and others to track him down. A highly-accomplished drummer, his instinctive partnership with Paul Hanley brought about some of the group's most legendary moments.

Jonnie Brown
Bass (1978)
Tony Friel's replacement. Chucked out after only a couple of weeks because of his heroin habit. Created the drawing on the cover of *Bingo-Master's Break-Out!*.

Eric McGann
Bass (1978)
Real name Anthony McGann (or possibly McGahan), also known as 'The Ferret' (he played in a band called The Ferrets) and Rick Goldstraw. Replaced Brown, but then bailed from the group on the eve of their first Peel session, allegedly because he was offended by conga player Steve Davies's Hawaiian shirt.

Yvonne Pawlett
Keyboards (1978-1979)

Replaced Una Baines after the group responded to her *NME* advert, and went on to make an important contribution to *Live At The Witch Trials*. It's often reported that she left the group because she had to look after her sick dog, but she explained it was because she felt that she didn't fit in.

Marc Riley
Bass, guitar, keyboards (1978-1982)

Appointed following McGann's departure. Only 16 years old, Riley had been acting as the group's unofficial roadie; he had also played in The Sirens with schoolmates Steve Hanley and Craig Scanlon. Made a significant songwriting contribution to many of the group's early 80s material, but found himself in increasing conflict with MES. This led to a notable confrontation in Australia that ultimately led to his dismissal. Went on to a successful broadcasting career which included co-hosting the Radio 1 breakfast show and a highly regarded evening slot on BBC 6Music.

Mike Leigh
Drums (1979-1980)

An unlikely choice for Karl Burns's replacement in 1979, given his Teddy Boy background and teetotal habits. Played on *Dragnet*, but left the following year citing the lack of regular gigs.

Steve Hanley
Bass (1979-1998)

Appointed as part of the reshuffle following Bramah's departure. Like Riley, had previously acted as an unpaid roadie for the group. Other than MES, the longest-serving member of The Fall. As Smith admitted, he simply *was* 'the Fall sound'. From 2014, played in Brix and the Extricated. He co-hosts the *Oh! Brother* Fall podcast series with his brother Paul.

Craig Scanlon
Guitar (1979-1995)

Promoted at the same time as his fellow ex-Siren Steve Hanley; only Hanley and MES himself had a longer stint in the group.

Largely abandoned music after being sacked by letter; has shunned publicity and had little to say about his time in the group since. The only dismissal MES ever publicly regretted.

Paul Hanley
Drums, keyboards, guitar (1980-1984)
Joined the group whilst in the middle of doing his mock O-levels; turned up to his first gig still wearing his school uniform. Left after Smith's aggressive dressing-down of the group following the theft of their gear in Cardiff in November 1984, although he filled in on drums a couple of times thereafter. After leaving the music industry for many years, he joined The Extricated alongside his brother Steve. Before writing *Have A Bleedin Guess*, he published *Leave The Capital*, a history of Manchester music. Co-host of the *Oh! Brother* Fall podcast series with Steve.

Brix Smith
Guitar, vocals (1983-1989, 1994-1996)
Had a whirlwind romance with MES after attending a Fall gig in Chicago in April 1983 and became his first wife three months later. Had a significant influence on the group's sound and fashion sense, and was part of The Fall's most commercially successful period. Also released her own records under the name The Adult Net. After separating from MES in 1989, she stepped away from music and for a while was best known for her relationship with violinist Nigel Kennedy. Made a surprise return to the group in the mid-90s, but left after the acrimonious 1996 tour. Went on to have a successful career in the fashion industry. From 2014 she fronted Brix and The Extricated with the Hanley brothers.

Simon Rogers
Bass, keyboards, guitar (1985-1986)
'The least likely musician ever to end up in The Fall.' Classically-trained Rogers was appointed – via his connection to Michael Clark – to cover Steve Hanley's paternity leave. He left the group after *Bend Sinister*, but subsequently made several performance and production contributions.

Simon Wolstencroft
Drums, keyboards (1986-1997)
Christened 'Funky Si' by Johnny Marr, Wolstencroft played in
early incarnations of both The Stone Roses and The Smiths. MES
poached him from support band The Weeds. Smith seems to
have been genuinely fond of Wolstencroft, and the two socialised
regularly. The drummer quit during the recording of *Levitate*,
principally – although not exclusively – because of financial
pressures. He published a well-received autobiography in 2014,
You Can Drum But You Can't Hide, and produced a podcast series
called *Funky Si's A-Z of Manchester*. He continues to play drums
for an assortment of Manchester bands.

Marcia Schofield
Keyboards (1986-1990)
New Yorker Schofield had previously played with Fall support
act Khmer Rouge. Was dismissed during the group's 1990
Antipodean tour along with her then partner Martin Bramah.

Dave Bush
Keyboards, 'machines' (1991-1995)
First worked with the group as a sound engineer on their 1990 tour,
and was promoted to full member the following year. Although
not a fan of The Fall's music to begin with, his electronics had
a significant impact on the group's sound in the first half of the
1990s. Gradually side-lined during the recording of *Cerebral
Caustic*, as Smith moved towards a back-to-basic garage rock
approach, before being sacked via letter at the start of 1995. He
later joined Elastica, and worked with MES again in 1999 when
Smith made a guest appearance on their *6 Track EP*.

Julia Nagle
Keyboards, guitar (1995-2001)
First worked with the group as a sound engineer on *Bend Sinister*.
Became Smith's girlfriend around the time she joined The Fall,
although she claimed that the relationship only lasted about eight
weeks. Was involved in the infamous post-Brownies altercation
in 1998 that led to Smith's arrest. After reverting to her original

surname Adamson, she founded the Invisiblegirl record label in 2006.

Tommy Crooks
Guitar (1997-1998)
Scottish artist who contributed artwork to The *"Twenty-Seven Points"* and designed *Levitate*'s cover. Left the group, along with Steve Hanley and Karl Burns, after the Brownies debacle.

Tom Head
Drums (1998-2000)
Head – real name Thomas Murphy – was an actor and also the brother of Smith's friend Steve Evets. A violent argument between him and Smith at the 1999 Reading Festival led to Nick Dewey's one-off appearance in The Fall. Died in 2015.

Neville Wilding
Guitar, vocals (1998-2001)
Had previously played in Welsh band Rockin' Gomez. Sang lead vocals on 'Hands Up Billy' from *The Unutterable*. Quit the group because of financial disagreements.

Adam Helal
Bass (1998-2001)
A friend of Wilding's. Helal was one of the longest-serving members of The Fall never to play on a Peel session. He left at the same time and for the same reasons as Wilding.

Spencer Birtwistle
Drums (2000-2001, 2004-2006)
Previously played in Manchester bands including The Bodines. Left in 2001 after a punch up with Ed Blaney in New York, but returned in 2004 to replace Dave Milner. Left the group again, along with Steve Trafford and Ben Pritchard, halfway through the ill-tempered 2006 US tour, during which MES threatened him with a corkscrew.

Ben Pritchard
Guitar (2001-2006)
A Prestwich native, he played guitar on 2000's 'Dr. Bucks' Letter',

but didn't join the group full-time until the following year. Like Steve Trafford and Spencer Birtwistle, left during the 2006 US tour because of Smith's behaviour.

Jim Watts
Bass, guitar, keyboards (2001-2003, 2004)
Played in Trigger Happy, who had been due to support The Fall in early 2001. Sacked as bassist by MES in 2003, he returned on guitar the following year before leaving once more, fed up with – amongst other things – Smith's arbitrary allocation of songwriting credits.

Dave Milner
Drums, vocals (2001-2004)
Another member of Trigger Happy. His demo track '8 Clothorn Road' formed the basis for 'Mountain Energei'; the lyric of 'Contraflow' was inspired by the journey through Snake Pass that the group had to take to pick him up. Left the group because of a combination of foot problems and a dislike for Ed Blaney's management style.

Eleni Poulou
Keyboards, vocals (2002-2016)
Greek-born Eleni (or Elena, Elenor or a multitude of other different spellings) first met MES in 1996 and became his third wife in 2001. Although she appeared on the cover of 2001's *Are You Are Missing Winner*, she didn't join the group until 2002, making her debut alongside one-off performer Ruth Daniel at the Blackburn *Touch Sensitive* DVD gig. Her simplistic but distinctive keyboard style and dispassionate vocals played an important role in The Fall's later work. The fourth longest-serving member of the group after MES, Steve Hanley and Craig Scanlon.

Steve Trafford
Bass (2004-2006)
Recruited by Ben Pritchard in a Manchester pub toilet. Responsible (although not officially credited) for the distinctive bassline of 'Blindness'. Quit The Fall during their 2006 US tour

along with Ben Pritchard and Spencer Birtwistle. Joined Brix and The Extricated on guitar in 2014.

Rob Barbato
Bass (2006-2007)
Bassist in LA band Darker My Love, Barbato was one of the three American musicians (collectively known as 'The Dudes') recruited for Smith by the Narnack label following Pritchard, Trafford and Birtwistle's sudden exit from the 2006 US tour. The first musician in The Fall to have a beard. He and the other 'Dudes' were due to play on 2008's *Imperial Wax Solvent*, but their US commitments made this impossible. Wrote at least part of '50 Year Old Man' but never received an official credit. Made a couple of guest appearances in 2013, and also contributed to 2015's *Sub-Lingual Tablet*.

Tim Presley
Guitar (2006-2007)
Another of 'The Dudes', also a member of Darker My Love. Appeared on stage with the group in 2011 and 2013, and also contributed to 2013's *Re-Mit* and 2015's *Sub-Lingual Tablet*. Has released several albums under the name White Fence.

Orpheo McCord
Drums (2006-2007)
The third 'Dude', drummer in (On) The Hill. Described by *The Fall Online* as the 'most jazzy Fall drummer ever'.

Pete Greenway
Guitar (2006-2018)
Like several others, recruited from a former support band (Pubic Fringe). Originally part of a 'squad-rotation' system for when 'The Dudes' couldn't appear. His distinctive, tremolo surf-rock style was a key component of the group's final decade. Formed Imperial Wax alongside Dave Spurr and Keiron Melling after Smith's death.

Dave 'The Eagle' Spurr
Bass (2006-2018)
Originally part of the 2006 'subs bench' alongside Greenway. His unmistakeable thick, heavy bass sound was another distinctive

feature of The Fall's final years. Part of Imperial Wax with Greenway and Melling, but left in 2021 when he relocated to Cornwall.

Keiron Melling
Drums (2006-2018)

Joined the 'subs bench' a couple of months after Greenway and Spurr. Some of the dual-drummer performances and recordings he made with Daren Garratt recaptured the energy and intensity of the Paul Hanley / Karl Burns years. Played in Imperial Wax.

Daren Garratt
Drums, vocals (2013-2015)

Like Pete Greenway, a member of Pubic Fringe. His first contributions to The Fall were as a backing vocalist. Covered for Keiron Melling's paternity leave in late 2013 before playing – highly effectively – as second drummer throughout most of 2014-2015. Also made a valuable contribution to *The Remainderer* EP.

'With…' / Guest Appearances / 'One Night Only'[433]

Steve Ormrod

Drummer on The Fall's first performance. Known for many years as 'Dave' until Dave Simpson unearthed his identity. Renowned for writing a pro-Tory song called 'Landslide Victory' that the group unsurprisingly rejected. After suffering from mental health issues, he committed suicide in 1994.

Jon Ormrod

Also known as 'Jon/John the Postman', he was a renowned figure in the late 70s Manchester punk scene, often jumping on stage at the end of gigs to perform impromptu a cappella versions of songs such as 'Louie Louie' (he appears on The Fall's performance of that song on *Live 1977*). His 1977 album *Jon the Postman's Puerile* features Smith's first appearance on record.

Steve Davies

Conga player and famed Hawaiian shirt-wearer, Davies played

---

[433] People who made some sort of noteworthy contribution to either the group's recorded output or live performances without being (by my admittedly vague criteria) 'proper' members of The Fall.

on the group's first Peel session and also stood in for Paul Hanley on the group's Dutch gigs in the summer of 1980.

Michael Adamson
The group's driver (son of Peter Adamson who played Len Fairclough in *Coronation Street*) is the voice declaring 'OK, studio, that's plenty' on 'Music Scene'.

Dave Tucker
Played clarinet on *Slates* and the group's fourth Peel session as well as several gigs in late 1980 and early 1981. Referred to in the lyric of 'Fantastic Life': a 'friend called David'.

Arthur Kadmon
Real name Peter Sadler, he was credited as 'Arthur Cadman' on the sleeve of *Room To Live*. Contributed no more than a few seconds of guitar to 'Hard Life In Country'.

Adrian Niman
Played sax on *Room To Live*'s title track. Apparently paid £26 for his efforts.

Alan Pellay
A friend of Smith and Carroll's, also known as Alana Pellay and Lanah P. Performed on the 15-minute version of 'And This Day' (recorded at Hammersmith Palais on 25th March 1982) that featured on *Hip Priest And Kamerads*.

Gavin Friday
Singer for Irish band Virgin Prunes, contributed to 'Copped It', 'Stephen Song' and 'Clear Off!' in 1984.

Phil Ames
Brix's guitar technician, he covered for her departure at a February 1989 gig in Munich that was broadcast on German TV. Every six months or so, someone posts a video of this performance on social media and asks, 'Who's the bloke with the long hair?'

Charlotte Bill
Played flute and oboe on *Extricate* and made a handful of live appearances in 1990-1991.

Kenny Brady
Played violin on *Extricate* and *Shift-Work* as well as Peel sessions 13 and 14 and several 1990–1991 gigs.

Cassell Webb
Contributed backing vocals to *Extricate*, *Shift-Work* and *Code: Selfish*. Sang the lead vocal on 'Free Range' B-side 'The Knight, The Devil And Death'.

Craig Leon
Cassell Webb's husband, he co-produced *Extricate*, *Shift-Work* and *Code: Selfish* as well as contributing guitar, keyboards and backing vocals.

Kevin 'Skids' Riddles
Filled in on keyboards for a handful of gigs in 1990 following Marcia Schofield's sacking. Described by Steve Hanley as 'eighteen stone of hairy-arsed Motörhead roadie'.

Mike Edwards
Singer/guitarist of Jesus Jones; played on the 1990 single 'Popcorn Double Feature'.

Stuart Carswell
Played drums (standing in for Dave Milner) on a March 1993 Granada TV performance. Learned the songs on the way there in Ben Pritchard's car.

Lucy Rimmer
Provided backing vocals on *Cerebral Caustic* and *Light User Syndrome* as well as lead vocals on 'The City Never Sleeps' (Peel session 19) and 'Birthday'.

Adrian Flanagan
Filled in on guitar for five gigs in 1996–97 after Brix's second and final departure. At the time he was Smith's sister Caroline's boyfriend. Fans were divided by his flamboyant guitar contributions.

Andy Hackett
Guitarist for Edwyn Collins; played on *Levitate*.

Sebastian Lewsley

Studio engineer who delivered the opening lines ('Awake at 5am / Mr Hughes was right in retrospect') on *Levitate*'s 'Hurricane Edward'.

Basil Nagle

Julia Nagle's son: performed the spoken word section that features on the 'single mix' of 'Masquerade'.

Damon Gough

Aka Badly Drawn Boy; recorded 'Calendar' with The Fall in 1998 following the infamous taxi/false teeth incident.

John Rolleson

Tour manager who contributed backing vocals to Peel session 21 in February 1998.

Stuart Estell

Over the years, hundreds of fans made vocal contributions to Fall gigs when handed the microphone by Smith. Estell is the possibly the only one who was handed a guitar. He did his best to play along to 'Industrial Estate' at Reading Alleycat in April 1998, which earned him a place in Dave Simpson's *The Fallen*.

Kate Themen

Drummer with Polythene, recruited in 1998 in the aftermath of the Brownies gig. Only played three gigs.

Karen Leatham

Recruited by Julia Nagle in 1998, Leatham had previously played in Wonky Alice. Played bass and keyboards. Quit after bottles were thrown onstage during her fourth performance, in Bristol.

Speth Hughes

Responsible for the 'special effects' on Peel session 22 in 1998, apparently.

Nick Dewey

After a violent argument between MES and Tom Head, Dewey was persuaded to stand in for The Fall's 1999 Reading Festival appearance. Did a fine job, despite not having played drums for several years and having only a couple of hours' preparation.

Kazuko Hohki

Singer from Japanese group Frank Chickens (and Grant Showbiz's wife); provided the distinctive vocals on 2000's 'Cyber Insekt' without ever meeting any of the group.

Roy Gittens

US tour manager in the 2000s, known as 'Cuz'n Roy'. Occasionally joined the group onstage for encores and played the washboard.

Brian Fanning

Played guitar on *Are You Are Missing Winner* and appeared at a handful of UK dates in the autumn of 2001. Quit because of the group's eccentric touring schedule.

Ruth Daniel

Recruited by Ed Blaney, Daniel played keyboards for part of the 2002 Blackburn gig captured on the *Touch Sensitive* DVD (also Eleni's debut).

Al Goldson

Roadie who read Smith's spoken-word piece 'Enigrammatic Dream' at Blackburn in 2002, captured on the *Touch Sensitive* DVD.

Steve Evets

Tom Head's brother, and a long-standing friend of Smith's. Filled in for the recently sacked Jim Watts at one gig in Turkey in March 2003. He also played on a two-song performance recorded for Granada TV (also in March 2003), had a backing vocal credit on *The Unutterable* and contributed on-stage backing vocals on several occasions – most notably the 2002 Blackburn *Touch Sensitive* DVD gig. MES and Evets also appeared together in the 1997 BBC drama *Diary of a Madman* and Mark Aerial Waller's films *Glow Boys* and *Midwatch*.

Stephen Beswick

A friend of Ben Pritchard who played keyboards on 'Recovery Kit'.

Simon 'Ding' Archer

Sound engineer on Smith's second spoken-word album, *Pander! Panda! Panzer!* Played a key role in reimagining *Country On The Click* into *Real New Fall LP* after the former's online leak. 'Loaned out' to PJ Harvey in 2004, but made several subsequent guest appearances as well as contributing to the production of several later releases at 6dB Studios in Manchester, which he established in 1990.

Dougie James

A friend of Smith's, and the leader of Manchester act Dougie James and the Soul Train, he joined the group onstage to perform backing vocals on several dates in 2004-2006.

Chris Evans

Steve Trafford and Spencer Birtwistle, stuck in traffic, failed to make the group's December 2004 gig in Bristol. Evans, drummer for support act Rag Week, filled in for Birtwistle. Like Nick Dewey, he did a remarkably good job given the circumstances.

Billy Pavone / Kenny Cummings / Phil Schuster

Members of New York band Shelby, they sang the vocals on 'Trust In Me', the final track on *Fall Heads Roll*.

Gary Bennett

Credited on the sleeve of *Reformation Post TLC* for rhythm guitar. All that's known about him is that he was a friend of Tim Baxter, a studio engineer at Gracieland Studio.

Nikki/Nicky

One of the group's roadies (surname unknown) who introduced several 2008 gigs by reading out a piece of MES-composed text.

Tamsin Middleton

Like 'Ding', a member of As Able As Kane, another Fall support act. She contributed startlingly intense vocals to 'Touchy Pad' from 2013's *The Remainderer*.

Paul Bonney

Drummer in The Australian Pink Floyd Show. Performed as part of a two-drummer line-up only twice, in July and October 2016.

Michael Clapham

The last ever new recruit, Manchester comedy promoter Clapham played keyboards on the last seven Fall gigs.

Production / Management

Kay Carroll

The Fall's manager from 1977 to 1983. Helped to cement MES's role as the group's lead figure. Her acerbic and aggressive management style played a key role in establishing and securing the group's independent, uncompromising attitude. Credited with vocals on *Dragnet,* vocals and kazoo on *Slates* and vocals and percussion on *Hex*. Severed her connections with the group during their 1983 US tour, shortly before Brix arrived on the scene. She died in 2020, aged 71.

Grant Showbiz

First met Smith at the 1978 Deeply Vale festival. Produced several Fall releases, including *Dragnet, Slates* and *The Unutterable*, and manned the desk at innumerable gigs over the years.

Geoff Travis

Founder of Rough Trade; co-produced *Grotesque* and *Slates*.

Richard Mazda

Producer on *Hex Enduction Hour* and the 'Lie Dream Of A Casino Soul' single; he played sax on the latter release. Instrumental in choosing The Regal for the recording of *Hex*.

Dale Griffin

Ex-drummer of Mott The Hoople and a childhood idol of Steve Hanley. Produced several of the group's Peel sessions.

Adrian Sherwood

Founder of the On-U Sound label; worked on the production of *Slates* and *Extricate*.

John Leckie

Veteran producer who, in the mid-80s, played a key role in making The Fall more commercially viable without sacrificing their independent, uncompromising spirit. Established a highly productive relationship with MES and the rest of the group during the recording of *The Wonderful And Frightening World* and *This Nation's Saving Grace*, although this soured during the *Bend Sinister* sessions.

Ian Broudie
Best known as the frontman of The Lightning Seeds, Broudie produced *I Am Kurious Oranj*.

Trevor Long
Became The Fall's manager in 1989, aiming to make them a bit more business-like. Long was given the responsibility of dismissing Bramah and Schofield in 1990. Smith became increasingly convinced that Long was embezzling The Fall's funds, which resulted in an unsuccessful court case in 1994. He was the subject of 'The Birmingham School Of Business School' and (possibly) 'Gentlemen's Agreement' and 'Married, 2 Kids'.

Rex Sargeant
Producer on *The Infotainment Scan* and *Middle Class Revolt*; also manned the mixing desk on several mid-90s performances. Warned by MES on *The "Twenty-Seven Points"* that he'd better get the sound 'sorted out'.

Mike Bennett
Co-produced *Cerebral Caustic* and *Light User Syndrome*; also sang on 'Cheetham Hill' and appeared live several times as backing vocalist. Produced and compiled many of the avalanche of dubious Fall compilations that appeared from the mid-90s onwards.

Rob Ayling
Head of Voiceprint Records, which, from the late 90s onwards, released an apparently endless stream of Fall live albums that varied hugely in quality.

Jason Barron
One half of D.O.S.E., who released 'Plug Myself In', with MES on vocals, in 1996. Also part of The Filthy 3, a track of whose formed the basis for 'The Crying Marshal'. Did some production and engineering on *Levitate* and *The Marshall Suite*.

Simon Spencer

The other half of D.O.S.E. Started production work on *Levitate* but was dismissed by Smith. Retaliated by releasing 'Inch' (under the name Inch), which featured some secretly recorded MES dialogue. Co-wrote 'Spencer Must Die', which, following his death in 2003, has become part of the MES 'pre-cog' mythology. Played keyboards at The Fall's pair of gigs at Jilly's Rockworld in Manchester in May 1997.

Keir Stewart

Spencer's production partner on *Levitate* before the duo's dismissal; also the other half of Inch. Played keyboards at the Astoria in February 1997.

Bernard MacMahon

Did some production and programming on *The Marshall Suite*. Possibly the source for the 'granny on bongos' quotation.

Steve Hitchcock

Produced and provided string arrangements on *The Marshall Suite*. Later known as Steve Sharples, he took Smith to court in 2015 regarding the royalties for 'Touch Sensitive'.

Ed Blaney

Played in Trigger Happy alongside Dave Milner and Jim Watts and was a long-standing friend of Smith's. He played guitar on *Are You Are Missing Winner*, contributed backing vocals at several gigs and was for some time the group's manager or 'broker'. Recorded an album with MES in 2008.

Pamela Vander

Smith's final partner and also The Fall's last manager. She designed the cover of *New Facts Emerge* and appeared onstage with the group in July 2017 at London's 100 Club.

Christophe Bride

Studio engineer on *New Facts Emerge*, he contributed backing vocals to the album's title track.

Cover Artists

Tina Prior
Mother of Saffron Prior (MES's second wife), she designed the 'spider' image that appeared on the cover of *Dragnet*.

Suzanne Smith
Smith's sister designed some of The Fall's best cover art, including the 'Fiery Jack' single and *Grotesque*.

Claus Castenskiold
Played in Banda Dratsing with Brix and in Khmer Rouge with Marcia Schofield. The intense, nightmarish imagery of his designs were a distinctive feature of many of the group's releases in the 80s, including *Perverted By Language* and *The Wonderful And Frightening World Of...*

Anthony Frost
Designed the bold, abstract covers of *Extricate* and *Imperial Wax Solvent*; also co-created the artwork for *Re-Mit* with Suzanne Smith. MES described his work as 'by far the best stuff I've ever been submitted'.

Pascal Le Gras
Described by Smith as 'a sublime genius', French artist Le Gras first met Smith at a Fall gig in Paris in 1990. He went on to be the most prolific of all The Fall cover artists, designing the artwork for the majority of the group's 90s output as well as many of the Voiceprint live albums.

Mark Kennedy
Manchester mosaic artist who worked on the cover art for *Reformation Post TLC*, *Your Future Our Clutter* and *Ersatz GB*.

Miscellaneous

John Peel
The Fall's most famous fan and – 'granny on bongos' aside – the source of the best-known quotations about the group. The Fall recorded a record-breaking 24 sessions for his Radio 1 show and were the only artist that had their own special section in his

enormous record collection. Despite this, he and Smith had only a distant, off-hand relationship. His voice featured on 'Symbol Of Mordgan' from 1994's *Middle Class Revolt*. Peel's untimely death in 2004 sparked a renewed interest in the group.

Sol Seaberg
Worked as the group's driver in the early 80s. Co-wrote 'The Man Whose Head Expanded' and was possibly the inspiration for the 'Jew on a motorbike' line in 'Garden'.

Michael Clark
Ballet dancer, Fall fan and friend of MES who memorably danced bare-buttocked to the group's performance of 'Lay Of The Land' on a 1984 episode of *The Old Grey Whistle Test*. His most famous collaboration with the group was the ballet *I Am Curious Orange*, performed at the Edinburgh Festival in 1988. Also appeared onstage with the group in 1998.

Saffron Prior
Ran the group's fan club, and became Smith's second wife in 1991. Simon Wolstencroft suggests that she stood in on keyboards for a few gigs following Schofield's sacking in 1990, but this seems unlikely and is contradicted by Steve Hanley. She and MES divorced in 1995.

Bec Walker
A 17-year-old aspiring singer who was doing work experience at Gracieland Studio whilst the group were recording *Fall Heads Roll*, she wrote the lyrics for 'Breaking The Rules'.

Bibliography

Paintwork: A Portrait of The Fall, Brian Edge
Omnibus Press, 1989

Hip Priest: The Story of Mark E Smith and The Fall, Simon Ford
Quartet Books Ltd., 2003

The Fall, Mick Middles and Mark E. Smith
Omnibus Press, 2003

A User's Guide To The Fall, Dave Thompson
Helter Skelter Publishing, 2003

Renegade – The Lives & Tales Of Mark E. Smith, Mark E Smith &
Austin Collings
Viking, 2008

The Fallen, Dave Simpson
Canongate Books, 2008

The Big Midweek – Life Inside The Fall, Steve Hanley and Olivia
Piekarski
Route Publishing, 2014

You Can Drum But You Can't Hide, Simon Wolstencroft
Route Publishing, 2014

The Rise, The Fall, and The Rise, Brix Smith Start
Faber & Faber, 2016

40 Odd Years Of The Fall, Tommy MacKay
2018

Have A Bleedin Guess, Paul Hanley
Route Publishing, 2019

The Annotated Fall http://annotatedfall.doomby.com/
The Fall Online http://thefall.org/index.html
The Fall Online Forum https://www.tapatalk.com/groups/thefall/
The Track Record https://thefallliveblog.wordpress.com/

Notes

Introduction

Smith's 'tongue of Satan' remark appeared in 'We Only Have This Excerpt: Mark E. Smith Of The Fall Interviewed', Kevin E.G. Perry, *The Quietus*, 24th November 2011.

His claim that Fall fans invented the internet is from 'Mancunian Candidate', Tony Herrington, *The Wire*, September 1996.

The 'envy of a lot of groups' comment appeared in 'The Fall: Fighting Talk', Tim Cumming, *The Independent*, 28th May 2004.

Before The Witch Trials

For a detailed account of Smith's formative years, see Simon Ford's *Hip Priest*, pp 1-11.

Smith's assessment of Bramah's frontman credentials and his description of The Fall's first recording session are taken from Mick Middle's *The Fall*.

His views on pot, punk, tarot and the origins of the group's name are provided by *Renegade*.

Much has been written about the Sex Pistol's early gigs in Manchester: the best account is David Nolan's *I Swear I Was There: The Gig That Changed the World*.

Dave Simpson's *The Fallen* provided the information about Steve Ormrod, The Fall's first gig and Tony Friel's departure.

The imaginary early setlist was posted on Tony Friel's now-defunct website in 2006. At the time of writing, it can still be seen at http://thefall.org/gigography/gig77.html

Martin Bramah's comments regarding 'Drugs Or Something' are from an (undated) online interview for Wicked Spins Radio.

Smith's account of his meeting with Tony Parsons and Julie Burchill is taken from 'The Man In The High Castle', an interview with Simon Dudfield, *NME*, October 1988.

Bernie Wilcox's description of the Stretford gig can be found on the *fall.org* gigography.

Smith's explanation of 'Hey! Student/Fascist's title change is based on interviews for *Temporary Hoarding*, no. 5, Spring 1978 (the paper/zine of Rock Against Racism) and 'United They Fall', Chris Brazier, *Melody Maker*, 31st December 1977.

Chapter 1: Live At The Witch Trials

Danny Baker's review of the Huddersfield Poly gig was published in *ZigZag* in February/

March 1978. (This is the interview that some suggest partly inspired the lyrics to 'Hip Priest'.)

Smith's comments about Siouxsie and the Banshees were made in an interview with Michael Lang for *BravEar* in 1986.

The reviews of *Short Circuit – Live At The Electric Circus* appeared in 'Conurbation Rock', Jon Savage, *Sounds*, 24th June 1978 and 'Various: Short Circuit', Adrian Thrills, *NME*, 22nd July 1978. Those of *Bingo-Master's Break-Out!* are from 'Rise of The Fall', Colin Irwin, *Melody Maker*, 12th August 1978 and Vivien Goldman, *Sounds*, 12th August 1978.

Smith's description of Danny Baker securing The Fall a record deal is from Mick Middles's *The Fall*, p100. Kay Carroll's comments on the deal were made to Simon Ford and Dave Simpson.

The accounts of the 1978 Deeply Vale festival appear on *The Fall Online* gigography page.

Smith made the claim that he wrote 'Frightened' at the age of 16 in an interview with Graham Lock: 'Stopping, Starting, and Falling All Over Again', *NME*, 7th April 1979. His description of the character John Quays was based upon, and his comments about the album's title track, are from the same interview.

The 'Beefhearty' quotation from Bramah regarding 'Mother-Sister!' was posted by 'wontonton' on the *Fall Online Forum*, and is reproduced on the song's *Annotated Fall* page.

Smith's description of 'Industrial Estate' is from *Renegade*.

Julian Cope's denial of drug dealing appeared in *Uncut*, September 2007.

Martin Bramah's comments on 'Music Scene' are from 'The Fall: album by album', *Uncut*, July 2019.

The album reviews are from 'The Fall Land On Their Feet', Graham Lock, *NME*, 24th March 1979 and 'The Fall Staying Ahead', Chris Westwood, *Record Mirror*, 31st March 1979.

Chapter 2: Dragnet

Smith's and Bramah's comments about the recruitment of Mike Leigh come from 'All Fall Down', Ian Penman, *NME*, 5th January 1980 and Simon Ford's *Hip Priest* respectively.

Martin Bramah's account of the making of *Dragnet*, 'Through A Glass Darkly', which includes his comments about songwriting credits on the album, can be seen at http://thefall.org/news/pics/MartinBramahsStoryofDragnet.pdf

The description of Hanley and Scanlon's recruitment is taken from *The Big Midweek*.

Andy Partridge's review of 'Rowche Rumble' appeared in *Smash Hits*, 20th October 1979.

Yvonne Pawlett explained her reasons for leaving the group to Dave Simpson in *The Fallen*.

Smith's comments about Grant Showbiz's production techniques are taken from 'Hobgoblins on the Loose', Bob Giddens, *ZigZag*, June 1980.

His explanation regarding the inspiration for 'Psykick Dancehall' appeared in 'Northern Uproar', Simon Goddard, *Uncut*, October 2003.

His comments on 'A Figure Walks' featured in 'Looking at the Fall Guise', Don Watson, *NME*, 1st October 1983.

The 'Branch on the tree of showbusiness' (also a phrase used in the lyric of 'Dice Man') quotation is from an interview of Smith by John Wilde, 'The Frightening World of the Fall', *Jamming*, November 1984.

Kay Carroll's comments about Bishop Abel Tendekayi Muzorewa appeared in a 1980 *NME* interview with Ian Penman, quoted on *The Track Record*. In the interview, she suggests that she wrote the lyric 'when pissed'.

Mike Leigh's praise for 'Flat Of Angles' is taken from *Reformation! Webzine*, issue 008.

The conflicting views of Paul Hanley and Smith regarding the use of out-of-tune guitars as a stylistic statement come from *Have A Bleedin Guess* and *Renegade* respectively.

The reviews of *Dragnet* are taken from 'Cryptic', Paul Du Noyer, *NME*, 10th November 1979

and 'Falling into the Eighties', Allan Jones, *Melody Maker*, 17th November 1979.

David Quantick's description of the album's production comes from *Q*, May 1999; Smith's is from *Renegade*.

Dave Thompson's evaluation of *Dragnet* is taken from *A User's Guide to The Fall*.

Chapter 3: Grotesque (After The Gramme)

Much of the information about The Fall's first US tour (and indeed about all of The Fall's tours up until 1998) comes from *The Big Midweek*.

Smith's comment about the tour appeared in 'Hobgoblins on the Loose', Bob Giddens, *ZigZag*, June 1980.

His description of the demo recording of 'New Puritan' was quoted by Richard Osborne, and appears in *Mark E. Smith and The Fall: Art, Music and Politics*, ed. Michael Goddard and Benjamin Halligan, Routledge, 2010.

Smith's comments about 'Fiery Jack' are from *Renegade* ('hard livers') and an interview quoted on the song's *Track Record* page ('the ageism thing').

His explanation of the move to Rough Trade comes from 'The Fall of Slick', George Kay, *Rip It Up*, September 1982.

The varying accounts of the reasons for Mike Leigh's departure are taken from *The Big Midweek, Have A Bleedin Guess* and the 'Mark E. Smith Self-Interview 1980' for *Tapezine*.

The 'self-interview' is also the source for Smith's comments about 'Elastic Man'.

Marc Riley told the tale of John Sparrow and his pipe in a 1999 BBC Radio 4 interview.

John Peel made his comments about 'New Puritan' during his Radio 1 show on 4th March 1986.

Mark Fisher's view of 'The N.W.R.A.' is from *K-Punk: The Collected and Unpublished Writings of Mark Fisher*, Repeater, November 2018. Smith's comment on the song was made in 'The Wit and Wisdom of Mark Smith', Andy Gill, *NME*, 10th January 1981.

The album reviews featured are 'Fall-ing in love again', Johnny Waller, *Sounds*, 15th November 1980 and 'Fall in a Pit', Graham Lock, *NME*, 29th November 1980.

Brian Edge's comment about the album is from *Paintwork: A Portrait of The Fall*.

Chapter 4: Slates
Dave Tucker's account of touring and recording with The Fall comes from *The Fallen*.

Smith's views about bootleggers were expressed in 'After the "Gram"', X. Moore, *NME*, 3rd April 1982.

Andy Gill's comment about *Slates'* format and his evaluation of the

release is from 'Gruff, tumble and Fall Boys', *NME*, 2nd May 1981.

Smith's criticism of Rough Trade is quoted from *User's Guide to The Fall* and *Renegade*.

His explanation of 'Prole Art Threat's narrative comes from *Hip Priest*.

The anti-London interpretation of 'Leave The Capitol' was put forward by 'MartinM' from the *Fall Online Forum*, and is quoted on *The Annotated Fall*.

Chapter 5: Hex Enduction Hour
Obviously, I am indebted to Paul Hanley's meticulous and detailed *Have A Bleedin Guess* for much of the information in this chapter.

Colin Irwin's account of the Iceland visit was published as 'The Decline and Fall in Iceland' in *Melody Maker*, 26th September 1981.

The article from the issue of the *NME* in which Smith first graced the cover was 'The Rise of Citizen Smith' by Barney Hoskyns.

Smith's comments about the move from Rough Trade to Kamera are taken from *The Big Midweek* and *Renegade*.

His explanation of the meaning of 'Lie Dream' appeared in 'Looking At The Fall Guise', Don Watson, *NME*, 1st October 1983.

Dave Tucker identified himself as the Dave mentioned in 'Fantastic Life' in *The Fallen*.

Smith's description of The Regal

is from 'Becks Induction Hour', John Doran, *The Quietus*, 2017. His comment about *Hex* possibly being the last Fall album is also from this article. Scanlon and Riley's statements on this issue are from *Have A Bleedin Guess*.

Smith's comments about *Hex*'s title and cover are taken from *Renegade*.

Stuart Estell's analysis of 'The Classical' is quoted on the song's *Track Record* page. Smith's comment on the message of the song is quoted on *The Annotated Fall*, attributed to 'Meijer Interview (July/August 1989)'.

The Danny Baker article mentioned in reference to 'Hip Priest's title is the same as referenced in Chapter 1.

The J Neo Marvin interview (for a punk fanzine) wasn't published at the time, but can be found at http://jneomarvin.com/ interviews-of-our-times/the-fall-unpublished-1981/

Smith cited Norman Mailer's *Deer Park* as an influence in 'Portrait of the Artist as a Consumer', *NME*, 15th August 1981.

The description of the second half of 'Winter 2' is taken from *Have A Bleedin Guess*.

The album reviews are from 'These Fallish Things', Richard Cook, *NME*, 13th March 1982 and 'The Manic Maze', Colin Irwin, *Melody Maker*, 6th March 1982. The *Sounds* review can be found at https://thefall. org/gigography/82hexad.html

Mark Storace expressed his dislike of the album in 'View From The Top', *Flexipop!*, March 1982.

Smith's evaluation of Hex is taken from *Renegade*.

The Stewart Lee quotation is taken from his introduction to *Have A Bleedin Guess*.

Chapter 6: Room To Live

Smith's comments about the passport-eating dog and the Antipodean tour are from *Renegade*. Much of the rest of the information about this tour (and the making of the album) is taken from *The Big Midweek*.

Roger Shepherd's account of his dealings with Smith regarding *In A Hole* can be seen in 'Roger Shepherd on The Fall's 1982 tour of NZ', *The Spinoff*, 25th January 2018.

Smith explained his 'instantaneous' approach to *Room To Live* in an interview with Helen Fitzgerald for *MasterBag* magazine, 1982. Paul Hanley's reaction to this approach is taken from 'INTERVIEW! in depth interview with drummer Paul Hanley on his days in The Fall', Rahman The Writer, *Louder Than War*, 3rd December 2016.

Smith's explanation of 'Joker Hysterical Face' appeared on the website *The Biggest Library Yet*, February 1997.

His comments about the Falklands War are from 'Mark E. Smith: wonderful and frightening', Nicholas Blincoe, *The Daily Telegraph*, 26th April 2008.

The album reviews are from 'White Rap Or Right Crap?', Amrik Rai, *NME*, 2nd October 1982; Dave McCullough, *Sounds*, 9th October 1982; and *Paintwork, A Portrait of The Fall*.

Chapter 7: Perverted By Language

The conflicting accounts of Marc Riley's removal from The Fall come from *The Big Midweek*, *Renegade*, and Riley's conversations with Dave Simpson in *The Fallen*.

Kay Carroll's reflections are taken from *The Fallen*. Marc Riley's comment about her is from 'Remembering Kay Carroll Of The Fall', Fergal Kinney, *The Quietus*, 9th June 2020.

Brix's perspective on her life in The Fall (in this and subsequent chapters) is taken from her memoir *The Rise, The Fall, and The Rise*. Description of the musicians' reaction to her arrival is largely taken from *The Big Midweek*.

The account of Smith's marriage proposal is from 'Personal File', *Smash Hits*, 20th May 1987.

The 'corruption and greed' comment regarding 'Kicker Conspiracy' is Simon Ford's. Smith's comment about leaving Kamera is also from *Hip Priest*.

Smith's description of *Perverted By Language*'s beauty and humour are from 'The Fall Guy', John Wilde, *ZigZag*, November 1983.

Paul Hanley's explanation of the 'brown baize' reference in

'Garden' appears in *Leave The Capital*, Route Publishing, 2017, as do his comments regarding 'Smile' and 'Tempo House'.

Brix's interpretation of the 'Jew on a motorbike' line from 'Garden' appears in 'The Surprising Jewish Story Behind Indie Rock Legend Brix Smith-Start', Michael Kaminer, *Forward*, 3rd September 2016. Smith's version is taken from 'After The Fall', Steve Lake *Melody Maker*, 21st April 1984.

Smith's comment about the lyrics of 'I Feel Voxish' appeared in *Tape Delay: Confessions from the Eighties Underground* (1987, SAF), a selection of interviews complied by Charles Neal.

The album reviews are from 'Words: Fall On Stony Ground', Jim Shelley, *NME*, 10th December 1983 and 'Speech Defects', Dave McCullough, *Sounds*, December 1983.

Chapter 8: The Wonderful And Frightening World Of...

The descriptions of John Leckie and his approach are taken from *The Rise, The Fall, and The Rise* and *The Big Midweek*.

Smith's account of his first sight of Michael Clark is taken from 'How we met: Michael Clark And Mark E. Smith', Glenda Cooper, *Independent on Sunday*, 16th November 1997.

Brix's comments about 'Lay Of The Land' and '2 x 4' come from the 2010 reissue CD booklet; those about 'Elves' are from *The Rise, The Fall, and The Rise*. She made the comments regarding Smith's obsession with *The Twilight Zone* and the Curly Wurly incident to dannyno on Twitter.

The album reviews are from 'Slang Kings', Richard Cook, *NME*, 13th October 1984 and 'World Domination', Andy Hurt, *Sounds*, 13th October 1984.

Smith's comments about *Wonderful And Frightening*'s change of sound are from *Renegade*.

Chapter 9: This Nation's Saving Grace
Much of the description of the events of 1984–85 is again taken from *The Big Midweek* and *The Rise, The Fall, and The Rise*.

Smith's assessment of John Leckie's production is from *Hip Priest*.

I am indebted to blogger and *Fall Online Forum* contributor thehippriestess for the eloquent 'single unit' summary of 'Quantifier'.

Simon Roger's description of the recording of 'Paintwork' appeared in the booklet accompanying the Omnibus edition of *This Nation's Saving Grace*; Smith's comments are from an interview with Edwin Pouncey in *Sounds*, 28th September 1985.

Brix identified the origins of 'Hey Mark! You're spoiling all the paintwork' in 'The Fall: album by album', *Uncut*, July 2019.

John Leckie's account of the recording of 'I Am Damo Suzuki' is taken from the booklet accompanying the Omnibus edition of *This Nation's Saving Grace*.

The album reviews are from 'Fall In!', David Quantick, *NME*, 28th September 1985 and 'Nationwide', Chris Roberts, *Sounds*, 28th September 1985.

Chapter 10: Bend Sinister
Comments by Simon Wolstencroft from this point onwards are, unless otherwise stated, taken from his memoir, *You Can Drum But You Can't Hide*.

The 'idiosyncrasies' quotation is from Simon Ford.

Smith's comment about 'standardised society' appears in an interview with Michael Lang, *BravEar* vol.3 issue 5, 1986. The one about the SS from 'Revolting Soul', Gavin Martin, *NME*, 30th August 1986.

His comment on 'R.O.D.' is taken from the 'Meijer Interview' referred to in the notes for Chapter 5.

The 'fairy tale book' comment about 'Dktr. Faustus' is from 'Revolting Soul', Gavin Martin, *NME*, 30th August 1986.

Smith's comment about 'Terry Waite Sez' is from a radio interview with Steve Barker, *On The Wire*, BBC Radio Lancashire, 1986; Brix's is from 'Brix Smith has just released her acclaimed autobiography: in depth interview', MacGabhann, *Louder Than War*, 31st May 2016.

Smith's explanation of the word 'riddler' appears in 'Revolting Soul', Gavin Martin, *NME*, 30th August 1986.

The album reviews are from 'Mind Rocker', Dave Haslam, *NME*, 4th October 1986 and 'Fall Guise', Simon Reynolds, *Melody Maker*, 4th October 1986.

Chapter 11: The Frenz Experiment
The 'beer mats/shoe box' anecdote is from Tommy Mackay's *Forty Odd Years of The Fall*.

The contrasting reviews of *Hey! Luciani* (the play) are from 'Cardinal Sins', Roy Wilkinson, *Sounds*, 13th December 1986; 'Gelli Babies Go Pope', Adam Sweeting, *The Guardian*, 12th December 1989; 'Say Hey, Say What, Say Nothing', *Melody Maker*, 20th December 1986; and 'Hey Luciani', Len Brown, *NME*, 20th December 1986.

Brix and Marcia's excitement regarding a possible *Top of the Pops* appearance is covered in *Hip Priest*.

Simon Roger's account of the origins of 'Hit The North' is taken from 'The Fall "Hit The North"', Tom Doyle, *Sound On Sound*, March 2015.

David Stubbs' review of 'Victoria' is from *Melody Maker*, 16th January 1988.

Smith's somewhat misleading statement about 'Victoria' comes from 'Victoria Falls', Danny Kelly, *NME*, 13th February 1988.

The description of how the group came to steal Spinal Tap's riff is based on the account in *The Big Midweek*.

Smith gave his account of his visit to Bremen in 'The Bug Eyed Pop Goblin' Roy Wilkinson, *Sounds*, 2nd January 1988 and 'Falling back to Berlin', Rachel Glassberg, *Exberliner*, 12th March 2016.

The reviews of *Frenz* are taken from 'Perverse, The Fall, The Frenz Experiment', Andy Gill, *Q*, 18th March 1988 and 'Totally Weird', Danny Kelly, *NME*, 5th March 1988.

Chapter 12: I Am Kurious Oranj
Reviews of the ballet come from 'Insect Power', Jann Parry, *The Observer*, 25th September 1988 and 'M.E.S. in Tutu Draw', Sean O'Hagan, *NME*, 1st October 1988.

Smith's explanation of the origins of 'Van Plague' is from '1989 – July/August – Meijer Interview', quoted on *The Track Record*.

He described how he took the word 'gibbous' from H.P. Lovecraft in 'The Fall's Mark E. Smith on Re-Mit, Playing for German Lawyers, and H.P. Lovecraft', William Van Meter, *Vulture*, 13th May 2013.

The album reviews are taken from 'Outspanding', Len Brown, *NME*, October 1988; *Paintwork: A Portrait of The Fall*; and *User's Guide to The Fall*.

Smith's claim of complete authorship of 'Wrong Place, Right Time' was made in *Mojo*, February 2015.

Chapter 13: Extricate

Smith's comments about leaving Beggars Banquet were made in 'Beggars Fall Out', *NME*, 10th December 1988.

Eddie the soundman and the seaweed anecdote occurred on The Fall's 1988 US tour and was related in Simon Wolstencroft's autobiography, which is also the source of 'from Salford, Mark would say...'

The reviews of *Seminal Live* are from 'The Big E', Richard Cook, *Sounds*, 10th June 1989 and 'Frenz Again', Andrew Collins, *NME*, June 1989; Marcia Schofield's brutal assessment is quoted in *Hip Priest*.

Smith's comments about 'Bill Is Dead' are from 'Mark E. Smith Extricates Himself', *Sounds*, 3rd February 1990.

Jonathan More's comment about 'Telephone Thing' appeared in 'Ring The Noise', *NME*, 20th January 1990; Bramah's come from 'The Fall: album by album', *Uncut*, July 2019.

Smith's supposed ignorance about Gretchen Franklin and his tale about phone tapping are quoted from 'Funky, Cold, Modern-ah', Andrew Collins, *NME*, 25th January 1990.

Bramah's unlikely tale regarding 'Hilary' and 'A Horse With No Name' appeared in *The Vinyl District*, 26th May 2016.

Smith's appreciation of 'And Therein...' appeared in 'Lyricists: Mark E. Smith', Phil Sutcliffe, *Q*, May 1992.

The album reviews are from Jon Wilde, *Melody Maker*, 17th February 1990 and 'Fall's Gold: Top Mark!', James Brown, *NME*, 17th February 1990.

Chapter 14: Shift-Work

Smith's tearful account of preparing to leave Edinburgh is taken from 'Funfair For The Common Man', Ian Gittins, *Melody Maker*, 3rd March 1990. His explanation of Bramah and Schofield's dismissal appears in 'Strife In A Northern Town', Andrew Harrison, *Select*, 1990.

The comments regarding Saffron Prior's keyboard skills are from *The Big Midweek*.

The *La Vanguardia* review was called 'Trapped in their Claws' by Karles Torra, 14th November 1990.

Dave Bush's 'Les Dawson' remark is taken from *Hip Priest*.

The reviews of 'High Tension Line' are both from *Sounds*, 8th December 1990.

Smith's clarification regarding his opposition to the Nazis is from 'Not Falling, Soaring', Stephen Dalton, *Vox*, June 1991.

His comment about Pascal Le Gras is reported in *Hip Priest*; his distaste for sportsmen releasing records and the Happy Mondays comes from 'Badmouth Strikes Again', Andy Peart, *Sounds*, 8th December 1990.

Smith's bemusement at his own lyrics for 'You Haven't Found It Yet' was reported in 'Lyricists: Mark E. Smith', Phil Sutcliffe, *Q*, May 1992.

Album reviews are from 'Quiet! Genius At Work...', Stephen Dalton, *NME*, 20th April 1991 and 'The Sinister Waltz', Jon Wilde, *Melody Maker*, 20th April 1991.

Chapter 15: Code: Selfish
The description of CaVa studio is taken from *You Can Drum But You Can't Hide* and *The Big Midweek*.

Smith's 'arm's length' comment is from 'Love, Love, Love, Love, Love Your Armani', Ian McCann, *NME*, 29th February 1992, as is his suggestion that 'Married, 2 Kids' refers to Trevor Long.

Stewart Lee's description of Craig Scanlon's 'Birmingham' guitar solo can be found in *The Wire Primers: A Guide to Modern Music*, edited by Rob Young, Verso 2009.

The 'chilling vision' quotation regarding 'Free Range' is from *A User's Guide to The Fall*.

The *NME*'s descriptions of 'Immortality' and 'Two-Face!' appear in 'Tales From the Cryptographic Ocean', Dele Fadele, 14th March 1992.

Peter Kimpton's anecdote regarding 'So-Called Dangerous' is taken from 'Readers recommend: songs about impermanence', *The Guardian*, 3rd April 2014.

Album reviews are from 'Tales From the Cryptographic Ocean', Dele Fadele, *NME*, 14th March 1992; Mathew Hyland, *Rip It Up*, April 1992; and David Cavanagh, *Select*, March 1992.

Chapter 16: The Infotainment Scan
The story about Levitation's removal from the Fall tour was published as 'Levitation Dropped by Fall!', *Melody Maker*, 28th March 1992.

Smith's rant about Phonogram's 'A&R guy' is from 'Alright?', Andrew Perry, *Select*, May 1993.

His explanation of the album's title is taken from '15 Years of Fame', Carol Clerk, *Melody Maker*, 1st May 1993.

The description of 'Ladybird's live performances is from *The Pseud Mag* issue no.12 (October/ November 2006).

Smith's distain for Sting was expressed in 'Peace Talks Collapse', Andrew Harrison, *Select*, January 1992; his comments on Suede are from '15 Years of Fame', Carol Clerk, *Melody Maker*.

The comment about bald heads was made by Ben Pritchard. http://www.markprindle.com/ pritchard-i.htm

Smith's explanation of 'A Past

Gone Mad' is taken from 'Alright?', Andrew Perry, *Select*, May 1993.

The album reviews are from 'Infotainment Tonight', Dave Jennings, *Melody Maker*, 24th April 1993; 'Radical Spangle', Stephen Dalton, *NME*, 23rd April 1993; and 'Manchester's old flames blaze again', Ben Thompson, *The Independent*, 2nd May 1993.

Smith's comment about leaving Phonogram is from 'The Great Infotainer', Anthony Noguera, *Indiecator*, 1993.

Chapter 17: Middle Class Revolt
Smith's disdain for Pavement was expressed in 'Counter Culture', Simon Price, *Melody Maker*, 18th December 1993; his thoughts regarding Nirvana are from the *NME*, 19th February 1994.

Chris Roberts and Johnny Cigarettes's comments about Smith's live performances are from 'Manc Outsiders', *Melody Maker*, 29th May 1993 and *NME*, 30th October 1993.

The 'bottle of Pils' comment appears in 'Manchester United', Ian Gittins, *Melody Maker*, 26th February 1994.

The Lori Kramer interview was posted on a blog that doesn't supply the source (although it appears genuine) – there's a link to it on the song's *Annotated Fall* page.

Smith's views on students were expressed in 'Mark E Smith:

Heroes & Villains', Ted Kessler, *NME*, 11th December 1993.

Dave Bush's views on the album are taken from *Hip Priest*.

Album reviews are from 'Revolting, Cock', Ian McCann, *NME*, 7th May 1994; Jim Sullivan, *The Boston Globe*, 8th September 1994; and Mark Jenkins, *The Washington Post*, September 9th 1994.

Chapter 18: Cerebral Caustic
Smith's explanation of Brix's return to the group is taken from 'The Smiths Reform', L. Verrico, *Vox*, May 1995, as are his comments about 'Don't Call Me Darling'.

The 'your life is a mess' comment is from *The Big Midweek*; Smith's account of the court case is from *Renegade*.

Smith's comments about Mike Bennett and the album's sound appeared in 'Northern Soul', *The Lizard* issue 4, May 1995. The 'endless possibilities' quote is from 'Fall Guy', Alastair Mabbot, *The Scotsman*, 15th March 1995.

Brix and Smith's comments about individual songs are mostly taken from the 'Mark E Smith & Brix Smith promo interview' included on the album's 2006 reissue.

John Harris's review comes from 'Carp Life!', *NME*, 4th March 1995.

Chapter 19: The Light User Syndrome

Dave Bush's account of his marginalisation comes from *The Fallen*, as does Craig Scanlon's claim that Smith asked him to return to the group.

Smith's regret regarding Scanlon's sacking and his explanation of *The "Twenty-Seven Points"* title appears in 'Cash For Questions', David Cavanagh, Q, February 2001.

His comments about 'The Chiselers' and those about Pete Waterman are from 'Gitpop now!', Sylvia Patterson, *NME*, 3rd February 1996 – as is his discussion of his alcohol use.

The review of 'Hostile' was included in *Reformation Post TPM* no. 3, Autumn 2008.

Smith's comments about 'Powder Keg' are from a TV interview (not broadcast) for VH1: https://www.youtube.com/watch?v=RTt64fsfzsM

John Mulvey's review is from 'Git on up!', *NME*, 8th June 1996.

The 'whisky perfume' and 'whisky-rash' comments are taken from *Renegade*.

Chapter 20: Levitate

The evaluations of Adrian Flanagan's guitar work both come from *The Track Record*, respectively gig reviews of Gloucester Guildhall, 30th January 1997 and London Astoria 2, 26th February 1997.

Smith's explanation of his dismissal of Spencer and Stewart as well as his renewed praise for Pete Waterman appear in 'The Outsider', Tony Herrington, *The Wire*, May 1999.

Steve Hanley's comment on 'Jungle Rock' is from *Perfect Sound Forever*, April 1998.

Damon Gough's description of the recording of 'Calendar' appeared in an interview with Mark Jenkins, *Washington Post*, 3rd November 2000.

The album reviews quoted are Steven Wells, *NME*, 11th October 1997 and '"An agent of chaos, fuelled by fire": stars' memories of Mark E Smith', *The Guardian*, 26th January 2018. The latter article also contains the tale of Damon Gough and the dentures.

Chapter 21: The Marshall Suite

Smith's description of the 'open rebellion' in Belfast is taken from 'Narky Mark', John Robinson, *NME*, 7th February 1998. The *Belfast Telegraph* article about the cancelled gig is 'Punk's fall was anarchy in the empire', 10th November 1997.

Dave Bush made his claim for authorship of 'granny on bongos' in 'The Fall: album by album', *Uncut*, July 2019.

The first explanation of Smith's black eye is taken from 'Mark E. Smith: This Nation's Misbehaving Disgrace', *NME*, 25th April 1998; the other is from *Renegade*.

Smith's description of Steve Hanley as 'the Fall sound' appears in 'Fall Guys', Frank Worrall, *Melody Maker*, 18th June 1983. His enigmatic comment about Karl Burn is from *Renegade*.

Jonathan Romney's review of the first post-Brownies gig is taken from 'He's Grim Up North', *The Guardian*, 1st May 1998.

Smith's enthusiasm about Tom Head was reported in 'The Outsider', Tony Herrington, *The Wire*, May 1999. This is also the source for his description of *The Post Nearly Man*, the concept behind the Marshall character, his dissatisfaction with Steve Hitchcock and his comments about 'The Crying Marshal'.

The description of Neville Wilding's first performance is by 'Gez', quoted in *Fall News*, 26th October 1998.

Smith's explanation of the 'three sides' idea was posted on *Fall News*, 20th September 1999.

His 'Elton John' comment regarding 'Touch Sensitive' is from *Renegade*, as is his proud description of the album as a 'glorious return'.

The live review of 'On My Own' is taken from the song's *Track Record* page.

The album reviews are from *The Guardian*, 30th April 1999; *Select*, May 1999; *The Times*, 1st May 1999; and *Uncut*, May 1999.

Chapter 22: The Unutterable

Justine Frischmann's description of working with MES is from '"The Menace" Unmasked!', *NME*, 27th February 2000.

The summary of *Midwatch* can be found on director Mark Aerial Waller's website: http://www.markaerialwaller.com/midwatch.html

The account of Nick Dewey's unlikely recruitment into the group is taken from *The Fallen*.

Julia Nagle's comments about 'Cyber Insekt' are taken from *The Annotated Fall*, although the link provided there is a dead one. Her explanation of 'Way Round's lyric is from the album's press release. Her comments regarding 'Ketamine Sun' are quoted from the song's *Track Record* page.

Ben Pritchard's description of the creation of 'Dr. Bucks' Letter' can be found at http://www.markprindle.com/pritchard-i.htm

Dave Simpson's album review is from *The Guardian*, 3rd November 2000; the others are all quoted from *Fall News*, 1st December 2000.

Chapter 23: Are You Are Missing Winner

Brian Fanning's comments about The Fall's touring schedule are taken from *The Fallen*.

The *Record Collector* interview quoted re 'Crop-Dust' is 'Smith's Moanin' Institution', Piper Terrett, 3rd February 2002; this is also the source of Smith's 'straight down the line' comment at the end of the chapter.

Stewart Lee's comment about 'Ibis-Afro Man' is from *The Sunday Times*, 25th November 2001.

The description of the recording of 'Reprise' is taken from *The Fallen* (based on Dave Simpson's conversations with Brian Fanning).

The album reviews come from *Q Online* (quoted on *Fall News*, 14th November 2001) and *The Wire*, February 2002.

Chapter 24: The Real New Fall LP Formerly 'Country On The Click'
Blaney's declaration that his friendship with MES was finished is from *Manchester Online*, quoted on *Fall News*, 8th November 2002. The article described it as a 'John and Yoko style rift'. Eleni's comment about the visa issue is taken from *Fall News*, 15th October 2002.

Ruth Daniel's account of how she came to play with The Fall is from *The Pseud Mag*, issue 11.

The account of Jim Watts' sacking is from defunct website *playlouder*, quoted on *Fall News*, 28th March 2003.

The description of 'I'm Going To Spain's revival is from *Fall News*, 22nd July 2003.

Smith's account of the events in Lisbon are from the full transcript of an interview for *The Independent*, conducted by Tim

Cumming at Malmaison Hotel Bar, Manchester, 14th May 2004. Published on Tim Cumming's blog and on *The Fall Online*.

The albums reviews are from *The Wire*, 3rd December 2003; *Mojo*, 3rd December 2003; *The Guardian*, 24th October 2003; and *NME*, 4th December 2003. Smith's comment is from *Renegade*.

Chapter 25: Fall Heads Roll
The description of Steve Trafford's recruitment is from *The Fallen*.

Sheila Ravenscroft's comments are from *Margrave of the Marshes*, Bantam, 2005.

Smith's comments regarding the *Newsnight* interview are from *Renegade*.

Stewart Lee's review of *Interim* is from *The Sunday Times*, 21st November 2004; the *Vox* review was quoted on *Fall News*, 22nd November 2004; *Pitchfork*'s review is by Joe Tangari, 30th November 2004.

Jim Watt's announcement about leaving The Fall is taken from *Fall News*, 7th January 2005.

The account of the 'mystery dancer' is by 'up2much' on the *Fall Online Forum*, 13th March 2005.

Ben Pritchard's comments about the recording of *Fall Heads Roll* and Smith's explanation of 'Blindness' are taken from 'The Fall Pick Up the Thread', Jeff Johnson, *Pitchfork*, 17th October 2005.

Smith's 'Eastern European fellas' comment regarding 'What About Us?' featured in an interview with Michael Stewart at the Huddersfield Literary Festival, 14th June 2009.

His vague explanation of 'Assume' is from a *Mixing It* interview, first broadcast 10th February 2006 on BBC Radio 3.

Jim Watts posted his description of 'Blindness's origins on the *Fall Online Forum*.

Simon Archer's comment regarding playing the banjo on 'Clasp Hands' is from an interview with Tony Thornborough, Salford City Radio, 2013.

Cummings and Schuster's description of their role in 'Trust In Me' is from a defunct website, quoted on the song's *Track Record* page.

The album reviews are from *The Daily Mirror*, 30th September 2005; *Sunday Times*, 2nd October 2005; *The Guardian*, 9th December 2005; Louis Pattinson, *NME*, 1st October 2005; *The Wire*, issue #260; 'Rolling Your Own', Stuart Maconie, *Word*, 5th November 2005; and 'Laughing Boy Returns', Mick Middles, *Record Collector*, October 2005.

Chapter 26: Reformation Post TLC
Ben Pritchard and Steve Trafford's comments about the 2005 UK tour and the meaning of 'TLC' are taken from *The Fallen*, as is

the story of Smith threatening Birtwistle with a corkscrew in America.

Smith's dismissive comments about the material recorded with Grant Showbiz in April 2006 appear in 'The Fall: On the rise again', Tim Cumming, *The Independent*, 22nd February 2007. The comments about 'Das Boat' are from the same source.

His comment about 'proper stubble' is from *Renegade*, as is his dismissal of the 'great lost album'.

The review of the 'Dudes' first gig comes from *Fall News*, 10th May 2006.

Smith's comments regarding the album's title are from '26th Album, Approximately. 346th new line-up. Still great', John Robinson, *Uncut*, 7th February 2007.

The description of the Rochdale pub is from the booklet by Daryl Easlea accompanying the 2020 reissue of the album.

Tim Cumming's comments on 'Coach And Horses' are from 'The Fall: On the rise again', *The Independent*, 22nd February 2007.

The album reviews are from Alexis Petridis, *The Guardian*, 9th February 2007; 'Work to Rule', Ian Harrison, *Mojo*, 7th February 2007; Joe Tangari, *Pitchfork*, 12th March 2007; and the John Robinson interview cited above.

Chapter 27: Imperial Wax Solvent
The reviews of *Tromatic Reflexxions* come from *The Guardian*, 18th May 2007 and Barry Nicolson, *NME*, 13th June 2007.

The collection of Fall-inspired short stories is *Perverted by Language: Fiction inspired by The Fall*, published by Serpent's Tail, June 2007.

John Doran's assessment of *Renegade* is from *The Quietus*, 28th April 2008.

The 'squirrel' interview with Ben Marshall appeared in *Uncut*, April 2008. The *Daily Mail* article was published on 9th April 2008.

Pete Greenway's description of the recording of *Imperial Wax Solvent* and Dave Spurr's explanation of the origins of 'Senior Twilight Stock Replacer' are both taken from an August 2018 interview by Jason Gross for the *Perfect Sound Forever* website: http://www.furious.com/perfect/fall/imperialwaxsolvent.html

The album reviews are from *The Guardian*, 25th April 2008; *The Independent*, 25th April 2008; and *The Quietus*, 24th April 2008. *The Quietus*' John Doran and Luke Turner also wrote an amusing track-by-track analysis on the site that's well worth a read: https://thequietus.com/articles/00017-the-fall-imperial-wax-solvent-track-by-track-analysis

Chapter 28: Your Future Our Clutter
The description of Smith's appearance at the Hay-on-Wye literary festival is taken from an article by Charlotte Higgins in *The Guardian*, 28th May 2008.

Smith's comments about the LP's title and his explanations of 'Bury', 'Mexico Wax Solvent' and 'Weather Report 2' are from 'theartsdesk Q&A: Musician Mark E Smith', Tim Cumming, *The Arts Desk*, 24th January 2018.

The comparison of 'Bury' to a 'muddy footprint' appears in an article by Nick Neyland in *Drowned in Sound*, 19th April 2010.

Brix's comments referred to with regard to 'Cowboy George' come from 'My life with Mark E. Smith', *NME*, 25th January 2018.

Smith told John Doran that Cowboy George was Pete Greenway in 'Funnel Of Love: Mark E Smith Of The Fall Interviewed', John Doran, *The Quietus*, 17th December 2010; his contradictory explanation is from the Tim Cumming interview mentioned above, as are his comments about 'heavy German medication'.

Greenway/Spurr/Melling's assertion that 'Cowboy George' was the song offered to *Twilight* was made via the Twitter account of their post-Fall band Imperial Wax.

Smith's 'thought about quitting' statement is also from the *Quietus* 'Funnel Of Love…' interview.

The album reviews are from *Pitchfork*, 7th May 2010; *Drowned in Sound*, 19th April 2010; the *Quietus* 'Funnel Of Love...' interview; and https://www.bbc.co.uk/music/reviews/mxnv/

Chapter 29: Ersatz GB

Smith's bizarre Q&A appeared in 'Q&A: Mark E Smith', Rosanna Greenstreet, *The Guardian*, 21st May 2011.

Ian McNay's comments about Cherry Red and The Fall appeared in 'The One Label That Was Not Out: The Fall and Cherry Red', Daryl Easlea, 21st October 2021.

Smith's moan about how slowly labels work and his complaint about his feet are from 'We Only Have This Excerpt: Mark E Smith of The Fall Interviewed', Kevin E. G. Perry, *The Quietus*, 24th November 2011.

The review of 'Cosmos 7' is from JViney, *Sputnik Music*, 22nd November 2011.

Soundblab's negative comments about 'I've Seen Them Come' were posted by Rich Morris, 28th November 2011.

The MES interview with *The Irish Independent* was 'Falling in Hate', Eamon Sweeny, 13th July 2012.

The album reviews are from *The Sunday Times*, 13th November 2011; *NME*, 12th November 2011; *Louder Than War*, 26th October 2011; *The Wire*, November 2011; *Uncut*, November 2011; *Pitchfork*, 1st December 2011; and 'A poor LP that proves that Mark E. Smith alone does not The Fall make', *BBC* website, 2011.

The 'wet slop' comment is taken from 'The Fall Albums From Worst To Best', Robert Ham, *Stereogum*, 12th February 2015.

Luke Turner's 'mediocrity' comment is from *The Quietus*, 18th November 2011.

Chapter 30: Re-Mit

The 'sharp, sober...' comment was made by 'Cod Shellfish' of the *Fall Online Forum*, describing the Cambridge performance on 15th November 2011.

The joint interview with Blaine Harrison was 'Heroes', Kevin EG Perry, *NME*, 14th April 2012.

Smith's views about Record Store Day were posted on *Fall News*, 22nd April 2012.

His cryptic 'glove' comment is taken from an interview for *Going Thru Vinyl* (a now-defunct website) quoted on *Fall News*, 28th March 2014.

The LCD Soundsystem/shop anecdote is related in Dorian Lynskey's review of *Tromatic Reflexxions* in *The Guardian*, 18th May 2007.

The *Lancashire Telegraph* interview is 'Mark E Smith speaks out as The Fall return to Clitheroe after 28 years', Tony Dewhurst, 12th April 2013.

The 'terrify people' comment is from 'Cash for Questions – Mark

E Smith', Ben Mitchell, Q, April 2013.

The album reviews are taken from Joe Kennedy, *The Quietus*, 14th May 2013; Stuart Berman, *Pitchfork*, 16th May 2013; John Robb, *Louder Than War*, 10th May 2013; J.R. Moores, *Drowned in Sound*, 16th May 2013; and 'Garbled Noise, Playful Blues and Whispery Echoes', Ben Ratliff, *New York Times*, 10th May 2013.

The 'daft history books' quote is from 'The Fall's Mark E. Smith on Re-Mit, Playing for German Lawyers, and H.P. Lovecraft', William Van Meter, *Vulture*, 13th May 2013, as are Smith's comments about the lyrics to 'Irish'.

Chapter 31: The Remainderer
Nick Hasted's live review is from *The Independent*, 20th May 2013.

The 'What I see in the mirror' article is from *The Guardian*, 14th December 2013. The John Doran interview was part of *Noisey*'s 'British Masters' series (*Noisey* is an off-shoot of *Vice* magazine.)

The Tamsin Middleton quotation appears (unattributed) on 'Touchy Pad's *Annotated Fall* page.

The reviews are from Niall O'Keeffe, *The Quietus*, 13th December 2103; Hayley Scott *The Line of Best Fit*, 9th December 2013; and Stuart Berman, *Pitchfork*, 12th December 2013.

Smith's comment about the EP's title was made in an interview for an Irish radio station that is apparently no longer online.

'Steadfast in its impenetrability...' is from *The Annotated Fall* page about 'Amorator!'

Chapter 32: Sub-Lingual Tablet
The Guardian's comment on Steve Hanley's book is from 'The Big Midweek: Life Inside the Fall review – up close with Mark E Smith', Barney Hoskins, 1st October 2014.

Digby Warde-Aldam's live review is from 'If the idea of disturbing kraut-punk sung by a troll appeals, you'll love The Fall', Digby Warde-Aldam, *The Spectator*, 4th October 2014.

The *Quietus* review of *You Can Drum But You Can't Hide* is taken from 'Drums Not Dead: An Interview With Si Wolstencroft', Mick Middles, 27th December 2014.

John Robb's live review appears in *Louder Than War*, 31st January 2015.

An example of the media's coverage of the 'Touch Sensitive' court case can be found in 'Fall lyrics "hard to hear", says judge in copyright case', *The Guardian*, 3rd June 2015.

Tim Cumming's live review is from 'A powerful sub-lingual assault on the senses', *The Arts Desk*, 26th April 2015.

The *Vice* interview is 'Mark E. Smith's Guide To Britain', Daniel Dylan Wray, 1st June 2015.

Smith's 'Barclays advert' comment appeared in 'NME's last ever interview with Mark E. Smith was a rip-roaring rant on class, music, manners and selfie sticks', Jon Bennett, *NME*, 25th January 2018.

His strange tale of online impersonators and Richard Madeley's technology comes from 'Mark E Smith', Ted Kessler, *Q*, July 2015, as does his explanation of his impaired urinary function.

The album reviews are from Jennifer Kelly, *Dusted*, 14th July 2015; Chris McCall, *The Skinny*, 6th May 2015; 'The Fall: Sub-Lingual Tablet review – predictable and surprising in almost equal measure', Michael Hann, *The Guardian*, 7th May 2015; Devon Fisher, *PopMatters*, 21st June 2015; Stuart Berman, *Pitchfork*, 8th June 2015; and Luke Turner, *The Quietus*, 25th May 2015.

Chapter 33: New Facts Emerge
The champagne on the trousers story is from 'Interview with Fat White Family' by David Sue, *Manchester Evening News*, 26th Feb 2016.

The Bognor Regis review is by Emma Finamore, *The Line of Best Fit*, 3rd November 2015.

The reviews of 'Wise Ol' Man' are from 'The Fall have summoned another EP that will please the faithful while baffling everyone else', John Garratt, *PopMatters*, 7th March 2016 and 'The Fall being messy and imperfect is better than no Fall at all', Hayley Scott, *The Line of Best Fit*, 2nd March 2016.

The BBC's erroneous report of Smith's death is covered in 'BBC apologises after accidentally announcing that Mark E Smith had died – on his 60th birthday', Katie Fitzpatrick, *Manchester Evening News*, 5th March 2017.

An account of the assault on Keiron Melling can be found at 'The Fall drummer "beaten to a pulp" in vicious train attack', Damon Wilkinson, *Manchester Evening News*, 3rd April 2017.

The *Counterfeit* review of the Belgrave Music Hall performance was written by Gary Sykes in May 2017; John Robb's account of the Transformer festival is from *Louder Than War*, May 2017.

The Cherry Red statement regarding 'Victoria Train Station Massacre's title appears in 'The Fall's New Song "Victoria Train Station Massacre" Is "Unfortunate Coincidence," Recorded Before Manchester Bombing', Chris DeVille, *Stereogum*, 30th May 2017.

Smith's Lee Brilleaux comment is from 'The 40 Years War', Ian Harrison, *Mojo*, September 2016.

His thoughts on Victoria Station's architecture appear in 'Mark E Smith's final Uncut interview: "The Fall is like a Nazi organisation...", Tom Pinnock, *Uncut*, 25th January 2018; this interview is also the source of the 'Mellotron' and 'they were the group in Paris' comments regarding 'Couples Vs Jobless

Mid 30s'; Greenway and Melling's description of the song's recording is from 'The Fall: album by album', *Uncut*, July 2019; Smith's explanation of the track appears in 'The 40 Years War', Ian Harrison, *Mojo*, September 2016.

Robert Brokenmouth's analysis of 'Second House Now' can be found at http://www.i94bar.com/albums/the-fall-new-facts-box-set

The description of 'Nine Out Of Ten's vocals as recklessly vulnerable is taken from 'The original and eternal post-punk Mancunian rumpus-maker returns', Javi Fedrick, *thearstdesk*, 24th July 2017; David Cavanagh's thoughts on the song's conclusion are from 'Mark E Smith: The Hip Priest Remembered', *Uncut*, April 2018.

The album reviews are taken from 'The Fall: New Facts Emerge review – bright pop riffs lift the eerie drama', Rachel Aroesti, *The Guardian*, 27th July 2017; 'The latest from The Fall: ever nastier, ever greasier, ever more hypnotically righteous', Harry Sword, *The Quietus*, 8th August 2017; Ian Harrison, *Mojo*, 28th July 2017; Marc Burrows, *Drowned In Sound*, 26th July 2017; and John Robb, *Louder Than War*, 28th July 2017. Robb's comment about 'Nine Out Of Ten' being a 'snark attack' is also from this review.

The 'grab-bag Fall album' comment was made by 'brownsocketspurpleseyes' on the 'Groundsboy' *Annotated Fall* page.

The description of the group's plans for their next album are from an interview with Denzil Watson in *Penny Black Music*, 24th December 2019.

Epilogue
Graham Eatough's comments about Smith's inability to participate in *No End to Enderby* appeared in 'Politics and pollution spark play that ends up blurring life and art', Neil Cooper, *Glasgow Times*, 3rd August 2017.

The description of Smith's appearance at the group's Wakefield gig was posted on *The Fall Online Forum* by 'Ersatz JP'.

Peter Ross's description of Smith's final entrance is taken from 'The Fall at Queen Margaret Union, Glasgow: a triumphant portrait of courage and commitment', *The Daily Telegraph*, 5th November 2017.

Adam Sweeting's comments are taken from 'Mark E Smith obituary: the Fall's driving force was poet, satirist and misanthrope', *The Guardian*, 25th January 2018; Dave Simpson's are from 'Legend of the Fall: Mark E Smith kept swinging to the end', *The Guardian*, 24th January 2018; Stewart Lee's are from an interview with Mark Radcliffe on BBC 6Music – https://www.bbc.co.uk/sounds/play/p05w2g4k

Appendix 1: The Fall's Peel Sessions (and other radio broadcasts)

The reviews of *The Complete Peel Sessions* are taken from Joe Tangari, *Pitchfork*, 12th June 2005; *Rolling Stone*, 16th June 2005; and Simon Goddard, *Uncut*, 5th May 2005.

Appendix 2: Fall Compilation Albums

The 'daft deals' comment is from 'Cash For Questions', David Cavanagh, Q, February 2001.

The reviews of *Sinister Waltz* are from 'Are You Still Doing What You Were Doing Two Years Ago? Yeah? Well Don't Make A Career Out Of It', Mark Luffman, *Melody Maker*, 10th February 1996 and, Mike Goldsmith, *NME*, 3rd February 1996.

Steve Hanley's comment about the 1999 *Peel Sessions* compilation is from *The Big Midweek*.

Acknowledgements

When I began the original *Fall in Fives* blog, I had only modest ambitions as to its readership, but Eric Smith was an early champion of my work, and I am hugely grateful for his enthusiasm, encouragement and sage guidance in securing a wider audience for my writing. Caroline McKenzie aka hippriestess – who writes about The Fall with true beauty and passion – was another staunch supporter from the very beginning and I am profoundly grateful for her advice and expert knowledge.

Many of the regular contributors to the *Fall Online Forum* have provided me with invaluable advice and constructive criticism. I am also very grateful for the encouragement I received regarding my various blogs via Facebook and Twitter. There are far too many people to mention without fear of offending someone by omission, but their support over the last few years has been most heartily appreciated.

Special thanks are due to Barrie Francis, who has provided me with an ongoing series of enjoyably beer-soaked evenings in Cardiff discussing Fall-related matters that have nurtured and sustained my passion for this project. I would also like to thank Conway Paton and Jonny Swift for their contributions.

Chris, aka 'bzfgt', is the architect of the utter wonder that is *The Annotated Fall* website, a resource upon which I relied heavily throughout this book. He is another long-standing supporter of this project, fuelled to no small extent by our shared love of extravagantly lengthy psych-rock wig-outs.

Thanks are also due to Steve Hanley, Simon Wolstencroft, Grant Showbiz and Ben Pritchard for their support and forbearance regarding my endless queries. I am also incredibly grateful to Paul Hanley for his constant support and excellent foreword. I would also like to thank Ian Daley and Isabel Galán from Route Publishing for their unwavering belief in this project and their consistently helpful expert advice.

This book strives, above all else, to tell The Fall's story with comprehensiveness and accuracy. This may ultimately be an unobtainable goal, but if it comes anywhere close, it is due to the assistance provided by dannyno's exceptionally dogged and analytical research skills. Dan proofread every single *You Must Get Them All* post and has constantly been on hand to correct every one of the blunders and misunderstandings in my various online projects. This whole project would literally have been impossible without him, and for that, as well as his good company and wonderfully dry humour, I am eternally grateful.

Above all else, I have to thank my wife Kirsty for her unending support, patience and resilience in putting up with the almost constant exposure to what she has been known to describe as 'the worst group ever'. Whatever she might think about The Fall's music, she recognises my passion for it and has been my biggest rock and most enduring supporter throughout. I couldn't have done this without her.

Steve Pringle, April 2022
www.thefallinfives.blogspot.com
Twitter: @TheFallinFives